ANTHROPOLOGY AT HARVARD

Peabody Museum Monographs ◆ Number 11
Peabody Museum of Archaeology and Ethnology
Harvard University ◆ Cambridge, Massachusetts

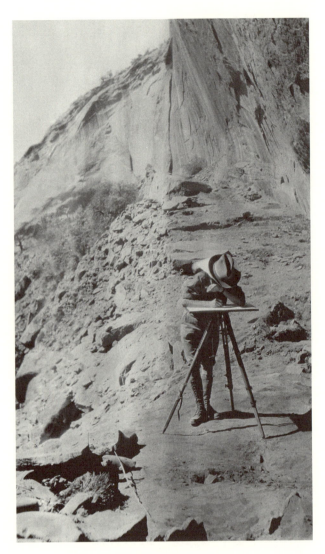

Alfred Vincent Kidder surveying in the
American Southwest, ca. 1914.

ANTHROPOLOGY AT HARVARD

A Biographical History, 1790–1940

DAVID L. BROWMAN & STEPHEN WILLIAMS

PEABODY MUSEUM PRESS
HARVARD UNIVERSITY
Cambridge, Massachusetts

Copyright © 2013 by the President and Fellows of Harvard College.
All rights reserved. This book, or any part thereof, may not be reproduced
in any form or by any means, electronic or mechanical, including photo-
copying, recording, or use in any information storage or retrieval system
now known or to be invented, without the permission of the publisher.

Editorial direction by Joan Kathryn O'Donnell
Design and composition by David Alcorn, Alcorn Publication Design
Editing by Jane Kepp
Production management by Donna Dickerson
Printed and bound in the United States by Maple Press, York,
Pennsylvania

ISBN 978-0-87365-913-0

Library of Congress Cataloging-in-Publication Data

Browman, David L.
Anthropology at Harvard : a biographical history, 1790-1940 / David L.
Browman and Stephen Williams.
    p. cm. — (Peabody museum monographs ; number 11)
Includes bibliographical references and index.
ISBN 978-0-87365-913-0 (cloth : alk. paper)
1. Harvard University. Dept. of Anthropology—History. 2.
Anthropology—Study and teaching (Higher)—Massachusetts—
Cambridge—History. 3. Anthropology teachers—Massachusetts—
Cambridge—History. 4. College teachers—Massachusetts—
Cambridge—History. I. Williams, Stephen, 1926– II. Title.
GN43.2.M4B76 2012
301.0710744'4—dc23
2012001176

Contents

List of Institutional Abbreviations *vi*

A Brief Chronology of Events Related to the History of Anthropology at Harvard *vii*

Preface *ix*

Introduction *3*

1. Harvard Contributions to the Origins of Americanist Archaeology, 1790–1860 *11*
2. The Lawrence Scientific School, the Museum of Comparative Zoology, and the Peabody Museum, 1847–1866 *23*
3. Frederic Putnam and His Student Cohort, 1859–1875 *47*
4. Development of the Peabody Museum and Its Collections, 1875–1890 *81*
5. The Influence of Other Professionals and the Archaeological Institute of America, 1865–1890 *141*
6. Development of the Harvard Anthropology Graduate Program, 1890–1900 *169*
7. Graduate Students, Faculty, and Others, 1890–1900 *197*
8. Putnam's Students at the American Museum of Natural History, 1894–1903 *245*
9. Professionals, Benefactors, and Supporters, 1890–1910 *277*
10. Peabody Museum Students and Faculty, 1900–1919 *297*
11. Growth and Professionalism in the Twenties *351*
12. An Explosion of Scholars, 1929–1939 *397*

Bibliography *459*

Picture Credits *557*

Index *563*

Illustrations follow pages *84, 212, 340,* and *436*

List of Institutional Abbreviations

AAA	American Anthropological Association
AAAS	American Association for the Advancement of Science
AAPA	American Association of Physical Anthropologists
AIA	Archaeological Institute of America
AES	American Ethnological Society
AMNH	American Museum of Natural History
ASPR	American School of Prehistoric Research
ASW	Anthropological Society of Washington
BAE	Bureau of American Ethnology
BIA	Bureau of Indian Affairs
BSNH	Boston Society of Natural History
CIW	Carnegie Institution of Washington
CWA	Civil Works Administration
MCZ	Museum of Comparative Zoology
NPS	National Park Service
NRC	National Research Council
ONI	Office of Naval Intelligence
OSS	Office of Strategic Services
PMAAE	Peabody Museum of American Archaeology and Ethnology
PMAE	Peabody Museum of Archaeology and Ethnology
SAA	Society for American Archaeology
USGS	U.S. Geological Survey
USNM	United States National Museum
WPA	Works Progress Administration

A Brief Chronology of Events Related to the History of Anthropology at Harvard

1636	"New College" created in Cambridge, Massachusetts, by Massachusetts colonial legislature; renamed Harvard College in 1639
1780	American Academy of Arts and Sciences founded in Boston
1812	Philadelphia Academy of Natural Sciences founded
1812	American Antiquarian Society founded
1821	Essex County Historical Society founded in Salem, Massachusetts
1830	Boston Society of Natural History (BSNH) established
1839	Lowell Institute lecture series initiated after institute is founded in Boston by a bequest from John Lowell Jr. (1799–1836)
1842	American Ethnological Society (AES) established
1845	*Scientific American* founded
1846	Smithsonian Institution founded
1847	Lawrence Scientific School founded at Harvard
1848	Essex County Historical Society merges with Essex County Natural History Society (founded 1833) to form the Essex Institute in Salem
1848	American Association for the Advancement of Science (AAAS) founded
1859	Museum of Comparative Zoology (MCZ) at Harvard (since 1995 part of the Harvard Museum of Natural History) opens under the direction of Louis Agassiz
1863	National Academy of Sciences founded
1863–64	Frederic Putnam and fellow students leave the Museum of Comparative Zoology in the "Salem secession"
1866	Peabody Museum of American Archaeology and Ethnology (PMAAE) founded at Harvard
1866	Peabody Museum of Natural History founded at Yale
1867	Peabody Academy of Science (the Peabody Museum of Salem after 1915) founded at Salem, Massachusetts (merged with the Essex Institute in 1992 to form the Peabody Essex Museum)
1867	*American Naturalist* founded
1869	American Museum of Natural History (AMNH) founded in New York City

1872	Harvard's first "Graduate Department" organized
1879	Harvard School for the Collegiate Instruction of Women (the "Harvard Annex") established
1879	Bureau of Ethnology (after 1897 the Bureau of American Ethnology, or BAE), established (becomes part of the Smithsonian Institution in 1965)
1879	U.S. Geological Survey (USGS) established
1879	Archaeological Institute of America (AIA) established
1879	Anthropological Society of Washington (ASW) established
1882	Section H, Anthropology, formed within the AAAS
1883	*Science* first published
1887	University of Pennsylvania Museum of Archaeology and Anthropology (the University Museum) established
1888	*American Anthropologist* established
1890	Harvard Graduate School of Arts and Sciences formally established
1890	Department of American Archaeology and Ethnology established at Harvard
1893	Harvard School for the Collegiate Instruction of Women becomes Radcliffe College
1893	Columbian Museum of Chicago (after 1905 the Field Museum of Natural History) established
1894	Frederic Putnam accepts appointment at AMNH, held jointly with his Peabody Museum curatorship, ending in 1903
1897	Peabody Museum formally merges with Harvard University
1902	Carnegie Institution of Washington (CIW) founded
1902	American Anthropological Association (AAA) founded
1910	International School for American Archaeology and Ethnology established in Mexico City
1915	Peabody Academy of Science renamed Peabody Museum of Salem
1916	National Park Service (NPS) established as part of the Department of Interior
1916	National Research Council (NRC) established
1916	George G. Heye founds the Museum of the American Indian
1923	Social Science Research Council founded
1928	American Association of Physical Anthropologists (AAPA) established
1934	Society for American Archaeology (SAA) established

Preface

THE INITIAL RATIONALE FOR THIS VOLUME WAS TO TRY to gain a deeper understanding of the origins and historical development of Americanist anthropology in the United States. By "Americanist anthropology" we mean to limit our discussion to American scholars—or American-trained scholars of different nationalities—doing research in the four fields of anthropology: archaeology, sociocultural anthropology, linguistics, and physical (or biological) anthropology. Our definition is somewhat broad. Frequently the term *Americanist* is limited to American scholars doing research in the Americas, but the Harvard anthropologists described in this volume studied cultures around the world. Our use of the term, then, refers to "American" research, wherever it was undertaken.

At the time we conceived the book, both of us were teaching the history of Americanist archaeology, and we found that we shared two major concerns. First, the general histories of Americanist anthropology and archaeology then available tended to emphasize events and people only later than about 1915. Second, whereas various writers (for example, Hinsley 1979, 1981; Judd 1967; Noelke 1974) had detailed the influence of governmental bodies such as the Smithsonian Institution, the U.S. National Museum, and the Bureau of American Ethnology in the nineteenth-century evolution of anthropology, the contributions of university and other nongovernment researchers to the early field had been neglected. Our idealistic plan was to bring balance to this picture by researching more of the nongovernment nineteenth-century contributors, identifying women and ethnic minorities who were important players, looking broadly at the contributions of American universities to the development of Americanist anthropology, and explicitly recognizing that the development of Americanist archaeology was an integral part of the broader development of anthropology in these venues.

To capture the nongovernmental components, our initial plan was to deal with the development of university anthropology at the four institutions where the subject was taught during the late nineteenth century—Harvard University, the University of Pennsylvania, Clark University, and the University of Chicago—and to include the people who worked closely with these institutions avocationally. We quickly found, however, that the universities' trajectories had been so different that we could not collapse them into a single, uniform, "university" thread. More important, Harvard's was the only successful anthropology initiative in terms of being maintained as a continuous program. Chicago, Clark, and Pennsylvania all had false starts: their first anthropological programs failed and had to be reinitiated in the twentieth century (Darnell

1998:106–110). Moreover, we found that an overwhelming amount of material existed for Harvard alone.

For reasons both intellectual and practical, then, it did not seem unreasonable to redefine our project, limiting it primarily to Harvard and the Peabody Museum of Archaeology and Ethnology, the only successful university and museum anthropology program that persevered and prospered. Indeed, when we looked at the reintroductions of anthropology programs at Chicago and Pennsylvania in the early twentieth century, we found that they were based on successful models developed at other institutions and drew in no small part on the success of the anthropology program at the Peabody Museum. In this regard, Chicago and Penn were not dissimilar to the scores of other American institutions that launched anthropology programs in the first half of the twentieth century.

As we began this project, we estimated that we would be detailing the contributions of perhaps several dozen scholars, expanding on previous treatments that mentioned only a handful. We never imagined that we would end up discussing the contributions of more than 500 persons associated with the Peabody Museum program before 1940. Had we recognized the magnitude of the record, we likely would never have tackled such an enormous project. As it turned out, the identification of cohorts of students and instructors proved invaluable, because their interactions and long-sustained networks profoundly influenced the development of anthropology. Yet their sheer numbers made it impossible to focus equitably on both the actors and the broad intellectual trends of successive periods.

Although we found it imperative to look at events such as the professionalization of the field and the development of graduate education, we ultimately decided, in the interest of keeping this treatise to a manageable size, to ruthlessly eliminate many of our discussions of broader national and global trends. We have tried, in the way we have organized the volume into chapters, to indirectly address some trends particularly relevant to anthropology, but fundamentally we have chosen to present an account structured in terms of biographies. This allows us to emphasize what we call the "cohort effect"—the way contemporaneous sets of students and professors interacted and influenced one another. Throughout the book we have tried to organize our biographical sketches not only thematically but also according to the way various cohorts of anthropology students at Harvard formed and overlapped.

In another sort of cohort, three people played indispensible roles in the creation of this volume: Al Gordon, Joan Tozzer Cave, and Greg Finnegan. Albert Hamilton Gordon received his A.B. from Harvard in 1923, graduating cum laude in economics. He went on to receive his M.B.A. from Harvard in 1925, graduating with distinction, and then into a successful career in business. As a member of the Visiting Committee of the Peabody Museum, Gordon worked closely with Stephen Williams during the decade when Williams was director of the Peabody Museum and continued his close association until his death in 2009.

Joan Tozzer Cave, who passed away in 2012, was a former U.S. figure skating champion and the daughter of Alfred M. Tozzer, a Mayanist archaeologist who taught and researched at the Peabody Museum for more than half a century. Cave came to know Williams almost as soon as he arrived at Harvard in 1954, and over the years she contributed materially to his research projects. Gordon and Cave provided funds that allowed us to make research trips to the archives at Cambridge, as well as assistance to the Peabody Museum Press for the publication of this volume. We are deeply grateful to them both.

Gregory Allan Finnegan, head of reference and associate librarian for public services at the Tozzer Library, Harvard University, as well as the managing editor of *Anthropological Literature,* the Tozzer Library's quarterly journal, was invaluable in our quest to track down rare publications and difficult sources. For some of our biographical sketches, he is truly an unsung, silent third author. We threw down challenges to his skills as a specialist in anthropological literature when we were at an impasse, and he never failed to winkle out a new and important resource for us. We could not have done it without his aid.

ANTHROPOLOGY
AT HARVARD

The Peabody Museum of American Archaeology and Ethnology, 1889.

Introduction

A FREQUENT TENDENCY IN SCHOLARLY WORKS THAT ATTEMPT to detail the historical roots of anthropological theory and practice has been to focus only on contributions from the last half century and ignore the scholarship of earlier scientists. Albert C. Spaulding, in his article "Fifty Years of Theory" (1985:307), lamented this neglect of intellectual antecedents in archaeology, observing that "archaeology was not practiced exclusively by idiots before 1962 (or 1950 or 1935)." One could appropriately substitute "anthropology" for "archaeology" in the quotation. This tendency to ignore or overlook earlier scholarship is exacerbated by new students coming into the field, who seem to feel that anything useful surely must have been said or written in the last quarter century or less. Good anthropological scholarship requires historical context, and clearly archaeology is a historical discipline, but recent syntheses seem at times surprisingly ahistorical.

For these reasons we have chosen, in exploring the origins of Americanist anthropology and archaeology at Harvard University and its Peabody Museum of Archaeology and Ethnology, to focus on events prior to World War II, or before roughly 1940. Although the majority of our coverage deals with events after 1859, we begin in the late eighteenth century, for the roots of anthropological interest at Harvard began to take hold at that time. Anthropological work burgeoned with the first students who studied with Louis Agassiz in 1859 and with the founding of the Peabody Museum in 1866, but Harvard professors and graduates first became involved in anthropological studies in the 1780s.

The story of anthropology at Harvard is much influenced by the nineteenth-century development there of scholarly interest in natural history and, as a subset, the "natural history of humans." By the mid-nineteenth century this had translated into a specific emphasis on archaeology. Sociocultural anthropology and physical anthropology achieved equal importance at Harvard only with the beginning of the twentieth century. Although by the early twentieth century the "four field" approach—encompassing archaeology, cultural and physical anthropology, and linguistics—became a frequently stated ideal for anthropology departments, Harvard did not develop a strong linguistics subfield on campus at the time, but rather sent its graduate students elsewhere, particularly to Columbia University, for linguistics training.

Because of the early focus by Harvard's staff and students on archaeology—especially Americanist archaeology—by necessity we end up concentrating more heavily in this book on the institution's archaeological contributions than on its advances in cultural and biological anthropology. Because of the strong archaeological component, we sought to see whether extant models for defining periods of intellectual events in the history of archaeology could help us organize our discussion. Over the years, various researchers have developed their own favorite schemata for dividing the intellectual growth of Americanist archaeology into periods. The best known is that of Gordon Willey and Jeremy Sabloff (1974, 1980, 1993), who, for the time segment of interest here, defined a Speculative period, from 1492 to 1840; a Classificatory–Historical–Descriptive period, from 1840 to 1914; and a Classificatory-Historical-Chronological period, from 1914 to 1940.

The Willey-Sabloff periods work fairly well for describing certain philosophical approaches in archaeology itself, but we decided to focus more on the actors involved in the early history of anthropology and archaeology at Harvard than on such broad intellectual trends. The resulting clusters from this focus on actors did not aptly replicate Willey and Sabloff's periods. Rather, an earlier breakdown of disciplinary development suggested by Clark Wissler (1942:190), consisting of four major periods before 1940, seemed more congruent with what we observed. Wissler's periods were the Exploratory or Survey period, from 1492 to 1800; the period of the discovery of research techniques, from 1800 to 1860; the Museum period, from 1860 to 1900; and the Academic period, from 1900 onward. Wissler's "discovery of research techniques" phase, for example, appropriately included the development of linguistic classification, comparative anatomical methods, stratigraphic excavation in archaeology, and ethnographic approaches, some of the issues we delve into in the following chapters.

As we began attempting our own breakdown of disciplinary ideas and intellectual schools into discrete periods, we rooted our phases more directly in the actors involved and in the events of their professional careers. These included events such as the entry of Frederic Putnam and his cohort of fellow students into the Lawrence Scientific School at Harvard in about 1860, the shift in American perceptions of history at roughly the time of the nation's first centennial, the establishment of the first American anthropology programs in about 1890, the reorganization of the intellectual field after World War I, and major government interventions during the Great Depression. We find these events to be much better markers of the trajectory of the anthropological and archaeological actors of our story than more "global" shifts in abstract intellectual philosophy.

What we hope to contribute with this book is, in part, a means of uncovering the biases of prior stories about Americanist anthropology and archaeology, as well as a means of inducing reflexivity about the goals and directions of our discipline. By providing a close analysis of the roots of the kinds of university "lineages" that affect the framing of research questions in any discipline, we hope to provide additional perspectives on contemporary intellectual traditions. As Timothy Murray (2002:238) observed for archaeology, in a comment just as appropriate for anthropology as a whole, "exploring new histories of archaeology can help us understand how the edifice of modern archaeology—its agendas, concepts, categories, patterns of socialization, and institutions—became established, and the processes which have underwritten its transformations."

There are several pitfalls in trying to do such historiography, and we have tried to avoid or navigate around them as much as possible. Jennifer Croissant (2000:195) has complained that books organized like ours, such as the histories by Willey and Sabloff, Bruce Trigger (1989), and Glyn Daniel (1981), often turn out to be mainly "chronological dictionaries" of the main characters. Although we understand that concern, we believe it is essential to treat the significant persons who have previously been omitted or overlooked and to flesh out the contributions of people who have previously been depicted one-dimensionally. Therefore, although we have tried to avoid writing only a chronological dictionary, some of our goals have led us necessarily in that direction, and this book is meant deliberately to be a *biographical* history. Before one can usefully generalize to the higher-order levels of abstraction sought by Croissant, one must understand and control the basic data sets. For us, that requires knowing the cohorts of actors involved.

We have identified more than 500 persons who contributed directly to the growth and development of anthropology at Harvard University and the Peabody Museum before 1940. Many of these people formed cohorts—contemporaneous networks of scholars who attended the same classes and scientific meetings, worked on the same projects, and debated issues of common interest, regardless of their subfield specialization. Cultural anthropologists and biological anthropologists were just as interested in, and just as aggressive about arguing over, archaeological issues as the archaeologists were in contributing to the research of their fellow students in other subfields. We believe it is impossible to understand the evolution of any of the three major subfields at Harvard—archaeology, biological anthropology, and sociocultural anthropology—without understanding the vigorous discussions that went on among students of the different disciplines. We call this the "cohort effect." We believe studies that concentrate on single individuals miss a significant part of the origin of ideas by ignoring the vibrant cohort with whom the designated "star" interacted. Far too many studies in our field focus on the contributions of one or two influential instructors and thus ignore the real context of intellectual development. Even the biggest names in anthropology have been tremendously affected by the cohort of persons with whom they trained and with whom they regularly came into contact during their careers.

Identifying these cohorts at Harvard has been one of our goals for this volume. Increasingly, at the annual symposia of disciplinary history groups at the meetings of both the Society for American Archaeology (SAA) and the American Anthropological Association (AAA), our colleagues have been rediscovering the important and underrecognized contributions of lesser-known intellectual ancestors of both American archaeology and anthropology. The focus on "superstars" is slowly but inexorably being replaced by an understanding of the critical importance of cohorts and the interplay between competing factions in the growth of our field.

For the period between the Civil War and World War I, relatively few actors were involved at Harvard, and so we are able to devote more space to the intellectual history of university anthropology at that time. For the decades between the two world wars, however, the sheer number of persons involved reduces us often to providing little more than biographical dictionaries. Only occasionally, as for the development of the role of women in the field (chapter 12), are we able to enlarge on some important themes for the later chronological periods.

One strategy we employ to help develop the context of anthropology at Harvard in the later nineteenth century is to focus on the contributions of Frederic Ward Putnam and the cohorts he recruited and interacted with during the phases of his career. We are fully aware of the risk of producing a hagiography, but that does not mean we should completely avoid acknowledging the contributions of leading figures. And in this case, Putnam serves as an excellent hub around which to construct others of our arguments and narratives. The literary device of employing Putnam as a hub means that although he is often involved indirectly in components of our argument, we have deliberately opted not to include a major biographical discussion of him, which has been done ably in other works (for example, Hinsley 1992). Rather, we try to employ his influence as part of our cohort argument.

Timothy Murray, in an article titled "The History, Philosophy, and Sociology of Archaeology" (1989:56–57), observed that most histories of archaeology had focused on the lives of "great" archaeologists but lacked context. His comments apply equally to histories of anthropology in general:

> The result of these shortcomings is that much of the history of archaeology reads as a kind of travel journal, an account of the slow journey out of the darkness of subjectivity and speculation towards objectivity, rationality, and science. In such histories the nature of archaeological knowledge transcends social and historical context, and the determinants of archaeological knowledge are themselves treated as ahistorical and acultural. Consequently, only on rare occasions are we presented with the detailed analysis of the taken-for-granteds of the history of archaeological practice, such as institutional structures, relations with governments and the general public, organizing concepts and categories, and archaeology's relationships with its cognate disciplines.

Murray (2002:235) later returned to his theme that historians of anthropology need to study, among other things, the institutions—universities, departments, museums, professional associations—that shape the intersection between anthropology and society. Our focus in this book on the Peabody Museum, Harvard University, the founding of anthropology departments at Harvard and elsewhere, and the development of anthropological associations does just that. We look especially at the institutional character of education at Harvard in the late nineteenth century and the way it influenced the evolution of anthropology there. We examine the way institutional changes in the early twentieth century similarly caused paradigm shifts in the conceptualization and execution of anthropology. One of these shifts was the early-twentieth-century "revolution in anthropology" that George Stocking (1989:3) identified, which transformed the discipline in many respects.

Analysis of the cohort effect also assists in dealing with the ever-troubling problem of "presentism" when writing about the intellectual history of a discipline. Now frequently called "unreflexive presentism," this issue was once known as Whiggism, a term derived from historians' tendency to write, as Herbert Butterfield put it (1950:v), "on the side of Protestants and Whigs, to praise revolutions provided they have been successful, to emphasize certain principles of progress in the past and to produce a story which is the ratification if not the glorification of the present." Whiggish history, then, describes the past with reference to the present. Such an intellectual history imagines that it has found the root of the modern world in the first mention of a concept. It too easily credits changes to a single person, and it has a tendency to see the resulting paradigm as progress (see Butterfield 1950:10–12, 40–45).

A presentist history of anthropology views the past in terms of the "winners"—those ideas and institutional settings that survived to find a place in contemporary anthropology. Thus most historians of anthropology have tended to be chroniclers of the progressive triumph of "truth" and less analysts of how successive structures of perception were adopted and used in the social organization of anthropology. Presentism seeks out past phenomena that seem to resemble those under investigation and then describes a simple lineage from one to the other. This is seen as "progress"; it assumes in advance the progressive character of historical change (Fahnestock 1984:8).

Regna Darnell (2001:2) argues that presentism is precisely what characterizes histories of Americanist anthropology today—that the current approach to intellectual history is a slavish adherence to the unilinear succession of dominant paradigms, portrayed as a reconstruction of scientific progress without reflection on the rationale of such evolution. Although Darnell is one of the principal spokespersons for Boas and Boasian anthropology, she clearly observes that when Boas emerged as the victor in the competition for organizational power in early-twentieth-century anthropology, he took advantage of his power base and rewrote the history of anthropology, giving no quarter to his intellectual or institutional competitors (Darnell 2001:11, 33, 35). She notes that not only Boas himself but early Boasians as well explicitly viewed themselves as rewriting the history of anthropology, in their view thus creating a professionally respectable and scientifically rigorous discipline. Boas and his students maintained control of the intellectual direction and social organization of North American anthropology and the origin stories of its heritage until at least the end of the Second World War.

The result, we believe, has been a general presentist history of sociocultural anthropology, if not of the entire field. The current perspective on the development of

Americanist anthropology has been deliberately skewed to lionize Boas and his students, while the "losers" of the battle for dominance, whether Frederic Putnam or others, have been effectively written out of the history of Americanist anthropology. We seek in this volume to resurrect an important historical thread in the heritage of Americanist anthropology and bring it back into the narrative of the development of our discipline, to counter the "Whiggish" history that currently dominates our field.

With respect to the archaeological component of the discipline, Marc-Antoine Kaeser (2002:171–72), writing about the international roots of archaeology, identified two major nineteenth-century research paradigms: an antiquarian approach, illustrating the life, manners, customs, and beliefs of ancient peoples, and an evolutionist approach, used by those with naturalist backgrounds and seeking to demonstrate the process of human evolution with respect to its social and natural milieu. Both trajectories are represented in our work. Some of the major university actors in our story were strong advocates of the evolutionist approach, but by including the cohort of avocational researchers who worked with the Peabody Museum and by integrating the contributions of the antiquarian approach, we develop a more robust picture of the events and actions that contributed to the nineteenth-century flowering of the field.

A natural science background gave the people associated with the Lawrence Scientific School (chapter 2) who became so important to the development of anthropology at Harvard, such as Asa Gray, Jeffries Wyman, and Frederic Putnam, access to a new paradigm. They had learned a scientific approach that gave them a greater breadth of understanding and taught them well how to judge data. These scholars' view of the place of science is sometimes difficult for either historians or sociologists to understand in their more limited views of "knowledge" and "truth." Science for this cadre of nineteenth-century researchers held as a tenet of faith that it was an ennobling pursuit only when it was unselfish, without self-seeking by its adherents.

We believe that a signal difference between Putnam's cohort and the Boasians was the former's view that if one were a good, solid scientist, self-promotion was unnecessary, because the science would speak for itself. Other observers of the history of Americanist anthropology (for example, Mark 1980) have also commented on Boas's self-promoting style as contrasted with Putnam's near reticence. Putnam's lack of public self-promotion was shared by Wyman, Gray, and many others associated with the origins of anthropology at Harvard. It is a notable feature of this cohort, and we address it further in subsequent chapters.

Many of the broader social and historical themes influencing the evolution of Americanist anthropology have been ably identified by previous researchers writing on the history of the field, eliminating the need for us to repeat them here. One broad intellectual trend, however, has been previously unaddressed in such histories and bears mention here. This is the so-called American renaissance, encompassing roughly the years 1865 to 1917, which seems to have influenced the perceptions of people outside of the academy regarding what American archaeology could or should be.

According to Richard Wilson (1979:11), the term *American renaissance* "concerns the identification by many Americans—painters, sculptors, architects, craftsmen, scholars, collectors, politicians, financiers, and industrialists—with the period of the European Renaissance and the feeling that the Renaissance spirit had been captured again in the United States." Thomas Bender (1993:34) argued that for urban intellectual life, the period between 1840 and 1875 was one of confusion, in which the previous paradigm was collapsing and a new direction had not yet been perceived. American intellectuals of this era looked about for viable institutional means of achieving social order, and the American renaissance became one of the concepts selected and emphasized for the next half century. The perspective was that "the art of the past could provide useful sources for the development of a national American art" (Wilson 1979:12). In seeking appropriate symbols for American civilization, artists and architects fixed on the European Renaissance and its Greco-Roman Classic past as the appropriate sources for deriving expression.

In terms of the events that unfold in the following chapters, the notion of an American renaissance helps to explain how the early strong interest in American Indian origins and mound cultures was overturned and why classical archaeology came to dominate much of public archaeological interest after the 1880s, until the First World War and even later. Wilson (1979:68) observed that the period was also characterized by a mania for the formation of organizations and institutions that advanced the American renaissance—a useful consideration in helping us understand the development of the Archaeological Institute of America and its fetish for classical archaeology (chapter 5).

A good deal of the modern history of anthropology has been written from the perspectives of Boasian and post-Boasian scholarship. If one wishes to enrich the discussion of the history of anthropology by investigating earlier, non-Boasian paradigms that have been forgotten or deliberately excluded, it is difficult not to appear to be "anti-Boasian." We do not intend to give that impression at all; we have benefited greatly by considering the works of that group of scholars. What we hope to do in this volume is to enrich the heritage of our disciplinary origins by taking up some additional threads of the fabric of our discipline that have been forgotten and providing a broader and more representative view of our disciplinary history. We are well aware that the ultimate story will involve the integration of the themes we develop in this volume with Boasian themes and other historical threads yet to be developed by other researchers.

I

Harvard Contributions to the Origins of Americanist Archaeology and Anthropology, 1790–1860

AMERICANIST ANTHROPOLOGY AND, ESPECIALLY, ARCHAEOLOGY—at Harvard as elsewhere in the young United States—grew out of interest in the natural history of humans in the Americas on the part of a few people educated in other fields and subjects. Some of the first Harvard scholars in this arena more or less stumbled onto the study of ancient human cultures, thanks to their interest in languages, comparative anatomy, or botany—or perhaps just because their houses sat near ancient Indian mounds. In this chapter we cover the somewhat arbitrary period from the 1780s, when Harvard-trained researchers began to study Indian relics in the Ohio Valley, to the late 1850s, when students at Harvard first received some training in things anthropological.

Harvard, first a college and later a university, was established in 1636. Governor Henry Vane of the Massachusetts Bay Colony decreed in Boston on September 8, 1636, that a college be launched with an initial subsidy from the colony of 400 pounds. The following year John Winthrop, the new governor, ordered that the college be built across the Charles River from Boston in the village of Newetowne, and a legislative act created a board of overseers for the new college. In 1638 the colonial legislature decided that Newetowne should be renamed Cambridge, and in 1639 it agreed that the college be called Harvard, in honor of John Harvard, deceased son of the college's first benefactor (Harvard University 1930:3).

From the start, Harvard was an American institution, created and governed through a series of colonial charters that established the roles of Harvard's president, fellows, overseers, and corporation but were never approved by the king of England. A contemporary volume, *New England's First Fruits* (1643:12), described the founding of the college as follows:

> It pleased God to stir up the heart of one Mr. *Harvard* (a godly Gentleman, and a lover of Learning, there living amongst us) to give the one halfe of his Estate (it being in all about 1700 [pounds]) toward the erecting of a Colledge, and all his Library; after him another gave 300 [pounds]; others after them cast in more, and the publique hand of

the State added the rest: the Colledge was, by common consent, appointed to be at *Cambridge* (a place very pleasant and accommodate) and is called (according to the name of the first founder) *Harvard Colledge*. (Quoted in Harvard University 1930:5)

Thus began the institution Harvard, America's first college. And long before any archaeological or anthropological training existed anywhere in North America, some Harvard graduates took up archaeological activities—simple and straightforward excavations like the early archaeological fieldwork being done all over Europe. Late eighteenth- and early nineteenth-century European philology focused mainly on classical archaeology, and for English antiquarians that included everything from Greco-Roman finds to exciting Egyptian tomb discoveries. A few scholars at Harvard were involved in similar research.

John C. Greene (Harvard Ph.D. 1952), in his *American Science in the Age of Jefferson* (1984), carefully described the general development of American sciences during the Jeffersonian period, the 1780s to the 1820s. Greene explained in his preface (1984:xxi) that his narrative presentation was not strongly analytical but instead provided readers with significant data about the actual findings and how they were discovered. He allowed readers to draw their own conclusions about the value of the results. We follow a similar path in our presentation here.

Greene's volume has three chapters covering what would now be called bio-anthropology, archaeology, and linguistics. Ethnography, anthropology's fourth field, is left out. In Greene's "archaeological" chapter (1984:343–75), readers are introduced to a rather negative inaugural address delivered in November 1780 by **James Bowdoin** (1726–90), Harvard class of 1745. As the new president of the American Academy of Arts and Sciences, Bowdoin called attention to the academy's stated purpose: "to promote and encourage the knowledge of antiquities of America" (Greene 1984:343). Bowdoin believed this could not be done among the "uncivilized" American Indians. Other Harvard graduates of the period would show how wrong he was.

In 1786, just six years after Bowdoin's address, a group of Massachusetts men formed the "Ohio Company of Associates" (Hurt 1996:155). Established to settle what was then called the Northwest Territory, the Ohio Company's members included three with Harvard degrees: Manasseh Cutler, Samuel Holden Parsons, and Winthrop Sargent. These men founded the company's settlement at Marietta, Ohio, in 1788, on an archaeological site—a piece of property covered with Indian mounds and an enclosing embankment (Greene 1984:344). James Bowdoin's son, James Bowdoin II (Harvard A.B. 1771) was an investor in the Marietta project (Kershaw 1999:273). Although theirs was certainly not the first discovery of a complex of Indian mounds and enclosures, this site would be studied in a way that would help shape American archaeology for the future. It was of interest not only to the new Ohio settlers, some of whom would continue archaeological investigations elsewhere, but also to two Ivy League college presidents—Ezra Stiles at Yale and Joseph Willard at Harvard—who discussed the Marietta finds in 1786 and 1787, and to a future American president, Thomas Jefferson, who learned of the discoveries and wrote to Stiles about them on September 1, 1786 (Greene 1984:344–45; Williams 1991:28–31).

Two of the Harvard-affiliated men contributed to the early mapping of the Marietta site. **Samuel Holden Parsons** (1737–89; Harvard A.B. 1756), who was Indian commissioner for the United States from 1783 to 1787, drew a poor-quality sketch map (Parsons 1793). A fine, finished map was made by Winthrop Sargent, chief aide to General Rufus Putnam, who was in charge of the whole operation, but it was not published until some years later (Sargent 1799).

Reverend **Manasseh Cutler** (1742–1823; Harvard honorary A.B. 1770) also visited the Marietta mounds. Cutler, who had a passion for botany, arranged to have a number of the largest trees on the mounds felled so he might count the tree rings as an estimate of minimum age for the mounds. He reported that the largest trees had between 300 and 400 rings, with one tree having at least 463 (Cutler 1888 [1798]). Hence, he estimated that the site was at least this old. His was the first published attempt in the United States to try to define mound antiquity in a scientific manner and the first use of dating based on tree rings in the New World.

Winthrop Sargent (1753–1820; Harvard A.B. 1771), the son of an old Boston-area family, was born in Massachusetts and entered Harvard College in Cambridge as a boy of only 13. He was no child prodigy; many, if not most, of the members of the class of 1771 were that age when they began college, and they would graduate at 17 or 18. After graduation, Sargent served in the American Revolutionary War, advancing to the rank of major. His activities introduced him to a number of notables in Philadelphia and elsewhere, including Thomas Jefferson and Benjamin Franklin. It was Franklin who encouraged Sargent to become a member of the American Philosophical Society before Sargent went west with the Ohio Company. Sargent had been commissioned in 1786 by Thomas Hutchins (1730–89), President George Washington's geographer of the United States, as one of eight surveyors to evaluate the public land of the Ohio River area. The surveyors sent back glowing reports of the new land, and five of them joined with Massachusetts investors to form the Ohio Company of Associates. Sargent was elected the company's secretary in 1787 (Hurt 1996:148–50).

The Ohio Company had decided on "Adelphia" (renamed Marietta within three months) as the location of its first settlement, and its members soon began to investigate the Indian mounds at the site. As the official surveyor of the settlement, Sargent drew a detailed map of the Marietta mounds that was sent to the American Academy of Arts and Sciences in Boston in 1799 but was not published for more than half a century (H. Bowditch 1855; Williams 1991:29–30). When he returned to Cambridge in 1788, Sargent brought back some turtles and other biological specimens from Ohio for Harvard's natural history collections.

Sargent was later sent to Cincinnati's military post, Fort Washington, as territorial secretary of Ohio, thus becoming the first secretary of the Northwest Territories. He lived on a hill, and as the town grew larger, some roadwork near his home cut through a prehistoric mound. On August 30, 1794, Sargent recovered 10 artifacts from one extended burial in the mound—copper ear spools, a panpipe, stone pendants, hematite and other minerals—drew them, and wrote a brief description of what we now know were Hopewell culture materials. Sargent published a newspaper article on these finds and sent a report to *Massachusetts Magazine* in Boston (Williams 1987:6). He also sent a report to Dr. Benjamin Smith Barton at the American Philosophical Society, where it was read into the record in May 1796 and published along with some well-executed illustrations in *Transactions of the American Philosophical Society* (Sargent 1799). For North American archaeology, Sargent's materials were "the first *excavated* archaeological finds published in the United States" (Williams 1991:37). Sargent sent the artifacts themselves to the American Philosophical Society, which eventually turned them over to the University Museum at the University of Pennsylvania (Williams 1991:36).

But Winthrop Sargent had larger political goals than could be realized in Ohio. In 1798 he was transferred from Cincinnati to Natchez, where he became the first governor of Mississippi Territory. He was removed from office in 1801. During his first year in Natchez he met and married Margaret McIntosh Williams, a well-to-do widow, and he spent the rest of his life on a handsome plantation called Gloster near that town.

Sargent did not give up on archaeological matters, and at some point he acquired from a local planter a handsome stone sculpture of a seated figure. We do not know the sculpture's provenience, other than that it came from the Natchez area, but a number of important nearby sites could have produced the artifact. Sometime after acquiring this Mississippian period object (A.D. 1200–1400), Sargent sent it to the American Antiquarian Society in Worcester, Massachusetts, of which he was a member, perhaps in the care of his son, George Washington Sargent (1802–64; Harvard class of 1820). The person in charge of the Antiquarian Society at this time, Samuel Foster Haven, was also a Harvard graduate.

This stone sculpture from the Natchez region would have an interesting history of its own. Many years later the American Antiquarian Society divested itself of all its archaeological materials, starting in the 1890s and completing the transactions by World War I, in order to transform itself into a library more than a museum. By good chance or purpose, the archaeological specimens were turned over to the Peabody Museum, and Sargent's stone sculpture ended up in Cambridge, a place its donor had known well. Indeed, it spent a decade or more on a shelf in Stephen Williams's Peabody office.

It was not only antiquities that drew some Harvard graduates' interest toward American Indians. In the case of **John Pickering** (1777–1846; Harvard A.B., A.M. 1796), of Salem, Massachusetts, his linguistic skills led in that direction. Pickering first joined his father, Timothy Pickering, in Philadelphia in 1796 to pursue a legal career. Timothy Pickering (1745–1829), a member of the Harvard class of 1763, served as postmaster general from 1791 to 1795 and as secretary of war from 1795 to 1800 in the cabinet of John Adams. Following his father into public service, John Pickering was secretary to the American legations in Portugal and England and then returned to Boston to practice law. He became a member of the Massachusetts State House of Representatives and later of the State Senate (Mitra 1933:91). From 1818 to 1842 he served Harvard as an overseer.

Pickering had achieved a mastery of Greek and French while at Harvard, although he turned down an offer of the Eliot Professorship of Greek at Harvard in 1806 (Greene 1984:397). Believing that a considerable amount of historical data could be secured from living Native American groups, he began studying Indian languages in 1810. Over the next decade he worked out a phonetic system for writing Indian languages, which was employed by scholars for many years. In 1820 he presented his system to the American Academy of Arts and Sciences (of which he later became president), and he published it that year as *An Essay on a Uniform Orthography for the Indian Languages of North America* (Pickering 1820).

Looking at what we would now call bioanthropology, we find **John Collins Warren** (1778–1856), who received his A.B. and A.M. from Harvard in 1797 and went on to become Hersey Professor of Anatomy and Surgery there. Warren also "studied anatomy, including some comparative anatomy, with the best teachers in Paris" (Greene 1984:336). In his 1822 *Comparative View of the Sensorial and Nervous Systems in Men and Animals,* the first American work on comparative anatomy, Warren addressed the problem of American Indian origins. He examined reports of skeletal remains excavated by various "scientists" and collectors, although he recognized that the problem of Indian origins could not be solved by physical comparison alone (Greene 1984:341). Among the materials he described were skulls from the Pacific coast that had artificial flattening. Warren argued that the brain could undergo substantial alterations in shape without any corresponding change in intellectual ability, a dramatic determination for his day. He also described human physical remains from sites in the Boston area and from the Grave Creek mound near Wheeling, West Virginia, first described by the founders of Marietta (Greene 1984:339).

The question of the racial identification of American Indians continued to interest him, alongside his successful career as dean and professor in the Harvard medical school. In 1837, for example, Warren presented a paper titled "Some Remarks on the Crania of the Mound Indians of the Interior of North America, as Compared with the Crania of the South American Indians of Peru" at a scientific gathering in Liverpool, England. Later he donated Peruvian skulls from the Lake Titicaca area as type-examples to the Boston Society of Natural History (E. Warren 1860, 1:328, 2:5).

Warren secured the first complete skeleton of an American mastodon from an amateur excavation near Newburgh, New York, in 1845. The Warren mastodon was reconstructed with advice from some of the leading naturalists of the day—Charles Lyell, Louis Agassiz, Jeffries Wyman, and William E. Horner (J. Warren 1855:8).

Warren's occasional ventures into direct archaeological work were limited mainly to the Old World. The Dutch firm of van Lennep and Company, which had license to trade with the Ottoman Empire, donated an Egyptian mummy, "Padihershef," to the Massachusetts General Hospital in 1823 as an anatomical specimen. (We know the mummy's name, occupation, and place of origin because Egyptologists at Boston's Museum of Fine Arts translated the coffin's painted hieroglyphics in the 1960s, although their work was not published until 1984.) For many years, Padihershef resided in the hospital's operating room. The mummy became famous when Warren, who was a surgeon at Massachusetts General Hospital, unwrapped its 25 thicknesses of bandages before an audience of scientific men in the hospital's operating amphitheater and then published an illustrated report in volume 1 of the *Boston Journal of Philosophy and the Arts* in 1824. Warren also used his position somewhat later, in 1856, to secure a dozen antique stone sculptures from the Assyrian site of Nineveh for the Boston Society of Natural History (E. Warren 1860, 2:279).

As Harvard moved into the nineteenth century, antiquities continued to exert their pull on some of its graduates. One such person, a member of the class of 1800, was **Timothy Flint** (1780–1840). Like most of the college's students in this period, he was from New England—North Reading, Massachusetts. He had attended Phillips Academy at Andover, Massachusetts, and entered Harvard in 1796. As his later travels indicate, he was something of a free spirit, although his career ambition upon graduation was the ministry. He served for a decade or more as a Congregational minister in his home state, but he eventually grew tired of it and in 1815 accepted an appointment as a Presbyterian missionary west of the Alleghenies.

Most of what we know about Timothy Flint comes from his own pen, for he became a well-known and often-read writer in the next decade. Although few people today have heard of him, his *Recollections of the Last Ten Years . . . in the Valley of the Mississippi* (1826) was a best seller at the time. It was followed in 1828 by *The Condensed History and Geography of the Western States, or the Mississippi Valley*. Modern historians consider him one of the most influential Western writers of his period (Lamar 1998:375).

The Harvard-trained Flint involved himself in archaeology in some interesting and surprising ways. The Ohio and Mississippi River valleys, major gateways to the West for all Easterners in the post–Revolutionary War years, were strewn with large, easily visible earthen monuments. The Ohio Company had settled in the midst of one of them at Marietta, as had Sargent at his home in downtown Cincinnati. People making the trip from Pittsburgh, on the Ohio, to its confluence with the Mississippi in Illinois could not miss them. For example, the Grave Creek mound in West Virginia measures 69 feet high and 295 feet in diameter. It became a well-known landmark and was attacked archaeologically very early on.

Despite all the literature about the mounds available then and now, Flint did several things that deserve comment. For a year or two he owned a small farm north of St. Louis, on the Missouri River near St. Charles. While working the land near some mounds on his property, he ran into a midden full of pottery:

> Directly back of my house, were two conical mounds of considerable elevation. A hundred paces in front of them, was a high bench, making the shore of the "Marais

Croche," an extensive marsh, and evidently the former bed of the Missouri. In digging a ditch on the margin of this bench, at the depth of four feet, we discovered great quantities of broken pottery, belonging to vessels of all sizes and characters. Some must have been of a size to contain four gallons. (Flint 1826:121)

A few pages on, he provided a more detailed description of the pottery: "I have examined the pottery, of which I have spoken above, with some attention. . . . It is evident, from slight departures from regularity in the surface, that it was molded by the hand and not by any thing like our lathe. The composition, when fractured, shows many white floccules in the clay that resemble fine snow, and this I judge to be pulverized shells" (Flint 1826:127). This description seems to be the earliest published reference to what is now called "shell tempering."

Flint went on to discuss the fact that pottery similar to this was often found along the banks of the Mississippi. At great length he described a pottery vessel in his possession. It was a gourd-shaped "drinking jug," smooth and gray, and could contain two quarts of liquid. On top of the vessel was the head of a "squaw" with an open mouth: "Although the finish was fine, the head was monstrous. There seemed to have been an intention of wit in the outlet. It was the horrible and distorted mouth of a savage, and in drinking you would be obliged to place your lips in contact with those of the madam, the squaw" (Flint 1826:127). We would now call this a "hooded bottle."

News of the mounds "out West," as well as general curiosity about the inhabitants of the continent, led the scholars of the day to decide that a more orderly means of data collection was desired. Learned associations such as the American Philosophical Society turned their attention to this problem. The job fell to **Thomas Jefferson** (1743–1826), who held a Harvard honorary LL.D. (1787). In 1799 Jefferson, then president of the American Philosophical Society, and several of his colleagues on a society subcommittee developed a circular that they sent to the leaders of all major exploring expeditions, as well as to smaller operations going west, asking them "to obtain accurate plans, drawings and descriptions of whatever is interesting (where the originals cannot be had), and especially of ancient fortifications, tumuli, and other Indian works of art; [and to ascertain] the materials composing them, their contents, the purposes for which they were probably designed, etc." They explained that

> the committee are desirous that cuts in various directions may be made into many of the tumuli, to ascertain their contents; while the diameter of the largest tree growing thereon, the number of its annulars and the species of the tree, may tend to give some idea of their antiquity. If the works should be found to be of masonry; the length, breadth, and height of the walls ought to be carefully measured, the form and nature of the stones described, and specimens of both the cement and stones sent to the committee. (Jefferson et al. 1799:xxxvii–xxxviii).

These instructions set the parameters of much of the archaeological research done in the United States for the next half century.

Thomas Jefferson is perhaps better known to archaeological historians for his burial mound excavation near his homestead, Monticello, carried out in about 1770 and reported in "Notes on the State of Virginia" (Jefferson 1784). Jefferson had been familiar with Indians since boyhood, had read everything he could concerning them, and had collected vocabularies and artifacts for many years. He believed the American Indians had reasonable antiquity, finding the most logical explanation for the large number of American Indian languages to be their having undergone diversification for a long period of time (Greene 1984:321–22).

In 1780, the king of France had sent a questionnaire to Jefferson, in his position as governor of Virginia, as well as to the governors of the other colonies, asking them about New World geography, zoology, botany, geology, and history. Its purpose was to help the French assess what they might do about their colonies in present-day Canada. Among the topics covered in Jefferson's reply to the king was his own mound exploration.

The specifics of Jefferson's work are modest from the perspective of modern archaeology. But we must remember that this was a "first." Indian burial mounds had been excavated earlier on the East Coast, but none had been detailed to any extent. Jefferson did not discover or collect artifacts of any kind—just human skeletal remains. His commentary, however, did detail his method of excavation, and it described the four strata he observed in the trench that his slaves excavated into the mound. Thus the third president of the United States made some of the first post-facto stratigraphic observations known in Americanist archaeology. But because his description was published in a political document, his pioneering work was largely overlooked by anthropological students for the next century and a half.

Jefferson's interest in archaeology was shared by others of his Harvard-affiliated colleagues. **Albert Gallatin** (1761–1849), Jefferson's secretary of the treasury from 1801 to 1803, during the fateful Louisiana Purchase, had some Harvard roots, having taught French there in 1782–83 (Harvard 1930:79). His important *Synopsis of the Indian Tribes,* mainly an ethnological and linguistic treatise, was inspired by contact with Alexander von Humboldt, the German naturalist and explorer. Gallatin first met Humboldt in 1804 and saw him again in Paris several times between 1816 and 1823, when Gallatin was U.S. minister plenipotentiary to France (Greene 1984:403). In 1836, after 13 years of research, he published his synopsis volume in *Transactions and Collections of the American Antiquarian Society.*

Gallatin and his friend John Russell Bartlett (1805–86) were the main movers behind the founding of the American Ethnological Society (AES) in 1842. The AES was an important clearinghouse for people interested in anthropological investigations at this period, and its officers became intimately acquainted with the state of research. Gallatin was president of the AES when Ohio newspaper editor and antiquarian Ephraim G. Squier (1821–88) came calling in 1846, to see whether the AES would publish the lengthy work on the Ohio mounds that Squier was writing with physician Edwin Hamilton Davis (1811–88). Gallatin and Bartlett agreed in 1846 to publish the results of Squier and

Davis's mound research, but only in a shorter, summary volume. Squier then went looking for alternative sources, trying the American Academy of Arts and Sciences and the American Antiquarian Society. These groups, too, expressed interest but could manage only the same sort of reduced coverage that the AES offered (Barnhart 2005:40). In the spring of 1847, Gallatin mentioned to Squier that Joseph Henry (1797–1878), the first secretary of the newly formed Smithsonian Institution, was looking for manuscripts in order to launch a publication series and might have the financial resources to publish the massive number of illustrations and descriptions that Squier and Davis had compiled. Their book *Ancient Monuments of the Mississippi Valley* (1848) became the Smithsonian's first published book.

Another person long associated with the American Antiquarian Society who made important archaeological contributions was **Samuel Foster Haven** (1806–81). Haven, born in Dedham, Massachusetts, entered Harvard with the class of 1826 but finished his undergraduate work at Amherst, receiving his A.B. there that year. When he received his A.M. from Harvard in 1852, Haven was granted a retroactive Harvard A.B. as well (Harvard 1930:227). After receiving his 1826 degree, he practiced law, but in 1837 he was offered the post of librarian at the American Antiquarian Society, a position he kept until shortly before his death in 1881 (Willey 1973:vii).

In this position, Haven wrote a number of books on New England history. For many years he edited the society's *Proceedings* and *Transactions*, often contributing papers on American history and archaeology. Like John Bartlett at the American Ethnological Society, Haven was often the institutional person visited by prospective explorers. For example, he encouraged Stephen Salisbury Jr. to travel to Yucatán to view Maya ruins and to publish the results of these travels in *Proceedings of the American Antiquarian Society* (Willey 1973:vii). Bartlett, similarly, had introduced the explorer John Lloyd Stephens to Maya studies, showing him the book by Jean-Frederic Maximillien, Count de Waldeck, on the ruins of Yucatán.

At the Antiquarian Society, Haven earned a reputation for his dedication to the institution and was admired for his scholarly achievements. In 1854, when the library had outgrown its first building in Worcester, he presided over the construction of the new building in Lincoln Square and oversaw its expansion in 1876. He also served as a member of the society's council from 1855 until 1881.

But Haven is best known for his influential summary of Americanist archaeology, based on research conducted by many people during his years as the Society's librarian. This 1856 volume, *Archaeology of the United States, or, Sketches, Historical and Bibliographical, of the Progress of Information and Opinion respecting Vestiges of Antiquity in the United States,* was the touchstone for researchers for many years thereafter. His study was "a model of reasoned description and discussion in comparison with the speculative works that had dominated the literature until then. Haven's archaeological outlook typified the new, increasingly professionalized descriptive trend, which was to dominate the period [1840–1914] by its close" (Willey and Sabloff 1993:44).

George Gibbs IV (1815–73), the last of the figures we treat in this chapter, overlapped temporally with those in the next two chapters, but his career trajectory fits more comfortably here. He was the older brother of Wolcott Gibbs (1822–1908), a chemist at the Lawrence Scientific School at Harvard whom we discuss in chapter 2. George Gibbs was born in Long Island, New York, and originally took a course of studies that his family hoped would lead to an appointment to West Point. He seems to have become intrigued with Americanist studies from his prep school days, when he stayed with the historian George Bancroft while attending Bancroft's Round Hills School (Stevens 1874:220).

Gibbs began law studies at Harvard in 1834 but left in 1836 to take a two-year break with his aunt, touring Europe (Beckham 1969:36). After receiving his law degree in 1838, he practiced law in a low-key manner in New York for the next decade. He began his first inquiries into antiquarian affairs with the exploration in early 1840 of a prehistoric burial found along Fall River near Troy, Massachusetts (Beckham 1969:41). He had joined the New York Historical Society in 1839 and became its librarian in 1843. In that position he began communicating with Albert Gallatin and John R. Bartlett at the AES on their shared interest in American Indian languages and ethnology (Beckham 1969:42, 234).

In 1849 Gibbs left New York to try his hand in the California gold rush. He had no luck in the gold fields but picked up employment with the government on a series of railroad and geological surveys over the next decade, working as a naturalist, geologist, and cartographer, mainly in Oregon, Washington, and California. He also spent a season with William H. Dall, whom we introduce in chapter 3, in Alaska, and he picked up a little support freelancing as a collector for Louis Agassiz, Asa Gray, and other eastern researchers (Beckham 1969:121, 364; Stevens 1874:222). Gibbs's own research during this period was focused primarily on linguistics, because one thing he wanted to do was to see whether he could discover the aboriginal migration route from Asia to North America via linguistic analysis.

Gibbs's reports to his government employers in 1853 and 1854 included significant information about the political organization of tribes and innumerable notes on the material culture and languages of Indian groups (Beckham 1969:143). This work brought him to the attention of explorer, geologist, and self-taught ethnographer Henry Rowe Schoolcraft (1793–1864), who was in the midst of completing a massive synthesis of information about American Indian tribes, and Schoolcraft wrote to Gibbs requesting information on the nature of Indian ruins in Oregon and Washington. Gibbs was clearly much more interested in the language of the surviving Indian groups, for his initial reports back to Schoolcraft were that there were "no antiquities in Oregon." Apparently, to Gibbs the antiquities of importance were mounds, and he reported in a series of letters to Schoolcraft in 1853 that there were no mounds in Oregon or Washington. In his last notice, he finally reported observing one mound on the Yakima River, which measured 50 yards in diameter and 1 yard in height, with some petroglyphs also to be found in the area (Gibbs 1855, 5:664–65).

When Gibbs left the Pacific Northwest after 11 years to return first to New York and then to Washington, D.C., he had notebooks full of ethnographic and linguistic data and a massive ethnographic artifact collection (Beckham 1969:224). Although he worked for the Smithsonian Institution for the next decade, Gibbs had no formal appointment there until 1867. For the first few years he apparently relied on "piecework" projects from Joseph Henry.

Henry saw the potential relevance of the method and theory being developed by researchers in Old World archaeology to the study of American antiquities, and he saw the Smithsonian's publication series as an excellent means to introduce these ideas to American researchers. Beginning in 1860 he initiated a series of five translated papers, summarizing important European advances, beginning with the work of Adolphe von Morlot (Bourque 2002:150).

Gibbs had been trying to convince Henry to hire him to create a master ethnological mapping scheme. Henry was reluctant. "To generate further interest and obtain additional information, Gibbs offered to author a philological circular and devise a set of maps to be sent out by the Smithsonian to assistants all over North America" (Beckham 1969:234 n. 19, Gibbs to Henry, November 7, 1862). He prepared two circulars with instructions in excavation methodology for private collectors wishing to secure materials for the Smithsonian and the U.S. National Museum (Gibbs 1862, 1867 [1863]).

Gibbs's instructions were quite sophisticated (Browman 2002b:244), particularly for a man who only a few years earlier had trouble finding archaeological sites. For example, he suggested that an excavator of a burial mound or shell midden should note whether it "exhibited any marks of stratification." If any artifacts were found, "the depth at which they were discovered" should be noted, and researchers should count the annual rings of any tree growing on a mound to get an estimate of its age (Gibbs 1862:395, 1867 [1863]:6). For cave excavation, Gibbs's instructions were even more avant-garde, suggesting that "the superficial earth should be carefully removed over a considerable space and results, if any, being kept separate and marked accordingly.... underlying materials should then be cautiously removed and sorted over, each layer being kept by itself. ... every fragment of bone or other evidence of animal life should thus be preserved and marked with order of its succession in depth" (Gibbs 1862:395–96).

The source of Gibbs's archaeological instructions was an enigma to us for many years, for he had little knowledge of archaeology. When we read the letter of November 7, 1862, from Gibbs to Henry (Beckham 1969:234 n. 19), the pieces finally fell into place. To secure access to the linguistic data at the Smithsonian, he agreed to create an archaeological circular for Joseph Henry. But to do so, he had to rely on the expertise of others. He used the European sources that Henry had been collecting, copying the cave excavation instructions from the work of William Pengelly and the mound excavation instructions from Adolphe von Morlot. The Smithsonian Institution ended up with some first-rate instructions for excavation, although, regrettably, collectors for the Smithsonian and the U.S. National Museum failed to follow them until nearly half a century later.

Gibbs's second circular included a substantial section on how to conduct philological and linguistic investigations. Although this was an area of particular interest to Gibbs, he apparently employed the assistance of William Dwight Whitney, from the Smithsonian Institution, in creating these instructions (Hinsley 1981:47). Gibbs had come to the Smithsonian with some 50 to 60 vocabularies he had collected on his own, and over the next decade he was given nearly carte blanche to research and codify materials that the Smithsonian had collected. He helped develop the vocabulary word list used by Smithsonian field-workers, later taken over by John Wesley Powell. According to Stephen Dow Beckham (1969:257), there are more than 100 vocabularies in Gibbs's handwriting in the Smithsonian archives, the additional 40 to 50 beyond his own having been based on his work for the Smithsonian from 1860 to 1870.

Like others of his era, Gibbs, although he conducted serious research, became interested in what we would now consider Americanist anthropology only avocationally. No training had yet been instituted in any aspect of anthropological research in the United States. Indeed, the association between the subjects of this chapter and Harvard University is almost incidental, for although it was one of the few places in the United States where able scholars were trained, it had not developed a research focus on Americanist prehistoric studies. The first half of the nineteenth century had seen a rapid expansion of the U.S. population beyond the Appalachian Mountains to the Pacific Ocean, with a concomitantly broader understanding of the variations of North American Indian cultures. This experience was reflected in part by the growing sophistication of the commentary on the continent's first peoples.

Willey and Sabloff (1993) saw this time as marking the shift from their Speculative period, in which the collection of archaeological data was incidental to other pursuits, to the Classificatory–Historical Descriptive period, with its new emphasis on the description of archaeological sites and materials. If Timothy Flint and Winthrop Sargent fall more into the incidental collection of data, then George Gibbs and Samuel Foster Haven certainly mark the beginning of this new descriptive phase. Perhaps the most important development in terms of the ultimate professionalization of the discipline was the interest of the learned societies, such as the American Academy of Arts and Sciences, the American Antiquarian Society, the American Ethnological Society, and the American Philosophical Society, in uncovering the roots of the original inhabitants of the continent.

2

The Lawrence Scientific School, the Museum of Comparative Zoology, and the Peabody Museum, 1847–1866

THE GROWTH OF ANTHROPOLOGY AT HARVARD in the second half of the nineteenth century stemmed from the interests and skills of the professional staff assembled at three interrelated Harvard institutions. The first was the Lawrence Scientific School, founded in 1847 as a separate arm of Harvard College, and the second was the allied Museum of Comparative Zoology, opened in 1859. The third—and ultimately the most important for anthropology—was the Peabody Museum of American Archaeology and Ethnology, as it was originally called, launched in 1866.

Among the staff members of these institutions, three were the most influential in training students and shaping the trajectory of anthropology at Harvard and elsewhere at the time: Asa Gray, Jeffries Wyman, and Louis Agassiz. All three had earned M.D. degrees—Agassiz in 1830, Gray in 1831, and Wyman in 1837—but none of them ever practiced medicine (Putnam 1888f:486). Their tenure overlapped closely. Gray taught in Harvard from 1842 to 1873, Agassiz from 1847 to 1873, and Wyman from 1847 to 1874 (Appel 1988:69).

In this chapter we recount the founding of the Lawrence Scientific School, the Museum of Comparative Zoology, and the Peabody Museum and the role played by each of these three men, with additional consideration of other actors in these and related events. What was each man's background, and how were his anthropological concerns expressed? A recurring theme is the interactions of the professional staff with the students who became involved in anthropological research through their influence, especially our central figure, Frederic W. Putnam, who came to Harvard to study at the Lawrence School under the renowned naturalist Louis Agassiz.

Jean Louis Rodolphe Agassiz (1807–73) had been born in Switzerland. After receiving both a Ph.D. and an M.D. at German universities, he went to Paris, where he studied for a year with Alexander von Humboldt and Georges Cuvier, with a focus on fossil fishes. In 1832 he returned to the University of Neuchâtel in Switzerland, where he studied fossil fishes, wrote one of the first expositions of glacial movements and deposits (to some, one of his most important contributions), and helped turn the university into a noted center for scientific study. His major paleontological work during this period, the five-volume *Recherches sur les poissons fossiles,* published between 1833 and 1843, was dedicated to von Humboldt (Guyot 1878:54).

Agassiz's work with fossils and glaciers had brought him into contact with the noted geologist Charles Lyell (1797–1875) in England. In 1841–42 Lyell had been involved in a successful lecture and research tour in the United States, and he was scheduled to embark on another tour in 1845–46 (L. Wilson 1998). In early 1845 Agassiz wrote to Lyell saying that he, too, was planning to go to the United States to give public lectures and asking Lyell's advice. Lyell immediately suggested that Agassiz investigate the lecture series sponsored by an organization called the Lowell Institute as a possible venue. In a classic example of the fruits of networking, Agassiz's association with the Lowell Institute would lead to the founding of the Lawrence Scientific School.

The Lowell Institute was run by **John Amory Lowell** (Harvard class of 1815), whom Lyell had come to know in Boston. Among other things, it offered a subscription series of public lectures on cutting-edge scientific discoveries of the day, and it was the locus for some early discussions of anthropological and archaeological issues. The geological specialist J. Peter Lesley (1819–1903), for example, gave a lecture series titled "Anthropology" in 1865–66, and the Reverend Ebenezer Burgess gave lectures on "The Archaeology of India" in 1865–66. In view of the tender age of the terms *anthropology* and *archaeology* for the disciplines at the time, these lecture titles make the Lowell Institute look avant-garde. Many of the important actors in this chapter, including Asa Gray and Jeffries Wyman, were frequent presenters during the first 30 years of the Lowell Institute (H. K. Smith 1895:726, 729).

Charles Lyell wrote directly to his friend John Lowell asking him to invite Louis Agassiz to speak (H. Smith 1895:724), and in May 1845 Agassiz wrote to Lyell with the good news that Lowell had asked him to give the lecture series for the winter of 1846 (Lyell was giving the fall 1845 series). Lyell wrote back cautioning him that the lectures had to be in English (L. Wilson 1998:145).

Agassiz's 1846 lecture series, "The Plan of Creation as Shown in the Animal Kingdom," drew 5,000 people for its first presentation, and Agassiz had to repeat his talks to the overflow audience on subsequent days (Bruce 1987:116). He included in these lectures the first use of the stereopticon at the Lowell Institute, which was much commented upon by the audience. So successful were Agassiz's lectures that John Lowell, wanting to keep him available as a speaker for the institute, became involved in a scheme to create a scientific institute at Harvard to provide a venue ensuring that Agassiz would come again in 1847.

In 1846 Harvard's new president, Edward Everett, prompted partially by his own German university experience, had called for the establishment of both a school of science and a graduate program at Harvard. Harvard professor Benjamin Peirce had previously made a similar suggestion for a scientific school and had drawn up a plan, which the faculty had discussed without taking action (M. James 1992:69). President

Everett and John Lowell together took the idea of a special, dedicated science program to the technology-conscious railroad and textile millionaire Abbott Lawrence (1792–1855), who agreed to fund an applied scientific school at Harvard. When founded in 1847, it became known as the Lawrence Scientific School. (Lawrence's grandson, Abbott Lawrence Lowell, would become Harvard University president in 1909.) Eben Norton Horsford was named to chair the new school, and Louis Agassiz joined him as the second member of the staff.

Eben Norton Horsford (1818–93) had grown up in New York state, where his father was a missionary to the Seneca Indians, so he had a long-standing interest in Indian matters and local history. After graduating from Rensselaer Polytechnic Institute he went to Germany, where he received additional training in chemistry. When Abbott Lawrence endowed the Lawrence Scientific School in 1847, Horsford was chosen to head it, in addition to becoming the third Rumford Professor for the Application of the Sciences to the Useful Arts, a chair transferred at the time from Harvard College to the Lawrence School (Dupree 1959:149; C. Elliott 1992:342; M. James 1992:69). Horsford was named dean of Lawrence in 1861, but he was by then becoming increasingly heavily involved in his private business affairs. In January 1863 he resigned to focus his energies full-time on his burgeoning industrial and agricultural chemistry business, Horsford Chemical Works, in Providence, Rhode Island, where he subsequently made a fortune (Bruce 1987:283).

In the 1870s Horsford became interested in looking for lost Viking villages in New England. By 1888 he claimed to have located "Leif Ericson's house in Vinland on the banks of the Charles not many blocks from his own home" in Cambridge, and he placed a presumed Viking settlement called "Norumbega" on a high point "overlooking the junction of Stoney Brook and the Charles, in Weston," just a few miles from Harvard (S. Williams 1991:207–8). Not everyone in Cambridge was happy about this. One contemporary writer criticized Horsford for the "most incautious linguistic inferences and the most uncritical cartographic perversions" (Winsor 1889, 1:88).

It was the renowned Louis Agassiz, though, who was seen as Harvard's prize catch upon the founding of the Lawrence Scientific School. The professionalization of science at Harvard with the establishment of the school was part of the emergence of a "self-conscious American scientific estate" (McCaughey 1974:266) in the mid-nineteenth century, a development that can also be seen in events such as the founding of the Smithsonian Institution in 1846 and of the American Association for the Advancement of Science (AAAS) out of the old Association of American Geologists and Naturalists in 1848, with Agassiz as one of its founders. Lawrence's initial wish for an applied scientific institute, however, was diverted as Agassiz changed the school into a research institute along the lines he had previously achieved at the University of Neuchâtel (Sinclair 1992:77).

Until 1871 the Lawrence Scientific School (1847–1906) was the only place at Harvard that offered advanced instruction in physical and natural sciences (Hughes 1930:413). By

1849 Lawrence had three of its own professors: Horsford, Agassiz, and Henry E. Eustis, in engineering. Working with them was an additional group of scientists with primary appointments in Harvard College, including Jeffries Wyman, Asa Gray, Benjamin Peirce, and Daniel Treadwell (Rossiter 1975:78). Although the school's focus was on science, it had no meaningful entrance exam, offered no courses common to all students, and required no special knowledge for the S.B. degree other than the study done under one professor. Its regulations required a minimum residence of one year to obtain a degree, although most students took two or three years to do so (Browman 2002a:212; Bruce 1987:328).

Louis Agassiz's great dream was to establish a research museum. It was fulfilled when the Museum of Comparative Zoology (MCZ) was built at Harvard and officially opened in 1859 under his supervision. In the way he organized the museum's exhibits, Agassiz would exert one of his most important influences over Frederic Putnam and his fellow students. Agassiz noted that all similar museums were arranged by supposed natural affinities—that is, by inferred lines of evolutionary descent—but he "intended to arrange the Cambridge Zoological Museum in a totally different manner, viz.: according to natural zoological provinces" (Agassiz 1859:191). Thus, his students were already being trained in a new method of museum arrangement nearly 30 years before Franz Boas made the case to the Smithsonian Institution that anthropological exhibits should be arranged by culture area (Boas 1887b, 1887c, 1887d). Historians of American sociocultural anthropology have often seen Boas's position as paradigm-shattering, but we suggest that it was fostered in part by his association in the late 1880s with Frederic Putnam, whom Agassiz had already trained in organizing and displaying scientific materials by natural provinces (Browman 2002d:517 n. 2).

Louis Agassiz contributed greatly to the growth of American natural sciences, as Edward Lurie well detailed in his 1960 biography of Agassiz. Lurie observed, however, that for all his greatness, Agassiz was unable to accept other naturalists on a level of equality, and as a result, he fell out with many of his European colleagues and almost all of his American ones. His approach to teaching students was similarly handicapped by his Germanic attitudes. Agassiz was a "fascinating lecturer, gifted with eloquence which won its way everywhere" (Billings 1889:158), so he was able to recruit students to his program, particularly after the MCZ was completed. But Agassiz patronized his students, telling them that as their professor, he knew they were not yet ready to set out on their own. This attitude would lead to a rift known as the "Salem secession," described in the next chapter, although Agassiz would make peace with his rebellious students. Asa Gray and Jeffries Wyman, in contrast, had been inculcated with the American ideal of egalitarianism and treated their students essentially as equals, encouraging their independence (Appel 1992:108).

During his American years, Agassiz shifted toward institutional development and political activism. His contributions are measured more by what he did "for" science in this country, such as working to establish the MCZ and the National Academy of

Sciences, which he helped start in 1863, than by what he did "in" science (Bruce 1987:233). It did not hurt that he was tied closely to the Harvard power structure through marriage (Story 1980:87). Agassiz's first wife had died in 1848, shortly after he came to the United States, and in 1850 he married Mary Elizabeth Cabot Cary, daughter of Thomas G. Cary. Mary Elizabeth Cary's sister had married Cornelius Felton, a Harvard professor of Greek who later served as Harvard College president. Elizabeth herself, after Agassiz's death, became involved in the founding of the School for the Collegiate Instruction of Women at Harvard in 1879, and when it changed its name to Radcliffe College in 1893, she became the first president of Radcliffe (Browman 2002b:222–24).

Agassiz's institutional focus continued in his later years. In 1868 he spent two months in Ithaca, New York, where he helped found Cornell University and saw two of his students, Burt G. Wilder and C. Frederick Hartt, appointed as faculty members there (Lurie 1960:360). In 1873 he established the nation's first biological summer field school—the Anderson School of Natural History—on the island of Penikese off the south coast of Massachusetts. The wealthy New York tobacco merchant John Anderson deeded the island to Agassiz, and he started his school there for 50 teachers—30 men and 20 women (Fry and Fry 1989:13; Holder 1910:162). Among the instructors were many of his former students, such as Frederic Putnam and Edward Morse (see chapter 3). The field school's pedagogical focus was unusual for the time, because original research was not then a part of the American college curriculum, except among Agassiz's group (Jordan 1892:722).

Despite his sometimes turbulent relations with colleagues and students, Agassiz was critical in recruiting several of the students who would become significant players in the development of anthropology at Harvard and other institutions in the later part of the nineteenth century, particularly men such as Putnam and Morse. Significantly for anthropology, he trained his students to consider assemblages in terms of geographical area rather than presumed evolutionary sequence, in a kind of historical particularism that Franz Boas would later borrow and popularize in sociocultural anthropology. Yet Agassiz's unstinting opposition to evolution alienated his students, and his racial theories later tarnished his reputation. Working with Samuel Morton, Josiah Nott, and George Gliddon, the primary authors of polygenetic theory, he spent years trying to prove certain components of its idea that Africans, Asians, American Indians, and Europeans were different species. In the process he collected thousands of comparative measurements of racial types and a number of skeletal remains, which were later transferred to the Peabody Museum (Ruffins 1992:524). In the end, Harvard students of the time learned most of their skills relating to anthropology from Jeffries Wyman and, to a lesser extent, from Asa Gray. Agassiz remains for us a paradoxical figure: key in recruiting many of the players and in putting Harvard on the scientific map, but in the long term having relatively less influence on his students than some of his quieter and more reticent colleagues, such as Wyman and Gray.

Jeffries Wyman (1814–74) was born in Chelmsford, Massachusetts, and graduated from Harvard College in 1833. Of his class of 56 students, 6 later became professors at Harvard (Gray 1875a:7, 1875b:98; Wilder 1910b:173). Wyman went on to get his M.D. in 1837 and following his graduation was appointed preparator and demonstrator of anatomy for John Collins Warren, the Hersey Professor of Anatomy, from 1838 to 1840 (Gray 1875b:99). Warren introduced Wyman to the Boston Society of Natural History in 1837; Wyman would later lead the organization as its president from 1856 to 1870 (Appel 1992:100). In 1839 John Amory Lowell offered Wyman the position of curator for the newly formed Lowell Institute, a position he held for three years, receiving a stipend of $500 a year (Wilder 1910a:176). From the spring of 1841 to the spring of 1842 Wyman studied at the University of Paris. From there he went to London for another two months of study. It was during his time in France and England that he made his first personal contacts with Charles Darwin, Charles Lyell, and several of the other leading scientists of Europe. It was also during this trip that he seems to have become aware of the nascent Scandinavian excavations in coastal shell mounds, which were just beginning to be discussed in European scientific circles.

In 1843 Wyman was appointed professor of anatomy and physiology at Hampton-Sidney College in Richmond, Virginia, and until 1847 he spent every winter and spring teaching there, returning to his home in Boston for the summer and fall (Gray 1875a:8; Packard 1878:83). The geologist Lyell met with Wyman at Hampden-Sydney College during Lyell's second trip to North America, in 1845–46; he referred to Wyman in his diary as "the best comparative anatomist in the United States" (L. Wilson 1998:175). Lyell visited Wyman first during a trip south in December 1845 and returned to accompany him on two field trips in May 1846 (L. Wilson 1998:174, 268).

In 1847 Wyman succeeded John C. Warren as the Hersey Professor of Anatomy at Harvard, by then affiliated with the newly formed Lawrence Scientific School. This was an endowed chair, and many contemporaries had assumed it would go to Oliver Wendell Holmes Sr. (Appel 1992:103), who held a related chair in anatomy at Harvard. That same year Wyman published the first scientific description of a gorilla, and he began his own Museum of Comparative Anatomy, at first in Holden Chapel, a small building shared with Asa Gray for use as an office and lecture hall. After Boylston Hall was completed in 1857, one wing became Wyman's lecture hall and office; the other, the chemistry laboratory of Joseph Parsons Cooke (1827–94; Harvard A.B. 1848); and the central portion, Wyman's museum. After Wyman's death the building was changed over primarily to a chemistry laboratory building (Appel 1992:105–6). Until the Peabody Museum was built, Wyman stored and displayed newly acquired archaeological and ethnological specimens at Boylston Hall. In the early 1870s Holmes (1874:611–12) reported that the second floor gallery was devoted to archaeological and ethnological objects, including artifacts from shell heaps in Denmark, Florida, and Massachusetts and bones of the dead that had been cracked open for their marrow. In 1872 Wyman had a new story added to Boylston Hall to accommodate the burgeoning anthropological displays (Wyman 1873:5).

An interesting sidebar is the part Wyman played during the succession of Joseph Cooke, his Boylston Hall colleague, to the Erving Chair of Chemistry and Mineralogy in place of the earlier chemist, John White Webster (1793–1850). On November 23, 1849, Dr. George Parkman, who had endowed the chair in anatomy held by Oliver Wendell Holmes Sr., disappeared. Subsequent investigations revealed that Parkman had gone that day to visit Webster, to see about collecting a debt of $2,432, in those days the equivalent of two years' salary for Webster. A week later, on November 30, 1849, Webster was arrested for the murder of Parkman, on the basis of a forensic examination of bones found in the ashes of the furnace of the Harvard Medical School building.

Both Holmes and Wyman were called in to examine the bones. The conclusion reached was that Webster had tried to "dispose of the corpse by various means, including fire, and the fragments of bone were identified by Wyman with characteristic skill and caution; his evidence related also to the manner of dismembering the body and to the determination of blood-stains" (Wilder 1910b:197). Webster was found guilty of murder on April 1, 1850 (Seitz 1911:28), and was hanged on August 30, 1850. Cooke was appointed his successor at the college, with a position in the Lawrence Scientific School. The victim, George Parkman, we should note, was the uncle of Francis Parkman, the well-known historian, who was later involved with the Peabody Museum in the early years of the Archaeological Institute of America, often being one of the few AIA members in favor of Americanist archaeology (see chapter 5).

Jeffries Wyman is a perfect example of the researcher who did not trumpet his accomplishments but let his works speak for themselves. His colleague Asa Gray (1875b:121) remarked, "He was one of the best lecturers I ever heard, although, and partly because, he was the most unpretending." Whereas Agassiz patronized his students, Wyman treated them as equals and encouraged independence (Appel 1992:108). Wyman played a major role in training Agassiz's students, men such as Frederic Putnam, Edward Morse, Addison Verrill, Nathaniel Shaler, Alpheus Hyatt, Alpheus Packard, Alfred Bickmore, Burt Wilder, Alexander Agassiz (Louis Agassiz's son), and Henry Bowditch (Appel 1992:108). While Louis Agassiz was making the headlines, Wyman and Gray in general carried the load of natural history instruction for Harvard College and were staff members of the Lawrence School mostly in name (Dupree 1959:314).

Charles Darwin relied on Wyman and Gray for information on natural history. Indeed, Darwin sent Wyman one of three advance copies of *On the Origin of Species*, because of his great respect for Wyman's work. By early 1861 Wyman had begun discussing the theory of evolution in his classes, initially by presenting two hypotheses, transcendental anatomy and progressive development, as alternatives (Appel 1988:85). He, Asa Gray, and several of their students were interested in evolution but adhered mainly to a neo-Lamarckian vision of it. Neo-Lamarckians did not accept Darwin's idea of evolution completely but instead argued for "acquired adaptive evolution," or the inheritance of characteristics newly acquired under the direct influence of the environment.

Wyman's interest in Americanist archaeology as a subset of his studies in natural history was born at least as early as 1846, when he began a correspondence with Ephraim G. Squier on mounds. Wyman's first documented shell mound excavations were conducted in 1852, when he began wintering in Florida for his health (Murowchick 1990:57). His initial interest in Americanist studies was not limited to the culture history of the United States. For example, in 1858–59 he took part in a major expedition to South America with Captain John M. Forbes and George Augustus Peabody, a relative of the George Peabody who founded the museum. From the coast of Argentina they traveled up the Río de la Plata and the Paraná River, across the Andes into Chile, and then north to Peru, collecting artifacts in all three countries (Gray 1875b:102). His chief anthropological interest, however, from his first excavations in Florida shell mounds in 1852, continued to be in the mound dwellers and their artifacts and in prehistoric Indian populations. At the Boston Society of Natural History, where he shared many of his early interests in archaeology, his earlier papers tended to focus on excavated human skeletal remains (Wyman 1854, 1856, 1857, 1866, 1867a, 1867i, 1874), but later they shifted more to cultural materials associated with the shell mounds that he dug along the Atlantic coast, particularly in Maine and Massachusetts in the north and Florida in the south (Wyman 1864, 1867b, 1867c, 1867e, 1867g).

Shell mound exploration apparently became sufficiently commonplace for Wyman and his students that they saw it as nothing important to write about, and they rarely mentioned these explorations in their commentaries. One student, Nathaniel Shaler, did leave a tantalizing glimpse of this component in his autobiography (Shaler 1909:105–6):

> [In] about 1860, I came into close relations with Jeffries Wyman, whose lectures I regularly attended, and in whose laboratory work I took a small share. In some ways he was the most perfect naturalist I have ever known. . . . A part of his quality was his certainty and the balanced judgment which enabled him unerringly to attain to it. As a proof of this quality, I note an instance. From an Indian mound I had obtained two lots of bone which were evidently fragments of human tibiae, though they were somewhat malformed. To make sure of this, though the determination seemed certain, I took them to Wyman, asking him what they were. To my surprise he said that he would examine them and let me know next week. When I said to him that he surely knew at a glance, he remarked that if I had brought him a human skull for inspection he would take time to [do] it.

In 1867 Wyman published his first major summary of the work on shell heaps in Maine and Massachusetts in the new national natural history journal put out by his former students, the *American Naturalist*. Later that year Wyman visited between 25 and 32 more shell heaps in Maine and Massachusetts, where he collected hundreds of specimens (Holmes 1874:618; Packard 1878:86; Wyman 1868a:11). In the 1860s he continued excavations on shell mounds in those two states and began work on mounds in Florida, his most important work there being conducted in the late 1860s and 1870s.

How much influence Wyman had on the excavation techniques later used by Frederic Putnam and his other students remains uncertain, partly because we still do not know precisely what techniques Wyman himself used. Although he had been excavating in mounds for nearly a quarter century before his death, in his writing he focused primarily on the results of his excavations rather than on the methods he employed. His later work seems to have been influenced by European methods as worked out by French excavators and popularized in two English translations of papers by Adolphe von Morlot, published by the Smithsonian Institution (von Morlot 1861, 1863). Wyman made specific reference to von Morlot's papers in various of his publications in 1867 and later (see Bourque 2002 for further discussion of von Morlot's influence).

We know that Wyman took particular care in his excavations. He made careful notes on the context from which artifacts derived, and he observed and recorded changes in strata as they correlated with artifact categories, noting that in some Florida mounds pottery occurred only in upper layers and was lacking in lower zones. His descriptions and analyses of ceramic technology and decoration were unmatched until the twentieth century. He made such careful zooarchaeological investigations that he was able to support an argument for possible human cannibalism at the Florida mounds through a correlation between the treatment of a set of excavated human bones and a set of butchered and boiled deer bones showing the same patterns (Murowchick 1990:60–61; S. Williams 1991:68; Wyman 1874).

Of particular note for the origins of Americanist archaeology is Wyman's 1867 report on an examination of animal species represented in New England shell heaps (Wyman 1867j). This report and a similar one by his good friend Othniel Charles Marsh at Yale (Marsh 1866) are two of the earliest cases of zooarchaeological studies on American mound sites of which we are aware.

The commentaries offered on presentations at the Boston Society of Natural History (BSNH) provide brief insights into other activities and arguments of Wyman and his students regarding their work in mounds. For example, Alexander Agassiz reported his studies of California shell mounds in his comments on an 1864 paper by Wyman. Frederic Putnam, in his discussion of an 1874 paper by Wyman, observed that the same sort of human bone fragmentation Wyman had identified as possible evidence of cannibalism in the Florida mounds was known from New England mounds. In addition to Putnam's own observations, his field man, Manly Hardy, of Brewer, Maine, had described bones recovered during excavations for the Peabody Museum in shell heaps on Great Deer Island, Penobscot Bay, in 1878. Hardy had reported the same kinds of fracture patterns that Wyman had interpreted as evidence of cannibalism (Thwing 1881:677). Later, Putnam's MCZ colleague and fellow student Edward Morse was to make the same suggestion of possible cannibalism (now rejected) for fractured human bones he found in his pioneering work on Japanese shell mounds (see chapter 4).

Wyman had several opportunities to pass his excavation methodology on to Putnam through actual field demonstrations. In addition to the other relationships the two had at the Lawrence School, Putnam worked with Wyman on excavations in Maine and Massachusetts in 1867 (Wyman 1868c), and the two stayed in active contact until Wyman's death in 1874. Writing about his own shell mound work, Putnam reported (1886a:479) that Wyman "at various times conducted similar explorations of shellheaps in Maine and Massachusetts, when it was several times my privilege to accompany him." In a previous volume (Browman and Williams 2002), we suggested that Wyman became enthusiastic about rigorous methods after reading von Morlot, as well as from his contacts during his European trips, and he passed these concerns on to his students in their field excavations. Our additional research supports this position.

At Wyman's death, his colleagues and students widely acknowledged his contributions. Burt Wilder (1875:355) wrote that American science had lost two of its greatest leaders within a year—Agassiz and Wyman. Alpheus Spring Packard Jr. (1878:110) wrote, "At the time of his death Wyman was indisputably the leading anthropologist of America, though he had published nothing upon myths, languages, and little on the social relations of the human races. But to the physical history of mankind, particularly of the American aborigines, he made important contributions."

Asa Gray (1875a:9) wrote in his memorial that Wyman had a special predilection for osteological investigations and a fondness for ethnological observation, which provided him with the skills the trustees of the new Peabody Museum were looking for when they selected Wyman as curator upon the museum's founding in 1866. Gray noted Wyman's particular dedication, reporting that "even last summer, when there was evidently no strength to spare, and a considerable amount of ancient Indian pottery had almost to be reconstructed from the separated fragments, when besought to call in skilled assistance, he replied that he would first see what he could do by himself" (1875a:10). It was time apparently well spent: "Wyman's posthumous monograph (1875) on the Shell Mounds of the St. Johns River in Florida was a virtuoso performance, with methods of analysis of the pottery in terms of technology and decoration that were not to be matched for nearly one hundred years" (S. Williams 1991:68).

Asa Gray (1810–88) was himself one of the key figures, along with Wyman, Agassiz, and several others whom we discuss later, in training the earliest students in anthropology and archaeology at Harvard. He was born in Sauquoit, near Paris, Oneida County, New York (Goodale 1889:193). He was initially self-taught in botany, reading Amos Eaton's *Manual of Botany* while snowbound on his father's farm in the winter of 1827–28 (Fry and Fry 1989:2). He was sent to Fairfield Medical School in New York City in 1829 and, after training with physicians living near Sauquoit, received his M.D. in 1831 (Farlow 1889:164).

While he was at home, Gray collected a good-size herbarium. He also began corresponding with John Torrey (1796–1873), a physician and eminent botanist in New York City, and Lewis C. Beck (1789–1853), a geologist and botanist at Rutgers College in New Jersey, regarding his materials. In late 1830, while still a student at Fairfield Medical School, Gray wrote to Torrey asking whether he might come study botany with him (Rodgers 1942:30). In 1833 Gray spent the summer teaching at Hamilton College in Clinton, New York, and then was given a one-term leave to be Torrey's assistant in chemistry at the College of Physicians and Surgeons in New York City. In the autumn of 1834 Gray was again Torrey's assistant, this time at the New York Lyceum of Natural History (later renamed the New York Academy of Sciences) (Rodgers 1942:96). In 1836 and 1837, through Torrey's influence, Gray was appointed curator of collections of the Lyceum, a job that one historian has called the first paid scientific position in the United States (Robbins 1968:561). Torrey and Gray, in their publications, were primarily responsible for the acceptance by botanists in the United States of the Linnaean classification system. As one author wrote (Rodgers 1942:309), "the nation owes to Torrey and Gray the commencement of an organized flora of North America, the beginnings of a completed system of American botany."

In 1836 Gray was approached by the federal government and agreed to accept the position of botanist on the United States Exploring Expedition, an around-the-world voyage of surveying and exploration organized by the U.S. Navy. The expedition, just then being put together, was ultimately led by navy lieutenant Charles Wilkes from 1838 to 1842. Only three weeks before the expedition was to sail, Gray received an offer of the first American professorship in botany at the nascent University of Michigan, and he withdrew from the project to accept the position (Eyde 1985:27). He would, in a sense, rejoin the expedition a decade later, accepting the responsibility for writing up part of its botanical corpus. Although Gray did not accompany the expedition, it was an important venture with effects on the development of linguistics, ethnography, biological anthropology, and archaeology. Because it is relatively little known, and because two other Harvard men played significant roles in it, we digress from our account of Asa Gray here to outline the story of the U.S. Exploring Expedition.

In 1836, three scientists were recruited to help plan and take part in the expedition—Gray as its botanist, James Dwight Dana, from Yale, as its geologist, and Charles Pickering, a Harvard graduate (A.B. 1823, M.D. 1826) then working in Philadelphia, as its zoologist and naturalist (Joyce 2001:15; Stanton 1975:43). A last-minute addition to the staff was another Harvard graduate, Horatio Hale (A.B. 1837). Wilkes, the expedition leader, opposed Hale's participation because of his extreme youth (Joyce 2001:23), but he was overruled, and Hale became the expedition's philologist and linguist. Together, Pickering and Hale provided the bulk of the anthropological specimens collected during the journey.

Charles Pickering (1805–78) was the son of John Pickering, the diplomat and avocational linguist whom we mentioned in chapter 1. Charles Pickering began practicing medicine in Philadelphia and became a member of the Academy of Natural Sciences of Philadelphia. In his funeral eulogy of Pickering years later, Asa Gray would describe him as "retiring and reticent," with an "encyclopedic and minute" grasp of science

(Joyce 2001:22). Pickering was extremely near-sighted, so the planners of the exploring expedition decided to add an assistant to help him—the artist-naturalist Titian Ramsey Peale, manager of the Philadelphia museum founded by his father, artist Charles Willson Peale (Stanton 1975:46). Peale took over much of the zoological collecting, freeing Pickering to focus more on anthropology during the voyage (Joyce 2001:22).

One of the charges of the U.S. Exploring Expedition was to collect specimens to test the "polygenesis" theory of human racial origins that was then being advocated by, among others, Louis Agassiz. This job fell particularly to Pickering. The expedition started out exploring South America, and when it stopped in Tierra del Fuego, Pickering excavated the first human remains for the expedition from a cave near Orange Harbor. He also collected ethnographic materials such as fish spears, bolas, quivers, arrows, paddles, guanaco wool items, and jewelry (Joyce 2001:19, 37–38).

When the expedition reached Lima, Peru, Pickering led a group of fellow scientists and officers to the pre-Columbian ruins of Pachacamac, situated on the coast 20 miles southeast of Lima, in search of skulls and other artifacts. He located a burial ground and collected eight skulls on June 28, 1839 (Joyce 2001:39). Pickering was more interested in the plant remains buried with the dead than in the skeletons. While the rest of the party rummaged through an Inca graveyard for intact skulls, pottery sherds, and scraps of cloth from the mummy burials, Pickering focused on archaeobotanical materials, writing that "what interested me more particularly were numerous vegetable substances. Here then was evidence of the existence of these vegetables here before the arrival of the Spaniards" (Pickering journal, June 28, 1839, quoted in Joyce 2001:40). Pickering's excavations are said to have been the only attempts at the scientific collection of archaeological materials of the entire 1838–42 expedition (Kaeppler 1985:144). Pickering found that he could not support the polygenesis hypothesis, and he wrote repeatedly during the trip to Samuel George Morton, a professor of anatomy in Philadelphia and one of the main champions of the idea that human races were actually different species, suggesting modifications.

Less collecting was conducted during the journey than the scientists had hoped. They continually complained about Wilkes's policy of stressing surveying and hydrography at the expense of other scientific pursuits such as exploring new terrain, interviewing natives, and collecting specimens and artifacts (Joyce 2001:123). When the expedition returned, Wilkes directed that the materials collected be put on display in the U.S. Patent Office—there not yet being a Smithsonian Institution museum—and Pickering was appointed to supervise the collections. After a few months he resigned this position in order to voyage to Egypt to do more collecting. After his return, Pickering devoted his research attention to ethnobotany and to geographical distribution—the correlation of the movement of humans and the dispersion of plants and animals—until his death in 1878.

The ethnographic and other collections from the expedition were severely compromised. Of the initial 20 tons of materials sent back by the expedition in 1841, nearly one quarter was marked "private." This portion included the choicest specimens, most of which were reserved by Titian Peale for his father's "American Museum" (Evelyn 1985:232; Kaeppler 1985:119). Even the remaining collections proved to be of reduced scientific value:

> Unbeknownst to the scientists on the expedition, . . . many of the boxes of specimens of every variety that had been shipped home during the course of the voyage had been tampered with. The boxes had been opened, in many cases, not by scientists but by politically appointed "curators" who often treated the collections as they would patronage, doling out specimens upon request to politically partisan gardener-botanists and private collectors. As a result, much of what was forwarded during the voyage was either lost or rendered useless by separating the descriptive identifying information from the specimens. (Joyce 2001:145–46)

Wilkes got Asa Gray to rejoin the research group in 1847 to write up the botanical materials and later was able to get Louis Agassiz on board to analyze the fishes. Gray published the first part of the botanical analysis in 1854, but his work was never completely published. At the official end of the project in 1873, 1,700 sheets of his analysis remained unpublished for lack of funds (Stanton 1975:362).

Nor did Agassiz's work turn out successfully. On Pickering's advice, and after long negotiations over fee and publication schedule, Agassiz agreed to work on the fish collection (G. Watson 1985:66). By 1861 he had completed a 2,000-page manuscript and 670 illustrations, but for the next six years, and after his spending nearly $4,000, nothing was submitted (Stanton 1975:354, 361). When the publishing committee finally did see Agassiz's manuscript, it was apparently not what they expected. First the manuscript was nearly lost in a train wreck in the Susquehanna River, and then the committee decided it was unacceptable. According to Wilkes (1978:544): "Among other accidents was one which happened to the drawings and mss. of Louis Agassiz which the Committee had ordered to be sent on from Boston by Express. I felt under some apprehensions that we might suffer loss, but Agassiz had somewhat irritated the Committee about his mss. as he naturally knew it could be of no use to them, written as it was in his usual way." Describing the baggage car wreck in the Susquehanna River (Wilkes 1978:544–45), he went on:

> The value of the drawings was great and we were sorely perplexed to think that in all probability all the drawings of Agassiz' fishes were lost, but it turned out otherwise. The Box was sent to the Room in the Capital occupied by the Committee, opened there and nothing removed from it, and in some weeks, it was ordered to be returned. . . . the very fact that no one of the Committee ever even examined the mss. is enough to show their want of interest and desire to ascertain. In fact it was like Greek to them. It was retained for some weeks and then it was requested that the whole mss, drawings and all, be returned to Agassiz, which was done. I was heartily ashamed of this action and Agassiz was mortified very considerably.

The other Harvard member of the U.S. Exploring Expedition, **Horatio Emmons Hale** (1817–96), also set about writing up his part of the results upon his return to the United States. His analyses were published in 1846 as *Narrative of the United States Exploring Expedition,* volume 6, *Ethnography and Philology.* Asa Gray, in a review of this volume, wrote that Hale's data would stand in the foremost rank of ethnological research.

Hale had been born in Newport, New Hampshire, the son of the noted poet Sarah Josepha Buell Hale. (Although she published 35 volumes of poetry, perhaps her best known work was "Mary Had a Little Lamb.") Horatio Hale had become interested in linguistics when a group of Indians camped near Harvard College for several months while he was an undergraduate. Intrigued, he spent some time learning their language and thus became an accidental "linguist" and philologist when he graduated from Harvard in 1837. It was these skills that secured Hale a position on the expedition.

After completing his part of the expedition reports, Hale shifted his career path into law. He moved to Clinton, Ontario, and practiced law in Canada from 1855 until 1880. He returned to his interest in linguistics and ethnology after a short period, beginning with work among the Iroquois in Ontario in 1867 (Fenton 1991:262). In 1881 he attended the meetings of the AAAS to debate Lewis Henry Morgan on the Iroquois and other issues, arguing for a cultural relativist perspective, in contrast to the cultural evolutionist position then dominant.

In 1884 the British Association for the Advancement of Sciences (BAAS) asked its seven Canadian members to conduct some salvage ethnography. Hale, as secretary of the BAAS Committee for the Study of the Northwestern Tribes of Canada, initiated a research program in British Columbia (Fenton 1991:263). It was through this project that Hale would leave his most significant mark on Americanist anthropology, in an unforeseeable way: he gave Franz Boas some of his earliest training in ethnographic fieldwork. Hale soon convinced the BAAS committee that the magnitude of the anthropological component of his program required assistance, and in 1888, he and the BAAS recruited the young German to continue their investigations in the Pacific Northwest. Boas at the time was working as an assistant editor at *Science* magazine. Hale recognized Boas's credentials as a geographer, but he and the committee did not think Boas's bona fides as an ethnographer or anthropologist were yet established, so Hale was delegated to provide him with instructions (Koelsch 2004:13–15). Hale guided and influenced Boas's work, training him to use and rely on native texts, a procedure that later became key in Boasian anthropology (Joyce 2001:156–58; Stanton 1975:377). Hale later made other intellectual contributions to Boas's theoretical stances. In 1888 Hale challenged the value of Darwinian evolutionary theory in explaining mental and emotional differences among races (Wissler 1942:194), following an argument he had made earlier, in 1881, emphasizing the cultural relativist position. Boas was later to take exactly the same stance. We cannot prove that Boas picked up the basis for his historical particularism from Hale or, as we mentioned earlier, his insistence on organizing museum displays by culture area rather than by cultural evolution from Frederic Putnam. Nevertheless, it is clear that Boas was exposed to cultural particularistic ideas from these two scholars in the mid-1880s, just when he was developing his anti-evolutionary arguments.

Horatio Hale gave Boas another contract for the summer of 1889, but he continued to be dissatisfied with Boas's progress and instructed him further in how to conduct fieldwork properly and effectively (Koelsch 2004:15). In 1890 Boas secured some funds from the Bureau of Ethnology, an alternative source of money that enabled him at last to go his own way, effectively ending his linkages with Hale and the BAAS (Gruber 1967:31).

Leaving the U.S. Exploring Expedition and returning to Asa Gray, we pick up with his having been appointed professor of natural history at the new University of Michigan in 1838. First, however, he arranged with the university to take a leave of absence for additional training in Europe. As it turned out, the neophyte University of Michigan was inadequately funded, could not cover Gray's salary, and had to let him go. Gray never activated his professorship there, although he was carried on the university's books until 1842.

In the spring of that year, having returned from Europe to Boston, Gray was appointed Fisher Professor of Natural History at Harvard, a title he held until his death in 1888, although he retired from lecturing in 1873. In July 1842 he also took a position at the Lowell Institute and lectured there as well until 1844 (Dupree 1959:114, 130). In his new positions, Gray was influential in helping to get Agassiz and Horsford appointed to the Lawrence Scientific School. Initially Gray was a strong supporter of Agassiz, even assuring his old mentor, John Torrey, that some remarks Agassiz made on race in 1846, referring to Africans as a separate species, had been distorted. This case was more difficult to maintain when, in 1847, Agassiz again referred publicly to Africans as a separate species, supporting Josiah C. Nott's and Samuel George Morton's views on polygenesis and racial purity (Bruce 1987:125). Initially, Gray and Agassiz remained good colleagues and worked together, joining others in the founding of the American Association for the Advancement of Sciences on September 20, 1848, at a meeting of the Academy of Natural Sciences of Philadelphia (Kohlstedt 1999:7).

After a decade, this situation had changed. One of both Wyman's and Gray's contacts in Europe was Charles Darwin; Gray had met him while in London in 1839. The heady and tumultuous years of the founding of the Museum of Comparative Zoology and the training of Putnam and his cohorts, from 1859 through 1864, marked the definition of a sharp split between Agassiz and other Harvard scholars who did not support Darwin's ideas and empiricists such as Gray and Wyman, who did.

Wyman had been elected president of the Boston Society of Natural History, a post he held from 1854 to 1870, and because Darwin had sent Wyman a prepublication copy of *On the Origin of Species* late in 1858, a debate on Darwin's work was set there early in 1859. Gray and Wyman argued that evolution was good theology and that "philosophical," or "transcendental," anatomy did not act as a barrier to the acceptance of evolution

(Appel 1988:83; Fry and Fry 1989:8). Philosophical anatomy placed an emphasis on discovering general laws of nature, even though it presupposed design in nature. It could readily be joined to a theistic view of evolution, such as that held by Agassiz, or to a neo-Lamarckian view, emphasizing the parallel between evolution and ontogeny, such as was held by several of Agassiz's students (Appel 1988:93–94). Although most of Agassiz's students were members of the BSNH, and the BSNH audience thus might have been expected to support Agassiz's position in opposition to evolution, in fact he lost the debate to Wyman's side. Later, at the American Academy of Arts and Sciences, which was more Gray's bailiwick, where scientific Boston as well as the Boston of society and literature met, Agassiz lost the evolution debate again (Dupree 1959:285).

Gray and Agassiz soon found themselves at opposite poles on almost every issue, and their once close friendship became seriously strained (Lurie 1960:338). The rift involved a group that became known to historians of science as the "Lazzaroni," of which Agassiz was an important member. This cadre had its beginnings as early as 1838 with an informal arrangement between Alexander Dallas Bache (1806–67), later superintendent of the Coast Survey, and the physicist and meteorologist Joseph Henry (1797–1878), who became the first secretary of the Smithsonian Institution in 1846. Bache seems to have become the kingpin of the group as it developed. He had gone to Europe in 1837–38 and become concerned about the differences in the way science was taught in Europe and the United States (Bache 1839). He recruited others who shared his concern into an informal association. Bache and his small group focused principally not on doing science but on raising funds for, organizing support for, and guiding scientific institutions (Bruce 1987:217).

During the late 1840s, Louis Agassiz, Benjamin Peirce (1809–80, Harvard professor of mathematics and astronomy), Cornelius Felton (1807–62, Harvard professor of Greek and Latin and later president of Harvard), Benjamin Apthorp Gould (1824–96, Harvard's Dudley Observatory astronomer), and Oliver Wolcott Gibbs (1822–1908, later Harvard University chemist) were added to the group. The Cambridge contingent began meeting "officially" in 1853, both on campus and through social clubs such as the Saturday Club. For a decade they exerted strong influence on the development of institutional scientific policy at Harvard.

Apparently, Bache's group originally referred to itself as the "Florentine Academy." In the 1850s the Cambridge contingent occasionally referred to itself jokingly as the "Scientific Lazzaroni" (*lazzaroni* is Italian for Neapolitan beggars or idlers), and historians of science have seized on the name Lazzaroni for this scientific cabal (Bruce 1987:217, 223). In our view, the Lazzaroni tended to be people who loudly trumpeted their excellence, as opposed to those who were content to let their science speak for them. Many prominent scientists did not join the group, including, significantly, Gray, Wyman, and most of Agassiz's other colleagues at the Museum of Comparative Zoology.

The year 1863 marked a rupture in the previous strong collaboration among Agassiz, Gray, and Wyman at the MCZ, which inevitably influenced the development of anthropological training of students in the MCZ natural history program. On the national level, the Lazzaroni had been able to get the National Academy of Sciences established, with Bache as its first president. In the selection of its first 50 members, conflict arose among the founding members from the MCZ. Agassiz and the other Lazzaroni were firmly opposed to the election of the naturalist Spencer Baird, assistant secretary of the Smithsonian, to the academy, because they thought he was only a descriptive scientist. Gray, Wyman, Joseph Henry, James Dwight Dana, and all the other naturalists associated with the MCZ supported Baird's nomination. Agassiz took personal offense against Gray and Wyman for supporting Baird and exchanged harsh words with them (Rivinus and Youssef 1992:103–4).

Later that year Agassiz had his revenge. Harvard had traditionally hired from within or from the local community, so when Eben Horsford, holder of the Rumford professorship in the Lawrence Scientific School, resigned from the school, the expectation was that Charles W. Eliot, a young assistant professor from a long Harvard lineage, would take over the endowed chair. Eliot was supported for this position by Gray and Wyman (McCaughey 1974:267). Lazzaroni members Agassiz and Peirce opposed Eliot's appointment and lobbied for the position to be given to one of their own, Oliver Wolcott Gibbs (Dupree 1959:317; Sinclair 1992:79). They were successful, and Gibbs took over as head of the chemistry department and dean of the Lawrence School. Eliot was forced out of Harvard altogether, going to MIT, although he returned six years later, in 1869, for a long and successful tenure as president of Harvard. During his presidency he would exert strong influence on the development of the Peabody Museum and its anthropology graduate program. The loss of Eliot in 1863 was a bitter defeat for Gray, who considered Agassiz's treatment of Eliot "shabby" (Lurie 1960:329–30).

Sparring between Gray and Agassiz continued for a few more years before it abated. Henry James Clark, one of Agassiz's first group of students, who had left Gray to study with Agassiz, was subsequently forced out by Agassiz in 1863, and Gray made known his opinion that Clark had been ill treated. In 1865 Gray wrote to a friend, advising him to have his son enroll in Harvard College rather than Lawrence Scientific School (the two were at this point separate entities), because, he said, Agassiz and Peirce had destroyed the quality school that he, Wyman, and Eliot had tried to develop (Dupree 1959:315).

By the end of the decade the rift had essentially been healed, but the conflict had obviously affected the students. Agassiz's "implacable hostility to natural selection and to Asa Gray extended to the students of both professors" (Livingstone 1987:28). Gray, meanwhile, had strengthened his power base outside of the MCZ, a strength soon to be demonstrated during the founding of the Peabody Museum, from which Agassiz would be deliberately excluded.

The story of the Harvard Peabody Museum of Archaeology and Ethnology begins with **George Peabody** (1795–1869), the benefactor whose gift founded the institution. Peabody was born in South Danvers, Massachusetts (now known as Peabody), on

February 18, 1795. As a youngster he apprenticed in a grocery store; later he became an assistant to his brother David, who ran a dry goods store. He then moved south and went to work for his uncle, who had a business in Georgetown, District of Columbia. With the onset of the War of 1812, he left to serve as a volunteer. After his war service, he joined a dry goods business run by Elisha Riggs Sr. in Georgetown. He rose rapidly in the enterprise, becoming manager in 1814 and soon thereafter Riggs's partner. In 1815, Riggs and Peabody moved to Baltimore. The business flourished through Peabody's energy and skills and grew larger over the years. On the retirement of his partner in 1829, Peabody found himself in charge of one of the largest mercantile concerns in the world, Peabody, Riggs and Company.

After 1837 Peabody left the United States and established himself in London as a merchant and money broker. He came to enjoy London and finally withdrew from his American business interests entirely in 1843. The American firm's transactions ended in 1848. In 1864 Peabody sold his holdings in his banking company to his partner, Junius Spencer Morgan, father of John Pierpont Morgan Sr., later a dynamo in the New York City and American banking industries.

Following his retirement from banking, Peabody became focused on philanthropy. He built homes for the impoverished in London and gave large monetary gifts to aid the needy in the United States, including considerable sums for his hometown of Danvers. He donated money to educational institutions and promoted an extraordinary education fund to support black schools in the South.

In 1862, wanting advice from a successful but conservative American businessman about his philanthropic plans for museums, universities, and charities in the United States, Peabody approached **Robert Charles Winthrop** (1809–94) for help (F. Parker 1971:154). Until this time Peabody and Winthrop had been known to each other only by name. Winthrop was a wealthy Boston businessman who had graduated from Harvard in 1828 and then studied law with Daniel Webster. He entered politics as a member of the Whig Party, served as a representative to and speaker of the Massachusetts House of Representatives from 1836 to 1840, became a U.S. representative (1841–47) and speaker of the U.S. House of Representatives (1847–50), and filled in a term as U.S. Senator from 1850 to 1852.

During this period Winthrop was closely associated with Abbott Lawrence, who later provided the funds for the Lawrence Scientific School at Harvard. Lawrence had been elected to the Massachusetts legislature as a Whig in 1834, and when he resigned because of business interests and poor health, Winthrop replaced him. Lawrence and Winthrop politicked together for the next decade, often being called the "Massachusetts Whigs" (Winthrop 1897:87). In 1850 Lawrence interceded to have Winthrop take over the U.S. Senate seat (Winthrop 1897:166).

In his later years Winthrop became increasingly involved with Harvard. He became an overseer in 1855 and frequently met with faculty members such as Oliver Wendell Holmes Sr., Louis Agassiz, and George Ticknor, another politically active Whig

(Winthrop 1897:214, 227, 233). Altogether, his political experience and connections and his strong links to the world of education and science made him an ideal person for Peabody to consult.

George Peabody developed the habit of seeking Winthrop's advice on his various educational foundations. In early 1866, perhaps as an inducement to secure Winthrop's help with his philanthropic work, Peabody gave the Massachusetts Historical Society, of which Winthrop was president from 1855 to 1885, the sum of $20,000, for which donation he was made an honorary member of the society (Hanaford 1870:201; Winthrop 1897:273, 315). Peabody and Winthrop continued to work together on their common interests, becoming close enough friends that they went jointly for a private audience with Pope Pius IX in 1868 (Winthrop 1894:100).

In 1861 George Peabody was considering a donation to Harvard that would enlarge its astronomical observatory. By the following year he had changed his mind and was contemplating his Harvard benefaction in terms of a school of art (F. Parker 1971:139, 199). Fortunately for the history of archaeology, Peabody was influenced a few years later by Winthrop and by his nephews Othniel C. Marsh and George Peabody Russell to make his donation to Harvard for a new museum for archaeology and ethnology instead. James Walker, the eighteenth president of Harvard (1853–60), concurred in the plan.

George Peabody Russell (1834–96), whose father, Jeremiah Russell, lived in Zanesville, Ohio, had apparently maintained a long interest in prehistoric mounds; shortly after the Peabody Museum was established, he donated a collection of artifacts from his personal exploration of a mound in Dunleith, Illinois (Wyman 1869:15). Othniel C. Marsh (1831–99) was a Yale graduate (A.B. 1851, A.M. 1862) who had become interested in mounds and antiquities under the influence of Charles Lyell, whom he met in London in 1862 (for more on Marsh, see chapter 5). With Russell, he made an exploratory visit to the famous mounds at Newark, Ohio, in the summer of 1865 (E. Brown 1949:217). Marsh was greatly impressed by the materials he saw there, and he wrote to George Peabody in October that year, urging him to establish a museum of American archaeology at Harvard. In a letter to Jeffries Wyman on October 6, 1866, Marsh wrote:

> The first idea of the Peabody Museum at Cambridge occurred to me in October, 1865, while digging in an ancient mound near Newark, Ohio, and that evening I wrote my uncle, Mr. Peabody, at London, urging him to establish such a museum. . . . My own interest in American archaeology was mainly due to Sir Charles Lyell, who had just published his "Antiquity of Man" and, when I saw him in London, urged me in the strongest terms to take up the subject in America as a new field for exploration. (Quoted in Putnam 1892:188)

On October 8, 1866, on the advice of Winthrop, Marsh, and Russell, George Peabody made a gift of $150,000 to fund the Harvard Peabody Museum of American Archaeology and Ethnology. He named as trustees Robert C. Winthrop, Charles Francis

Adams, Francis Peabody (another relative), Stephen Salisbury II, Asa Gray, Jeffries Wyman, and George Peabody Russell, all residents of Massachusetts. Two weeks later, on October 22, he made a second gift of $150,000 to found the Peabody Museum of Natural History at Yale, naming Winthrop again as a trustee, along with James Dwight Dana, James Dixon, Benjamin Silliman, George Jarvis Brush, Othniel C. Marsh, and George Peabody Wetmore, all Connecticut residents (Hanaford 1870:166, 170). Yale rewarded Othniel Marsh for bringing in the museum by giving him the chair of geology and paleontology at Yale's Sheffield Scientific School.

Not long afterward, in February 1867, George Peabody gave $140,000 to Essex County, Massachusetts, to establish the Peabody Academy of Science, renamed the Peabody Museum of Salem in 1915 (F. Parker 1971:155). It shared many of the same board members with the Harvard museum—a tight circle of friends was involved—but Winthrop was not on this set of trustees. He was, however, named a trustee of George Peabody's Southern Education Fund, to which Peabody had given $3 million to help in the post–Civil War reconstruction of the South (Hanaford 1870:278; Winthrop 1897:274). Winthrop and the other trustees of this fund used part of Peabody's money to found the George Peabody Normal College in Nashville, Tennessee, in 1875, a college that is now part of Vanderbilt University.

Significantly, because of the rift between Louis Agassiz and many of his colleagues, Agassiz was not made a trustee of the Harvard Peabody Museum, even though the museum was envisioned as (and ultimately physically became) part of the larger MCZ complex. Toby Appel (1988) has argued that the disagreement over evolution had more influence on Agassiz's exclusion from the Peabody Museum than most people realized:

> Wyman's anthropological writings, undertaken in the latter part of his career, gave evidence of the antiquity of man in America, and Wyman explained the primitive habits of the mound builders by reference to evolution. The Peabody Museum of Archaeology and Ethnology, of which Wyman became the first curator, was founded in 1866 with an evolutionary purpose in mind. The letter accompanying the deed of gift called for the search in America for evidences of man in earlier geological eras, such as evolutionists had already uncovered in Europe. Wyman and Gray, both evolutionists, were made trustees of the Peabody Museum, while Agassiz had no official relation to the institution. (Appel 1988:88)

Winthrop (1878:178) indicated that the final deal for the Harvard museum came together rather quickly. On June 1, 1866, Peabody and Winthrop first met to discuss the changes in the proposed Harvard endowment. On June 4, Winthrop, Peabody, and Peabody's nephews Othniel Marsh and George Peabody Russell met at the Massachusetts Historical Society to work out more of the details. On July 6, Winthrop, after consulting with Harvard officials, gave Peabody the college's blessing to proceed with the museum endowment. The necessary paperwork was not completed until September 24, at which time Winthrop, Peabody, Marsh, and Russell met again to finalize the project.

On September 28, a meeting of the proposed trustees was called to order. The instrument of trust was signed on October 18, and the first formal meeting of the trustees was held on November 3. On the emphatic recommendation of former president Walker, on December 1, 1866, Jeffries Wyman was named the museum's first curator (Winthrop 1878:180).

The terms of the instrument and its codicils, as worked out by Peabody, Winthrop, Marsh, and Russell, gave Harvard a good deal of latitude in operating the museum. But they also set the agenda that the museum followed rigorously for the next half century. Peabody wrote:

> Aside from the provisions of the instrument of gift, I leave in your hands the details and management of the trust; only suggesting, that, in view of the gradual obliteration or destruction of the works and remains of the ancient races of this continent, the labor or exploration and collection be commenced at as early a day as practicable; and also, that, in the event of the discovery in America of human remains or implements of an earlier geological period than the present, especial attention be given to their study, and their comparison with those found in other countries. (Quoted in Hanaford 1870:171)

Provisions were also made for the establishment and maintenance of a Peabody professorship of American archaeology and ethnology, the holder of the chair to be appointed by Harvard, with the concurrence of its overseers, in the same manner as other professors. The Peabody Professor "shall have charge of the above-mentioned collections, and shall deliver one or more courses of lectures annually, under the direction of the government of the university, on subjects connected with said departments of science" (quoted in Hanaford 1870:173).

Peabody also made provisions for the orderly replacement of trustees, a policy that was followed for the next 30 years and was modified only when the museum became integrated with the college in 1897. The trustees were to be chaired by Winthrop, whose replacement would be the president of the Massachusetts Historical Society. Francis Peabody's replacement would be the president of the Essex Institute, an organization in Salem, Massachusetts, that had begun as the Essex County Historical Society in 1834; Salisbury's, the president of the American Antiquarian Society; Gray's, the president of the American Academy of Arts and Sciences; and Wyman's, the president of the Boston Society of Natural History (Hanaford 1870:174).

Robert C. Winthrop remained a trustee of the Peabody Museum until his death in 1894. He had resigned from most of his other institutional board positions in 1885, but he maintained his position at the Peabody Museum, as his son reported (Winthrop 1897:318), because of "the interests of which, in conjunction with his friend, Jeffries Wyman, he had done so much to foster in the beginning, in connection with which he ultimately founded a scholarship." Winthrop's keen interest in the museum was particularly exhibited in his efforts to help Wyman secure the first major collections for the Peabody. Although for the most part Winthrop seems to have been content to provide advice and guidance to Wyman and his successors, he became actively involved when a specific need arose. In 1866 a committee consisting of Winthrop, Wyman, and Gray developed a circular listing the museum's collection needs, which they distributed widely. It asked for donations of the following items, from any part of the world (excerpted from Hanaford 1870:181):

1. *Lithics*: axes, gouges, chisels, clubs, pestles, sinkers, tomahawks, mortars, arrowheads, spearheads
2. *Ceramics*: vases, pots, pipes, bowls, figurines
3. *Ethnographic*: bows, arrows, quivers, spears, rattles, drums, shields, snowshoes, knives, lodges, medicine bags, tobacco pouches, cooking utensils, articles of dress
4. *Somatology*: mummies, skeletons, particularly skulls and long bones
5. *Antiquities*: images, sculptures, casts from Peru, Mexico, Chile, Central America
6. Articles made by or relating to Eskimos, and the Fuegians or Patagonians

Because Europe was then the center of anthropological inquiry, Wyman was eager to establish a comparative collection of European materials. Winthrop moved easily among the scientists of the day, both European and American, and was able to help. Among other connections, being distantly related to Mary Lyell, the geologist Charles Lyell's wife, he had befriended the couple when Lyell came to the United States to deliver lectures at the Lowell Institute in the early 1840s. During the Peabody Museum's second year of existence, Wyman, with Winthrop's assistance, added to the museum collections roughly 3,000 items from Gabriel de Mortillet's collections of Paleolithic tools, 1,600 items from Wilmot J. Rose's collections from Denmark, and 865 items from the Swiss lake-dwelling excavations of a Dr. Clement, a noted antiquary from St. Aubin, Switzerland (Browman 2002d:509). In regard to the Mortillet collection, acquired during Winthrop's third major trip to Europe, when Wyman asked that he act as the agent for the Peabody Museum, the Swiss-born geologist Jules Marcou (1896, 2:164), a protégé of Louis Agassiz's, wrote that "Robert C. Winthrop visited me in Paris, and asked my help in the purchase of de Mortillet's collection. The transaction was successfully made, and I superintended the packing of the collection."

Over the years, Winthrop provided invaluable aid in fund-raising for the museum as well. In 1886, for example, he helped organize a successful fund-raising effort by the trustees in response to a letter from then curator Frederic Putnam—"An Appeal for Aid in the Explorations," dated August 6, 1886 (Putnam 1887e)—detailing a "crisis" in museum accessions and field explorations. A few years later, when Putnam was in desperate need of aid for graduate students, Winthrop's son stepped up and, on December 31, 1894, established the Robert C. Winthrop Scholarship in American Archaeology and Ethnology in honor of his father. Initially worth $200 a year, it was later increased and helped support many graduate students at the Peabody in the twentieth century (Winthrop 1897:318).

George Peabody was honored for his works as well. Queen Victoria of the United Kingdom offered him a baronetcy, although he declined it. In 1867 the U.S. Senate awarded him a special vote of thanks for his benefactions to his native land. Peabody died in London on November 4, 1868. After lying in state briefly at Westminster Abbey, his body was carried back to America on a British warship. In Boston, American soldiers carried his casket, which was then taken by train to Danvers, where he was buried, apparently with military honors. There is no question that George Peabody was one of the most significant American philanthropists of his time, somewhat before that of better-known figures such as the Rockefellers and Carnegies.

Louis Agassiz, Jeffries Wyman, Asa Gray, and the other men mentioned in this chapter formed the critical teaching and support faculty and staff for the eager and precocious students who were attracted to the rapidly growing scientific community at Harvard. These men were critical not only in the intellectual development of the generation of students to follow but also in doing anthropological research themselves and in developing the support facilities necessary for the growth of university anthropology. Jeffries Wyman was developing an interest in things anthropological two decades before he became the first curator of the Peabody Museum. But it was not just the professional staff that was important. Without the avocational contributions of people such as George Peabody and Robert Winthrop, the Peabody Museum program likely would never have come together.

3

Frederic Putnam and His Student Cohort, 1859–1875

IN THE MID-NINETEENTH CENTURY, wrote archaeologist Andrew Christenson (1985:236), "Boston was the center of American science. Harvard University, with its medical school and with Louis Agassiz, was the major producer of naturalists in the United States, and the Boston Society of Natural History was an important forum for research, discussion, and publication in all fields of natural history." A considerable amount of the activity relating to the development of anthropology took place at the Lawrence Scientific School and its associated Museum of Comparative Zoology (MCZ), then the centers of natural science at Harvard.

One person, **Frederic Ward Putnam** (1839–1915), was especially critical to the growth of university anthropology in the United States. Indeed, reading the standard histories of our field, one sometimes gets the feeling that Putnam developed anthropology in splendid isolation. But although we use him as the centerpiece around which to build much of our argument, Putnam was only first among a large cohort of students who contributed in one fashion or another to the growth of the field. To fully understand why anthropology succeeded at Harvard but failed at other universities during the latter half of the nineteenth century, the intellectual context and contributions of this entire cohort are important. Many people were crucial and many intellectual trends were significant to Putnam's ultimate success in founding the first continuing anthropology program in the country.

In discussing the development of science at the Lawrence School under Agassiz, the geologist Jules Marcou (1896, 2:51), who had moved to the United States in 1861 to join Agassiz at the MCZ, perceived two useful divisions of students: those who trained at Lawrence prior to the construction of the Museum of Comparative Zoology in 1859 and those who trained there after it existed. Among the first cluster of students were young men such as Louis Agassiz's son, Alexander, James M. Barnard, Henry James Clark, William Jones, John L. Le Conte, Joseph Le Conte, Theodore Lyman, James McCrady, James E. Mill, William Stimpson, Richard Wheatland, and Frederic Putnam. As might be expected, Putnam, who entered the Lawrence School in 1856 to study natural history with Louis Agassiz, had more interactions with Marcou's second group, and we examine them in detail subsequently. But at least three of the men in Marcou's first group were also relevant in the development of Putnam's career or of anthropology at Harvard in general: Clark, Lyman, and Alexander Agassiz.

Henry James Clark (1826–73) was born in Easton, Massachusetts, and received his A.B. from the City University of New York in 1848. He taught for a short period in White Plains, New York, where he entered into correspondence with Asa Gray about botany. As a result, he became a student of Gray's at Harvard in 1850 (Dupree 1959:257; Packard 1877:319). He shortly transferred over to work with Agassiz, becoming the third (Marcou 1896, 2:52–53) or fourth (Lurie 1960:177) advanced student in Agassiz's program. He received an S.B. from Lawrence Scientific School in 1854 and became Agassiz's right-hand man—his favorite student or favored assistant—for the next 12 years. Agassiz viewed Clark as the most skilled microscopist in the country, and after taking over most of Agassiz's work at the microscope, Clark did much of the work in histology and embryology for the four volumes (of the originally proposed 10) of Agassiz's *Contributions to the Natural History of the United States* (Dupree 1959:321). With Agassiz's support, Clark received a five-year appointment as adjunct or assistant professor of zoology in the Lawrence Scientific School in 1860. The title apparently carried with it no salary directly from Harvard, but Clark was paid by funds Agassiz had at the MCZ (Lurie 1960:241; Wayman 1942:100).

Some of the other students at the MCZ were becoming restive under Agassiz's increasingly heavy hand, and young Alexander Agassiz, writing to a colleague, praised Clark as Louis Agassiz's only "loyal" worker (Lurie 1960:313). When Agassiz's *Contributions* was published to great acclaim, however, Clark was stunned to find that what he considered his co-authorship was not acknowledged in any fashion, nor had Agassiz even acknowledged Clark's intellectual contributions. Clark made his bitterness known in a pamphlet, "A Claim for Scientific Property," which he circulated in 1863, and he began to criticize Agassiz at that point for his failure to embrace evolution (Dupree 1959:257; Marcou 1896, 2:54).

Agassiz did not take the criticism kindly. Judge Ebenezer R. Hoar, a member of the Harvard College Corporation and the Saturday Club and a good friend of Agassiz's and the Lazzaroni's, helped ease Clark out of the MCZ in November 1863, although Clark maintained some institutional rights until the end of his five-year appointment in 1865 (Lurie 1960:321). After being asked to give lectures for the Lowell Institute in 1864, Clark became a professor of botany, geology, and zoology at the Agriculture College of Pennsylvania State University in 1866. In 1869 he moved to the University of Kentucky, where he was chair of natural history, and finally went to the veterinary science department at Massachusetts Agricultural College at Amherst in 1872 (Packard 1877:322).

Clark, then, was the first of Agassiz's students forced out by what the students saw as increasingly autocratic treatment, setting the way for the Salem secession rebellion against Agassiz, which began the month after Clark left. As we discuss later, Putnam and a number of other students all left the Lawrence Scientific School and ended up taking positions in the museums at Salem, Massachusetts, whence the name of their revolt. Agassiz's behavior toward Clark only increased the friction that already existed between him and Asa Gray and Jeffries Wyman (Lurie 1960:330).

Theodore Lyman (1833–97), the independently wealthy son of a Boston mayor, was a member of the Harvard College class of 1855 and thus a classmate of Alexander Agassiz's, whose brother-in-law he later became (G. Agassiz 1927:150). Apparently, he was also a cousin of Charles W. Eliot, future Harvard president (Hawkins 1972:47). He socialized with other elite men of Harvard and Boston at the Saturday Club, and he eventually became a member of the U.S. House of Representatives. Lyman received his S.B. from the Lawrence Scientific School in 1858, became a trustee of the Museum of Comparative Zoology in 1859, worked as Agassiz's assistant from 1860 to 1861, and served in the Civil War from 1863 to 1865, mustering out with the rank of colonel. He held an appointment as professor of zoology at the Lawrence School from 1863 to 1887 and served as treasurer of the MCZ from 1865 to 1876. From 1868 to 1888 he was an overseer for Harvard College (Harvard University 1937:37–38, 308). Thus Lyman was either a fellow student or an instructor of most of the MCZ cohort whom we discuss later.

Lyman interacted with men such as Frederic Putnam in a variety of venues. For example, in 1868 he excavated aboriginal shell mounds with former Harvard student Edward Morse for Wyman and Agassiz at Cape Cod and at Damariscotta, Maine (Wyman 1869:17–18). When Louis Agassiz set up his first summer field school at Penikese in 1873, Lyman was on its faculty, along with Alexander Agassiz, Joel Asaph Allen, Count Francois Pourtales, Alpheus Packard, Frederic Putnam, Nathaniel Shaler, and Burt Wilder, all former Agassiz students (Lurie 1960:380). In 1885 Lyman would offer strong support for Putnam's nomination to the Peabody professorship, the chair endowed by George Peabody in 1866. Alexander Agassiz, however, citing Putnam's lack of credentials and a paucity of public demand for anthropology, initially sidetracked the nomination, causing a two-year delay. Thanks to the strong support of Lyman, Asa Gray, and Robert C. Winthrop, Putnam's nomination ultimately passed (Casler 1976:53–60).

Alexander Emmanuel Rudolph Agassiz (1835–1910) was the oldest of Louis Agassiz's three children by his first wife, the other two being Ida, born in 1837, and Pauline, born in 1841 (Fry and Fry 1989:12). He was a classmate or professional colleague of many of the people who contributed to the growth of anthropology at Harvard. Not only did he receive his degree as a colleague of Lyman's in the class of 1855, but he also rowed crew with Charles W. Eliot, the later Harvard president, as an undergraduate (G. Agassiz 1927:32).

After completing his A.B. in 1855, Alexander and his sister Ida helped their mother, **Elizabeth Cabot Cary Agassiz** (1822–1907), open a school for girls and young women on Quincy Street, a school that continued for eight years and had nearly 500 students during that time (Marcou 1896, 2:61). At age 20, Alexander taught German, French, and other subjects at his mother's school (G. Agassiz 1913:23–25). This school provided the administrative background for Elizabeth Agassiz to accept the presidency in 1879 of the School for Collegiate Instruction of Women, known colloquially as the "Harvard Annex," which subsequently became Radcliffe College. Frederic Putnam, James Dixon, and others of the early Harvard anthropology program began teaching special sections at the Harvard Annex in the late nineteenth century, a program that by the mid-1920s had developed into a combined graduate degree program at the Peabody Museum (Browman 2002a:222–24).

After receiving his A.B. in 1855, Alexander Agassiz earned an S.B. in engineering, geology, and chemistry in 1857 under Eben Horsford and another S.B. in comparative zoology and natural history in 1862 under his father at the Lawrence Scientific School. He served as a Harvard College overseer from 1873 to 1878 and again in 1885, and he was a Harvard College fellow from 1878 to 1884 and from 1886 to 1890. For the MCZ he served as business agent from 1860 to 1863, lecturer from 1863 to 1865, curator from 1875 to 1898, and director from 1892 to 1898. He was director of the University Museum, the buildings housing the MCZ and the Peabody Museum, from 1902 to 1910 (Harvard University 1937:9, 38, 100; Mayer 1910:419).

In 1859–60 Alexander Agassiz went to California on a job with the U.S. Coast Survey under Alexander Dallas Bache. After he returned to the MCZ, he obtained through his friend J. M. Forbes the presidency of some coal mines in Pennsylvania in 1863 (G. Agassiz 1913:53). Although he later sold them, he maintained an active interest in mines. From April 1865 to the summer of 1866, while Louis Agassiz headed an expedition to the Amazon funded by Harvard overseer and museum supporter Nathanial Thayer (1808–83)—the most important of the MCZ's expeditions during that period (G. Agassiz 1930:404)—Alexander was left in charge of the MCZ. After his father's return from Brazil, Agassiz took a vacation and went to Michigan to see its copper mines. He and his brother-in-law Quincy Adams Shaw bought into the Calumet and Hecla Mining Company (G. Agassiz 1913:57; Goodale 1913:295). Agassiz made significant improvements to the mining procedures, ultimately controlling about two-thirds of Michigan copper production. Alfred Goldsborough Mayer, in an obituary for Agassiz (1910:423), observed, "It is due more to him than to any other man that this mine has produced the largest profits ever divided by any corporated mining company, for the dividends up to December 31, 1907 amounted to $105,850,000." The mines made Agassiz a millionaire several times over. He gave more than three-quarters of a million dollars to the MCZ and considerably more than a million altogether to Harvard (Goodale 1913:297; Morison 1936:379)

Like many of the other students who studied with Jeffries Wyman, Alexander Agassiz developed a side interest in anthropology. In 1864, in a commentary on a presentation given by Wyman on explorations of shell mounds in Atlantic coastal areas, Agassiz noted that he himself had explored similar aboriginal shell mounds in California while working for the U.S. Coast Survey in 1859–60 (Wyman 1864:72).

In the fall of 1874 Agassiz planned a trip to Chile and Peru for the purpose of visiting copper mines, exploring Lake Titicaca, and collecting antiquities for the Peabody Museum (G. Agassiz 1913:131). In February 1875 he attempted the first dredging operations to try to secure Tiwanaku and Inca copper, silver, and gold offerings that had been thrown into Lake Titicaca between Copacabana and Isla de Sol, but mud soon clogged the dredge. He wrote to Oliver Wolcott Gibbs on March 3, 1875, that "I myself made two trips on the lake in the small steamers which are run by the Peruvian Government between Peru and Bolivia. During the trips I devoted myself mainly to sounding and to collecting what few antiquities I could pick up at the different ports" (G. Agassiz 1913:147). He was disappointed in the returns around Lake Titicaca, but on the coast his explorations "yielded a rich harvest of Peruvian mummies, Inca relics, and implements of the modern Indians." These he gave to the Peabody Museum (G. Agassiz 1913:149). Frederic Putnam, by then the museum's director, was delighted to receive the materials, writing, "The most important collection received, and, I believe, the largest donation ever made to the Museum, is that from Peru and Bolivia, collected by Mr. Alexander Agassiz and his Assistant, Mr. S. W. Garman. This collection was made at the personal expense of Mr. Agassiz, by whom it was not only presented to the Museum, but delivered in Cambridge free of all charge for transportation from Peru" (Putnam 1876:9).

In the late 1870s Alexander Agassiz began a campaign to explore the oceans of the world, becoming one of the founders of the new science of oceanography and pioneering new methods of dredging. He also continued collecting archaeological and ethnographic materials over the next 35 years, in the United States (principally near his mines in Michigan but also in the Southwest), Panama, Mexico, the Caribbean, Peru, Chile, Africa, and several Pacific islands, as documented in the collections catalogue at the Peabody Museum. Frederic Putnam, in his annual reports for the museum, singled out the donations from the Pacific Islands: "Among the gifts of more than ordinary importance, I may mention the ethnological collection made by Dr. Agassiz during his recent trip to Australia" (Putnam 1896a:244). A few years later he wrote: "The most valuable single gift received by the Museum, during the past year, is the large ethnological collection from the South Sea Islands collected by Dr. Alexander Agassiz and Dr. W. McM. Woodworth, while on the expedition of the U.S. Fish Commission S.S. Albatross in 1899–1900, and presented by Dr. Agassiz" (Putnam 1901a:299). As another indication of Agassiz's interest in archaeology and ethnography, his name was carried on the roster of the Boston chapter of the Archaeological Institute of America from the 1880s onward as a "Life Member."

Putnam and Alexander Agassiz thus not only were old schoolmates but also shared an interest in anthropology from at least as early as 1860. Agassiz inherited his father's autocratic personality, a trait that, together with his donations and leadership positions at Harvard, provided him with the means to make his personal views known about all aspects of science and education. He frequently questioned the way geologist and ethnologist John Wesley Powell, first director of the Bureau of Ethnology (later the Bureau of American Ethnology), was running that office (Champlin 1944:144). After being appointed a Harvard fellow in 1877–78, he gave his old classmate Charles Eliot trouble about the way he was operating Harvard College as its president (Morison 1936:359). Agassiz questioned the scholarship of his former classmate Nathaniel Shaler, particularly after Shaler was made a Harvard dean (Hawkins 1972:69). When Agassiz openly doubted, in 1885, whether there was sufficient interest in anthropology to create a professorship for Putnam, his position reflected his strong and often-voiced opinions on how to run the college and his concern, as a Harvard overseer, over the college's being eclipsed by Johns Hopkins, Clark University, and other institutions in graduate work. Agassiz presumed that these other institutions required any new professor to have a Ph.D., which Putnam did not. There is no evidence that bad blood existed between Agassiz and Putnam, so Agassiz's opposition to the appointment must be seen in the light of his belief that as an overseer he had a duty to guide the institution.

Despite Agassiz's delaying his professorship, Putnam continued to work well with Agassiz, who in 1890 was put on the Peabody Museum's visiting committee and, in 1895, on the museum's board of trustees, both at Putnam's request (Brew 1966a:4; Putnam 1895a:226). In the annual report for 1910, Putnam wrote:

> It is with sad realization of our loss that I begin the records of the past year with an allusion to the death of Dr. Alexander Agassiz, our honored Director of the University Museum. Dr. Agassiz was constantly aiding the objects of this department of the Museum. He was interested in its various activities, and always expressed his gratification when its friends gave their aid toward its advancement. During his extended travels to distant countries, he secured and gave to this Museum many large and important ethnological and archaeological collections. Especially is this the case with those which he obtained in South America, Africa, and the Pacific islands. To our library he gave many volumes and a number of albums of photographs of anthropological importance.
>
> Dr. Agassiz was in full sympathy with those who considered the museums for research and instruction important parts of the University. He hoped to see the completion of the great natural history museum as planned by his father, thus uniting all the sections of the University Museum under one roof, and furnishing the necessary room for the development of the section of anthropology. (Putnam 1911:220)

Of the group of students with whom Putnam was first associated, clearly Clark, Lyman, and Alexander Agassiz all had significant effects on the development of Putnam's later research.

Putnam himself entered Harvard as a teenager on the personal invitation of Louis Agassiz, thanks to training Putnam had received from **Henry Wheatland** (1812–93), of the Essex Institute in Salem, Massachusetts. Wheatland, a member of the Harvard class of 1832, had been one of the founders of the Essex County Historical Society in 1833 and an officer of that society, through its various permutations as it developed into the Essex Institute, from 1835 to his death in 1893. Wheatland was also a founding member of the American Association for the Advancement of Science (AAAS) in 1848 and in his position there was instrumental in helping Putnam become the permanent secretary of the AAAS in 1873. Putnam held that position for the next 25 years, and it gave him significant influence over the direction of development of the AAAS and American science during that period. Wheatland served on the Peabody Museum's board of trustees from 1867 to 1893, in which position he had influence on Putnam's selection as director of the Peabody in 1876, as well as the subsequent directions in which Putnam took the museum after becoming curator. Wheatland was thus a key figure in Putnam's life, not only in terms of the young man's initial recruitment into science and archaeology but also in providing continuing guidance and support through the Essex Institute, the AAAS, and the board of trustees of the Peabody Museum (Browman 2002a:210).

Putnam had begun studying natural history under Wheatland's tutelage in January 1856 through an apprenticeship that included work in the local museum of the Essex Institute. Louis Agassiz visited the museum while working on a chapter on embryology for the first volume of his *Contributions* and was so struck by Putnam's grasp of the museum specimens that he invited the young man to come study with him at Harvard. On February 14, 1860, Putnam wrote to his family:

> A few days after[ward] I concluded to accept his invitation to go to Cambridge and see his Museum. . . . In the meanwhile Dr. Wheatland had written to him and it was arranged that I was to go and see him, and if the visit was satisfactory I should make arrangements to study with him. . . . He said if I would come and study with him for a term, he would see what I could do and agreed with Dr. Wheatland to take me without charging me the usual fee for tuition. (Putnam Papers, Peabody Museum Archives)

After Putnam's initial meetings with Agassiz in 1856, it was agreed that he would enter the Lawrence Scientific School the next January, 1857, and would be provided with a rent-free room and a salary of $200 a year (Browman 2002a:211). He was 17 years old.

Putnam studied at Lawrence from 1857 to 1864, primarily with Louis Agassiz, Asa Gray, and Jeffries Wyman and occasionally with chemistry professor Joseph P. Cooke. At the time, students learned science as part of an apprentice-style system. With Agassiz's establishment of the MCZ in 1859, Putnam came to entertain hopes of rapid advancement to a professorship. That fall he wrote his family telling how he, Albert Ordway, and Nathaniel Shaler had helped Agassiz prepare a report on the proposed development of the MCZ to be delivered to the Harvard Corporation and the board of trustees. He wrote excitedly:

> I shall get my appointment soon from the Museum, as an assistant, and that will be quite a step toward a professorship. In the plan which we gave in last night it was stated that three professorships would be needed as soon as possible in the Museum,

> one as a professor of embryology, which [Henry James] Clark will have; one as professor of invertebrates, which will not be filled until [Albert] Ordway is old enough to take it; and the other professor of vertebrates, which I suppose will come to me, in fact Professor [Agassiz] has told me that that is his idea about the matter. (October 21, 1859, Putnam Papers, Box 1.7, Peabody Museum Archives)

Clearly, Putnam believed he was on the inside track to a Harvard professorship, and it was not professional degree credentials that mattered but the word of Louis Agassiz. This helps explain why Putnam did not bother to finish his degree work, an issue that would come back to haunt him a quarter century later when he was finally made Peabody Professor (Browman 2002a:212).

Together with Clark, Lyman, and Alexander Agassiz, Putnam was one of Agassiz's first cohort of students, who served the developing program in a variety of ways. Of this first group of students, during the years of transition before and after the founding of the Museum of Comparative Zoology, Alexander Agassiz served as business manager, Clark was an adjunct professor of zoology, Lyman worked on Ophiuroidea, or the echinoderms known as brittle or basket stars, and Putnam was put in charge of fishes and vertebrates (Marcou 1896, 2:88). As someone in whom Agassiz had more confidence because of his seniority, Putnam was also put in charge of the new student residence for the second cohort of students at the MCZ, the "Zoological Club" or "Zoological Hall," next door to the MCZ.

This second group developed a tremendous esprit de corps. Several of its members contributed to the ultimate growth of anthropology, both at Harvard and elsewhere. Part of the group's cohesiveness seems to have derived from the students' not only working and studying together at the MCZ but also living together in Zoological Hall. The residence made such an impression on its occupants that two of them, Edward Morse and Nathaniel Shaler, described it in some detail in their memoirs. Because of its importance to the group and because both Shaler and Morse were Harvard contributors to the development of anthropology in the last quarter of the nineteenth century, we take a closer look at Zoological Hall.

In 1855, Engineer Hall on Kirkland Street was converted to a zoological research facility (Lurie 1960:191). While the MCZ was under construction, the collections were housed in this wooden building, which at that point stood near the chemical lab of the Lawrence Scientific School. Shaler (1909:97) described the building as follows:

> Agassiz's laboratory was then in a rather small two-storied building, looking much like a square dwelling-house, which stood where the College Gymnasium now stands. The structure is still extant, though in forty-six years it has three times changed its site and uses, having been first a club-house for his students on Divinity Avenue, where the Peabody Museum has been built; it went thence to a site on Jarvis Street, where it served as the club-house and theatre for the Hasty Pudding Club; from there a little further west to its present location, where, after being long the habitation for the

department of French, it came to be a part of the little establishment for teaching students astronomy. Agassiz had recently moved into it from a shed on the marsh near Brighton bridge, the original tenants, the engineers, having come to riches in the shape of the brick structure now know as the Lawrence Building. In this primitive establishment Agassiz's laboratory, as distinguished from the storerooms where the collections were crammed, occupied one room about thirty feet long and fifteen feet wide—what is now the west room on the lower floor of the edifice. In this place, already packed, I had assigned to me a small pine table with a rusty tin pan upon it. Of other students, all somewhat older than myself, there were: Alpheus Hyatt, F. W. Putnam, A. E. Verrill, E. S. Morse, Richard Wheatland, Caleb Cook, and a person by the name of Lamb. Hereto also came from time to time but not regularly Theodore Lyman and [William] Stimpson. There was also in some narrow quarters a translator, a Swede, whose name is gone from me [It was Hansen], and a sterling old person, Gugenheimer [Guggenheim, according to Morse], who served as a preparator. Agassiz's artist [Jacques Burkhardt, according to Lurie] generally worked at his near-by dwelling or at his place in Nahant. One of the small rooms upstairs was a sleeping-place for Putnam, who served as keeper of the establishment.

In December 1859 the MCZ was nearly enough finished that the students transferred the collections from the old wooden building to the new facilities, where they set up new displays. By mid-January 1860, the student's room in the MCZ was completed. Morse wrote on January 15, 1860, that this room had two new blackboards, and "last Monday all the students collect in the Student's room for the first time. There was Mr. [Thomas] Barnard, Mr. [Theodore] Lyman, [Samuel] Scudder, [Alpheus] Hyatt, [Frederic] Putnam, [Richard] Wheatland, [Albert] Ordway, [Addison] Verrill and myself" (quoted in Wayman 1942:84).

The old lab structure was then moved opposite the north wing of the newly finished museum and placed where, according to the plan, the south wing of the MCZ was to be built, the site where the Peabody Museum is now situated (Marcou 1896, 2:85). Agassiz had the building refitted at his personal expense, arranged as a sort of boarding house for the use of the assistants and students of the new MCZ (Marcou 1896, 2:85). Student expenses were mostly covered: Boston philanthropist Nathanial Thayer paid salaries for some of the museum assistants, and Agassiz both paid for the renovation and other costs of Zoological Hall personally and gave all his students free tuition to Lawrence (Lurie 1960:314). Besides giving Putnam rent-free quarters and a stipend, he recruited Morse and Shaler, among others, in the fall of 1859 with the promise of a $25-per-month salary and free board and lodging to be furnished once the house could be renovated (Wayman 1942:64). Shaler (1909:102) wrote:

> As soon as Agassiz's collections were removed to the new museum, the old building (now to be known as Zoological Hall) was put on rollers and taken across lots to its second station on Divinity Avenue. It was then given over to what was called the Zoological Club, an association of about a dozen students who were working with

him. It was so arranged as to provide bed-rooms, a dining-room, and a room in the centre of the upper story with which the bed-rooms connected, to serve as the meeting placed of the Zoological Club, which was organized at this time and became the centre of our life. I had the good fortune to receive in the allotment a sleeping-place and a study therewith.

Edward Morse kept a diary during his first few years at Harvard, excerpts from which, published by Dorothy Godfrey Wayman (1942:106–7), provide a glimpse into the ambiance of the place:

> February 26 [1860]. Our rooms are papered, and tomorrow Ad [Addison Verrill] and I go in to buy carpets. Now I want you to send my bed and bedding by next Thursday. Putnam and [Albert] Ordway have their rooms filled up and are in them. Mr. and Mrs. [Albert and Katie] Glenn [the house supervisors] are all settled downstairs and in a week we shall have our breakfasts and suppers furnished us and it will not be long before we shall have our dinners also in the same way.
>
> March 1. Our carpets are being put down and Verrill and I have been busy buying things, furniture etc., for our rooms.
>
> March 4. Send immediately pillows, pillowcases, sheets, blankets, comforter and towels. I shall buy me a bedstead and mattress. Prof. [Louis Agassiz] gave us sixty dollars apiece to furnish our rooms and we have fixed them up in style. On our study we have a splendid dark green carpet, $1.00 a yard. Our paper is very handsome. We have a nice large new black walnut bookcase, a lounge, two cane chairs and black walnut tables. In our bedroom we have a large wardrobe bureau with six drawers; wash stand and so forth.
>
> March 11. We have a splendid black walnut bookcase, two nice black walnut tables, a black walnut mantel and a lounge, two nice large armchairs in our study. Our carpet is a dark green and black check and looks tiptop. We have nice chintz curtains.

Rooms on the second story opened onto a large central room. Soon after the students were situated, by early March 1860, this room became the venue for meetings of the "Agassiz Zoological Club" every Thursday night. Professor Agassiz attended these meetings, and the students took turns giving papers (Morse 1902:416). Shaler (1909:179) described the students' routine:

> It was my custom to get to my work by eight in the morning, and to keep at it until one o'clock; we then had dinner, and expected to be again at our desks by half-past two, working there usually until dark, or at least until five o'clock. We then went to the gymnasium or had boxing-matches, as we fancied, for half an hour. At six we supped, and then got to work in our rooms. We managed to get about seventy hours a week of pretty solid business. Once a week, or oftener, we had our club-meetings, and after them—they usually ended about midnight—we had dance-music from an old piano in our common room and a Virginia reel with shouts to wake the dead.

New museum labs, camaraderie in dedicated living quarters—life at first seemed idyllic. It was not to last. The first seeds of trouble germinated in the first year, and ultimately little problems in the training program culminated in what has been called the Salem secession. But during the first few months at Zoological Hall, life was rosy. The students plowed up a garden behind the house to raise tomatoes and squashes (Wayman 1942:118). They threw themselves into learning. Putnam, himself made a member of the Boston Society of Natural History by the Lawrence School staff, proposed Verrill, Morse, and James L. Foley for membership in December 1859 (Wayman 1942:59–60, 74). Foley was from Kentucky and had joined Cooke, Hyatt, Morse, Ordway, Putnam, Shaler, and Verrill as student assistants in 1859–60. He roomed with Shaler but dropped out of school at the beginning of the Civil War to join the army and never returned. Shaler then moved in with Hyatt (Shaler 1909:119).

The first issue developed in the summer of 1860. Morse recounted the incident in his diary (Wayman 1942:126–29):

> July 2, 1860. Cooke and I were with Putnam and Ordway in their room when Katie Glenn, our cook, came up crying. Putnam and Bertie Glenn had gotten into a fight over size of butter pats; Katie defended students to her husband Bertie and got into fight. Bertie Glenn despised by Guggenheim, Owen, Hansen, Verrill, Foley and Katie, in fact by all. [Owen is not mentioned in other records as a student. We think the Owen to whom Morse refers was Ellen Elizabeth Owen, later his wife.] The uproar was carried up to Agassiz. Agassiz stripped Cooke, Foley, Ordway and Putnam of their room keys on July 3. Putnam and Ordway engaged rooms outside of the building, and Morse moved in with a friend in North Cambridge on July 6, but Putnam's family told him to move back in, and he did so on the next day, July 7. After further negotiations, on July 9, Agassiz agreed to let all the students move back into the building, but decreed they had to find boarding arrangements outside.

Although seemingly a minor incident, this appears to have been the first in a series of irritations to the students that led them to rebel three years later.

During the 1860–61 school year, Albert Bickmore, Alpheus Packard, and William H. Niles joined the group at Zoological Hall (Marcou 1896, 2:86; Morse 1902:415). Charles Pickering Bowditch, although not a resident of Zoological Hall, also participated in events there frequently (see chapter 9). Altogether, during the time Putnam was a student at the Lawrence Scientific School, Louis Agassiz employed 19 assistants (G. Agassiz 1930:402): Henry J. Clark, Theodore Lyman, and Alexander Agassiz, whom we have already profiled; the early Zoological Hall residents Albert S. Bickmore, Caleb Cooke, Alpheus Hyatt, Edward S. Morse, Albert Ordway, Alpheus S. Packard Jr., Frederic W. Putnam, Nathaniel S. Shaler, and Addison E. Verrill; and Joel A. Allen, James M. Barnard, William James, John McCrady, Samuel H. Scudder, and William Stimpson (Browman 2002a:212). In the rest of this chapter we look more closely at Putnam's cohort in Zoological Hall and at the others of his contemporaries who maintained the strongest interests in the "natural history of humans"—anthropology and archaeology—throughout their careers. Some of them worked together, belonged to the same scientific organizations, and corresponded and collaborated over the years. Some of them, too, were about to rebel. They were coming to see themselves as underpaid, undervalued, and intellectually and professionally trammeled.

Jules Marcou (1896, 2:92), who stayed at the MCZ after the student rebellion against Agassiz, believed the crisis was brought on by new "Regulations for the Museum of Comparative Zoology" that Agassiz issued for the assistants in the MCZ, which were formalized on November 19, 1863. Rules 4 and 5 prohibited the assistants or students from having private collections and from working for any other institution (Lurie 1960:317). Most of the students, if not all of them, had taken additional positions during their apprenticeships with Agassiz, both for needed additional funds and for the experience. Some of the students had begun to publish on their research outside of the MCZ. To stop these practices, Agassiz forbade his students from publishing without his permission, from working on their own research during museum hours, and from holding any outside position (Cockerell 1920:192; Conklin 1944:30). Addison Verrill later complained to a friend that "exceedingly arbitrary and tyrannical rules . . . have been imposed . . . by which all intellectual independence is taken away" (quoted in Bruce 1987:292).

Another complaint was that although the minimum residence required for an S.B. at the Lawrence Scientific School was one year, students of Agassiz's who had entered Lawrence expecting to secure a degree within a year or two were taking much longer. University students could get Ph.D. degrees in Germany in one year, and no extant scientific degree program took more than a few years. Most of the students who were soon to rebel and leave the MCZ had been there for four years or more, because Agassiz was reluctant to see them as "ready," especially to publish scientific papers on their own. He complained that the students were pressuring him to be allowed to publish papers and that they had not consulted him about taking outside jobs.

The new regulations, which apparently all the students viewed as oppressive, resulted in what Ralph Dexter (1965, 1966a) called the Salem secession. In late 1863 and the first months of 1864, almost all of Agassiz's students left the MCZ (Dexter 1965:37; Lurie 1960:240, 316). Agassiz had become particularly furious that Bickmore, Hyatt, Packard, Putnam, Scudder, Verrill, and others had arranged for positions elsewhere, without his knowledge or permission. For this reason, in December 1863 he decided not to recommend permanent appointment of these students as museum assistants, despite his previous promises to them (Lurie 1960:315–16). Unsurprisingly, these students then left. None of the students, however, faulted Agassiz as a teacher. All of them made statements such as Edward Morse's later comment (1923:275), "I must emphasize the fact that Agassiz was a wonderful teacher."

Putnam had already established a base at Salem, Massachusetts, through his work with Henry Wheatland at the Essex Institute. Now, in 1864, the institute named him a curator; later he became director, until 1870. Cooke, Hyatt, Morse, Packard, Scudder, and Verrill soon joined him there. After the Peabody Academy of Science (later the Peabody Museum of Salem) was formed under the endowment from George Peabody in 1867–68, Putnam became superintendent of that museum in 1867 and director from 1868 to 1875 (Browman 2002a:214; Dixon 1930:277; Tozzer 1936a:126). Putnam also continued his association with the Essex Institute, serving as its vice president from 1871 to 1894 (Anonymous 1915).

Almost immediately, the former students put together a publishing venture. On November 22, 1866, Putnam, Morse, Packard, and Hyatt founded the scientific journal *American Naturalist,* which subsequently became the flagship journal of natural science in the Americas. They often published on anthropological topics. Packard was editor and wrote many of the articles for the first issue, of which 250 copies were printed. Hyatt was in charge of business affairs and book reviews. Morse made most of the drawings and oversaw mailing and subscriptions. Caleb Cooke also assisted in various tasks with the journal. Putnam, Packard, Morse, and Hyatt were all joint editors of the first three volumes. By the time volumes 4–7 were produced, Hyatt and Morse had left, and Putnam and Packard remained as editors. By the time of volume 8, the journal had been sold to paleontologist Edward Drinker Cope (Dexter 1956:210; Wayman 1942:214–15). When Putnam left the editorial staff of *American Naturalist* in 1875, upon his move to the Peabody Museum at Harvard, he remarked in his parting editorial that the journal had been

> started under the auspices of the Essex Institute by four of us who were unpaid officers of the Institute and with the simple and pure idea of doing missionary work in science. . . . After about one year from the start Mr. Peabody gave money to found the Peabody Academy of Science in Salem and we four editors of the magazine were made officers of the new academy and put on salary. We, therefore, turned out the Magazine in the name of the Academy. (Quoted in Dexter 1956:224)

It was in his position as editor that Putnam first made contact with many of the people who later became significant contributors to his program at the Peabody Museum in Cambridge (see chapter 4), when they sent him articles to consider for publication. In addition to co-founding the journal, Putnam established a printing office, known as the Salem Press, Printing, and Publishing Company, where the early issues of *American Naturalist* were printed. The proceedings of the AAAS were also printed there during Putnam's tenure as permanent secretary of that organization, along with works by many of Putnam's colleagues. Thus the Salem Press acted as a jobber, publishing not just natural history but also archaeological monographs. One example is William Bleecker Potter and Edward Evers's 1880 volume, *Contributions to the Archaeology of Missouri by the Archaeological Section of the St. Louis Academy of Science,* part I: *Pottery,* published on behalf of the Naturalists' Bureau of Salem. Unsold copies of that volume were still to be found in the basement storerooms of the Peabody Museum in the 1960s.

Because of this group of enthusiastic young workers at Salem, the AAAS held its annual meeting there in 1869 (L. Howard 1937:8). Putnam served as acting permanent secretary of the AAAS that year and shortly thereafter became permanent secretary. With his election as permanent secretary, the AAAS moved its national headquarters to the Peabody Academy of Science in 1873. It remained there until 1876, when it moved to a room over the Merchants Bank in Salem. By that time, although Putnam was still handling part of the publishing responsibilities for the AAAS through his Salem Press, he had accepted the curatorship at the Harvard Peabody Museum and left the Peabody Academy of Science (Whitehill 1949:81).

These young rebels went on to lead American science. Morse was the first of the group to achieve the presidency of the AAAS, in 1886, and Putnam later served as president, too. Verrill and Packard were elected to the National Academy of Science in 1872, Hyatt in 1876, Scudder in 1877, Putnam in 1885, and Morse in 1887 (Howard 1937:9). Morse remained associated with the Peabody Academy of Science for much of his career. Hyatt went to the New England Museum of Natural History (and the Boston Society of Natural History, MIT, and finally the MCZ); Packard, to Brown; and Verrill, to Yale (Wayman 1942:219, 277).

One of the students from the 1859–61 period drops out of our picture quickly, so we profile him before turning to the others. **Albert Ordway** (1843–97) was an active participant in the Putnam cohort for the short time that he was at the MCZ. In the fall of 1859, Agassiz thought highly enough of Ordway that he considered suggesting him for one of three new professorships in the MCZ. Agassiz had scheduled Ordway, Verrill, Morse, and Richard Wheatland to go on a collecting trip to Labrador and Hudson's Straits in the summer of 1860, but it was cancelled because of the war and lack of funds (Wayman 1942:93). In February 1861, Ordway, Verrill, and Putnam left for Washington, D.C., to consult with Joseph Henry and Stephen Baird at the Smithsonian Institution and collect some specimens to bring back to Cambridge (Lurie 1960:304; Wayman 1942:163). Ordway, Hyatt, and Morse led a discussion of Darwin's 1859 book, a subject that was a sore point for Louis Agassiz, during the January 1861 meeting of the Zoological Club (Dexter 1979:148), and Ordway had begun to publish his work on trilobites (Ordway 1862). Shortly after the Civil War began, however, he joined the Union Army, mustering out in 1866 as a brevet brigadier general (Bruce 1987:280). He never returned to science after the war. Instead, he stayed in Washington, D.C., and became involved in ordnance manufacture and politics. Between 1880 and 1883 he published a general index to the journals of the first 16 Congresses, those of 1789 to 1821. He became involved in the National Guard and was a commander in it at the time of his death in 1897.

Turning to the Salem secession students, **Alpheus Hyatt** (1838–1902) was one of Putnam's classmates at the Lawrence School who stayed involved in Putnam's life for several decades. Hyatt was the son of a leading merchant in Baltimore and had entered Yale in 1856. In 1857 his mother sent him to Rome to study for the priesthood, but Hyatt was able to convince his family to let him enter Harvard in 1858 to study with Agassiz (Putnam 1902b:414). Living in Zoological Hall, Hyatt went with Nathaniel Shaler and Addison Verrill on many field trips. They spent the summer of 1860 collecting on Mount Desert Island, Maine, and returned to the field together in 1861 on Anticosti Island in the Gulf of St. Lawrence, under Jules Marcou's guidance (Livingstone 1987:28; Marcou 1896, 2:92).

Hyatt took much of his coursework with Jeffries Wyman and Asa Gray. He received his 1862 S.B. retroactively from Harvard with high honors in 1864 (Packard 1903:717) and later followed Putnam to Salem. As a student of Gray's, Hyatt, along with Shaler and several of the other Lawrence students, disagreed with Agassiz over Darwin's ideas, which might have been another factor in the student's break with Agassiz. Indeed, Hyatt subsequently emerged as head of the American neo-Lamarckian school of biology (Livingstone 1987:28).

Hyatt served in the Civil War shortly after leaving Harvard, mustering out at the end of the war as a captain in the Union Army, before moving back to Salem (Putnam 1902b:414; Wayman 1942:66). In 1867 Putnam set up 10 scientific sections at the Peabody Academy of Science, with Hyatt as curator of three of them: geology and paleontology, protozoa, and ethnology. Hyatt remained in charge of these areas until 1870, when he returned to Boston as curator for the Boston Society of Natural History, a position he held until his death in 1902 (Putnam 1902b:414; Whitehill 1949:63). During this time he was also curator (1875) and assistant curator (1885–1901) in paleontology at the MCZ. He was one of two founders of the Boston Teachers' School of Science, becoming its manager. He was the principal founder of the American Society of Naturalists in 1883 and its first president; he taught at MIT from 1870 to 1888 and at Boston University from 1877 to 1902; and he was one of the founders of the Marine Biological Lab at Woods Hole, Massachusetts (Harvard University 1937:269; Packard 1903:717–18; Wayman 1942:67).

Hyatt is best known in the scientific world for his neo-Lamarckian (or American school of evolution) ideological position, which retained Agassiz's predetermined sequences along with Darwin's theory of evolution (Livingstone 1992:157–58). He shared this theoretical stance with other naturalists such as Morse, Packard, Edward D. Cope, William H. Dall, Clarence King, Joseph Le Conte, Henry F. Osborn, John A. Ryder, and Joel A. Allen, and with anthropologists such as Herbert Spencer, Lewis H. Morgan, John Wesley Powell, Lester F. Ward, and William J. McGee (Livingstone 1987:59–61). He and Edward Cope became the proponents of a well-known piece of neo-Lamarckian evolutionary theory called the "Hyatt-Cope Law of Acceleration and Retardation" (Packard 1903:722). Hyatt had a chance to spread his ideas most widely through his summer biological schools, which he started in 1880 at Annisquam on Cape Ann, Massachusetts, but moved in 1888 to Woods Hole (Dexter 1974:157–58, 1979:154).

Hyatt's most direct contributions to anthropology probably relate to his position as curator of ethnology for the Peabody Academy of Science from 1868 to 1870. He maintained his interest in material culture later, and in 1879 we find him serving as discussant at the meeting of the Boston Society of Natural History for Putnam's paper on archaeological work in Tennessee (Putnam 1879c:333). Hyatt made occasional donations of artifacts to the Harvard Peabody Museum over the years, such as materials from Newfoundland in 1887 (Putnam 1888a:13) and from Trenton, New Jersey, in 1888 (Putnam 1889a:35).

Addison Emery Verrill (1839–1926) was another of the students who came to Lawrence school in 1859 and left in 1863–64. Born in Maine, he was a boyhood friend of Edward Morse's (Wayman 1942:70) before they both came to Lawrence, and he was Morse's roommate the first year in Zoological Hall. With Shaler and Hyatt, he spent part of his first two summers as a Lawrence student dredging and collecting specimens from Mount Desert Island and Anticosti Island (Livingstone, 1987:28–29). Verrill and Hyatt became such good friends that Verrill named his first son, born in 1871, Alpheus Hyatt Verrill. During the 1862–63 school year, Verrill, along with Samuel Scudder and Frederic Putnam, was responsible for providing training, particularly with respect to Mollusca and other natural science specimens, to William Healey Dall (1845–1927), to whom we return later in this chapter (Bartsch, Rehder, and Shields 1947:3).

Verrill became one of Agassiz's favorite students. Agassiz sent him with Putnam and Ordway to meet with Henry and Baird at the Smithsonian to get specimens for the MCZ in 1861, and he offered Verrill an assistantship in the MCZ for 1862–63 and 1863–64 (Harvard University 1937:441; Wayman 1942:163). Late in 1863, however, a sharp disagreement arose over the amount of money Agassiz owed Putnam and Verrill for labors performed and over their desire to publish the results of their investigations. Agassiz refused to grant them permission to publish, stating that any work done by personnel at the MCZ would be considered the intellectual property of the MCZ (Lurie 1960:314–15). Agassiz apparently became particularly furious with Verrill and Putnam because of the great trust he had put in them, and in December that year he refused to recommend the permanent appointments as museum assistants that he had previously promised them (Lurie 1960:315–16).

Verrill went with the others to Salem (Wayman 1942:212), but only briefly. He seems then to have held an equally brief position with the Smithsonian (Conklin 1944:30; Marcou 1896, 2:100), but soon he was offered a position in zoology at Yale, where he taught from 1864 until his retirement in 1907. Apparently, Verrill's job offer at Yale caused a temporary rift between Agassiz and James Dwight Dana at Yale (Lurie 1960:342). Agassiz knew that Dana had encouraged students like Verrill and Albert Bickmore in their display of independence during the museum revolt, and after encouraging Verrill to leave Agassiz, Dana had hired him. Moreover, Dana was an ally of Asa Gray's.

Once the "secession" tempest blew over, as it quickly did, Agassiz and these students, including Verrill, got back together and worked harmoniously on various projects. Agassiz was apparently instrumental in nominating Verrill, along with Packard, to the National Academy of Science in 1872 (L. Howard 1937:9). Verrill joined his former Harvard colleagues in teaching for Agassiz at the Anderson School of Natural History on Penikese Island in 1873, and he was involved in subsequent summer biological field stations such as that at Woods Hole in 1875, where he and Dall, among others, taught Clinton Hart Merriam (1855–1942), who worked later with Putnam to establish a department of anthropology at the University of California–Berkeley (Merriam 1927:36).

Caleb Cooke (1836–80), too, was a resident of Zoological Hall who moved to Salem with the "secession" group. In the summer of 1859, Agassiz sent Cooke to Para, Brazil, to collect for the MCZ; Agassiz himself was to go there later (Dexter 1970:112). During the 1859–60 academic year, Cooke was one of the students who moved the collections into the new MCZ and refurbished Zoological Hall. He was also among the half dozen students whom Agassiz initially threw out of the house when they got into the squabble with the Glenns (Wayman 1942:111, 126, 127).

In November 1860, Cooke left on a major collecting trip for the MCZ, a trip that would ultimately last four and a half years. He collected in Zanzibar and Madagascar in Africa and also made some collections from the Far East (Dexter 1970:112; Wayman 1942:135). Apparently, Agassiz was opposed to the length of Cooke's collecting trips, which led to Cooke's joining the exodus to Salem. He moved to Salem when he returned to the United States in 1865 (Dexter 1970:112; Shaler 1909:106; Wayman 1942:135).

Cooke was officially appointed a member of the Peabody Academy of Science staff in 1867. He had just received an appointment at the MCZ for 1867–68 as an assistant curator (Harvard University 1937:165), so he finished his obligation there before transferring his allegiance to Salem. Cooke helped Putnam put out *American Naturalist* and performed other, miscellaneous duties for the museum (Dexter 1970:117). Among them was helping Packard dredge for Atlantic marine specimens for the museum in 1871 and 1872 (Whitehill 1949:75).

In September 1875 Cooke became curator of Mollusca at the Peabody Academy of Science, and Alpheus Packard was made curator of invertebrates, mineralogy, geology, paleontology, and botany. Each was to be paid $1,000. At the same time, Putnam was reappointed director of the museum and curator of vertebrates, archaeology, and ethnology—but without compensation. Putnam, however, already had an offer from the Peabody Museum at Harvard and almost immediately went to Cambridge (Whitehill 1949:82). In 1876 Packard established the biological field school of the Peabody Academy of Science, which he headed together with Cooke, Putnam, and Morse (Dexter 1974:156). "Mr. C. Cooke will have charge of the dredging parties" (Dexter 1957b:22). But Caleb Cooke, the "tall, gaunt red-headed Curator of Mollusca, who had devotedly done most of the drudgery of the museum since 1867," died suddenly from typhoid malaria, which he had contracted in Africa, in June 1880 (Whitehill

1949:87). Because of his early death, Cooke might seem to have been a minor player in the anthropological component of the MCZ-Salem group, but he made significant contributions to the development of the Peabody Academy of Science and to helping establish *American Naturalist*.

Edward Sylvester Morse (1838–1925) was born in Portland, Maine, where he met Addison Verrill and Alpheus Packard in 1859 (Wayman 1942:50, 53, 62, 70). After high school he took a job as a draftsman for the Portland locomotive works; his drafting skill is evident in many of his later publications in anthropology and zoology (Howard 1937:3). In July 1859, he and Alpheus Packard conducted some excavations at an aboriginal shell mound on Goose Island, Casco Bay, Maine, observing both Indian artifacts and shell species, which Morse later published (Morse 1863, 1867a, 1867b).

By the fall of 1859 Morse finally had enough money to enter Lawrence Scientific School, against his father's religious and economic objections and after five years of debate. His father acquiesced because Morse was to receive a salary of $300 a year as an assistant to Agassiz, with board and lodging to be furnished when Zoological Hall was renovated (Wayman 1942:64, 66). Until this time Morse had carried out a seven-year, solitary study of freshwater and land shells in Maine. At Lawrence he trained primarily under Agassiz, although he took courses with Wyman, Gray, and Joseph Cooke as well, from 1859 to 1862.

Morse moved into the academic scene rapidly. Putnam proposed him for membership in the Boston Society of Natural History on December 7, 1859, along with Addison Verrill and James L. Foley, and they were elected on December 21. On that date, in a letter home, Morse wrote: "Putnam, the assistant, told me yesterday that Prof. [Agassiz] told him I was to be the assistant in the Museum" (Wayman 1942:79). In the early spring of 1860 Agassiz scheduled Morse for the collecting trip to Labrador and Hudson's Straits that was later cancelled (Wayman 1942:93, 117).

After the quarrel with the Glenns over meals at Zoological Hall in the summer of 1860, Morse and Foley moved out and shared a room in the Harvard College residence halls. Apparently, this was the period when Morse spent a bit more time working with Wyman as well (Wayman 1942:128–41). Seeds of Morse's eventual rupture with Agassiz are evident as early as January 1861, when he, Ordway, and Hyatt presented the positive discussion of Darwin's new book at the Zoological Club meeting.

Morse had an extra concern, as he had found a girlfriend. He planned to get married and needed a predictable income, so he was particularly upset when Agassiz, in early 1861, paid the students' stipend three months late (Wayman 1942:165). Morse also perceived some nepotism or favoritism on Agassiz's part, writing in his diary, when Alexander Agassiz got his degree from Lawrence in 1862, that it was a put-up job. He subsequently had bitter words with Agassiz about salary and decided to leave the MCZ for more money as well as other issues. In his diary Morse mentioned spelling out his angst to William Stimpson, one of the pre-MCZ students, who wrote back supporting his decision to leave (Wayman 1942:181–82).

Because of his shortage of funds, Morse had taken a part-time position as curator of the Portland (Maine) Society of Natural History in 1861, a job he kept until 1866. This was one of the part-time, outside positions that so irritated Louis Agassiz. In 1862 Morse took academic leave to enter the Union Army, in which he served as an assistant surgeon (Howard 1937:6). Morse left military service in 1863 and was planning to return to the MCZ when Agassiz issued his infamous November decree. Morse joined Putnam and the others in resigning his MCZ position (Howard 1937:7). Morse also married his girlfriend in 1863, in Gorham, Maine, where he continued working part-time as superintendent of the Portland Society of Natural History. When fire destroyed the society's buildings in 1866, Morse, who had been a member of the Essex Institute since 1864, transferred to Salem to work full-time with Putnam (Whitehill 1949:55). Like Putnam, Morse left Harvard without securing an official degree, a situation that remained unrectified until he received an honorary A.M. in 1892.

At the Peabody Academy of Science, Morse was named curator of Radiata and mollusks in 1867. He also employed his drafting and artistic skills in creating illustrations for *American Naturalist* (Dexter 1956:210). His interest in archaeology and ethnology continued to grow, and he excavated with Theodore Lyman at the Damariscotta shell mounds in 1868, publishing comments on that work in 1869.

Salem was too small to support Putnam's dynamic group for long, and in the early 1870s most of the original members left for larger and more imposing venues. Morse left in 1871 to return to Maine, becoming a professor of zoology and comparative anatomy at Bowdoin until 1874 (Dall 1926:158). As was so often the case, the position carried a small salary, so Morse also lectured in zoology at Harvard in 1872–73 (Harvard University 1937:336) and at Maine State College in Orono in 1870–71, and he joined Agassiz and other former and current MCZ students in running the biological field school on Penikese Island in the summers of 1873 and 1874 (Wayman 1942:227). Although Asa Gray had recommended Morse for a position at Princeton in 1872, Morse turned it down after reviewing the offer (Wayman 1942:228).

Morse continued picking up part-time teaching jobs (reminding one in some ways of today's so-called gypsy scholars). In the summer of 1876 he taught at the biological field station Packard had established at Salem (Dexter 1957b:21), and in 1877 he did a little work in Kentucky. Later that year, however, Morse made a major career move when he went to Japan at the invitation of Sotoyama Seiichi, a professor at the Imperial University of Tokyo, to give some lectures on zoology at the newly founded institution. Sotoyama had studied at the University of Michigan in 1872 and had met Morse, who was on lecture tour, at that time (Ko 2003:30–31).

Morse left San Francisco for Yokohama in late May 1877. On the day after his arrival in June he saw the shell middens at Omori from the train as he journeyed to the capital (Howard 1937:11). "As the result of his field work in Maine and North Carolina, he identified the formation instantly as a prehistoric kitchen midden. . . . Archaeology, until that moment, had not existed in Japan" (Wayman 1942:236).

Three weeks after he arrived, he was offered and accepted a two-year contract to establish a department of zoology at the new Imperial University of Tokyo. He became the first professor of zoology at the university, a position he kept until 1880 (Dall 1926:158). He established the Enoshima field station, one of the first marine biology labs in the world, based on the models from his years in New England (Howard 1937:12). In his teaching, Morse, like most of his former classmates from the 1859–64 period, was a neo-Lamarckian.

When the university resumed session in September 1877, Morse inaugurated the first course of lectures in zoology ever given in the country, established Japan's first scientific societies, and began excavating the shell mounds at Omori (Wayman 1942:242). In his diary he referred to having two Japanese university students working with him on the mounds in 1877–78, the first Japanese students thus trained in scientific archaeology (Wayman 1942:250). As he was excavating these mounds, Morse found some indications of human bone modification like those Wyman had interpreted as evidence of prehistoric cannibalism in New England and Florida. When he published this finding in his volume on the Omori shell mounds, it created a local sensation, for the Japanese press interpreted his observation as a pejorative comment on the Japanese character.

Morse had considerable influence on the U.S.-Japanese intellectual dynamic and indeed is viewed by some as the surrogate father of Japanese anthropology. On leave in the United States in 1879, he collected 2,500 books and pamphlets for the Imperial University library (Howard 1937:12). He introduced scientific methods in the study of biology, archaeology, and ethnology, as well as evolutionary theory, to students and faculty of the Imperial University of Tokyo. He taught Japanese scholars collections management, how to publish university bulletins, and how to institute professional exchanges of specimens and publications (Ko 2003:32). He strongly influenced Tsuboi Shogoro (1863–1913), the "principal founder" of Japanese anthropology, who had worked on Morse's Omori excavations (Ko 2003:29, 34–36). Morse's 1879 book on that project, *Shell Mounds of Omori*, was the first academic publication of the Imperial University of Tokyo and thus the first in Japan, for it was the only university in the country at the time. The Japanese saw Morse as an expert in zoology and archaeology but also in ethnology, because of his publications on aspects of Japanese material cultural such as dwellings and ceramics (Ko 2003:33).

Not least, Morse helped bring other influential scholars to Japan. At his request, the art historian Charles Eliot Norton, head of the fine arts department at Harvard, sent his best student, Ernest F. Fenollosa (Harvard A.B. 1874), to Tokyo to teach Western art (Wayman 1942:286). On the basis of his early work with Morse in Japan, Fenollosa went on to become an expert in Asian art history at the Boston Museum of Fine Arts. In 1882 Morse brought William Sturgis Bigelow (Harvard A.B. 1871, M.D. 1875) to Japan, and he later enticed Perceval Lowell (Harvard A.B. 1870), Charles Goddard Weld (Harvard A.B. 1879, M.D. 1881), and Denman Waldo Ross (Harvard A.B. 1875) to come there to teach (Wayman 1942:271–81). Bigelow (who later became vice president of MIT) and

Weld contributed to medical training, Ross investigated the fine arts, and Lowell contributed to astronomy.

In 1880, at the end of his tour in Tokyo, Morse received an offer to return to the Peabody Academy of Science in Salem as director of its museum, an offer he accepted. He kept the position until his retirement in 1914. His time in Japan had stimulated his anthropological interests, which were reflected in his publications from 1880 onward. He donated most of his collection of more than 5,000 Japanese ceramics—the largest of its kind (Ko 2003:30)—to the Boston Art Museum. He gave a major portion of his ethnographic materials to the Peabody Academy of Science, but he also gave some materials to Putnam at the Harvard Peabody Museum (Howard 1937:12).

When Morse took over as director of the Peabody Academy of Science museum in 1880, he modified it, designing an alteration of the hall to place the ethnological collections on the first floor. He had space added on the second floor for archaeological collections (Whitehill 1949:172). Alpheus Hyatt had originally arranged the anthropological collections in 1867 according to the generic character of the objects, in a kind of evolutionary scheme. Morse, following what Putnam was now doing at the Peabody at Harvard, abandoned that format and instead arranged the collections according to the culture area from which the objects came (Whitehill 1949:89).

Morse's interest in and contributions to anthropology persisted after he took the job at the museum in Salem. He continued his interest in shell middens, working, for example, at a site near Friendship, Maine, in 1886 (Putnam 1888a:13). Having become interested in the bow and arrow after viewing Ainu technology in Japan, he began giving papers on the topic at the AAAS, the Boston Society of Natural History, and the Essex Institute and started publishing on bow and arrow technology in general in the mid-1880s. He began an extensive correspondence with well-known anthropological scholars including Zelia Nuttall (see chapter 4), Frank Hamilton Cushing, and Daniel Brinton about arrow release problems and bow technology (Wayman 1942:309, 310, 345). In 1887 he gave a paper on the Danish shell midden work of Johannes Steenstrup in Copenhagen, after giving several papers on bow release at the British Association for the Advancement of Science. The following year Morse returned to Europe, having been nominated to represent American ethnology at the International Congress of Americanists (Wayman 1942:319, 337, 340). He was asked to judge the Asian pottery exhibit at the 1904 Louisiana Purchase Exposition in St. Louis and reluctantly agreed to do so, noting in a letter of August 28, 1904 (quoted in Wayman 1942:389), "The only thing that tempted me was the opportunity of getting material for another paper on Arrow Release. . . . The head of the anthropological department, Prof. McGee, is an old friend of mine and every opportunity will be had for what I want." He retained his interest in shell middens throughout his life; his last published work, in *Science Monthly* in October 1925, was "Shell-mounds and Changes in the Shells Composing Them." The larger scientific community recognized his contributions by electing him president of the AAAS in 1886, as well as conferring on him other honorary positions and degrees.

The last of the original residents of Zoological Hall who left in 1863–64 was **Samuel Hubbard Scudder** (1837–1911), of Williamstown, Massachusetts. He entered Williams College in 1855, received his A.B. there in 1857, and earned an A.M. in 1860. He was acquainted with Alpheus Packard at least as early as January 1858, when the two met to talk about entomology (Cockerell 1920:188). He entered Lawrence Scientific School in the 1859–60 year and was there in time to help move specimens into the new MCZ and to be at Zoological Hall, but he left with several others in late 1861 to work in the war effort (Wayman 1942:84, 180). He apparently returned to Harvard rather soon from the war, for he was awarded his S.B. in 1862. He served as an assistant and university lecturer for Agassiz from 1862 to 1864 and then, with most of the rest of his group of students, left the MCZ (Harvard University 1937:398; Wayman 1942:99). But unlike the larger contingent, who went to Salem, Scudder stayed in Boston and changed his association to the Boston Society of Natural History (Wayman 1942:99).

In 1877 Scudder became one of several of Agassiz's former students to be named to the National Academy of Sciences. He served as assistant librarian at Harvard from 1879 to 1882 and was named president of the Boston Society of Natural History in 1880, a position he held until 1887 (Harvard University 1937:398; Wayman 1942:99). Because of his experience as both librarian and scientist, he was selected to become editor of the reborn journal *Science* in 1883. In its first iteration, *Science* had been funded by Thomas Edison from 1880 to 1882, but then the magazine had collapsed. With additional funding from Alexander Graham Bell it was reborn on February 9, 1883, under Scudder, and he remained editor until 1884 (Kohlstedt 1999:36). This was during the time Putnam was permanent secretary of the AAAS, and Putnam used that position to assist in establishing *Science*. He not only helped Scudder become editor but a short time later also helped arrange for a relatively unknown German scholar, Franz Boas, to get an assistant editor's job at the journal. Scudder remained involved with *Science* even after he left the editor's post. The journal's masthead in 1899, for example, listed a committee of editorial consultants that included, among others, John Wesley Powell for anthropology, Edward C. Pickering for astronomy, Samuel H. Scudder for entomology, John Le Conte for geology, Henry F. Osborn for paleontology, Henry P. Bowditch for physiology, J. McKeen Cattell for psychology, and C. Hart Merriam for zoology.

Like all of Jeffries Wyman's students, Scudder had some familiarity with ethnography and archaeology. For instance, Scudder and Hyatt were among those who had comments to make on the early archaeological explorations in Tennessee that Putnam and Curtiss reported at the Boston Society of Natural History (Putnam 1879c:333). During most of the years from 1880 to 1897, Scudder served as a member of the board of trustees of the Peabody Museum, thus advising Putnam as well as endorsing his decisions in anthropology (Putnam 1912:217).

Albert Smith Bickmore (1839–1914) was one of the students who came to the Lawrence Scientific School in 1860 and joined the remaining original residents of Zoological Hall. He, too, left when Agassiz enacted the new rules late in 1863. Bickmore was from Tenants Harbor, Maine, and became interested in American Indians when he was eight years old, when several families of Penobscot Indians came back to their annual camping place on one of the Bickmore family beaches (Hellman 1968:11). Bickmore graduated from Dartmouth in 1860 in chemistry, geology, and mineralogy and then went to study with Agassiz, who appointed him assistant in charge of Radiates and mollusks. In the fall of 1863 Agassiz made known his displeasure that Bickmore had taken a position in New York City without his knowledge. Bickmore had also gone so far as to solicit a popular subscription for a private research project of his own, a trip through the Malay Archipelago and Indonesia. In December 1863 Bickmore became another of the students for whom Agassiz refused to recommend reappointment.

After a tour with the Union Army during the Civil War, Bickmore made his delayed trip to Malaysia and Indonesia, returning after 16 months and writing his only book, *Travels in the East Indian Archipelago* (1868). He took a teaching job at Madison University (now Colgate) in Hamilton, New York, as a professor of zoology and geology. As early as 1867 he began to solicit support for a new museum to be based in New York City—the American Museum of Natural History (AMNH). Among the potential donors he interested were William E. Dodge Jr., a Phelps-Dodge copper scion and shell collector who had helped underwrite Bickmore's trip to Indonesia and Malaysia, Isaac N. Phelps and A. G. Phelps-Dodge, bankers Morris K. Jesup and J. Pierpont Morgan, businessman Theodore Roosevelt Sr., and merchant John D. Wolfe, who subsequently became the first president of the AMNH (Hellman 1968:18–19).

The official founding meeting of the AMNH was held on December 30, 1868, and it was officially incorporated on April 6, 1869. Bickmore resigned his position at Madison University to become the first superintendent (a title later changed to curator) of the museum, and he remained in that job until 1884 (Kennedy 1968:12).

Bickmore was certainly important in the beginnings of the ethnographic and archaeological collections at the AMNH, but the rest of the Lawrence cohort seems not to have taken well to him. The first indication of their dislike is a comment Morse made in his diary for October 5, 1860, noting that Putnam, Cooke, Foley, Morse, and Charles Bowditch had ganged together in Cooke's room and "endeavored to smoke Bickmore out, a student who makes himself particularly disagreeable to us all" (Wayman 1942:140).

Bickmore's reputation among scientists also suffered because of his relationship with showman Phineas T. Barnum (Hellman 1968:23; Kohlstedt 1986:177). Bickmore had collected for Barnum in Bermuda in 1862 and continued his relationship with the impresario later at the AMNH. In 1871 he solicited a fur seal, a giraffe, and a baboon from Barnum for the AMNH collections. Edward Cope, in a letter to Putnam on June 27, 1896, complained that the AAAS had gone downhill lately, and one reason was "the permission granted to a man like Bickmore to exhibit pictures, without a particle of science" (quoted in Dexter 1982b:113). Bickmore, then, seems not to have been well respected by his fellow students and never became a significant player in their group.

Unlike Bickmore, **Alpheus Spring Packard Jr.** (1839–1905)—another participant in the Salem secession—remained close to Putnam and other peers throughout his career. Born in Brunswick, Maine, Packard began collecting shells in 1853 and studying comparative anatomy in 1857, when he entered Bowdoin (Wayman 1942:54). In July 1859, Edward Morse, a native of Portland, Maine, brought Packard along for some exploring of Goose Island, Maine. They excavated a shell mound, where they recognized "Indian deposits," although Morse was more interested in some unusual shellfish species found in the mound (Morse 1863; Wayman 1942:61–62). Thus even before Morse and Packard entered the MCZ, we find them exploring archaeological sites together.

Packard's university training was split between Bowdoin and Harvard. His father was a professor of Greek and Latin at Bowdoin, and Packard received an A.B. there in 1861, an A.M. in 1862, and an M.D. in 1864 (Cockerell 1920:181, 191). After receiving his A.B., he took a position as an assistant to the Maine Geological Survey in 1861–62. He also entered the MCZ in the fall of 1860, moving into the room his friend Morse had vacated in Zoological Hall. In October 1861 he asked Agassiz for an appointment as entomological curator at the MCZ, at $300 a year, but he did not receive the appointment until the fall of 1863, for the 1863–65 period (Cockerell 1920:191–92; Harvard University 1937:350). Because Packard left with the group of disgruntled students, he did not receive a degree while at the Lawrence Scientific School, but he and classmate Albert Bickmore both got retroactive "special" S.B. degrees in 1901, as members of the class of 1864. During the Civil War, Packard, in addition to Morse and Burt Green Wilder (1841–1925), another former Agassiz MCZ student, served as an assistant surgeon in the Union Army (Howard 1937:6).

Alpheus Packard and Frederic Putnam became close friends during their MCZ days, and when Putnam became superintendent of the museum of the Essex Institute in Salem in 1864, Packard was one of those he brought with him as assistants. There, with Putnam, Hyatt, and Morse, Packard helped found the journal *American Naturalist* in 1866. When the Peabody Academy of Science was established in Salem in 1867, Packard was appointed its curator of Articulata. With the reorganization of the museum in 1875, he was named curator of invertebrates, mineralogy, geology, paleontology, and botany, at a salary of $1,000. In 1876 he became director of the museum, a position he held until 1879 (Whitehill 1949:63, 82, 173).

American Naturalist was an important vehicle for Packard for two decades. He served as editor and staff writer when it was first founded in 1866 (Wayman 1942:214–15). As the others slowly drifted away from the journal, Packard stayed with it, and when Putnam sold his interest to Edward Cope in 1875, Packard was retained as co-editor. He continued as co-editor of the journal with Cope for another 10 years, until volume 19. Under Packard's direction, the pages of the journal included a number of articles relating to evolution, that issue of dispute between Louis Agassiz and his students. Like Morse, Cope, and others, Packard took the slant of "neo-Lamarckism," a term he is credited with having introduced in 1884, although he had been publishing on this theory in the journal since the 1870s (Dexter 1979:163).

At the 1869 AAAS meetings, which were held in Salem, Packard and Putnam were especially involved in the special meeting of "microscopists," with a display of instruments. The meetings were well attended, by 275 members out of a total of about 700. Noteworthy for our focus is that two new sections of the AAAS were formed at this meeting (Dexter 1957a:260–61)—one on microscopy, as a result of the enthusiasm shown in the "microscopical gathering," and the other on archaeology and ethnology. This was the beginning of what was to become Section H, the vehicle that Putnam particularly, but also others of the MCZ cohort, used to expound his views on the nascent field of anthropology.

Once the spat between Louis Agassiz and his students had cooled, Packard was among those who helped their former professor in his first biological field school. After Agassiz died late in 1873, his son Alexander took over direction of the Anderson School for 1874. When Alexander himself became ill, Putnam and Packard took over the running of the research school for him. In a letter to Wolcott Gibbs on August 8, 1874, Alexander Agassiz wrote that "Putnam and Packard who had charge have done admirably and worked most faithfully. Everything has run to the satisfaction of all the pupils and there has not been a word of grumbling from anybody" (G. Agassiz 1913:130). When Packard took over as director of the Peabody Academy of Science at Salem in 1876, he founded its own summer school of biology, with Putnam, Cooke, Morse, and John Sterling Kingsley (1854–1929) on staff (Cockerell 1920:198; Dexter 1957b:22, 1974:156). This field school continued until 1881.

Packard collaborated with Putnam on other ventures as well. In 1874 Putnam was appointed an assistant in the Geological Survey of Kentucky, of which Nathaniel Shaler had become head in 1872. Packard worked with Putnam there, and the two subsequently published a series of jointly authored reports on their findings from Salts, Saunders, and Mammoth Caves (Abbott 1886:695; Putnam 1875b:410). Among the materials they reported on were imprints of sandaled feet, large numbers of cast-off sandals, pieces of finely woven bark cloth, bundles of faggots tied up with twisted bark, cane reeds from ancient torches, fragments of large gourds, and dried human excrement (Putnam 1875d:49–50). We tend to forget a century and a quarter later that these kinds of perishable materials were being observed, collected, and curated at the time.

Packard also had a part-time appointment at the Maine College of Agriculture at Bowdoin from 1871 to 1877. After receiving a full-time appointment as professor of zoology and geology at Brown University in 1878, he resigned his position at Salem and taught at Brown for the next 27 years, until his death in 1905. Because of his strong focus on zoology, his interest in anthropology during this time has been overlooked or eclipsed. But he still taught occasional classes in anthropology and was recognized by his students for his focus in that area. Theodore Cockerell (1920:199) reported that "in 1904 the class in anthropology presented him with a loving cup, the first that had ever been given at Brown." So Packard, who had excavated his first aboriginal shell mound with Morse in 1859, was still pursuing anthropology with sufficient vigor to receive an award 45 years later. A quick scan of his more than 570 publications turns up several with anthropological topics, such as "Our Aryan Ancestors" (1884), "Notes on the Labrador Eskimo and Their Former Range Southward" (1885), "Tertiary Man" (1887), "Among the Prehistoric Monuments of Brittany" (1891), and "The Java 'Missing Link'" (1895).

Among the original residents of Zoological Hall, one stands out for *not* having joined the student revolt. **Nathaniel Southgate Shaler** (1841–1906) was born in Newport, New York, but the family later moved west. Shaler came to Harvard from Kentucky in 1859, entering as a sophomore. He began in classical studies (Greek and Latin), but after taking one course with Agassiz, he shifted to the Lawrence Scientific School (Livingstone 1987:26; Shaler 1909:90). He moved into Zoological Hall and roomed first with James L. Foley, who was also from Kentucky. When Foley dropped out of school to join the army, Shaler moved in with Alpheus Hyatt for the next year (Shaler 1909:119).

Shaler learned lab procedures from **William Stimpson** (1832–72), a member of the pre-MCZ student cadre. Stimpson took Shaler dredging for mollusks in the Atlantic Ocean for the first time in 1860 (Shaler 1909:128, 130). Once trained, Shaler, Hyatt, and Addison Verrill made many collecting trips together, including the expeditions to Mount Desert Island in 1860 and Anticosti Island in 1861 that we mentioned previously (Livingstone 1987:29). In 1862 Shaler defended his senior thesis after Wyman examined it and found it sufficient to bring to defense. The committee consisted of the Lawrence School faculty—Louis Agassiz, Joseph Cooke, Asa Gray, Eben Horsford, Joseph Lovering, Benjamin Peirce, and Jeffries Wyman—and Harvard College president Cornelius C. Felton, previously a Harvard professor of Greek (Shaler 1909:189). This type of defense was typical of the day.

After completing his S.B. summa cum laude in geology in 1862, Shaler went to Kentucky to serve on the Union side of the Civil War for two years, despite his mother's having come from a long-established slave-holding family, and then he returned to Harvard (Livingstone 1992:149). In 1863, the students who left for Salem urged Shaler to join them, but he decided not to, saying that he had just put down one secession and did not want to be part of another (Conklin 1944:30). Almost immediately, Agassiz made Shaler his assistant in paleontology. When Agassiz left on the Thayer Expedition to Brazil the next year, Shaler took over his classes, and when Agassiz became ill upon his return, Shaler continued to teach. He thus was an assistant, a lecturer, and finally a professor in paleontology and geology from 1864 to 1906 (Harvard University 1937:400; Livingstone 1987:30–31; Shaler 1909:361). Shaler is credited with suggesting to Agassiz, in December 1872, the idea of a summer biological field school for teachers, which materialized as the field station on Pekinese Island (Lurie 1960:379).

Appointments at Harvard—and at other institutions of the day—often were not full-time. Although Shaler stayed on the Harvard faculty lists from 1864 to 1906, he frequently was not in residence during the early years. He went on leave to England in 1872 and while there was offered and accepted the position of head of the Kentucky Geological Survey. Thanks to his old classmate, Putnam held a temporary position with the survey in 1874, running its first field school and, with funds from the Peabody Museum, collecting specimens for Wyman from mounds there (Livingstone 1987:34; Putnam 1875b:410, 1875d:47). In the meantime, Shaler found time to keep his position at Harvard and to finish his doctorate (S.D.) in natural history there in 1875.

Shaler retained his interest in anthropology in part through his continued association with geology. In 1881 he was on leave in Europe because of poor health, and when he returned to the United States in 1882, he took a job with the U.S. Geological Survey (USGS). In 1884 John Wesley Powell appointed him director of the Atlantic Coast Division of the USGS (Livingstone 1987:36–37). From the inception of the USGS, Shaler had been a loyal supporter of Powell and the survey, and he defended Powell assiduously against attacks from Alexander Agassiz, even telling Othniel Marsh that he would go to Washington, D.C., to testify on Powell's behalf if necessary (Livingstone 1987:39, 43). Powell, as we describe in chapter 5, was a colleague of Putnam's and much interested in anthropology.

Shaler kept his linkage with Harvard strong. He and Justin Winsor, chief librarian at the Widener Library at Harvard, were good friends, and Shaler wrote the physiographic introduction for Winsor's *Narrative and Critical History of America* in the late 1880s. In 1886 Winfield S. Chaplin became dean of the Lawrence Scientific School, strongly supported by Shaler. Chaplin brought the school's enrollment up from 14 to 118 by the time he left five years later to become chancellor at Washington University in St. Louis. Shaler was then appointed as Chaplin's successor, serving as dean from 1891 until 1906, when he retired (Livingstone 1987:46).

Shaler was an early convert to Charles Eliot's system of elective courses (described in chapter 6) and believed strongly in student-faculty contact. In the 1890s Raphael Pumpelly, who taught at Harvard for a short period (see chapter 5), said that informal contact with professors was the key to good teaching, and the only American university professor who did this was Nathaniel Shaler, whose popular geology courses at Harvard thus attracted large numbers of students (Champlin 1994:17). Shaler was indeed a charismatic teacher, and his teaching impressed Gordon McKay, a mining tycoon, who subsequently left a large sum of money to Harvard for the Lawrence Scientific School (Hawkins 1972:212; Rossiter 1992:21). David Livingstone (1992:150) noted that Shaler's "famous Geology 4 class had some five hundred students packed into the lecture hall to hear him wax lyrical in his depiction of the wonders of the natural world." On the other hand, Alexander Agassiz and A. Lawrence Lowell, among others, were unhappy with Shaler's approach, and in 1903 a Harvard faculty committee criticized the course as a "gut" or "soft" lecture course (Fleming 1986a:72; Hawkins 1972:69). Shaler initiated a curriculum to train high school science teachers and created the Harvard Summer School as a vehicle to influence teachers in all fields (A. Powell 1980:22). He raised the enrollment of the Lawrence School to 187 by 1900 and in 1901–2 argued that it should be enlarged into a Harvard division, to compete with MIT. Alexander Agassiz, in a letter to Eliot, vigorously opposed the idea (Livingstone 1987:271, 1992:151–52).

During the 1890s, while he was dean of Lawrence Scientific School, Shaler had time to expand his writings in anthropology, but in a direction that today we find unfortunate. He became a convert to polygenism—also espoused by his mentor Louis Agassiz—a theory that provided for multiple creations of humans. Shaler was convinced of the biological reality of several different human species, which correlated with skin pigmentation. In 1890, in *Atlantic Monthly,* Shaler published the article "Science and the African Problem," in which he argued that sub-Saharan African populations were less evolved than the European species. In 1891 he published "Nature and Man in America," a typical sort of anthropogeography of the day, which again focused heavily on black and white "races." In it Shaler championed the idea that temperate climate was necessary for civilization to develop. In 1892, in his "Story of Our Continent," he devoted a chapter to American Indians, in which he argued that their "social retardation" was due to environmental reasons (Livingstone 1987:130–45). Shaler did like Putnam's ideas about the colonization of the New World from the Old World during the last glacial epoch, and he accepted the Calaveras skull (now long discredited) from California as evidence for this (Livingstone 1987:235).

Shaler's interest in polygenetic origins at least shows his continuing interest in anthropology since his days in the 1859–66 student cohort, and it reflects a significant trend of the day. The great anthropologist Daniel G. Brinton, for example, was also a convert to polygenism (Baker 1998). In any case, Shaler was part of a cohort at the Lawrence Scientific School that has been previously unappreciated in terms of its contributions to the development of anthropology in the late nineteenth century.

Finally, we mention another naturalist of importance among the first cohorts of students at the MCZ, **William Healey Dall** (1845–1927). Dall was the son of a Harvard graduate, Charles Henry Appleton Dall (1816–86, class of 1837). His mother, Caroline Wells Healey Dall (1822–1912) was an important worker for women's rights and one of the founders, in 1865, of the American Social Science Association. William Dall trained for one year at the Lawrence Scientific School, in 1862–63, with Agassiz, Putnam, Scudder, Verrill, Wyman, Joel Asaph Allen, Charles Frederick Hartt, and Hermann A. Hagen as teachers and associates. He received intensive training in the collecting of mollusks and other natural science specimens (Bartsch, Rehder, and Shields 1947:3). He did not finish his degree work there, but went on to the Chicago Academy of Sciences (Merriam 1927:347).

Dall's trail, however, continued to cross that of Putnam and the other members of the 1859–64 Lawrence School cohort. He was elected a member of the Boston Society of Natural History in 1863 and became a member of the Essex Institute in 1866. He became a member of the AAAS at the Salem meetings in 1869 and vice president (the AAAS term for chair) of Section H, Anthropology, in 1885 (Bartsch, Rehder, and Shields

1947:12–13). In 1875 he was again associated with several of the old Lawrence School group when he took part (along with later luminaries such as David Starr Jordan and Clinton Hart Merriam) in the summer biological field school at Woods Hole directed by Addison Verrill (Merriam 1927:347).

Dall saw himself as a naturalist writ large, so during his career he worked in anthropology, archaeology, botany, ethnology, geography, geology, hydrology, ichthyology, mammalogy, meteorology, ornithology, paleontology, parasitology, and tidal currents, as well as specializing in conchology, or malacology (Merriam 1927:346; Woodring 1958:92). He joined with Shaler, Hyatt, and others whom we have discussed in becoming an ardent neo-Lamarckian.

In 1865 Dall began research in coastal Alaska and the Aleutians, working with a private firm but moving to the U.S. Coast Survey and the Smithsonian after 1871. In 1884 he shifted to working with John Wesley Powell at the USGS. Significant for the development of archaeological method by Putnam and associates is a series of post-facto stratigraphic observations that Dall published (1877a). On rainy days in the Aleutians, when the weather was too inclement to conduct other field research, he had his men cut trenches in local shell mounds, exposing a relatively vertical face from the surface down to sterile soil. This procedure allowed Dall "to distinguish between the different strata and their contents" (1877a:47) as he walked through the cuts at the end of the day. He reported that "the several strata shown to exist correspond to actual stages of development in the social history of the people who formed the shell-heaps" (1877a:91). Dall's observations allowed him to define three chronological periods linked to the strata. He was also one of the first to recognize the influence of environment on the differential development of culture in his three stages.

Although Dall's work was not true stratigraphic excavation, it mirrored the methodology advocated by Wyman and Putnam during the MCZ period a decade earlier. We believe this indicates a strong interest in archaeological evidence on the part of the students of Wyman, Gray, and others during that period, which ultimately resulted in what we call the "Peabody Museum method" of excavation. Anthropology was part of the active research interests of many of this cohort.

In addition to his comments on stratigraphic sequences in the Aleutians, Dall published other papers on anthropological topics beginning in 1870 and continuing throughout his career. After he shifted to the Smithsonian Institution, he and paleontologist Fielding B. Meeks hired a budding young artist, William Henry Holmes (1846–1933), to do specimen drawings for them, starting in 1872 (Swanton 1937:224). Holmes would become a noted geologist and anthropologist, remaining with the Smithsonian and the U.S. National Museum, the Bureau of American Ethnology, and the National Gallery of Art throughout most of his long career. From 1880 onward, Dall was a regular contributor to Section H of the AAAS, where he commented on papers by Morse, Powell, Putnam, and Peabody Museum assistant Cordelia Studley, among others. Morse kept up a long friendship with Dall, from the MCZ days through the early 1900s; as late as 1901 he asked Dall to proofread one of his manuscripts (Wayman 1942:384).

Dall seems to have been most active on the anthropology scene in the late 1870s and 1880s. In 1877 he edited and contributed some articles to *Tribes of the Extreme Northwest*, the first volume of Powell's eight-volume series, *Contributions to North American Ethnology*, published between 1877 and 1893. In the late 1880s Dall became involved in the dialogue begun by the German immigrant Franz Boas on the proper means by which to collect and display ethnographic information (Boas 1887c:589). And in 1890 Putnam asked Dall to accompany him to investigate the location of an alleged Paleolithic pendant reported from northern Delaware by Hilborne T. Cresson, an amateur excavator and collector who was supplying objects to the Peabody Museum (Putnam 1890b:269; S. Williams 1991:121–27; and see chapter 4).

William Dall, then, despite the short time he spent at Harvard, well deserves to be included among the first cohort of Lawrence Scientific School students who contributed over the years to the growth of several strands of anthropology. These students' later career trajectories demonstrate the basic intellectual interests and probably the training that derived particularly from Jeffries Wyman. Dall and the other members of this cohort also illustrate the intricate and extensive sets of interrelationships Frederic Putnam, our central character, maintained with his colleagues.

It is during the Salem period that we see Putnam's developing archaeological interests. In addition to first publishing his work on the shell mounds near Salem in 1865—work carried out for the Essex Institute—Putnam, along with Edward Morse and Caleb Cooke, assisted Jeffries Wyman in excavating shell mounds near Eagle Hill, Ipswich, in 1867 (Wyman 1868c:568). From 1868 until 1876, when he began publishing his work through the Peabody Museum, Putnam published 32 additional papers on archaeological investigations (Tozzer 1936a:140–44), mainly in *American Naturalist, Proceedings of the Essex Institute,* and *Proceedings of the Boston Society of Natural History.*

Besides the MCZ, the Essex Institute, and the Peabody Academy of Science, two other scientific organizations were important in the evolution of Putnam's thinking from the 1860s through the early 1890s. He was elected to membership in both at the very beginning of his career: to the Boston Society of Natural History in 1856 and to the American Association for the Advancement of Science in 1857.

At the Boston Society of Natural History (BSNH), Putnam served as curator of ichthyology in the 1860s and as vice president and president several times during the later part of the nineteenth century. There he found a ready venue for exploring his new interest in anthropology. His first publication on archaeology, "On an Indian Grave Opened on Winter Island, Salem," detailing his work with Wyman, appeared in the *Proceedings* of the BSNH for 1865. His developing interest in the archaeology of the mounds of the Ohio Valley was reflected in his description of his 1871 investigations in the Wabash Valley (Putnam 1872a). Putnam made more than a dozen short archaeological contributions to the BSNH proceedings before 1885.

The American Association for the Advancement of Science was full of people with whom Putnam became associated. Louis Agassiz had been one of its founders in 1848, and Jeffries Wyman was named first permanent secretary that year. The first AAAS meeting that Putnam attended, at the age of 18, was the 1857 session in Montreal. It is from there that we have the first recorded indication of Putnam's later interest in archaeology, for he reported from the meetings:

> On Sunday, August 16th, [1857] while strolling along the side of Mount Royal, I noticed the point of a bivalve shell protruding from roots of grass. Wondering why such a shell should be there and reaching to pick it up, I noticed, on detaching the grass roots about it, that there were many other whole and broken valves in close proximity—too many, I thought, and too near together to have been brought by birds and too far away from water to be the remnants of a musk-rat's dinner. Scratching away the grass and poking among the shells, I found a few bones of birds and fishes and small fragments of Indian pottery. Then it dawned upon me that here had been an Indian home in ancient times and that these odds and ends were the refuse of the people—my first shell-heap or kitchen-midden, as I was to learn later. (Putnam 1899b:226)

We emphasize that this is the first *recorded* indication, because Putnam clearly recognized the potsherds as prehistoric Indian remains, something unlikely unless he had had previous experience with this enigmatic category of materials as a younger lad in Salem.

By 1869 the rift between Louis Agassiz and the students who had resigned from his program at the MCZ had healed, and he made peace with Asa Gray as well (Bruce 1987:357). Agassiz and his former students even shared a dinner of reconciliation in 1869, and it was with his support that the AAAS meetings were held in Salem that year. Putnam substituted for Joseph Lovering as secretary during the Salem meeting and the following year substituted for Charles Frederick Hartt as general secretary. In 1871 he was elected general secretary, to begin in 1872, the first of five five-year terms he ultimately served in this position. He was then elected president of the AAAS for 1898–99 (Browman 2002a:215). Putnam established a room at the Peabody Academy of Science in Salem as the national headquarters for the AAAS, and there he stored the proceedings, the official records, and the association's library. These records were transferred to the University of Cincinnati in 1896, but unfortunately, most of the official papers seem to have been lost in later transfers as the AAAS grew and evolved (Dexter 1982b:107).

A special group called Subsection C, Archaeology and Ethnology, was formed at the Salem meeting in 1869, becoming the third subsection created within the AAAS. At the later Detroit meetings, this subsection was reorganized as Subsection D, Anthropology, with Lewis Henry Morgan as chair and Putnam as secretary. It was reorganized again as Subsection E, Anthropology, in 1879, and in another reorganization of the AAAS in

1882, it became a regular section, Section H, Anthropology, as it remains to this day. Putnam was intimately involved in the initial founding and the subsequent reorganizations of this section. As permanent secretary he accepted the papers for the section and organized its agenda, up through the end of his term in 1897. As we show in later chapters, he continued to use Section H to pursue his vision of anthropology and to help found the American Anthropological Association in 1902.

The permanent secretary of the AAAS had "to care for the details of the meetings, to supervise the programs and pamphlets of information, to edit the proceedings, in all several hundred pages of printed matter, in addition to the correspondence incidental to assembling of such large numbers" (Ritchie 1898:659). It was a massive job, but one that gave Putnam considerable influence over the direction of American science. Although he presented papers at most of the AAAS meetings during his 25-year tenure, and he published abstracts and entire copies of many of the papers given by his peers in the anthropology sections and subsections of the *Proceedings,* his modesty prevented him from publishing his own contributions in the *Proceedings* other than simply by title. This is frustrating for us as historians of science, because it was in the papers he gave at the AAAS in the late 1870s and early 1880s that he first explicitly spelled out his new excavation methodology, which was to revolutionize Americanist archaeology. Thus we miss, for the most part, the critical development phase of this new paradigm as given in his own words.

Several commentators have noted Putnam's generosity. Alfred Kroeber (1917:717), for example, remarked that Putnam "was always and instantly ready to reciprocate with equally generous measures of his own hours." A report in *Science* (Anonymous 1915:639, possibly written by J. McKeen Cattell) observed that Putnam "was ready always to give unstintedly of his time, and so far as he was able, from the pocket, to any one who asked his aid." John Ritchie (1898:660), discussing Putnam's tenure at the AAAS, reported that Putnam "has manifested throughout his career a marked executive ability as well as a broad and thorough scientific knowledge in many branches of natural science. In personal character he is most genial and winning, the most modest and generous of men, and he has hosts of friends."

This generosity not only was reflected in Putnam's work with several early students of archaeology at the Peabody Museum but also was critical for the survival and success of the AAAS and of many other individuals' research projects. Ralph Dexter (1982b:111) noted that Putnam often subsidized the AAAS in its early years. In 1877 he paid $1,714.11 for printing, for which he was not reimbursed, and he paid for an office assistant out of his own pocket. For many years he received no salary for his work for the AAAS; finally he was paid a pittance, which was doubled to $250 a year in 1881. It is clear that in terms of today's dollars, Putnam carried the AAAS himself for nearly two decades. A. L. Kroeber's comment (1917:714) that Putnam was "even more deeply influential upon the destiny of scientific endeavor in the New World than is generally recognized" is even truer today than when Kroeber penned it nearly a century ago.

In 1875 Putnam moved from the Peabody Academy of Science at Salem to the Peabody Museum at Harvard, taking over the position of curator from Asa Gray, who had been serving as interim curator after Jeffries Wyman's death. Gray was in temporary charge from September 1874 to January 1875, but because of his obligations elsewhere on campus, he wrote that to keep the museum running, "I therefore availed myself of the permission granted at a former meeting of the board, and engaged the valuable assistance of Mr. F. W. Putnam, of Salem, who is better acquainted than any one else with the museum, and with Dr. Wyman's method and arrangements, having been much associated with him both in exploration and publication" (quoted in Abbott 1886:695). Hence Putnam was in many ways the de facto curator upon Wyman's death. The position involved administration, collections management, curation, fund-raising, and, later, teaching.

With Putnam's appointment as curator of the Peabody Museum came a shift in its emphasis from archaeology alone, as had been the case under Wyman's direction, into ethnology and physical anthropology as well. Putnam forged Native American archaeology, ethnology, linguistics, and somatology together. Importantly, he began insisting that the term *anthropology* be used in the museum's annual reports, to encompass all four fields.

Before getting into the business of running the museum, Putnam had to wind up his other obligations. He had finished his work for the Kentucky Geological Survey. He resigned his position as editor of *American Naturalist* and his position at the Peabody Academy of Science. He finished up an obligation to the Smithsonian Institution, where in 1876 he had been appointed assistant to the U.S. Engineers in what became known as the Wheeler Survey, a survey of territory west of the one-hundredth meridian led by First Lieutenant (later Captain) George Montague Wheeler between 1872 and 1879. Putnam wrote up the archaeological collections made during the survey, an undertaking he did not finish until 1879. In the process, he wrote the first summary of California archaeology, including some commentary on the Southwestern cultures (Putnam 1879d; Putnam et al. 1879). This work is rarely cited today, although it demonstrates the breadth of Putnam's archaeological knowledge when he took the Peabody Museum job.

The first task Putnam had to address before he could initiate his own research agenda was properly housing the collections the museum had amassed. This was done by constructing the first part of the current museum building on Divinity Avenue. The work began in 1876 and was finished in late 1877, and the building was inaugurated in 1878. Putnam worked zealously to increase the museum's holdings, and by the time the new building opened to the public, the inventory had grown from roughly 8,000 items at the time of Wyman's death in 1874 to more than 30,000 items. Putnam also worked tirelessly to build the library, so that near the time of the museum's fortieth anniversary in 1906, the library held the largest anthropological collection in North America, with 6,000 items—roughly 3,000 books and 3,000 pamphlets. Today this collection and thousands more items, still the country's largest anthropological collection, are housed in the Tozzer Library (Browman 2002d:509).

As Joan Mark (1980:14–15) observed, Putnam brought to anthropology the careful, painstaking scientific methods he had learned at the Lawrence Scientific School under Agassiz, Cooke, Eliot, Gray, and Wyman. He also employed the principles of museum collections organization he had learned from his work at the Museum of Comparative Zoology with Agassiz. Thus he arranged ethnological and prehistoric collections by geographical area rather than by evolutionary schema or industry, the practice followed by other leading institutions at the time, such as the Smithsonian Institution and the Bureau of Ethnology (Mark 1980:22). Exhibits, as Putnam wrote (1899b:235), were to provide a true picture of the local culture. "A strictly geographical arrangement is, therefore, the primary principle which should govern the exhibition of anthropological collections."

The differences in approach between Putnam and the government museums in terms of organizing collections were also reflected in differences in collecting methods. One of Putnam's necrologers (Anonymous 1915:638) wrote: "He was one of the earliest to realize the need of archaeological and anthropological exploration, and to insist that careful field notes and data are equally important with the specimens themselves." By the mid-1880s Putnam spoke regularly of the need for "thorough" and "systematic" methods as he argued for a developing rigor of methodology (Hinsley 1999:147). For archaeologists, the results of Putnam's work in developing systematic research techniques are best known as the "Peabody Museum method" and the "Chicago method" of excavation (Browman 2002a, 2002d), which we detail in later chapters.

Putnam did not arrive at this point in his career alone. Throughout his formative years as he developed into an anthropologist, he was part of a cohort of students who shared many of his interests. Many of the people we have profiled in this chapter are known best for their contributions in natural history, zoology, and botany. Putnam was included in this cohort of natural scientists as one of their own, only gradually shifting his interest from fish to humans. The coming university-based revolution in anthropology was not just the work of Frederic Putnam but can perhaps be best visualized as the product of a cohort of disciplinary advocates who spread the message from Harvard. Their gospel had been learned from historical giants such as Wyman, Gray, and Agassiz, but equally from the intellectual interactions of thoroughly engaged fellow students who learned from and enriched one another's experiences.

4

Development of the Peabody Museum and Its Collections, 1875–1890

The period following the Civil War was a time of great intellectual growth in the United States. Several scholars trying to capture the essence of this post-Enlightenment trend have spoken of it as the "American renaissance," although little agreement seems to exist about the precise time frame or definition of the term. Perhaps the clearest definition was offered by Richard Guy Wilson (1979:11), who began his American Renaissance period with the first centennial in 1876 and ended it with the United States' entry into World War I: "The term 'American Renaissance' concerns the identification by many Americans—painters, sculptors, architects, craftsmen, scholars, collectors, politicians, financiers, and industrialists—with the period of the European Renaissance and the feeling that the Renaissance spirit had been captured again in the United States." The United States had become a major world power during this time frame, and "the American Renaissance, by definition and action, was intensely nationalistic" (R. Wilson 1979:12).

Anthropology and archaeology were substantially affected by this fervor, and the contributors discussed in this chapter were part of that tradition. The increasing crescendo of anthropological participation at national expositions, perhaps culminating in the United States with the 1904 Louisiana Purchase Exposition in St. Louis, was part of this tradition as well. One of us observed the same trend in Americanist archaeology, proposing a "golden age of American archaeology" from roughly 1870 to 1895:

> Never before and never again would so many Americans really care about archaeology, especially the home-grown variety. It was a time of the rise of natural history societies and museums throughout the country, and archaeology was a part of it too. Gentlemen scholars, lawyers, doctors, and even business men studied birds and shells, Indians and dinosaurs, arrowheads and muskrats. There were few "professionals" in any of these disciplines, and bright-eyed and energetic "amateurs" could and did do excellent field collecting in all these areas of research. More than that, they published what they found and shared data via newly inexpensive photographic prints. (S. Williams 1987:18)

Many avocational scholars wrote to both the Smithsonian and the Peabody museums, offering their collections and their services. Frederic Putnam, at the Harvard Peabody Museum, often made more direct use of them than his counterparts at the Smithsonian. Putnam contacted the writers and usually either visited sites himself or commissioned a Peabody Museum associate to do so on his behalf. Putnam also made use of his position as secretary of the American Association for the Advancement of Science (AAAS) to have its annual meeting shifted to a different city each year, in order to meet local citizens who had contacted him. It was standard practice for Putnam in the 1870s and 1880s to travel with local collectors to visit sites and even conduct some test excavations after every AAAS meeting.

Associated with the American renaissance was an exposition mania and the associated formation of organizations and institutions that advanced the ideals of the renaissance. Many historians of the period have observed this acceleration of national and international expositions, but usually not with an eye for things anthropological.

The patterns that Nils Muller-Scheessel (2001) identified for the French Exposition Universelle seem to apply also to the United States. The French exposition of 1867 demonstrated the great potential of archaeological research and won archaeology wide support. By 1878 archaeology, as a subdiscipline of anthropology, had become fully established in France, and in 1889 archaeologists used all their newly gained scientific weight to contribute to the show of progress at the Exposition Universelle. Prehistoric archaeology received not only its own building but also premier billing. In the United States, Putnam achieved much the same results at the 1893 World's Columbian Exposition in Chicago, where archaeology was used to show American progress and had its own building. By the time of the 1900 Exposition Universelle in Paris and the 1904 Louisiana Purchase Exposition, however, although prehistoric objects were still displayed, archaeology and anthropology no longer had their own display buildings. From that time onward, archaeological objects played no significant role in such international exhibitions.

The 1900–1905 period was a turning point for anthropology at expositions. Coverage of the field at fairs had grown rapidly during the last quarter of the nineteenth century but decreased dramatically after 1905. Muller-Scheessel (2001) argued that the display of archaeological and ethnographic artifacts at the international exhibitions and fairs depended on three ideologies: those of progress, racism, and nationalism. When the ideology of progress was challenged and the notion of a superior, universal, Western civilization lost credibility in the first quarter of the twentieth century, such exhibits lost two of their most important rationales and ceased to be featured prominently at international fairs.

We return in a later chapter to some of the issues raised by expositions, but here we look at the American renaissance as it played out at the Peabody Museum of American Archaeology and Ethnology at Harvard between the end of the Civil War and the 1893 World's Columbian Exposition. With what objectives was the museum created? Whom did Putnam hire to staff it during its first quarter century of existence? What patterns of development can we can begin to identify for this period?

George Peabody's "letter of gift" of October 8, 1866, which established the Peabody Museum, included specific suggestions about the direction research at the institution might take (see chapter 2). He singled out the "exploration and collection" of the "works and remains of the ancient races of this continent" and the comparison of ancient human remains in America "with those found in other countries" (Peabody 1868a). In his "instrument of trust" he gave further directions for the way the museum should develop. First, the trustees should invest $45,000, "the income of which shall be applied to forming and preserving collections of antiquities, and objects relating to the earlier races of the American Continent." They should invest a second $45,000 for "the establishment and maintenance of a Professorship of American archaeology and ethnology in Harvard University." Until the professorship was filled, or at any time it might be vacant, the income from the funds should be devoted to the "care and increase of the collections." The trustees were to invest the final $60,000 of Peabody's gift "as a Building Fund" (Peabody 1868b).

Altogether, Jeffries Wyman, the museum's first director, and subsequently Putnam had five objectives established for them before they could expand into other areas: form a museum; acquire collections from other parts of the world for comparative study; explore the remains and works of the American Indians; pay particular attention to finding evidence of the earliest inhabitants of the Americas, especially of late Pleistocene times; and form a working library.

Wyman, recruited from the Lawrence Scientific School at Harvard, where he taught anatomy and had his own small Museum of Comparative Anatomy, held the curatorship of the Peabody Museum from 1866 until his death in 1874 (see chapter 2). His focus during the early development of the Peabody Museum was essentially on archaeology, a field in which, as we have shown, he took great personal interest. He concentrated on the first two charges of Peabody's bequest, the formation of a museum and the acquisition of comparative collections, and after his first few years also began working on the third charge, exploration of the remains and works of American Indians. Frances Mead (1905:67), later the collections administrator under Putnam, noted that the museum opened with only about 50 items in a cabinet, collected from various places on campus. Wyman set about obtaining additions to the collections from the Boston area, securing 36 donors in the first year (Brew 1966a:7), with items from the Boston Athenaeum, the Massachusetts Historical Society, the Smithsonian Institution, and several individual collectors.

During his first years as curator, Wyman tried to develop the museum's comparative collections of artifacts rapidly. He moved quickly to obtain a collection of European Paleolithic, Mesolithic, and Neolithic materials. He secured 264 items from northern Europe in the first year, and during the second year he purchased roughly 3,000 items from Gabriel de Mortillet's collection of Paleolithic tools, 1,559 items from the Wilmot J. Rose collections from Denmark, and 865 items from Clement's Swiss Lake dwelling assemblage (Browman 2002c:209). He purchased these collections in order to meet what he saw as a critical need: to gather the "means for making direct comparison between the implements of the stone age of the old world and the new" (Wyman 1869:11). No other American museum had such collections in 1869, and few have them even today.

The Peabody bequest was structured such that a museum building was not envisioned until after the principal and accrued interest reached a critical plateau, so Wyman did not start off working on a building design. In any case, the collections were at first too small to warrant a new building. Five years later, the collections had grown large enough that in order to continue housing them in the museum's temporary home—Wyman's old Museum of Comparative Anatomy in Boylston Hall—a new story had to be added to the hall to accommodate the displays (Wyman 1873:5).

It soon became evident to Wyman that for many areas of North American archaeology and ethnography, no collections of sufficient size or coverage were available to be purchased. If he wanted to obtain specimens from those areas, he would have to commission collectors to work on the museum's behalf. After the first few years, Wyman's annual reports increasingly refer to collections of North American materials made by many individuals, with evidence that the more important collections acquired had been formed in part with museum funding. Wyman was also using museum funding to support part of his own shell mound excavations in Maine, Massachusetts, and Florida, for he was now donating the materials to the museum collections. Among the outside collectors, six men—Rev. Edward Osborne Dunning, Professor Charles Frederick Hartt, Dr. Carl Hermann Berendt, Professor Ebenezer Baldwin Andrews, Henry Gillman, and Dr. Charles Conrad Abbott—seem to have been particularly important for Wyman's plans to secure broader representations of North American artifacts. We offer brief biographies of these major donor-collectors and summarize their contributions.

Edward Osborne Dunning (1810–74), a Congregational minister who resided in New Haven, Connecticut, became involved in mound exploration after the Civil War. He was listed as "Field Assistant in Tennessee" in some of the museum paperwork and conducted excavations for Wyman at several places in Tennessee between 1869 and 1871. For his first season, Wyman (1870:7) reported that Dunning had been employed to conduct excavations at Brakebill Mound, Turner's Mounds, Nashville Mounds, and two caves in Tennessee. In his second season, Wyman (1871:7) noted that Dunning had continued excavations in eastern Tennessee on behalf of the museum, working at Mahee Mound, and in his third season, he remarked (1872:11–12) that "under the direction of the Museum," Dunning continued working in eastern Tennessee at Brakebill and Lick Creek mounds, with most of the materials coming from the main Lick Creek mound, where Dunning put in a trench 10 feet wide in the center of the mound. It was from these excavations that Dunning secured the first Southeastern Ceremonial Cult shell gorgets for the Peabody (Wyman 1872:15–16).

Dunning became ill during the exploration of the mounds but continued his work until a few months before his death in March 1874. In addition to his reports on

Plate 1

Harvard College, 1726.

Plate 2

Jean Louis Rodolphe Agassiz, 1847.

Louis Agassiz, ca. 1860.

Frederic Ward Putnam, 1858.

Asa Gray.

Plate 3

Jeffries Wyman, 1865.

Jeffries Wyman.

Wyman's Anatomical Rooms, Museum of Comparative Zoology, Boylston Hall, 1875.

Plate 4

George Peabody, whose gift founded the Harvard Peabody Museum in 1866.

Charles Eliot Norton, president of the Archaeological Institute of America.

Charles William Eliot, president of Harvard College.

Plate 5

The Peabody Museum of American Archaeology and Ethnology, 1881.

Frederic Ward Putnam, 1882.

Plate 6

Elizabeth Cabot Cary Agassiz, president of the School of Collegiate Instruction of Women.

Alexander Agassiz, director of the University Museum.

William Sturgis Bigelow, Kyoto, ca. 1882.

Robert Charles Winthrop, Peabody Museum trustee.

Plate 7

Henry Wheatland, Peabody Museum trustee.

Stephen Salisbury, Peabody Museum trustee.

Lucien Carr, assistant curator of the Peabody Museum.

Samuel Hubbard Scudder, Peabody Museum trustee.

Plate 8

Zelia Maria Magdalena Nuttall, "Special Assistant in Mexican Archaeology."

Cordelia Adelaide Studley, the Peabody's first official physical anthropologist.

Alice Cunningham Fletcher, "Special Assistant in American Ethnology."

Plate 9

Alice Fletcher with two Winnebago women, Winnebago Reservation, Nebraska, 1888.

Fletcher (far left) talking to a group of Nez Perce men, Idaho, ca. 1889–1892.

Plate 10

Henry Haynes, advocate of Americanist studies in archaeology.

Joseph Lovering, secretary of the American Association for the Advancement of Science.

Charles Conrad Abbott, "Field Assistant in Archaeology in New Jersey."

Justin Winsor, chief librarian at Harvard's Widener Library.

Plate 11

Teobert Maler, photographer and explorer of the Maya area.

Ernest Volk, 1903.

Edward Herbert Thompson and dredge, Sacred Cenote, Chichen Itza, ca. 1902.

Plate 12

Frederic Ward Putnam,
Chillicothe Mounds, Ohio,
ca. 1890.

Putnam, Serpent Mound, Ohio, 1888.

Plate 13

Left to right: John Cone Kimball, unidentified, Putnam, and Charles Lewis Metz, Turner Mound group, Ohio, ca. 1890.

Ernest Volk, Hilborne Thompson Cresson, and unidentified, Turner Mound group, ca. 1890.

Putnam in his Peabody Museum office, 1890s.

Plate 15

Putnam with his portrait gallery on the wall, 1890s.

Marshall Howard Saville and Putnam, ca. 1890s.

Plate 16

Room 35 at the Peabody Museum, with a model of El Castillo, Chichen Itza, 1893.

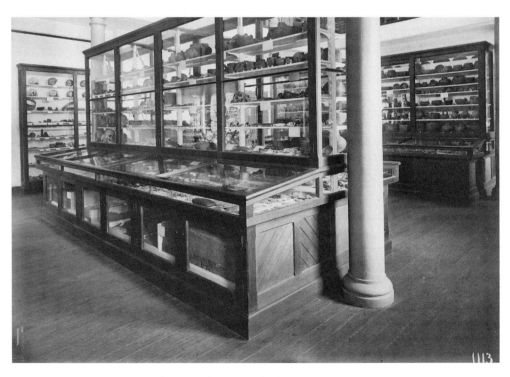

The Mound Room, Peabody Museum, 1893.

work for the Peabody, Dunning published a summary for the Smithsonian Institution (Dunning 1872). Putnam used Dunning's Tennessee ceramics as comparative materials when he studied the Swallow collection from Missouri in 1875, and Lucien Carr, assistant curator at the Peabody Museum, whom we discuss later, used Dunning's collection of crania from Tennessee mounds in his 1878 study of Tennessee burials.

Charles Frederick Hartt (1840–78) was a native of Nova Scotia and obtained his A.B. there in 1860. He then spent three years as a graduate student training with Louis Agassiz at Harvard before returning to Nova Scotia to serve as assistant to the geological survey in New Brunswick in 1864–65. He came back to the Museum of Comparative Zoology as an assistant, serving as the geologist for the Thayer Expedition to Brazil in 1865–67 (Harvard University 1937:245). After the expedition ended, he accepted a position teaching at Cornell University in 1868.

Hartt embarked on three more expeditions to Brazil from Cornell between 1868 and 1871. On his fourth expedition, he listed a series of research goals, among them exploration of the Marajo Indian mounds and a continuation of his study of the native dialect, Northern Tupi (Anonymous 1871:448–49). Wyman (1873:20) reported that "Prof. C. F. Hartt, having organized a geological exploration in Brazil in 1871, kindly offered to aid the Museum in making archaeological collections, and for carrying out his plans an appropriation was made by the Trustees." He noted that Hartt's description of the freshwater shell mounds of the interior of Brazil seemed much like that of the Florida mounds that Wyman himself had investigated (Wyman 1876:281). In 1874 Hartt took leave from Cornell to become director of the Geological Survey of Brazil. He published a number of papers on the archaeology and ethnography of Brazil (for example, Hartt 1871a, 1871b, 1872a, 1872b, 1875a, 1875b, 1875c). Work in Amazonia was dangerous, however, and Putnam (1878a:192) reported Hartt's death from yellow fever in 1878.

Carl Hermann Berendt (1817–78) was born in Danzig, Prussia. After completing his medical training and pursuing an early career in medicine in Europe, he immigrated to Nicaragua in 1851. He became interested in ethnographic research while practicing medicine there and maintained that interest when, because of civil unrest, he moved to the Yucatán Peninsula in 1853. Over the next two decades he spent a good deal of time in the Maya region (Brinton 1884:206; Wolfe 1982:2).

Berendt is best known for his work in linguistics. During his time in Middle America he collected 175 grammars, vocabularies, and dictionaries, many of which Daniel Brinton purchased in 1871 and used as the basis of his own writings on the Maya (Brinton 1884:210; Wolfe 1982:4). Berendt also collected ethnological and archaeological artifacts. During a trip to Providence, Rhode Island, in 1864–66, he made contact with Edwin H. Davis, with whom Ephraim Squier was studying prehistoric mounds in Ohio, and sold him a number of the artifacts he had collected from Maya sites (Barnhart 2004:79). From 1865 to 1867 the Smithsonian Institution provided funds for Berendt to secure collections for it from the Maya region (Wolfe 1982:3).

Berendt also collected for Jeffries Wyman and the Peabody Museum. Wyman first made his acquaintance with Berendt in 1860 through his colleague Asa Gray, the botanist at the Museum of Comparative Zoology, when Berendt collected and sold Gray a series of moss specimens from Mexico for his herbarium. Although Berendt had been working for the Smithsonian, Wyman had the executive committee of the Peabody Museum make an appropriation during the first year of the museum's operation, in 1867, to have Berendt acquire "antiquities, crania, and objects of ethnologic and archaeologic value" for the Peabody (Wyman 1868a:18). Berendt used these funds in part to purchase a group of Middle American materials from a "Dr. Kellar" in 1868, which he provided the museum that year. In 1870 Wyman reported that still further materials were expected from Berendt (Wyman 1869, 1871:8).

The years 1865–70 marked a brief time when Berendt devoted particular attention to archaeological remains. He is also said to have actually mapped a Maya site in 1869 while collecting for the Peabody (Wolfe 1982:9). He apparently saw his work as a kind of salvage ethnology and archaeology, for he is quoted as saying, "We must have museums, in which the plastic remains of the ancient American civilizations, either original, or in faithful imitations, shall, in as large numbers as possible, be collected, and duly grouped and labeled, according to the place and circumstances of their discovery" (quoted in Salisbury 1876:60).

Berendt may have helped recruit other collectors for the Peabody Museum. Earl Flint, to whom we return later, was a colleague of Berendt's in Nicaragua, and apparently it was through his linkage with Berendt that Flint began collecting for both the Smithsonian and the Peabody (Whisnant 1995:293).

Ebenezer Baldwin Andrews (1821–80) was born in Danbury, Connecticut, and died in Lancaster, Ohio. He attended the seminary at Princeton, from which he graduated in 1845, and was ordained as a Congregationalist pastor; hence he is occasionally referred to as "Rev. Andrews." However, he is also identified as "Prof. Andrews" because he was appointed professor of natural science at Marietta College, Ohio (where his brother had been president), from 1851 through 1869. After leaving Marietta, Andrews became assistant geologist with the Geological Survey of Ohio, working on coal and oil resources, and ultimately produced an introductory book on the geology of the upper Midwest (1878).

It was during work for the geological survey that Andrews became involved in investigating Ohio mounds. He wrote to Wyman offering his services, and Wyman named him "Field Assistant in Ohio" for the Peabody Museum, a position continued by Gray and Putnam, from 1874 to 1876 (Putnam 1881a:13). Putnam reported on the receipt of collections from Andrews during the middle 1870s, explicitly noting his museum funding: "[Andrews] has continued his exploration of mounds in Ohio, acting under the appropriations of last year . . . during the last two years" (Putnam 1877:10). Thus Andrews was recruited under Wyman's leadership but did most of his work for the Peabody after Putnam took over as curator. Putnam published two of Andrews's reports of his excavation work (Andrews 1877a, 1877b). Putnam was probably less than satisfied with the rather crude methodology Andrews employed, which Andrews (1877b:51) described as "tunneling," but Putnam no doubt was gratified that Andrews took considerable care in preserving and labeling the articles he recovered (Putnam 1881a:13). Andrews died shortly thereafter, and Putnam wrote a short obituary of him in the 1880 Peabody Museum annual report.

In spite of some of his crude excavation techniques, Andrews did save floral and faunal specimens, a field procedure followed by others of the collectors from this period whom Putnam instructed. We presume that in this matter, Putnam was following his own natural science training under Wyman, Gray, and Agassiz. Wyman, in his last reports of shell mound excavations in the 1860s and early 1870s, had begun to include analyses of animals used at archaeological sites. Gayle Fritz and Bruce Smith (1988:7) commented that Andrews's report on Ash Cave, Ohio (1877a), "is now recognized as the first report on archaeobotanical materials in the Eastern United States." In this report, based on his 1876 excavations, Andrews reported finding 16 liters of seeds of the genus *Chenopodium* in a storage pit. Asa Gray had identified the seeds when the samples were sent to the Peabody Museum. A small sample of this collection, in a sealed glass bottle, was still extant in the Peabody Museum more than a century later, and Fritz and Smith verified its identification as *Chenopodium*. More important, they ran a radiocarbon-based, accelerator mass spectrometer (AMS) date on the seeds, which yielded an uncorrected date of 1720 B.P. (Fritz and Smith 1988:7).

Henry Gillman (1833–1915) was listed as "Field Assistant in Southeastern Archaeology" beginning with Wyman and continued in this position through Putnam's early years as curator. Gillman was a gentleman naturalist who had gathered a 2,000-specimen herbarium and stocked his cabinet with private mineralogical and archaeological collections from the shores of Lake Superior (Hinsley 1999:144). His earliest professional paper (Gillman 1870) dealt with his herbarium collections.

Gillman conducted a series of excavations on mounds at the head of the St. Clair River in Detroit, under an appropriation made by the Peabody Museum trustees in 1872 (Wyman 1873:12). Again using museum funds, he explored mounds in northern Florida in 1878 (Putnam 1879d:466). Early on he was particularly interested in the physical characteristics of the human burials he found (see Gillman's works from 1871 to 1879 in the bibliography; also Wyman 1873:13–19). Gillman was assisted with his investigations of the skeletons by David Mack (Harvard M.D. 1863), who had earlier consulted with Wyman about crania he had collected from mounds in Washington state while working as a surgeon for the U.S. Navy (Putnam 1886a:484; Wyman 1869:16). Gillman was one of many people who wrote to Charles Darwin regarding natural history information. In 1871 Gillman sent Darwin details of the burials he had found in the mounds, together with Jeffries Wyman's comments on his finds.

Gillman was an active participant at the Second International Congress of Americanists, held in Luxembourg in 1877, and at the annual meetings of the AAAS throughout the 1870s. And although he conducted mound excavations for the Peabody in both Michigan and Florida, he was also interested in ethnographic work. In October 1876 he wrote to Putnam about the need for salvage ethnography, commenting that he had a collection of Ojibwa materials, but it would be difficult to get more because the Indians were dying out (cited in Conn 1998:95).

In the late 1870s a national economic depression became more severe, and Gillman was forced to sell his collections. According to Curtis Hinsley (1999:145), Gillman moved to Florida to set up a citrus business and did not return to Detroit until 1882. We have found sources in which Gillman lists Detroit as his home from 1879 to 1885, so it appears likely that during this period Gillman spent his summers in Detroit and wintered at his place near Waldo, Florida. In the later 1880s he stopped sending material from Michigan to the Peabody, a termination that Hinsley (1999:145) attributed to Putnam's perception of the poor quality of his work. However, we have found that the Peabody continued to receive materials from Gillman, now from a new venue. From 1886 through at least the mid-1890s, Gillman was the U.S. consul in Jerusalem, and he excavated and collected many "Holy Land" artifacts, which he donated to the Peabody Museum, the Smithsonian Institution, and other U.S. museums. In his later years he even wrote a novel (Gillman 1898) with details based on his time in Palestine.

Charles Conrad Abbott (1843–1919) began his association with the Peabody Museum during Wyman's tenure, although what we know best about Abbott's relationship with the museum dates to his subsequent work during Putnam's tenure. Abbott made his initial gift in 1871. Wyman reported, "The Museum is indebted to the generosity of Dr. Charles C. Abbott of Trenton, New Jersey, for a very valuable gift of more than eight hundred specimens of implements of stone obtained from the immediate neighborhood to Trenton, by Mr. Morgan and partly, also, by Dr. Abbott" (Wyman 1872:27). These materials included relatively recent arrowheads, axes, pestles, and pottery but also "several implements which, as Dr. Abbott states, very closely resemble the celts of the drift period of Europe, especially those found at St. Acheul, two or three of which, except for their material, could hardly be distinguished from them." Wyman referred his readers to two articles by Abbott on the "Stone Age of New Jersey," in the March and April issues of *American Naturalist* for 1872. Putnam was one of the editors of *American Naturalist* at this point, so he clearly was involved in the acceptance and publication of these articles.

Thus began a long and sometime tempestuous relationship between Abbott, the Peabody Museum, and particularly Putnam. Abbott had studied under Dr. Joseph B. Leidy (1823–91), professor of anatomy at the Academy of Natural Sciences in Philadelphia, and received his M.D. from Pennsylvania in 1865. He soon realized that he had little interest in practicing medicine and instead began to study natural history (Kraft 1993:2). Abbott and Putnam had known of each other during Putnam's earlier naturalist phase, when the two shared an interest in collecting ichthyological specimens (Abbott to Putnam, April 26, 1860, Peabody Museum Archives).

Abbott then shifted his interest to archaeology, beginning his surface collecting and later his excavations in the Trenton gravels of New Jersey as early as 1867. He began sending information about his excavation project to Putnam while Putnam was still at the Peabody Academy of Science in Salem (Abbott 1872, 1873). As Putnam later reported (1886a:481), "at one time before this he had sent specimens to the [Harvard Peabody Museum], he had in the meanwhile given his archaeological material to the Peabody Academy of Science at Salem. On my leaving that institution to take the position offered me in this, its Trustees transferred the larger part of the Abbott collection to this Museum." Thus, whereas Abbott's association with the Peabody Museum at Harvard began with Wyman in 1871, his archaeological association with Putnam was at least as early through the museum in Salem.

Putnam took seriously the five charges that George Peabody had set out in his bequest. Abbott's claim to have found artifacts in "glacial drift," of the same style and presumed antiquity as the Paleolithic finds at St. Acheul and other places in western Europe, clearly fit the enabling bequest's mandate that the museum pay special attention to evidence of the earliest inhabitants of the Americas. Thus it is no surprise to see Abbott listed as a museum "Assistant in the Field," and as "Field Assistant in Archaeology in New Jersey," from 1875, when Putnam became curator, until 1889, when Putnam helped Abbott get a job as curator at the new University of Pennsylvania Museum of Archaeology and Anthropology. This 15-year period was a time of exceedingly good relations between Abbott and Putnam, an association that decayed to acrimony on Abbott's part only in the late 1890s and early 1900s, when he was unable to get reaccredited at the Peabody Museum (see S. Williams 1991:116–21).

Abbott's position at the Peabody Museum from 1875 to 1889 carried no salary, but the museum did give him credit for his work. Putnam published several of his reports (for example, Abbott 1877, 1878), and special appropriations were made from time to time to cover his expenses (Putnam 1879a:466, 1884a:352, 1889:11, and others). Putnam, almost immediately after he became curator at the Peabody Museum, arranged for Nathaniel S. Shaler, his former classmate and close colleague, to visit the Trenton gravel site in 1876 to ascertain the antiquity of the glacial drift (Shaler 1877). A codicil to Abbott's appointment, which applied to everyone hired by the Peabody Museum during this period, was that no private collections were to be kept by any member of the Peabody staff. Hence, from 1875 to 1889 Abbott donated most of his materials to the museum.

Putnam was an ardent supporter of Abbott's. Through his position as vice president and later president of the Boston Society of Natural History, he arranged for special symposiums sponsored by that group, bringing together the experts of the day on early inhabitants of the Americas in sessions on January 19, 1881; December 21, 1887; and December 10, 1888. The 1881 session included, among others, papers by Abbott on the Trenton material and by Putnam on Paleolithic tools from Massachusetts and Trenton (*Proceedings of the Boston Society of Natural History* 21 [1881]:122–49). For the

1887 meeting, Abbott continued to provide information on his Trenton work, and Putnam compared materials in the Peabody Museum's de Mortillet collection with Abbott's finds (*Proceedings of the Boston Society of Natural History* 23 [1887]:421–49). The 1888 meeting was much the same.

Once the first part of the new Peabody Museum building was completed, Putnam had a special room developed to display these materials and had Abbott come up from Trenton to arrange them (Putnam 1886a:491). This period seems to mark the apogee of goodwill between Abbott and Putnam—for example, Abbott wrote a laudatory piece on Putnam's contributions to Americanist anthropology in *Popular Science Monthly* that year (Abbott 1886). In order to secure more specimens for the Peabody Museum, Abbott employed his son, Richard M. Abbott, to help him out, as was referred to in the annual reports for 1883 and 1888 (Putnam 1884a:351, 1889:41). Presumably Richard Abbott helped at other times as well. Abbott's formal relationship with the Peabody Museum came to an end in 1889, when he was appointed to a new full-time curatorial position at the University of Pennsylvania.

Putnam's letter to Penn's president, William Pepper (1843–98), is seen as having been critical in Abbott's appointment there (Horan 1992:30). When the Department of Archaeology and Paleontology was organized at Penn in 1891, Charles Abbott, as curator of American collections, was its only full-time, salaried employee. In 1893 Abbott resigned from the department after conflicts of opinion with Pepper, Daniel Brinton, Stewart Culin, and the overseeing board over, among other issues, whether the direction of the University Museum ought to be to secure objects for display or to engage in research. Abbott and Pepper clashed over Pepper's perceived indifference to the American collections and Pepper's threat to sell a collection of paleontological materials in 1890 and 1891. Henry Chapman Mercer, who subsequently replaced Abbott (Browman 2002d:190), and Frank Furness, the architect for the new building being planned for the University Museum, defended Abbott to Pepper and Culin on more than one occasion between 1891 and 1893, but in the end they were unsuccessful, and Culin forced Abbott out (Horan 1992:33–34).

Abbott became increasingly convinced that his finds from the Delaware gravels near Trenton represented examples of Paleolithic tools similar to those being reported in Europe. Putnam continued to require reassurance about the integrity of the evidence, wishing to have the finds replicated by other scientists besides Abbott. He asked Nathaniel Shaler to visit the site for the Peabody Museum in 1876. Putnam himself visited the site in 1880 and also took Abbott with him to investigate several New Jersey coastal shell mounds (Putnam 1880a:715). Later in 1880 Putnam and Asa Gray asked George Frederick Wright (1838–1921), from Andover, along with Henry Carvill Lewis (1853–88), a young geologist with the Pennsylvania Geological Survey, and the visiting English expert Sir William Boyd Dawkins, who was giving a course at the Lowell Institute, to inspect the site again, to see whether the associations of the presumed paleoliths could be firmly tied to the glacial drift (Wright 1919:451). Neither Putnam,

Shaler, Boyd Dawkins, nor the other experts who visited the Trenton gravel sites found additional examples of the reputed Trenton Paleolithic tools in situ.

When Abbott took up his new position at the University of Pennsylvania in 1889, Putnam was still enamored of the possibility of finding Pleistocene evidence at Trenton, so he hired Ernest Volk (1845–1919) to replace Abbott and continue explorations in the Trenton gravels for the Peabody Museum. Some recent histories suggest that Volk was hired because Putnam had lingering doubts about Abbott's veracity and reliability. After all, Abbott's detractors had accused him of salting his dig, for none of them had found an example of the famed paleoliths in the glacial drift when they visited the site. Putnam's disenchantment could be argued on the basis of his sending Shaler to investigate the site in 1876, and Wright, Lewis, and Boyd Dawkins in 1880, as well as making his own trip there. But the change from Abbott to Volk seems to have been more straightforward: Abbott had accepted a new position, and the Peabody simply needed someone to continue working the Trenton gravels.

No wavering of support by Putnam for the Trenton materials is apparent in any of his statements, and the Peabody Museum continued to support Volk's excavations at the site for 20 years, until Volk resigned in 1909. When Abbott was fired from Pennsylvania and tried to get Putnam to take him back to replace Volk, friction did develop between Abbott and the Peabody Museum. Putnam saw no reason to dismiss Volk, and Abbott became increasingly bitter about Putnam's failure to reinstate his Peabody Museum support.

The collectors we have just profiled were recruited mainly by Jeffries Wyman. Upon Wyman's death in September 1874, the trustees appointed one of their own board members, the renowned botanist Asa Gray, to serve as interim curator at the Peabody Museum. Gray was busy with his own teaching and herbarium duties and stepped in only to provide continuity until a new curator could be found. Putnam was appointed a few months later, in January 1875. Gray clearly saw himself as a caretaker, writing that "during the short period in which I have endeavored to act as temporary curator, while I have given to it such attention as I could, it was soon evident that the lack of time and of the requisite technical knowledge would prevent me from personally carrying on the work which had to be done. I therefore . . . engaged the valuable assistance of Mr. F. W. Putnam, of Salem, who is better acquainted than any one else with the Museum, and with Dr. Wyman's method and arrangements, having been much associated with him both in exploration and publication." But Gray is significant as a transitional figure for several reasons. He represents a continuation of the natural science training genre that dominated the Peabody for its first half century; he was, along with Wyman, an old professor of Putnam's; and he served as a key member of the board of trustees not only in the initial appointment of Putnam as curator but also in pushing in 1885 for the naming of Putnam as the first professor of anthropology, an appointment finalized in 1887.

Frederic Ward Putnam began a new chapter in the work of the Peabody Museum in many ways. The museum building fund had reached a critical level, and he was able to initiate the construction of the first phase of the museum during his early years as curator. Once this component of the building was finished, Putnam embarked on a new period preeminently of exploration and research (Putnam 1886a:480). He continued and intensified Wyman's plan for securing comparative collections, North American materials, and materials from the earliest inhabitants by having the museum subsidize outside collectors. "He was one of the earliest to realize the need of archeological and anthropological exploration, and to insist that careful field notes and data are equally important with the specimens themselves" (Anonymous 1915:638). He also focused on building the library collections. It is under Putnam, too, that we see the first teaching in anthropology at Harvard. The training of undergraduate students began in 1875, and that of graduate students in 1881, both critical steps in American archaeology.

Looking first at the development of the museum's collections, we see that Putnam continued working with people first contracted by Wyman, including Dunning, Gillman, Hartt, Andrews, and Abbott. Initially Putnam seemed much in favor of this procedure for securing materials, and during the first decade of his term as curator he greatly increased the number of subsidies, adding a new coterie of persons who were paid by the museum to conduct excavations and otherwise obtain specific collections. Among those identified by Putnam himself as most important were Paul Schumacher, Edward Palmer, Edwin Curtiss, Earl Flint, and Hilborne T. Cresson, on whom we elaborate later.

In his review of his first 10 years as curator in 1885, Putnam identified two major periods of collecting focus for the Peabody Museum, which seem to relate to differences in the procedures required (Putnam 1886a:481–84). He listed the most important people involved in making these collections, among them Charles Abbott in New Jersey; Albert Phelps in Maine; David Mack and Henry Gillman in Florida; Ebenezer Andrews and Charles Metz in Ohio; Lucien Carr in Virginia and Kentucky; Edwin Curtiss in Arkansas, Kansas, Missouri, and Tennessee; Henry Coe and Alice Fletcher in the Dakotas; Edward Palmer and Charles Parry in the Southwest; Palmer and Paul Schumacher in California; Palmer in Mexico; Earl Flint in Nicaragua; and himself in Maine, Massachusetts, Rhode Island, New Jersey, Ohio, Kentucky, Tennessee, Illinois, Missouri, and Wisconsin. The list was augmented during Putnam's second decade at the Peabody, so there are many people whom we must identify, if only briefly, in order to show the direction of growth of the Peabody collections during the museum's first three decades. But before we outline these collectors, we look at Putnam's unsung assistant curator during this period, Lucien Carr.

The contributions of **Lucien Carr** (1829–1915), assistant curator of the Peabody Museum for nearly two decades, were critical for the development and functioning of the museum during Putnam's tenure, but strangely, he has been essentially forgotten by American archaeologists. For example, Gordon Willey and Jeremy Sabloff, both Peabody

Museum staff members at the time they wrote their *A History of American Archaeology*, did not mention Carr even in passing. Carr started out as assistant in American archaeology and ethnology in 1875 but was promoted to assistant curator in 1877 and held the position until his resignation in November 1894. Carr ran the museum when Putnam was away on field trips and was a critical part of the maintenance of the Peabody's program from 1891 to 1893, while Putnam was in Chicago organizing the anthropology exhibits for the World's Columbian Exposition. During his tenure he contributed more than a dozen significant books and articles on American archaeology, physical anthropology, and ethnology.

Carr was born in 1829 in Troy, Missouri, a short distance north of St. Louis. He studied at St. Louis University, where he received his A.B. in 1846 (Thayer 1915:92). He then turned to a brief career in journalism. His stepfather, Adam B. Chambers, owned the St. Louis *Missouri Republican*. Carr worked for the newspaper for a few years but then resigned and moved to a rural area to become a gentleman farmer. Bushwhackers and other terrorists during the Civil War caused him to move from his farm back to the safety of St. Louis, and in 1867 he moved from there to Cambridge, Massachusetts. He apparently began exploring mounds in Tennessee and the mid-South in 1871–75, which no doubt brought him to Putnam's attention (Mainfort and Demb 2001:1).

According to William Roscoe Thayer (1915:92), in a memorial he wrote upon Carr's death, "having early taken an interest in the study of the Indians and of American archaeology, he was soon recognized as an expert in that field. . . . During this period he pursued his investigation of the Indians, collected a great deal of material and published various papers and short monographs, which gave him high rank among the then few authorities on the subject." Carr contributed a volume on Missouri for the American Commonwealth series published by Houghton, Mifflin and Company, wrote reviews of books on American Indians for the *New York Nation* for more than a quarter century, and was a member of the Anthropological Society of Washington, the American Antiquarian Society, and the American Academy of Arts and Sciences (Thayer 1915:93–94). He was one of five experts (along with Putnam, Henry Haynes, Daniel Brinton, and Joaquín García Icazbalceta) whom Justin Winsor listed as having consulted in writing his summaries of American Indian materials for his seminal *Narrative and Critical History of America* (Winsor 1889, 1:444). These kinds of credentials should have made Carr a well-known anthropologist. Yet he apparently was content to leave the politicking, meeting-going, and networking to others, which seems to have sealed his fate with the anthropological community of the day.

In the annual report of the Peabody Museum for 1875, Putnam (1876:8) took particular notice of the "important and special assistance I have received from Mr. Lucien Carr of Cambridge, who, with the exception of the time he was absent in Kentucky during part of the summer, has been constantly at work in the Museum as a voluntary assistant." A page later he noted, in reference to making the annual catalogue of acquisitions, "In this work I have been very materially assisted by Mr. Carr." He reported with approval the work Carr had undertaken in Kentucky: "During the absence of Mr. Carr in the summer, when he was attached to the Kentucky Geological Survey, he had an opportunity to make an excavation of a mound in Kentucky, and to examine several caves near the Cumberland Gap" (Putnam 1876:13).

Lucien Carr was officially appointed assistant curator at the board of trustees' meeting on January 17, 1877. For the year leading up to that appointment, Putnam reported even greater contributions by Carr to the museum, noting that thanks to "Mr. Carr's nearly uninterrupted labor," they had been able to catalogue all the 1,665 new artifact acquisitions, 78 books, and 97 pamphlets. "The great value of Mr. Carr's voluntary labor, and the fact that he can give nearly all of his time to the Museum while the detail work now required is more than I could accomplish unassisted, lead me to request that he be appointed Assistant Curator of the Museum, in which capacity he has acted during the year" (Putnam 1877:8).

Besides the work Carr did in Cambridge, Putnam reported that "Mr. Lucien Carr, acting under an appropriation granted at the last annual meeting, and in connection with the field party of the Kentucky Geological Survey . . . opened a mound in Lee County, Virginia" (Putnam 1877:11). Attached to the annual report for that year were two papers by Carr—a report on the crania received during the year (Carr 1878) and a "Report on the Exploration of a Mound in Lee County, Virginia" (Carr 1877)—showing that in addition to his fieldwork and museum work, Carr had been able to complete the analyses of his field data and publish his findings quickly. One might question his excavation techniques—he sank a shaft in the center of the mound and then carried out side excavations in a trench four feet wide (Carr 1877:77)—but this was not unusual for the day. Such excavations carried considerable risk. Lucius H. Cheney, who from 1873 to 1876 was the first president of what today is Southeastern Missouri University in Cape Girardeau, was a Harvard Summer School of Geology student in 1876. Spectators watching him excavate a burial at the mound crowded too close to the edge of the excavation, the wall collapsed, and Cheney was killed (Carr 1887b:78).

In addition to the publication he wrote on his mound excavation, Carr and Nathaniel Shaler wrote a report on the lithic collection in the possession of the Geological Society of Kentucky. The report was based on a "quite large" collection of stone tools, previously made mainly by Shaler for the Kentucky Geological Survey (Carr and Shaler 1876:20). The major portion of the report was by Carr, describing the materials and the prehistoric cultures of Kentucky; Shaler wrote a short section on the geological sources of stone for the tools. Carr warmed here to a theme he developed in greater detail a few years later—that of the identity of the mound builders with modern Indian groups. Carr noted that because of the size of mounds, many people ascribed them "to a mythical people" named the "Mound Builders" (Carr and Shaler 1876:4). He provided a brief review of the evidence and determined that "if any conclusion at all can be drawn from these facts, it is certainly not favorable to the existence here of two civilizations, but rather of one, and that one the Indian's" (Carr and Shaler 1876:7).

The stone tools in his analysis, Carr carefully noted, "are all what are technically known as 'surface finds.'" He observed them to be similar to tools used, for the most part, by recent Indian groups (Carr and Shaler 1876:9). His co-author, Shaler, took a step in a direction different from Putnam's on the issue of Pleistocene habitations, observing that "years of search, on the part of the director of the Survey among the river gravels, have failed to show a single indication of great antiquity. In our caverns the search has been but begun, yet there have been a good many sections made through their floors, so far with a negative result. At Big Bone Lick the excavations have failed, as yet, to show a trace of man along with the extinct mammalia of the country" (Carr and Shaler 1876:30–31).

The chair of the Peabody's board of trustees, in the annual report for 1877, recognized "the laborious work of transferring our collections to this new building, and arranging them," performed by Carr (Winthrop 1878:183). Putnam (1878a:194) seconded this acknowledgment in his curator's report, saying that "much work on the collections has been accomplished during the year by Mr. Carr and myself, and for a few weeks we had the assistance of Mr. Lucien Carr Jr., who devoted himself to repairing broken pottery in a skillful manner, and to painting, very neatly, the catalogue numbers on several hundred articles." In addition, Carr, assisted by museum staff member Jennie Smith, continued measuring the new crania acquired that year (Putnam 1878a:221), and he contributed a paper appended to the report, "Observations on the Crania from the Stone Graves in Tennessee" (Carr 1878), mainly an analysis of the crania excavated by Putnam and Edwin Curtiss in Kentucky the previous year.

In the 1879 annual report, Putnam noted that Carr and Smith had continued to analyze crania, this time those collected by Paul Schumacher during a California shell mound survey, which Carr published in the annual report as a research paper, "Measurements of Crania from California" (Carr 1879a). Putnam (1879a:479) observed that Carr had been "a most faithful" assistant, and his son, Lucien Carr Jr., was "special temporary assistant for a few months in the early part of the year." In the summer of 1879 Carr took a trip to Europe, with museum funding, to learn additional skills for analyzing crania. He got materials and received training from Professors John Evans, George Busk, and Sir William H. Flower in London and from Doctors Paul Broca and Paul Topinard in Paris. Putnam (1880a:729) enthused: "By the European trip of the Assistant Curator, Mr. Carr, the Museum has been brought into direct communication with several of the leading archaeologists and ethnologists abroad, which already has resulted in mutual advantage." Thus Carr followed the path Wyman had blazed to some noted institutions.

For 1880 Putnam reported (1881a:9, 26) that Carr continued doing cataloging, wrote a paper on the crania of New England Indians for a memorial volume from the Boston Society of Natural History (BSNH), and was well into his research on historical evidence for the connection of known Indian tribes with the mound builders. Carr also gave a paper at the BSNH on Abbott's Trenton gravel tools; Carr and J. D. Whitney had gone to Trenton and recovered several of the alleged paleoliths (Wright 1893:66). During 1881 Carr continued working on the relationship of contemporary tribes to mound builders, focusing on the historical evidence of agriculture associated with mounds. He presented portions of the argument as it developed in sessions of the BSNH (Putnam 1882a:70). In 1882 Carr prepared a paper on the social and political position of women among the Huron-Iroquois tribes for the Peabody's annual report (Carr 1883b). The following year Putnam (1884a:366) noted that "Mr. Carr has continued his historical researches during the year and is engaged in tracing out several of the customs of the Indians during the early years of their contact with the whites."

It was also in 1883 that Carr published the results of his research on linkages between the historically known Indian tribes and the mound builders:

> In a paper upon the Prehistoric Remains of Kentucky, published in the first volume of these Memoirs, I have expressed the opinion that it was impossible to distinguish between a series of stone implements taken from the mounds in the Mississippi Valley, and a similar series made and used by the modern Indians. . . . Nor does this similarity stop with objects made of stone. On the contrary, it is believed to extend to all the articles, of every kind whatsoever, that have thus far been taken from the mounds . . . and all the mound constructions known are well within red Indian abilities. . . . This conclusion, together with its corollary as to the origin of these structures, is neither new nor original; and yet, in spite of the simple explanation it gives of the mound question, or, perhaps, it might be more correct to say on account of this very simplicity, it has made its way but slowly. (Carr 1883a:3)

Carr (1883a:4) reviewed previous beliefs about the mound builders, lamenting that popular writers who had molded public opinion had approached mound building from one side only (that is, as exotic), had declared Indians unequal to the task of having constructed the mounds, and thus had invented an extinct race responsible for mound construction. On the subject of women's status, Thomas Wentworth Higginson, writing in *Harper's* (1883:23), reported confirmation of "the theory of that careful student, Mr. Lucien Carr, that the early position of women among the Indians was higher than has been generally believed."

Carr began his review of the evidence by addressing the question of agriculture, pointing out that one assumption made by those who thought the Indians were incapable of building mounds was that they did not have agriculture. To refute this error, Carr dedicated the first section of his book to showing that several prehistoric Indian groups were agriculturalists. He then devoted a long section to the types of mounds constructed, seeing first a division between mounds, on one hand, and embankments and enclosures, on the other. He then subdivided mounds into three main varieties: temple or truncated mounds; animal or effigy mounds; and simple conical mounds. He offered a good examination of literature sources, reviewing several direct observations of historic Indian settlements with mounds by early European explorers.

Historians seem to have read Carr's work, whereas anthropologists have forgotten it. One set of historical experts, Anne Paolucci and Henry Paolucci (1995:134–35), have argued that Carr's work "is the most elaborate collation of the accounts of the early travelers, and of others coming in contact with the Indians at an early day, which has yet been made, and his foot-notes are an ample bibliography of this aspect of the subject." They also observed that at the time Carr wrote his review, he was out of step with the "big name" anthropologists of the day, such as Brinton, who thought the mound builders were peoples different from the Indians and had been driven south, out of what is now the United States.

Even Carr's boss, Putnam, was split in his support. In the year Carr's monograph came out, Putnam noted a report by Francis La Flesche, an ethnographer at the Bureau of Ethnology, on a burial mound made for an Omaha chief by his tribe in about 1825, but he cautioned that

> these facts do not prove that all mounds are recent, or that all were made by the immediate ancestors of the Indian tribes which still erect mounds over their noted dead. . . . There are so many kinds of mounds in this country, that it shows a limited experience in their investigation when a writer here and there asserts that they are all the work of the present Indians, or their immediate ancestors; and an equal disregard of known facts, when another as confidently asserts that they were all made by a people unlike and superior to the Indian race, and of great antiquity. (Putnam 1883a:168)

Again the next year Putnam wrote, "That many Indian tribes built mounds and earthworks is beyond doubt, but that all the mounds and earthworks of North America were made by these same tribes, or their immediate ancestors, is not thereby proved. Mr. Carr, in his recent paper published by the Kentucky Geological Survey, has taken up the historical side of the question, but it must not be received for more than he intended" (Putnam 1884a:346).

The reviewer of Carr's volume for *Science* (Anonymous 1884a:152) agreed with Putnam's stance that even though Carr showed some of the mounds to have been built by Indians, it did not follow that there could have been no separate mound-builder culture that erected most of the mounds. Carr, in a book review of his own for *Science* (1885:177), took issue with those who thought the mound builders were not the ancestors of current Indian tribes. The editor of *Science* added a disclaimer: "The editor gladly inserts this review, written at his solicitation, but he does so without committing himself to the advocacy of the views therein expressed."

One issue that bothered Putnam was the possibility that all mounds would be seen as recent, which might jeopardize his hope for the great antiquity of the first Americans: "Of late years several writers have brought forward many arguments showing anew, what every archaeologist of experience knows, that many of the mounds in the country were made by the historic tribes. This has been dwelt upon to such an extent as to make common the belief that *all* of the mounds and earthworks are of recent origin" (Putnam 1890c:701).

Putnam was also concerned about the idea that some generic people known as the Mound Builders had existed. Regarding a lecture he delivered in Pittsburgh, it was reported that

> Prof. Putnam was received with great hand clapping. He illustrated his address by charts, hung upon the canvas at the rear of the stage. He said that there were mounds all over the world, in Asia, Africa, Europe, and America, built by many races, so that it was foolish to use the term "mound builders." He said: "You have no more right to call a certain class of people mound builders than you have to call the white men of today railroad builders." (Anonymous 1896a)

In his address upon his retirement as president of the AAAS, Putnam suggested that the term mound builders be completely abandoned, because it obfuscated rather than clarified. He argued: "Many peoples in America, as well as on other continents, have built mounds over their dead, to mark important sites and great events. It is thus evident that the term so generally applied is of no value as a scientific designation."

He further observed that the term lost explanatory value because it was applied even to refuse piles and shell heaps. Coastal shell heaps could not, he argued, "be regarded as the work of one people. The same may be said in regard to the mounds of earth and of stone so widely distributed over the country. . . . Thus it will be seen that the earth-mounds, like the shell-mounds, were made by many peoples and at various times" (Putnam 1899b:232).

Carr's work on mounds seems to be almost completely unknown to Americanist archaeologists. Carr was not the first to argue that the mounds were constructed by the ancestors of the historically known Indian tribes, but his argument is powerful. It is clearly not the case that Cyrus Thomas was the pristine myth breaker in his well-known work of a decade later, *Report on the Mound Explorations of the Bureau of Ethnology* (1894). The reaction to Carr's volume shows the tenor of the day. If we follow Franz Boas's statement (quoted in Tozzer 1909:286) that there were three great late-nineteenth-century anthropologists—Daniel Brinton, J. Wesley Powell, and Frederic Putnam—then we see that Brinton, at the time, was arrayed against Carr's position, and neither Putnam nor Powell had yet come out wholly in favor of it. The editor of *Science* found Carr's position so controversial that he had to dissociate the magazine from it.

The publication of the 1883 volume in some ways marked the apogee of Carr's association with the Peabody Museum. Although Putnam described Carr's work with great appreciation in every annual report through the one for 1883, mentions of Carr's contributions appear in only two reports of the subsequent 10 years, aside from his listing on the masthead. In the annual report for 1886 Putnam noted that Carr again had compiled the list of new acquisitions that accompanied his curator's annual report, and he commented that Carr continued to work on historical studies (Putnam 1887a:567).

In the annual report for 1888 Putnam recorded that Carr had made the index for the third composite volume of the annual reports (the fourteenth through the twentieth, 1880–86). After that point, the annual reports are mute on Carr's contributions. When he resigned in 1894, Putnam made no mention of it, offering neither thanks nor reasons for Carr's leaving. The Peabody's annual report for 1915–16 gave only a short note telling of Carr's death in January 1915, at age 86, mentioning that he had worked for free as the first assistant curator at the museum for 20 years (1875–94) and had published various reports in the annual reports (Willoughby 1917:254–55). No smoking gun indicates clearly why Carr and Putnam gradually disengaged. Whatever the reason, Carr resigned when the anthropology program at the Peabody Museum started in a new direction after 1890 (see chapter 6).

In addition to Carr, Putnam was materially assisted in running the museum by three women: Jennie Smith (who later shifted to the use of her formal name, Jane, in her writings), along with Alice Putnam, and Frances Mead. Curtis Hinsley (1999:144) has suggested that **Jennie Smith** (1850–?) began working for Putnam in 1875, although our record search indicates that she was not listed officially as a staff member until March 1878. At Putnam's suggestion, she was elected a member of the AAAS at its twenty-ninth annual meeting in 1879, and she remained a member throughout Putnam's tenure as secretary (1873–97) and president (1898–99). She resigned from the AAAS in 1899, at the end of Putnam's term, so part of her work seems to have been closely linked with assisting Putnam in conducting his activities for the AAAS.

After being appointed an "Assistant in the Museum" in 1878, Jennie Smith was carried on the museum's masthead in that position for the next three decades. She reduced her workload to half-time when Putnam retired in 1909, and she retired completely in 1915 when Putnam died. Putnam referred to her work primarily in secretarial capacities, but she also helped out with the library, and early on she assisted Carr with his osteological analyses, washing bones and measuring skulls. We presume she was hired while relatively young and so was comfortable being listed as "Miss Jennie Smith" for many years, until 1891, when she changed her listing to "Miss Jane Smith."

Alice Edmands Putnam (1865–1963) was first listed as an "Assistant in the Museum" in 1886. She was one of three children (the others being Eben and Ethel Appleton Fiske) whom Frederic Putnam had with his first wife, Adelaide Martha Edmands, before she died in 1879 (Tozzer 1936a:125). Although his first wife seems not to have been involved in Putnam's work, after his second marriage, to Esther Orne Clarke in 1882, occasional mention is made of both his children and his wife participating in archaeological work. For example, three days after Putnam married Esther Clarke in Chicago, they left on their honeymoon for excavations at the Ohio mounds with Charles Metz. In the archival papers of Frederic Putnam, as well as in the Peabody's annual reports, references appear to his son Eben's accompanying him on field investigations from Maine to Wisconsin.

The child involved most in Putnam's archaeological work, however, was not his son but his daughter Alice. After being hired in 1886, she worked with Putnam in both official and unofficial capacities for nearly a quarter century, until his resignation in 1909. The Alice Putnam papers at the Peabody Museum contain a number of letters from Alice to her father, discussing archaeological issues and detailing communications with various of her father's colleagues from professional scientific meetings she attended for him. She essentially served as her father's eyes and ears at these meetings, especially once his health began to fail (Putnam Papers, Box 1.2, Peabody Museum Archives).

Frances Harvey Teobert Mead (1847–1932) came to the museum in 1888 and was named an assistant there in 1889, officially replacing Alice Putnam, who had been the assistant from 1886 to 1889. Mead served in an important way as Putnam's personal assistant during the early 1890s, when he was involved in the correspondence and arrangements for the 1893 World's Columbian Exposition in Chicago. She continued to be listed as his assistant until her official retirement at the time of Putnam's death in 1915. Effectively, she retired when Putnam did in 1909.

Mead (1894) wrote detailed reports of various state exhibits at the 1893 Chicago exposition. At Putnam's urging, because he was serving as one of the journal's associate editors at the time, she wrote a piece on the Peabody Museum's displays for *Records of the Past* (Mead 1905), providing an interesting glimpse of what the museum looked like a century ago. She produced the first detailed bibliography of Putnam's work in her article for the *Putnam Anniversary Volume,* a book edited by Franz Boas and others (1909) and presented to Putnam on his seventieth birthday. She collected historical and environmental notes on the Conejos Canyon area of Colorado, where she took her vacations for more than 40 years, materials that were edited and published posthumously (Mead 1984).

Returning to the individual collectors whom Putnam recruited during this period, let us turn first to **Paul Schumacher** (1835?–1913?), who was briefly associated with the Peabody Museum in the late 1870s. Schumacher had worked for the Smithsonian Institution collecting in California and Oregon from 1873 to 1876 (see Schumacher works through 1877c in the bibliography). Putnam recruited him to work for the Peabody in 1877 and 1878, after running into him during his own work writing up the California artifacts collected for the Smithsonian during the Wheeler Survey (chapter 3). Putnam secured "special appropriations" from the Peabody Museum trustees for Schumacher to make artifact collections from shell mounds in Oregon and California (Putnam 1878a:200, 1879a:466) and then published reports from Schumacher on his work and his artifact analyses (Schumacher 1878, 1879a, 1879b). After this intense period of working for the Smithsonian and the Peabody during the 1870s, Schumacher disappeared from the scene, with one last paper on his work in Sonora in 1882.

Another of Putnam's recruits was **Charles Christopher Parry** (1823–90). Parry had come to the United States as a child in 1832, living in upstate New York. He obtained his A.B. in 1842 from Union College in that state and his M.D. from Columbia University in 1846. Parry moved to Davenport, Iowa, that year and opened a medical office. After practicing medicine for only a short while, he shifted to the study of botany. He began participating in expeditions as a botanist after 1848 while retaining his home base in Davenport (Stanton 1991:73). He began collecting ethnographic specimens in the U.S. Southwest in the mid-1870s.

Parry had taken classes with the well-known nineteenth-century botanist John Torrey while at Columbia and had maintained a lively botanical correspondence with Torrey, Torrey's protégé Asa Gray, and George Englemann. During his explorations in the Southwest, Parry had the opportunity to name some geographical features. In 1861 he named a set of twin peaks Torrey and Gray, and a nearby peak, Engelmann. A decade later, in 1872, Gray passed by this area on his way to Yosemite and made a side trip to climb Gray's Peak (Rodgers 1942:281–82).

In 1874, apparently at Gray's suggestion, Parry began sending ethnographic materials to the Peabody Museum. In 1875 he opened a mound on the Santa Clara River near St. George, Utah, by methods perhaps typical of the time: he diverted an irrigation ditch through the mound and collected the washed-out artifacts, which he sent to the Peabody (Jeter 1990:54; Putnam 1876:12). In 1876 and 1877 he collected other artifacts from California, Arizona, and Utah, which he donated to the museum.

Parry was part of a small archaeological controversy of the time, involving one of the early women interested in ruins, Julia J. Wirt, who was a corresponding member of the Davenport (Iowa) Academy of Natural Sciences. She sent a paper to Parry about excavations near Utah Lake, asking him to read it for her at the academy's meeting of October 27, 1876. He did so, in addition to delivering two papers on his own findings of Southwestern pottery (Jeter 1990:57; Wirt 1878). The collector Edward Palmer, whom we introduce next, questioned Wirt's interpretations in a paper given at the Davenport Academy's meeting in 1877, and Wirt later retracted her claim about finding wheat in the ruins (Jeter 1990:60).

Later Parry went from Davenport to Cambridge, Massachusetts, where he provided Putnam with additional information on his field materials. He then joined Edward Palmer for a joint Palmer-Parry Expedition to Mexico in 1877–78. Materials from that expedition—ethnobotanical as well as archaeological specimens—were sent to the Peabody Museum. Putnam seems subsequently to have shifted his support from Parry to Palmer; at least, no additional anthropological materials were received from Parry. We suspect this was because of Parry's rather destructive method of artifact recovery.

Edward Palmer (1829–1911) was born in England, where his father was a florist and horticulturist, which clearly influenced Palmer's career choice (Safford 1911:341). He came to the United States in 1849, studied medicine and biology with Dr. Jared Kirtland (1793–1877), an accomplished botanist and horticulturist, and became "perhaps the nineteenth century's greatest botanical and natural history field collector" (Jeter 1990:3, 41).

Marvin Jeter's biography (1990) gives the most complete picture of Palmer's work and contributions. Palmer began his collecting career in 1852–53 while serving as a biological collector on a U.S. Navy expedition to Paraguay. He studied at the Cleveland Homeopathic College in 1856–57 and then moved to Kansas to practice medicine. In 1859 he left Kansas for Colorado, to get involved in the gold rush there. In 1861 he had a job with the U.S. Geological Survey in California; in 1862 he served for the Union Army as a surgeon; and after the war, in 1865, he continued working for the army, collecting ethnographic items from the Apaches in Arizona but also picking up archaeological specimens from the ruins known as Montezuma's Castle. In 1867 Palmer left the army to collect Apache, Pima, and Papago materials on his own. By 1869 he had made the transition from amateur to full-time collector, working for Spencer Baird and the Smithsonian Institution (Jeter 1990:42–48).

Baird was a major patron of Palmer's. The association began with the Paraguay expedition of 1852–53, an expedition outfitted by Baird. Palmer continued sending Baird items through the 1850s and 1860s, and by 1869 Baird had commissioned Palmer as a general collector in the West. Their relationship intensified during the 1870s, particularly after Baird replaced Joseph Henry as secretary of the Smithsonian in 1878 (Jeter 1990:9–11).

It was during this early period, in 1869–70, that the U.S. commissioner of agriculture had Palmer collect in Arizona, New Mexico, and Utah for the U.S. National Herbarium (Safford 1911:345). Palmer summarized the results of this work in 1871 in a report titled "Food Products of North American Indians," which Jeter (1990:51) called the first ethnobotanical article in the United States. Later Palmer published follow-up reports on ethnobotanical studies (Palmer 1874b, 1878b). The year 1871 also marked Palmer's first extensive excavations in Southwestern ruins. Walter Hough (1911:173) wrote that "Dr. Palmer made the first exploration of an ancient pueblo ruin in 1871, a mound at St. George, Utah, which he thoroughly searched, preserving every fragment of evidence that came under his trowel and carrying out the exploration with a skill and perfection of method that have not been surpassed in that field. This work was followed by archaeological excavations on the lower Verde River in Arizona."

Palmer had a long and rich history with the Smithsonian, but we are concerned here mainly with his interactions with nongovernmental institutions such as the Peabody Museum. Beginning in about 1872 he collected marine invertebrates in New England for Louis Agassiz and the Museum of Comparative Zoology (Safford 1911:347). In 1872–73, one of his projects was the excavation of a shell mound near Harpswell, Peak's Island, Maine, the collection from which he donated to the Peabody Museum in 1877 (Putnam 1878a:198). During 1872–73 he met Putnam, then editor of *American Naturalist*. Putnam encouraged Palmer to write up some of his work for the journal, and the first articles appeared in 1873 and 1874. In 1877, when Palmer was in Cambridge on other business, he completed four more articles for the magazine.

Palmer served as "Field Assistant in Southwestern Archaeology" for the Peabody Museum from 1875 to 1881, when he was named field assistant for the Division of Mound Exploration at the Bureau of Ethnology. From 1875 to 1877 he worked in Utah, where he met the Davenport, Iowa, botanist Parry. The first archaeological collections that Palmer made for the Peabody were received in 1876 (Putnam 1877:10). The next year Putnam wrote that "Dr. Edward Palmer, acting under the special appropriation for explorations made at the last annual meeting, has made a careful examination of several mounds in Southern Utah, from which numerous articles of pottery, bone and stone were obtained. The notes and descriptions furnished by Dr. Palmer, show that most of these mounds in Utah are in reality the remains of adobe or mud houses" (Putnam 1878a:198). Palmer wrote a separate report on other work in Utah, "Cave Dwellings in Utah," which was attached to the Peabody Museum's annual report for that year (Palmer 1878).

Palmer was at Harvard for a short period in 1877, both to write up this work and to prepare for the joint Palmer-Parry Expedition to Mexico in 1877–78. During that expedition Palmer sent a series of ethnobotanical and archaeological specimens to the Peabody Museum and, when he returned, assisted in cataloguing more than 800 of the items (Putnam 1880a:716). Palmer made another trip to northern Mexico, and also to eastern Texas, in 1879–80, but the Peabody Museum ran short of funds to support the operation. Putnam ruefully reported, "It is to be regretted that, for want of funds, Dr. Palmer will be obliged to discontinue his investigations when so much of importance could be obtained by extending his field work into southwestern Texas and the adjoining parts of Mexico" (1880a:720).

Palmer apparently continued to collect on his own after Peabody funds dried up, and Putnam observed in the subsequent annual report (1881a:21) that "although from want of funds it became necessary to recall him from the field, he found the means to continue his work for a few months longer, and having received information of some old burial caves in the state of Coahuila, he went to the place" and continued collecting. Furthermore, Putnam observed (1881a:22): "As has been the case in all his explorations, Dr. Palmer procured such natural productions from the vicinity of the caves as would help in determining the material of which the old things were made, and we are thus enabled to exhibit the leaves, fibres, and other vegetable productions from which the cloth, baskets, and numerous other articles were constructed by the people who placed their dead in the caves."

Palmer returned to Cambridge in mid-1880 to catalogue his collections and continued work there until the spring of 1881, writing up a short report on his work (1882). Later in 1881 he secured his new position from Baird on the Bureau of Ethnology mound survey project. Palmer's work for the Peabody was brief but important, particularly in terms of the greater context he provided with his broad collecting technique.

Palmer began surveying for the Bureau of Ethnology in the southeastern United States and devoted himself full time to that work, collecting materials from mound excavations in Alabama, Arkansas, Georgia, Indiana, Mississippi, North Carolina, South Carolina, and Tennessee over the next few years, before returning to Mexico and the Southwest in the mid-1880s and early 1890s. Palmer had worked with Edwin Curtiss, the next of Putnam's recruits whom we profile, for the Peabody Museum in

1879 (Jeter 1990:84), so Palmer was aware of the finds Curtiss had been making in Arkansas. Curtiss had just died in December 1880, terminating the funded Peabody Museum projects in Arkansas and leaving an opening for Palmer to move in on behalf of the Bureau of Ethnology, which he did immediately upon beginning work on the mound survey project.

The new directives Palmer received reflected the work he had been doing for the Peabody. Now Baird, in a letter dated January 13, 1881, directed Palmer: "In view of the increased scope of our museum, I shall want not simply antiquities & illustrations of modern life, & food, but also all the industrial products derived from the vegetable kingdom in the way of gums, roots, dyes, etc." (Jeter 1881:81). He elaborated on these instructions in a letter of February 23, 1881: "Please give me a sketch of several of the different regions you would like to explore, either singly or successively, the object being in the first place, to increase our important archaeological collections; & then the botanical and zoological." Clearly, Palmer's charge was not simply to find the "origins" of the mound builders but to provide a detailed description of their lifeways. Now it was expected that a field archaeologist would collect more than just lithics and ceramics.

Edwin Curtiss (1830–80), born in New York, served as "Field Assistant in American Archaeology" for the Peabody Museum from 1877 to 1880, conducting excavations in Arkansas and Tennessee and also making some collections from Alabama, Kansas, and Kentucky. Curtiss had begun his adult life as a tailor, and in 1863 he joined the Union Army to work for the Commissary Department. During this time he also began working for the U.S. Army Corps of Engineers, and immediately after the war he worked for the government as an independent contractor on the same types of projects, including building railroads, levees, and bridges along the Mississippi River (Putnam 1881a:12). His construction work allowed him to scout potential archaeological sites. He relied on railway agents and railroad engineers to identify local landowners of mound sites, and he began to buy local archaeological collections (Mainfort and Demb 2001:2).

In the summer of 1877 Curtiss was working for a collector in Tennessee, General Gates P. Thurston (Kevin E. Smith, personal communication, 2003). A few years earlier, Frederic Putnam had become interested in the Tennessee mounds, particularly through the avocational archaeological work of a medical doctor in Nashville named Joseph Jones. Jones and his brother, Charles Colcok Jones Jr., made several collections in Tennessee and Georgia, which were later purchased for the museum by William H. Claflin (see chapter 11). In August and September 1877, the annual meeting of the AAAS was held in Nashville, and Putnam attended. During the meetings, Putnam, together with John Wesley Powell, of the Bureau of Ethnology, began exploring the local mound sites. The Nashville *Daily American* ran a column on the activities of the AAAS and noted on September 2, 1877, that Putnam, Powell, and several others "opened an Indian grave out near Fort Zollicoffer yesterday afternoon and procured several skulls and bones, and some specimens of pottery. One of the most curious obtained was what might be termed a small copper breast-plate, which was evidently beaten out to its present shape four or five hundred years ago. Prof. Putnam believes that the people who made such ornaments antedated the Indians who were found here by the first white settlers." Powell and Putnam continued collaborating during the approximately three weeks in which Putnam remained in the area, at times working on the same sites (K. Smith 2003). Putnam reported that "Major Powell was engaged in making equally extensive explorations in close proximity to my own, so that we had the advantage of each other's work" (1878a:203).

Putnam hired Edwin Curtiss to work with him on these initial Tennessee explorations. Needing to return to his museum duties, Putnam made arrangements with Curtiss (sometimes listed in the annual reports as Curtis) to carry on the mound exploration work that fall, hiring him on September 22, 1877, to work for "$3.00 a day for his services and his traveling expenses and what he pays out for labor and boxes is to be allowed him on receipt of specimens with item bill" (Putnam, quoted in K. Smith 1999:5).

The keeping of potsherds and animal bones was not a common practice in archaeological projects of the time, even in Europe, but Putnam had Curtiss keep these materials as well as take notes on every burial, draw maps of all the sites, and carefully pack the materials for shipment back to Cambridge (S. Williams 1991:69). Putnam's correspondence with his "field men" in Tennessee gave them clear instructions about recording stratigraphy, albeit at an emergent level, and his employees thus frequently recorded different "tiers" of graves in the mounds (Kevin E. Smith, personal communication, 2003).

For the next season, Curtiss continued the work in Tennessee for the museum during breaks from his business, following directions sent to him by Putnam (Putnam 1879a:469). By the third season, the summer of 1879, Putnam wrote that Curtiss had "continued in the regular employ of the Museum" and was now working on mounds in Tennessee, Kansas, Missouri, and Arkansas (Putnam 1880a:717–19), for which he was paid $75 a month (Mainfort and Demb 2001:7). Putnam was particularly interested in the chambered burial mounds Curtiss had opened, and he reported on this aspect of Curtiss's work at a fall meeting of the BSNH (Mason 1880:217). The early part of the field season was spent working in Tennessee, from February to May 1879. Curtiss then shifted to working on a railroad project for the next few months, returning when that job was finished to continue working for the museum, now in Arkansas, from October 1879 through March 1880 (Kevin E. Smith, personal communication, 2003).

An interesting sidebar to this work is the involvement of perhaps the first black regular archaeological field technicians, George Woods (1842–?) and his brother Joseph Woods, who began working for Curtiss in 1878. Curtiss referred to these men in his communications to Putnam as two of the most skilled excavators available. When Curtiss began working in Arkansas for the Peabody Museum, he wrote Putnam that he was so disgusted with the sloppy workers there that he had sent back to Nashville for the Woods brothers (Kevin E. Smith, personal communication, 2003).

Curtiss died in Nashville in December 1880, and the last notice of his affiliation with the Peabody Museum is the short obituary note that Putnam penned for the next annual report (Putnam 1881a:11–12). Putnam then hired George Woods to continue Curtiss's work at the mounds in Tennessee for the 1882 and 1883 seasons (Putnam 1884a:351)—certainly a first for the Peabody, if not for all American research institutions.

The next two of Putnam's recruits whom we mention were both minor figures in collecting for the Peabody Museum. **John Francis Patch LeBaron** (1847–1935), chief engineer for the St. John's and Indian Rivers Railroad, resided in Titusville, Florida, at the time he first appeared in the museum records. Putnam recruited him in 1878, noting in his annual report for 1879 that for the last two years LeBaron had "been engaged in making a reconnaissance of the archaeological remains in eastern Florida for the Museum" (Putnam 1880a:722). Soon afterward LeBaron disappeared from the Peabody Museum records. A search of Internet sites shows that he later took a position with the U.S. Army Corps of Engineers, for which he surveyed a possible route for a cross-Florida canal. While working for the Corps of Engineers, LeBaron found additional artifacts, which were reported in the Smithsonian Institution's 1881 annual report. A later Smithsonian letter file records his work in Nicaragua sometime between 1889 and 1908, and in 1912 he penned an article on Maya ruins in Nicaragua (LeBaron 1912). Although most of his support apparently came from his skills as a civil engineer, he maintained an avocational interest in archaeology from 1878 to 1912.

John W. Emmert Jr. (1841–1917) worked for Putnam during only one field season, and we mention him largely because of his later involvement with the "Bat Creek stone." Emmert was a Civil War veteran, born in Bristol, Tennessee, who had served with the Confederate Quartermaster Department. Because his leg had been badly wounded in the battle of Drury's Bluff in 1864, he mainly directed excavations rather than doing the work himself (Kirk 2001). In 1883 he worked for the Peabody Museum in Tennessee and North Carolina, at the same time the Woods brothers were doing mound work for Putnam in Tennessee. He excavated a burial mound on Joy Creek in North Carolina, a riverbank midden on the Walango River in Custer County, Tennessee, and two small burial caves in Sullivan County along the Holston River in Tennessee (Emmert 1891), collecting the artifacts for the museum (Putnam 1884a:339). In one of the caves he claimed to have found an extraordinary suite of artifacts spanning the entire known archaeological sequence, a claim subsequently shown to be implausible (Mainfort and Kwas 2004:765; Peabody Museum Accession 83-14-10). Putnam did not rehire Emmert the following year.

Between 1883 and 1889, however, Emmert worked as a field assistant for the Bureau of Ethnology and the Smithsonian Institution, mainly in eastern Tennessee (Mainfort and Kwas 1991). In February 1889 Emmert reported a fantastic artifact, the "Bat Creek stone," bearing ancient Hebrew or Cherokee script, from one of his new mound excavations. Perhaps this was an attempt to ensure his continued employment, which was on shaky ground after a drinking problem caused his reputation as a field archaeologist to slip (Mainfort and Kwas 2004:766). Although Cyrus Thomas published the find in his great work on mounds in 1894, most archaeologists of the time ignored it.

Only after Cyrus H. Gordon, a scholar of ancient Middle Eastern languages who taught at Brandeis University in the early 1970s, "rediscovered" it at that time did it briefly gain some notoriety (Mainfort and Kwas 1991, 2004). The Bat Creek stone did not save Emmert's job. He was dismissed by the Bureau of Ethnology and soon disappeared from the archaeological scene.

We turn next to one of the more important colleagues whom Putnam recruited—**Alice Cunningham Fletcher** (1838–1923). Fletcher began a correspondence with Putnam in 1878, seeking information for a lecture series she was preparing on American Indians. During the first year of her speaking tour, in 1878, she presented four "Lectures on Ancient America" in New York, Boston, and other East Coast cities, titling them "The Ancients—Here and Elsewhere," "The Lost Peoples of America," "Ceremonies of the Moundbuilders," and "Antiquities of Coast and Cave." She illustrated the talks with hand-drawn pictures of artifacts and sites in the Ohio and Mississippi Valleys (Mark 1988:32). In 1879 she expanded her lecture series to 11 topics and traveled to Ohio, Illinois, Wisconsin, and Minnesota (Browman 2002a:225–27; Mark 1980:63, 1988:32).

Fletcher was first associated with the Peabody Museum as a researcher in 1880, when she shifted her work to ethnographic studies of the Omaha and Sioux Indians, and in 1882 she was appointed "Special Assistant in American Ethnology." A prolific contributor on the anthropological scene of the time, she immediately took advantage of her appointment by publishing five separate papers as part of the museum's annual report for 1883. She remained a consistent contributor to the Peabody's annual reports and to the proceedings of the AAAS from 1882 onward, focusing initially on the Omaha and Sioux and shifting later to the Nez Perce. Thanks to strong support from Putnam, she was the first holder of the Peabody Museum's Mary Copley Thaw Fellowship in American Archaeology and Ethnology, which was established in 1890, and thus was also the first woman to hold any fellowship at Harvard. She gave occasional talks at the Peabody Museum (Putnam 1895a:224), but when not in the field she lived in Washington, D.C.

Because of her appointment title, Fletcher is often referred to as the first Peabody Museum ethnologist, but at first she was also much involved in archaeology. She participated in the excavation of shell mounds in Maine, Massachusetts, and Florida beginning in 1878, under Putnam's aegis. In 1885 she made a collecting trip to Alaska and came back with artifacts she collected there, as well as materials from William Dall's work.

Fletcher also helped Putnam in his attempts to develop national awareness of the need for archaeological site preservation. In 1886–87 she helped him solicit funds to purchase Serpent Mound in Ohio. In 1887 and 1888 Fletcher and Matilda Coxe Stevenson (1850–1915) served as representatives of the Women's Anthropological Society of America (WASA) and of the AAAS to lobby for a bill in Congress to have Mesa Verde, in Colorado, and ruins on the Pajarito Plateau, in New Mexico, declared national parks (Fletcher and Stevenson 1889). Although this bill failed, their work laid the foundation for the later successful effort, funded partly by Mary Hemenway, to preserve Casa Grande and for the Antiquity Act of 1906.

On Putnam's suggestion, Fletcher joined the fledgling Archaeological Institute of America (AIA) in 1879. She was a major influence in the research directions taken by the AIA after 1899, when the organization became involved in establishing research in the U.S. Southwest, and she was a key player in helping to found the AIA's School of American Archaeology in 1908–9 (Mark 1980:80–84, 1988:319–23). In 1891, in an article regarding women in science, Sarah Underwood (1891:698) wrote: "In ethnology and archaeology shine such bright names as Alice Fletcher, Erminie [sic] Smith and Amelia B. Edwards." Two of these three worked with Putnam—Fletcher and Erminnie A. Smith (1836–86), Putnam's cousin, who, after marrying Simeon H. Smith at age 17, trained as a geologist in Germany. After Putnam got Erminnie Smith into the AAAS in 1876, she shifted her interests to the Iroquois and worked for the Bureau of Ethnology.

Alice Fletcher was one of the original members and officers of the Women's Anthropological Society of America, where she gave several papers as well as establishing archaeology as one of six subsections. A number of women interested in archaeology met with this group, including, besides Fletcher, Phoebe Apperson Hearst, Zelia Nuttall, and another of the group's original 10 cofounders, Sarah Scull, who wrote on Greek archaeology, as well as women from families of prominent men with North American archaeological interests, such as Caroline Wells Healey Dall, Mary Porter Tileston Hemenway, Anita Newcomb McGee, and Emma Dean Powell (Browman 2002a:230). Fletcher served as president of the combined Women's Anthropological Society of America and Anthropological Society of Washington in 1903. Until the turn of the century, the Anthropological Society of Washington had been nearly exclusively a male organization.

In addition to serving on the planning committee and the judging committee for awards at the 1893 World's Columbia Exposition in Chicago, Fletcher sat on the advisory committee that oversaw the establishment of the museum and department of anthropology at the University of California–Berkeley in 1901, along with Putnam, Nuttall, Hearst, and Benjamin Wheeler. She served as president of the American Anthropological Association in 1904 and of the American Folklore Society in 1905, and she became a significant player in the AIA. Fletcher held several positions in Section H, Anthropology, in the AAAS, including that of president in 1909. When Section H became involved in founding the new version of the journal *American Anthropologist* at the turn of the century, in order to make the journal more representative of the entire field, Fletcher was named to its 10-member editorial board. Her list of accomplishments does not end there; we refer readers to the excellent works by Joan Mark (1980, 1988) for a full appreciation of Fletcher's contributions.

A perhaps less significant contributor, but someone still typical of the people who worked with Putnam during this period, was **Samuel Kneeland** (1821–88). Kneeland was a member of the Harvard College class of 1840 and subsequently received his A.M. and M.D. degrees from Harvard in 1843. He was a demonstrator in anatomy at Harvard

Medical School from 1851 to 1853, served as an overseer for Harvard College from 1856 to 1861, and worked as a professor of zoology and physiology at MIT from 1869 to 1878. After retiring from MIT, he apparently began traveling around the world and collecting ethnographic and archaeological specimens. Putnam reported the Peabody Museum's receiving donations of ethnographic materials from Kneeland from the Pacific Islands, the Philippines, and India during the 1880s, as well as materials from closer to home, including items from a historical burial near Fall River in Massachusetts (Putnam 1883a:184, 1886a:485, 1887a:543, 1889:39). Kneeland's interest in ethnology extended to his publishing a series of articles on the tribes of the Philippines in *Science* in the 1880s.

Leon Stacy Griswold (1865–1940), apparently originally a Michigan resident (documents place him there in 1890 and 1912), graduated from Harvard in 1889 in geology and physical geography. He worked at the MCZ with Alexander Agassiz in the 1890s, serving as assistant and instructor in geology and physical geography from 1892 to 1896. Agassiz sent him in 1895–96 to study the geology and corals of Florida, which he wrote up for an MCZ report. Griswold wrote about the geographical and geological features of the San Francisco mountains and the Grand Canyon in 1895, described the geology of Helena, Montana, in 1898, and served as a professor of geology at the University of Missouri in 1909–10. His archaeological work was mainly on stone sources used by American Indians for whetstones, to judge from his publications on this topic written immediately after he received his A.B. (Griswold 1891, 1892, 1893a). His other linkages to the Peabody Museum relate to donations from stone quarries and associated artifacts from Arkansas, which were made over several years at the end of the nineteenth century.

Because Putnam was able to make short trips out from Cambridge to work at locations in New England himself, we see less in his annual reports about his recruiting local New England collectors to work with the Peabody Museum, although he did not ignore opportunities to engage such assistance. In Massachusetts, he mentioned **David Dodge,** of Wakefield, from whom he purchased a small collection of lithic tools in 1880 (Putnam 1881a:16, 24). Dodge, "acting as an agent for the Museum," continued to collect stone tools in the area in 1881, and in later years Dodge and George B. Frazer, of Marshfield, together made additional lithic collections for the Peabody (Putnam 1882a:57; 1884a:374; 1886a:485; 1902a:273; 1908:290).

In Maine, **Manly Hardy** (1832–1910), **Abram Tarr Gamage** (1838–1913), **F. S. Knowlton** and his son **James E. Knowlton** (1837–?), and **Albert Irving Phelps** (1861–?) were all local collectors whom Putnam recruited to make collections for the museum along the Damariscotta coastal inlet. Putnam first worked with the local amateur naturalist and fur dealer Manly Hardy, of Brewer, Maine, in 1878, continuing to perhaps 1880, on excavations of shell middens on Great Deer Island in Penobscot Bay, but nothing seems to have been written up from Hardy's work (Bourque 2002:154; Thwing 1881:677). Hardy's daughter, Fannie Pearson Hardy Eckstorm (1865–1946), picked up her father's interests and became a well-known early contributor on Maine's Indians and their music, as well as on regional ornithology (James 1971:549).

Putnam's associations with Gamage, the Knowltons, and Phelps were more productive. His first reference to their work was in 1882, when he mentioned, "While I was in Damariscotta, it was my good fortune to meet several gentlemen interested in local archaeology" (Putnam 1883a:161), although he noted that he had known Gamage from a previous visit, presumably when he visited Hardy. Putnam continued working with these men the next year, making "an extensive exploration in their company" (Putnam 1884a:353). He noted particularly that Gamage and Phelps had donated their entire collections to the museum. The Knowltons, father and son, did not donate their whole collections at once but over the period 1882–87 donated the majority of their materials from the Damariscotta shell heaps (Putnam 1883a:163, 1885a:409, 1886a:508, 1889:12).

In 1884 Putnam hired Phelps to continue the excavation work they had begun the previous year: "In that work Mr. Albert I. Phelps was employed as an assistant and a plan was discussed with him for more extended exploration along the coast from the Damariscotta to the Penobscot river. As other duties prevented me from conducting the proposed explorations in person I arranged with Mr. Phelps to take charge of the field work, which he did with thoroughness and obtained most satisfactory results" (Putnam 1885a:408).

Phelps was replaced by Gamage in 1886; Putnam noted that he had "arranged with Mr. Gamage, who was associated with me in my former explorations, to watch the excavation day by day, and secure everything of archaeological interest." The excavations in question were those of a fertilizer company that had purchased the great shell mounds in the Damariscotta area in order to process the shell deposits for commercial fertilizer. Putnam made an arrangement with this company "to keep Mr. A. T. Gamage on the spot to look after everything connected with the structure of the heap, and to secure all objects found during the carting away of the shells" (Putnam 1887a:546). He lamented that "to-day, owing to the purchase of many of the sites of the heaps along the coast of Maine for summer residences, places where we could have explored to any extent two years ago are now leveled or built upon" (Putnam 1887a:547).

Samuel Walton Garman (1843–1927) was born in Pennsylvania and spent much of his youth doing survey work for the Milwaukee, St. Paul, and Pacific and Union Pacific railroads (*National Cyclopedia* 1900; Clark 1931:154). He returned to Illinois State Normal University, where, after a break to take part in the 1868–69 Colorado Exploratory Expedition with John Wesley Powell, he received his A.B. in 1870. He took a one-year job as professor of natural science at Ferry Hall Seminary in Lake Forest, Illinois, in 1871 (Summers and Koob 1997:lii). In 1872, after starting the season working with Edward D. Cope looking for fossils in Wyoming, he met up with Louis Agassiz on the S.S. *Hassler* in San Francisco Bay and became a student at the Lawrence Scientific School, although the only degrees he received there were an honorary S.B and an honorary A.M. a quarter century later. He was appointed assistant in herpetology and ichthyology at the MCZ in 1873, a position he held for the next half century.

Garman first comes to our notice with respect to the Peabody Museum in a report by Putnam on the receipt of the large Peruvian and Bolivian collections made by

Alexander Agassiz with Garman's assistance during their expedition to Lake Titicaca in 1874–75 (chapter 3). Considering Putnam's own interest in ichthyology, along with the fact that the MCZ was situated adjacent to the Peabody Museum, Putnam would have known Garman since 1872, when he first arrived at the MCZ. Putnam and Garman in fact co-authored a paper on sharks and skates for the 1874 AAAS meetings (Putnam and Garman 1875), which was one of Putnam's last works in ichthyology. Regarding the ethnographic and archaeological collections of 1874–75, Putnam commented on some of the lithic items that Garman collected, such as a "beautiful arrowhead" from Isla del Sol and a large grooved maul found near Juli (Putnam 1876:11).

This trip to the Andes seems to have whetted Garman's interest in American Indian artifacts, for shortly thereafter he penned a short piece on Indian medicine (Garman 1882). Putnam noted that in 1882 Garman visited various American Indian tribes and donated "several interesting stone and iron specimens" that he obtained from them (Putnam 1883a:178). Garman seems to have had a particular interest in prehistoric American uses of metals. Not only did he collect iron artifacts, as Putnam noted, but he subsequently wrote two short pieces on Andean metallurgy (Garman 1888, 1889), based on the materials from his trip to Peru and Bolivia with Alexander Agassiz. Thereafter, however, Garman devoted himself to his first love, ichthyology.

Earl Flint, M.D., of Rivas, Nicaragua, became an "Assistant in the Field in Central American Archaeology" in 1878, a position he held through 1891. Flint had practiced medicine in Nicaragua from the 1850s onward and had begun collecting artifacts for the Smithsonian Institution in 1866. When the Smithsonian ran low on funds to continue supporting work in Nicaragua in the summer of 1877, Spencer Baird suggested to Flint that he contact Putnam for work, which he did in the fall of that year. After some negotiating over salary (Whisnant 1995:484), the two must have reached an agreement, for Putnam reported having made a special appropriation in 1878 to Flint, "an enthusiastic archaeologist and careful collector," for shell heap work in Nicaragua (Putnam 1879a:468). In 1880 Putnam reported that Flint continued his explorations in Nicaragua, had sent many ceramic and lithic items from mounds and caves, and was now writing this material up for a special report for the museum (Putnam 1880a:716). As was so often the case, however, the report apparently was never completed.

Collections by Flint are mentioned in succeeding Peabody Museum annual reports. On March 7, 1881, Putnam wrote that "last winter, word was most reluctantly sent to Dr. Flint, who has for some time been so zealous in his explorations in Nicaragua, that the income of the Museum would not permit further expenditure for explorations at present," and Flint would send on what he had collected to date (Putnam 1881a:17). When Putnam received a new cash infusion in the exploration fund he developed in response to this shortfall, the first three people to receive cash to renew fieldwork were Charles Abbott, Charles Metz (whom we profile shortly), and Flint (Putnam 1883a:159, 1883g:288). Putnam reported the next year (1884a:354) that for six years Earl Flint had been an enthusiastic worker in Nicaragua for the museum, exploring caves and burial mounds and digging shell heaps. He indicated that Flint had made a great collection of ceramic vessels and idols, observing that "the taking of idols and other antiquities from the country has now been prohibited by law, but, thanks to the President [Chamorro] of Nicaragua, a special permit was given to Dr. Flint to continue his work for the Museum for the present" (Putnam 1884a:355).

On December 24, 1883, Flint notified Putnam that he had found fossil human footprints of great antiquity (Putnam 1884a:355). These so-called Acahualinca footprints, from the El Cauce quarries on the southern edge of Lake Managua, engaged Flint for the next several years (see bibliography). Putnam almost immediately reported this find in *Science*, describing Flint's work in Nicaragua in general and adding: "But the most interesting discovery is what Dr. Flint believes to be human footprints in clay under several layers of lava-rock, on the borders of Lake Managua. Under date of Dec. 24, 1883, Dr. Flint writes that he has cut out several of these footprints, which, with fossil leaves from the same stratum, are now on their way to the museum" (Putnam 1883g:288).

Although the footprints had first been reported in 1874, Flint was the first observer to write a careful descriptive account of them. He argued that because they came from a depth of 16–24 feet, under a dozen different strata, they would have to be between 50,000 and 200,000 years old (Flint, cited in Brinton 1889). Years later, Alan Bryan (1973:147) reported that although he had hoped for greater antiquity, the footprints were associated with radiocarbon determinations indicating a maximum age of 5,950 radiocarbon years.

In the 1885 museum annual report, Putnam (1886a:494) noted that "although our means have not allowed of any extensive explorations in Central America during the past year, Dr. Flint has been on the watch to do what he could for the Museum," having sent another cast of the footprints as well as some pottery specimens. Flint kept after Putnam for additional funds for more mound exploration, telling Putnam that he was in "readiness to explore a few burial mounds which are still intact, if the means can be furnished" (Putnam 1887a:548).

The relationship between Putnam and Flint broke down shortly after that. Flint's last collections for the museum seemed to have been made in 1888, and in 1890 Flint wrote to another Putnam collector, Hilborne T. Cresson, for assistance:

> I want to call the attention of scientists to this neglected spot in Nicaragua, and convince them that man existed here long prior to the glacial era. Will some of the scientists in the United States do me the favor to look over the few shells sent by me to the National Museum. These specimens will tell the exact time [geologically] when man lived here in the caves, and subsisted on the very oysters [the shells of which had been found]. The specimens may be seen among those I forwarded a few years ago, and which are now in some part of the National Museum. (Flint 1890:32)

Flint sought other patrons, sending, for example, additional molds of footprints to Daniel Brinton in 1889 (Anonymous 1889), but without success in locating a new museum-based supporter.

Putnam sought to replace Flint in Nicaragua by making arrangements with **John Crawford,** the state geologist in León, Nicaragua, during the early 1890s. Crawford was named government geologist in about 1888, to assist Nicaragua in developing gold mining claims along the Mosquito Coast (Karl Offen, personal communication, 2002). Like many geologists of the day, Crawford ran into archaeological ruins and developed an interest in them as a part of his field geology. Crawford had publicly supported Flint's version of the antiquity of the Nicaraguan footprints (Bryan 1973:146), a fact Putnam obviously liked.

Putnam had Crawford report on his discoveries at the Boston Society of Natural History (Crawford 1891a, 1893c). As he did with many of the field people he recruited, Putnam convinced Crawford to become a member of the AAAS, which Crawford joined in 1890, remaining a member for at least the next two decades. He attended meetings of the AAAS and occasionally gave papers on his work in Nicaragua (for example, Crawford 1895c, 1895d). Crawford made donations to the Peabody Museum, but although he published a number of papers relating to archaeology, ethnology, and linguistics (see bibliography), he seems never to have developed into a major source for Putnam.

In part this was because by the mid-1890s Putnam had changed strategy. He was beginning to rely almost completely on materials generated by his students, to the exclusion of his former network of avocational fieldworkers. Thus Putnam had his own expedition in the field in Honduras, under the direction of his graduate student John Owens, bypassing the need to recruit people like Crawford.

Zelia Maria Magdalena Nuttall (1858–1933) was born in San Francisco but raised in Europe. She studied at Bedford College, London, before returning to San Francisco in the late 1870s (Browman 2002a:228). She met Alphonse Louis Pinart (1852–1911) in 1878, when he made a trip to California, and they were married in 1880 (Parmenter 1971). Pinart, in addition to having ethnological and linguistic interests, collected archaeological specimens along the Pacific coast from Alaska to Peru in the 1870s and 1880s. Because of Pinart's interests, some biographical sources have suggested that he was responsible for Nuttall's training, but this seems unlikely. Within only a few months of their marriage, Pinart left on a voyage of such long duration, and was so out of touch with Nuttall, that he was unaware for many months of the birth of their only child in April 1882. They were effectively separated by the end of 1881, and by the end of 1883, if not sooner, Pinart had run through all his inherited wealth as well as Nuttall's money (Parmenter 1971). Because of the procedures of the time, Nuttall did not receive a formalized deed of separation until 1884, and their divorce was not finalized until 1888.

Thus, during the period 1880–88, Zelia Nuttall was usually referred to as Mrs. Nuttall-Pinart, and her first works in archaeology were published under that name. Other than a short trip the couple made to the Spanish West Indies in 1880–81, however, she was not in the field with Pinart. Rather, it appears that although Pinart might have introduced Nuttall to the general notion of anthropology, her archaeological contributions derived wholly from her own work. In 1884–85 she went to Mexico, her mother's birthplace (Chinas 1999:559), for five months, along with her mother, younger brother, sister, and daughter. During this time she worked for the national museum in Mexico City and collected terra-cotta heads from Teotihuacan, the analysis of which she wrote up for her first publication, in 1886. Putnam appointed her an unpaid "Special Assistant in Mexican Archaeology" at the Peabody Museum in the same year, a position she held for the next 47 years. Putnam had tried to get her to accept the more intensively involved position of "Curator of Central American Archaeology," but she declined (Parmenter 1971:640). During part of her tenure at the Peabody Museum, Nuttall, like Fletcher, was a Thaw Fellow.

Although Nuttall had an appointment with the Peabody Museum, she moved from Mexico to Europe in 1886 and lived in Dresden from then until 1899 or 1900, making short field excursions during that period. Thus, although she was listed as a member of the Peabody Museum staff, she functioned the way Putnam's field collectors did, sending material back to the Peabody from time to time. Putnam referred to her work on the Aztecs, Mexican studies, various codices, and the like in his annual reports, but he always mentioned that she was doing this from Europe (for example, Putnam 1887a:566, 1893a:207). He talked Nuttall into preparing a major display on Middle American codices for the 1893 World's Columbian Exposition and had her serve as one of the five women judges for the exposition.

Nuttall had her first paper published in the *American Journal of Archaeology* in 1886. She was made a fellow of the AAAS, one of the handful of women so honored in its early years, and published a half dozen papers in its *Proceedings*. Later her works focused on the Mexican codices, but not exclusively, as can be seen through a scan of the works by Nuttall that we include in the bibliography. She and Alice Fletcher worked together on a variety of projects, and both were part of the lobby for increased Americanist studies at the AIA. Nuttall and Phoebe Hearst became good friends, and Hearst subsidized Nuttall's work in Europe. Nuttall was also key to convincing Hearst to fund Max Uhle in his archaeological work in Peru (Jacknis 2000:51).

Putnam's work to establish a museum and anthropology department at Berkeley was spurred by Nuttall's return to San Francisco in 1900. The founding meeting of the University of California–Berkeley Department of Anthropology was attended by the university president, Benjamin Wheeler (a Greek philologist), Putnam, Nuttall, Fletcher, Hearst, Alfred Kroeber, and, apparently, archaeologist George H. Pepper, of the American Museum of Natural History, who had accompanied Putnam to California (Jacknis 2000:64). After participating in the founding of the department and museum, Nuttall moved to Mexico, where she lived from 1902 until her death in 1933, all the while continuing to be the "Special Assistant" in Mexican archaeology for the Peabody Museum.

Hilborne Thomson Cresson (1848?–94) is another of the quixotic individuals whom Putnam recruited, primarily because of Cresson's claim of having found evidence of Pleistocene habitation in the Americas. He was one of the few collectors, along with

Charles Metz, whom Putnam tried to train in the period immediately before he initiated a graduate program in anthropology and began to train his own students (see also S. Williams 1991:122–28). As Cresson himself described his introduction to antiquities, in a letter written in 1889: "My early education was artistic rather than scientific—I came in contact with scientific men by illustrating for them with my pencil the primitive endeavors of early man to decorate pottery and chip out his stone implements, and figurines" (quoted in Meltzer and Sturtevant 1983:341).

Between 1864 and 1870 Cresson allegedly was involved in excavations at a series of sites in northern Delaware, including a fish weir and a rock shelter on Naaman's Creek. He did not report on his reputed excavations until the late 1880s and early 1890s, however, because from the mid-1870s through 1880 he was in France, where he had gone to study at the Ecole des Beaux Arts and Ecole d'Anthropologie. He said he had found no opportunity to write the work up until he returned from France (Cresson 1890:117). It was the Delaware sites that interested Putnam, for they appeared to provide evidence for both Pleistocene occupation and a previously unknown type of habitation, which Cresson initially compared to Swiss lake dwellings.

It was the report of the Naaman's Creek "lake dwellings" that brought Cresson to Putnam's immediate attention (although he seems to have known of Cresson since 1883) and led to Cresson's being named an "Assistant in the Field" for the Peabody Museum. He soon gained greater notoriety with a report in 1889 on the so-called Holly Oak shell gorget, which bore an incised mammoth design. This shell artifact has been soundly discredited as a fraud, but at the time it was first reported it generated considerable interest. Cresson reported the circumstances surrounding the artifact in a letter to Putnam of January 30, 1890, which Putnam summarized in a report in the *Proceedings of the Boston Society of Natural History* (Putnam 1890b). Cresson said it was then owned by a Mrs. Fred Spencer of New York, but it had been found a few miles from Naaman's Creek in 1864 by two laborers who worked on Cresson's father's farm. Cresson's tutor, M. Suralt, recognized it, pulled it out of the muck the laborers were digging, and shared the find with his student. In an 1892 report to the U.S. National Museum, however, Cresson said the artifact had been owned at the time of donation by a Mrs. Bessie D. Spencer of Brooklyn, New York (Weslager 1941:11).

Except for Cresson, none of these people has been verified. Cresson's critics (Griffin et al. 1988; Meltzer and Sturtevant 1983) believe he invented them all. In addition, they argue that he deliberately backdated his discovery to 1864 so that he could say the piece was found before the date when a mammoth tusk from La Madeleine, France, engraved with the image of a woolly mammoth, was first published, in 1869. Modern archaeologists believe Cresson's artifact is a forged copy of the La Madeleine find.

Cresson's report of lake dwellings along the Delaware similarly caused some furor. In his original report in *American Antiquarian* in 1887, Cresson compared the wooden stakes he had found to those of the lake dwellings recently reported in Switzerland, but he soon backpedaled. By the time he published his paper "Supposed Aboriginal Fish-Weirs in Naaman's Creek" in 1890, he alleged that Henry Williamson Haynes, who cited his 1887 report in a book chapter Haynes published in 1889, had garbled his report, and that was because the editor of *American Antiquarian,* Rev. Stephen D. Peet (1831–1914), had garbled it originally in the journal. This brought angry retorts from both Haynes and Peet. Haynes (1890b) wrote, "Mr. Cresson's memory has played him false in regard to what he wrote to me: he clearly said 'pile-structures' and so they were cited." Peet (1890) denied having changed Cresson's words and provided quotations from Cresson's original letter, where he referred to "river dwelling sites." Cresson, as tended to be his habit, distanced himself from the original discovery, saying that a local fisherman had found the site and brought it to his attention. In subsequent reports he maintained that he had originally identified these structures as fish weirs (in itself an important addition to American archaeology of the time), and not as lake dwellings.

Cresson also claimed to have found Paleolithic tools along Naaman's Creek, as well as in Indiana (Abbott 1888b:104; Cresson 1888a, 1888b, 1889a, 1889b; Putnam 1890c:698). In 1889 Putnam wrote: "Mr. Cresson's investigations have also been carried on in relation to the palaeolithic implements found in the gravel, and he has been so fortunate as to discover two specimens in situ in the older gravel near Claymont, Newcastle Co., Del. He also, in company with Mr. W. R. Thompson, made a visit to Indiana and examined the gravel on White River above Medora in Jackson Co. Here he was so fortunate as to find a large palaeolithic implement of grey flint" (Putnam 1889:45). Subsequently, Putnam and William Dall went to visit the locations of reputed finds of Paleolithic tools along the Delaware, but found none (Putnam 1890b).

Despite these controversies, Putnam maintained faith or hope in Cresson's findings for several years, keeping him on as an "Assistant in the Field" at the Peabody Museum until 1892. Clearly, Cresson needed field training, and Putnam sought to provide it. Initially he sent him out to work with Charles Abbott—some might have called this the blind leading the blind—to collect paleoliths along the Delaware River (Putnam 1890a:75). During the next summer season, 1890, he sent Cresson out to Ohio with Ernest Volk to learn excavation techniques from Charles Metz. In June, with Marshall Saville as supervisor, Cresson and Volk, along with Putnam's graduate student George Dorsey (see chapter 7), worked at the Turner Mound group on the Little Miami River. In July, Putnam arrived, and with Dorsey as his chief assistant, he, Metz, and Cresson all moved over to excavations on Cline's Run (Putnam 1891:93–96). Later Cresson was placed in charge of the exploration at Cline's Run and continued excavations there until the end of September. Cresson reported finding a possible structure during the excavations and "made numerous sketches and notes of the singular structure, and Mr. Saville took a number of photographs as the work of exploration progressed" (Putnam 1891:97).

Cresson continued working in the field for the Peabody Museum for the next few summers, and in the winters he worked up his collections. He also spent the better part of his time pursuing an M.D. at Jefferson Medical College, where he received his degree on April 15, 1891 (Meltzer and Sturtevant 1983:341).

During this period, a long-standing interest of Cresson's in Mexico continued to grow. As early as 1883 he had made an amateur study of prehistoric Mexican musical instruments found in Philadelphia museums and published a journal article on them, which Putnam noted in a short piece in *Science* (Putnam 1883f). In 1887 he had visited Teotihuacan and collected artifacts that he donated to the Peabody (Putnam 1889:39). This interest continued unabated and led to friction with the rest of Putnam's fieldworkers in the early 1890s. Putnam had just appointed Saville, who was then one of Putnam's first students, to go to Yucatán to collect material for the upcoming World's Columbian Exposition. According to Ralph Dexter (1982a:28), Cresson spread rumors trying to discredit Saville, hoping to secure the appointment for himself. As a result, Metz wrote to Putnam in April 1891 complaining about Cresson's behavior, saying that he had "many proofs that Dr. Cresson is untruthful and that he is not a man to be trusted."

This apparently did not convince Putnam to cut Cresson loose. He appointed Cresson and Warren K. Moorehead field assistants for the Columbian Exposition in September 1891, assigning them to collect artifacts from Ohio for him. Only a few months later, however, on December 4, 1891, Putnam fired Cresson from the exposition payroll for theft of artifacts from the Hopewell site excavation (Warren K. Moorehead, diary, December 16, 1891, cited in Griffin et al. 1988 and Meltzer and Sturtevant 1983:343). Nevertheless, he apparently let Cresson's appointment as field assistant simply continue on the rolls of the Peabody Museum staff until it lapsed at the end of the reporting year in 1892. Putnam, it seems, let his desire to identify a late Pleistocene human occupation of the Americas cloud his judgment. He appears to have been willing to hang on to what we would characterize as "losers" if they claimed to have early archaeological materials.

Afterward, Cresson turned to pursuing his Mesoamerican interests, with funding from a small family endowment (Augney 1892). He spent much of the next two years on the Gulf coast of Mexico and Guatemala (Powell 1897:xxvi) and wrote several papers on Maya hieroglyphs. He returned to the United States in 1894 and shot himself to death in a park in New York City on September 6 of that year. He had been having hallucinations, believing that U.S. Secret Service detectives were secretly dogging him, according to a report in the *Philadelphia Inquirer* of September 8, 1894 (S. Williams 1991:125).

One of the men with whom Cresson worked on the Ohio mounds, **Charles Lewis Metz** (1847–1926), a medical doctor, was an Ohio resident who became interested in the aboriginal earthworks during his horseback trips to see patients in surrounding hamlets. Local people gave him tips about a pottery field in Madisonville (present-day Mariemont), where he unearthed bones and vessels. In late 1878 and early 1879 Metz hired Matthias Britten to excavate mounds on Charles Stites's property, and he located what became known as the Ferris Cemetery, or the Madisonville Ancient Cemetery. Metz was one of the founders of the Madisonville Literary and Scientific Society in 1879. Between April 1879 and August 1881, the society supported excavations by its members at the cemetery and divided up the finds. They developed a "Chart of the Prehistoric Monuments of the Little Miami Valley," plotting local sites discovered in the late 1870s and 1880s. The Cincinnati Society of Natural History and the Madisonville Literary and Scientific Society began joint excavations in late 1879, sharing costs and dividing the collections between the two societies (Ford and Ford 1881:874).

Putnam first wrote to Metz in April 1879 after seeing articles by Charles F. Low, secretary of the Madisonville Society, reporting on some of the artifacts the group had excavated (Dexter 1982a:24). The Cincinnati Society published the findings of the two groups' joint venture, again attracting Putnam's attention. Metz was the nominal supervisor of the excavations, which involved 40-foot-wide trenches and almost no recording of spatial data. In response to Putnam's request, Metz sent him a progress report in 1880 (Putnam 1881a:15).

Putnam made two site visits to Madisonville in 1881 and purchased part of the collections, but he was forced to suspend support to Metz for further fieldwork owing to a shortage of funds. Thus, in the summer of 1881 many of the original supporters also decided not to continue, but Metz and Low continued to underwrite the work into the spring of 1882. The other members of the group tried to sell their portion of the collections to the Smithsonian, the U.S. National Museum, and the Cincinnati Museum in 1882, when it appeared that the Peabody Museum was out of the picture (Drooker 1997:110). Putnam, however, maintained an active interest in Madisonville. Immediately after he married Esther Clarke in Chicago in 1882, the couple left for Ohio and spent their honeymoon excavating at Madisonville.

Putnam also inspected the Turner Mound group, near the Little Miami River, that season, but "as the time at my disposal was insufficient for a proper exploration of the group, I arranged with Dr. Metz to continue the work for the Museum" (Putnam 1883a:170). Metz conducted the excavations, this time taking careful notes and making sketches. At Putnam's suggestion he employed a civil engineer, J. A. Hasbrook, to make a map of the mounds (Putnam 1883a:170, 174). Leonard P. Kinnicutt, an assistant in chemistry at Harvard College, conducted the analysis of metal items from the mounds, including objects of both meteoritic iron and copper (Putnam 1883a:172).

When the new Peabody Museum Exploration Fund was started in 1883, Putnam immediately resumed funding of Metz's work and once again became involved in the excavations. In the 1884 annual report, Putnam wrote that he had "great pleasure in stating that he [Metz] has identified his archaeological interests entirely with those of the Museum and has made over to it the extensive private collection which he had formed during the past ten years," much of it from Madisonville (Putnam 1885a:407–8).

For a period, the mound explorations in and around Madisonville became Putnam's seasonal training camp. Metz and sometimes his brother Julius Metz ran the local arrangements. In 1889 Putnam had Marshall Saville trained there, and in 1890 he put Saville in a supervisory position and sent Hilborne Cresson, Ernest Volk, and George Dorsey for training. In 1897 he sent Ingersoll Bowditch, Roland Dixon, and John Swanton, and from 1907 to 1911 he sent Raymond Merwin and Bruce Merwin (Drooker 1997:112; Putnam 1890a:76, 1891:93; see chapter 7 on Dorsey, Dixon, and Swanton, chapter 9 on Bowditch, and chapter 4 on the Merwin brothers). The excavations between 1897 and 1911 represent the best of Putnam's fieldwork, according to Penelope Drooker (1997:117): "While he directed the Peabody Museum, Putnam strenuously championed the idea that all artifacts and remains excavated from a given archaeological component . . . should be kept together," so among other records, grave lots and proveniences were carefully saved. In contrast, during the late nineteenth and early twentieth centuries, workers from the Smithsonian and other institutions had a tendency to collect and save artifacts by type, not by excavation provenience within a site.

Metz strove to please Putnam, taking potshots at the Smithsonian's excavation techniques in several of his letters (see Dexter 1982a for examples). In addition, learning of Putnam's fascination with possible Pleistocene artifacts and sites, he went looking for paleoliths along the Ohio rivers and alleged that he found two (Abbott 1888:104; Putnam 1890c:698). Warren Moorehead (1893b), however, was openly skeptical, writing, "So far as Ohio goes, I think I am safe in saying, Dr. Metz is the only thorough archaeologist who claims to have found paleoliths in the drift. . . . How is it that those of us who spend all of our time in archaeologic work cannot find them? . . . Dr. Cresson—strong in 'paleolithic faith'—never found one specimen while he was for four months in my camp in Paint Valley, Ross County."

The last excavation work Putnam did with Metz appears to have been a project Putnam sponsored in 1895 under the auspices of the American Museum of Natural History, where he had recently helped establish an anthropology department (Drooker 1997:112; and see chapter 8). Putnam had initiated his graduate program at the Peabody Museum by that time and no longer relied to any great extent on the gaggle of correspondence volunteers he had collected over the preceding two decades. But Putnam was loyal to his volunteers, supporting their efforts long after some of his colleagues suggested he cut them loose. Metz was still a relatively young man at the time, in his forties. We believe Putnam terminated his reliance on Metz because Metz had a drinking problem—something remarked on in some of his correspondence and which some of the students from Harvard mentioned (Wesley Cowan, personal communication, 2002). Putnam then directed his energies toward developing professional programs to train students, not only at Harvard but also at the AMNH and Berkeley.

The beginnings of the 1890s marked a clear change in Putnam's approach to securing collections. After more than two decades spent trying to recruit outside volunteers and tying them to the museum by paying for certain minimal expenses, he began training his own students. With the exception of a few special correspondents, particularly in Mesoamerica and the Andes, he thereafter relied on his students increasingly heavily, moving away from dependence on enthusiastic but untrained amateurs. Putnam was interested in archaeological context and by the mid-1880s had developed a rigorous excavation methodology with a focus on both broad horizontal associations and vertical stratigraphic control. He had tried to impart this methodology to recruits such as Metz and Cresson, but with limited success. For the most part, Putnam focused in the 1890s on ensuring that his methodology was employed by teaching it to students enrolled in the department. As their advisor, he had the coercive ability to make sure these practices were carried out on Peabody Museum projects conducted by the students. The shift was not instantaneous, though, and during the transition years in the very early 1890s, Putnam made a few last attempts to expand anthropology by recruiting people such as Ernest Volk, Edward Thompson, Teobert Maler, and David Scott Moncrieff.

Ernest Volk (1845–1919) was one of the handful of such people whom Putnam recruited and subsidized in the field in the late 1880s and early 1890s, just before he shifted direction with his official departmental program. Volk was appointed in 1889 to take over the Trenton field operations when Charles Abbott moved to take the curator's job at Pennsylvania. Putnam tried to give Volk appropriate training. In June 1890, Volk arrived at the Turner Mound group on the Little Miami, where, under Metz and Putnam, he received excavation training. In August Volk left Ohio to return to his operations on the Delaware (Putnam 1891:93–95).

Volk lived in Trenton and, after beginning in 1889, worked for the Peabody Museum for the next 22 years. He published the results of his excavations in the AAAS *Proceedings* and the *Memoirs of the International Congress of Anthropology*, both in 1894, and he published a wrap-up paper in 1911, but he was never able to find the elusive evidence of glacial-age human occupation that Putnam had hoped was there.

Edward Herbert Thompson (1856–1935), a native of Worcester, Massachusetts, seems to have come to Putnam's attention through his work for the American Antiquarian Society. The society had supported the exploration work of Augustus and Alice Dixon Le Plongeon in Yucatán in the late 1870s and 1880s but had grown wary of their "fantastic archaeology" theories. Thompson became interested in the Mayas in the 1870s after reading the volumes by John Stephens and Frederick Catherwood. He became a member of the American Antiquarian Society, and society member Stephen Salisbury Jr., who shared his interest in the Mayas (see chapter 9), provided Thompson with funding to work in the Maya area beginning in 1885. Later, when the society cut its ties with the Le Plongeons, it offered Thompson funds to carry on work in Yucatán. Society members Salisbury, Charles Bowditch, and Senator George Hoar of Massachusetts managed to get Thompson appointed consul for Yucatán, giving him an official power base.

Thompson, who served as the American consul in Yucatán for many years, began to explore Maya ruins as a pastime at least as early as 1887. He sent annual reports of his work to the American Antiquarian Society, of which Putnam was also a member, and apparently came to Putnam's attention through these reports. Extensive correspondence between Putnam and Thompson, from 1891 through 1905, is curated in the Harvard

University archives, suggesting that Thompson's formal linkage with the Peabody Museum may not have come until 1891 and ended after 1905, although Thompson still played host to Peabody personnel working in the area.

Putnam seems to have become concerned about Thompson's procedures, and when he sent graduate student Alfred Tozzer to work on his doctoral dissertation research in Yucatán in 1902, he asked Tozzer to monitor Thompson's techniques and report back. Tozzer soon became disenchanted with Thompson, and after Thompson involved Tozzer in 1905 in smuggling gold and jade illegally dredged from the Sacred Cenote at Chichen Itza back to the Peabody, Tozzer apparently was instrumental in ending the Peabody's support for Thompson (M. McVicker 2005:78, 108, 118, 128).

The annual reports of the Peabody Museum for 1891, 1892, and 1893 all mention purchases of casts and artifacts from Thompson, apparently mainly for the anthropological exhibits at the Columbian Exposition, although after the exposition the casts came home to the Peabody. During the period of his association with the Peabody, Thompson prepared two reports on his work, which the museum published (Thompson 1897, 1904). In 1895 Thompson was also funded by Allison V. Armour, patron of the Columbian Museum of Chicago (later the Field Museum of Natural History), to collect artifacts for that museum as well (M. McVicker 2005:58). Thompson spent most of his efforts at Chichen Itza, but he also explored Palenque, Labna, and other Maya sites (see bibliography).

Teobert Maler (1842–1917) was born in Rome, Italy, and traveled from Europe with Archduke Maximilian's forces to Mexico in 1864 (Riese 1991:442). Like Thompson, Maler became enthralled with the ruins that had been reported by Stephens and Catherwood and spent much of the rest of his life in the Yucatán-Maya area of Mexico. Maler had sent occasional materials to the Peabody Museum from 1875 onward, but it was not until Mayanist and museum benefactor Charles Bowditch (chapter 9) provided funding that Maler began more intensive exploration work for the museum. Although Maler did a little excavation, by far most of his work was nondestructive documentation through photographs, maps, scale drawings, and careful descriptions of buildings (Riese 1991:443).

Bowditch had the idea that a clue for the translation of Maya hieroglyphs might be found in the Petén and Usumacinta areas or among the little-known and isolated Lacandón Mayas of Guatemala. To this end, in the late 1890s and early 1900s he provided the museum with money through the Central American–Mexican Subscription Fund to hire Maler to conduct surveys in those areas (Putnam 1899a:266, 1904:280). Tozzer met Maler while carrying out his Lacandón research for his Ph.D. dissertation (Tozzer 1904). When Putnam slowly withdrew from the day-to-day operations of the museum and Tozzer took over, he maintained the Peabody's links with Maler. Maler suddenly resigned in 1910, and although his name comes up occasionally because of his work in the Maya area, he was not as closely integrated into the Peabody Museum network as other Maya specialists of the period.

David Scott Moncrieff Jr. (1865–93) was among the last of the nonprofessional collectors whom Putnam recruited for the Peabody Museum, along with those he employed in 1892 and 1893 under the aegis of the World's Columbian Exposition. Moncrieff, born and raised in Scotland, took his initial training in medicine, receiving the "triple degree" in 1888 from the Royal College of Physicians of Edinburgh, the Royal College of Surgeons of Edinburgh, and the Faculty of Physicians and Surgeons in Glasgow (Moncrieff Sr. to Putnam, July 2, 1894, Putnam Papers). He served briefly as a ship's surgeon on the steamer S.S. *Armenia* and, after visiting various ports, became interested in Russia. He came to Harvard, received another M.D. in 1889, and made his first contact with Putnam. He then became assistant surgeon for the Canadian Northwest Mounted Police for two years. In 1891 he resigned that position and accepted an interim position as surgeon for the Fourth Regiment of the U.S. Calvary (Moncrieff Sr. to Putnam, July 2, 1894).

During this period Moncrieff was also employed by Putnam to try to link Pacific Northwest Coast cultures to coastal cultures of Siberia. In April 1893 Putnam appointed him to work for the Peabody Museum on a two-year collecting trip to Siberia, funding him in part through monies from the Columbian Exposition. Putnam wrote:

> Dr. Moncrieff had been employed for the preceding two years as an assistant in the Department of Ethnology, in which capacity he had made important ethnological and archaeological observations and collections on the northwest coast of America. As it is of special importance to trace the connection between the peoples of the northwest coast of America and those of the opposite coast of Asia, Dr. Moncrieff decided to pass some years in this study and accepting the position of honorary assistant in the Peabody Museum he went to Siberia for this purpose. (Putnam 1894:221)

Moncrieff arrived on the Russian coast in June 1893. In August he put to sea on a collecting trip off the coast of Sakhalin Island in an unfamiliar native boat. It capsized, and he was drowned. As we will see again in chapters 7 and 8, doing anthropological research for the Peabody Museum sometimes had fatal consequences.

The foregoing summaries cover the people mentioned most frequently in the Peabody Museum's annual reports and others of Putnam's writings and those whom he explicitly mentioned hiring or funding to provide materials for the Peabody. But the annual reports before the 1890s are a rich source of information about Putnam's attempts to secure collections from other areas, his continued interest in the possibility of finding Late Pleistocene human occupation sites, and his references to persons who later became significant through contact with a host of other avocational contributors. For example, Putnam tried for years to secure a trustworthy collector for the Dakotas. He worked initially with George W. Sweet (1823–98), a local resident with an interest in Indian relics and history (for example, Sweet 1894). In 1879 and 1880 Sweet provided the museum with a collection of artifacts from two seasons of mound exploration along the

Missouri River in the Dakotas (Putnam 1880a:720, 1881a:15), but Putnam did not afterward work with Sweet again. In 1885 he turned to another Dakota resident, reporting that "at a small expense for hired labor, Dr. Henry Waldo Coe, of Mandan, Dakota, acting for the Museum, has thoroughly explored a mound of that place, and has obtained information of interest in relation to its structure and contents. . . . this exploration by Dr. Coe is the only one that has been conducted in a proper manner. For a first attempt it is a most creditable piece of work" (Putnam 1886a:495). Clearly the qualifying words are "for a first attempt," because later Putnam credited the work of George Will and his colleagues in 1905 as being the first scientific excavations in the Dakotas.

The annual reports are filled with references to well-known people who provided materials, and many of them are dealt with elsewhere in this volume. To offer a flavor of the kinds of items they sent to the museum, we mention two. In 1883, at the annual meeting of the AAAS, Putnam heard a paper presented by Frances Eliza Babbitt (1824–91) on her reputed Late Pleistocene quartz tools from Little Falls, Minnesota. This resulted in the initiation of a correspondence between Babbitt and Putnam, wherein Putnam secured quartz tool samples for the Peabody Museum (Putnam 1884a:353–54). The correspondence continued later with Putnam encouraging Babbitt to do more work to verify the site's antiquity. That story is best told by Hilary Lynn Chester in her article "Frances Eliza Babbitt and the Growth of Professionalism of Women in Archaeology" (2002). In 1888 Alfred Kidder, of Marquette, Michigan, donated historic artifacts from a grave on the Dead River, two miles north of Marquette, along with a series of prehistoric obsidian materials from the Obsidian Cliff locality in Yellowstone National Park (Putnam 1889:39). This donation was the beginning of a long association between the Kidder family and the museum, one eventual result of which was that Alfred Kidder's sons, Alfred Vincent and Homer, as well as his grandson Alfred II and great-grandson Tristram Randolph Kidder, entered Harvard and became archaeologists.

The beginning of the 1880s seems to have marked a shift in Putnam's approach to collecting materials and information. He began wanting people who collected for the museum to obtain more than just artifacts. His natural science bent prompted him to begin requesting paleoethnobotanical and zooarchaeological specimens from projects in which he had relatively great confidence or involvement in the excavations. Putnam was thus something of a pioneer in the fields of zooarchaeology and paleoethnobotany.

Putnam had followed this interest himself during his excavations in the Cumberland Gap area of Kentucky in 1877, subsequently pursued for him by Edwin Curtiss, as well as during the Ohio mound studies, when he insisted on collecting plant and animal ecofacts. Putnam sent samples of maize from the Peruvian excavations of Alexander Agassiz and Samuel W. Garman to Dr. E. Lewis Sturtevant for analysis in 1878, the results of which Sturtevant published in 1885. Putnam sent him additional corn samples from George Dorsey's excavations in 1894, which Sturtevant published later that year.

Similarly, summarizing the museum's recent work in 1884 at Damariscotta and the Little Miami sites, he reported with satisfaction that the museum now had more than "7,000 bones of animals from the explorations of the shellheaps of the coast of Maine, and more than 8,000 from the mounds of the Little Miami valley. These are important in the study of the vertebrate fauna of the two places during the times they were occupied by the respective peoples in whose refuse piles the bones were found. Similar collections have been made in former years from other places" (Putnam 1885a:418).

Although Putnam himself did not conduct extensive zooarchaeological identifications, he made sure that his students had zooarchaeological training in his later programs, in the 1890s. For example, in a letter to Harvard president Charles Eliot on April 4, 1894, Putnam acknowledged a particular debt to Dr. Daniel Denison Slade: "The latter has had considerable to do with the students who have been with me, as they go to the Zoological Museum to examine the osteological collection under his charge, and he often comes to this Museum in connection with his own studies" (Putnam-Eliot correspondence files, Harvard University Archives, Pusey Library). Slade was a professor of applied zoology and lecturer in comparative osteology at the Bussey Institute from 1871 until his death in 1896.

Putnam began to interpret archaeological features in his excavations as well, using a bit of ethnoarchaeology. He had been puzzled by the occurrence of a number of ash pits at the Little Miami site. In his annual report for 1881 he noted that he had found more than 400 such pits and had spent much time exploring them, but "the purpose for which they were made is still, I think, a mystery" (Putnam 1882a:65). At his request, "Miss Fletcher had visited the ancient cemetery at Madisonville, and personally explored some of the singular ashpits of that place" in the summer of 1883 (Putnam 1884a:356). After pondering the issue for a time, Fletcher wrote to Putnam on January 15, 1884, suggesting, on the basis of her work with Omaha Indians, that the pits he was finding at Madisonville were abandoned storage pits, subsequently filled with trash (Putnam 1884a:357). Putnam hesitated at first to accept this explanation, but in his subsequent reports the features were so identified. Today the idea of storage pits backfilled with trash is standard first-year field school lore.

With the new excavation methods Putnam championed, features such as post holes also were identified and plotted. Drooker (cited in Browman 2002b:253) reported that in 1885, Putnam's student William Nickerson was the first person working on the Little Miami mounds to map rows of post holes. Putnam lost no time in integrating this new mapping technique into his work. In the 1886 summary of the excavations at Marriott mound number 1, Putnam reported that the identification of post holes indicated the presence of a wooden structure on the mounds (Metz and Putnam 1886:466). In 1887 Putnam reported finding 19 house floors and associated post holes at Madisonville (Stoltman 2004:18).

The 1880s mark the time when Putnam developed a rigorous archaeological methodology emphasizing the need for systematic, scientific excavation procedures, later known as the Peabody Museum method. His thinking on how to secure materials for the museum seems to have reached a critical point in 1881 or 1882. From 1883 onward, he made a point of stressing in his writings the need for systematic, controlled excavations. In one report on his mound work for 1883, Putnam (1885b:6) noted, "What should be done before conclusions of importance can be drawn, is to make careful and thorough explorations of several of the group . . . by cutting trenches their whole length and width, and digging at least two feet below the surface on which the mound rests . . . [The site should be] systematically examined, by a series of trenches through each mound, and not simply by sinking a shaft in its centre." Putnam employed these new procedures in the excavations of Marriott mound 1, where, when he was not present, he made sure that Charles Metz continued to give each artifact recovered a separate catalogue number.

In his 1884 annual report to the trustees, Putnam spelled out more of his methodological philosophy as employed at Madisonville, with details he apparently usually avoided for such a general audience (Putnam 1885a: 401–2):

> The systematic explorations we thus far have been able to carry on have given a clew to the sequence of events which have taken place in that region. . . . While it is of the utmost importance to explore any mound in a thorough manner and to get from it a complete record of its construction, contents, and relation to other works,—digging holes in a hundred places and obtaining here and there a few implements or ornaments, which by themselves are simply implements or ornaments and nothing more, is not working for scientific ends and should be discouraged by all scientific societies and by all owners of land upon which earthworks exist. . . . Thorough exploration followed by careful study of the results should be the method of all explorers, and a conscientious record of the whole should be kept to be published eventually in some permanent form accessible to all workers in the science. The various objects obtained during such exploration should never be scattered or separated from the associated articles, nor should they be trusted to the vicissitudes of private collections. . . . It is upon this plan and by such a method, that the explorations in Ohio have been carried on by the workers of the Museum.

In subsequent pages Putnam emphasized the importance of taking numerous photographs, making an abundance of diagrams of features, profiles, artifacts, and other archaeological items, and employing the comparative technique as an analytical tool to help work out time and space attributes.

At the Boston Society of Natural History in 1883 we see an early mention of the recording procedures that were to dominate Putnam's presentations in succeeding years: "Mr. Putnam illustrated his remarks by diagrams showing the structure of the mounds and by numerous photographs" (Putnam 1883b:358). The correspondent reporting on the 1884 meeting of the AAAS noted:

> A very long and extremely interesting account was then given by Mr. F. W. Putnam, of the explorations which he and Dr. Metz had carried on under the auspices of the

Peabody Museum at Cambridge. These investigations had been chiefly devoted to the study of a group of mounds near Madisonville, Ind. [sic], known as the Turner group. The very careful manner in which the exploration of the mounds had been carried on—the earth taken away and examined shovelful by shovelful—was shown, and the results of the work enumerated and illustrated by diagrams and photographs in great number. Neither time, labor, nor money has been spared in the prosecution of the work; and as a result one of the most remarkable series of objects ever discovered in America had been obtained, and also many new facts respecting the structure of the mounds themselves. (Anonymous 1884b:344)

For the 1885 meeting of the AAAS, the correspondent reporting on the anthropology papers noted that "Mr. F. W. Putnam gave some very practical and detailed directions as to the proper exploration of mounds, pleading earnestly for thorough work in all explorations; and illustrated its value by several examples from his own recent investigations" (Anonymous 1885a:234). Putnam's zealous lobbying for the new technique was having an effect. For example, Frank Hamilton Cushing lauded Putnam's new rigorous methodology in an 1886 letter to Alpheus Hyatt (Hinsley 1999:147).

We have been unable to determine when Putnam made his first stratigraphic excavations, but it appears to have been at least as early as 1880, for in the 1886 annual report of the National Academy of Sciences—covering Putnam's inaugural lecture, after he was elected a member in 1885—the meeting reporter noted, "F. W. Putnam, in a paper on 'Archeological explorations in the Little Miami valley,' illustrated by elaborate drawings and photographs, showed that the exhaustive method adopted during the past five years is the only one that can possibly give results of any value relative to the early occupants of this continent" (Anonymous 1886b:449). At this meeting Putnam indicated that he had explicitly been trying to develop a rigorous methodology in the Ohio mound work since 1880. What is unclear is how much earlier than the Ohio work he had begun to think about this problem.

By the mid-1880s Putnam had developed his method far enough and championed it widely enough that he was beginning to feel comfortable criticizing others for using less adequate recovery techniques. For example, he reported that George H. Squier, a local Wisconsin collector, had excavated two mounds near Trempealeau, but "it is to be regretted that the examination of the mounds was only partial, owing to his having followed the old and unsatisfactory method of digging a hole in the centre, instead of removing the whole mound, section by section" (Putnam 1885a:415).

In an August 6, 1886, appeal for further exploration funds, Putnam again stressed the Peabody Museum's new direction in the "systematic exploration" of mounds in Ohio, "to which I have given all the time possible each year since 1881. This work has conclusively shown the necessity of conducting such explorations on a systematic plan and an extensive scale" (Putnam 1887e:532). Among the new procedures Putnam introduced was the use of photography to record features and artifacts in situ, to which end he had his student John C. Kimball begin to attend Metz's excavation projects for the entire season in order to photograph materials as they were exposed (Putnam 1887a:549).

Because Putnam was not officially a member of the Harvard faculty until the Peabody Museum was integrated into the university in the 1890s, he gave self-organized lectures at the museum, at the so-called Harvard Annex (later Radcliffe College), and at other, similar venues, but he was unable to offer regularly scheduled classes through Harvard College. As of 1883 he had developed a short course on American archaeology arranged around six lectures: "1. Ancient mounds, earthworks, and fortifications in the United States; 2. Explorations of ancient towns; 3. Stone graves of the Cumberland valley, and their contents; 4. Ancient pottery; 5. Altar-mounds and their contents; 6. Burial customs, and the arts of the ancient Peruvians" (Anonymous 1883a:236).

By 1885 Putnam was offering a series of 38 public lectures (Putnam 1886a), divided roughly into two coherent "courses," and a group of other, stand-alone lectures. Putnam noted: "The first fifteen lectures are planned to give in a continuous course a review of the prehistoric peoples of America," the topics including lithics, pottery, metals, and burial mounds, among others (Browman 2000b:218). The second course, of 10 lectures, approached the archaeological material from a different perspective, detailing the various periods of sociocultural development that Putnam saw in the Americas, from humans' first entry onto the continent through two phases of hunters and gatherers, based on lithic types, up to agricultural groups. The third group, 13 lectures, included a range of topics from rock art to excavation methods; many of these were potentially stand-alone presentations.

Of specific importance for our argument is the topic "The Proper Methods of Exploration," listed as lecture 38 in an 1886 brochure (see Browman 2002a:218–19 for the complete list). This lecture was delivered to the newly formed graduate school at Johns Hopkins in 1885 and was summarized by an anonymous audience member in a December 15, 1885, paper titled "On the Methods of Archaeological Research in America." The correspondent reported:

> Trenching and slicing, he said, could be used to express in general terms the method followed in field work. For instance, in exploring a mound, a trench is first dug at the base of the mound. . . . The wall is the first section of the exploration, and its outlines should be drawn or photographed and its measurements noted. . . . After this first section is made, the work is carried on by slicing, or cutting down about a foot at a time, always keeping a vertical wall in front, the whole width of the mound. Each slice thus made is a section, and whenever the slightest change in the structure is noticed or any object found, that section should be drawn or photographed, and measured as at first, and the exact position noted of any object, ash bed, or change in the character of the structure of the mound. (Putnam 1886b)

The 1887 annual report on Putnam's work at the Little Miami mounds in Ohio described excavation by just this method, giving a bit more detail:

> We started the exploration of this place by making a trench along the edge down to the hard-pan. The earth was then removed along the front line of the trench, always going down to hard-pan, and thrown by hand. In this way, a vertical wall was always in front of the diggers, and the bottom of the trench was kept clean of loose dirt for the space of two or three feet, so that any former disturbance of either the soil in front or of the hard-pan below could be detected at once. (Putnam 1887a:550)

For another mound, Putnam reported (1887a:551) that "the work of exploration was begun by digging a straight trench down to the clay hard-pan across one edge of the mound and another on the opposite side. The mound was then cut down in slices, throwing the earth behind and always keeping a vertical wall in front."

Control was kept "by drawing a line north and south and another east and west through the center" of the mound. When the excavators discovered a feature, "this was examined, removing it inch by inch with small flat trowels" (Putnam 1887a:552). Otis T. Mason (1888:525) was impressed that in Putnam's procedure, "every ounce of earth passed backward through a screen or sieve." Troweling and screening in the 1880s are startling indeed. Some Smithsonian Institution collectors at the time were reported to be opening mounds by using dynamite. Only a decade earlier, even one of Putnam's field collectors, Charles Parry, had collected for the museum by diverting an irrigation ditch and collecting the artifacts that washed out.

The same attention to detail and control of context can be seen in Putnam's explanation of how one should excavate burials, published in 1886:

> If a skeleton is in dry earth or gravel, and is very dry and crumbling, the proper mode of procedure is to uncover the bones with great care, loosening the earth with the point of a small flat trowel and removing it from the bones by means of a small broom, or clothes brush, then let the moist air come in contact with the bone, or, if the air is very dry and hot, sprinkle the bones with water and let them absorb all they will. In this way the particles of bone swell and interlock, and after a while the bone can be safely taken up by avoiding force in removing it from the earth. In case the bones are in wet clay or earth the matrix must be removed with great care. In such cases the bones are soft and spongy and they must be allowed to remain in place until they have dried off; but they must not be exposed to the full heat of the sun, otherwise they will crack and splinter as they dry. (Putnam 1886c:1026)

Putnam had come to appreciate that the indiscriminate collecting done previously in the name of the Peabody Museum was inadequate. In his 1886 pitch for more funding for field research he said, "The time has passed when the mere haphazard gathering of antiquities was considered the end and aim of the archaeologist. That was the work of the curiosity seeker, the pioneer of the student. Now the time has come for thorough work, carefully planned, and systematically executed. Archaeology has become an acknowledged branch of science, aiming at far-reaching results, and it is necessary that none but scientific methods should be pursued" (Putnam 1887e:533). He reiterated this point in a letter of July 12, 1888 (reprinted in Putnam 1889:55), in which he stated, "Our methods of thorough exploration have set an example which others are following, so that American archaeology can no longer be regarded as consisting of an indiscriminate collection of relics of the past." Regrettably, Putnam was a bit too optimistic; it would be another three decades before the majority of American archaeologists could be said to follow such procedures.

To accomplish his goals, Putnam had not only to develop the methods of recovery—the Peabody Museum method—but also to find the funds to run the excavations and the appropriately trained people to staff the operations. He was clearly anticipating the time when he could train his own students, viewing the collector as but "the pioneer of the student." He first tried to obtain outside help instead of teaching students himself, attempting to secure an assistant professor to help in training and fieldwork. He immediately ran into difficulties with this approach, however, reporting in September 1888 (Putnam 1889:33–34) that "only a month or two since[,] I was requested to name a young man for the position of an assistant professor of anthropology, and although I soon after consulted with several of the leading anthropologists in the country we could not name an individual capable of filling the required position, who was not already holding a life situation, or else too old for such an assistant professorship." Putnam was unable to solve this problem until he established his own graduate program and provided the necessary training himself.

It was at this time that Putnam also began pleading for laws to preserve important archaeological sites. Visiting Serpent Mound in Ohio for the first time after attending the AAAS meetings in Chicago in August 1883, he came away awed by the mound but fearful for its future:

> Shall Fort Ancient, Fort Hill, Hopeton, The Serpent, and many other ancient works in various parts of Ohio be obliterated? Shall such vandalism, such shame, be laid to Americans of this century? If the state will not take action, cannot the cities, or counties, or local societies become preservers of ancient monuments? And Cahokia, the largest of all the tumuli of the Mississippi valley, must not be omitted when this work of preservation shall begin. Will the great state of Illinois permit this monument of another race to be leveled to furnish ballast for a railroad, its inevitable fate if left in private hands? (Putnam 1884a:350–51)

Thus, as we discuss in the following chapters, Putnam not only took on the task of training students to become skilled field-workers but also began a "salvage archaeology" program attempting to either preserve or salvage archaeological resources in imminent danger of destruction. All this required funds, an issue that soon sidetracked Putnam temporarily from realizing his objective.

During the decade-long transition from volunteer collectors to trained field-workers, Putnam still relied heavily on the stable of collectors he had recruited to provide specimens for the museum. Soon he found himself strapped for funds to support these people. In the museum's annual reports he noted with alarm the need to terminate various field projects, with remarks such as, "It is to be regretted that, for want of funds, Dr. Palmer will be obliged to discontinue his investigations" (Putnam 1880a:720), and "Last winter, word was most reluctantly sent to Dr. Flint, who has for some time been so zealous in his explorations in Nicaragua, that the income of the Museum would not permit further expenditure for explorations at present" (Putnam 1881a:17).

For this reason Putnam convinced the board of trustees to send to prospective donors a funding request for "Archaeological Research in America." By the end of the 1881 reporting year, $3,350 special funding donations had been received, and Putnam reported with pleasure (1882a:55) that explorations that had reluctantly been suspended two years earlier had been resumed. By the end of 1884 the "exploration" fund stood at $5,433, but then donations tailed off. Putnam wrote to Robert Winthrop, chair of the trustees, for assistance, and a new "Appeal for Aid in the Explorations" was made (Putnam 1887e), with part of the money earmarked for the purchase of Serpent Mound. In his summary for 1890 Putnam reported (1891a:106–7) that the special exploration fund had received a total of $27,801, including $8,738 for the Serpent Mound purchase. This amount did not include $500 contributed to establish a new Visiting Committee Fellowship, which was given to Marshall Saville (see chapter 7). This new fellowship highlights the direction in which Putnam's fund-raising went for the next few years, as he shifted his focus to securing fellowships and other funding for students in the newly formed Department of American Archaeology and Ethnology, soon retitled the Department of Anthropology. As a point of reference, a literature review suggests that an adequate professor's salary at this time would have been $2,000.

A far-reaching step that Putnam undertook was to initiate the training of students—made possible for undergraduates at Harvard College only after 1869, when President Charles Eliot introduced the new system of elective courses, and for graduate students only after the reorganization of the graduate school at Harvard in 1890 (see chapter 6). Putnam became involved in training undergraduates almost as soon as he was named curator of the Peabody Museum, with his first student in 1875. He made his first attempt at training post-A.B. students in 1883–87, but the program failed for lack of funds as well as structure. Thus the first successful training program for graduate students was really his second generation of such students, beginning in 1890.

The first undergraduate Putnam trained, beginning in 1875—just as he was finishing labeling the old Wyman collections and getting ready to develop the new museum—was **Ernest Jackson** (1857–1913). A member of the Harvard class of 1878, Jackson was the nephew of Asa Gray, again showing the strong linkage between Putnam and his old professors. Regarding the training program, Putnam wrote (1876:8), "To Mr. Ernest Jackson, of the sophomore class, I am also indebted for considerable assistance. While thus giving his aid in the preparation of specimens, Mr. Jackson is gradually attaining the general knowledge in archaeology which was his desire when offering his services."

Part of Jackson's training involved working with the collections from Peru and Bolivia that Alexander Agassiz and Samuel Garman had donated. Many of the artifacts had been broken or damaged during transport, and Jackson spent a good deal of time, under the guidance of Lucien Carr, repairing them (Putnam 1876:12).

Jackson went on to get an A.M. from Harvard, "with final honors in the classics," in 1879 (Anonymous 1913b). He spent much of his life as a private tutor but maintained a lifelong interest in collecting artifacts. More important, he kept clear documentation of proveniences, a procedure learned under Putnam at the Peabody. He stayed interested in archaeology, joining the AIA in 1879, immediately after its founding (Anonymous 1913b). He also continued to do volunteer work at the Peabody Museum. In his twenty-fifth class report he noted that in addition to having been elected secretary of the Boston Society of the AIA since 1895, he had "given much of his time in helping to help arrange the collections of the Art Museum in Boston and those of the Peabody Museum in Cambridge." He added, "I spend my spare time and money in collecting, in an amateurish way, the implements, etc, of the savage and semi-civilized races of mankind" (Jackson 1901:59–60). In his last class report before his death (Jackson 1908:46), he wrote, "My regular business and the work of the Archaeological Institute have kept me very busy for the last few years."

According to his nephew, Patrick Jackson, Ernest Jackson acquired his interest in part from his aunt, Jane Lathrop Loring Gray (1821–1909), who had accompanied her husband, Asa Gray, on nearly all his field trips. Jane Gray's interest in antiquities was known to the Peabody, to which she contributed items from time to time (Putnam 1881a:15). Patrick Jackson provided additional details:

> Mrs. Asa Gray was deeply interested in the Indians of New Mexico and Arizona, and each year used to receive a considerable consignment of baskets, blankets, weapons, costumes, etc., which she would dispose of by holding a Fair and returning all proceeds to the Indians over and above expenses. My Uncle [Ernest Jackson] helped her in this and soon, probably in the early 80's, he began his Indian collection by buying only the best things. His taste was excellent and he studied what literature he could get on the subject, so that he knew what was good. He joined the Archeological Society and became its secretary for most of his life.
>
> His connections with Indian matters broadened and he corresponded with various traders and agencies, picking up pieces here and there. In the 90's he became interested in South Sea, Indonesian, and African art and weapons, also Alaskan and South American Indian, and started new lines to his collection. He began by interviewing ship captains in Boston, getting them to buy weapons, etc., in the course of their voyages and getting him in touch with original sources. Several of these articles were also being sold at Boston auctions and the auction rooms and antique dealers often had a few pieces on hand that could be bought....

He lived with his family at 383 Beacon Street, Boston, and every inch of wall space in his room and in all the halls was covered with the collection. He also had various cabinets filled with it, trunks and cases also full up. He kept a catalogue closely up to date that contained a full description and drawing with measurement of every piece he owned. He also built up a considerable library on these subjects. (Patrick T. Jackson to Donald Scott, December 23, 1946, Peabody Museum Accession Files 46-78)

The detailed catalogue, which was transferred to the Peabody in 1946, was a collections requirement no doubt imparted to Jackson by Putnam.

Whereas Jackson was Putnam's first undergraduate student, three other people can be identified as the first cohort of advanced students whom Putnam recruited for specialized training in what later became the graduate program.

Because the Department of American Archaeology and Ethnology (later Anthropology) was not officially established as part of Harvard College until 1890, our fellow historians of science have assumed that Putnam did not begin teaching students until that date. But we find evidence of his first undergraduate in 1875, the year he was hired to take over the museum, and of his first advanced students in 1882 to 1884—as much as 15 years earlier than most sources seem to be aware of concerning this component of Putnam's career. In his annual reports to the trustees, Putnam explicitly applied the term "students" to three people whom he recruited between 1883 and 1887, listing them as "student assistants" and "special students," the latter term having specific institutional significance with respect to rights and privileges in Harvard College. The three were Cordelia Studley, John Kimball, and William Nickerson.

Cordelia Adelaide Studley (1855–87) was a medical student who had trained first at Boston University and then at the University of Michigan, where she hoped to take her degree (Putnam 1888e:420). She had taken medical leave from her schooling and was recuperating in Boston when Putnam recruited her to work on the osteological collections that Edward Palmer had donated to the Peabody Museum from his excavations at Coahuila, Mexico. She quickly accomplished this task, and her paper "Notes upon Human Remains from Caves in Coahuila, Mexico" (Studley 1883) is one of the earliest such studies in Americanist human osteology.

Putnam reported that Studley began work as a volunteer in October 1881 and as an official "assistant" in 1882: "By the liberality of a few friends, the services of Miss C. A. Studley as an assistant in the Museum have been secured without encroaching upon the limited means derived from the Museum funds. Miss Studley was at the Museum for three months of the past year, as a special student in craniology, and commenced work as an assistant on the first of January last" (Putnam 1882a:71). As the assistant in somatology she became the first official physical anthropologist at the museum (Brew 1966a:30). In addition to working in osteology and managing the osteological collections, she "aided in various ways in Museum work" (Putnam 1883a:190), including helping in the library and cataloguing.

During Studley's tenure, besides analyzing the Coahuila materials, she worked up some of the osteological remains excavated by Putnam and Metz from the Turner Mound group and other mounds at Madisonville, Ohio, and presented the results at the annual meeting of the AAAS in 1883 (Anonymous 1883c:344; Browman 2002a:232). She excavated shell mounds at Marion and Northborough, Massachusetts, in 1884 and 1885 (Putnam 1885a:413, 1886a:493) and conducted some of the first work for the museum at the large shell mounds at Damariscotta, Maine, in 1885 (Putnam 1888a:38).

In July 1886 Studley left the museum, citing financial reasons (Putnam 1887c:420, 1888a:38). Putnam reported that first he had lost his student William B. Nickerson for financial reasons, and then

> the second to leave us is Miss Studley, who had been with us, first as student and afterwards as assistant in special charge of osteological collections of the Museum, for nearly five years. During this time Miss Studley was engaged in a study of the human skeletons contained in the Museum.... Unfortunately, just at a time when cases were ready for completing the detailed arrangements of the large collection of crania and skeletons, which she had so well begun, she felt the necessity of obtaining an addition to her income, beyond our means to provide, and therefore accepted another position where she could still continue in scientific work. (Putnam 1887a:568–69)

A little more than a year later, Putnam sadly reported Studley's unexpected death in December 1887 (Putnam 1888e:420).

John Cone Kimball (1857–?) was listed as a "Student Assistant" for the Peabody Museum from 1883 to 1887 and, on internal documents, as "Field Assistant in Southeastern Archaeology" (Brew 1966a:8). Putnam seems to have had a close relationship with Kimball, referring to him as "his friend and pupil" (Putnam 1885b:4). He placed particular confidence in Kimball's judgment, on occasion sending him into the field alone to assess collectors and sites, so that Putnam could ascertain whether a follow-up visit might be worthwhile. During his first year working for Putnam, in 1883, Kimball visited several collectors in Brookfield and other Boston suburbs and acquired specimens for the museum (Putnam 1884a:352). Putnam took the young man along on many field trips to serve as expedition photographer, as shown by the frequent mention of his photographic contributions in the annual reports for 1884–89.

In August 1883, after the annual meeting of the AAAS in Chicago, Putnam, his son, Eben, John Kimball, and Rev. Stephen D. Peet, editor of *American Antiquarian,* visited several of the effigy mound sites in Wisconsin and Illinois (Putnam 1884a:346). In September, Kimball and Putnam met Charles Metz for their first inspection of Serpent Mound in Ohio. Throughout the visits and negotiations over the purchase of Serpent Mound in the next few years, Kimball seems to have served as Putnam's right-hand man in the field.

In the summer of 1884, after reading a newspaper story about some relics found by schoolboys near Scioto, Ohio, Putnam wrote, "I requested Mr. Kimball to go to the place and make inquiries relating to the specimens," and "the result of his visit impressed me with the importance of making a comparative study of the group of mounds" (Putnam 1885a:400, 403). This began Putnam's association with excavations run by Metz for the museum at the Turner Mound group in Ohio.

In 1884, William Nickerson, who would also become a student at the Peabody, contacted Putnam to see whether he could secure aid in work at mounds near Elgin, Illinois. Rather than visit Nickerson himself, Putnam sent John Kimball to Elgin to assess the archaeology and the archaeologist. When Kimball reported back on the site and Nickerson's work, Putnam was impressed. He wrote to Nickerson in November requesting a full written report of his work and inviting him to continue his contact (Browman 2002b:253).

Kimball took advantage of the trip to Illinois to make additional collections for the museum: "To Mr. John Cone Kimball, who has been for several years my companion in field work and a volunteer assistant in the Museum," Putnam wrote, "we are indebted for the thorough exploration of three mounds on the bluffs of the Mississippi, in Atlas township, Illinois. This work was carried on at his own expense" (Putnam 1885a:412–13). In addition, "during Mr. Kimball's visit to Pike county, Illinois, he was able to secure from several friends and by his own efforts a fair representation of the stone implements." The mounds in Atlas township became known as the Adams mound group, and the first season apparently led to subsequent investigations. In the next year's annual report Putnam referred to "explorations conducted for the Museum by Messrs. F. W. Putnam, John Cone Kimball, and Eben Putnam" at mounds on land belonging to Captain J. G. Adams in Pike County, in September after the AAAS meeting in Ann Arbor, Michigan (Putnam 1886a:495). On the basis of this Illinois mound research, Putnam for the first time subdivided mounds into two types: those in the American Bottoms, like those in Ohio, and those on the river bluffs above the Mississippi (Putnam 1886a:499).

Putnam's curator's report in the annual report for 1885 noted continued work by Kimball: "Mr. Kimball has, as in former years, given voluntary assistance in various ways, particularly in photographic work. He has accompanied me on many archaeological excursions, during which his skill as an amateur photographer has proved of great service" (Putnam 1886:494). Later in the annual report, reference was made to the excavation of a series of burials and collection of burial goods by Kimball and his friends from Watson's Hill, Plymouth, Massachusetts.

Kimball continued making trips with Putnam to various of the museum's projects, including another visit to Serpent Mound in 1886 (Putnam 1887a:564). In the summers of 1886 and 1887 Kimball seems to have worked on the museum's mound excavations in the Little Miami Valley in Ohio, both when Putnam was there and when he was not, functioning, among other things, as the official photographer (Putnam 1887a:549, 1888a:42). Whereas the reasons for Cordelia Studley's and William Nickerson's leaving the museum were discussed in some detail in the annual reports, the end of Kimball's relationship is signaled by a single line in the report for

1889 (Putnam 1890a:66), with the staff listing now modified to "John Cone Kimball, Student Assistant, 1883–87."

Putnam's secretary wrote years later that John Kimball "never accepted anything from the Museum, not even his traveling and camp expenses," and "when this man had his attention diverted into a new channel, he asked to have his name taken off the staff list, and since that time he has not taken the least interest in the Museum or in American Archaeology" (Mead 1915:1). During the period when he was associated with the museum, a Mrs. Clara B. Kimball of Boston gave the museum $100 yearly for research, a significant sum in that day, but her donations stopped abruptly after 1887 when Kimball left—more than a coincidence, it seems. Despite what Mead wrote, Kimball seems to have kept aware of events at the Peabody Museum, for he was partly responsible for a major donation of materials to the museum from the estates of his father and uncle, David and Moses Kimball, in 1900 and 1901 (Putnam 1900a:276, 1901a:300). The Kimball brothers had helped form the Boston Museum in 1841, and after it was damaged by a fire in 1899, the Peabody Museum had purchased more than 1,400 items from its collections at its "fire sale."

The earliest communication we have located between Putnam and **William Baker Nickerson** (1865–1926) is the letter of July 1884 in which Nickerson asked Putnam for funds to continue a mound survey in the Fox River Valley near Elgin, Illinois (Browman 2002b:253–57), which prompted Putnam to send John Kimball to visit Nickerson that fall. Nickerson had been working as a railroad employee and in 1885 was transferred east, where he seems to have been stationed alternately in Millbury, Massachusetts, and Meriden, Connecticut. He continued to send archaeological specimens to the Peabody Museum, now from work in Massachusetts and Connecticut, and arranged visits with Putnam at the museum beginning in April 1885.

Putnam set up a meeting between Metz and Nickerson in the summer of 1885, and Nickerson worked with Metz on the Turpin site that summer (Browman 2002b:253). The list of personnel at the Peabody Museum in that year's annual report includes "W. B. Nickerson. Student-Assistant. 1885." The next year Putnam wrote (1886a:494) that "for about a year Mr. W. B. Nickerson has been engaged as a volunteer assistant in field work for the Museum. In March, 1885, he partly explored a group of burial mounds in the Fox River valley, near Elgin, Illinois. . . . afterwards he was associated with the work in Ohio, and prepared a map of a portion of the Little Miami valley." The list of new donations to the Peabody Museum for that year includes materials collected by Nickerson from the Fox River mounds, from Scapell Hill at Millbury, Massachusetts, and from Anderson township, Newton, Ohio.

Nickerson continued to work directly for Putnam in 1886, taking part in an exploration of a shell heap near New Haven, Connecticut, for the museum, as well as working in Ohio under the direction of Metz and Putnam (Putnam 1888a:12, 1888a:37). Later during that year he ended his direct association with the museum. Putnam wrote that two of our former collaborators have been obliged for pecuniary causes to seek other fields of labor, and the loss of their assistance is one of the reasons that has led me to suggest the possibility of the foundation of a form of scholarships, by which means might be at hand for the support of deserving students or assistants.... The first called from us is Mr. Nickerson, a young man, who, during the time he was associated with us in our work of special explorations in the field, evinced an aptitude for archaeological research which I greatly regret could not have been further encouraged by providing a small salary for his support. (Putnam 1887a:568)

Nevertheless, Nickerson seems to have made one last foray to Ohio for Putnam. The 1888 curator's annual report (Putnam 1888a:37, 42) refers to the museum's having received a collection of artifacts from Newton, Hamilton County, Ohio, made by Nickerson.

Nickerson maintained his archaeological interests for the next few decades, supporting himself by working in railroad positions and obtaining occasional small donations from Putnam to assist in excavations during his vacations. In the late 1880s and early 1890s, he conducted mound excavations near railroad stations in Michigan and Illinois. In 1898 Putnam reported (1898a:249–50): "Mr. W. B. Nickerson, who was a student in the Museum several years ago, but was obliged to withdraw and take a business position, has never lost his love for archaeological investigations. He continues to devote his vacations and such time as he can take from business to exploration in the vicinity of his home in Galena, Ill. He has during the past few years explored a group of mounds in a most through and scientific manner." When Nickerson was looking for a more permanent archaeological position, Putnam wrote to his distant cousin, Edward K. Putnam (1868–1939), at the Davenport Academy of Natural Science, that Nickerson "has done some first rate work in archaeological exploration for this museum. Every summer I have sent him a sum of money that he might explore a mound during his vacation" (July 5, 1901, quoted in Herold 1971:27).

The railroad moved Nickerson in early 1894 to the Portage Curve Station, near Galena, Illinois, where he spent much of the next decade. Apparently Putnam continued making a practice of visiting as many of his field collectors as possible, for in a letter in 1894 Nickerson suggested that when Putnam took "his annual trip," he should stay a few days in Galena. Nickerson spelled out in great detail the excavation method he was going to employ, asking Putnam if he had remembered all the details correctly and thus providing us with one of the most explicit statements of Putnam's methodology of the period. After Nickerson's death, detailed notes from the Galena excavations fortuitously fell into the hands of a field crew headed by Paul S. Martin and John Blackburn under the direction of Fay-Cooper Cole, the new assistant professor of sociology and anthropology at the University of Chicago. Martin and Blackburn soon abandoned the primitive techniques they had been using and took over Nickerson's methods. Within a few years, the new "Chicago method" of excavation was being widely heralded around the country as one of the best in the field. Ironically, it was nothing more than Putnam's original Peabody Museum method, resurrected and refurbished (Browman 2002b:257–63).

During the 1890s and early 1900s Nickerson sought Putnam's aid in securing full-time archaeological employment. He asked for a job with Putnam at the World's Columbian Exposition in Chicago and over the next few years asked him for help in finding positions with researchers including the University of Wisconsin geologist and later university president Charles R. Van Hise (1857–1918); Edward Putnam at the Davenport Academy of Natural Science; Frederick Skiff (1851–1921) and George A. Dorsey (1868–1931) of the Field Museum of Natural History; Frederick Starr (1858–1933) at the University of Chicago; and even Putnam himself at the new Department of Anthropology at the University of California–Berkeley. But Nickerson was frustrated in all these quests. The only job that arose from his inquiries was a single field season working for Edward Putnam in Iowa.

Nickerson came increasingly to view himself as an archaeologist, publishing a series of articles summarizing his work in Illinois in the journal *Glimpses of the Past* from 1908 through 1912. In addition to the field season in Iowa doing excavations for Edward Putnam and the Davenport Academy in 1908, he conducted fieldwork in southwestern Manitoba for the Geological Survey of Canada between 1912 and 1915. When money for his work in Canada was interrupted by World War I, Nickerson was hired by the Minnesota Historical Society to conduct archaeological surveys in that state in 1913 and 1916. He also continued his own privately funded fieldwork in Iowa and Illinois through 1921. Thus Nickerson had nearly a 40-year career in Americanist archaeology, from at least as early as 1884 through 1921 and perhaps even until his death in 1926, with much of the early part funded by Putnam.

After losing all three of his advanced students—at least two of them, Nickerson and Studley, because of lack of financial support—Putnam decided he needed to develop a more structured program with stronger financial backing. Thus began a major shift in his activities. Although he kept in contact with his coterie of field collectors, during the period 1887 to 1890 he began putting in place the elements of an entirely new approach. He had clearly recognized that to achieve the greater control and documentation he now wanted in field research, he would need to work with better-trained people. This meant, in short, graduate students. During this transition period he obtained the Thaw and Hemenway Fellowships to support students in training for the museum; he lobbied for and secured the position of Peabody Professor at the museum; and with the reorganization of the graduate school in 1890, he seized the opportunity to create the first anthropology graduate program in the country, a program under which he recruited his second generation of students.

In 1887 Putnam petitioned the trustees for fellowship support, after reminding them that he had just lost the help of his first cohort of students due to a lack of funds:

> If several scholarships could be secured for special students by which they could be made student-assistants, and thus enabled to aid in the work of the Museum while carrying on their special studies, a number of properly trained assistants might be gradually obtained.

> To do this, however, and to provide for the care of the collections, a larger income in some form is essential, and the establishment of student-assistantships in the Museum is believed to be a feasible way of securing a portion of the funds needed for the purpose. (Putnam 1887a:536)

By 1890, when the Harvard University faculty was reorganizing the graduate school and with it voting to officially establish the Department of American Archaeology and Ethnology in order to offer instruction for the A.M. and Ph.D. degrees (Putnam 1891:98), Putnam already had in place a special Visiting Committee Fellowship. The next year he added two more financial fellowships, the Thaw and the Hemenway, and in the following year, a third and a fourth (because the Visiting Committee Fellowship seems to have been only a temporary measure), the Winthrop and the Austin. By the turn of the century he was able to fully support all his graduate students. In the next chapter we detail the new program with the second set of students, which began in 1890, starting with two graduate students, George Dorsey and John Owens, and three undergraduate students, Marshall Saville, Frank Gerrodette, and Allan Cook.

During the early years, Putnam thus employed a variety of strategies to develop anthropology at the Peabody Museum. One of the mechanisms he adopted, maximized, and then abandoned was to recruit an educated but independent cadre of collectors to help build the museum's collections. These people ranged from gentleman collectors whose passion was archaeology to university-trained natural and physical scientists who became involved in anthropology as a career adjunct, and they included some of the first professional women scholars in the field. Putnam's natural science background no doubt led to his pioneering efforts with members of his network who were involved in zoo-archaeology, paleoethnobotany, human osteology, and the like. During the first decade and a half of Putnam's tenure as museum director, he was loyal to his network of volunteers, supporting their efforts long after their disappointing production suggested that he really should cut them loose.

As time progressed, Putnam came to recognize that collections without proper context were of relatively minor value. Hence we see early on his efforts in trying to upgrade the quality of fieldwork. By the early 1880s this thrust led him to develop a more rigorous recovery methodology. Explicit stratigraphic excavation was a major means by which to achieve context. In order to properly control the field situation, so that appropriate archaeological information could be recovered, Putnam saw that he would have to train his own students. He had tried to teach proper field methodology to some of his more enthusiastic amateur volunteers, such as Metz and Cresson, but he lacked a way to enforce their compliance with his new standards. When this approach failed, he tried to recruit a set of volunteer students such as Kimball,

Nickerson, and Studley, but a lack of appropriate infrastructure frustrated his initial efforts in that direction. In the next chapters we explore the ways in which Putnam sought to build the country's first viable department of undergraduate and graduate education in anthropology and provide the necessary infrastructure for the orderly growth of the discipline.

5

The Influence of Other Professionals and the Archaeological Institute of America, 1865–1890

THE GROWTH OF ANTHROPOLOGY AT THE PEABODY MUSEUM involved other professionals who were less directly involved than those discussed in the preceding two chapters but whose contributions were still critical to the direction the museum took during its first quarter century. We turn to those people in this chapter. All of them worked with Putnam and his colleagues, and most of them also contributed to the growing collections at the Peabody Museum. Some of these professionals were major figures in their own right, although they are often overlooked in syntheses of the period.

In addition, during this time Putnam began to actualize his recognition of the need for broader institutional support, becoming involved in transforming the American Association for the Advancement of Science and founding the Archaeological Institute of America. In spite of his concerted efforts, Americanist archaeology lost out to classical archaeology on the national scene, owing in part to the broader philosophical enlightenment movement of the period. These events, too, helped shape the direction of the program at the Peabody Museum and must be integrated into our story. But first let us turn to some of the important players who should be added to the mix.

We start with two figures, Raphael Pumpelly and Wills DeHass, whose influence was perhaps more on Putnam the man than on the Peabody Museum. Pumpelly was a contemporary of Putnam's, and their common interest in natural history led their paths to intersect at the AAAS and elsewhere. DeHass was one of the first people to explicitly style himself a "professional archaeologist," and his research trajectory intersected with Putnam's during much of the later nineteenth century.

Raphael Pumpelly (1837–1923) was an interesting late-nineteenth-century naturalist who, like so many of the other natural history students of the time, became involved in anthropology. Pumpelly attended the Yale prep school, known as the New Haven Collegiate and Commercial Institute, in 1853–54 but then decided he wanted to attend school in Germany. He left New Haven in 1854, did some exploring along the way, and finally enrolled in 1856 at the Freiberg Mining Academy, where he stayed through 1860 (Champlin 1994:7, 9; Willis 1934:31). Louis Agassiz had seen to it that his young

French protégé, Jules Marcou, had been appointed geologist for the American Thirty-Fifth Parallel Survey, led by army lieutenant Amiel W. Whipple in the 1850s; Pumpelly had wanted to join this or another, related western survey and saw mining expertise as a vehicle for doing so (Champlin 1994:35).

By 1865–66 Pumpelly had begun working for Alexander Agassiz at the copper mines Agassiz had purchased in Michigan (see chapter 3), thus establishing contact with Louis Agassiz and Lawrence School students as well. Louis Agassiz had been largely responsible for the establishment of the School of Mining and Practical Geology at Harvard in 1864, by having Josiah Dwight Whitney brought onto the faculty to establish the institute. Whitney then invited Pumpelly to become professor of mining in the new school, an appointment Pumpelly accepted early in 1867, although he did not actually teach there until the 1869–70 term (Champlin 1994:80–81; Land 1933:169). During the winters of 1869–70 and 1870–71 he lectured on mining deposits at the School of Mining and Practical Geology. He integrated smoothly into the faculty and became a regular at the prestigious Thursday Club, along with Agassiz, Oliver Wolcott Gibbs, Benjamin Peirce, and others (Land 1933:178). He resigned from the Harvard mining school in 1871. Its closure in 1875 was due largely to his resignation and to Whitney's frequent absences while he conducted fieldwork in California (Champlin 1994:74).

Pumpelly then embarked on a series of jobs that took him around the country and indeed the world. He occasionally excavated a mound or two; Putnam's report on Peabody Museum activities for 1880 refers to aboriginal crania received from an excavation Pumpelly had made in Oswego, New York (Putnam 1881a:10). Pumpelly worked for the U.S. Geological Survey briefly in the early 1880s and again in 1884 under John Wesley Powell, in a position he kept for the next eight years. Although most of his research for Powell was in geology, he also worked alongside the archaeologists Powell had hired and was up-to-date on archaeological arguments. Pumpelly's position was tied to Powell's rise and fall. When Powell lost a major institutional battle in 1892, Pumpelly was one of several employees he had to let go (Champlin 1994:142).

For the next decade Pumpelly was involved in non-anthropological activities, but he returns to our pages because of his major excavation project at Anau, then in Russian Turkestan (now in Turkmenistan), which was funded by the Carnegie Institution of Washington (CIW). The CIW was founded in 1902 as a research organization in the sciences, humanities, and social sciences, and Pumpelly's excavations at Anau in 1903–4 were the first project it sponsored (Willey 1967:301). His 1903 season was to be dedicated primarily to seeking evidence of geological changes in association with ancient civilizations, and the 1904 season was to be aimed at excavating old dwelling sites.

The excavation was trendsetting in being the first widely recognized, large-scale, multidisciplinary excavation project. Pumpelly involved a variety of specialists in the field excavations, each responsible for components of the project. When he brought the materials back for analysis, he continued this procedure, recruiting another series of specialists to help him in the technical components of the research.

As Peggy Champlin (1994:174), Pumpelly's biographer, argued, Pumpelly knew that including an experienced archaeologist was crucial to his expedition's success. For the 1903 season he invited Richard Norton, son of Charles Eliot Norton, whom he had known at Harvard, to accompany him. Richard Norton had taught the history of fine arts at Bryn Mawr and was then the director of the American School of Classical Studies in Rome. But Norton did not return for the 1904 season, and Pumpelly turned to Hubert Schmidt, curator of ceramics for the Museum für Völkerkunde in Berlin, who had studied and worked with Wilhelm Dorpfeld at Troy. The ultimate success of the Anau expedition is said to have owed much to Schmidt's planning and excavation strategies (Champlin 1994:186; Schmidt 1908). Pumpelly also brought along his son, **Raphael Welles Pumpelly** (1881–1949), a Harvard undergraduate who had studied with Nathaniel Shaler, for both seasons. The younger Pumpelly was allowed to invite some of his friends along as archaeological assistants, one of whom was Homer Kidder, the older brother of archaeologist Alfred V. Kidder (on both Kidders' careers, see chapter 10).

A plague of locusts descended on Anau in the middle of the 1904 season, attacking crops and causing the provincial governor to recall many of the Anau workers to help destroy the insects. This loss of labor effectively brought an end to the excavation work. Pumpelly vividly described the locusts' effects on the project's work. "The whole surface of the oasis became at once covered with an endless insect army, always twenty or more per square foot, and all marching southward," he wrote (Pumpelly 1918, 2:732). He continued:

> When they came to our shafts, they descended the sixty or ninety-foot depth and, failing to climb the opposite wall, fell back and piled up on the bottom. These shafts were sunk for my son to study the character of the strata and to collect pottery. In one he stood knee-deep [in locusts]. . . . At last, when they accumulated in our excavation pits faster than the men could shovel them out during the day, we had to stop work and flee from the growing stench that rendered the air unbearable. (Pumpelly 1918, 2:733)

Pumpelly believed that collecting and analyzing animal bones, which to his knowledge no Middle Eastern archaeologist had done before, would provide evidence to support his thesis that the people of Central Asia had originated animal domestication. Putnam and some other North Americanist archaeologists had been collecting animal bones since the 1860s, but not with the domestication issue in mind. The inclusion of a range of specialists for analyses had been practiced on a small scale in several of the Americanist projects we have reviewed, but not at the magnitude of the Anau project:

> In a move that was very unusual in archaeology at the time, Pumpelly called on several specialists to analyze materials . . . and to contribute reports to the Carnegie volumes. These specialists were Yale chemist and metallurgist Frank A Gooch, who analyzed metal objects; comparative anatomist J. Ulrich Durst of the University of Bern, who

spent three years studying and classifying the many animal bones Pumpelly collected; physical anthropologists Giuseppe Sergi of the University of Rome and Thomas Mollison from the Zurich Anthropological Institute, who studied human skulls and bones; and Swiss botanist H. C. Schellenberg, who determined that grain hulls, straw, and chaff from cultivated varieties of wheat and barley had been used in pot making. (Champlin 1994:185)

Three-quarters of a century later, Lewis Binford and other "new" archaeologists would again raise the call for more interdisciplinary projects, leading the unsuspecting neophyte to believe that such projects were the invention of New Archaeology, or processual archaeology. Perhaps they were a reinvention, but Pumpelly and others were doing them long before the 1970s.

The Peabody Museum was given part of the Anau materials. Pumpelly himself donated various type specimens in 1906–7 (Putnam 1908:297), and in 1934–35 his son, Raphael W., donated a much larger series of materials (Scott 1936:322).

Another quasi-professional archaeologist with whom Putnam interacted occasionally during the 1860s and 1870s, largely through the AAAS, was **Wills DeHass** (1817–1910). Born in Washington County, Pennsylvania, DeHass was educated at Western University and Washington County's Jefferson College, where he received his M.D. degree (Anonymous 1911:815). He lived a good part of his early life in Moundsville, West Virginia, not far from the Grave Creek mound. During research for his volume on the history of western Virginia (DeHass 1851), he became interested in prehistoric mounds and the mound-builder question in general. He became particularly interested in the alleged Grave Creek mound tablet (on this pseudo-artifact, see S. Williams 1991:82–87). According to Terry A. Barnhart (1986:124n), the legendary stone was in DeHass's collection when he died in 1910 but has since been lost.

At the 1858 AAAS meeting, in Baltimore, DeHass was selected to be a member of the committee set up to "study ancient monuments and their distribution" (Williams 2000:7). Despite its apparent early support from the AAAS, this committee seems to have done little for nearly a decade after its formation. In March 1868 DeHass traveled to St. Louis, where he met with members of the St. Louis Academy of Science and visited the mounds in the city of St. Louis and at Cahokia. His announced purpose for this trip was that he was initiating a general survey of ancient mounds in the West, mapping and measuring them, collecting vestiges of art, and excavating many of the smaller mounds for a planned "superbly illustrated volume"—at last following up on the charge from the AAAS a decade earlier (DeHass 1868a). DeHass followed this notice with a short addendum saying that his first report was too cursory, and he had found a rich mound assemblage in Illinois, where he had already collected information on more than 200 mounds. He asserted that his explorations were "the most important and extensive yet made in the West," and the artifacts he had recovered proved that "the original occupants of the fine alluvial opposite St. Louis were agricultural as well as hunters and fishermen" (DeHass 1868b).

DeHass also reported on this trip to St. Louis in the 1869 report of the work of the "Committee on Mound Survey" to the AAAS anthropology section (DeHass 1869a, 1869b). There DeHass acknowledged that the charge to conduct a survey had been made a decade before, but, he explained, the Civil War had intervened. As a result, only the chair, DeHass, had done any work, mainly in the Ohio and Mississippi River valleys, especially at Cahokia, on which he was reporting at the current meeting. These brief commentaries of 1868 and 1869 seem to be the sum of the reports of work done by the AAAS committee. DeHass was in St. Louis when its "Big Mound" was being destroyed, and he sent a photo and sketch of the "long-nosed god mask" from that mound in a letter to Putnam, whom he apparently knew through the AAAS connection and who was then at the Peabody Museum in Salem (Williams 2000:8). DeHass subsequently donated other materials he collected from the Big Mound to the Peabody Museum at Harvard after Putnam moved there (Putnam 1875d:15).

In the spring of 1877 DeHass gave a series of archaeological lectures at Syracuse University. Otis T. Mason (1877:626) viewed the proposed talks with perhaps some skepticism: "Prof. Wills de Hass has issued a Syllabus of a course of Lectures on American Prehistoric Archaeology before the College of Fine Arts, Syracuse University. This being the first attempt to popularize in this manner the whole subject of prehistoric archaeology in our country, we would congratulate his hearers if the richness of the lectures bear any comparison with the luscious bill of fare." This was a one-time event—DeHass gave no subsequent lectures at Syracuse or any other university on archaeology.

The years 1879 to 1881 seem to have been the brightest period of DeHass's archaeological career. In February 1879 he, Otis Mason, Dr. Joseph M. Toner, and Col. Garrick Mallery drafted a constitution for a newly proposed "Archaeological and Ethnological Society of Washington." At the subsequent founding meeting, when the organization was renamed the Anthropological Society of Washington (ASW), John Wesley Powell was elected president, and DeHass, Mallery, and Toner, vice presidents (Lamb 1906:565; Mason 1880b:813). Later that spring DeHass gave the fifth paper at the meeting of the Anthropological Society of Washington, titled "Progress of Archaeological Research in the United States" (Williams 2000:8).

Powell and DeHass had fought together as officers at the Battle of Shiloh, where Powell was wounded, in April 1862. They knew each other from their military service as well as from their AAAS and ASW connections. At first blush, the fact that soon after the Bureau of Ethnology (later the Bureau of American Ethnology, or BAE) was founded in 1879, with Powell as its director, DeHass became one of Powell's first employees, heading up the Division of Mound Exploration in 1881–82, looks as though it was the result of this long-standing acquaintance. But in reporting later on the founding of the bureau, Powell wrote (1894:xl):

> When the Bureau of Ethnology was first organized the energies of its members were devoted exclusively to the study of North American Indians, and the general subject

of archeology was neglected, it being the dominant purpose and preference of the Director to investigate the languages, arts, institutions and mythologies of extant tribes rather than prehistoric antiquities; but certain archeologists, by petition, asked Congress to so enlarge the scope of the Bureau as to include a study of the archeology of the United States.

Powell noted, however, that for the fiscal year 1881–82, Congress had placed a rider on the bureau's funding bill, earmarking some of the monies exclusively for investigation of the origins of mounds. For that year, "in compliance with the terms of the statute the work of investigating the mounds of the eastern half of the United States was at once organized, and Mr. Wills de Haas [sic] was placed in charge, as he was one of the men who had interested himself to have the investigation enlarged" (Powell 1894:xli). Powell's wording implies that DeHass's appointment was not a happy one for Powell, and indeed, DeHass was fired after the first year.

As a member of the staff of the Bureau of Ethnology, DeHass gave short papers at meetings of the AAAS on the progress of his work (see bibliography). Powell (1884:xxiv) listed him as carrying out investigations in West Virginia and adjacent portions of eastern Ohio at this time and indicated that the bureau's and Smithsonian's collections contained materials from DeHass's earlier visit to Missouri and Ohio. DeHass believed the mound builders were a separate race, and in one of the papers he gave at the AAAS (which he had also read at the ASW), he attacked the idea espoused by Lewis Henry Morgan, Lucien Carr, Powell, and others, that the mounds were built by the ancestors of modern Indians (DeHass 1881b).

Powell terminated DeHass at the end of his first year in charge of the Division of Mound Exploration and replaced him with Cyrus Thomas. Williams (1991:65) has referred to "early bungling" of the survey by DeHass and observed, "What is in the published record is that DeHass got very little done. He certainly was not a good field person" (2000:10). Jon Muller (2002:100) suggested a more intriguing picture, writing that Powell dismissed DeHass under mysterious circumstances, with the relevant documents deleted from the incoming mail and the copies of outgoing letters razored out of the letter books at the National Anthropological Archives.

DeHass did leave a legacy. Muller noted that in Cyrus Thomas's landmark volume on mounds (1894), he ultimately included a good deal of the material from a 256-page manuscript that DeHass had been compiling—"The Mound Builders: Their Monumental and Art Remains" (National Anthropological Archives manuscript 2430, U.S. Museum of Natural History). After being let go by Powell, DeHass largely dropped out of sight in archaeology, although he maintained his interest in mounds and American archaeology, giving a few reports in the anthropology section of the AAAS (DeHass 1886a, 1886b, 1888) and exploring a few ruins when he was named U.S. consul in Yucatán.

The year 1879 was one of major institutional events in Americanist anthropology. The most prominent scientific organization of the country, the AAAS, for the first time elected an anthropologist, Lewis Henry Morgan, as its president. Congress authorized the establishment of the Bureau of Ethnology, and two national anthropological organizations were established: the Anthropological Society of Washington, in Washington, D.C., and the Archaeological Institute of America, in Boston.

Although the Harvard crowd was involved with the AAAS, and some of its graduates to a lesser extent with the BAE and ASW, it is the AIA that is most directly relevant to our theme. In the spring of 1879 a letter signed by a dozen persons, mainly with Harvard linkages, went out to people in the Boston area who might be interested in forming a "Society for Archaeological Research." The letter was soon followed by a circular that gave its recipients the following rationale for forming the new society:

> It is proposed to establish a Society for the purpose of furthering and directing archaeological and artistic investigation and research.
>
> The increasing interest in archaeological science as its relations become better understood, the importance of the historical and artistic results of properly conducted explorations, and the immense extent of the field of work, embracing the sites of ancient civilization in the New World as well as in the Old, make it plain that such a Society is needed, in order to encourage and aid the efforts of individual explorers, and to send out special expeditions such as no individual could readily undertake.
>
> As yet America has taken small part in work of this sort, and has reaped but small benefit from it. Her own territory is imperfectly explored, she has had little share in the splendid work of rediscovery of the early civilizations of the Old World.
>
> The services which investigations undertaken under the direction of a Society such as is proposed may render, not only to the science of archaeology, but to classical and Biblical studies, and to the fine arts, by quickening the interest in antiquity and by increasing the resources of our Universities and Museums, are obvious. (Quoted in Donohue 1985:3)

After receiving 108 positive responses, the group moved ahead, and the official founding meetings of the Archaeological Institute of America were held on May 10 and 17, 1879 (Dort 1954:196). The initial circular called for research in both the New and Old Worlds, but that aim was almost immediately subverted.

Charles Eliot Norton had had one of his first students, **Harold North Fowler** (Harvard A.B. 1880) write and address the several score copies of the invitation that were sent out (Dort 1954:195). Fowler was in the classical archaeology camp; he was a student at the American School of Classical Studies in Athens in the first year of its existence, in 1882, under the directorship of William Goodwin. In 1885 he offered the first Harvard presentation in Greek archaeology—on the antiquities of Athens and Olympia—so he has been credited with starting the teaching of classical archaeology at Harvard (Chase 1930:130; Turner 1999:410). Fowler continued teaching Greek archaeology there until he moved to Phillips Exeter Academy in 1888. He later served as editor of the *American Journal of Archaeology* from 1907 to 1916 (Chase 1930:132).

This initial letter and circular for the AIA went out over the sponsoring names of Alexander Agassiz, Thomas G. Appleton, Martin Brimmer, Charles W. Eliot, William C. Endicott, William W. Goodwin, Ephraim W. Gurney, Henry P. Kidder, Augustus Lowell, Charles Eliot Norton, Charles C. Perkins, and Frederic W. Putnam. Besides Agassiz, Eliot, and Putnam, whom we have already introduced, who were the signers? Profiles of these men help in understanding why, in spite of lobbying by Putnam and Powell, among others, the AIA began with an almost exclusive devotion to classical archaeology, and why it maintains that bias today.

Thomas Gold Appleton (1812–84) received an A.B. from Harvard College in 1831 and an honorary A.M. in 1877. He was an amateur painter and writer, a collector, and a long-time patron of Boston museums, donating a number of Greek and Roman art objects, collected during his time as an aspiring artist in Europe, to the Boston Museum of Fine Arts. The Appleton family had links to later Peabody Museum personnel—Putnam's mother was an Appleton, and Alfred V. Kidder later married Madeline Appleton. Thomas Appleton's immediate linkage to the AIA seems to have been his interest in Greco-Roman heritage, which was based on his years in Europe and his friendship with Charles Eliot Norton, who was the principal champion of the AIA's focus on classical archaeology (Emerson 1918:222).

Martin Brimmer (1829–96) was a Boston merchant who, like almost the entire founding group, had substantial ties to Harvard. He had graduated with an A.B. in 1849, and he served as a fellow of the college in 1864–68 and 1877–96 and as an overseer in 1870–77 (Harvard University 1937:9, 37, 135). When the AIA was organized in 1879, Brimmer was elected vice president and served in that position during most of the organization's formative years. He also served as an officer of the Boston chapter of the AIA from its founding until his death (Annual Reports, Archaeological Institute of America, 1880 to 1896). Norton (1903:355) credited Brimmer, along with AIA executive committee member Francis Parkman, with providing the funds that allowed the AIA to succeed in its first few years.

Brimmer was more even-handed in his support of archaeology than several of the other officers of the new group, such as its president, Norton. When Putnam needed funds to help purchase Serpent Mound in Ohio, both Parkman and Brimmer added their endorsements to the subscription drive being circulated, at Putnam's suggestion, by Alice Fletcher and the women's groups she had recruited in Boston to help secure funds. In short order, more than $6,000 was raised (E. Brown 1949:225; Putnam 1888a:14, 1890d:872). Brimmer also provided major financial support for the Peabody Museum once its graduate program was approved in 1890 (Putnam 1895a:223).

On the other hand, Brimmer was equally if not more interested in classical archaeology. He had a long friendship with Norton, had taken care of Norton's business affairs when he left to go abroad in 1855, and had worked with him to establish the New England Loyal Publication Society in 1863, supporting the Union side of the Civil War (Turner 1999:125, 179). Brimmer served on Norton's board of trustees for the American

School of Classical Studies at Athens (Lord 1947:340) and assisted Appleton in securing classical specimens for the Boston Museum of Fine Arts. He published in classical archaeology, writing a book with his niece, Minna Timmins Chapman, on the history, religion, and art of ancient Egypt (Brimmer and Chapman 1892), based on his own travels in Egypt. The book was favorably reviewed by one of the principal Egyptologists of the day, Amelia B. Edwards (1892).

William Crowninshield Endicott (1826–1900) received his A.B. from Harvard in 1847 and then went into law. He served as a Harvard overseer from 1875 to 1885 and was a Harvard fellow from 1884 to 1895 (Harvard University 1937:9, 38). He was heavily involved in political life, serving as a judge from 1873 to 1882 and as secretary of war in President Grover Cleveland's cabinet from 1885 to 1889. He was also engaged with the Peabody Academy of Science at Salem, being one of the original nine members of its board of trustees in 1867 (Whitehill 1949:59) and, from 1869 until his death, vice president of the board. In addition, he was a member of the Peabody Educational Fund and the Massachusetts Historical Society. In these last activities one might expect him to have leaned slightly toward Americanist rather than classical archaeology, but if that was the case, it was never an important factor in his influence on the direction of the AIA, of which he became a life member.

William Watson Goodwin (1831–1912) was a member of the Harvard faculty. He received his A.B. from Harvard in 1851, having taken some courses with Agassiz, Gray, and Wyman, and then went to Germany, obtaining a Ph.D. in philology at the University of Goettingen in 1855 (Grandgent 1927:214). After returning to Harvard, he served as a tutor from 1856 to 1860, when he was appointed Eliot Professor of Greek Literature, a position he held until 1901. After his retirement he was an overseer from 1903 to 1909 (Harvard University 1937:40, 206). As a professor, Goodwin interacted with Putnam, teaching along with him in the Harvard Annex when it was first founded (Eliot 1924:7) and also giving one of the early series of Peabody Museum lectures to Harvard anthropology graduate students (Putnam 1895a:224). Goodwin sat on the executive committee of the AIA from its founding through its first decade. He became the first director of the AIA's American School of Classical Studies in Athens in 1882, setting up the first classes with seven graduate students and serving on the supervising committee of the school for the next several years (Turner 1999:298, 320). He also later served as vice president of the Egyptian Exploration Fund (Grandgent 1927:217), so his commitment to classical archaeology was clear.

Ephraim Whitman Gurney (1829–86) received his A.B. from Harvard in 1852, went on to serve as a tutor from 1856 to 1863, was appointed McLean Professor of Ancient and Modern History in 1863—a position he held until his death—and served as a fellow of Harvard Corporation from 1884 to 1886 (Harvard University 1937:9, 206). He was an old friend of Norton's, taking over as editor of *North American Review* when Norton went to Europe from 1868 to 1872 (Turner 1999:221). He was material in helping Eliot expand and professionalize Harvard College, particularly in the development of departments, and served as the first dean of the Harvard College faculty (Eliot 1924:7; Emerson 1918:443). Gurney became a life member of the Boston chapter of the AIA, and although his academic duties kept him from playing a particularly active role, his field of interest, history, biased him in favor of classical archaeology for the group.

One could wish that **Henry Purkitt Kidder** (1823–86) had been a recruit for the Americanist cause. His relatives A.V. Kidder, Homer Kidder, Alfred Kidder II, and Tristram R. Kidder, all Harvard graduates, later contributed in important ways to Americanist archaeology. Henry P. Kidder, however, seems to have been more interested in European archaeological work. He started out in the banking business with John E. Thayer and Brothers, later Nathaniel Thayer and Brothers, and subsequently bought out Thayer, establishing Kidder, Peabody and Company in its reorganization (Stafford 1941). According to a brief mention in the Harvard College president's report for 1885–86 (Harvard University 1886:4), "Mr. Kidder was not a college graduate; but he took a strong interest in institutions of education and religion." Kidder did provide some service to Harvard College, serving as an overseer from 1881 to 1886 and as a member of the Peabody Museum Visiting Committee (Brew 1966b:4; Harvard University 1937:40).

In addition to becoming a life member of the AIA in its second year, Kidder served as a member of the committee to solicit subscribers for AIA projects. He subsidized an excavation season for William J. Stillman in Crete and made a donation of artifacts from Crete to the Boston Museum of Fine Arts (AIA 1881:25, 32, 33).

Joseph Augustus Peabody Lowell (1830–1901) received his A.B. from Harvard in 1850. He was a member of the executive committee of the Massachusetts Historical Society (along with Eliot, Norton, and Perkins) and vice president of the American Academy of Arts and Sciences. More important, perhaps, he was the second trustee of the Lowell Institute from 1881 to 1900, taking over from his father, John Amory Lowell. (He was succeeded by his son, Abbott Lawrence Lowell, who was not only the grandson of Abbott Lawrence, founder of the Lawrence Scientific School, but also became president of Harvard in 1909 [M. Green 1966:53]). It is unclear whether Augustus Lowell had any bias for or against New World cultures, although he was linked closely with Norton and Perkins, who held strong biases in favor of Old World research.

Charles Callahan Perkins (1823–86) received his A.B. from Harvard in 1843 and an A.M. in 1846. He took further training at the American Academy of Arts and Sciences and at the Ecole des Beaux Artes in Paris. He was an amateur painter, art collector, and critic, a founder of the Boston Museum of Fine Arts in 1870, and president of the Boston Art Club from 1869 to 1879. His interest in archaeology was strictly classical in focus; he gave lectures on Greek and Italian art at the Lowell Institute in 1873–74 and 1879–80 (H. K. Smith 1895:728). At the first annual meeting of the AIA in 1880, when John Wesley Powell argued for support of North American studies, Perkins strongly opposed him, arguing that the group should focus exclusively on Old World sites to acquire materials for museums (Hinsley 2003:4).

Charles Eliot Norton (1827–1908), who became the first president of the AIA, was perhaps the most influential member of this founding group. Norton received his A.B. from Harvard in 1846 and an A.M. in 1849, and he actually evinced a brief interest in North American prehistory right after graduating. Francis Parkman suggested that Norton contact Ephraim G. Squier, with the aim of writing a review of Squier and Davis's 1847 volume on mound builders (Seitz 1911:19; Wade 1942:303). Norton did so and wrote a moderately favorable review (Norton 1849). For the most part, however, Norton was single-minded in his pursuit of European-based cultural artifacts.

Harvard president Thomas Hill asked Norton to deliver a course in a new university lecture series he instituted in 1863. Norton gave courses to auditors in this provisional graduate program in the spring term of 1864, but when Hill asked him to continue teaching the next term, Norton declined, instead continuing to take trips to Europe, to write for the *North American Review*, and to conduct similar personal business (Turner 1999:180). In 1874, when the Department of Fine Arts was established, Harvard president Charles Eliot named his cousin, Charles Eliot Norton, to run it (Harvard University 1937:345; Morison 1936:352). Norton held this position until he retired in 1898, when he became an overseer of Harvard from 1899 until his death in 1908.

Norton was enormously important in establishing the history of art as a discipline in American academia. Because he was well known among the faculty and students, he was the person to whom former "Salem secession" student Edward Morse turned in 1878 when the Japanese asked him to find someone to teach art in Japan (see chapter 3). One reason Norton had a large number of undergraduate students in his classes was that the coursework was undemanding. His ambition was to reach as many students as possible, and this goal was aided by a reputation for easy grades. In his first class, in 1875, he had 34 students, but by 1885 he had 125 of Harvard's 1,080 undergraduates in his course, making it among the largest courses. By 1889 his class had an enrollment of 250, and by 1895 this introductory class had 446 students, nearly a third of the undergraduates at Harvard (Rudolph 1977:175; Turner 1999:316). As Martin Green (1966:135) observed, "his courses in the history of art were large and popular, but that was apparently because they were easy to pass."

Norton's evaluators, although acknowledging the tremendous effect he had on the development of art history in the United States, have not always been kind to the content of his discourses. Laurence Veysey (1965:223) observed that his teaching was often irrelevant to his subject, sometimes consisting of little more than lengthy digressions about current events. Green (1966:139) commented more critically that Norton's influence and power in art history "must be judged in many ways destructive," because he exhibited an overwhelming nostalgia for European features and eschewed American things. Certainly in his decade as president of the AIA (1879–90), he managed to effectively exclude Americanist studies from the organization's research agenda.

From the very founding of the group, Norton had a vested interest in one area—Greek classical archaeology. The year before, in early 1878, Norton had asked the Greek government to allow a few recent Harvard graduates to excavate at Delphi, but he was turned down (Turner 1999:278). Thus, as he wrote many years later, "the chief motive which had led me to undertake this task [accepting the presidency of the AIA] was the hope that, by the establishment of such a society, the interests of classical scholarship in America might be advanced, and especially that it might lead to the foundation of a school of classical studies in Athens" (Norton 1903:351).

The deck was thus stacked against Putnam and the Americanists from the beginning. Out of the dozen men who signed the circular for the creation of the new archaeological society, only Putnam and perhaps Agassiz had clear Americanist interests. By far the bulk of these people had interests especially or only in classical archaeology. Nevertheless, Putnam and his allies tried to get the AIA to live up to its initial high-sounding statement of intent.

During the AIA's first annual meeting, in Boston in 1880, Putnam, Powell, and executive committee member Francis Parkman argued strongly for the support of Americanist studies. Other founding members, such as Charles Perkins, opposed them. They argued for the sole use of funds to acquire Old World artifacts for American museums, denigrated the usefulness of Americanist artifacts for display, and insisted that the need to buy classical antiquities required postponing any Americanist research indefinitely. They saw the function of the AIA as being to "improve the people and repay expenditure," so they saw no point in collecting "where the civilization was inferior to our own instead of superior." Racism prevailed. When Parkman rose to argue that what was needed was the "acquisition of knowledge and not the acquisition of objects or works of art," the classical archaeology supporters replied that the knowledge wanted "was not that of barbarians but that of cultivated races which had preceded us." Norton told the group that "while the archaeology of America offers many instructive analogies with the prehistoric archaeology of the Old World, it offers nothing to compare with the historic archaeology of civilized man in Africa, Asia, and Europe." He held that "what we might obtain from the Old World is what will tend to increase the standard of our civilization and culture" (Hinsley 1993:112, 2003:4–5; Snead 2002:124; Turner 1999:286).

In a concise summary, the classical archaeological scholar Phoebe Sheftel (1979:4) described the events at the May 15, 1880, meeting:

> By the time of the annual meeting (May 1880) the debate had accelerated and, despite the Institute's declaration of support for American study, Norton's presidential report fairly bristled with disparaging comments about the remains of his native land. He attempted to dismiss the controversy by stating, "Probably little of essential importance in respect to the character of the remains of aboriginal life lies undiscovered." Disdaining this pursuit of knowledge as merely "legitimate curiosity," he gave a scathing and highly personal assessment of the field. "The study of American archaeology relates, indeed, to the monuments of a race that never attained to a high degree of civilization, and that has left no trustworthy records of continuous history. It was a race

whose intelligence was for the most part of a low order, whose sentiments and emotions were confined within a narrow range, and whose imagination was never quickened to find expression for itself in poetic or artistic forms of beauty. From what it was or what it did nothing is to be learned that has any direct bearing on the progress of civilization."

Later during the same year Norton confessed his true feeling in a letter to Thomas Carlyle, dated July 26, 1880. "I don't care much for our American Archaeology (though as president of the society I must say this under my breath).... My interest in this new Archaeological Institute of ours springs from the confidence that it may do something to promote Greek studies among us."

Because Norton was eager to establish an American school of classical studies in the Mediterranean area, he saw any diversion of interest or funds to Americanist causes as a danger. With AIA backing, he was soon successful in establishing the American School of Classical Studies in Athens in 1882 (Sheftel 1979:4). Putnam wrote to Lewis Henry Morgan on January 31, 1880, complaining about Norton's attitude: "To my knowledge he has never been inside the Peabody Museum, and he has not the slightest idea of what I have been doing or am trying to do. If you can get him interested in the exploration of the remains of the ancient peoples of America you will be doing a good thing" (Hinsley 2003:5). But this was to no avail.

When the AIA was organized, with Norton elected president and Brimmer vice-president, the executive committee consisted of Agassiz, Goodwin, Parkman, Henry W. Haynes, and William R. Ware. Although Oliver W. Peabody was elected treasurer, and Edward H. Greenleaf, secretary (Thwing 1881:673), it is the president and executive committee that are mentioned in the archival documents as having made the critical decisions. Peabody and Greenleaf seem not to have been major players in the overall direction of the early AIA.

Was there any hope for Americanist archaeology in this executive group? We have already reviewed the interests of Agassiz, Brimmer, Goodwin, and Norton and seen little reason for Americanist encouragement. What about Ware, Parkman, and Haynes?

William Robert Ware (1832–1915) was a member of the Harvard class of 1852 and thus a classmate of Ephraim W. Gurney's. He went on to get an S.B. from Lawrence Scientific School in 1856. In 1861 he became the first head of the Department of Architecture at MIT, a position he held through 1881. At MIT he was interested in, among other things, the renaissance of the Greek revival style. He did not lose his allegiance to his alma mater but served on examining committees at the Lawrence School from 1859 onward and as a member of the visiting committee for Lawrence from 1870 onward. Later he designed Harvard buildings, notably Memorial Hall and Sanders Theater in 1865. Ware served as a de facto manager of the American School in Athens for several years, together with Norton, Goodwin, and John William White (1849–1917), a Harvard professor of Greek (Turner 1999:320). Ware, then, was clearly a member of the classical archaeology camp.

Francis Parkman Jr. (1823–93) received his A.B. in 1844 from Harvard, where he had become a good friend of Norton's (Wade 1942:319). He was the nephew of George Parkman, the professor who, as we mentioned in chapter 2, was the victim in a murder case in which Jeffries Wyman did some early forensic anthropology. Francis Parkman and his cousin, Quincy Adams Shaw (Alexander Agassiz's brother-in-law), went on a trip west in 1846 and came into contact with Lakota Sioux and other American Indian groups (Jacobs 1991:9, 30). Parkman began writing about the indigenous tribes in his 1849 journal of the trip, "The California and Oregon Trail," and continued his interest in Indian affairs with his 1851 book, *History of the Conspiracy of Pontiac.*

Parkman engaged in a lively correspondence with Ephraim Squier between 1849 and 1851 over the origins of the mound cultures. He was instrumental in getting the Lowell Institute to recruit Squier to give lectures on his Peruvian exploration work in 1866 (Seitz 1911). Parkman later had considerable correspondence with Lewis Henry Morgan over Morgan's 1851 book *League of the Ho-dé-no-sau-nee, or Iroquois,* particularly because he challenged many of Morgan's ideas (Doughty 1962:315). Parkman was aware of Putnam's work at the Peabody Museum, too, writing to Morgan in 1877 that "there are the beginnings of an archaeological museum here and I hope something will come of it" (Doughty 1962:314). With these credentials, Parkman was one of the few potential supporters of the Americanist position in the AIA.

Although a well-respected scholar, Parkman was not the most active of advocates at this time. He was beset by illnesses, apparently both real and imagined, according to his biographers (Doughty 1962; Jacobs 1991; Wade 1942). He suffered partial blindness in 1849, which prevented him from returning to the field and caused him to cut back on his historical research. One result was a shift to an interest in horticulture, and in 1866 he penned *The Book of Roses,* apparently still seen as a classic by gardeners. Over the next few years he wrote several other tracts on horticulture, and he served as president of the Massachusetts Horticultural Society from 1875 to 1878. Thus, at the time of his AIA service, he was as well known for horticulture as for history.

Parkman became more involved in Harvard over the years, serving as an overseer from 1868 to 1871 and from 1872 to 1875 and then as a fellow from 1875 to 1888. In 1869 he was credited by Eliot himself as being critical in breaking the deadlock among the overseers regarding the next president of Harvard and getting Eliot elected. As an overseer he helped Eliot enact his far-reaching educational reforms (Doughty 1962:317). In response, in 1871 Eliot named him professor of horticulture at Harvard's Bussey Institute, although Parkman resigned after a year in this position. During this time, some of the politicking went on in the prestigious Saturday Club, where Parkman interacted with Appleton, Brimmer, and others who were later part of the AIA group (Doughty 1962:293).

The AIA executive committee asked Lewis Henry Morgan to give a speech at its first meeting in 1880, capitalizing on the fact that Morgan had just been elected president of the AAAS that year. Morgan gave a presentation on his work titled "The Houses of the American Aborigines" (Turner 1999:286). After this talk, as a sop to the Americanist interests represented by Parkman, the AIA executive committee decided to engage Adolph Bandelier to continue Morgan's research in the U.S. Southwest, not only because of Parkman's urging but, more important, because of Parkman's promise of complete financial support. Bandelier worked on this project for the next five years. Parkman seems to have taken an active interest in the Southwest at this time, for he provided the funds not only for Bandelier's expeditions but also to help preserve the national monument site of Casa Grande, near Tucson, in 1889 (Fowler 1986:142). He also gave considerable financial assistance (Doughty 1962:316; Wade 1942:434) to Captain John Gregory Bourke (1846–96), whose writings on the Apaches and Hopis he called "studies from life" (Jacobs 1991:138). Powell published some of Bourke's work in the BAE reports, and Powell and Parkman collaborated in encouraging Bourke's research.

Henry Williamson Haynes (1831–1912), who rounds out our discussion of the executive committee of the early AIA, proved to be a surprise to Norton and his colleagues. Because Haynes later became a significant figure in some of the American archaeology debates, we offer here a few relevant observations about him in 1879 and return shortly to his evolving Americanist interests. Suffice it to say for the moment that Haynes had taught Latin and Greek from 1867 to 1873 and had spent much of the time from 1873 to 1878 investigating the archaeology of Europe, so he might have seemed a sure bet to fall into the classical archaeology camp. Much to Norton's chagrin, Haynes was undergoing a metamorphosis in his interests and, while he was in the AIA, spent a good deal of his time as one of the lone voices for Americanist studies, rather than championing classical archaeology as Norton had expected.

After providing the bit of eyewash "official" support for work by Adolph Bandelier in the Southwest, to satisfy the demands of Haynes, Morgan, Powell, Putnam, and others, Norton took the AIA completely into classical archaeology, a position that has remained essentially unchanged since his day. A brief review of the AIA's financial expenditures reconfirms its increasingly classical bent. In 1882, for example, the AIA received $5,620 for classical archaeology from the general membership drive, versus only $200 for Americanist archaeology. That year the AIA spent $10,267 on classical archaeology, principally for the new school in Athens, while Parkman's donation provided almost all the $2,457 given to Bandelier that year (Allen 2002:10).

Although the AIA retained some of the materials from its classical archaeology field schools in the early years, its leadership wanted no part of the Americanist materials and immediately turned over objects from Bandelier's excavations, as they came in from the field, to the Peabody Museum. Putnam wrote after the first season (1881a:24): "By the action of the Executive Committee of the Archaeological Institute of America, the American collections obtained by Mr. Bandelier, under the direction of the Institute, will be made over to the Museum as a permanent deposit." In subsequent reports he acknowledged receipt of the materials from the later work Bandelier did in the Southwest.

Putnam and his colleagues were defeated by the Euro-American ethnocentrism or bigotry of Norton and his friends, and most of the Americanists soon dropped out of the AIA. The organization became a hotbed of the late-nineteenth-century "philhellenism" that was taking literary circles by storm. It remained for a competing society, also founded in the spring of 1879, in Washington, D.C., to focus on the inhabitants of the Americas. This group, the Anthropological Society of Washington, was to establish *American Anthropologist,* the journal that in a later iteration became the flagship journal of the American Anthropological Association.

Putnam was lured to rejoin the AIA in 1899 when, because the group had become moribund, it proposed a new Americanist agenda as a strategy to increase its membership. Putnam became a member of the AIA's Standing Committee on American Archaeology, initially with Charles P. Bowditch as chair and, as the third member, a new recruit to the AIA, Franz Boas (Archaeological Institute of America 1899b). As we recount in a later chapter, this committee was enlarged twice, because from the perspective of the AIA leadership, Putnam, Bowditch, and Boas had unacceptably big plans to involve the AIA in Americanist archaeology. The tactic employed by the classical archaeology leadership was not to try to remove the trio, for they were important figures in Americanist studies by that time, but rather to pack the committee with other people who disagreed with them. Boas, Bowditch, and Putnam subsequently dropped out of the AIA after being outmaneuvered by the AIA leadership. Alice Fletcher, from her power base on the reconstituted Standing Committee on American Archaeology, would later become the chair and chief architect of the School of American Archaeology when the AIA established it in Santa Fe, New Mexico, in 1907.

Looking at some other professionals who were relatively indirectly involved with the Peabody Museum, we next return to Henry Williamson Haynes. Like so many of the other people we have covered relating to the AIA, Haynes was born in New England—in Bangor, Maine—and was a Harvard graduate, in the class of 1851. He taught for a few years, then studied law and was admitted to the bar in Boston in 1856. He received an A.M. from Harvard in 1859 and continued in law until 1867 (C. Peabody 1913:336). He then went to the University of Vermont, where he was a professor of Latin from 1867 to 1870 and of Greek from 1870 to 1873. (Because of his interest in languages, Henry Williamson Haynes has been confused by some researchers with Henry Harrison Haynes, Harvard class of 1873 and Harvard Ph.D. in philology 1899, who taught Semitic languages at Harvard from 1901 to 1907.)

Haynes became interested in archaeological and historical investigations during this period and resigned his professorship in 1873 to give his entire attention to such research. He spent much of the time from 1873 to 1878 in Europe studying antiquities and making collections from historic, prehistoric, and Paleolithic sites in Greece, Italy, Switzerland, Austria, Hungary, Denmark, Sweden, France, England, and Ireland and participating in international congresses (Putnam 1913:216). He spent the last winter before he returned to the United States, in 1877–78, in Egypt, doing surveys to look for Paleolithic sites. He presented a paper on his Egyptian work at the International Congress of Americanists in Paris in 1878 and published a version of it in the AAAS *Memoirs* (Haynes 1881a).

When Haynes returned from his European excursions, he joined a number of learned societies in order to exchange ideas with colleagues about his prehistoric interests. He became a trustee of the Boston Athenaeum, a member of the Massachusetts Historical Society, a member and later vice president of the Boston Society of Natural History, a fellow of the AAAS, a member of the executive committee of the AIA, a fellow of the ASW, a fellow of the American Academy of Arts and Sciences, and later a fellow of the American Anthropological Association.

Seemingly to everyone's surprise but his own, Haynes developed a new field of interest in archaeology when he returned from Europe, throwing himself enthusiastically into North American archaeology and becoming keenly interested in a question dear to Putnam's heart—the question of "Palaeolithic" occupations in the New World. Haynes also maintained his interest in Old World archaeology, writing short summaries for the AIA. One example comes from the nineteenth-century annual reports of the AIA in the Tozzer Library at the Peabody Museum, which were Haynes's own copies that he later donated to the library. In a handwritten note found in the margin of his copy of the sixth annual report, for 1885, Haynes indicated that he was actually the author of the archaeological summary on pages 27–47, a fact nowhere else noted in that publication. He apparently wrote similar sections for AIA annual reports in other years. And although Haynes shifted his interest primarily to Americanist archaeology in the next few decades, he did not give up teaching in Old World studies completely. Professor David G. Lyon, who founded the Semitic Museum at Harvard, reported that Haynes could be found occasionally teaching a course for that museum, beginning in 1900 (Lyon 1930:235).

Haynes kept a museum at his house that included most of the specimens he collected over the years—collections he transferred to the Peabody Museum shortly before his death. Putnam noted in his obituary for Haynes (1913a:216): "The only specimens in this country of the much discussed flints or "pseudo-eoliths" from Theney are also in the [Haynes] collection. His archaeological collecting trips in Europe began in 1873 and continued nearly to the time of his death. In August, 1911, he brought home the last specimens to be added to his already large museum which overflowed one good-size room in his home."

But it is Haynes's Americanist research and collections that are most relevant for our purposes. The 1880s were a busy decade for Haynes. He went looking for evidence of the antiquity of humans in New England, inland in Maine, Vermont, and New Hampshire as well as in coastal shell mounds and other sites. He reported on his find of a possible early stone "chopper" (Haynes 1882a) and his take on Abbott's materials from Trenton, Frances Babbitt's lithics from Little Falls, and other possible contenders for American

Upper Paleolithic tools (Haynes 1881b). He argued that the American Indians were latecomers to the Americas, in comparison with the human colonization of Europe, and that mound builders were the ancestors of the prehistoric tribes found historically in the area. He became interested in Edward Morse's arguments about the bow and arrow and wrote about evidence from New England for this technology (Haynes 1886a, 1888). He also wrote about later tool assemblages in New England, discussing agricultural implements and the quarrying and fabrication of soapstone bowls (Haynes 1883a, 1883b, 1886b).

Haynes became interested in the claim of possible cannibalism among shell-mound peoples, which was current in Americanist archaeology discussions of the time. To investigate the issue he excavated shell heaps on Mt. Desert Island, Maine, in the summers from 1878 to 1881. He reported that human bones were found in the same trash, and broken in the same manner, as the bones of moose, deer, bears, dogs, beavers, otters, seals, dogfish, geese, and great auks. He noted that his observations were the same as those reported by Manly Hardy in Maine, as well as those made by Putnam and Wyman in earlier reports (Haynes 1882b:60–62, 68; 1893a).

Haynes became interested in the complex civilizations of highland Mexico and wrote up the summary of them for volume 2 of Justin Winsor's *Narrative and Critical History of America* (Haynes 1886c). He wrote two crowning summaries of Americanist archaeology, one for the decade of the 1880s, for the tenth annual report of the AIA (Haynes 1889b), and the other an omnibus summary of North American archaeology for Winsor's *Narrative and Critical History of America* (Haynes 1889a). Haynes's stature in North American archaeology was emphasized elsewhere in Winsor's volume, in which Winsor reported (1889, 1:144) that he had relied on five experts for his information on American Indian cultures—Haynes, Daniel Brinton, Lucien Carr, Frederic Putnam, and Joaquín García Icazbalceta, a Mexican historian and specialist on the Aztecs.

In the 1890s Haynes's research attention seems to have turned almost wholly to the question of "Paleolithic man" in North America. He contributed an appendix on "Tertiary man" to *Man and the Glacial Period,* by George Frederick Wright, a book that engendered much controversy. He also wrote about Hilborne Cresson's supposed Paleolithic fish weirs in Delaware (Haynes 1890a, 1890b) and Paleolithic tools from Ohio (1890c, 1893c).

Haynes was particularly incensed at comments about his writings made by William H. Holmes (1893:135), then with the Bureau of Ethnology, who said that Haynes's 12 papers on paleoliths had only "two lines and a quarter of text" on actual data and that Professor Wright, whom Haynes vigorously championed, had not found a single item in glacial gravels. Therefore, discussion of the possibility of an American Palaeolithic should be entered into only with "real investigators" (Holmes 1893:136) such as Abbott, Cresson, and Metz, and not with what Holmes viewed as pretenders such as Haynes and Wright. Haynes responded bitterly (Haynes 1893b, 1893c, 1893d, 1893e, 1893f), among other things complaining that "there has been put forth by a little knot of men, principally connected with the U.S. Geological Survey," adverse commentary with little scientific basis (1893b:66). "The great difficulty about Mr. Holmes's discussion of this subject," wrote Haynes (1893e:291), "is that he has no correct appreciation of what a Paleolithic implement really looks like. This is not to be wondered at when we reflect that his studies in 'archaeology' have been limited to investigations of the subject of 'native art.'"

Clearly Haynes had no hesitation about leaping into the fray and questioning Holmes's credentials. In hindsight, however, Haynes was on the wrong side of the argument. Some of his other criticisms were better founded. He challenged Brinton's claim that Paleolithic man had pottery (Haynes 1894:161) and in doing so demonstrated good control of sources in the literature such as William Pengelly's work in 1859 showing the first proven associations of Upper Paleolithic fauna and human tools and the Marques de Nadaillac's excellent summary of American archaeology (Nadaillac 1884). He responded to some people's doubts about whether there actually were shell implements in shell heaps, detailing the shell artifacts he had found in his 1878–81 excavations at Frenchman's Bay on Mt. Desert Island (Haynes 1895).

Haynes's broad familiarity with these arguments provided him with the database from which to draw when he wrote his second 10-year summary of Americanist archaeology for the AIA in 1899 (Haynes 1900). Charles Peabody (1913:338) later observed that this report and Haynes's 1889 summary chapter were the two most important articles Haynes ever wrote.

Haynes had direct contact with the Peabody Museum in addition to that resulting from his interest in and support of Putnam's search for Paleolithic sites in the United States. As Putnam noted (1913:216), Haynes "was sincerely interested in its [the museum's] work and development and served on the Museum Visiting Committee from the time that committee was appointed by the Board of Overseers in 1890" until his death in 1912. He provided significant support for building up the holdings of the museum's library. "For several years," Putnam wrote (1913:216), "Professor Haynes had given to the Museum fifty dollars annually for binding serials in the library. By his will he left $1,000 as a fund, the income of which, by vote of the Museum Faculty, will be devoted to the same purpose."

Haynes had collected archaeological materials for more than 40 years but had donated items to the Peabody Museum only occasionally (Putnam 1888a:34). By his will, however, he bequeathed to the museum his private collection of prehistoric stone artifacts and his books and pamphlets relating to archaeology and ethnology. He left his Greek and Roman materials to the Fogg Art Museum at Harvard, his Egyptian collection to the Boston Museum of Fine Arts, and his fossil and mineral collection to the Boston Society of Natural History (Peabody 1913:342; Putnam 1913:220). Putnam had been alerted to the bequest shortly before Haynes's death, and he arranged for museum staff member Charles Peabody to catalogue the lithic specimens from Europe and North America that were destined to come to the museum while it was still possible to secure

Haynes's commentary on the items (Peabody 1913:340; Putnam 1913:220). Peabody (1913:342) wrote with pleasure that "in spite of his wide interests abroad, Professor Haynes by no means neglected his own immediate neighborhood, as witness the hundreds of archaeological specimens from New England included in the collections in the Peabody Museum."

Haynes, then, had been recruited by Norton for the AIA executive committee in 1879 because of his Greco-Roman interests but quickly revealed a strong interest in Americanist issues. He was nearly the lone voice for Americanist studies in most of the first quarter century of the AIA, because people like Putnam and Powell soon dropped out when they saw the direction in which Norton was taking the group. And Haynes was important in helping bring Putnam, Bowditch, and Boas into the AIA at the turn of the century, to staff a new Americanist initiative.

Justin Winsor (1831–97), whose name has come up a few times in this chapter and elsewhere in this book, merits a brief note here. He was another Harvard graduate, class of 1853 (although his A.B. was not awarded until 1868; Harvard University 1937:469), and was superintendent of the Boston Public Library from 1868 to 1877 (Koelsch 1983:59). In 1876 he helped organize and became president of the American Library Association, a position he held until 1885. In 1877 he was elected to the Massachusetts Historical Society, a prestigious organization at that time. Also that year he was appointed chief librarian at Harvard by an old classmate, Harvard president Charles Eliot. Winsor served in that position for the next 20 years, until his death. His research as a historian of "discovery," which resulted in his being recognized as an expert on early cartography and geography, began only after he became librarian at Harvard (Koelsch 1983:58). In 1884 he was a founding member and temporary president of a new group, the American Historical Association (Van Tassel 1960:175).

Winsor's eight-volume *Narrative and Critical History of America* (1884–89) is a work without equal in Americanist studies. Clarence Frederick Jewett, a noted Boston publisher, had brought out several local histories before he approached Winsor to do a history of Boston. After that three-volume project was successfully completed, Jewett was delighted and suggested a new project, a history of the United States (Van Tassel 1960:169). Winsor accepted the job as editor and set about getting experts to write chapters for the project. He ended up with 66 narrative essays written by 39 contributors, most of whom were also members of the Massachusetts Historical Society. Winsor is formally credited with at least 10 of the essays, but he did substantial editing of most of the others. Only the two essays by Nathaniel Shaler on the physiography of North America appear to have escaped Winsor's annotative spirit entirely (Koelsch 1983:62–63). In addition to the work he had Haynes and others do regarding American Indians, Winsor wrote his own chapter, "The Progress of Opinion Respecting the Origin and Antiquity of Man in America," a 40-page summary that is remarkable in its breadth and depth. It is the best single source we know of on the researchers of that period. Regrettably, few anthropologists today know of this masterful work.

We mentioned another of Putnam's professional contemporaries in chapter 2: **Othniel Charles Marsh** (1831–99), one of the nephews of George Peabody who influenced him in his decision to found the Peabody Museum. Marsh completed his undergraduate training at Yale in 1851 and continued with postgraduate training there in the Sheffield Scientific School, where he received his A.M. in 1862 (Schuchert 1939:5–6). In November that year Marsh visited Sir Charles Lyell in London and gave him a copy of a paper on fossil vertebrates. Lyell read the paper for Marsh at the Geological Society of London in December and published it in the society's proceedings in 1863. He put Marsh up for membership in the society in 1863 as well, a signal honor for such a neophyte scholar (Schuchert 1939:7). Lyell strongly urged Marsh to get involved in the study of mounds and of the antiquity of humans in North America, a piece of advice Marsh seems to have taken to heart (Grinnell 1910:291).

In 1863, after George Peabody worked out a preliminary plan for a scientific museum at Yale—the future Peabody Museum of Natural History—Yale rewarded Othniel Marsh for helping to bring in the museum by giving him the chair of geology and paleontology at the Sheffield Scientific School (F. Parker 1971:142). Marsh hoped to start his job at Yale in 1864, but Yale asked for a delay of a year, so he traveled in Europe and, in the summer of 1865, went to visit Ohio with his cousin George Peabody Russell. It was during this trip that Marsh and Russell visited the mounds at Newark, the visit that prompted Marsh to urge his uncle to direct his philanthropy at Harvard toward anthropology.

In February 1866 Marsh gave a paper on his explorations at the Ohio mounds to the Connecticut Academy of Arts and Sciences. He published the paper in the *American Journal of Science and Arts,* detailing, because of his interests, the animal species used in the archaeological assemblage (Marsh 1866:7–8). This made it one of the first zooarchaeological reports in the Americas. When he was finally appointed professor of paleontology at Yale's Sheffield Scientific School in July 1866, it was the first such chair in the United States. He kept the job at Sheffield until 1879, when he was transferred to Yale College (Schuchert 1939:8).

Marsh continued his interest in archaeology, although his emphasis was on paleontology, and maintained a correspondence with Frederic Putnam while Putnam was still at Salem. In reviewing Putnam's work with Alpheus Packard on Mammoth Cave in 1872, Marsh chided Putnam, writing to him, "I am only sorry you don't believe in Evolution, as all naturalists should who hope for liberation. You will come to it yet" (quoted in Dexter 1979:172). By 1874 Putnam was a reluctant evolutionist, and by the time of the AAAS meeting in Detroit in 1875, Putnam was called "an ardent evolutionist" (Dexter 1979:172). Ralph Dexter has argued (1979:171) that "Putnam's greatest contribution to evolutionary doctrine was its application to the evolution of man and primitive cultures he explored as one of the founders of American archaeology." Marsh, along with several of Putnam's colleagues, such as Hyatt and Powell, became a neo-Lamarckian.

When Jeffries Wyman died in 1874, Asa Gray first offered Marsh the job of curator of the Peabody Museum at Harvard, but Marsh turned it down (Schuchert and

LeVene 1940:230). However, Marsh had "Archaeology" added to Mineralogy, Geology, and Zoology as sections of the Yale Peabody Museum of Natural History in 1877, the same year he became president of the AAAS (Grinnell 1910:307; Schuchert and LeVene 1940:90). George Bird Grinnell (1910:305), commenting on Marsh's continuing interest in archaeology, wrote:

> On his return from Europe in 1866, he saw the importance of beginning a collection of American antiquities, and both before and during his western expeditions large numbers of ancient implements found their way to New Haven. Purchases were also made from collectors in various states, and through the liberality of friends of Yale many specimens have at various times been added. . . . Notable in this collection are the thousands of specimens from the Province of Chiriqui, Panama, mainly from prehistoric graves.

Marsh not only collected pottery from the Chiriqui area of Panama but also gave a paper in Putnam's Anthropology section at the AAAS meetings in 1878 titled "Ancient Pottery from Chiriqui, Central America" (Marsh 1879). In 1898 Marsh gave his collections to the Peabody Museum of Natural History, collections that contained not only vertebrate and invertebrate fossils and minerals but also fossil footprints, recent osteological specimens, and American archaeological materials (Grinnell 1910:304). The American materials included a number of collections from the lower Mississippi Valley, especially southeastern Missouri.

Another important professional who consulted and collaborated with Putnam and the Peabody Museum—in this case for nearly three decades—was **John Wesley Powell** (1834–1902). In the anthropological literature it is usually Powell's work in linguistics and ethnology that are mentioned, and justifiably so, but here we are equally interested in his contributions to archaeology.

Powell was born in Mt. Morris, now part of New York City, but the family soon moved to Ohio and then, when he was about 10 years old, to Wisconsin. Powell began his archaeological and natural history collections in the Midwest during his boyhood. "There were Indian mounds in Wisconsin as well as in Ohio, and there were the remains of much more recent aboriginal settlements and encampments. When the boy was about fourteen, he began to assemble a little museum of artifacts, as well as collections of flowers and insects" (Elman 1977:161).

His father, Rev. Joseph Powell, a Methodist minister, was named a trustee of the new Wesleyan college at Wheaton, Illinois, in 1851, and the family moved there when J. Wesley Powell was 17. Powell did not begin his formal scientific education until his twenties. In 1855 he entered the scientific department at Illinois College in Jacksonville, Illinois. In his hometown, the Illinois Institute, soon to be reorganized as Wheaton College under the Congregational Church, had also begun offering science, and Powell took courses there for a short while before entering Oberlin College, in Ohio, in 1858 (Elman 1977:162). He stayed there only briefly, however, and did not finish a degree program.

Also in 1858, Powell, along with Cyrus Thomas, later his employee at the Bureau of Ethnology, helped organize the Illinois State Natural History Society. Powell was named curator of conchology and secretary of the society, and Thomas served as president (Muller 2002:101). That same year Powell began a barnstorming tour of Illinois to urge the inclusion of science in the school curriculum, and as a result he secured a job teaching in the Hennepin, Illinois, public schools. In 1860 he was appointed superintendent of the Hennepin school system and took his lecture tour promoting science throughout Kentucky, Tennessee, and Mississippi (Jeter 1990:13). In addition, Powell had begun excavating mounds in Illinois, Missouri, Indiana, and Ohio in 1858–60 (Powell 1894:xxxix).

With the outbreak of the Civil War, Powell enlisted in the Union Army in May 1861. Even during the war he continued his archaeological explorations. He reported surveying and excavating mound sites in Missouri, Tennessee, and Mississippi from 1861 to 1864, as well as a cemetery of stone box graves near Nashville (Powell 1894:xl).

At the battle of Shiloh, on April 6, 1862, Captain John Wesley Powell, Battery F112, 2nd Illinois Artillery, lost his right arm. Among his fellow officers in the battle, as we mentioned earlier, was Lt. Col. Wills DeHass, who would later become Powell's first full-time employee dedicated to mound survey. Powell mustered out at the end of the war in 1865 as a major and returned to teaching, accepting a professorship in geology at Illinois Wesleyan University at Bloomington. Among the topics on which he lectured was the evidence for prehistoric humans (Elman 1977:192).

In 1866 Powell transferred to Illinois State Normal University, also in Bloomington, where in 1867 he secured funds to begin a museum and served as its first curator (Elman 1977:168). In 1866–67 he successfully sought state support for a revitalized Illinois Natural History Society and was named its curator. It was from the base of his university position and the natural history society that he began his justly famous explorations of the Colorado River area in 1867. During his later explorations (1869–73), supported by federal funding, Powell held the official title of director of the "Geological and Geographical Survey of the Colorado River of the West and Its Tributaries" (Stenger 1954:18–19).

In his 1867–73 fieldwork, Powell collected vocabularies of the Ute and Shoshone Indians, recorded their myths, social institutions, dress, religious ceremonies, customs, and art, and made ethnographic (and some archaeological) collections for the Smithsonian, Peabody, Illinois Normal, and other museums. For example, the 1873–74 Peabody Museum accession catalogue records a "collection of 22 specimens of seeds and fruits used by Paiutes, from Major J. W. Powell" (Putnam 1875a:16).

Powell was able to collect so much ethnographic information in part because he had a policy of having two or three Indians accompany him in the field, so he could quiz them as the expedition traveled (Hallowell 1960:32). "Powell was the first observer to systematically record details of the customs, practices, and beliefs of many of the Indians of the Canyon Country and the Great Basin," and he "called attention to the anthropology of the Canyon Country—the silent ruins of past cultures, as well as the historic tribes—and to the need for systematic study of these cultures and peoples" (Fowler and Fowler 1969b:22, 28). With respect to archaeology, Powell reported the ruins he observed and the broken pottery, stone tools, and basketry fragments recovered from eight prehistoric sites he explored in the Grand Canyon (Euler 1969:8).

In the late 1860s and 1870s, four great western geological surveys, run by Ferdinand V. Hayden, Clarence King, John Wesley Powell, and Lt. George M. Wheeler, respectively, ultimately contributed to the growth of government archaeology. For analyses of his survey's research findings, Powell began to focus on developing his own government agency, with particular expertise on Indians. In 1876 he hired two philologists, Rev. J. Owen Dorsey and Albert S. Gatschet, to work for his Rocky Mountain Survey (Fowler and Fowler 1969a:6). Dorsey had been an Episcopal missionary to the Ponca Indians of Iowa, and Gatschet had been a member of the Wheeler Survey.

In 1877 Powell added to his program. He hired Harry C. Yarrow, who had also worked on the Wheeler Survey, to work on Apache and Paiute ethnography, and Hayden's topographer and artist, William H. Holmes, who had previously spent three years studying Southwest Indian ruins while working for Hayden (Noelke 1974:24–25). In 1879 the components of the four western geological surveys were consolidated into the U.S. Geological Survey (USGS). At the same time, the Bureau of Ethnology was officially created, with Powell as its head and a staff of 11, 5 of them co-opted from his competitors (Noelke 1974:57). By 1881 Powell was head of the USGS as well.

In the late 1870s Powell continued his earlier interest in archaeology. For example, in 1877 he and Putnam enthusiastically explored mounds together in Tennessee (Putnam 1878a:203). At Putnam's request, Powell went up to Boston in 1879 to lobby the newly formed AIA to give equal time to Americanist archaeology.

In the spring of 1879 Powell was instrumental in helping establish the Anthropological Society of Washington, of which he was elected the group's first president, eventually serving nine terms (1879–87, 1895). He continued to exhibit a strong interest in anthropology, presenting the third largest number of papers at ASW meetings during the nineteenth century. As president he suggested in 1880 that the society explore and map shell heaps and other aboriginal remains along Chesapeake Bay and its tributaries (Lamb 1906).

When Powell took the position of head of the new Bureau of Ethnology in 1879, the Smithsonian's Spencer Baird asked him to report on what he had been doing in this arena over the last decade. He responded that his ethnographic studies had "heretofore embraced the following subjects," which he listed by number: "1. Somatology; 2. Philology; 3. Mythology; 4. Sociology; 5. Habits and customs; 6. Technology; 7. Archaeology; 8. History of Indian affairs" (Powell to Baird, April 2, 1880, quoted in Judd 1967:3).

Thus, although linguistics and ethnography are often seen as the principal goals of Powell's research, what he told his boss was that his work covered a much broader spectrum of anthropological interests. What he told the public, if we can judge by the words of Otis Mason, might have been somewhat different. Mason (1880a:218) reported that Powell had set up six goals for the Bureau of Ethnology: (1) preparing a history of Indian affairs, including an atlas of treaty cessions; (2) carrying on an exhaustive investigation concerning the languages of the North American Indians, including a series of grammars and dictionaries and a bibliography; (3) collecting of a complete synonymy of North American Indians as material for an encyclopedia or classical dictionary of every tribe known to have lived on the continent; (4) investigating sign language, something to be carried out by Garrick Mallery; (5) detailing Indian mythology or philosophy, under the special direction of Major Powell; and (6) studying the arts and industries of all tribes, something that included the work of James Stevenson, Frank Cushing, and Jack Hillars in the Southwest. In this last goal Powell explicitly included both prehistoric and contemporary artifacts, so there is no question that from the beginning of the work at the Bureau of Ethnology, Powell had an interest in archaeology.

Powell was a doctrinaire cultural evolutionist, much to the later dismay of Franz Boas. For example, a brief report of the 1882 meetings of Section H of the AAAS noted that "a most thoughtful and able paper was then read by Major Powell, on three culture periods—savagery, barbarism and civilization. The evolution of man was dwelt upon very earnestly by the speaker" (Anonymous 1883c:345).

Powell was also an early supporter of the idea that mounds were the constructs of surviving North American indigenous tribes. Thus his later assigning of Cyrus Thomas to do the research for what some have considered the government's "position paper" on mound origins, the classic 1894 report of the Bureau of Ethnology, is now interpreted more as a political move to satisfy his critics in Congress than as an endeavor of discovery. We can find many statements by Powell, written years before Thomas's work, that support this interpretation. For example, in 1881 he wrote:

> With regard to the mounds so widely scattered between the two oceans, it may also be said that mound-building tribes were known in the early history of discovery of this continent, and that the vestiges of art discovered do not excel in any respect the arts of the Indian tribes known to history. There is, therefore, no reason for us to search for an extra-limital origin through lost tribes for the arts discovered in the mounds of North America. (Powell 1881:74)

Moreover, at the November 20, 1883, meeting of the ASW, Powell reported that the work of the Bureau of Ethnology and the Peabody Museum "combined to show that the 'Moundbuilders' could not be classed as a people distinct from the historic Indians occupying those localities where such remains are still found" (Powell 1885:2, quoted in Williams 2000:11). In 1890 he wrote, "No fragment of evidence remains to support the figment of theory that there was an ancient race of Mound-builders superior in culture to the North American Indians" (Powell 1890a:492).

Powell had other views to share on the state of archaeology as well. He was unsure about the evidence for Upper Palaeolithic settlements in the Americas. On one hand, he noted that "in river deposits, in filled lakes and ponds, and in late glacial drift, a few stone implements have been discovered here and there, of rude type. It is thus we trace the presence of man in the United States back nearly to the middle of the Glacial Epoch" (Powell 1890a:500). On the other hand, he cited the work of William H. Holmes showing that the purported turtlebacks found in these deposits were quarry performs, observing that instead of being tools of great antiquity, "it is now known they have other explanations." He added: "During late years of investigation of this subject, many a hoax has been played, many a fraud perpetrated, and many an error committed" (Powell 1890a:502).

Powell believed that aboriginal languages and institutions sprang from many independent centers of origin throughout North America, and "the primal problem of American archaeology is in part geologic and in part cultural" (Powell 1890b:638–39). He argued, "It appears that the North American Indians were not largely migratory, but that the same peoples occupied the same districts of country from generation to generation, and that such permanency of habitat extends far into the past"(1890b:646). Therefore, in conducting research on artifacts, "first, they should be studied by tribes, or groups of cognate tribes, as far as this is possible; and, secondly, the material should be classified by arts, and the evolution of each art carefully traced" (1890b:645). On the basis of his research to that point, Powell thought that for North America including Mexico, "perhaps there will be from 80 to 85 great culture groups to be studied. Concomitant with these there may be an equal number of archaeological districts" (1890b:648). He could not keep from again expressing his displeasure over the disservice Norton had done to Americanist archaeology at the AIA, observing, "Our archaeologic institutes, our universities, and our scholars are threshing again the straw of the Orient for the stray grains that may be beaten out, while the sheaves of anthropology are stacked all over this continent; and they have no care for the grain which wastes while they journey beyond the seas" (1890b:652).

The collaboration between Putnam and Washington-based archaeologists such as Powell became a bit strained, however, as competition heated up between the Smithsonian Institution and U.S. National Museum, on one hand, and university museums such as the Peabody, on the other, in the attempt to secure the best comparative artifact collections. In a later chapter we remark on the zealous competition between Putnam, Powell, George Dorsey of the Field Museum, and other museum curators to tie field collectors to their respective institutions. Thus the spirit of equal collaboration of the 1870s gave way to somewhat more restrained relations in the 1880s. Putnam, for example, in a letter to Asa Gray on August 15, 1884, complained of the decision by Powell's Bureau of Ethnology staff to excavate mounds near his project in the Little Miami Valley, saying that he had been working there since 1880, and certainly the bureau could have found someplace else to work (Meltzer 2002:86 n. 8). Yet this irritation did not prevent Putnam from supporting Powell for an honorary LL.D. from Harvard in 1886, a special year, its 250th anniversary. All told, 42 other people received LL.D.s from Harvard that year, including such figures in our account as Spencer Baird, James Dwight Dana, and Othniel C. Marsh. In addition, Powell and Putnam frequently exchanged materials between their two museums throughout this period.

In 1890, a bitter rivalry between Edward Cope and Othniel Marsh over fossil collecting in the West, which became known as the Bone Wars, spilled over into the BAE and Powell's life. In 1882 Powell had appointed Marsh to act as his chief of vertebrate paleontology, a position Marsh kept until 1892. Marsh and Cope competed head-to-head over many discoveries of new paleontological fossils during this decade, and federal backing resulted in Marsh's eventual "victory" in the conflict. Cope took his frustration out in a full-page ad against Marsh and Powell published in the *New York Herald* in 1890 (Schuchert 1939:14).

Most commentators discuss the effect the Cope-Marsh conflict had on the scientific community, but another domino-like effect it had was to give Powell's detractors additional support for attacking his work and his agency in Congress. In the scientific world, zoologist Alexander Agassiz was one of Powell's severest critics (Champlin 1994:144). His Harvard colleague Nathaniel Shaler, however, was a loyal supporter of Powell's, after having served as director of the Atlantic Coast Division of the USGS in 1884. In 1894 he offered to go to Washington, D.C., to support Powell and Marsh in congressional hearings (Livingstone 1987:36, 43). Powell had already upset a number of powerful western land interests, and the public controversy surrounding Marsh and Cope added another factor, resulting in a 30 percent cut in the Bureau of Ethnology's budget in 1892, the consequent discharge of Marsh and many geologists, and the de facto end of Powell's active western research (Schuchert 1939:14, 26). The loss of support resulted in Powell's resigning as director of the USGS in 1894, although he kept his position as head of the Bureau of (American) Ethnology until he died in 1902. After 1894, however, he spent increasingly less time running the bureau and more on his philosophical and ethnographic writings.

The first two decades after Putnam became curator of the Peabody Museum thus saw him working primarily with fellow professionals as well as volunteer collectors in the field in his attempt to develop anthropology at Harvard. He found some collaborators, such as his Harvard colleagues Justin Winsor and Henry W. Haynes, who seemed to share his goals. He was frustrated by some presumed peers, particularly those in the AIA, who did not share his broad-based vision of what the study of human history involved. In addition to addressing the ethnocentrism of this group, he was beginning to address the critical need for more professional and rigorous research strategies, rather than the widely accepted casual collecting that characterized anthropology at the time. The competition in presumed salvage ethnology, as well as salvage archaeology—particularly with Powell at the Smithsonian Institution—made it more difficult to institute such new procedures.

Putnam's first attempts at recruiting students and establishing support organizations such as the Archaeological Institute of America were unsatisfactory. In the ensuing years, as we detail in the next chapters, he shifted his energy toward developing educational programs in universities. He established anthropology programs at Harvard and Berkeley and played important roles in launching a program at Columbia and revitalizing one at Pennsylvania. He also devoted significant energy to establishing specifically anthropological (and sometimes Americanist archaeological) organizations. He had learned the hard way that his endeavors in broader-based scientific organizations could be thwarted by people with competing political agendas.

6

Development of the Harvard Anthropology Graduate Program, 1890–1900

THE DEVELOPMENT OF EDUCATIONAL PROGRAMS, especially graduate programs, is a topic little known among students of anthropology. It is widely recognized that the existing paradigm has not always prevailed, but little real understanding exists about how anthropology as a discipline and, particularly, research-based graduate studies in anthropology originated. In casual conversations with colleagues we found an almost complete lack of knowledge about the basic development of universities' current elective systems and of graduate work in American schools. We believe that in order to explain the development of anthropology at Harvard in the 1890s, we need first to describe the development of the dominant education paradigm in American graduate education. In this chapter, therefore, we depart somewhat from our usual format and discuss several themes in American education that we consider relevant to the growth of anthropology, before looking specifically at developments at Harvard.

Dorothy Ross (1979) made the argument that the emergence of the social sciences at the end of the nineteenth century was due to three factors: the influence of advocates of social and educational reform in the 1870s; academic pioneers of the 1870s (such as Putnam at the Peabody) who introduced social sciences into the curriculum as independent subjects; and a cadre of German-trained Ph.D.s who took the lead in defining new disciplines in the 1880s. Here we are particularly interested in the development of anthropology at the Peabody Museum in the context of these three factors, as well as others that we develop.

In terms of the social and educational reform component, Thomas Bender (1993:34) argued that inclusive diversity of urban intellectual life in the eighteenth-century city was replaced in the twentieth century by the city of "closed social cells." In the transition period, between roughly 1840 and 1875, he argued, confusion reigned among intellectuals, who saw the end of one standard but did not yet clearly see the succeeding paradigm. As the old pattern collapsed, intellectuals looked for viable institutional means of achieving social order. In the United States, Bender argued, the solution was achieved through the development of graduate education.

Harvard was a leader in part of the educational reform, but not in all of its aspects. Before 1860, essentially no post-A.B. educational opportunities existed in the United States. The first true graduate schools in the country were established only after the Civil War, as the country's need for specialized expertise expanded. In 1870 there were fewer than 50 graduate students in U.S. universities; by 1900, there were nearly 6,000 (Oleson and Voss 1979:xii). In the 1870s, research played no important role in American higher education. By 1880 this had begun to change, and by 1890 research had become one of the dominant concerns of American higher education.

Before 1860, pure research-based degrees were offered in Germany but not in France or England (Veysey 1965:127). German universities thus had developed a reputation in research, and it was partly this prestige that drew American students to them for graduate degrees. Harvard president Thomas Hill, Charles Eliot's predecessor, had noted in 1868 that a major problem for Harvard and other American universities was that "a University, richly endowed with chairs of pure science . . . does not exist in the country; it is a national want, and its need is testified by the multitudes of young men from America who are found in German universities" (quoted in Pusey 1969:vi–vii).

Some pragmatic reasons also drew American students to Germany. German universities imposed fewer admissions requirements than American institutions, and in most cases there were no examinations, which made it relatively easy to obtain a Ph.D. (Caullery 1922:22; Oleson and Voss 1979:xx, n. 12). The German Ph.D. was designed to train European "gymnasium" teachers, so only a brief dissertation in three subjects (such as history, geography, and mathematics) was required (Higham 1979:11). Earning the degree was also relatively inexpensive. Even as late as 1889, one year's study in Germany was cheaper by a third than a year of graduate work at Johns Hopkins, Harvard, or Cornell—and this included all the costs of travel from the United States to Germany (Veysey 1965:130). The low cost, ease of admission, and short term of study all made the German Ph.D. attractive. The peak year for study in Germany by American students wanting graduate degrees was the 1895–96 school year, when 517 American students were enrolled in Ph.D. programs at German universities (Veysey 1965:130).

When the Ph.D. degree was established in the United States, the American colleges converted the degree from its German format into an advanced degree for students specializing in one field. The tradition of "pure research" was adopted from Germany, but it was institutionalized in a new ambience, in newly formed departmental settings. The American professor was required to teach and hence lacked the leisure and freedom of the German university "Privatdozent" (Shils 1979:30). The American focus on departments fostered an entirely different sort of academic relationship from that in Europe, with its limited professoriate.

Because of the reconfigured emphasis on teaching and research in the American conception of a Ph.D. degree, after the mid-1890s the number of American graduate students studying in Germany declined steadily (Higham 1979:12; Veysey 1965:131). Whereas the degree in Germany required only one year, by the late 1890s it took an

A.B. (which required minimally three years), two years of additional study, and a dissertation to obtain a Ph.D. from an American institution. The American Ph.D. was thus more rigorous (Reingold 1986:145). When Frederic Putnam established the graduate program in anthropology at Harvard in 1890, he instituted a requirement of three years beyond the A.B. for the Ph.D., which made his the most rigorous program in the United States—hence the almost immediate high reputation of any anthropology Ph.D. from Harvard.

The redesigned German-style Ph.D. degree program was first adopted in 1861 by Yale, where Arthur William Wright received the first American Ph.D. By the mid-1870s there were Ph.D. programs at Cornell, Harvard, and Johns Hopkins (Reingold 1986:136). Harvard introduced the D.Sc. degree along with the Ph.D. in 1872, but the D.Sc. was later converted into an honorary degree only (Higham 1979:12). Johns Hopkins University (in 1876), Clark University (in 1887), and the University of Chicago (in 1892) were established primarily as graduate schools, although they were later forced to add more undergraduate teaching than they had originally anticipated (Shils 1979:28). By 1893, some amount of graduate work was required to secure a permanent teaching appointment at nearly every major university. By 1900 a Ph.D. was often expected and nearly mandatory (Veysey 1965:176).

Referring to Charles Eliot, president of Harvard from 1869 to 1909, Hugh Hawkins (1972:288) wrote, "Specialization is the term that represents the tendency of Eliot's educational reforms most completely." Eliot was faced with showing how specialization functioned for the university, no matter how unegalitarian it seemed. Specialization went hand in hand with the expansion and modernization of universities and the development of departments. Before the 1870s or 1880s, teaching had been the principal emphasis, and colleges had not recognized research as a necessary part of professors' scholarly function. This pattern changed by the end of the century.

The major period of department formation was the 1890s. Harvard moved in this direction in 1890, Chicago was organized around departments in 1892, and Columbia, Yale, and Princeton all reorganized into departments later in the decade. Other major universities rapidly followed suit, so that shortly after 1900 the establishment of new departmental fields tapered off (Veysey 1965:320–21). The new focus on research in academia changed the intellectual environment, and governmental scientific institutions such as, in anthropology, the Bureau of American Ethnology and the Smithsonian Institution, which had previously been the primary domains of research, began to lose their position of dominance in scholarly issues. In the academic realm, the new pattern of secular control and the specialized, department-based studies that evolved broke the pattern of sectarian-sponsored, fixed-curriculum colleges that had dominated American education during the eighteenth and most of the nineteenth century (McCaughey 1974).

Johns Hopkins University initially was able to turn its research focus into a tremendous lead in graduate training. It opened in 1876 with an enrollment of 54 graduate students and 12 undergraduates, and between 1878 and 1889 it awarded 151 Ph.D.s and

S.D.s. Yale, in contrast, awarded 101, and Harvard only 55 (Hawkins 1972:65; Reingold 1986:138). Johns Hopkins took the early lead in establishing quality controls as well. In 1877–78 it formalized its requirements for the Ph.D. to two years beyond the A.B., in one main subject and one subsidiary subject, supported by a disciplinary dissertation.

But by 1915 Hopkins was a follower, adopting the shift previously initiated by Harvard and other major universities toward increasing the time required for the degree to three years (Higham 1979:11). After the first surge of interest in the Hopkins program, the novelty wore off, and Hopkins ran into financial trouble. By 1892, Harvard, Columbia, and Chicago had taken the lead in producing Ph.D.s (Hawkins 1979:291; Veysey 1965: 165). For the years between 1898 and 1915, the top graduate schools in terms of numbers of Ph.D.s produced were, in rank order, Columbia, Chicago, Harvard, and Yale, with Johns Hopkins coming in fifth (Caullery 1922:95).

Nevertheless, Hopkins had a major influence on American academia in the late nineteenth century. By 1891, 184 out of 212 Hopkins Ph.D.s were teaching in American universities (Reingold 1986:139). The number of Ph.D.s granted by Harvard exceeded the number granted by Johns Hopkins for the first time in only 1900. Initially, the majority of Harvard Ph.D.s went to students whose undergraduate degrees had also been awarded by Harvard; not until 1904 did more than half the graduate students enrolled in Harvard programs come from other colleges (Hawkins 1972:58).

Before 1865, in terms of programs, little related to a social science existed independently. With the expansion of the universities in the 1870s and 1880s, psychology, anthropology, economics, sociology, and political science began to emerge, although they did not all completely crystallize their separate identities until after 1920 (Ross 1979:107; Shils 1979:39). In the social sciences, as in other areas, the development of departments transformed heterogeneous and somewhat embryonic bodies of intellectual activities and beliefs into disciplines. At Harvard, President Eliot's early appointment in the 1870s of individuals who became founding figures helped to establish strong, autonomous departments in anthropology, psychology, economics, and history (Ross 1979:124).

Most social scientists were in academia. Only in anthropology was there the significant possibility of working for the government or in museums. As higher education began to expand in the 1890s and the traditional curriculum was displaced, a market for academics in the social sciences began to emerge. By 1896, a quarter of the graduate students in the United States were taking training in the social sciences. Most new academic fields had emerged by this time and had been established as separate departments (Veysey 1965:173, 321).

As the young, research-oriented scholars gained prominence, the influence on the directions of university studies by the old, established academic elites, mainly humanists, gradually weakened. This change led in some instances to rearguard sniping by the elder statesman scholars, displaced from their position of dominance, who were less enamored of the new focus on research and specialized disciplines. In this respect, a quotable member of the old guard—the humanists who had ruled colleges for more than 200 years—is James Russell Lowell (1819–91), the American poet, critic, and editor of the *Atlantic Monthly* and later the *North American Review*. Lowell, a member of the Harvard class of 1838 and a Harvard professor from 1855 to 1886, was uncomfortable with science, as were many humanists. He said of science, "I hate it. I hate it as a savage hates writing, because I fear it will hurt me somehow" (quoted in Green 1966:175). Of the new focus on research, Lowell opined that "mere scholarship is as useless as the collecting of old postage stamps" (quoted in Veysey 1965:201). Other humanists derided the new research-oriented scholars as pedants or intellectual spinsters, saw the publication of research papers as a mania, and reserved special scorn for the social sciences as "demi-sciences."

A corollary of the development of departments was the replacement of local learned societies and academies of generalists by national associations of specialists. These organizations began to develop in the 1880s around the new specialized disciplines represented in the departments (Oleson and Voss 1979:xiv; Shils 1979:35). Universities encouraged the emergence of such professional associations because they offered good venues in which to discover candidates for faculties (Hawkins 1979:298). Within the social sciences, economics, anthropology, psychology, and political science had formed professional journals by the 1880s, and sociology followed in the 1890s (Ross 1979:108). Academics increasingly looked to the new, discipline-specific associations for intellectual support. Between 1876 and 1905, 13 major scholarly societies were established in the United States, including the American Historical Association in 1884, the American Economic Association in 1885, the Geological Society of America in 1888, the American Psychological Association in 1892, the American Anthropological Association in 1902, the American Political Science Association in 1903, and the American Sociological Association in 1905 (Bender 1987:278).

The direction of anthropology at Harvard was influenced to some extent by the development of graduate education at Clark University, in Worcester, Massachusetts, by G. Stanley Hall, its first president, and by the anthropology taught there by Franz Boas and Albert F. Chamberlain. In the fall of 1876, more than a decade before Clark University was established, **Granville Stanley Hall** (1844–1924) entered the Department of Philosophy at Harvard to work with William James in psychology. He received his Ph.D. from Harvard in June 1878, the first Ph.D. in the department and the first Ph.D. in psychology to be given in the United States (Ross 1972:62, 77, 79). In the fall of 1880, President Eliot of Harvard offered Hall a lectureship in pedagogy and the history of philosophy, aimed primarily at teachers in Boston (Hawkins 1972:252). But even before Hall finished his first series of lectures, President Gilman of Johns Hopkins offered him a new position there as guest lecturer, which he accepted and began in January 1882, advancing to staff lectureship in 1883 (Ross 1972:112, 134). Hall organized the psychological laboratory at Johns Hopkins when he arrived in 1882 and founded the *American*

Journal of Psychology from there in 1887. Unfortunately, he also ran into some personality differences, driving away from Johns Hopkins two of the department's strongest students, James McKeen Cattell and John Dewey (Ross 1972:145).

After 15 years, the excitement of the new graduate education focus at Johns Hopkins was waning, and the institution began experiencing financial troubles (Veysey 1965:164). Millionaire magnate Jonas G. Clark, of Worcester, Massachusetts, was in a position to exploit this situation. In November 1885 Clark's old California friend U.S. Senator Leland Stanford Jr. launched a new university bearing his name. Clark then became excited about starting his own institution and in 1886 discussed the idea of forming a new university with a strong graduate emphasis with Andrew D. White, president of Cornell, and Charles W. Eliot, president of Harvard (Koelsch 1987:6). To serve on his board of trustees, he secured a number of graduates, trustees, and overseers from Harvard, as well as some other local donors, including Harvard-related people such as Stephen Salisbury II, the wealthiest man in Worcester, a bank president and landowner, president of the American Antiquarian Society, and a trustee of the Peabody Museum; John D. Washburn, from the Harvard Law School; and U.S. Senator George Frisbie Hoar, later a member of the Harvard Board of Overseers (Koelsch 1987:7–8; Ross 1972:188). These trustees were successful in luring Hall away from Johns Hopkins to become president of the new university, which was envisioned as a "purer" Johns Hopkins–style, graduate-focused institution (Veysey 1965:164).

When Clark University opened in Worcester in 1889, it had a faculty of 18, along with 34 graduate students, 12 of whom already had Ph.D. degrees. By the end of the first year there were 52 faculty members, 19 of whom had studied in Germany and 15 of whom Hall had attracted away from Johns Hopkins, taking advantage of its financial woes (Hawkins 1979:287; Koelsch 1987:24). Hall was also head of the department of psychology at Clark, a department with five other staff members, which offered training in anthropology, education, neurology, and philosophy as well as psychology (Koelsch 1987:29; W. Ryan 1939:57).

Hall had developed an interest in anthropology sometime earlier, and he gave a lecture course in psychological anthropology at Johns Hopkins at least as early as 1887 (Ross 1972:164). For the staff anthropologist at Clark, hired at the level of a "docent," G. Stanley Hall recruited Franz Boas. The two had met on a train while traveling to Cleveland to attend the AAAS meetings in September 1888, when Boas was geography editor of *Science*. In August 1889 Hall offered Boas the docent's position at Clark, telling Boas that he wanted teaching on myths, customs, and beliefs rather than craniology and prehistoric remains and industries (Koelsch 1987:29; Ross 1972:196). The docent position was intended for young scholars, often untried, who would teach only one course of lectures. The position was essentially designed to be only half-time, with a commensurately low salary. Hall got full-time faculty work from Boas, however, by making him direct students and laboratory work in addition to the lecturing that the position officially called for (Ross 1972:197, 216). According to Dorothy Ross (1972:31), "the promise of unlimited laboratory and library facilities and of plenty of time (including full summers) for research moved Boas to accept Hall's offer of a docentship in anthropology, the first such non-museum appointment in that discipline in America, at a salary of only $1,000 a year, half what he had been getting at *Science*."

Boas's first course in anthropology at Clark, titled "The Psychology of Language, Myth, Custom and Belief Anthropologically Considered," was offered in May 1890. With the new academic year, anthropology was set up as a subdepartment of psychology, and Boas gave courses in physical anthropology and the anthropology of Africa. In the spring of 1892 he added a course in the application of statistics to anthropology (Chamberlain 1894:52). One of Stanley Hall's Ph.D. committee members from Harvard, Henry Pickering Bowditch, had been interested in anthropometric measurements of schoolchildren, and Boas seems to have been influenced by Hall to become involved in this research (Boas 1891). It later became the basis for Boas's studies of human growth and form. In the fall of 1891, local newspapers such as the *Worcester Telegram* attacked Boas's plan to take physical measurements of the city's schoolchildren, apparently in part because Boas was simultaneously sending his students to measure the heads of "insane people and idiots" in New England asylums in 1890 and 1891 (Koelsch 1987:33; Ross 1972:210, 218).

Jonas Clark, as it turned out, failed in his promise of funding the infant institution, and by 1892 Clark University was in financial crisis. In January that year, Boas's colleague Charles Otis Whitman tried to get William Rainey Harper to hire seven Clark instructors, including Boas, at the newly organized University of Chicago, but Harper refused to take Boas, apparently because Boas lacked any national visibility at that point (Ross 1972:220). Owing to the financial crisis, two-thirds of the faculty and 70 percent of the students left Clark in the spring of 1892, half of them going directly to Chicago. For example, of the 16 biologists at Clark in 1892, all but 4 went to Chicago. At the start of the fourth year at Clark, in the fall of 1892, only 12 faculty and 40 students remained (Ross 1972:220; Ryan 1939:63; Veysey 1965:167). Although Hall complained of what he considered the unethical recruiting actions of Chicago's Harper, the complaint, as William A. Koelsch (1987:24) pointed out, rang hollow, considering that Hall had similarly raided Johns Hopkins three years earlier when he was staffing Clark.

Alexander Francis Chamberlain (1865–1914) was the first "fellow" appointed in anthropology at Clark, in June 1890; his first course, "The Relation of Linguistics to Psychology and Anthropology," was given in the spring of 1891. In November 1890, Dr. Gerald M. West was appointed as the second fellow. He was named assistant in anthropology in 1891 and in the spring of 1892 gave the course "The Growth of School Children," based on investigations in the public and private schools of Worcester, a project begun and continued under Boas (Chamberlain 1894:52; Ryan 1939:71–72). Boas resigned in the spring of 1892 because of the financial crisis at Clark and went to work with Frederic Putnam at the World's Columbian Exposition in Chicago. Gerald West, too, resigned; he left for the University of Chicago, where he was appointed a docent in

1893 (Chamberlain 1894:53). Chamberlain, Boas's first Ph.D., was appointed lecturer in anthropology in the fall of 1892, to succeed Boas.

Chamberlain had been born in England, but his family emigrated to New York when he was a child and later moved to Canada. There Chamberlain entered the University of Toronto, receiving an A.B in 1886 in modern languages and ethnology. At Toronto he was a student of **Sir Daniel Wilson** (1816–92) (Gilbertson 1914:337), who in 1854 taught the first course including ethnology to be offered in Canada (Levin, Avrith, and Barrett 1984:1), as part of the curriculum of his courses in history. Wilson was also the first English speaker to use the term *prehistory*. Frederic Putnam commented with appreciation on Wilson's coining of "that most useful word, prehistoric" (Putnam 1899b:227) and, writing about Wilson's 1851 archaeological work, said, "I think we may fairly reckon the beginning of a new epoch in archaeological investigation as coincident with the introduction of this new term, prehistoric" (Putnam 1973 [1898]:160).

Wilson became interested in "antiquarianism" in 1842 and conducted his first dig in Scotland in 1851. In 1853 he accepted an offer to chair the Department of History and English Literature at University College in Toronto. He became the second president of University College in 1880 and the first president of the reorganized University of Toronto, which included University College, in 1887. He simultaneously served as chair of history and ethnology from 1884 to 1892 (Chamberlain 1894:51; Hale 1893:259).

Alice Kehoe (1998) believed Wilson's contributions had only recently been appreciated, but a quick survey of nineteenth-century sources indicates that his work was widely read at the time. However, Wilson is remembered in Canada mainly for his work in promoting higher education. Bruce Trigger (1966:26, 1992:57) argued that Wilson's contemporaries saw him essentially as a skillful administrator, an educational reformer, and the champion of the University of Toronto, but not as a scholar. Consequently, they viewed what little he said about archaeology as "that of a dilettante" (Trigger 1966:4), and they viewed his studies in anthropology mainly as a hobby (1966:26). Trigger also argued that Wilson's role in teaching the first anthropology in Canada was of little importance because he never trained any specialized students of his own in anthropology (1966:26).

Trigger, we believe, was in error in this characterization. Alexander Francis Chamberlain stands out as an excellent example of a student trained by Wilson, and he clearly acknowledged Wilson as his mentor (Chamberlain 1894:52). Under Wilson's guidance, for example, he wrote a short paper as an undergraduate in the early 1880s titled "Contributions towards a Bibliography of the Archaeology of the Dominion of Canada and Newfoundland." In 1889 he followed this up with a paper written under Wilson's guidance, "The Archaeology of Scugog Island."

Chamberlain, however, while working on his A.M. with Wilson, initially found employment in languages rather than ethnology. He was appointed a fellow in modern languages at University College, Toronto, from 1887 until 1890, serving as examiner in German, French, and modern languages (Gilbertson 1914:338). His initial post-degree role in languages perhaps led Trigger to dismiss Wilson's influence. But it was also during this period that Chamberlain began working as a graduate student under Wilson's guidance with the Mississagua Algonkian Indians, studying their language and customs. He received his A.M. on this topic from the University of Toronto in 1889. In addition, Chamberlain wrote several ethnographic papers derived principally from his Mississagua work, possibly the most important of which, from a career standpoint, was "The Relationship of the American Languages," published in *Science* in 1887. That was during the time when Franz Boas was assistant editor at *Science,* and it apparently was Boas's introduction to Chamberlain.

In 1890 Chamberlain accepted the fellowship in anthropology at Clark University, where he went to work with Boas. He received his Ph.D. there in 1892, on the language of the Mississagua Indians (Gilbertson 1914:338). Chamberlain was appointed lecturer to replace Boas in 1892 and was sequentially promoted through the ranks to full professor in 1911. During this time Chamberlain served as editor of *Journal of American Folk-Lore* (1900–1908); associate editor of *American Anthropologist* and *American Journal of Archaeology;* co-editor, with G. Stanley Hall, of *Journal of Religious Psychology;* vice president of the American Anthropological Association; and secretary of Section H of the AAAS (Gilbertson 1914:339).

Frederica de Laguna (1960:455) noted that "Chamberlain and Hall made Clark University a center for investigations into childhood and adolescence to judge from book reviews, the titles of papers read at meetings, and the dissertation, 'The Adolescent Girl among Primitive Peoples,' presented by Miriam van Waters for her Ph.D. in anthropology." But this research strength was not enough to save anthropology at Clark. Harvard and Columbia accused Hall and Clark University of admitting students with inadequate preparation and of granting Ph.D.s for inferior work merely to augment the number of students (Veysey 1965:424). During the 1911–12 school year, for example, 67 percent of all Clark grades were As and Bs, compared with 27 percent at Harvard (Koelsch 1987:104). Anthropology at Clark withered and disappeared after Chamberlain's death in 1914 and Hall's retirement in 1920.

Yet the early development of a graduate program at Clark University strengthened the arguments being made contemporaneously at Harvard, Pennsylvania, Chicago, and elsewhere about the need to incorporate anthropology into the graduate curriculum. Clark's proximity to Harvard as a possible competitor for graduate students from elite New England schools may well have helped convince the Harvard University faculty to approve Putnam's petition to include anthropology there during the major curriculum reform conducted on campus in 1890. But because Clark's reputation and influence rapidly waned, its importance to our story can probably be limited to Boas, Chamberlain, and the indirect support the anthropology program at Clark gave to Putnam in the creation of an anthropology graduate program at Harvard.

Returning specifically to Harvard, we find that it contributed richly to the early development of American higher education and later influenced the directions it took. One of the most important individuals for our argument is **George Ticknor** (1791–1871). Ticknor was one of the early American professors to earn a Ph.D. in Germany, having gone to the University of Goettingen in 1814–15 to study Spanish language and literature. He returned to Harvard in 1819 to assume the Smith professorship of French and Spanish languages and literature.

Ticknor was critical of the academic programs at Harvard and other American universities relative to those at European institutions. Harvard was, "in Ticknor's words, a high school" (Green 1966:29). Ticknor "brought back the German ideal he had found exemplified at Goettingen, saw how far short of it the American college fell, and worked out a series of proposals that would have advanced Harvard toward that ideal. Had those proposals been accepted, Samuel Eliot Morison says, Harvard would have been put a generation ahead of every other American college" (Green 1966:90).

Ticknor suggested many changes, a large number of which eventually became the basis of college training today. He proposed that the following new procedures be implemented at Harvard: that classes be divided up into groups according to ability instead of being taught as a single unit; that the hearing of recitations be replaced by formal teaching; that individual tutorials be instituted; that a final examination be instituted to test what had been learned; that better entry screening be instituted so that less remediation would be required; that separate departments of specific studies be formed; that a graduate school be founded; that Harvard construct a much larger library and require of its students more reading; and that the "off" or vacation term be moved to the summer instead of its then winter break time (Green 1966:91; Rudolph 1977:76).

Ticknor lobbied in vain to get his colleagues to accept these revisions as part of Harvard's new "College Laws" of 1825, although he managed to get a few changes made. He was able to upgrade the methods of teaching foreign languages at Harvard, and he saw the introduction of the concept of elective courses. But because few of the Harvard faculty at the time shared Ticknor's ideals, the establishment of elective courses was made optional for each department (nascent departmental organization being another part of Ticknor's plan). As a result, few elective courses were available. By 1843 a faculty reaction against the elective principle had taken place that was not reversed until Charles Eliot became president. Harvard undergraduate teaching did not get back to where it had been headed under Ticknor until 1883 (Rudolph 1977:79).

Ticknor was successful in introducing at least the idea of some post-A.B. study at Harvard in the newly created "resident graduates" program of the College Laws of 1825. Under the program, alumni of Harvard and other colleges could become enrolled as resident graduates for a fee, which allowed them to attend any lectures they liked and to use the library. Ticknor intended the program to include specific postgraduate instruction, but none was provided. Although Harvard invited graduates of other colleges to enter the program, only Harvard alumni could obtain an A.M., by being enrolled in the program for three years (no quota was set for the number of classes to be taken) and by paying a $5 fee (Hawkins 1972:54). The number of resident graduates was never more than 15 and often was many fewer. In the program's first year of operation, 1826–27, there were five resident graduates, among them Ralph W. Emerson from Harvard, Edward Mellen from Brown, and Alexander Rives from Hampden-Sidney (Green 1966:237). Among those who took advantage of the program later were some men who became members of the Harvard College faculty, such as William Watson Goodwin, Charles Eliot Norton, and Charles Sanders Peirce. The resident graduates program was ended in 1886 (Ryan 1939:7).

Ticknor resigned from Harvard in 1835 to focus on his research in Spanish literature, but he remained involved in the intellectual life of Boston. He helped found the Boston Public Library, served as trustee and vice president of the Boston Athenaeum, and later became a trustee of the Museum of Comparative Zoology. For our argument it is perhaps most important that Ticknor's work planted the seeds for academic renovation that his nephew, Harvard president **Charles William Eliot** (1834–1926), implemented four decades later.

Eliot returned to the college reform package when he became president in 1869 and made several changes to the Harvard curriculum, changes he fine-tuned and expanded on throughout his long term in office, until his retirement in 1909. He changed the way Harvard College was organized, made its credentials more professional, and shaped it into a more universalistic establishment. In terms of the coursework itself, Eliot's most important contribution was, arguably, the college "elective" principle, which ultimately dominated American universities as they emerged in the late nineteenth century.

Charles Eliot's predecessor as president from 1862 to 1868, **Thomas Hill** (1818–93), paved the way for many of the reforms that Eliot successfully brought about. In the year before Eliot's election, Hill had written that in order to succeed as an institution, Harvard "must devise stimulants to original investigation, research, and experiment," and he suggested more research-oriented electives as the means to do this (Pusey 1969:vi). He encouraged the development of graduate studies through a plan for "terminable fellowships," or scholarships for resident graduates, "to be given to young men of ability who should remain in Cambridge pursuing studies" and receiving advanced degrees (Land 1933:142). Hill identified the need for better admissions requirements for undergraduates (Land 1933:207), and he proposed a partial elective system, whereby students would have free choice in selecting courses except for those deemed necessary. Hill noted in 1866, however, that "as a practical matter in the present state of the College Treasury, the Elective System is limited both by the paucity of teachers and paucity of rooms" (quoted in Land 1933:147). He attempted to address the latter issue by encouraging a building program and a hiring policy that began Harvard's shift from a college to a university format (Land 1933:123). Although Hill had many good ideas, it remained for Eliot, with his administrative skills, to actualize the new directions.

In his inaugural address in 1869 Eliot argued for instituting an electives program, particularly as a means to create more skilled and competent students. He observed that the prep school–like requirement format then current at Harvard was an artifact of "an unintelligent system of instruction from the primary school through the college, [which] is responsible for the fact that many college graduates have so inadequate a conception of what is meant by scientific observation, reasoning and proof" (Eliot 1969 [1869]:2). To change and improve upon this situation, he argued, an elective system would provide "an accurate general knowledge of all the main subjects of human interest, beside a minute and thorough knowledge of the one subject which each may select as his principal occupation in life" (Eliot 1969 [1869]:3).

Three years later, having initiated his elective system, Eliot wrote to a friend that "with regard to the college proper, the one thing which we are doing at Cambridge is the introducing of a true University freedom of studies under the name of the 'elective system' . . . I believe that Harvard is doing a great service to American education by leading the way in this reform" (quoted in Hawkins 1972:92). Hugh Hawkins (1972:80) observed, "It was a tribute to Eliot's effectiveness as a spokesman for academic reform that the public associated his name with student freedom of course election as if the idea had been uniquely his and the reform uniquely Harvard's. Actually, electivism had been tried at several colleges, and at Harvard it was in partial effect before Eliot's presidency."

Up through the 1868–69 school term, essentially all courses were prescribed, and Harvard College resembled the small college-prep school of today. Samuel E. Morison (1936:344) reported that there were only 23 faculty and 529 students at Harvard that year. The number of students and faculty one counts varies, however, depending on who gets included as teaching staff and whether one lists just Harvard College students or includes special students, Lawrence Scientific School students, and so on. Hence, instead of corroborating Morison's figures, Donald Fleming (1986b:77) wrote that there were 45 instructors and 570 undergraduates in the 1868–69 year. Of the 45 instructors, 21 were permanent faculty, professors or associate professors (Handlin 1986b:112). Nathan Pusey (1969:viii) cited the figures of 63 faculty and 1,050 students for 1869. Regardless of which figures one uses, the point is the same: Harvard was a small, intimate institution at this time, quite different from the international powerhouse it became in the twentieth century.

By Eliot's time, the anti–elective course mood of the 1850s had passed, and Ticknor was once again a curricular hero. In response to Eliot's initiative, the Harvard catalogue of 1870–71 was reorganized from "class studies," organized by class year, to list courses by field or discipline. "In 1870–71, these 'studies' became 'courses' with Arabic numerals attached, and were divorced from the classes; in 1872–73 the student was informed for the first time who would give the course. Each year thereafter, some of the required courses became electives, and every new subject added became an elective automatically" (Morison 1936:345).

By 1872 seniors were freed from all requirements, and by 1875, required courses were gone for upperclassmen, with only a few freshman courses such as English, chemistry, physics, and either French or German required (Hawkins 1972:95–96). Eliot, reflecting on this change in 1908, commented, "The largest effect of the elective system is that it makes scholarship possible, not only among undergraduates but among graduate students and college teachers" (quoted in Oleson and Voss 1979:xi).

Departmental identities began to be clearly recognized. Establishment of definitive departments in association with the elective courses led to rapid professionalization of the faculty at Harvard.

Admission requirements were steadily raised during Eliot's administration by requiring greater accomplishment in classics, mathematics, and modern languages and by adding new requirements in English, history, and science. By 1886 only one in eight Harvard students was the son of a Harvard graduate, unlike the case before Eliot's tenure (Hawkins 1972:172). Eliot's overhaul of the undergraduate educational program, begun in 1869, was completed with the acceptance in 1906 of College Entrance Examination Board (CEEB) rankings (established in 1900) and the stipulation in 1908 that graduation with cum laude, magna cum laude, or summa cum laude recognition required a thesis and an oral examination rather than simply meeting a grade point prescription (Morison 1930:xlvi, 1936:369).

Eliot also is credited with the first public proposal, made in 1877, for establishing a standardized examination board for college admissions, which was actualized as the New England Board in 1879. Eliot proposed a national board in 1894, and the CEEB was organized in 1900. That Harvard did not adopt its rankings until 1906 was partly due to its leadership of the local New England Board (Hawkins 1972:178).

By 1880 Harvard undergraduates were clearly using the college library in greater numbers for research purposes; by 1890, research had become one of the dominant concerns of Harvard as well as of American higher education in general (Veysey 1965:175). Whereas other New England colleges were losing enrollment in the 1870s, Harvard began growing because of its new education programs (Ryan 1939:69). By 1877 Harvard had its first entering class of more than 200. By 1892 the figure had risen to more than 300, by 1896 to more than 400, by 1904 to more than 500, and by 1906 to more than 600 (Morison 1930:415). By 1909, when Eliot retired, there were 194 instructors and 2,277 undergraduates in Harvard College (Fleming 1986b:77), with a total enrollment in the university of roughly 3,900 (Pusey 1969:viii).

The elective system underwent an overhaul with the inauguration of President Abbott Lawrence Lowell in 1909. The idea of a college "major" had been developed by David Starr Jordan, first as president of Indiana University and then more fully when he became president of Stanford University when it opened in 1891. At Harvard, Lowell had championed the idea of establishing a major in faculty meetings beginning in 1903, in response to the fact that a review of the coursework of the class of 1898 showed abuse of the elective system, with 55 percent of the class members taking nothing but elementary courses (Fleming 1986b:93). The end of the free elective system occurred in the fall of 1909, when Lowell became president. Students now had to declare majors and minors and were required to take various classes in a distribution system (Hawkins 1972:85, 278).

Before turning to the development of graduate education at Harvard, we want to look briefly at the diversity of the undergraduate student body that developed during this period. Some writers (e.g., Kehoe 1998; Patterson 1995), referring to Harvard College during the growth of the anthropology program in the last quarter of the nineteenth century and first quarter of the twentieth, have portrayed the school as an elite, effete, Eastern establishment limited to rich, white, Anglo-Saxon males. To the contrary, we agree with Harvard historian Samuel Morison (1936:416) that "Harvard has never been socially homogeneous since President Dunster's day" (Dunster was president from 1640 to 1654). President Eliot noted in his inaugural address (1969 [1869]:15) that "Harvard College has always attracted and still attracts students in all conditions of life. . . . There are always scores of young men in this University who earn or borrow every dollar they spend here." Major scholarship funds established as early as the 1850s supported students in need, regardless of ethnic or religious status.

Eliot particularly, during his term in office from 1869 to 1909, worked to maintain what today is popularly called cultural diversity at Harvard. Although Harvard College had admitted freed slaves as students before Eliot became president, during his tenure Harvard actively sought a multiplicity of backgrounds. The university admitted Negroes and other minorities from the United States, as well as students from China and other Asian countries, something unthinkable at most other New England colleges of this period (Veysey 1965:288). Morison (1936:416) noted that "Southerners avoided Harvard after the Civil War because it admitted Negroes on the same terms as Whites, allowing them to eat at Memorial Hall, room in college dormitories, and participate in debating and athletic contests." The concerns of the Southern parents were so great that Eliot regularly sent letters to them after 1899, explaining why Negroes were attending Harvard.

Eliot also played a part in the establishment of Radcliffe College. It was he who gave Arthur Gilman and his executive board permission to approach members of the Harvard faculty to ask them to repeat their courses for "young ladies" in the "Harvard Annex" (the School for the Collegiate Instruction of Women), and it was he who later worked with Elizabeth Agassiz when Radcliffe College was officially founded (Comstock 1943:17).

In 1870, the year after Eliot had become president, only seven Catholics and three Jews were officially listed at Harvard College (Handlin 1986a:60). By the early 1890s, owing to Eliot's liberalization policies, significant numbers of Catholics began attending Harvard, and Jewish enrollment climbed after the turn of the century, reaching almost 7 percent in 1908 and more than 21 percent by 1922 (Dinnerstein 1994:84; Fleming

1968b:79). With Eliot's blessing, the Harvard Catholic Club was founded in about 1893, and the Menorah Society in 1906 (Hawkins 1972:128, 190). In contrast, at other New England colleges, such as Princeton, students of Jewish origin found it impossible to gain acceptance in the late nineteenth century (Veysey 1965:287, 417). Hence Laurence Veysey (1965:283) argued that one could identify three patterns of student bodies in American colleges by the late 1890s: ethnically homogeneous Eastern colleges such as Princeton, Yale, and other small New England schools; a few ethnically heterogeneous Eastern universities, such as Columbia, Harvard, and Pennsylvania; and the ethnically heterogeneous Western universities.

Harvard under Eliot was too democratic in its admissions policy for some of its constituents, and after Eliot retired in 1909, Harvard moved closer to Yale, Princeton, and other Ivy League schools in limiting diversity (Veysey 1965:92, 111). We should stress that we are detailing only official undergraduate admission practices here. In chapter 11 we outline a different perspective for admission of graduate students of Asian and African origin at this time.

Under the administration of A. Lawrence Lowell, who held the presidency of Harvard from 1909 until 1933, an empirically observed shift took place in undergraduate admissions procedures. That nearly a quarter of the undergraduate student body was Jewish apparently concerned some of Lowell's advisors, and in 1922 he proposed a Jewish student quota of 12 percent, the same quota being used in European universities at the time (Keller and Keller 2001:41). Quotas were in the American public mind just then because of quota-based immigration laws of 1921 and 1924, which were being put in place at the national level.

In part this "quota hysteria" had to do with a shift in immigration patterns. In the century before 1890, official immigration to the United States was 15.4 million persons, mainly from northern and western Europe. Less than 2 percent of that group was Jewish. Then, in the quarter century from 1890 to 1914, another 16.5 million immigrants arrived, this time mainly from southern and eastern Europe, and more than 10 percent of them were Jewish (Dinnerstein 1994:58). This shift in the number and ethnic composition of immigrants appears to have had an effect on the American social order. Leonard Dinnerstein (1994:77) argued that the Jews among the new immigrants tended to be discriminated against by some segments of American society, not only because of perceived "cultural" traits but also because of their presumed association with Bolshevism. Dinnerstein saw this as part of a general, countrywide "Red scare" of the decade, owing to the popularity of socialist ideologies in the eastern European countries at the time.

The Harvard College faculty soundly rejected Lowell's call for a formal quota for Jewish students. Nevertheless, Lowell quietly instituted an unofficial admissions policy that had the staff place an asterisk by the name of each Jewish student. Admissions officials were told to cap the number of "asterisked" students admitted at 10 percent. At the same time, Lowell was concerned about Harvard's growing too rapidly, and he limited the size of the incoming freshman class to 1,000 students.

Only 10 percent of the entering undergraduate class in 1930 was Jewish, compared with almost 25 percent in 1924. This unofficial quota was kept in place at Harvard until 1946 (Keller and Keller 2001:42, 51). Dinnerstein (1994:87) believed a similar unofficial quota was in place at American universities on the number of Jewish faculty members. He reported that in 1927, Yale, Princeton, Johns Hopkins, Chicago, and the University of Texas had only one Jewish faculty member apiece. There were two each at Berkeley and Columbia, three at Harvard, and four at City College of New York.

Similarly, Morton Keller and Phyllis Keller (2001:59) have asserted that a de facto quota existed at Harvard for Catholics, who made up about 20 percent of the American population at the time but were restricted to about 7 percent of the Harvard classes under Lowell's administration. In 1922 Lowell also called for a new policy of excluding blacks from freshman dormitories (Titcomb 1993).

In addition, Lowell has been characterized as seeking to eliminate women students from Harvard between 1929 and 1933 (Comstock 1943), because of his lobbying for the complete separation of Harvard and Radcliffe. Under such a split, students from Harvard and Radcliffe would no longer have shared either faculty or classrooms. Ada Louise Comstock (1943:16), president of Radcliffe at the time, reported that with the help of the Harvard faculty, Radcliffe defeated this attempt to separate the two institutions.

Under Lowell, then, Harvard's undergraduate student body did change from the relatively culturally diverse group of a generation earlier to a much more restricted ethnic grouping by the beginning of the Great Depression.

Among the other Ivy League schools, only Columbia University seems to have tried to achieve a social diversity similar to that espoused by Charles Eliot. Seth Low, president of Columbia from 1890 to 1901, wanted the student body there to represent the social and cultural composition of New York City itself (Bender 1987:287). He pointed out to his college deans that the public included both men and women, and by the end of his term of office, 14 percent of candidates for higher degrees in the graduate division were women (Bender 1987:283). But as happened at Harvard, a new president, Nicholas Murray Butler, who held office at Columbia from 1901 to 1945, terminated Low's admission reforms. Like Lowell at Harvard, Butler employed the notion of "selective admission" to limit Jewish enrollment. From 1917, when Butler enacted this policy, to 1921, the proportion of Jewish students at Columbia declined from 40 percent to 22 percent, and the decline continued during the next decade (Bender 1987:289).

The Harvard College of 1925 to 1950 offered a different social environment from that of Harvard College from 1875 to 1925, the time of the major development of anthropology there. Characterizations of Harvard such as Alice Kehoe's (1998) and Thomas Patterson's (1995) have, regrettably, a ring of truth in terms of the undergraduate college during the second quarter of the twentieth century, but they apply less well to what was a quite culturally diverse situation in the last quarter of the nineteenth century and first quarter of the twentieth. Moreover, as we hope to show, such a portrayal is incorrect for the graduate school, particularly in anthropology, for all periods in its history.

Charles Eliot traced the official beginning of graduate work at Harvard not to George Ticknor's resident graduates program of the early nineteenth century but to President Thomas Hill's later "University Lecture" program (Haskins 1930:453; Ryan 1939:7). Hill, in response to a suggestion by Louis Agassiz, had initiated the University Lecture series in 1863. In its first year, 126 people registered for this graduate series, paying $5 each for the privilege, but there was no specific structure or direction to the degree program (Land 1933:140).

When Eliot took office, he attempted to upgrade the University Lecture program by adding some structure, offering a special graduate "University Course of Instruction" in 1869–70. It included one course in philosophy and one in modern literature. But competition with the public lectures of Boston's Lowell Institute was intense, attendance was small, and Eliot admitted failure for this graduate program initiative and terminated it in 1871 (Hawkins 1972:55).

He then set up a "Graduate Department" in January 1872 for A.M., Ph.D., and S.D. degrees, under the direction of an Academic Council. Until that time, no facilities had existed at Harvard for graduate education. Until 1863 there had been an A.M. degree program at Harvard College, but only Harvard alumni could obtain the degree, by being enrolled in the program for up to three years. No quota had been set for the number of classes to be taken; candidates had obtained their degrees by paying a $5 fee (Hawkins 1972:54). From 1863 to 1869 the A.M. program had been run through the University Lecture series, again with the $5 fee (Land 1933:140). From 1869 to 1872, the A.M. degree required, for the first time, an examination under Eliot's University Course of Instruction, but no specific program was designated (Harvard University 1930:163).

With the new Graduate Department program of 1872, the A.M. degree required a year's postgraduate study and an examination. The Ph.D. and S.D. degrees required additional study, another examination, and a dissertation. The first doctorates were awarded within a year, in 1873, when two Ph.D.s were granted, to William Elwood Byerly and Charles Leavitt Beals Whitney, and one S.D., to John Trowbridge. The Ph.D. training was slow to grow. In 1880, 5 Ph.D.s were granted, and in 1890, only 8, but finally in 1900, 36 doctorates were awarded.

The early years of the graduate school were anything but rigorous. The students chiefly took elective studies they had been unable to take in the college A.B. program; the first courses "primarily for graduates" were not listed in the catalogue until 1875–76 (Haskins 1930:344). The continued failure of Harvard and other schools to provide the necessary training for American students opened the door for the establishment of the major graduate training programs with the founding of Johns Hopkins University in 1876 and later the founding of Clark and Chicago, with their heavy emphasis on graduate training.

It was principally the competition from Johns Hopkins that ultimately resulted in Harvard's upgrading its programs. Graduate fellowships, which had been reluctantly introduced in the 1870s and limited to Harvard College graduates, were greatly expanded in the 1880s to include graduates from other colleges, in an attempt to compete with Johns Hopkins and Clark. Between 1885 and 1892, more than 40 percent of Ph.D.s went to non–Harvard College graduates (McCaughey 1974:305). Charles Eliot, in an address at the twenty-fifth anniversary of Johns Hopkins, on February 21, 1902, wryly observed that "the graduate school of Harvard University, started feebly in 1870 and in 1871, did not thrive until the example of Johns Hopkins forced our faculty to put their strength into the development of our instruction for graduates. And what was true of Harvard was true of every other university in the land which aspired to create an advanced school of arts and sciences" (quoted in Ryan 1939:3–4).

In 1890 Eliot turned Harvard's rather amorphous graduate program into the Graduate School of Arts and Sciences, through a reorganization of Harvard College. The faculty of Lawrence Scientific School was combined with the faculty of the college to form the Faculty of Arts and Sciences, and the provision was made that henceforth all courses at Lawrence and Harvard College could be taken interchangeably. Graduate courses now were to be offered only through the Faculty of Arts and Sciences. Morison (1936:335) argued that "the establishment of the Graduate School was one of Eliot's most vital and far-reaching reforms."

Although the initial graduate school reform included only members of the Lawrence School and Harvard College, and not the female students of the Harvard Annex (soon to become Radcliffe), by 1894 women were admitted to all Harvard graduate courses. Eliot, frustrated at the resistance to educating women by Harvard College, had lent his support to the annex experiment from its beginning in 1879 (Browman 2002a:222–24; Hawkins 1972:194–95).

In 1890, at the time of the formation of the Faculty of Arts and Sciences, the combined faculty numbered 62 members, divided into 12 divisions. These divisions were broad fields of studies that sometimes included one department, sometimes two or three. Anthropology was included in what Harvard defined as "Division XIV." Each division controlled its own honors degrees and graduate programs, and the "default" examining committee for such students consisted of faculty members selected from the division. The departments handled other matters. Departments had existed since the 1825 reforms but had been at best loosely organized. With the reforms of 1890, they took on new life. The reorganization also affected courses. A three-group system of courses went into effect, with the lowest group primarily for undergraduates, the middle group for undergraduates and graduates, and the highest group primarily for graduates (Morison 1936:383). By 1909 Arts and Sciences had grown nearly threefold, to 164 faculty members (Hawkins 1972:74).

Although the minimum residence term for a Ph.D. in the Graduate School of Arts and Sciences was officially one year, most students in programs university-wide took much longer. For example, for the 145 Harvard Ph.D.s granted in 1912–14, 13 percent of the students completed the requirements in 2 to 3 years, 40 percent took 4 to 6 years, 27 percent took 7 to 10 years, and 20 percent were in their programs for more than 10 years before finishing their degrees (Haskins 1930:451). Thus the reality of time spent "in grade" was not that much different from that of today in anthropology.

At the Peabody Museum, still a quasi-independent entity when the Graduate School of Arts and Sciences was established, Frederic Putnam required a minimum of three years for a Ph.D. Putnam, as we have seen, began his teaching in the mid-1870s and 1880s according to the methods employed in his own education, principally by mentoring individual students, as he had been mentored by Henry Wheatland, Louis Agassiz, Asa Gray, and Jeffries Wyman in a sort of internship system, and through public lectures. After dedicating the first few years of his curatorship to the construction of the initial museum building, Putnam began to expand his teaching activities, using the same kind of mentoring or apprentice system to train his first "students," Ernest Jackson, Cornelia Studley, John Kimball, and William Nickerson.

The other teaching method Putnam employed most often in the early years of his incumbency was the public lecture series, which capitalized on the popularity of what has become known as the Chautauqua system in New England at the time. He began giving regular public lectures in the Peabody Museum by 1881, open to both Harvard students and the general public. For that year, he reported that popular demand

> induced me last spring to offer a free course of four explanatory lectures in the several halls of the Museum, when I had the gratification of finding that more people wished to attend the lectures than could well be accommodated. . . .
>
> This preliminary course has led to my offering another of six gallery lectures on Thursday afternoons, which commenced yesterday. For this course, free tickets to the number of one hundred and fifty have been given out on application, this being the largest number which our rooms could accommodate. . . . The demand for admission to these lectures was so far in excess of the accommodation that the course was repeated on the following Saturdays. . . . The subjects to be discussed in this course are as follows: first the Mounds and their contents; second, the Pottery from the Mounds; third, Ancient and Modern Pueblos; fourth; Mexico and Central America; fifth; South America; sixth Ancient Peruvian Art. . . .
>
> I have also just concluded a free course of nine lectures before members of the classes for Private Collegiate Instruction for Women in Cambridge. (Putnam 1882a:70–71)

In addition, he gave public lectures at the Boston Society of Natural History, the American Academy of Arts and Sciences, the Essex Institute, and the Harvard Natural History Society (Putnam 1882a:69).

For the following year, 1882, Putnam observed:

> In the last Report I mentioned a course of ten lectures, about to take place at the Museum. Those were delivered in the months of February and March last, and were attended to the full capacity of the rooms in which they were given. As already mentioned, another special course was given during the past fall, beside these, lectures have

been given to a class from the State Normal School at Framingham, to the scholars of two private schools from Boston, and to a party of the members of the Young Men's Christian Union. . . . Twenty-five free lectures were thus given at the Museum during the year 1882. (Putnam 1883a:191)

By 1886 Putnam had developed a series of 38 lectures, mainly on American archaeology, organized into three major clusters, which he advertised in a promotional brochure (see Browman 2002a:218–19). Some of these lectures were worked up into short pamphlets that were put on sale at the museum—for example, "Remarks on Chipped Stone Implements" in 1885 and "Conventionalism in Ancient American Art" in 1887.

On June 24, 1885, the Harvard Corporation, acting on the recommendation of the trustees of the Peabody Museum, named Putnam the Peabody Professor at the museum (Anonymous 1885b; Brew 1966a:14). The nomination had to be confirmed by the Harvard Board of Overseers before it became official. At the overseers' regular October meeting that year, Asa Gray moved and Theodore Lyman (Charles Eliot's cousin) seconded the nomination (Casler 1976:53), but Putnam was not confirmed as Peabody Professor by the overseers for another 15 months, until January 1887. He did not become a completely official, full member of the faculty of Harvard College until the Peabody Museum changed its quasi-independent status and merged with the university in 1897.

The reason for the overseers' delay in confirming Putnam involves a misunderstanding of long duration. Years ago Ralph Dexter (1965, 1966a) wrote that Alexander Agassiz convinced the overseers to deny Putnam the professorship until 1887 because of ill feeling over Putnam's involvement in the student revolt against Louis Agassiz nearly a quarter century earlier. Since then other writers have picked up and repeated Dexter's story (e.g., Casler 1976). We find no support for this account. By the mid-1860s Louis Agassiz and the rebellious students had made their peace, and every one of the students remembered him later, in written tributes, with admiration and affection. Alexander Agassiz himself recruited Putnam to head the work at the Penikese Island field station in 1873 and 1874, and the two worked collaboratively as directors of the Peabody Museum and Museum of Comparative Zoology for three decades. Any tension between the Agassiz family and Putnam was long gone by the 1870s.

The real reason for the delay was that by the late 1880s, doctorates were common enough among the faculty at Harvard that Putnam's lack of one—indeed, of any degree at all—required a full explanation (Rossiter 1992:21). It would be only a few years later, in the early 1890s, that all new appointments to professorships at Harvard held an A.M. or a Ph.D. When Gray and Lyman nominated Putnam for the professorship at the October 1885 meeting, the overseers viewed the nomination through this lens and expressed concern over Putnam's lack of degree credentials. A special committee was formed, consisting of Alexander Agassiz, Moorefield Storey, and Roger Wolcott, to investigate the nomination (Board of Overseers Records 12:182, 1885). Agassiz said on record that he believed there was no demand for anthropology on the part of either the public or the students at Harvard College (Casler 1976:54). The committee reported back on December 9, 1885, and recommended that Putnam's nomination for professor not go forward.

Putnam was taken aback at this rejection. In a handwritten comment on the Peabody Museum's copy of the overseers' report, he remarked that the overseers were "ignorant or jealous" when they turned him down (Casler 1976:56). Putnam's long-time colleagues and friends were equally surprised. Alpheus Hyatt and Samuel Scudder wrote asking the overseers to reconsider, and Asa Gray wrote to his fellow board members urging them to support Putnam's nomination (Casler 1976:56, 58). From the records, it appears that Gray, Lyman, and Robert C. Winthrop—all of whom were deeply involved in the Peabody Museum—were Putnam's main supporters on the Board of Overseers.

The nomination came up for reconsideration at the January 12, 1887, meeting of the overseers. Morrill Wyman, the brother of Jeffries Wyman and a good friend of Putnam's, moved to send the nomination back to committee, but the motion lost. The overseers then went ahead with the main motion, and Putnam was finally approved as Peabody Professor (Board of Overseers Records 12:246, 1887). It was clearly a sign of their esteem for Putnam and their confidence in his abilities that they ultimately confirmed him as professor, despite his lacking even the S.B. he was granted retroactively in 1898 for his work at the Lawrence Scientific School. Morrill Wyman, Alexander Agassiz, and the other overseers who had questioned his nomination appear not to have done so for personal reasons; they simply believed that Harvard faculty should have postgraduate degrees.

Because the museum and the college were still institutionally separate in 1887, Putnam's appointment as professor at first carried with it no additional teaching duties. He had done some teaching through the museum, and his experiences with his first three advanced "students," Studley, Kimball, and Nickerson—all of whom had to leave for financial reasons—helped him develop his later formal academic program, particularly its emphasis on student funding.

At a meeting of the Faculty of Arts and Sciences on October 8, 1890, Putnam proposed a three-year curriculum for a Ph.D. in anthropology at the university. The program was described as entailing studies in "Laboratory Work, Museum Work, Comparative Archaeology, the Evidence of the Antiquity of Man, Ethnology, and Field Work" (Putnam 1891:98–99). On December 9, 1890, the faculty gave its approval to the establishment of the Department of American Archaeology and Ethnology, for the purpose of giving instruction in these subjects in preparation for the A.M. and Ph.D. degrees.

Financial aid for students in the new department was one of Putnam's critical concerns. In his report to the visiting committee in 1890–91, he listed as one of his points of vital importance "the establishment of fellowships or student-assistantships, by means of which students wishing to pursue anthropological studies could be aided and the Museum receive their labors. In this way a corps of assistants would be trained for work in the Museum. This I regard of the utmost importance for the future of the Museum, as you can easily realize that it is now impossible for the Curator, with the slight aid he can procure with the means at his command, to do all that is required" (Putnam 1892:103).

In anticipation of the new program, Putnam solicited Charles P. Bowditch (see chapter 9) and Dr. Francis M. Weld for fellowship funds in 1889, and they agreed to provide $1,500 for a three-year fellowship. **Francis Minot Weld** (1840–93) was a member of the Harvard class of 1860. He went on to get his M.D. in 1864 and an A.M. by title in 1871. He apparently practiced medicine for only a short while before taking over the family cotton mills. He served as a Harvard College overseer from 1882 to 1889 and the following year was named head of the newly reorganized Visiting Committee of the Peabody Museum. Weld and Bowditch's scholarship donation became known as the Visiting Committee Fellowship; it seems to have been awarded only once, in 1890.

Putnam secured other funds as well. In addition to the standard Faculty of Arts and Sciences scholarship funds, he developed long-term, continuing fellowships limited specifically to anthropology students. The first two of the special museum fellowships were the Mary Copley Thaw Fellowship, established on October 1, 1890, and consisting of $1,050 for "work and research relating to the Indian race of America, or other ethnological and archaeological investigations," and the Mary E. Hemenway Fellowship, established on June 1, 1891, and consisting of $500 awarded to a graduate student for study of American archaeology and ethnology. The "J. Huntington Wolcott and Huntington Frothingham Wolcott Research Fund," named for the late father and brother, respectively, of its donor, Joshua Roger Wolcott (later a Massachusetts governor), was also established on June 1, 1891. (Hereafter we refer to this simply as the Wolcott Fund.) In 1895 the Robert C. Winthrop Scholarship in American Archaeology and Ethnology was added, in the amount of $200, to be given to a student of American archaeology and ethnology from the Peabody Museum, "over which [Winthrop has] presided since its organization." Before the end of the decade, the Austin Fellowship for teaching was also in place (Anonymous 1895a:73; Dorsey 1896:97; Harvard University 1895:557–8; Putnam 1891:98). These awards were soon augmented by others.

Putnam's graduate degree program was a good deal more rigorous than other training programs of the period. Frederick Starr (1892:291), writing about the developing field of anthropology in the United States, quoted the following description of the initial advanced anthropology curriculum from a Harvard brochure:

> A course of special training in archaeology and technology, requiring three years for its completion, will be given by Prof. Putnam. It will be carried on by work in the laboratory and museum, lectures, field-work, and exploration, and in the third year by some special research. The ability to use French and Spanish will be necessary. For this course, a knowledge of elementary chemistry, geology, botany, zoology, drawing, and surveying is required, and courses in ancient history, ancient arts, and classical archaeology are recommended as useful.

In the Peabody Museum's annual report for 1893–94, Putnam (1894:223) wrote that "with the beginning of the college year, 1894–95, a course in General Anthropology was offered to graduates, and to undergraduates by permission. One graduate and four undergraduates have regularly entered the course, and two graduates, an undergraduate, and a special student are also taking it as an extra." He went on to report that he had officially requested that Harvard change the department's name from "American Archaeology and Ethnology" to "Anthropology" that year.

A description of the program for the 1895–96 school year published in *Science* magazine (Anonymous 1895a:72–73) indicated that the curriculum would be taught by Putnam and graduate student George Dorsey, with two main courses:

> The first course in general anthropology is intended to give students a general knowledge of the subject and to be preparatory to advanced work in physical anthropology, ethnology, sociology and history. The first part of this course will be devoted to the study of somatology or physical anthropology; the second part to ethnology, with special reference to the origins and development of primitive arts and culture; and the third part to archaeology and ethnography, in which man will be considered in relation to his distribution over the earth from geologic to the present time, and his division into groups. Each group or variety of man will be studied separately, special attention being given to American groups. These subjects will all be studied with the aid of work in the laboratory and museum.
>
> A second course is announced, entitled *Research Course,* which will be conducted under the immediate supervision of Professor Putnam and will require three years for its completion. This course will be carried on by work in the laboratory and museum, lectures, field work and explorations, and in the third year by some special research.
>
> This course is in the first place intended for graduate students who are candidates for the degree of Ph.D., but it is also open to students who have taken Course I, or its equivalent, and who may be competent to undertake it.

The *Science* article added that the Peabody Museum library now had 1,400 volumes and 1,700 pamphlets, making it one of the largest anthropology libraries in the world.

By the 1896–97 term, two new courses had been added (Dixon 1930:211), and 10 undergraduate and 6 graduate students were now enrolled in four Harvard College courses: General Anthropology, American Archaeology and Ethnology, Somatology, and Advanced Somatology (Putnam 1898a:4; Willoughby 1923b:501). By 1898 two more courses had been added, with three instructors: Putnam, Frank Russell, and Roland B. Dixon (Putnam 1898a:9). The increase in staff was due partly to a change in policy by Harvard University. Until 1898, all instructional staff in anthropology had been paid from the museum's budget. On January 1, 1897, with a new agreement, the museum was officially incorporated into the university, which gave it access to new resources. The president's report for 1898–99 announced, "In 1898–99, the College assumed for the first time the payment of the salary of an Instructor in anthropology. The amount of instruction given in connection with the Museum is increasing, and it engages more and more the interest of the students, both graduate and undergraduate" (Harvard University 1899:38).

Because the Peabody Museum did not officially become an integrated part of Harvard University until the beginning of 1897, some six years after the Department of American Archaeology and Ethnology was established in December 1890, Putnam at first had the freedom to develop a program in anthropology without the need to conform to other college regulations. The program he developed was much more extensive than the college norm. Putnam required of his graduate students rigorous prior training, and his program offered a more thorough education than the general Ph.D. scheme at Harvard or anywhere else in the country at the time. Although he required at least three years of work for the degree, rather than the additional one year after the A.B. officially required by Harvard, the actual norm for Putnam's students in this period was four years (Mark 1980:52). The first major Ph.D. program that developed to compete with Harvard's was the one Boas established at Columbia in the early 1900s, and the popularity of his program was due partly to the fact that he fashioned it along the lines of the less intensive model of the day. His students at Columbia could receive the Ph.D. only two years after the A.B., taking fewer courses and writing shorter dissertations, a much less rigorous program than that required by Harvard (Darnell 1998:188; Mark 1980:52).

The first official listing of anthropology class attendance in the *Harvard Bulletin* was in 1894–95, when anthropology had five students. The official counts, however, often underestimated the actual number of students, because of varying mechanisms for enrolling in courses. As we noted earlier, Putnam in fact had five regular students and four special or other students that year, for a total of nine rather than five.

The issue of "special students" is complex and difficult to evaluate accurately, for early documentation on them is incomplete. Eliot reintroduced the program of special students, who were allowed to take courses without being candidates for a degree, early in his administration. This option became popular in the Lawrence Scientific School, and from 1880 to 1894, special students outnumbered regular students (Hawkins 1972:350, n. 14). According to Hugh Hawkins (1972:325), after 1894 Harvard for a short time allowed any instructor who had faculty approval to teach a special course for a fee, which he collected himself. The Harvard catalogues for 1890, 1895, and 1900 indicate that the distinction between special students and regular students was that special students did not have to pass the usual examination for admission to the college and thus were not candidates for degrees, but they had to pay the same tuition as regular students. If they completed the course of study, they could, at commencement, be awarded a certificate instead of a diploma. Occasionally a student was referred to as a "private" rather than a "special" student; perhaps these were the people who, after 1894, could be charged the special fee that the professor could keep for himself.

The growth of Harvard's anthropology program was astounding. According to the official figures in the Harvard University reports, the number of students enrolled in anthropology had increased from the original 5 in 1894–95 to 279 in 1904–5. Another

29 students were enrolled in anthropology through Radcliffe, for 308 students in all. That year William C. Farabee had 159 Harvard College students in Anthropology 1, 4 students in Anthropology 2, and 15 students in Anthropology 4. He had 29 additional students through Radcliffe College enrollments. Roland Dixon had 71 students in Anthropology 5, 24 students in Anthropology 7, and 3 students in Anthropology 8, and Putnam had 3 graduate students in Anthropology 20.

The 1912–13 course listings included 11 courses for undergraduates and graduates (Anth 1, General Anthropology; Anth 2, Somatology; Anth 4, Ethnography of Europe; Anth 5, American Archaeology and Ethnography; Anth 7, Ethnography of Oceania; Anth 8, American Indian Languages; Anth 9, Archaeology and Hieroglyphic Systems of Central America; Anth 10, Archaeology and Ethnography of Mexico; Anth 11, Ethnography of Asia; Anth 12, Primitive Sociology, a History of Institutions; and Anth 13, Primitive Industries and Arts). Six research courses were primarily for graduates (Anth 20a, American Archaeology and Ethnology; Anth 20b, Advanced Somatology; Anth 20c, Studies in American Languages; Anth 20d, General Ethnology; Anth 20e, Central American and Mexican Archaeology and Hieroglyphics; and Anth 20f, South American Archaeology and Ethnology). In addition, "attention is called to the following courses" elsewhere on campus: one course each in economics, botany, and German literature; two courses each in Egyptology, classical archaeology, philosophy, comparative philology, and zoology; three courses each in comparative literature and the history of religions; and six in geology. Several of these other relevant courses were taught by professors in other departments who served as readers on the anthropology department's doctoral dissertation committees of the period.

In 1913, while Dixon was away on leave for a year, Putnam's former assistant and good friend Franz Boas, who was then an anthropology professor at Columbia University, was hired for one term to cover the teaching gap. Boas and the Harvard faculty were much closer than many researchers have realized. For example, Boas and Alfred Tozzer collaborated in running the International School of American Archaeology and Ethnology in Mexico City during its existence from 1911 to 1914. Boas served as director of the school for the 1911–12 term, and Tozzer for the 1913–14 term. The two worked together on many of the political events that arose as the American Anthropological Association grew and as anthropologists sought to secure federal funding in the 1910s and 1920s. Tozzer and Boas remained close friends throughout the rest of Boas's life; Tozzer made a special trip to New York City to visit Boas just before his death.

That semester at Harvard in 1913, Boas taught somatology and linguistics and introduced a special graduate seminar in theory called "Aims and Methods," which enrolled three graduate students. Two years later the department made the theory course part of its regular offerings, now listed as "Field Methods in Anthropology" and team-taught by Dixon, Tozzer, and Earnest Hooton. By 1915–16 there were 14 courses in anthropology offered at Harvard, divided over a two-year cycle, as well as 6 courses in Egyptology, for archaeologists who wanted additional training (Caullery 1922:69).

Although we reviewed class enrollments by professor for the first 20 years they were published, we failed to identify any useful patterning, such as whether one professor was more popular than others, perhaps because he was an easier grader or a more dynamic lecture. One of the few anomalies that appeared was a blip in the enrollment for Anthropology 5, North American Archaeology and Ethnology. Enrollment in Anth 5 from the time it was first offered in 1899 through the rest of the first 20 years ordinarily averaged about 15 students, but for the short period of 1903 to 1907, it suddenly boomed, with an average of 75 students per year. Frank Russell had been the instructor in 1902, and Roland Dixon became the instructor in 1903, but the boom apparently was not due to Dixon's taking over the course. He was also the instructor in 1908 and later, when the enrollment dropped back to about 15. Harvard made no changes in graduation requirements relevant to this course or its division, so its surge in popularity seems to have been attributable to some external cause. A likely one was the hundredth anniversary of the Lewis and Clark Expedition, which resulted in a lot of popular press on American Indians and their history.

Frederic Putnam actively recruited women students and minorities into his anthropology program. Elsewhere, Browman (2002b) has outlined Putnam's extensive support for women who conducted research in archaeology before 1900. Putnam also made sure that anthropology classes were available to the women students of Radcliffe. By 1893 President Eliot had arranged for members of the Faculty of Arts and Sciences to serve officially as "Visitors" for what was to become Radcliffe, letting them offer repeat versions of their Harvard College courses for the women in the Harvard Annex (Hawkins 1972:195). Putnam quickly took advantage of this to offer classes for the women students there. For example, Anth 1, General Anthropology, had an enrollment of 13 undergraduates in Harvard College in 1899 but was repeated for 5 Radcliffe students. In 1900 this class had 20 Harvard College male students and was repeated for 10 Radcliffe College female students. Female graduate students had a different status, so that in the 1900–1901 school year, the Primitive Religions course had three Harvard male students, but a Radcliffe graduate student took the class with them (Mead 1914:6). Thus the women graduate students seemed to have had access to more resources than their female undergraduate colleagues. Undergraduate Radcliffe women could not take the same class in the same room with Harvard men, but apparently that restriction did not apply to graduate women.

Because Harvard University offered the first successful graduate program in anthropology in the Americas, and because it trained a large number of the first cohort of anthropologists staffing museums and universities at the turn of the century, we believe the foregoing details of its initial courses provide essential background for understanding the development of the field. In addition, the Harvard pattern of greater rigor and more intensive training ultimately became the pattern for graduate training in anthropology in the United States, winning out over Boas's two-year program, which was popular at the beginning of the twentieth century.

Putnam's own teaching was limited, because his position as curator of the Peabody Museum involved him in many other activities outside the museum. The Harvard College president's report for 1898–99 (Harvard University 1899:38) gave some of the explanation for Putnam's situation: "As it is impossible for the University to pay for the whole time of the curator, he gives half his time to the service of the American Museum of Natural History in New York City." We note elsewhere in this volume his contributions to the growth of anthropology at Columbia, Berkeley, and the American Museum of Natural History and his involvement in the founding of the American Anthropological Association and other anthropological institutions during this period.

The lack of funding for the curator was a continuing problem over the next decade or so. Putnam (1908:296) wrote in his last official annual report, for 1907–8, that the income from George Peabody's gift provided only about $4,000 to run the museum and only about $2,500 for the salary of the Peabody Professor and the curator of the museum. To put this in context, a Harvard professor's salary in 1863 had been $2,400 but was raised that year by President Hill to $3,000. Eliot raised it to $4,000 in 1869, then to $4,500 in the mid-1890s, and by another $500 in 1905 (Hawkins 1972:24, 61, 67). Clearly, the endowment provided only a half salary for the Peabody Professor. Although the problem was temporarily solved in the teens, it came back to haunt the museum again half a century later.

Some historians of our discipline have suggested that Putnam's program encompassed only archaeology and lacked a broader anthropological focus. That is incorrect. Although Putnam himself was particularly interested in archaeology, he encouraged study in all fields of anthropology. A good indication of the program's breadth can be seen in the fields of the first seven Ph.D. dissertations, completed under Putnam's guidance between 1894 and 1904: two each were in archaeology, physical anthropology, and linguistics, and one was in ethnography. Harvard training was strong in archaeology, ethnology, and somatology (physical anthropology). If the resources were unavailable at Harvard, then Putnam sent the graduate student to receive additional training elsewhere (as we do today). Hence he sent his two linguistics Ph.D. students to get additional training at Columbia with Boas.

Putnam's innovative educational contributions through Peabody Museum programs have often been overlooked by disciplinary historians. When he initiated the preliminary phases of his training program, at least as early as the 1880–81 academic term, it was not an isolated event. At Harvard itself, Charles Eliot was championing the transformation of the college from the previous almost preparatory-school format into a true university model. Undergraduates now had a choice of electives and could choose to major in specific disciplines. Graduate education was developed, with the first American doctorate programs put in place at Harvard and other East Coast institutions.

Putnam paid a good deal of attention to the development of his program. For example, he effected a major redesign of his approach after receiving feedback from his first generation of students. And when the college gave him permission to initiate his doctorate program, Putnam launched a format requiring much more rigorous training for Ph.D. students than any other early American university anthropology curriculum. This situation continued for at least the next quarter century, contributing to the rapid recognition of Harvard as one of the leading programs during the florescence of the discipline in the early twentieth century.

7

Graduate Students, Faculty, and Others, 1890–1900

The first formal students at the Peabody Museum, those who entered as the first university-recognized class, were actually the second generation of students for Putnam, as we saw in chapter 4. These students were a hardy, daring bunch, choosing a major that was just being defined—indeed, just being invented. Where were the jobs? What were the career opportunities? Until this time, people who thought of themselves as being in anthropologically related careers worked mainly for government agencies, with a few finding museum positions. Working for universities or elsewhere had not yet become a possibility. Thus, the majority of those who trained with Frederic Putnam during this first decade headed for museum positions upon completion of their work. It would take another decade before teaching positions began to dominate.

Although Putnam had been appointed Peabody Professor in 1887, his first formal students were not to be found until 1890, when Harvard College officially recognized the Department of American Archaeology and Ethnology and approved its curriculum as part of the general reorganization of Harvard undergraduate and graduate education that year. In his report for 1890, Putnam (1891:98) reported that "during the present year, three private students have been in attendance for laboratory instruction, and two from the Graduate School of the University have entered for a three years' course preparatory for the degree of Ph.D." The three undergraduates were Marshall Saville, Frank Gerrodette, and Allen Cook; the two graduate students were George Dorsey and John Owens. In the next few years Putnam recruited other students, such as George Gordon, John Swanton, Roland Dixon, Charles Peabody, Frank Russell, and Charles Willoughby—who would become director of the Peabody Museum after Putnam's death—into his program.

In the rest of this chapter, we profile first the three undergraduate and two graduate students, followed by a look at students added to the program later and the teaching support faculty during the first decade of the program.

Marshall Howard Saville (1867–1935) was originally from Rockport, Massachusetts, where he had become interested in archaeology as an amateur collector in his high school years (Wissler 1944:647). After graduating from high school, he clerked for six years in the Boston area, but he also took some night courses at the Massachusetts Institute of Technology and read some anthropology at the Boston Public Library. In 1889 he wrote to Putnam, "I would like to know if I can pursue a special course at Harvard with the intention of fitting myself to became an intelligent archaeologist" (D. McVicker 1992:147).

Putnam apparently agreed, for Saville began working for Putnam, receiving training in excavation at the Turner Mounds on the Little Miami River in Ohio with Charles Metz in the summer of 1889 (Putnam 1890a:76). In the fall of 1889 Saville came to the museum as a special student assistant (Dorsey 1896:90). He was admitted as an undergraduate when the anthropology program was established in 1890 and was supported in his studies at Harvard during the 1890 through 1892 terms by the special Visiting Committee Fellowship established by Francis M. Weld and Charles P. Bowditch (Putnam 1892:193). The fellowship seems to have been created especially to support Saville; we find no other recipients of it mentioned later in the annual reports.

Saville learned field methods quickly under Putnam. In the summer of 1890, at the end of his first year as a special student, the Turner Mounds project "was placed in charge of Mr. Marshall H. Saville on the first of June" (Putnam 1891:93). For a short time that summer Saville was in charge of training George Dorsey on the Turner Mounds. He also had responsibility for photographing the excavations at both the Turner Mounds site and the Cline's Runs mound excavations (Putnam 1891:94, 97). The next summer Saville was again working in Ohio, this time as a supervisor for Allen Cook at the mounds at Fort Hill (Putnam 1892:193). During the 1892 season he excavated with Cook, Metz, Warren Moorehead, and Harlan I. Smith on other Ohio projects (Putnam 1893a:201).

With the aid of Charles Bowditch (1840–1921), the Peabody Museum secured a decree from the government of Honduras in 1891 giving the museum exclusive right to explore the ruins of that country. John Owens was appointed to head up the first expedition, in 1891, and Saville was engaged as the chief assistant and photographer (Dorsey 1896:85, 90; Hinsley 1984:64c). Putnam (1893a:207) wrote that "Mr. M. H. Saville, the holder of the Visiting Committee's fellowship, was on the Honduras expedition from November, 1891, to May 1892, the remainder of the time he has been at work in the Museum or in the field, as a student assistant of the Museum." Saville thus gained additional experience on excursions to Labna and Uxmal in Yucatán (D. McVicker 1992:147; Starr 1893:611).

Part of the business of the expedition was to collect artifacts and take photographs for the 1893 World's Columbian Exposition in Chicago for Putnam. Saville may have begun this aspect of the work as early as on a trip to Mexico in 1890 (D. McVicker 1989:120; Wissler 1944:648), although he was not put on the exposition payroll until 1892. He collected other materials for the exposition as well. For example, in 1893

T. J. Case found a cache of soapstone vessels in his quarrying work near Bristol, Connecticut, and informed both the Smithsonian Institution and the Peabody Museum. "Marshall H. Saville of the Massachusetts [sic] Museum came promptly, took a lot of photographs of the quarry nests [caches of soapstone vessels], and in the course of careful examination about the ledge disclosed four new" caches. He "induced Mr. Case to cut a section of the nests [of vessels] from the quarry which will be sent to the Columbian Exposition" (Anonymous 1893).

The Mesoamerican experience was a turning point for Saville, who thereafter dedicated his career to working in Latin America. He was put in charge of developing and constructing the Mexican and Central American exhibits at the Columbian Exposition (Wissler 1944:648) and then returned to the Peabody, where he remained as an assistant curator for about a year, until he was hired, on Putnam's recommendation, by the American Museum of Natural History (AMNH). Putnam had nominated Saville to be the assistant curator in the anthropology division there in 1893, a job he began in 1894, the same year Putnam, too, accepted a position at the AMNH, which he held concurrently with his Peabody curatorship until 1903 (see chapter 8).

Saville's interest was primarily in collecting objects. He "owed" Putnam (and Charles Bowditch, the financial backer of the Copan expedition to Honduras) reports on the Copan work, but he never finished them. He soon came into conflict with one of Putnam's other appointees to the AMNH, Franz Boas. Saville was able to continue his collecting activities, however, because by 1895 he had secured the financial sponsorship of New York businessman Joseph Florimond Loubat (Cole 1999:232; D. McVicker 1992:149; and see chapter 9). In February 1903 Saville managed to have himself appointed the first Loubat Professor of American Archaeology at Columbia University, in spite of Boas's strong opposition and his lack of advanced degrees. Although Loubat lost interest in archaeology and left New York, his endowed chair of archaeology still existed, and Saville held it until his death in 1935. For most of that time he offered no courses but spent his time in the field collecting.

By 1906 Saville had recruited another wealthy New York businessman, George Gustav Heye (1874–1957), to help support his collecting, now with a new focus on South America and later with a strong link to Heye's Museum of the American Indian, founded in 1916. With Heye's money, Saville worked in Ecuador with George Pepper, another former student of Putnam's, and later in Guatemala, Honduras, Belize, and Costa Rica. In 1918 Saville terminated his last departmental links with Columbia University to become a full-time researcher at the Museum of the American Indian (Kidwell 1999:247).

Marshall Saville remained chiefly a museum collector throughout his career. Even though his primary appointment from 1903 to 1916 had been as a professor at Columbia University, he had few students. Donald McVicker (1989, 1992) wrote that this was because Saville disliked teaching and deliberately avoided attracting students to the department. Moreover, he took extended leaves of absence in which to conduct excavations and make collecting trips to Latin America or even attend international conferences, which resulted in his canceling lectures and entire semester-long courses. Indeed, Clark Wissler (1944:648) reported that Saville's last official class at Columbia was in 1908. Nevertheless, Saville won recognition among his colleagues, being elected president of the American Anthropological Association for the 1927–28 term, and he was widely acknowledged as an expert on artifacts and their distribution in the Andes and Mesoamerica.

Frank Honore Gerrodette (1866–1951), listed in Putnam's 1890 report as "Francois Gerrodette," officially entered the program at the museum as an undergraduate that year. He graduated cum laude in 1892 and then entered the graduate program for an A.M. degree. Putnam (1892:193) listed him as "the new and third graduate student." The following year Putnam (1893a:207) wrote that "Mr. Gerrodette entered the Department for a year's study for the degree of A.M. and having given considerable time in his senior year to laboratory work in this department, he was employed in making a general review of the whole subject of American archaeology, and afterwards in preparing a map and special account of the native tribes of Central America, working through the larger part of the vacation for this purpose." Part of this work was included in Gerrodette's paper (1892), now in the Tozzer Library at Harvard.

Putnam helped Gerrodette get the job as first director of the Carnegie Museum of Natural History in Pittsburgh when it opened in 1896. Gerrodette began his first and last excavation for the Carnegie Museum on July 18, 1896, at McKees Rocks Mound, an Adena site, just downriver from Pittsburgh. An accusation of "grave-robbing" of non-Indian burials was made against Gerrodette in some local newspapers, a trumped-up scandal that escalated into a "ratings war" between the newspapers on either side of the issue (Swauger 1940:8, 24). Although Putnam even came to Pittsburgh to defend him, the pressure from the Carnegie Museum's trustees was such that Gerrodette resigned on September 19 of that year and subsequently went into a career in law.

Allen Cook (1874–1900) was born in Barnstable, Massachusetts, the son of a schoolteacher. Cook first appears in the Harvard College archive records in 1890 as a private student, and from 1891 to 1893 he is recorded as a special student in the Lawrence Scientific School. Like his pioneer undergraduate classmates, Saville and Gerrodette, Cook continued his interest in anthropology after his undergraduate years.

In 1892 Putnam (1892:193) wrote that Cook, a "private student," was working as an archaeologist at Fort Hill, Ohio, with Marshall Saville. In 1893 Putnam (1893a:207) reported that "Mr. Allan [sic] Cook, a special student in the Scientific School, has been doing regular laboratory work in this department during term time, and has been engaged in field work under my direction during the vacation." Among the field projects Cook was involved in were excavations in Ohio with Metz, Saville, Moorehead, and Harlan Smith, as well as his own brief study of a burial place in Maine (Putnam 1893a:201).

Only a few years later, however, in a short note in his curator's report for 1900, Putnam (1901:10) wrote: "It is with regret that I record the death of Mr. Allen Cooke [*sic*] at Iloilo, Philippine Islands on March 23d, 1900. Mr. Cooke was a special student in 1891–93, and he had an abiding love for archaeology. He enlisted for the Spanish war and served in Cuba, and later in the Philippines, where he hoped to be of service to the Museum in making an ethnological collection." In the list of war dead, Cook was identified as a Private, Company L, 26th Massachusetts Infantry Volunteer Battalion, Fifth Army Corps (Peterson 1958:26). Thus Putnam lost another potential recruit for the field.

George Amos Dorsey (1868–1931), born in Hebron, Ohio, was one of Putnam's first two graduate students, entering the program in 1890. He received his first A.B. degree in 1888 from Denison College in Granville, Ohio, where he also received an LL.D. in 1889. He then enrolled at Harvard, receiving his second A.B. in 1890. Putnam (1891:94) sent Dorsey to excavate at the Turner Mounds in Ohio that year. There he acquired some initial training under Marshall Saville, and later that season he moved to the Cline's Runs mounds, where he was chief assistant to Hilborne Cresson (Putnam 1891:96).

After an additional year of graduate training, Dorsey was sent by Putnam to the Andes in May 1891, "to carry on archaeological and ethnological researches as a special assistant of the Ethnological Department of the World's Columbian Exposition." Dorsey acquired materials from Bolivia, Chile, and Peru and conducted doctoral research on the ruins at Ancon, Peru, which was to become one of the most important archaeological sites in that country in the early twentieth century. Putnam appointed Dorsey "Superintendent, Section of Archaeology, World's Columbian Exposition," when he returned. Dorsey not only had several display cases of artifacts but also presented a large floor display of his excavations at Ancon. He wrote that for his display, "two large sections of the main floor have been fenced off, and within have been reconstructed shallow graves, in which have been placed bundles or packages containing the desiccated bodies. Around them are the earthenware vessels and calabashes of food, work-baskets, looms, implements of various kinds, tablets, etc." (Dorsey 1893:374).

In 1894, with the defense of his dissertation, "The Necropolis of Ancon: An Archaeological Study Based on a Personal Exploration of Over One Hundred Graves at the Necropolis of Ancon, Peru," Dorsey became Putnam's first Ph.D. student to finish the program. He was then appointed an instructor in the anthropology program at Harvard. Because Putnam had no university funds with which to hire instructors, Dorsey was supported during his last year of graduate work and his two years of teaching at Harvard primarily by a Hemenway Fellowship, which he held from 1893 to 1896. Putnam reported that, thanks to Dorsey's joining him as an instructor, the department was now able regularly to offer two team-taught, graduate-level courses: "Anth 1. General Anthropology, with special reference to American Archaeology and Ethnology," the contents of which were actually one-third somatology, one-third ethnology, and one-third archaeology, and "Anth 20. Research Course. A course in research in archaeology and ethnology requiring three years for its completion" (Putnam 1896a:242).

Dorsey, however, resigned his position at Harvard in 1896, shortly after he had begun teaching, in order to accept the position of curator at the Columbian Museum of Chicago (after 1915, the Field Museum of Natural History), and Frank Russell was appointed to take over part of his classes (Mead 1914:4). Commenting on the move, Putnam (1897:246) noted that "Dr. Dorsey is the fifth man trained in the Peabody Museum, who has been called to fill a place of responsibility elsewhere as a professional anthropologist."

Early in his time at the Columbian Museum, in 1897–98, Dorsey was asked to identify human remains in the "Luetgert case," a sensational Chicago murder trial. He is thus credited with doing some of the earliest forensic anthropological work and as being the first known anthropologist to testify in court on forensic science (Ubelaker 1999:764).

Dorsey soon changed direction toward collecting ethnological materials, conducting "whirlwind collecting trips" (Calhoun 1991a:153). During his first years at the Columbian Museum, Dorsey felt himself to be in a contest with the AMNH, the Smithsonian, and other museums, doing "salvage ethnography" to collect what he thought was the vanishing American Indian ethnographic and archaeological record. The Columbian Museum obtained money for ethnographic collections in the late 1890s "largely through Dorsey's aggressive fund-raising techniques." He used the specter of museums in other cities outdoing Chicago as one of several themes to extract money from wealthy Chicago donors. The files in the museum are "thick with his cajoling, flattering and insistent letters to potential donors" (Rabineau 1981:32).

As Tristan Almazan and Sarah Coleman observed (2003:90–91), "Dorsey was more interested in having a large number and [variety] of objects from a particular tribe or culture area to exhibit at the Museum than he was in gathering objects and information for research purposes. Few field notes remain for the collecting activities of Dorsey and his assistants from 1897 to 1901." It was during this period that he penned the following note to his assistant, Stephen Simms, on January 31, 1900, a note that has been reprinted in several places, indicating Dorsey's initial slapdash collecting techniques: "When you go into an Indian's house and you do not find the old man at home and there is something you want, you can do one of three things: go hunt up the old man and keep hunting until you find him; give the old woman such price for it as she may ask for it running the risk that the old man will be offended; or steal it. I tried all three plans and have no choice to recommend" (Almazan and Coleman 2003:89).

In 1901 Dorsey made a significant change in his collecting procedures. He and other proponents of salvage ethnography had been subjected to increasing criticism from Putnam, Boas, and other colleagues for losing sight of the aims of research in their fierce competition to secure as many ethnographic items as possible. For example, at the AMNH, Boas wrote to Morris Jesup on January 9, 1902, that both the University of Pennsylvania Museum and the Columbian Museum were "simply bringing together material without any serious attempt to preserve the scientific and historic significance of the objects collected and for this reason I consider their activity destructive" (quoted in Bernstein 1993:22). In response, Dorsey began to change his procedures. For example, he "began to ask his assistants to collect more than just objects. On numerous occasions, he wrote to those working for him in the field and asked that they write down as much information as they were able about a culture, its religion, games, objects, and so on" (Almazan and Coleman 2003:91).

Thus, Don Fowler (2000:224) has argued that even though Dorsey was an aggressive and flamboyant showman, his 1901 and later collections documentation policy set a new standard by requiring sufficient documentation on each specimen "to make its use, history, origin, material, etc. available in a scientific journal" if required. Yet it took Dorsey a long time to live down his previous haphazard approach. His successor, Berthold Laufer, in a letter to Boas of April 13, 1908, wrote, "According to the Dorsey method . . . it is possible for every ethnologist to work in any territory; he photographs a little bit, buys indiscriminately everything he can get his hands on, has a good time with the people, and that settles the matter" (quoted in Wilcox 2003b:42 n. 4).

From January 1903 through April 1904, Dorsey took a leave of absence from the Columbian Museum to work in the Indian Department of the Fred Harvey Company, which operated hotels, gift shops, and tours along railroad routes in the U.S. Southwest (Pardue 1996:102). "The Indian Department employed ethnologists like George A. Dorsey to acquire objects and to write catalogs to make their collections scientific, authentic, and salable" (Pardue 1996:106). Dorsey wrote a lengthy handbook describing the Indians of the Southwest for the Atchison, Topeka and Santa Fe Railroad, and he arranged the Alvarado Indian Museum for the Harvey Company at its railroad hotel in Albuquerque, New Mexico (Howard 2002:61, 68). He also collected and sold ethnographic and archaeological specimens to the American Museum of Natural History, the Columbian Museum, the University of Pennsylvania Museum, and the U.S. National Museum during this period, mediating between commerce and science apparently to supplement his low salary at the Columbian Museum.

When George Dorsey was hired by the Columbian Museum, he immediately applied for a part-time teaching job, in April 1896, with the University of Chicago, but Frederick Starr initially blocked his request (Darnell 1998:113; N. Evans 1987:64). Dorsey finally obtained a part-time appointment to teach physical anthropology at Chicago in 1905, an appointment he kept until 1915, but owing to continuing personal difficulties with Starr, he taught only a few classes at the very beginning of this period (Miller 1978:54–55; S. Murray 1988:383). He also occasionally taught courses in physical anthropology and comparative anatomy in the dental school at Northwestern University from 1900 to 1913 (Calhoun 1991a:153; F-C. Cole 1931:413).

During the first years of the twentieth century Dorsey served as a member of the AAAS-sponsored organizing committee that formally founded the American Anthropological Association (AAA) in Pittsburgh on June 30, 1902 (W. McGee 1903). He subsequently served as one of the first two secretaries of the AAA (Anonymous 1906c:442). He took another leave of absence from what was by now the Field Museum from 1909 to 1912, in order to serve as foreign correspondent for the *Chicago Tribune*

(Calhoun 1991a:154); apparently his commitment to museum anthropology had begun to wane. He served at the museum another few years but resigned in 1915 to become a lieutenant commander in the U.S. Navy and later assistant naval attaché in Spain (1917–19) and Portugal (1919–21). He remained in the navy until 1921 (Cole 1931:413; Ubelaker 1999:765). During this period he became involved with the Office of Naval Intelligence, helping to run a series of agents in Portugal. After returning to the United States, Dorsey made a living as an independent writer and scholar in New York City. He became partially reinvolved with anthropology when he was named a director and occasional lecturer at the New School for Social Research in 1925 (*National Cyclopedia* 1932:200), but otherwise he dropped out of the anthropology scene.

John Gundy Owens (1865–93), the second graduate student who entered in 1890, was a native of Lewisburg, Pennsylvania. He attended Bucknell College in Lewisburg from 1883 to 1887, obtaining both an A.B. and A.M. In the fall of 1887 he took a job teaching in the natural and mental sciences department of the South Jersey Institute in Bridgton, New Jersey, where he introduced the study of astronomy and zoology. In the summer of 1888 he enrolled at the marine laboratory at Wood's Hole, and in 1889 he came to the Harvard summer school in marine biology, where he met Jesse Walter Fewkes (see chapter 9), who was working there as an instructor for the Museum of Comparative Zoology. Fewkes lost his MCZ job at Harvard that year but was hired by the Hemenway Southwestern Archaeological Expedition, and on the basis of his work with Owens at the marine biology institute, he recruited Owens to work as his assistant on the expedition. Thus Owens joined the Hemenway Expedition for 1890 and 1891, working among the Zunis, Hopis, Navajos, and White Mountain Apaches (Hinsley 1984:64C, 1992:134; Putnam 1894:215).

After the first summer, at Zuni Pueblo, Owens decided he needed more anthropology background, and he was the perfect student for Putnam to enroll in his new program, for the 1890–91 school term. Owens was supported as the first recipient of the Hemenway Fellowship, which he held for the next two years (Putnam 1890a:77, 1891:98–99, 1894:215).

At the end of this first year of graduate studies, Owens left for a second season with Fewkes on the Hopi Mesas, doing mainly ethnographic research. He was initiated as an Antelope priest in the Hopi Snake ceremony (Fewkes 1892a:3; Fewkes, Stephen, and Owens 1894:81–82) and wrote a series of ethnographic observations on Hopi ceremonies (Owens 1892; Fewkes and Owens 1892; Fewkes, Stephen, and Owens 1894). He also helped Fewkes set up the Hemenway exhibit for the Madrid portion of the 1892 quartocentenary of Columbus's voyage (Fowler 2000:162; Putnam 1893a:207).

In addition, Owens conducted some archaeological fieldwork during his time with Fewkes. He measured and mapped the site of Casa Grande, near Tucson, Arizona, in April 1891 for Mary Hemenway, in her successful push to get Casa Grande designated the nation's first national monument (Fewkes 1892b:193). After locating some old Zuni archaeological sites in 1890 (Fewkes 1891:9), Owens had asked to conduct additional archaeological explorations on some cliff ruins near Flagstaff, Arizona, but Fewkes refused him permission to do so (Hinsley 1983:64).

When Owens returned from his second season in the Southwest, in the fall of 1891, he was at Harvard finishing up his reports for only a month when Putnam put him in charge of the first Peabody Museum expedition to Copan, Honduras, in 1891–92, with Marshall Saville as his assistant. The immediate aim was to gather artifacts for display at the Chicago exposition (Putnam 1893a:207). Before leaving for Copan, Putnam sent Owens to get some training in anthropometry from Franz Boas, then at Clark University (Hinsley 1992:135). This was the first of a series of collaborations in training students between Putnam and Boas.

Owens returned from Copan in the summer of 1892 with a number of massive plaster replicas of stelae for the exposition. He left for the second season at Copan in the fall of 1892, with George Byron Gordon replacing Marshall Saville as his chief assistant. Shortly after arriving in Honduras on this trip, Owens contracted yellow fever and died in February 1893. He is said to have been buried "before one of the huge stone altars in the grand square of the ruins of Copan, where he had done so much in the cause of science and with which his name will ever be associated" (Putnam 1894:215). A sad end to a potentially significant career in archaeology.

In 1893, someone named Owen, not Owens, worked for Putnam as well. Because at least one source has conflated these two, we want to clarify who this Owen was. **Charles Lorin Owen** (1861–1927) began his archaeological work that year with Putnam and then moved to work with Putnam's former student Dorsey at the Columbian Museum of Chicago. Owen was born Ohio and had received his A.B. from Denison in 1885; Dorsey received his degree there in 1888, so the two overlapped for at least one year. Owen had initially found work as a civil engineer, but in 1893 Putnam recruited him to secure collections for the Columbian Exposition, and Owen, who had an avocational interest in archaeology, shifted his career from engineering to archaeology.

The changeover took a while to get settled. After the collecting job for Putnam, Owen returned to work as a civil engineer until 1898, when he secured a position as a pest control "poisoner" for the Columbian Museum. In 1900 he became assistant curator of archaeology, under Dorsey's direction. He then led archaeological excavation projects in Arizona, California, and Ohio for the museum and worked in its collections department until he retired in 1925 (Almazan and Coleman 2003: 93; Rabineau 1981:34, 37). Charles Owen was yet another "professional" archaeologist who got his start with Putnam and continued in the discipline.

After this start with his first class of "official" students, Putnam recruited growing numbers of students to his educational programs during the rest of the decade. Some of these people he trained more in museum studies, some more as archaeologists and field men, and others as first-rate ethnologists and general anthropologists.

George Byron Gordon (1870–1927), born in Perth, Prince Edward Island, Canada, was one of those who almost immediately joined the cluster of first formal students at the museum. He had started college at the University of South Carolina in the 1888–89 term but then transferred to Harvard, where he enrolled at Lawrence Scientific School as an engineering student (King and Little 1986:19). While there, he was recruited by Putnam to go as the surveyor on the Peabody Museum's second Copan expedition, in 1892–93. When Owens, the expedition director, died, Gordon ended up taking over the project. Upon his return to Harvard, after securing his S.B. in engineering in 1894, he shifted to archaeology for his graduate work.

Gordon subsequently led several more expeditions to Honduras between 1894 and 1900. Putnam supported the Copan work through a variety of means. During Owens's period, he used funds from the 1893 Columbian Exposition operations. In 1894 he used the new position he had just accepted at the AMNH to get Morris K. Jesup to subscribe $1,000 to the project in order to acquire materials for the AMNH (Putnam 1895a:222). Later, he talked Charles Bowditch into providing a major portion of the fieldwork support (Putnam 1898a:243).

By 1899 George Gordon was listed among the Peabody Museum staff as "Assistant in Central American Archaeology" (Putnam 1900a:271). In his final years at Harvard he was supported by a Winthrop Scholarship, in 1901–2, and a Hemenway Fellowship, in 1902–3. He defended his dissertation, "The Serpent Motive in the Ancient Art of Mexico and Central America," in 1903. Because Harvard did not yet have a large anthropology faculty, Gordon's Ph.D. examining committee included faculty from the broader Harvard academic division as well. From the Peabody Museum there were Frederic Putnam, Frank Russell, Roland Dixon, and Francis Lowell, and from the larger Division XIV, David Lyon, and George Goodale. We discuss most of these people later in this chapter; on Francis Lowell, see chapter 9.

After completing his doctorate at Harvard, Gordon took the job of assistant curator of the University of Pennsylvania Museum. Stewart Culin had just resigned from that position to take a job at the Brooklyn Museum. Putnam had first suggested William C. Farabee (see chapter 10) as a replacement for Culin, but when Farabee withdrew his candidacy because Harvard offered him an instructorship in anthropology for the 1903–4 term, Putnam suggested Gordon. Gordon began the job in September 1903 (King and Little 1986:21; Putnam 1904:283).

Gordon took with him to the University Museum Putnam's ideas about how anthropology should be constituted. Elin Danien (1999:287) noted that "during his first year at the museum, he urged the university to offer a program of instruction in anthropology that would include courses in somatology and linguistics as well as archaeology and ethnology." This statement closely mirrors a comment by Eleanor King and Bryce Little (1986:24) that Gordon sought approval in November 1903, two months after he had been hired, "for a broad-based approach to anthropology, to include somatology, and later linguistics, with archaeology and ethnology." This request was approved, and Gordon offered courses in anthropology as electives in the spring term of 1904. In 1907 the Department of Anthropology was officially established at the University of Pennsylvania, with Gordon appointed assistant professor as well as chair. He taught in the department until 1915, when his duties as museum director more severely limited his time (LeGrain 1927:355).

In 1910 Gordon was named the first director of the University Museum. His interest in trying to link the museum to academic departments soon ran Gordon into problems with some of the older collectors at Pennsylvania, and he spent a good deal of time arguing with them over the functions of a museum (Kuklick 1996:136–39). Gordon's plan for the development of the University Museum seems to have mirrored in many ways the plans followed by the Peabody, the AMNH, the Field Museum, and others at the time—conducting salvage ethnography and archaeology, securing comparative collections, and providing the Euro-American public with evidence of its roots. In a letter of September 13, 1913, Gordon spelled out his three-part plan for the museum (Conn 1998:100–101):

> The first [method], because the most urgent, is to assemble the best available examples of the handiworks of the various peoples known to history and geography, and left behind, as it were, in the march of events. The second method is to assemble, either by excavation or by purchase, collections of the relics which precede the records of the earliest civilization and which carry the history of man backwards a hundred thousand years and more to the beginning of his life on the planet. The third method consists in assembling examples to illustrate the great civilizations of antiquity to which our own civilization is more directly indebted, namely, Egypt, Babylonia, Greece and Rome.

In 1908, at the International Congress of Americanists, Putnam and Boas had roped Gordon into discussions about the possibility of starting an international school for anthropology in Mexico City. As director of the University Museum, he was the official representative of the University of Pennsylvania in September 1910 when Eduard Seler, for Prussia, Louis-Joseph Capitan, for France, Boas, for Columbia, Dixon, for Harvard, and Ezequiel A. Chávez, secretary of public instruction and fine arts, for Mexico, signed a formal agreement to found the school (Ruiz 2003:154–55). The directorship of the new International School of American Archaeology and Ethnology was established on a one-year, rotating basis, but before Gordon's turn came up, the school failed in 1914, during the Mexican Revolution.

Except for two collecting expeditions to Alaska in 1905 and 1907 with his brother Maclaren, George Gordon conducted no more active fieldwork after the Copan excavations. The 1907 expedition was partially funded by George G. Heye, and the materials, which were initially curated at Pennsylvania, were moved to New York in 1917 with the completion of Heye's Museum of the American Indian (King and Little 1986:31, 44; Madeira 1964:35). Gordon spent the bulk of his career after 1903 in museum administrative duties, until his unexpected death in 1927, a result of his falling and hitting his head on a marble step (Harrison 1927:6; Madeira 1964:40). In the years just before his death he had taken over the museum's involvement in Mediterranean and Middle Eastern expeditions and was in overall charge of expeditions at Ur and Beisan when he died (Anonymous 1927; Legrain 1927:355).

Joining Putnam's program shortly after Gordon was **Frank Russell** (1868–1903). Born in Fort Dodge, Iowa, Russell began his training at the University of Iowa. He took part in a collecting expedition to the Canadian Northwest under Prof. Charles Cleveland Nutting of Iowa and received his B.S. from Iowa in 1892 on the basis of an analysis of zoological collections from this project. He then took off on his own to do research in the Canadian Arctic from the fall of 1892 to May 1894; he received his M.S. from Iowa on the basis of this work in 1895 (Hodge 1903:738). He next enrolled at Harvard, in 1895, continuing his work on the Subarctic. In the summer of 1896 he was listed as a member of the teaching staff for a larger party from the University of Pennsylvania going to Labrador: "The professors will give lectures daily on their various subjects, illustrated by the specimens procured, and thus the excursion will be made a valuable training school for young naturalists" (Anonymous 1896b:54).

Russell received a second A.B., in anthropology, from Harvard in 1896, an A.M. in 1897, and a Ph.D. in 1898. His dissertation, defended in front of an examining committee composed of Putnam, Bowditch, Lowell, Lyon, and Goodale, was titled "A Study of a Collection of Eskimo Crania from Labrador, with Observations on the Prevailing System of Craniometry." He was supported in his first year of graduate work by the Winthrop Scholarship and during the next two years by the Hemenway Fellowship.

In 1896, shortly after Russell enrolled, George Dorsey resigned his teaching position at Harvard to take the curatorial post at the Columbian Museum of Chicago. Russell, with his newly minted Harvard A.B. but also with an Iowa M.S., was recruited to take over Dorsey's course, Anthropology 1. Russell was appointed assistant in anthropology in 1896 and instructor in anthropology in 1897, thus serving as one of three anthropology faculty instructors at this time, the others being Putnam and Roland Dixon (Dixon 1930:211; Putnam 1898a:251). In the 1897–98 year, Russell introduced the first course in physical anthropology—"Somatology"—into the curriculum, and in 1898, having been reappointed without a time limit and made a member of the Faculty of Arts and Sciences, he added "Advanced Somatology" (Mead 1914:4; Putnam 1899a:274, 1904:285).

Russell had contracted tuberculosis during his years working with Inuit people in the Subarctic. A desire to sojourn in the dry, sunny Southwest to treat the disease seems to have been the reason for a 700-mile bicycle tour of Arizona and New Mexico he made in the summer of 1898. During this trip he stopped to visit George Pepper, another student of Putnam's, at his excavations at Pueblo Bonito (see chapter 8), and he visited the Jicarilla Apache reservation with an eye to future research possibilities (Putnam 1899a:272). Russell made another trip to Arizona in the summer of 1900, but his planned archaeological research on the Hopi reservation was cut short. The Office of

Indian Affairs had already given George Dorsey, at the Columbian Museum, a permit to work with the Hopis that season and thus rejected the Peabody Museum's application for an excavation permit (Putnam 1901a:295; Snead 2001:43, 53).

Putnam encouraged Russell to become involved in discipline-wide activities, and it was during this period that he served as vice president of Section H, Anthropology, for the AAAS. "Vice president" was the official AAAS term for the chair of each of the scientific sections. This was before the AAA was formed, so Russell was essentially the national leader of all anthropologists outside the Washington, D.C., orbit during his term of office. He subsequently became one of the 24 councilors named to the newly formed American Anthropological Association in 1902, and he was also elected president of the American Folk-Lore Society that year (Hodge 1903:738).

Although today it might seem strange for an archaeologist to have been president of the folklore society, in the late 1890s and early 1900s this group had a strong archaeological component. Russell's presidential address at the American Folk-Lore Society was published, giving us a further window into his views. He noted in the address that anthropology, which he believed should be considered "the crown and completion of the sciences" (Russell 1902:562), was now taught in 30 colleges in the United States, and it "equips the student who is to become a merchant, physician, attorney, with a practical knowledge of the motives of his competitors and clients" as well as being a good field for training for the diplomatic service and for legislators, lawmakers, and jurists (Russell 1902:570). We also learn a bit about his teaching style, for he noted that discussions in his Harvard classes were "sometimes adjourned to the home of the instructor" (Russell 1902:566).

Russell was sufficiently unwell that he took medical leave from his teaching duties at Harvard for the 1901–2 year. He returned to the Southwest for medical reasons but supported himself by securing a contract as field assistant with the Bureau of American Ethnology (BAE), doing archaeological and ethnographic work with the Pima and Papago Indians (Putnam 1902a:272, 1904:285). He felt recovered enough to return to Harvard for the 1902–3 year and took on a strenuous teaching load.

It is from one of his lectures in Anthropology 4, Prehistoric Archaeology—European Ethnology, in November 1902 that we have the first documented evidence of the actual teaching of stratigraphic excavation methods to undergraduates in the classroom at an American university, from the notes of an anonymous student, now in the Peabody Museum archives. The student wrote (Russell mss 1902) that Russell said that proper excavation procedure in caves required one to "divide the cave into blocks one foot deep and three feet square." This was the same excavation methodology that Pengelly had begun in Europe in 1859 and Putnam had adopted at the Peabody Museum. Putnam had passed on such methods by personal letter, by example, and through the "Chautauqua or Lyceum method" (Stocking and Montague 1979:16) of public lectures, but using full-term college class lectures to this end was a new and different approach, which took Putnam longer to develop. All of Russell's archaeological training had taken place at

Harvard, where we see him presenting possibly the first explicit instructions in scientific excavation in a formal classroom situation by detailing the archaeological methods advocated by Putnam.

During the spring Russell served on the examining committee for George B. Gordon's Ph.D., along with Lowell, Dixon, Lyon, and Goodale. Later that spring Russell again felt so unwell that he took medical leave in mid-term, departing in March 1903 to return to the Southwest. James H. Woods, whom Putnam had hired to teach for Dixon while Dixon was on leave in 1901–2, was then hired to take over the remaining portion of Russell's General Anthropology course, giving lectures with the notes Russell had prepared. The two graduate students in the course were allowed to complete their coursework by correspondence with Russell (Mead 1914:6). In Arizona, Russell spent his time digging irrigation ditches for a homestead that summer, but his health continued to worsen, and he died from tuberculosis at Chloride, near Kingman, Arizona, in November 1903 (Putnam 1904:285). Putnam appeared to have been grooming Russell to be a major player in the field of Americanist archaeology. As with Owens, disease had taken from Putnam and from the profession a promising ally.

John Reed Swanton (1873–1958) was born in Gardiner, Maine, and entered Harvard as an undergraduate in 1893, apparently having previously developed an interest in American Indians. In the summer of 1894 he went back to Maine with Charles Willoughby on an archaeological expedition; the next summer he worked with Ernest Volk at the Trenton site in New Jersey (we profile Willoughby later in this chapter; on Volk, see chapter 4). After receiving his A.B. in the spring of 1896, Swanton was sent with Roland Dixon and Ingersoll Bowditch (see chapter 9) to work that summer with Charles Metz at the Ferris Cemetery site at Madisonville, Ohio (Putnam 1897:249). The following winter Swanton was assigned to the analysis of skeletons and associated artifacts as part of duties apparently associated with his receipt of the Winthrop Scholarship. The work formed the basis of his 1897 A.M. degree, but he was less than enthusiastic about it, later complaining that he had spent half the winter washing skeletons in the museum basement (Kroeber 1940:1). Following that, Putnam sent him to work for the next five months with George Pepper at Pueblo Bonito (Putnam 1899a:272).

Swanton had earlier joined the Harvard College Folklore Society with Dixon, and this seemed partly to define his changing interests (Dorson 1980:612). After working at archaeological sites in Maine, New Jersey, Ohio, and New Mexico for four years running, Swanton had developed something of an antipathy for archaeology. Hence in the fall of 1898, at Putnam's suggestion, he went down to the AMNH and Columbia University with Dixon to take additional training with Boas on Indian languages and ethnology (Putnam 1899a:272). While at Columbia, Swanton met Alfred Louis Kroeber (1876–1960), who had come to take classes with Boas as well. Boas had Dixon, Kroeber, and Swanton in the field in the summer of 1899, studying the languages of West Coast ethnic groups. Swanton's research was the basis of his 1900 Ph.D. dissertation at Harvard,

"Morphology of the Chinook Verb." Swanton's Ph.D. examining committee included Putnam, Bowditch, Lowell, Lyon, and Goodale.

Swanton was then hired immediately by the BAE, where he worked until his retirement in 1944. During this period he served as associate editor of *American Anthropologist* from 1910 to 1923, with a one-year term as editor when Frederick W. Hodge took a break in 1911. He was president of the AAA in 1932, vice president of Section H of the AAAS, and a member of the Social Science Research Council and the National Research Council. In 1913 he won the second-place Loubat Prize for publications in ethnology (see chapter 9) and in 1948 the Viking Fund Medal in Anthropology. He published more than 200 articles and 20 monographs, the majority of them dealing with the U.S. Southeast, covering ethnography, ethnological theory, ethnohistory, folklore, and linguistics (Fenton 1959:663–64).

Despite his involvement in anthropological organizations, Swanton tended to be a loner. For example, when archaeologist Philip Phillips (chapter 11), knowing that Swanton had been trained at Harvard and thus might be helpful in Phillips's research in the Mississippi Valley, contacted Swanton and went to Washington, D.C., to discuss Swanton's well-known 1939 DeSoto report, Swanton was short with him and provided little assistance (S. Williams 2003:xxv). Other researchers reported similar treatment.

In his early years Swanton had been interested in spiritualism and had avidly followed experiments on ESP. Later in life he wrote colleagues urging them to learn the truth about anthropology via parapsychology, suggesting that he had learned much from using a ouija board and other psychic phenomena (Fenton 1959:667; S. Murray 1991b; S. Williams 1991:296). This quirk has led some recent scholars to view much of Swanton's later work with skepticism, with some reason.

Roland Burrage Dixon (1875–1934), born in Worcester, Massachusetts, forms an integral part of the archaeological heritage of the Peabody Museum, although many of his contributions to the museum belong to the post-1905 time frame; indeed, he was recognized as a giant in the field in the first quarter of the twentieth century. Because he directed that his files, notebooks, and other materials be destroyed when he died, it is more difficult to get at Dixon than some of his fellow students. Not only was information about his personal history lost, but so was a tremendous amount of ethnographic field data. For example, Bruce Bernstein (1993:21) reported that by 1908 Dixon had filled 78 notebooks with ethnographic observations, 38 of them relating to the Maidu, all of which were destroyed at his death.

Dixon was recruited into the anthropology program by Putnam, starting out as a student in ethnology. Dixon was clearly in at the beginning of Putnam's course development at the Peabody Museum. He took Anthropology 1, General Anthropology, in 1894–95 with only two other undergraduates and one graduate student, although one graduate and four other students took the course as an "extra" (Mead 1914:4).

Like all of Putnam's initial graduate students, Dixon was required to take field training in archaeology. Thus, after he received his A.B. in the spring of 1897, he and John Swanton were sent out to Ohio to work on the mounds at Madisonville under the supervision of Charles Metz, with their expenses supported by monies from the Wolcott Fund (Putnam 1897:249). Dixon spent the fall of 1897 sorting through the collections from the first field season (Putnam 1899a:272) and was sent out again, funded as the Hemenway Fellow, to continue work the next season (Putnam 1899a:274). In contrast to Swanton, who grew to detest archaeology, Dixon continued a lively interest in the topic throughout his career.

These Harvard crews did good fieldwork. Penelope Drooker (1997:117) wrote that it was not until the excavations by Dixon and Swanton in 1897—along with later excavations by Raymond Merwin, also of the Peabody Museum—that "adequate" archaeology was done at Madisonville. She stated that the methods employed by the Putnam-trained Peabody Museum crews of Dixon, Swanton, and then Merwin provided for the first modern, well-provenienced artifact recovery, tied in by grid system and depth.

After George Dorsey left for Chicago in 1896, leaving Putnam with a teaching staff problem, Dixon, with only an A.B., was appointed an "Assistant in Anthropology" to help teach the courses Dorsey had been scheduled to teach with Putnam for the 1897–98 school year. Dixon did not receive his A.M. until May 1898. Putnam, through his position at the AMNH, secured Dixon a place with the Jesup North Pacific Expedition to British Columbia, directed by Boas, for the rest of that year. During the 1898–99 school year, Dixon commuted from Boston to New York to take Boas's courses at Columbia. At the same time, he was teaching his new course, Anthropology 3, Primitive Religions, at Harvard. In 1899, using funding available through the AMNH, Putnam and Boas sent Dixon to California to study Maidu ethnology (S. Murray 1991a:149; Putnam 1900a:274). Dixon received his Ph.D., with a dissertation titled "The Language of the Maidu Indians of California," in 1900, his dissertation committee consisting of Putnam, Bowditch, Lowell, Lyon, and Goodale.

After having served as an assistant in anthropology for four years, Dixon, with Ph.D. in hand, was finally appointed an instructor. He was soon sitting on Ph.D. students' committees, the first degree being George Gordon's in 1903. Dixon rapidly worked his way up through the academic ranks, becoming a full professor in 1916. He continued a distinguished teaching career at Harvard, with significant contributions and publications in archaeology, linguistics, physical anthropology, and sociocultural anthropology.

Dixon almost immediately settled into the pattern that he was to continue for the next two decades. He spent a good deal of time in the field or in foreign institutions doing research, employing his own funds, and only part of his time in Cambridge at the university. Thus Putnam observed that because Dixon was going to Berlin to do more work in early 1901, James Woods had to be appointed instructor in anthropology to take over Dixon's primitive religion course (Putnam 1901a:299). Dixon did occasionally take students with him. In the summer following the receipt of his degree, he took

Plate 17

The North American Hall at the Peabody, 1893.

Sculptures from Copan, Central American Room, Peabody Museum, 1899.

Plate 18

John Gundy Owens, 1890. Putnam's handwritten inscription on this portrait reads, "A noble man and thorough student."

George Byron Gordon, who became director of the Copan expedition after Owens's death.

Owens in Copan, Honduras, 1893, with porters carrying casts of Maya sculpture for shipment to the Peabody Museum.

Plate 19

Gordon at the Hieroglyphic Stairway, Copan.

Gordon perusing a plan of Copan in his field office.

Roland Burrage Dixon, a founding member of Harvard's anthropology faculty.

Charles Clark Willoughby, director of the Peabody from 1915 to 1928.

George Henry Chase, professor of classical archaeology.

George Grant MacCurdy, founding director of the American School of Prehistoric Research.

Egyptologist Sarah Yorke Stevenson, Putnam's "God-daughter in Science," 1896.

Putnam with some of his staff for the World's Columbian Exposition, ca. 1891–92. Standing, left to right (tentative identifications marked "?"): Warren K. Moorehead (?), unidentified, Stewart Culin, Antonio Apache, Charles Willoughby, and Charles L. Metz (?). Seated, left to right: Harlan Smith (?), George A. Dorsey (?), Putnam, Frances Mead (?), and Alice Fletcher (?).

Antonio (Anthony) Apache.

Plate 23

Maya casts in the Peabody exhibition, World's Columbian Exposition, Chicago, 1893.

Reconstructed stone grave from southern Ohio, another Peabody exhibit at the World's Columbian Exposition, 1893.

Plate 24

Mary Porter Tileston Hemenway,
Peabody Museum benefactor.

Mary's husband, Augustus Hemenway.

Frank Hamilton Cushing, first director of the Hemenway Southwestern Archaeological
Expedition, with Zuni men in Boston, 1882.

Plate 25

The Hemenway exhibit at the Columbian Historical Exposition, Madrid, 1892.

Pottery exhibit cases in the Hemenway Room at the Peabody, 1899.

Plate 26

Jesse Walter Fewkes, second director of the Hemenway Expedition.

Francis Cabot Lowell, Peabody Museum trustee.

Stephen Salisbury Jr., Peabody Museum trustee.

Joseph Florimond, duc de Loubat, 1899.

Plate 27

Bowditch at Comayagua,
Honduras, March 1890.

Charles Pickering Bowditch, a trustee, faculty member,
and benefactor of the museum.

Plate 28

Adela C. Breton, artist and archaeologist.

Breton copying the frescoes in the Painted Chamber at Chichen Itza.

Plate 29

Raymond E. Merwin (right) and Robert Berger, Trench A, Madisonville site, Ohio, 1907.

David Ives Bushnell Jr.

Plate 30

William Curtis Farabee, seated at far left, in camp on the Tambopata River, Peru, 1907. Other members of the ethnological expedition were (left to right) Dr. Edward Franklin Horr and Harvard College students Louis Jean de Milhau and John Walter Hastings. Local guides stand at left and right.

Franz Boas, Alfred Tozzer, and Zelia Nuttall at Xochimilco, Mexico, ca. 1911.

Plate 31

Alfred Marston Tozzer in Guatemala, 1909–10.

Tozzer with his crew in camp during the 1909–10 Peabody expedition to map Tikal, Holmul, and Nakum.

Plate 32

Breaking ground for the expansion of the Peabody Museum building, spring 1913. Left to right: Charles Peabody and his son Alfred, Alice Putnam, Mrs. F. W. Putnam, Frederic W. Putnam, Samuel Henshaw (director of the Museum of Comparative Zoology), Charles C. Willoughby, and Samuel J. Guernsey.

Alfred M. Tozzer, who had just received his A.B. that spring and who, like Dixon, was a Winthrop Scholar, to California to continue studies on the Maidu language. Dixon was in California from August 1900 to January 1901, then went to Germany to do comparative material studies, and in the fall of 1901 went on to do further studies in Mongolia and Siberia (Putnam 1902a:271).

Dixon spent six field seasons working in California before moving his ethnographic research elsewhere. In his first few seasons, on Boas's directions, he collected plaster face casts and anthropomorphic measurements, predominantly from males. Some evaluators of Dixon's work have taken a dim view of the first few years of his collecting of Maidu material culture. Bernstein (1993:25) alleged that "like many Boasian anthropologists who would follow him, Dixon collected objects more like a tourist than a trained anthropologist." On the other hand, Bernstein (1993:20) credited Dixon's pioneering work in California with the production of the seminal ethnographies on the Shasta and Maidu; the identification of two major California Indian linguistic stocks, Hokan and Penutian; a dissertation on California Indian languages; a monograph on Maidu myths and folktales; two of the first academic publications on basketry; and 650 Maidu artifacts for the AMNH. In all, Dixon published 3 books and 28 articles based on his California fieldwork.

Boas was as pleased as Putnam was with Dixon's California work. Boas had been overseeing the work of Kroeber, Swanton, and Dixon in the classroom and in the field in 1898 and 1899. When the California Academy of Sciences in San Francisco wanted a curator, Boas recommend Dixon to its director, David Starr Jordan, in a letter of January 27, 1900. Jordan ended up giving the position to Kroeber when Dixon declined it, but Kroeber kept the job for only five months before the job ended (Jacknis 2002:524).

For the first decade of his teaching at Harvard, Dixon, who spent most of his time doing ethnographic research, nevertheless kept his hand in on the prehistoric component of ethnography as well. In 1905 he supervised the beginning of excavation work on a Mandan site in North Dakota by Herbert Spinden (class of 1906) and George Francis Will (class of 1907), to whom we return in chapter 10. In 1907, using Wolcott Fund support, Dixon embarked on an expedition to the Nez Perce area for linguistic, ethnological, and archaeological research with Spinden and Robert Hellman (class of 1906). Hellman became sick, but otherwise they had a successful season (Putnam 1908:298–300). In the following summer, 1908, Dixon joined a Harvard crew including Tozzer, Sylvanus G. Morley, and A.V. Kidder (see chapter 10) for the last three weeks of excavations for the Archaeological Institute of America (AIA) directed by Edgar L. Hewett on the Rito de los Frijoles, New Mexico (Putnam 1909:300). In addition to Dixon's participation in archaeological fieldwork in the Southwest, on the Pacific Coast, and in the Great Plains, archival materials at the Tozzer Library at Harvard indicate that he took a keen interest in archaeological work in the Southeast as well.

Part of Dixon's continuing interest in archaeology no doubt derived from his intense love of the outdoors. His first publication (Dixon and Drew 1897) was based on the natural history observations he made during a field trip to the Berkshires in the spring of 1897. Dixon's former student George Will noted in his tenth reunion report to his classmates that he had spent his summer vacation of 1907 with Dixon, Hellman, and Spinden on a five-week camping trip to the Olympic Mountains in Washington. Several of the Peabody Museum's annual reports also note this kind of activity. Alfred Tozzer and Carleton Coon (1943:xi) observed that "with pack trains [Dixon] spent several summers in the Olympics, the Cascades, and the Sierras of the Pacific Coast, and he knew every camping site in the White Mountains." Dixon was truly, as Alfred Kroeber wrote (1936:297), "a naturalist translated into a scholar in the field of culture history."

Roland Dixon continued to integrate prehistory into his ethnographic studies throughout his life, but his last major explicit statement on archaeology was his extraordinary (but little cited) presidential address to the AAA in December 1913, "Some Aspects of North American Archeology." In it he speculated on the origins of the American Indians, but more important, he called Americanist archaeologists to task for their methodological shortcomings. In the address, we can see one of the first explicit position statements for the "direct historical approach" in archaeology. Dixon argued for the

> advantage of carrying out our archaeological investigations not only in a more systematic manner, but in one which rests firmly on an ethnological and ethnographical basis. The time is past when our major interest was in the specimen, the collection, the site itself; our museums are no longer cabinets of curiosities. We are concerned with the relations of things, with the whens and the whys and the hows; in finding the explanation of the arts and customs of historic times in the remnants which have been left us from the prehistoric; in tracing step by step the wanderings of tribes and peoples beyond history, beyond tradition; in attempting to reconstruct the life of the past from its all too scanty remnants. (Dixon 1913:565)

Putnam's training had put a heavy stamp on Dixon; Putnam's archaeological interests were also Dixon's throughout his life. Nearly a decade and a half after the presidential address just quoted, a time when most researchers presume Dixon was doing only ethnographic research, we find him still taking an interest in Putnam's long-term quest for early human occupations in the Americas. In 1927 Dixon wrote to Clark Wissler: "At Hallowell's suggestion I am trying to get up a similar symposium on early man in America," referring to the formation of a symposium for the AAA to review the current state of "early man" studies (Dixon to Wissler, November 27, 1927, reproduced in Reed 1980:153).

Dixon had assumed other duties in the anthropology department at the Peabody Museum by that time. Originally there was no separate librarian; Putnam had been running the library with the help of Jane Smith (Browman 2002a:237–38). As Putnam began shedding some of his responsibilities, Dixon, as a member of the faculty, became the official librarian of the museum in 1906 (Putnam 1907:294). In that capacity he oversaw the growth of the library's 3,138 volumes and 2,908 pamphlets in 1904 to 17,075 volumes and 10,788 pamphlets in 1934 (Tozzer and Coon 1943:ix). Dixon established the Peabody system of cross-listing articles in serials by author, subject, and geographic location, three entries for each, making the Peabody Museum catalogue without question the best bibliographic tool in the world for anthropological researchers for decades; it is now available online. When Putnam informed the faculty on May 12, 1909, that he had decided to resign as Peabody Professor and curator of the Peabody Museum at the end of the year, he suggested Dixon as his replacement, and Dixon was appointed chair of the division (Putnam 1910:276).

Dixon also played an important role in founding the International School of American Archaeology and Ethnology. At the International Congress of Americanists in Mexico City in 1910, where the final papers were signed, Dixon and Tozzer represented the department and the museum while also serving as official U.S. delegates at the founding of the National University of Mexico.

Dixon maintained his heavy commitment to ethnographic research during this time. For example, in the summer of 1909 he worked in New Zealand and Australia (Putnam 1910:271). In 1910–11 he was on leave for the last half year to work with Indian tribes for the U.S. Census (Putnam 1912:222). In 1912–13 he was on leave to travel in South and Southeast Asia to develop material for his new course on the ethnography of Asia, being absent for 14 months (Putnam 1913:220, 1914:225).

Although Frederic Putnam had officially retired in 1909, he still held the title "honorary curator," continued to file the museum's official reports, and was not replaced as director until he died in 1915. At that time, Dixon, as head of the division, became acting director of the Peabody Museum, serving from August 14 until Charles Willoughby was appointed director on November 29 (Willoughby 1917:251). During World War I, Dixon's expertise was tapped by the government, and he worked on "special investigations" for the State Department (Willoughby 1919:240). In 1919 he was a member of the U.S. delegation to the Paris Peace Conference, which wrote the Treaty of Versailles (S. Murray 1991a:150).

Dixon was seen as "driven to organize and interpret masses of fact" (Kroeber 1936:294). He had an intense interest in comparative ethnology, learning Russian and Scandinavian languages in addition to French, German, and Italian, in order to read everything he could (Tozzer and Coon 1943:ix). He traveled extensively in Asia and Europe as well as the Americas, making ethnographic observations; his knowledge of geographic environments and ethnography was immense.

Three of Dixon's books are usually singled out as his most important. The first, *Oceanic Mythology* (1916a), presented hypotheses about the origins of the Polynesians and the sequence of their migrations, in addition to summarizing their mythology. The second, *Racial History of Man* (1923), was Dixon's attempt to understand the physical variation of humankind. In this volume he divided all human crania into eight categories, in spite of advice from Earnest Hooton not to do so (Tozzer and Coon 1943:x).

The third book, *The Building of Cultures* (1928a), was Dixon's foremost contribution. Its fundamental approach was geographical-historical, not descriptive, looking at both the natural and the cultural environment. In its preface Dixon wrote that it was a volume on the relationship between the environment and the origin and diffusion of culture, based on a Harvard course he had been offering for a quarter century. The volume expresses his philosophy of anthropology and his ideas concerning environmental influence, diffusion, and independent invention. Today we might categorize it as belonging to the "age and area method" of characterizing cultural groups that was so popular with Dixon, Kroeber, Wissler, and others of the period.

After 34 years of service to Harvard, Dixon died in 1934, at the age of 59. His obituary writers noted that he was a man of great reserve and few intimacies, but also one of the most erudite scholars of all time (Tozzer and Coon 1943; Tozzer and Kroeber 1936).

Charles Peabody (1867–1939) was a long-time colleague of Dixon's and the other turn-of-the-century museum staff members. He was born in Rutland, Vermont, the son of Richard Singleton Peabody (1837–1904, Harvard class of 1857), who in 1901 established the Department of Archaeology at the Phillips Academy, Andover (later the R. S. Peabody Foundation), to house his collections, and the grandnephew of the George Peabody who founded both the Yale and Harvard Peabody Museums. R. S. Peabody had become interested in archaeology as a boy, exploring sites around his hometown, Andover, Massachusetts (Anonymous 1904:745). His son Charles obviously inherited this interest.

Charles Peabody earned an A.B. from the University of Pennsylvania in 1889. He received an A.M. from Harvard in 1890 and a Ph.D. in philology (his dissertation was titled "De Saturnio Versu") in 1893, the same year George A. Reisner, an expert in Egyptian archaeology whom we discuss later, also received his Harvard Ph.D. in philology. Robert McCaughey (1974:313) observed that 11 of the 13 recipients of Ph.D.s granted in the United States in 1892–93 went on to careers in academic life, but only two of them were at Harvard, and both were in archaeology: Charles Peabody and George Reisner. We have some difficulty with McCaughey's numbers, because the records for the 12 Ph.D.s granted at Harvard alone that year show them accepting teaching positions at Harvard, Texas, Kansas State, Beloit, Iowa, Michigan, Chicago, and Berkeley in 1893; perhaps they later dropped out of academia. But whether or not McCaughey's totals are correct, his observation clearly highlights the importance of Harvard's archaeological tradition.

Charles Peabody and Frederic Putnam almost immediately began working together, establishing exhibits for the 1893 World's Columbian Exposition. Peabody was appointed chief of the Department of Liberal Arts at the fair, while Putnam handled anthropology. Both of them had originally been shoehorned into the Manufacturer's Building, but they convinced the organizers that their exhibits required separate spaces and buildings (Dexter 1966c:322). Following the exposition, Peabody went to study at the American School of Classical Studies in Athens.

After a short lacuna—we have yet to find out what he was doing in these half dozen years—Peabody returned to take additional graduate work at Harvard with Putnam in 1900–1901 (Putnam 1902a:271). Putnam sent Peabody in 1901–2 to conduct excavations at the Oliver site in Mississippi, where he was assisted by William C. Farabee, who had just received his A.M. in anthropology from Harvard in 1900. Peabody had his own financial resources, so he "kindly undertook on his account to equip an expedition for archaeological exploration" of the two mounds (Putnam 1901c:467, 1902a:271). He subsequently assumed the entire cost of publishing the report of his work in *Papers of the Peabody Museum of American Archaeology and Ethnology* (Putnam 1905:301).

Ethnomusicologists still take note of Peabody's work in Coahoma County, Mississippi, for it was during this time that he collected the first documented ragtime music from his workmen (Peabody 1903:148). Archaeologists take note of his work because it represents clear evidence of the continuing spread of Putnam's rigorous excavation methodology. Peabody reported setting up a grid system dividing the mounds into five-foot squares; "the system of excavation was that practiced by the Peabody Museum" (Peabody 1904:28). Within the five-foot grid system, the method was "that of making successive cuttings down to the level of the surrounding ground, and thus, by throwing the soil from each new cutting into that preceding, making possible a thorough examination of the distance excavated, yet leaving the ground more or less in its original condition. At each five feet, descriptions of the wall of soil in front of the excavators were taken" (Peabody 1904:23). Thus, although his initial Ph.D. work was not done directly through Putnam, Peabody had later studied with Putnam long enough to learn his method of careful stratigraphic excavation and went on to employ it in his excavations in North America and Europe.

Charles Peabody also employed a metric version of this technique, not only in his later work in Europe but also in the United States. For example, in a cave excavation in Missouri in 1903 he employed a one-meter grid system, using letters and numbers on opposite axes. He excavated across the site in vertical sections, keeping running vertical profiles, as had been suggested by Putnam (Peabody and Moorehead 1904:13). He employed the metric system as well in a mound excavation in North Carolina, where he employed a two-meter grid, also making cross-section profiles at every two meters (Peabody 1910:427–28).

From his earlier research, Peabody had developed an interest in European archaeology, and he became involved in the AIA, for which he took over the occasional review of updates of American archaeology from Henry Haynes (for example, see Peabody 1905; and see chapter 5). When William Farabee taught Anthropology 4, Prehistoric Archaeology–European Ethnography, in 1904–5, he invited Peabody to give several lectures (Mead 1914:8). Putnam nominated Peabody as a member of the Peabody Museum Visiting Committee in December 1905, although the following June Putnam secured sufficient funds to offer Peabody an instructorship in European archaeology and ethnology, and Peabody had to resign from the committee (Putnam 1907:295). Peabody served as an instructor for the next two years. Then, to allow himself more research freedom, he cut back on teaching to become assistant in European archaeology in 1908, and from 1913 to 1932 he was curator of European archaeology for the museum.

Although he focused primarily on Europe, Charles Peabody maintained an interest in American archaeology. He had worked in Mississippi for the Peabody Museum, but during the first decade of the twentieth century he worked in Missouri, Maryland, and North Carolina on behalf of the Department of Archaeology at the Phillips Academy, of which he had been named director at the time his father established it. In 1909 Peabody and his wife first excavated in Texas for a few months and then made a trip to France to continue their studies (Peabody 1912:416; Sterns 1918b:2–3). Peabody returned to excavate a set of mounds in North Carolina in the spring of 1910 (Putnam 1911:225). He took over from Putnam the responsibility for supporting Ernst Volk in the search for paleoliths at Trenton (see chapter 4). Peabody and another benefactor, Joseph F. Loubat (chapter 9), provided most of the support for Volk from 1910 through 1913 (Putnam 1912:219, 1913:215, 1914:224). After the Trenton project was terminated, Peabody contributed funds to support several other Peabody Museum excavation projects over the next two decades. In addition, Peabody Museum director Charles Willoughby (1916) mentioned a substantial contribution that Charles Peabody made to ensure the completion of the last wing of his great-uncle's museum at Harvard.

When Henry Haynes became terminally ill in 1912, Peabody returned from Europe, where he had been most of the year, to spend a good deal of time with Haynes in the preparation of notes on the specimens in the Haynes collection, which was to be donated to the Peabody Museum (Putnam 1913:216, 220). Peabody was able to completely catalogue the European stone specimens and part of Haynes's American lithic specimens during this time (Peabody 1913:340). Following Haynes's death, Peabody returned to making European trips to collect artifacts for the museum (Putnam 1914:225), but with the outbreak of World War I he was prevented from working in Europe and returned to cataloguing the Haynes collection (Dixon 1916b:256). During the war he was commissioned a first lieutenant in the equivalent of the Reserve Officers Training Corp (ROTC) and taught military science to recruits on campus (Willoughby 1919:240). He seems even to have conducted one short archaeological field season in Mississippi for the R. S. Peabody Foundation in 1918, just at the end of the war.

After the war Charles Peabody became interested in establishing a foundation to conduct prehistoric research in France. He spent a good part of 1919–20 working on this project, in collaboration with committees from the AIA and the AAA (Bricker 2002:279; Willoughby 1921:242). The culmination of this work was his co-founding of the American School of Prehistoric Research (ASPR) with George Grant MacCurdy, with whom he had conducted research in France in 1908 and 1912, and Leon Henri-Martin (Bricker 2002:278). Peabody spent the 1921 season excavating in France and Belgium and became director of the second season of ASPR work in France in 1922 (Willoughby 1922:275, 1924:260). In 1923 Peabody moved permanently to France, and for the next decade he continued excavating, ultimately passing his Peabody Museum French excavation mantle to Homer Kidder (chapter 10). Even from France, Peabody kept his hand in the Americanist sphere, retaining his position as director of archaeology for the Phillips Academy until his death in 1939.

Another of Frederic Putnam's organization, although he was never formally a student in the anthropology department, was **Charles Clark Willoughby** (1857–1943). Willoughby was born in Winchendon, Massachusetts, but later moved to Augusta, Maine. He opened an art store, C. C. Willoughby's Art Rooms, in Augusta in 1882 and helped found the Kennebec Natural History and Antiquarian Society in 1891–92 (Spiess 1985b:125). Earnest Hooton (1943:235) noted that Willoughby had two principal hobbies at that time: parquetry work—making beautiful inlays in furniture and small picture frames—and archaeological explorations in the shell mounds of Damariscotta, Popham, and elsewhere. Both hobbies stood him in good stead when he later was recruited by Putnam.

As Bruce Bourque (2002:153–57) has pointed out, Putnam developed an interest in Damariscotta and other Maine shell mounds possibly as early as his excavation work with Wyman in the late 1860s; certainly it was well established by the early 1880s. Willoughby was one of the amateurs who had worked at Damariscotta. He had written a pamphlet, "Antiquities of the Kennebec Valley," in 1891 (published in 1892) for the Kennebec Natural History and Antiquarian Society, which made him stand out among the amateurs who were working on these mounds (Spiess 1985:44).

Putnam recruited Willoughby in 1891–92 and sent him for training with Metz and Peabody Museum personnel on the Ohio projects (Hooton and Willoughby 1920:7; Willoughby and Hooton 1922:7, 11, 14). In 1892 he hired Willoughby to begin excavations at Soper's Knoll at Orland, Androscoggin Valley, Maine. The excavations, conducted under Putnam's direction, were aimed at collecting materials for the 1893 Columbian Exposition in Chicago (Putnam 1894:220).

Willoughby employed the grid method advocated by Putnam, using a 10-foot grid at Orland and a 12.5-foot grid at Bucksport in 1892 (Willoughby 1898:402, 415). His first-year methods were the same as those he detailed for his 1894 excavations at Ellsworth, where he noted that the "ground to be explored [was] taken off into sections ten feet square . . . [with] workmen throwing the earth behind them as they advanced, keeping a perpendicular wall of gravel in front." He employed this method to locate artifacts and features with respect to east-west and north-south measurements from the grid, and their depth below surface (Willoughby 1898:390).

Putnam appointed Willoughby an "Assistant, Department of Anthropology," for the 1983 Columbian Exposition and asked him to make a model of the Orland excavation, in order to display the Peabody Museum excavation techniques. This model is the first good graphic example of Putnam's method of excavation, and Putnam wanted to make sure it was widely visible. In his editorial note introducing Willoughby's report (Putnam 1898b:387), Putnam wrote that Willoughby's work "was so admirably carried out in accordance with the Museum methods, that it was decided to use the material from the Orland site to illustrate the 'Methods of Archaeological Research by the Peabody Museum'" at the Chicago exposition. In addition to a display of photographs, sketches, field notes, and copies of specimens, a plaster model was constructed for the exhibit that included scale stakes set on the 10-foot-square grid system, details of stratigraphic working faces, and the like. Putnam described this special exhibit in the Liberal Arts Building as

> a case illustrating the Museum method of archaeological exploration in the field and its method of arranging collections. This special exhibit contained the field notes, drawings, and photographs relating to the exploration of an ancient Indian burial place in the Androscoggin valley, Maine, conducted under my direction by Mr. C. C. Willoughby. Every object found in the graves was arranged as found, while a series of photographs showed the position of the objects before they were taken from the graves. The method of exploration was further illustrated by a small plaster model made by Mr. Willoughby, showing the excavations. Taken altogether this little exhibit was most creditable to Mr. Willoughby and to the Museum, and it was much commented on by archaeologists. (Putnam 1894:220)

For an illustration of this exhibit, see the frontispiece in Browman and Williams 2002 or the less clear image in Putnam's introduction (1898b:388). Following the exposition, the model was moved back to the Peabody Museum, where it was on display for many years (Putnam 1899a:267).

At the close of the exposition, and with the retirement of Lucien Carr, the long-time assistant curator at the Peabody Museum, Putnam named Willoughby chief assistant in the museum in 1894. Willoughby then began to design and produce what Hooton (1943:236) described as "the series of exquisite small scale ethnographical models that are one of the most useful and attractive exhibits in the Museum and were later developed and made famous by Guernsey and Pitman." Willoughby, with Samuel J. Guernsey (see chapter 10) as his assistant, created all the exhibits in the new wing of the Peabody Museum when it was completed in 1913 (Hooton 1943:236).

Willoughby, perhaps because he never had a college education, was little involved in the teaching program at the Peabody Museum, even though Putnam had him appointed the Austin Teaching Fellow from 1899 to 1901 (Putnam 1900a). As Hooton (1943:236) noted, Willoughby was "essentially a museum and specimen man." He retained his interest in art and artifacts from his first years at the Peabody, when he wrote a joint publication with Putnam on American Indian art styles (Putnam and Willoughby 1896), until his retirement. Following his Maine excavations, he had little opportunity to conduct fieldwork, although the annual report for 1913–14 noted that Mary Hemenway's son Augustus had funded another expedition to the Southwest, under the Hemenway Southwestern Expedition's name, and Willoughby had directed the project in Arizona, assisted by then visiting committee member as well as graduate student Robert Fuller, and he had explored Mesa Verde and sites in the Chinle Valley (Putnam 1914:223).

Willoughby moved up in museum positions from chief assistant to assistant curator in 1899, to assistant director in 1913, and to director in 1915, a position he kept until he retired, after 35 years of service with the museum, in 1928. Although he was not directly involved in recruiting undergraduate or graduate students, Willoughby's long association with the museum made him a significant aspect of the development of anthropology at the Peabody Museum and, by extension, the development of the discipline, in the first quarter of the twentieth century.

Turning to students who arrived in the late 1890s, we look next at **Albert (Albertus) Lovejoy Dakin** (1879–1933). Dakin was born in Hudson, Massachusetts, and entered the Peabody Museum as a "private student" in 1896–97. In the early days of the anthropology program at the museum, students could enter training either officially as Harvard undergraduate or graduate students, in which case one can find documentation for them in the Harvard College archives, or unofficially as "special" or "private" students, through the individual programs, in which case the official archives have no student records for them. Such is the case for Dakin, which handicaps our ability to thoroughly evaluate his contributions.

Putnam (1898a:251) reported that during Dakin's first year at the museum, he assisted in arranging the Indian collections. A few years later Putnam (1899a:272) reported that Dakin, now listed as a "student assistant," had left to enlist as a volunteer in the Spanish-American War, had served in Puerto Rico, but had returned to resume his studies. And in 1900 Putnam (1900a:296) reported that Willoughby was "being assisted in his work by Albertus L. Dakin, a student assistant, who is obtaining practical knowledge of museum work for his future. Mr. Dakin has made a card catalogue of the photographic negatives the museum owns, and a subject catalogue of the papers on American archaeology and ethnology." (This catalogue still exists at the Peabody.) Dakin was officially carried on the masthead of the 1899–1900 and 1900–1901 Peabody Museum annual reports as a student assistant, but after 1901 he was no longer listed as a staff member.

It appears that Dakin might have become involved in archaeological field excavations for a few years after that date. Alanson Skinner (1908:702) reported that Dakin explored the Wilbraham Hills steatite quarry in 1903. Skinner identified him as a "Harvard student" and said that Dakin obtained and donated a good series of specimens illustrating the manufacture of steatite vessels to the Springfield (Massachusetts) Museum. In 1905 Putnam (1905:302) reported that Dakin, supported by the Henry C. Warren Fund, conducted an archaeological exploration in the Connecticut Valley that season and during the project excavated an Indian burial place at Ipswich. According to notes in the Biographical Files of the Peabody Museum (loose-leaf file folder, Peabody Museum Collections Department), Dakin later resigned and entered business to make a living, but in a letter to the museum in December 1915, he wrote that he hoped soon to land a job at the U.S. National Museum. As far as we have been able to ascertain, Dakin never found subsequent employment in the museum world or in anthropology.

Edward Kirby Putnam (1868–1939) was a distant cousin of Frederic Putnam's. His family had been associated with the Davenport Academy of Natural Sciences in Iowa, doing archaeological exploration since as early as the late 1870s. His father, Charles Edwin Putnam, mother, Mary Louisa Duncan Putnam, and brother, Joseph Duncan Putnam, had all been presidents of that society during the late 1800s (Browman 2002a:240–41), a time when the so-called Davenport Tablets were widely publicized (S. Williams 1991:90–96).

After receiving an A.B. at Illinois College in 1891, Edward Putnam did newspaper work until 1896. He entered graduate school at the Peabody in 1898 and received his A.M. in anthropology in 1900. With the A.M. in hand, he landed a job as an instructor of anthropology at Stanford University from 1901 to 1906 (*Who Was Who in America*, 1:1002, 1943). When he returned home to Davenport, Iowa, in 1906, he took on duties at the Davenport Academy of Sciences and its museum for the next three decades, until his death, serving as its director and trustee. His sister Elizabeth Duncan Putnam served as its treasurer during much of this time, overseeing the transition from the Davenport Academy of Sciences Museum to the Davenport Public Museum (Harvard University 1930:668). Edward Putnam was active more widely in the field as well, serving as president of the Iowa Anthropological Association in 1907, being a spirited member of the AIA and Section H of the AAAS, serving as a director of the American Association of Museums, serving two terms on the council of the AAA between 1915 and 1935, and serving on the board of the American School of Prehistoric Research in 1922 (*American Anthropologist* 9(2):445, 1907; 24(1):105, 1922).

George Grant MacCurdy (1863–1947) was a graduate of Harvard, although he did not study directly with Putnam there. Because of his later association with Charles Peabody, as well as his part in the founding of the American School of Prehistoric Research, which subsequently became a part of the Peabody Museum, as required by a codicil of MacCurdy's will, we add a quick review of MacCurdy's contributions here.

MacCurdy was born in Warrensburg, Missouri, and trained at Missouri State Normal School in Warrensburg to be a public school teacher. By the time he entered Harvard in 1891, at the age of 28, he had already taught at schools in rural Missouri throughout the 1880s (Bricker 2002:265). He finished his work for his A.B. in 1893 in the Lawrence School and his A.M. in 1894, writing two master's theses, one in geology and one in zoology (Bricker 2002:266). Immediately after receiving his A.M., he spent part of the summer as a research assistant at Alexander Agassiz's marine laboratory in Newport, Rhode Island.

MacCurdy had met Putnam and others from the Peabody Museum while at the MCZ. He noted in his autobiography that Putnam "loves to talk of his profession . . . and almost persuades me to enter his field of research" (unpublished autobiography, 1946:18, quoted in Bricker 2002:266). But there is no substantial evidence that MacCurdy contemplated archaeology as a profession while he was a Harvard student.

It was during subsequent postgraduate study in Europe that MacCurdy became interested in Paleolithic archaeology and paleoanthropology. While training with Marcellin Boule and Albert Gaudry at the Ecole d'Anthropologie, he was also being mentored from Yale by Othniel Marsh, a good friend of MacCurdy's aunt, who was funding his school training. Marsh suggested that MacCurdy attend the International Zoological Congress in Leiden, Netherlands. The scientific highlight of the meetings for MacCurdy was a paper on *Pithecanthropus* by Eugene Dubois, who had just returned from Java. MacCurdy became enamored of paleoanthropology and was sent by Marsh to complete additional work in prehistoric archaeology at Munich and Vienna (Bricker 2002:267–68).

After three years in Europe, MacCurdy was offered an appointment as an instructor in prehistoric anthropology in the graduate school at Yale in 1898, and he returned to the United States. At the same time he began teaching, he started work on a Ph.D. dissertation dealing with the controversial subject of "eoliths" in Europe. He explored the question of whether chipped lithic objects of late Tertiary and early Quaternary age were truly the products of human workmanship that defined an Eolithic stage preceding the Palaeolithic stage. He received his Ph.D. from Yale in 1905 (Bricker 2002:272–73).

MacCurdy became active in anthropology as soon as he returned to the United States. He served as secretary for Section H of the AAAS and was elected its chair in 1905–6 (McCown 1948:519). On the basis of his activism in Section H, he also became a founding member of the AAA in 1901–2. He went on to serve as secretary of the AAA from 1903 to 1916 and as its president in 1931 (Bricker 2002:274; McCown 1948:516). He produced the major American book in paleoanthropology in the first part of the century, his 1924 *Human Origins: A Manual of Prehistory*, a nearly thousand-page compendium of Old World prehistory and human paleontology.

MacCurdy was one of the main founders of the American School of Prehistoric Research. During two of his trips to Europe, in 1908 and 1912, his traveling companion had been Charles Peabody. MacCurdy recounted the founding of the ASPR in his autobiography:

> My old friend, Dr. Charles Peabody, now doing post-war work for a Franco-American Committee writes from Paris on March 12, 1919, inviting me to spend the summer in France. . . . On May 3, another letter comes from Peabody, enclosing one from Dr. Henri-Martin, whose epoch-making discoveries at La Quina (Charente) are now well known. The latter suggests that a school of prehistoric studies, somewhat after the plan of our American schools of classical studies in Athens, Rome and Jerusalem, might be established in France. This to me is not a new idea, for ever since my student days in Europe, I have been hoping to see a prehistoric link formed that would bind the New World to the Old World. (Unpublished autobiography, 1946:150, quoted in Bricker 2002:279)

Leon Henri-Martin's suggestion was strongly supported by Charles Peabody as well. At Peabody's and MacCurdy's urging, in January of 1920 Clark Wissler, president of the AAA, appointed a committee to act jointly with a committee from the AIA to study the feasibility of founding an "American School of Prehistoric Studies in Europe." This became the original name of the ASPR; it was not changed to American School of Prehistoric Research until 1927. The AAA committee members were MacCurdy, Charles Peabody, and Aleš Hrdlička. The formal founding of the school took place in February 1921, MacCurdy was named its director, and its first field school was held that summer at Henri-Martin's site of La Quina, with an operating budget supplied by co-founder Charles Peabody, who became the field director during the second year (Bricker 2002:280). Subsequently MacCurdy served as field director of the ASPR until 1931, when he retired from Yale. He continued as director of the ASPR until he resigned in 1945, and he continued his work in European paleoanthropology until he was killed in a car accident in New Haven, Connecticut, in 1947. The ASPR then came under Peabody Museum control when Hugh Hencken became its next director (see chapter 12), and it became an official division of the museum in 1972, when Hencken retired.

Putnam and his growing staff received assistance in training the students in the new program from other faculty on the Harvard campus. Some of these people were interested in archaeology—for example, Crawford Toy, David Lyon, Daniel Slade, Charles Lanman, Albert Lythgoe, George Reisner, and George Chase—but several others, such as George Goodale and James Woods, were recruited on other bases. For the most part, these men also served as members of doctoral dissertation committees for Peabody Museum students during the program's first quarter century.

Crawford Howell Toy (1836–1919) received his A.M. from Virginia in 1856 (Morison 1936:381). He was named Harvard Divinity School's Hancock Professor of Hebrew and Oriental Languages from 1880 to 1909. According to Hugh Hawkins (1972:68), Toy and Charles Lanman (along with Frederick D. Allen) were the first of the new cohort of professors at Harvard, beginning in 1880, who were appointed on the basis of their specialized scholarship and research, rather than according to the previous practice in which appointments were based on the way someone fit into Harvard's academic culture. Although Toy was appointed initially in the Divinity School, he later was responsible for starting the Semitic department (Lyon 1930:231).

Putnam worked closely with Toy and had him, Lanman, and David Lyon deliver lectures at the Peabody Museum in the mid-1890s (Putnam 1895a:224). Along with Putnam and Goodale, Toy served as a member of the examining committee for honors and higher degree students for Division XIV, until they were officially replaced in 1909 by Lanman, George Chase, and William Z. Ripley (Putnam 1910:276). Unlike Goodale, Toy served as an examiner for only one of Putnam's Ph.D. students, John Swanton, but Toy was clearly a good friend of Putnam's; he served as the presiding official at Putnam's retirement Festschrift at the Somerset Hotel in Boston, a retirement commemoration led by Harvard president Charles Eliot (Tozzer 1909:285).

Toy's former student **David Gordon Lyon** (1853–1935), from Benton, Alabama, who finished his Ph.D. in Leipzig, was appointed Hollis Professor of Divinity at Harvard in 1882. He held the position until 1910, when he became, until 1922, the Hancock Professor of Hebrew and Other Oriental Languages, after Toy's retirement (Lyon 1930:231). Lyon seems to have served as Toy's proxy on Ph.D. dissertation committees for Division XIV; he is listed as a member of the defense committees for Russell, Dixon, Swanton, Farabee, Gordon, Tozzer, and Spinden—that is, with two exceptions, for every Ph.D. dissertation in anthropology through 1909 (Dissertation Title Pages, Pusey Archives, Harvard University).

Lyon was regarded as an Akkadian specialist and Assyriologist (Kuklick 1996:100) and in this capacity had begun securing Babylonian cuneiform tablets and other artifacts in 1887. He gave a series of Lowell Institute seminars on "Ancient Assyrian Life" in 1887–88, based on this work (H. K. Smith 1895:729). Lyon began the Semitic Museum in 1890 and was appointed its first curator from 1891 to 1922. Because the Semitic Museum had no home, Putnam had the trustees of the Peabody Museum offer a gallery in the Peabody as a temporary home for the Semitic collections in 1891. The temporary Semitic Museum remained in the Peabody Museum building until 1903, when the new Semitic Museum opened across Divinity Avenue (Lyon 1930:237). Many years later, in the 1960s, the collections were again stored at the Peabody Museum while the Semitic Museum was being renovated. David Gordon Lyon, unlike many of his classical studies peers, actually conducted some archaeological excavations in the Middle East, directing explorations in Samaria from 1908 to 1910.

George Lincoln Goodale (1839–1923) was the other main dissertation committee member from Division XIV between 1890 and 1909, serving on the same committees as Lyon, in addition to Spinden's. Goodale received his M.D. from Harvard in 1863. He was a professor of botany from 1872 to 1888, then Fisher Professor of Natural History from 1888 to 1909, and director of the botanical gardens from 1879 to 1909.

The year 1909 marked the official retirement of Goodale, Toy, and Putnam, in some ways turning over a new leaf on the constitution of the committee and in expectations for the anthropology graduate students. Putnam and Goodale had brought with them strong backgrounds in natural history, which no doubt affected the training of doctoral candidates. Both had been members of the MCZ, and they had served simultaneously as officers for the Boston Society of Natural History. Dissertation committees after 1909 became increasingly composed solely of anthropology professors who had received their degrees in the early twentieth century and thus had another vision of the world than Goodale's and Putnam's.

Daniel Denison Slade (1823–96) received his A.B. at Harvard in 1844, as a classmate of Francis Parkman's (chapter 5), and his M.D. from Harvard in 1848. After practicing medicine for many years, he turned to academia and served as professor of applied zoology at Harvard from 1871 to 1882, when he resigned. He accepted the position of lecturer in comparative osteology at the MCZ in 1885 and kept that position until his death. Putnam wrote in a letter to President Eliot of April 4, 1894, covering departmental issues, that Slade "has had considerable to do with the students who have been with me, as they go to the Zoological Museum to examine the osteological collection under his charge, and he often comes to this Museum in connection with his own studies." Until Frank Russell was hired, Slade seems to have served as the expert for anthropology students on zooarchaeology and human osteology.

Charles Rockwell Lanman (1850–1941), a professor of Sanskrit at Harvard from 1880 to 1926 as well as the Wales Professor from 1903 to 1926, was one of the new anthropology Ph.D. committee members from Division XIV after 1909. It was only after Toy retired, and Lyon thus no longer substituted for him, that Lanman began serving on the Ph.D. committees of Peabody students, starting with Raymond Merwin in 1913 and including others later such as Homer Kidder, Frederick Sterns, and Edward Handy (see chapter 10). Although Lanman gave some lectures for Putnam at the Peabody in the 1890s, he seems not to have been much integrated into the Peabody Museum sphere, except in his obligation to serve on dissertation committees for Division XIV.

Albert Morton Lythgoe (1868–1934) received his A.B. from Harvard in 1892 and his A.M. in 1897. Although he had some earlier experience in Greek archaeology (Jacknis 2000:59), he was hired as an instructor of Egyptian archaeology from 1898 to 1899 and as an instructor in Egyptology from 1904 to 1906. He subsequently was recruited by George Reisner, a former colleague from Harvard, then at Berkeley, to be Reisner's chief assistant on the Phoebe Hearst–funded Egyptian Expedition of the University of California, from 1899 to 1904 (Reisner 1930:241).

In 1904–5 Lythgoe returned to Harvard, where he resumed his position as an instructor of Egyptology, giving two courses, one on Egyptian art and the other on Egyptian archaeology, although he was still in part associated with the Berkeley project. For the 1905 year Lythgoe was promoted to assistant professor of Egyptology, while Reisner had returned to Harvard that year as assistant professor of Semitic archaeology. A new Joint Egyptian Expedition of Harvard University and the Boston Museum of Fine Arts was created, with Reisner as director and Lythgoe as field director (Reisner 1930:242). During the 1905–6 field season, however, Reisner and Lythgoe had serious interpersonal conflicts, and Lythgoe resigned from Harvard and went to the Metropolitan Museum of New York (Kuklick 1996:104). Although Putnam had Lythgoe give lectures to his students, and the Harvard Anthropological Society hosted Lythgoe as an honored speaker (Tozzer 1908:758), his contributions to the Peabody Museum program were cut short by this conflict.

James Haughton Woods (1864–1935) was a member of the Harvard class of 1887. He entered Harvard's graduate school following his A.B., studied there from 1887 to 1888, and then went to the Episcopal Theological Seminary in Cambridge, where he received a bachelor of divinity degree in 1890. He enrolled again in Harvard with the new graduate program in 1891 and continued his studies through 1894, when he left and went to Germany. He received his Ph.D. there in 1896. Woods returned to Harvard, where he was listed yet again as a postgraduate student from 1897 through 1901.

We have yet to pin down precisely what post-Ph.D. work he was engaged in, but it was during this time that Woods wrote two volumes on comparative religions (Woods 1899, 1906). Part of his research was done in the Peabody Museum, where he became well known to Putnam and the others working there. Hence, in 1901–2, when Roland Dixon received a leave of absence to travel and do research in Berlin, Woods was appointed instructor to take over Dixon's primitive religions course. At the beginning of the spring term that year, Frank Russell's illness had progressed to the point that he took medical leave to go to Arizona, and Woods took over Russell's general anthropology course, giving lectures with the notes Russell had prepared (Mead 1914:6; Putnam 1901a:299, 1901b:528). In 1901–2 Woods was reappointed instructor in anthropology, teaching the general anthropology course for both terms, because Russell was still ill.

Now that Woods had his foot in the door as a teacher at Harvard, he also received an appointment as instructor in philosophy in 1901–2. For the 1902–3 year he went on leave to study the religion of the Malayan peoples, and when he returned he once again received an appointment as instructor in philosophy for 1903–4. Dixon cancelled his own primitive religions course in the anthropology program for that year because Woods was giving a duplicate course in the philosophy department (Mead 1914:7). Woods continued teaching comparative religions in the philosophy program, being promoted to full professor in 1913 and retiring in 1934. With his new departmental affiliation, he no longer worked closely with the anthropology staff at the Peabody, but some of the students took his courses over the years.

George Andrew Reisner (1867–1942) was born and raised in Indianapolis, Indiana. He went to Harvard for his college education and received his A.B. in 1889, his A.M. in 1891, and his Ph.D. in philology, with a dissertation titled "A Review of Grammatical Development of Noun-Endings in Assyro-Babylonian," under David Gordon Lyon's guidance, in 1893. Reisner held a Harvard traveling fellowship for research in cuneiform and Egyptian studies from 1893 to 1896. He spent most of that time studying under Adolf Erman and Kurt Sethe in Berlin and became the assistant in the Egyptian department of the Royal Museum of Berlin in 1895–96 (Bartlett 1939). Reisner was named instructor in Semitic languages at Harvard in 1896–97, and he took advantage of this position to offer the first course in Egyptian hieroglyphics there.

Reisner left Harvard to work for the International Catalogue Commission of the Khedivial Museum in Cairo in 1897. His work had become known to Sara Yorke Stevenson, of the University of Pennsylvania Museum, through her work with the Egypt Exploration Society; Stevenson was one of several women whom Putnam encouraged to become involved in archaeology (Browman 2002a:231–32). Consequently, when her friend Phoebe Apperson Hearst wanted to set up a joint University of Pennsylvania and University of California–Berkeley expedition to Egypt in 1897, Stevenson recommended

Reisner to her (Jacknis 2000:58). Phoebe A. Hearst (1842–1919), who was searching for someone to head up the five-year expedition, was the multimillionaire widow of California Senator George Hearst (1820–91) and the mother of the later well-known newspaper publisher William Randolph Hearst (1863–1951). Reisner also had an offer from Yale in 1897 but decided to accept the Hearst offer, because "I thought there was a chance to develop the scientific method of excavation and scientific methods of recordings which before had been haphazard" (quoted in Bartlett 1939). By 1899 Reisner had shifted his association completely to Berkeley and the University of California, apparently tired of Stevenson's "meddling" in the execution of his work (Jacknis 2000:59). He stayed there until 1905, occasionally teaching some courses as the Hearst Lecturer in Egyptology from 1902 to 1905. He kept his ties with Harvard, however, hiring Lythgoe from Harvard to work for him in Egypt from 1899 to 1904 (Reisner 1930:241).

In 1905 Reisner left Berkeley to return to Harvard, where he was appointed to a position in Semitic archaeology, Lythgoe already having the position in Egyptology there. He also headed a new Joint Egyptian Expedition of Harvard University and the Boston Museum of Fine Arts, again with Lythgoe as his assistant (Reisner 1930:242). Reisner was on campus teaching for only a year before taking leave to continue field projects. Although he later spent most of his time in Egypt, he conducted fieldwork in Nubia from 1907 to 1909 and in Samaria in 1909–10. In the summer of 1908 the workmen not immediately needed for Reisner's fieldwork were sent to a Peabody Museum graduate student, Oric Bates (chapter 10), to assist him in his excavations in Nubia (Reisner 1930:242).

Reisner did not return to Harvard from his field projects until 1911, when he took over the post in Egyptology (Lyon 1930:234) and began offering six courses: Egyptian Language for Beginners; Advanced Course in Egyptian; History of Egypt; History of Egyptian Art; Egyptian Archaeology; and, the most important course for the Peabody Museum students, Egyptology 6, Archaeological Field Work: Theory and Practice of Archaeological Field Work as a Branch of Historical Research (Reisner 1930:243). Unfortunately for the museum students, Reisner was gone again for most of the next decade, being on campus only for the spring and fall terms of 1911. He left for the field in 1912 and did not return to teach until the spring of 1921 (Reisner 1930:243, 245). He kept his post in Egyptology until his death in 1942.

Reisner's "Archaeological Field Work" course was critical for many of the classical archaeologists, but it was also the key course for A.V. Kidder (chapter 10) in the development of his methodology. Kidder no doubt was the origin of the comment made in Reisner's death notice in *American Antiquity:* "From Dr. Reisner's courses in Egyptology, given intermittently at Harvard, came the germ of the stratigraphic technique that was adapted and first used in America on a large dig at Pecos" (Anonymous 1942:180). In 1954 Kidder reminisced that he thought Reisner's course was the best single course that I ever took. I think I have covered the principal elements of it [ceramic analysis] in recording and chronological correlation with cultures through traded material or introduced material. I came back from the field [1907–8] all het up about pottery and I was delighted to find in my reading and in Reisner's course ... that pottery was an important element in archaeology and which I didn't know anything about before at all. (Kidder, unpublished 1954 biographical memoir, "Rambling Reminiscences," pp. 4–5, quoted in Givens 1992:51)

Kidder was one of the major figures in helping to popularize excavation by natural stratigraphy in Americanist archaeology after 1915, partly on the basis of ideas he had encountered in Reisner's course (Browman and Givens 1996).

Other Peabody students also learned methodology from Reisner. For example, Kidder's undergraduate as well as graduate colleague Sylvanus Morley took Reisner's method course the same year Kidder did. Morley, indeed, had originally come to Harvard as an undergraduate because of Reisner: "From boyhood much interested in antiquities, especially hieroglyphic systems of writing, he'd made the transfer in order to study Egyptology under G. A. Reisner" (Kidder, unpublished tape-recorded transcript, "Personal Remembrances," 1957:53, quoted in Givens 1992:133). George C. Vaillant received training from Reisner in Egypt in 1923–24, as well as from Kidder in the Southwest, before embarking on his Mexican archaeological research (Kidder 1945:591; Strong 1945:115). The linkages between Reisner and the Peabody were strong in other ways as well. For example, in 1912–13 the income of the Mary Hemenway Fund for Archaeology was used in part for the salary of the Hemenway Assistant, in part for the Egyptian collection from Reisner, and in part to pay for Kidder's explorations in Mexico (Putnam 1914:226).

Because of his long association with Harvard, Reisner may well have been influenced by Putnam's great concern with excavation methodology. Reisner is credited with bringing stratigraphic excavation to work in the Middle East, but this was a decade after Putnam had made it standard methodology for his students at the Peabody Museum. Reisner initiated his first stratigraphic excavation at Deir el-Ballas in 1900 (Lacovara 1981:120) and introduced it into Egypt by 1902. He had modified his method to explicitly excavate "debris layer by layer" in Samaria by 1908 (Reisner 1910:254).

Reisner's peers credited him with bringing methodological rigor to excavation in the Middle East. Stephen B. Luce (1942:412) credited him with "revolutionizing" fieldwork, and John W. Crowfoot (1943:123) noted that his methodology had been adopted as the standard for Middle Eastern archaeology, not only by American but also by British, French, and German excavators. Dows Dunham's comments (1942:410, 412) encapsulate the evaluation of Reisner's contributions by his colleagues in classical archaeology: "Reisner developed scientific methods of field work to a higher point of perfection than any other previous worker. . . . He has revolutionized field work by the adoption of strictly modern scientific research methods, including the minute recording of all evidence and the completion of tasks undertaken irrespective of results in museum material."

Another classical archaeologist, **George Henry Chase** (1874–1952), received his A.B. from Harvard in 1896 and went on to get an A.M. in 1897 and a Ph.D. in philology in 1900. He was appointed instructor in Greek in 1901 and then was shifted over to instructor in classical archaeology in 1904. He was named the John E. Hudson Professor of Classical Archaeology in 1916, a position he held until his retirement in 1945, and he served as dean of the Graduate School of Arts and Sciences from 1925 to 1939.

Because of his appointment to the Division XIV doctoral review committee in 1910, Chase served on a number of examining committees for anthropology doctoral students for the next decade, including Spinden, Merwin, Kidder, and Sterns. But his interest in classical archaeology must have been more for classics and art history and less for archaeology, because he seldom shows up in connection with the Peabody Museum archaeologists. Like all the other classical archaeology faculty, he was asked by the Harvard Anthropological Society to give a talk on his work (Tozzer 1908:758). Douglas Givens (1992:21, 25) credited Chase with providing A.V. Kidder with training in ceramic design analysis in his course Classical Philology 49, History of Greek Vase Painting, in 1907–8, when Kidder would have been a senior, which was reflected in his Ph.D. work. But in general, Chase is perhaps notable by his absence from comments on the training of Peabody Museum archaeologists.

Of particular significance to the trajectory of the development of anthropology is the formation of the first student anthropology organization in the country, at Harvard in 1898. In May of that year Frank Russell, who was just finishing his Ph.D., and Walter S. Andrews founded the Harvard Anthropological Society, for the "promotion of interest in the study of the natural history of man and of the history of human culture" (Barber 1900:95; Tozzer 1908:757). **Walter Scott Andrews** (1852–1929) was a member of the Harvard College class of 1877 and hence a classmate of Jesse Walter Fewkes. He received his LL.B. at Columbia University in 1883. After working as a lawyer for several years in New York City, he returned to graduate school, first to Cornell for a short stint, where he studied horticulture, and then to the Peabody Museum, where, besides his anthropology graduate curriculum, he took an outside class in botany and wrote his A.M. paper in 1898 with an ethnobotanical slant. After completing this degree, Andrews had another shift in his career and went back to New York to sell real estate insurance, as he recounted in the class of 1877's twenty-fifth anniversary report.

We have not found a complete roster for the Harvard Anthropological Society in its first year, but we do have one for the second year, when William C. Farabee was president and Alfred M. Tozzer was secretary and treasurer. Members included Putnam and Russell from the faculty as advisors or honorary members, four graduate students in anthropology—Roland B. Dixon, Edward K. Putnam, Percy C. Miller, and Farabee—and a dozen undergraduates, including Tozzer and William Jones (Barber 1900:95). Of the graduate students, Dixon and Edward Putnam we have covered in this chapter, and we profile Farabee in chapter 10. That leaves **Percy Chase Miller** (1879–1967?), a member of the Harvard class of 1899. After completing his A.B., he continued with graduate work in anthropology at the Peabody, receiving his A.M., along with Farabee, in 1900. Apparently finding no work to his interest in anthropology, Miller then became an Episcopal church organist and choirmaster until 1920, when he retired at an early age.

The undergraduates in the club were extraordinary in quality. Walter Conrad Arensberg went on to graduate work in English and became a major American poet; his nephew, Conrad M. Arensberg, later got his Ph.D. in anthropology from Harvard in the 1930s. Freeman Dodd Bosworth, Arthur Hallan Crosbie, Robert John Graves, and Harvey Field Newhall went on to get their M.D. degrees at Harvard; Norman Fisher Hall received an A.M. in Spanish; Ralph Revere Kent proceeded to graduate work in geology at the MCZ; and Augustus Hunt Shearer got his Ph.D. in history from Harvard. As we detail in the next chapter, William Jones earned a Ph.D. in anthropology at Columbia, and Alfred Tozzer, a Ph.D. in anthropology at Harvard. Putnam, Dixon, and Russell were attracting top-notch undergraduate students in anthropology.

During its first decade, members of the Harvard Anthropological Society met once a month during the fall and spring academic terms, at which time papers were presented and discussed and the current anthropological literature was reviewed. After the first few years of success of this Harvard College group, a companion Radcliffe Anthropological Club was founded in 1903, along the same lines. Membership in the Harvard group averaged about 40 during the first decade, and for the Radcliffe group, about 25. For the first seven years, two or more public lectures were given each year by eminent anthropologists in one of the Harvard lecture halls, under the auspices of the Harvard Anthropological Society (Putnam, "Anthropology at Harvard," HUD 3146, Putnam Papers, Peabody Museum Archives). After the first seven years, rather than offering public lectures, the student group switched to having two dinners annually with a guest of honor who delivered a topical address (Tozzer 1908:757).

"Honorary" members of the club in its tenth year were Putnam, Franz Boas, Alice Fletcher, Charles P. Bowditch, and Alfred C. Haddon. Among the public lecture and dinner speakers in this first decade were Boas, Bowditch, Chase, Culin, Fletcher, Haddon, Kroeber, Lythgoe, Putnam, and Saville, as well as Dr. James M. Bell, Edward B. Drew, Prof. George F. Moore, Prof. John Murdoch, Prof. Edward H. Nichols, and Prof. Leo Wiener (Tozzer 1908:758).

Among the latter group of speakers, James MacKintosh Bell (1877–1934) had received his Ph.D. from Harvard in 1904 in geology, but during his fieldwork in Canada he became knowledgeable about the Chippewa Indians. Edward Bangs Drew (1843–1924) received his A.B. in 1863 and his A.M. in 1869 from Harvard and then went on to a 40-year career in customs posts in China, leaving China for the last time in 1908.

Drew was responsible in 1879 for helping to recruit Ko Kunhua of Ningpo, who taught the first Chinese language courses at Harvard (Harvard University 1879:46). Alfred Cort Haddon (1855–1940) was on the MCZ staff and specialized in the Pacific Islands. George Foot Moore (1851–1931) was Frothingham Professor of the History of Religion, teaching from 1894 until 1928, and a colleague of David G. Lyon and Charles R. Lanman, whom we met earlier. John Murdoch (1852–1925) received his Harvard A.B. in 1873 and his A.M. in 1876. He worked for the Smithsonian Institution and the Bureau of Ethnology in the 1880s and 1890s, leading an expedition to Point Barrow and writing an ethnography of the Inuit there. Edward Hall Nichols (1864–1922) graduated with the Harvard class of 1886 and then enrolled in the medical school, where he received his M.D. in 1892. He was a professor of surgical pathology and clinical surgery from 1896 to 1922, as well as being one of the first members of the Harvard College Baseball Hall of Fame and coach of Harvard baseball for 30 years. Leo Wiener (1862–1939), an expert in philology and folklore and a professor of Slavic language at Harvard from 1896 to 1930, was later involved in "fantastic" archaeology (S. Williams 1991:251–53). These speakers helped provide the majors and graduate students at the Peabody Museum with a wide range of specialists and certainly an impressive group of distinguished experts.

Garnering support for his engaged, high-caliber students was one reason Putnam became involved in organizing the 1893 World's Columbian Exposition in Chicago, an event commemorating the four-hundredth anniversary of Columbus's landing. Putnam had been continually handicapped in developing his programs by a shortage of funds. He had lost his first cadre of students for lack of financial resources to support them, and he had had to mount several funding drives to help support his ambitious museum excavation projects. The 1893 World's Columbian Exposition offered him a golden opportunity. If he could use it as a vehicle to capture the public's and sponsors' attention, it would no doubt provide funding for a series of collecting missions, with obvious benefits to the growth of the Peabody's own holdings. Indeed, such funding supported Putnam's first Ph.D. student, George Dorsey, and a number of his other students in the mid-1890s. The exposition would also allow Putnam, for the first time, to put university-based anthropology on a par with government-based anthropology. At the First Centennial in 1876 and other earlier expositions, the Smithsonian Institution and the U.S. National Museum had monopolized the display spotlight. The Chicago exposition was at last a chance for university-based anthropology to show what it was all about. As well, the exposition offered Putnam an opportunity to bring anthropology to the attention of the general public, creating an interest base, he hoped, that he could turn to in the future.

In early 1890 Putnam wrote to George R. Davis, director-general of the exposition commission, proposing that Putnam and the Peabody Museum help in developing a major anthropological display. No previous major American exposition had had such a coordinated set of exhibits, although there had been some at Paris and other European expositions. Putnam believed the time was right for this to occur in the United States.

Putnam was already on an institution-building push. Part of his pitch to the fair's board of directors was that he would not merely supervise the collecting of a few miscellaneous artifacts, "but if I were asked to collect a permanent exhibit I would go into it with all my heart and soul" (Dexter 1966c:319). That is, he proposed using the exposition to build a permanent collection for a new museum to be established in Chicago, designing his wish list for what ultimately became the Field Museum of Natural History.

After an extended correspondence, Putnam's proposal was officially approved on February 5, 1891. Putnam was appointed "Chief of Department M, the Department of Ethnology and Archaeology" by Director-General Davis, acting for the commissioners of the fair and the board of directors (Dexter 1966c:316). Putnam thus was required to spend a good deal of time away from the Peabody Museum from 1891 to 1894, recruiting personnel, developing displays, and dealing with the politics of the exposition. He hired Franz Boas as his primary assistant, and he integrated into his plans nearly 100 students and colleagues as staff members. The largest cohort consisted of 75 students he recruited from Harvard and other universities. They were specially instructed in ethnological and somatological work and were employed to go among the American Indian tribes to secure somatological measurements for Boas as well as ethnological materials (Mead 1914:3).

Department M was initially meant to be situated in the Manufacturers and Liberal Arts Building, but as Putnam's collections grew, it became evident that he needed more space. Whereas George Davis was director-general of the World's Columbia Commission, Harlow Niles Higinbotham was president of the World's Columbian Exposition, which was incorporated separately to produce the fair under Davis's direction. Higinbotham was unsympathetic to Putnam's plans, and Putnam had to fight him nearly every step of the way (Dexter 1966c:317). Higinbotham, formerly an executive with Marshall Field and Company department stores, was more concerned with the commercial exhibits than the scientific ones. Putnam's promised space was reduced by more than 60 percent, and he had to move his office nine times in eight months (Hinsley 1999:150).

By October 1892 Davis was convinced of the need to move Putnam out of the Manufacturers Building and into a building of his own. He wrote to Putnam on October 3: "I am very much in hope that we shall be able to provide a separate building either for you or Dr. [Charles] Peabody [chief of the Department of Liberal Arts] in which event our distress regarding these exhibits will be very much relieved" (quoted in Dexter 1966c:322). By December 1892 Putnam had finally convinced Higinbotham, too, to erect a separate building for Department M. It was to be completed by March 15, 1893, in time for the opening of the exposition on May 1, but in fact the Anthropology Building was not completed until July 4. Because of the delay, some private exhibitors withdrew their collections, and some of the state exhibits for anthropology were transferred to the respective state buildings (Dexter 1966c:325).

It had originally been agreed that Department M would be strictly scientific, and the Bureau of Indian Affairs (BIA) would handle living Indian exhibits through a demonstration of modern Indians in an Indian school. However, Davis forced on Putnam an Indian rights political activist named Emma Sickles, as a political favor for Senator James H. Kyle of South Dakota, in return for Kyle's help in passing the appropriations bill for the exposition. Sickles had once been a teacher on the Pine Ridge Reservation for the BIA, and at the time of the exposition she was chair of the Universal Peace Union's Indian Committee. She was officially hired by the exposition on October 15, 1891, to work among the Dakota tribes. Putnam was sorely distressed when Sickles announced that she was preparing her own Indian exhibit. He made it clear that Department M was "to illustrate the Indian in his primitive condition. The Government [i.e., BIA exhibit] proposes to show the Indian on his road to civilization."

Putnam fired Sickles on February 29, 1892, because she continued working on her own agenda, ignoring Putnam's instructions. In retaliation, she wrote to the *New York Times* about the allegedly racist way Indians were being displayed by Putnam. She attacked him for showing uncivilized Indians and keeping modern Indians away. Her friend Senator Kyle threatened to vote against the bill to provide souvenir coins for the exposition unless Sickles was rehired. Much to Putnam's dismay, Davis restored her to his staff (Dexter 1966c:327–28). Clearly, battles like this handicapped Putnam's ability to work effectively in developing the exhibits.

Another problem for the exposition was finding a space for the living Indian exhibits. As the Indians were shifted from place to place, they complained about the frequent moves. They were also distressed because the goods they had been instructed to bring to vend were not selling well, and they were afraid they would not meet their expenses. Originally the Indian exhibits had been scheduled for the "Midway Plaisance," which had been slated to be educational and at first had been listed as part of the BIA's and Putnam's venue. But by early 1892 the Chicago Exposition company needed to improve its financial situation, and the fair management shifted the Midway Plaisance to a San Francisco entrepreneur, Sol Bloom, to run as entertainment. It ultimately became a successful amusement area (Badger 1979:80–81). As a result, the ethnographic exhibits were turned into kinds of carnival sideshows.

Putnam tried to intervene in this issue, although any authority had been stripped from him. His input seems to have been limited primarily to the contacts he was able to make through one of his assistants, a man known as Antonio Apache, whom we treat at length in chapter 8. Putnam had employed Apache in the spring of 1892 to collect ethnological materials and take anthropometric measurements of Apaches and Navajos for Franz Boas. Apache had secured other funds to help recruit some Indians from the Southwest to come as "living exhibits" for the Midway Plaisance. Although Putnam lacked official authority, as an anthropologist he felt a responsibility to assist the Indians with their increasing problems at the exposition. He found Antonio Apache useful in making contacts with the living exhibit Indians, helping them reduce the adverse effects of their inclusion in the Midway Plaisance, now reconfigured as a sideshow (Bancroft 1895, 2:663).

Putnam displayed his new view of archaeology as a science at the fair, clearly signaling his shift from reliance on securing collections from well-meaning amateurs to a new reliance on a directed research focus, in which careful field notes and data were as important as the specimens themselves. Warren K. Moorehead recognized this, writing in wonder in his article about a "new science at the Fair" that previously "nobody spent several thousands of dollars in a single season's exploration of Ohio Valley mounds and village sites," but that Putnam had done this, and the spectacular results were to be seen at the exposition (Moorehead 1893a:508). Putnam "desired to do away with the prevailing erroneous impression concerning mound-building tribes" (Moorehead 1893a:509), and the exhibits were viewed as successful in accomplishing that goal.

Anthropology at the 1893 exposition is really a book-length story; here we can touch on only a few more highlights. In addition to the student collectors, Putnam assembled a major group of experts, as can be seen in the list on page 236. Several of the people on the list we have met or will meet in the pages of this book. The rest will have to await another venue for elaboration.

The eight rooms of laboratories in the north end of the Anthropology Building, organized by Franz Boas and staffed by several of the experts Putnam had enlisted, offered fairgoers comparative craniology, anthropometry, and "exhibits referring to the development of the white race in America." To hype anthropology even more, Putnam had helped arrange for a special "International Congress of Anthropology" to be held during the exposition, integrating the presentations into the exhibits and laboratories of the Anthropology Building. An extract from the introduction to the published proceedings of the congress gives a flavor of the meeting:

> In addition to the papers read, and to the Introductory address by the President, Dr. Daniel G. Brinton, addresses were given by Dr. Franz Boas, Professor Henry H. Donaldson and Professor Joseph Jastrow, on the Anthropological Laboratories of the Department of Ethnology; by Mr. Stewart Culin, Captain John A. Bourke, United States Army, and Mr. Frank Hamilton Cushing, on the Collection of Games in the Anthropological Building; by Professor F. W. Putnam, on North American Archaeology; by Professor Otis T. Mason, on North American Ethnology; by Mr. Frank Hamilton Cushing, on "A Zuni Dramatic Ceremonial," and on "The Cliff-Dwellers"; by Mrs. M. French-Sheldon, on "Customs among Nations of East Africa"; and by Dr. Ulrich Jahn, on the Ethnological Collection in the German Village on the Midway Plaisance. (Wakeland 1894:viii)

At the end of the exposition, Putnam seemed pleased with the exhibits, in spite of all the politics, the delayed opening of his building, and other issues. In his analysis in October 1893 of the activities of Department M of the exposition, Putnam (1893b) wrote:

Partial List of Putnam's Assistants at the World's Columbian Exposition, 1893

Dr. Charles C. Abbott, New Jersey, Archaeology

Anthony Apache

Franz Boas, chief assistant and in charge of Physical Anthropology

Stewart Culin, in charge of Games, Religions, and Folklore

Capt. Cornelius C. Cusick, in charge of Living Indians

James Deans, British Columbia Ethnology

Dr. Henry H. Donaldson, in charge of Neurology

George A. Dorsey, South American Archaeology

Miss Alice C. Fletcher, Indians of Western United States

Dr. Sheldon Jackson, Expedition to Alaska and Siberia

Dr. Joseph Jastrow, in charge of Psychology

Prof. Leslie A. Lee, Labrador Ethnology

Miss Frances H. Mead, secretary to Dr. Putnam

Dr. Charles Metz, Ohio Archaeology

Dr. David Scott Moncrieff, Indians of the Pacific Northwest

Warren K. Moorehead, Ohio Archaeology

Miss Zelia Nuttall, Mexican Archaeology

Lt. Robert E. Peary, Expedition to North Greenland

Marshall Saville, North American and Central American Archaeology

Miss Emma C. Sickles, Indians of Western United States

Harlan I. Smith, Ohio and Michigan Archaeology

Edward H. Thompson, Yucatán Archaeology

Ernest Volk, New Jersey and Ohio Archaeology

Charles Staniland Wake, Librarian

Dr. Gerald M. West, assistant in Physical Anthropology

Charles C. Willoughby, draftsman and general assistant

Prof. G. Frederic Wright, Ohio Archaeology

Sources: Bancroft 1895; Dexter 1966c.

> This is the first time in the history of world's expositions that anthropology has been ranked as one of the great departments and given a departmental building. My plans for scientific research and exploration were, thanks to the local directory, carried out, and the several expeditions sent out under my direction were markedly successful. ... never before has so much new material in anthropology been brought together as is now exhibited in this department....
>
> There is one thing more that I should like to see done before I leave Chicago and that is the establishment of the Columbian museum upon a broad and scientific basis.

After the exposition closed, Putnam arranged for the anthropology collections to be transferred to a new Chicago institution. He was one of the incorporators of the Columbian Museum of Chicago, eventually the Field Museum of Natural History, in 1893 and expected to be made a trustee of the museum. Edward Everett Ayer was named president of the board of trustees, but Putnam's old nemesis Harlow Higinbotham was chair of the executive committee and became president of the board of trustees when Ayer resigned in 1898 (Dorsey 1900:247). As well, Frederick J. V. Skiff, a member of Higinbotham's exposition staff, with whom Putnam also had had run-ins, was named director of the new museum. Thus Putnam's hope of becoming a trustee was moot, and the politics grew intense. After ensuring that Franz Boas would stay on in charge of the collections, Putnam left. Shortly thereafter, Boas was eased out by William H. Holmes, who left Washington from 1894 to 1897 to serve as curator at the Columbian Museum. Putnam was responsible for the fact that the collections remaining from the exposition after it closed became the basis for the anthropology department of today's Field Museum, but for a number of political reasons, he was quickly shown the door.

This did not end Putnam's institution-building. Almost immediately after resigning from his Columbian Exposition and Columbian Museum positions in 1894—on the rebound, as it were—Putnam became involved in developing the anthropology department at the American Museum of Natural History in New York City, accepting a joint appointment there from 1894 until he resigned in 1903. Farther away still, in 1901 he began talks with the University of California–Berkeley, resulting in his joint appointment there in developing the department and museum from 1903 until his retirement in 1909. In addition, he found time to advise the Academy of Natural Sciences of Philadelphia on developing its anthropological expertise.

But it is his contributions through the American Association for the Advancement of Science (AAAS) that are of particular concern at this point. Putnam had always been interested in publishing anthropology. He was a co-founder of *American Naturalist* and was critical in starting and maintaining the Peabody Museum publication series. But perhaps nowhere in American science was his influence more important than in the establishment of the journal *Science* as the major voice for scientists in the United

States. It was between 1890 and 1905 that he engineered this feat, and as his retirement approached, he was finally able to exit the publishing business.

Putnam and several other contributors to the Harvard anthropological community had a long history with the AAAS during the late nineteenth century. The organization had been founded at the Academy of Natural Sciences in Philadelphia on September 20, 1848, and Putnam had joined in 1856, at Louis Agassiz's suggestion. The first AAAS meeting that Putnam attended was the 1857 session in Montreal, and from there comes the first recorded indication of Putnam's later interest in archaeology. During these meetings he reported visiting a shell heap at Mount Royal, then on the outskirts of Montreal, and observing some artifacts mixed in with the shell deposits (Putnam 1899b:226).

The AAAS was brought back to a central position in American scientific life after the Civil War. Under the leadership of Frederic Ward Putnam, permanent secretary from 1872 to 1897, the association became a stabilizing force for the scientific community in a turbulent environment. In an important sense, Putnam *was* the AAAS for nearly a quarter century, and he used his position there to build both science in general and anthropology in particular.

In 1869 Putnam substituted for one year for long-time AAAS permanent secretary Joseph Lovering, who held the job from 1854 to 1868 and from 1870 to 1872 (Kohlstedt 1999:40). By this time the rift between Louis Agassiz and his students over evolution had healed, and with the support of Agassiz, Henry Wheatland, Jeffries Wyman, and other colleagues, Putnam was elected permanent secretary in 1872, the same year his former professor and now colleague Asa Gray was elected president. Putnam began serving his first five-year term in this position in 1873 and was subsequently elected for a total of five five-year terms.

In 1873, after Putnam's election as permanent secretary of the AAAS, the organization's national headquarters was moved to the Peabody Academy of Science at Salem, where Putnam was then situated. The AAAS office remained in the museum there until 1876, when Putnam moved it to a room over the Merchants Bank in Salem, because he now had taken the job of curator at the Peabody Museum at Harvard and could no longer use his former liaison with the Salem museum for AAAS purposes.

Putnam did all of the AAAS's staff work. He arranged for speakers at annual meetings, negotiated presidential and other officers' nominations, handled all official correspondence, and managed the membership records and budget of the AAAS (Kohlstedt 1999:37–46). He assumed responsibility for publishing the proceedings of the AAAS meetings through the Salem Press, which he had organized. Thus for a quarter century Putnam ran the AAAS single-handedly, with only one official staff member, Caroline A. Watson, during his entire tenure. He did get the Peabody Museum trustees to provide funds to hire a second assistant, Jane Smith, to assist him when he had AAAS work to do in Cambridge.

Putnam struggled his entire tenure to maintain the financial base of the AAAS and enlarge its role in promoting a research agenda for science. The AAAS was initially so cash-strapped that it could not afford even an official incorporation fee. Putnam solicited some local donors for assistance. In 1873, New York philanthropist Elizabeth Rowell Thompson (1821–99) stepped forward, providing a $1,000 grant that allowed Putnam finally to file incorporation papers for the AAAS in Massachusetts in 1874 (Kohlstedt 1999:37). Thompson was enrolled thus as the first patron of the AAAS. Money was so tight initially that when Putnam needed an assistant in 1874, he had to pay Caroline Watson's salary from his own pocket. Later the AAAS was able take over payment of her salary. Watson handled the association's affairs at the Peabody Academy of Science and Salem Press for 21 years, from 1874 to 1895, when she retired. In Cambridge, Putnam hired Jane "Jennie" Smith in 1875 to handle the AAAS business that came to Putnam there, and she continued handling his Cambridge AAAS business until 1897 (Browman 2002a:238). Smith's work for the AAAS was paid for by Peabody Museum–Harvard funds.

Putnam provided important stability for the AAAS for a quarter century. It had a continuous home at the Merchants Bank building in Salem and at the Salem Press from 1873 through 1897. The stability of the AAAS was further helped when, after a series of short moves once Putnam left the presidency, the offices were situated for 40 years at the Smithsonian Institution, from 1907 to 1946 (Lewenstein 1999:112).

Putnam did not ignore his AAAS position as a potential basis of power for anthropology. He was instrumental in forming a special Subsection C, Archaeology and Ethnology, at the Salem meetings in 1869—the third subsection to be created at the AAAS. This subsection went through two more iterations under Putnam's guidance before anthropology finally became a full-fledged scientific section of the AAAS, Section H. It was during his tenure that Erminnie Smith, in 1883, became the first woman to serve as a secretary of any section in the AAAS and that Alice Fletcher, in 1896, became the first woman to serve as the head of any AAAS scientific section—both in Section H. Thanks to their elections, Putnam could be seen as a leading advocate for women scientists. He helped his friend, sometime anthropologist Edward S. Morse, become president of the AAAS in 1887.

After 25 years as permanent secretary, Putnam served as president of the AAAS for the 1898–99 term. He used this position to his advantage in the founding of the American Anthropological Association and its official publication, *American Anthropologist*. In 1898, representatives of the AAAS met with members of the Anthropological Society of Washington (ASW) and agreed that the AAAS would pay off the debts of the old series of *American Anthropologist* and would provide the mechanism for continuing the journal (the "new series") as long as the ASW ceded control to a new group being formed under the aegis of Section H of the AAAS. This new group ultimately became the American Anthropological Association.

Perhaps one of the most important things for which Putnam was at least partly responsible during his tenure with the AAAS was seeing that *Science* got to its feet and became the leading journal for science in North America, by co-opting it to become the official journal of the AAAS, replacing its *Proceedings* series. During the first half century of the existence of the AAAS (1848–98), the primary publication outlet for its members had been the annual *Proceedings,* published for much of the period through Putnam's Salem Press. The weekly journal *Science* had been founded in 1880 with John Michels, a New York journalist, as editor and Thomas Alva Edison as funder of the venture. When Edison withdrew financial support late in 1881, Alexander Graham Bell took over funding in 1882. In 1883, Bell and Gardiner Greene Hubbard purchased the journal, and Putnam's old Lawrence School colleague Samuel H. Scudder became editor. As a stand-alone journal, however, *Science* had continual trouble securing adequate financial support. By the time Scudder resigned in late 1884, the journal had lost $40,000, and Scudder's young, virtually unknown assistant, Nathaniel Dana Carlisle Hodges (1851–1927), was named editor and took over *Science.*

Hodges was a Harvard A.B. from the class of 1874. He had been teaching at Worcester Polytechnic Institute for the 1882–83 term when Scudder recruited him as assistant editor. In anthropology, he is best remembered for his job offer to Franz Boas: it was Hodges, alerted by Scudder and Putnam, who made Boas the two-year contract offer to become geographic editor of *Science* from January 1887 to January 1889, Boas's first long-term entry into the American scientific scene. Hodges ran the journal from 1885 to 1894, at which time, because of continued financial losses, he sold it for $500 to James McKeen Cattell of Columbia University (Kohlstedt 1999:36; Kohlstedt, Sokal, and Lewenstein 1999:171; Sokal 1999:52–53).

Putnam thought it was critically important to have a major scientific journal in the United States. To investigate the issue, he organized a committee chaired by his good friend W. J. McGee, who was then working for the Bureau of Ethnology in Washington, D.C. McGee's committee recommended that the AAAS provide financial assistance to help support the existing journal, *Science.* Hence Putnam was able to provide Cattell with a significant subsidy to get the new version of *Science* back in production. Not coincidentally, the AAAS now had a vested interest in the journal's success (Kohlstedt 1999:47). By 1896 Putnam had arranged the situation so that *Science* was publishing the bulk of AAAS manuscripts and news. Later that year the AAAS voted to cut back dramatically on its own publications and to issue only a condensed version of its annual *Proceedings,* since most AAAS materials were now being published in the weekly *Science* (Sokal 1999:55). Within a few years the *Proceedings* series had completely atrophied, and it was terminated in 1910. Putnam thus got out of the business of publishing the *Proceedings* at his Salem Press and was able to transfer the responsibility to the new, improved journal. In 1900 the AAAS entered into an agreement with Cattell to make *Science* the official journal of the AAAS, although Cattell retained ownership of the magazine. Only on his death in 1945 was formal ownership of *Science* finally transferred officially to the AAAS (Kohlstedt, Sokal, and Lewenstein 1999:171).

Putnam then turned his labors to several other things, among them developing anthropology programs at other institutions and getting a federal preservation program—the 1906 Federal Antiquities Act—in place, using the vehicle with which he was most familiar, Section H of the AAAS. In the next chapter we detail some of Putnam's work at the AMNH. But while holding down leadership positions both there and at Harvard, he also helped establish anthropology at the University of California–Berkeley campus.

Putnam had first become engaged in California archaeology when he took on the responsibility for writing up the archaeological portion of Lt. George M. Wheeler's geographical survey between 1876 and 1878 (Putnam et al. 1879). In 1900 Putnam became involved in talks with University of California president **Benjamin Ide Wheeler** (1854–1927) and **Phoebe A. Hearst** (1832–1919), one of the university's regents, about establishing an anthropological program there. Putnam had known Hearst from consultations with her and encouragement of her in her previous dealings with the development of archaeology at the University of Pennsylvania Museum and during his activities in helping to advise the Academy of Natural Sciences of Philadelphia on developing anthropological expertise (Browman 2002a:235).

President Wheeler was also someone Putnam knew from Harvard and archaeology. After receiving his Ph.D. in classics and philology in 1885 from Heidelberg, Wheeler had taught at Harvard for one year, in 1885–86. He then went to Cornell, where he taught classical philology, including classical archaeology, from 1886 to 1899. He also taught at the American School of Classical Studies in Athens in 1895–96, while on leave from Cornell. Wheeler became president of the University of California–Berkeley from 1899 to 1919, during the period of its greatest development, when students and faculty increased fourfold and 20 new departments were created (Jacknis 2000:59). In 1901 Wheeler established an advisory committee to pursue the development of an anthropology department for Berkeley, consisting of himself, Hearst, and Putnam, along with three of Putnam's colleagues—Boas, Fletcher, and Zelia Nuttall—and assisted by the paleontologist John C. Merriam from the Berkeley campus (Thoresen 1975:266).

The founding of the Berkeley department marked one of the few times when Boas and Putnam acted not in concert but toward different goals. Boas had recommended to Hearst that she fund four fellowships in ethnology at Columbia and two fellowships in archaeology at Harvard for a period of five years and then, after the fellowship holders had trained for five years, choose appropriate persons on the basis of their acquired skills for her new department in California. There, Boas proposed, he himself would direct the new program (Jacknis 2000:63). Putnam and the rest of the committee did not want to wait that long. The Berkeley committee hired Alfred Kroeber to run the program and Pliny Earle Goddard (1869–1928) as his assistant, with Putnam in a supervisory position. Kroeber was Boas's first Ph.D. at Columbia, having received his degree in 1901. Goddard was a former missionary to the Hupa Indians of California who had entered Berkeley in 1900 as a graduate student to study linguistics and philology with Wheeler, finishing his Ph.D. there in 1904, after the department was organized.

Boas, who had been directing field research in California since 1899, viewed Putnam's appointment as an intrusion into his territory (Jacknis 2002:524). Boas had been put on the executive committee of the department at Berkeley in 1901, but a year later, after that committee had gone ahead with Putnam's plan, Boas dropped off it. Nuttall and Fletcher, too, soon resigned to pursue other objectives (Jacknis 2002:524). Boas was also upset with Kroeber, whom he told in a letter of May 20, 1902 (quoted in Jacknis 2002:524), that graduate training and fieldwork should take precedence over undergraduate instruction, whereas Kroeber had opted to focus on undergraduate training. Boas's idea of focusing initially on graduate students was similar to what Putnam had done earlier at Harvard. After a short time, Boas believed, some of the graduate students should know enough to become assistants in the department and take over the instruction of undergraduates.

Phoebe Hearst, who particularly had wanted a department at Berkeley as soon as possible, rewarded Putnam for his help, as we can see in the annual report for the Peabody Museum that year: "When did man first appear in California? Mrs. Phoebe A. Hearst, at my suggestion, has generously provided the means for continuing this most important investigation for five years in connection with the work of the Department of Anthropology of the University of California. This Department was organized while I was in the state, and an advisory committee, of which I have the honor of being Chairman, was appointed by the Regents of the University" (Putnam 1902a:271).

At this point Putnam was commuting between Cambridge and both New York and San Francisco, running three departments, although most of his California work was limited to the summers of 1902 and 1903. After the Harvard administration expressed concern about his availability at the Peabody Museum, Putnam cut the time he spent away from Cambridge during the academic year down to one week per month, instead of his previous two weeks per month. At the end of 1903 he resigned his position at the AMNH to take on just the Berkeley duties (Putnam 1904:285). In addition, he was granted time off from his Harvard responsibilities: "In January, 1904, the corporation granted to the Peabody Professor a leave of absence for three months. This time was spent in performing his duties at the University of California as head of the Department of Anthropology in that University. During the summer vacation he was again in California looking after the installation of the Department in its temporary quarters at the affiliated Colleges in San Francisco" (Putnam 1905:301). The one-quarter time off for his work in Berkeley was also granted in subsequent years. Putnam retained the Berkeley situation until 1909, when he resigned both this and his Harvard position because of increasing ill health.

Anthropologists trained at Harvard during the last decade of the nineteenth century were to become a major force in the development of anthropology in the United States in the first half of the twentieth century. Coming from a department with a strong museum background, many of them went on to establish museums. The majority of them also became involved in creating academic departments, in undergraduate training, and in graduate programs in anthropology at the major universities and museums around the country.

The educational thrust of Frederic Putnam's vision for American anthropology now involved him in institution-building. His extensive involvement with the 1893 World's Columbian Exposition in Chicago taught him lessons about the need for establishing proper infrastructure. Thus, although he and his protégé Boas ultimately lost out in the development of anthropology at the Field Museum in Chicago, Putnam was much more successful in his plans for anthropology at the University of California–Berkeley and, as we show in the next chapter, at the American Museum of Natural History. He used his powerful position at the AAAS to assist in the founding of the AAA and to help initiate federal legislation for resource protection.

In the time period we have covered in this chapter, one can also begin to see the effect of the student cohort on the career trajectories of several anthropologists who are better known in the history of our discipline. Anthropologists such as George Dorsey and Roland Dixon did not develop in isolation. Rather, an exciting cohort of advanced undergraduates and graduate students already existed in anthropology, whom we have assembled here. These were the people who helped their peers hone their views of the field. And there was a generally unsung group of other Harvard professors who assisted Putnam and the anthropology department with the training of these students. Many of the people whom we have addressed in this chapter were subsequently recognized as leaders in the field by election to the presidency of the American Anthropological Association—Putnam in 1905–6, Dixon in 1913–14, Farabee in 1921–22, Saville in 1927–28, and Swanton in 1932–33.

8

Putnam's Students at the American Museum of Natural History, 1894–1903

We have seen Frederic Putnam's struggles at Harvard to establish both an undergraduate and a graduate degree program in anthropology. Putnam quickly capitalized on his hard-won experience by first helping to reestablish a strong anthropology program at the American Museum of Natural History (AMNH) in New York City and, only a short time later, founding the anthropology department at the University of California–Berkeley. During his AMNH years, Putnam was particularly active in working with people who had American Indian or First Nations heritage. Besides looking at his training of anthropologists at the AMNH in this chapter, we explore his work with these people.

After Putnam's difficulties following the 1893 World's Columbian Exposition at Chicago, where local politics derailed his expectation to be involved in the continuing development of anthropology through the Columbian (Field) Museum, Putnam turned his attention to New York and the AMNH. In 1894, almost immediately after resigning from his exposition and Columbian Museum positions, he accepted an appointment at the AMNH, to be held jointly with his position at the Peabody Museum. At the AMNH he had responsibility for developing the anthropology department, a job he held until 1903. Although the roots of AMNH's Division of Archaeology and Ethnology had been established in 1889, anthropology became central to the program only after Putnam came on staff. One of his first acts was to rename the division "Anthropology," in order to be more inclusive (Darnell 1998: 140). Because the arrangements for Boas at the Columbian Museum also collapsed soon after Putnam left Chicago, putting Boas out of a job, Putnam hired him as his assistant at the AMNH in 1894. By 1896 he had succeeded in getting Boas a joint appointment with the AMNH and Columbia University.

One aspect of Putnam's interest in expansion outside the Peabody Museum, first to the AMNH and later to Berkeley, was financial. He reported for 1890, for example, that the endowment of the Peabody Museum provided a little over $2,000 a year for the salary of the Peabody Professor and a comparable sum for the museum's expenses, including salaries of assistants, heating, lighting, water, postage and shipping, printing, and maintenance (Putnam 1891:102). The situation did not change rapidly; almost two decades later, in his report for 1908, he wrote that the income from Peabody's gift provided only about $4,000 to run the museum and only about $2,500 for the salary of the Peabody Professor and curator.

Because of the lack of adequate compensation, Harvard gave Putnam permission to spend only half time at the Peabody Museum. In the president's report for 1898–99 (Harvard University 1899:38), it was related that "as it is impossible for the University to pay for the whole time of the curator, he gives half his time to the service of the American Museum of Natural History in New York City." Putnam not only used this job to enhance his income but also noted that his position at the AMNH had enabled him "to place in the field several students in this department" (Putnam 1897:242). Putnam was both building an independent program at the AMNH and using resources from the AMNH to help support students from the Peabody such as Roland Dixon, George Pepper, Marshall Saville, and John Swanton.

In this chapter we are particularly interested in the trajectory of the core group of students Putnam recruited into anthropology at the AMNH. Although he recruited professionals such as Franz Boas, Roland Dixon, Aleš Hrdlička, Alfred L. Kroeber, and John Swanton to work on projects during his tenure there (Dexter 1976:306) and was a key player in the development of the Jesup North Pacific Expedition, which began 1897, it is the cadre that some biographers have called "Putnam's boys" on which we particularly focus (Fenton 1991:16; Hertzberg 1978:128, 1979:53; Porter 2001:58).

"Putnam's boys" referred to the students and other interested colleagues, many of whom had American Indian ancestry, who met regularly in the New York City parlor of Harriet Maxwell Converse to discuss anthropology. The main group included William Jones, Mark Raymond Harrington, Arthur Caswell Parker, Alanson Buck Skinner, Frank Gouldsmith Speck, Udo Joseph Keppler, and John William Fenton, as well as earlier recruits of Putnam such as Harlan Ingersoll Smith and George Hubbard Pepper. Many of these young men had started out as naturalists, like Putnam, and gradually shifted their interest to anthropology, although the early naturalist bent remained throughout their lives. Some, such as Harrington, Skinner, and Speck, continued making contributions to natural history as well as anthropology in their later professional careers (Fenton 1991:16).

Harlan Smith's association with Putnam actually predated Putnam's AMNH years, but it was the job Putnam secured for him at the AMNH in 1895, which Smith kept until 1910—overlapping Putnam's 1894–1903 association with the AMNH—that makes him part of this grouping. **Harlan Ingersoll Smith** (1872–1940) was born in East Saginaw, Michigan (Wintemberg 1940:63), and had started out collecting Indian artifacts in the Saginaw Valley in the late 1880s (Marquis Who's Who 1950:1143; Smith 1894a). His initial contact with and subsequent recruitment by Putnam replicates a typical pattern of Putnam's support for enthusiastic but little-schooled amateurs. Putnam was impressed enough by Smith's activities that he arranged for him to work with Charles Metz on the Peabody Museum excavations at Madisonville, Ohio, in the summer of 1890. The following summer, Smith was again working in Ohio for the Peabody Museum, this time as a supervisor for Allan Cook at the mounds at Fort Hill (Putnam 1892:193). During the 1892 season he participated with Cook, Metz, Marshall Saville, and Warren Moorehead on other Ohio excavations (Putnam 1893a:201).

According to Douglas Cole (1999:192), Smith "continued working intermittently under Putnam's supervision, while pursuing erratic study at the University of Michigan," where he had the title of curator of anthropological collections, from 1891 to 1893. Smith was involved in the first coursework in anthropology at the University of Michigan. He reported that this work was for the second semester of the 1891–92 year, the semester before the University of Chicago opened, and was "a course in museum laboratory work in American Archaeology" (Smith 1894b:98, 1894c). The apparently self-taught course had an enrollment of two students—Smith and another, unnamed person—who did work for themselves and for the newly formed museum.

The two students constructed two large display cases, set up an anthropology lab in one of the museum rooms, and spent much of the rest of their time securing existing collections from donors in the area. In addition to soliciting local contributors, Smith secured a collection of materials from the St. John's River in Florida from Clarence B. Moore. Under the joint auspices of the University of Michigan and the Detroit branch of the Archaeological Institute of America, Smith also began survey work in 1892 on the so-called Garden Beds near Kalamazoo, mapping two large sets of earthworks. He continued work on this site and another set of earthworks, near Madison, Wisconsin, in 1893 (Smith 1895:352; Wintemberg 1940:63).

At this same time, in 1891–93, Putnam employed Smith in making collections for the World's Columbian Exposition at Chicago. Before the exposition opened, Smith worked along with Cook, Metz, Moorehead, and Saville, collecting materials from the Ohio mounds for display (Putnam 1893a:201). During the exposition itself, Smith was appointed to help Putnam as "Assistant in Ohio and Michigan Archaeology."

In 1895 Putnam hired Smith to be assistant curator for North American archaeology at the AMNH. Ralph Dexter (1984:121) quoted Putnam as writing on December 25, 1895: "At last I have got Boas appointed as Assistant in Charge of Ethnology and Physical Anthropology at a salary of $3,000 a year and I have Harlan Smith appointed Assistant in the department and also a Mr. Pepper." In the same letter Putnam referred to having created an exceptionally strong team, consisting of himself, Boas, Pepper, Saville, and Smith, and with satisfaction reported, "I have the best equipment of any anthropological museum in the country and I'll show Chicago I can go them one better" (Dexter 1984:122). Clearly, his poor treatment at the hands of the empire builders in Chicago still rankled.

Smith began excavations at Fox Farm in Kentucky with an AMNH crew, with Putnam himself initially paying a portion of Smith's salary (Cattell 1910:431; Cole

1999:176, 186, 192). Smith subsequently took part in excavations in British Columbia for the Jesup North Pacific Expedition, serving as its official archaeologist from 1897 to 1899. During this period he assisted Putnam in other venues as well—for example, serving as an officer in Section H of the AAAS in 1897 and 1902 and as a founding member of the AAA in 1902 (Cattell and Brimhall 1921:627; Dyck 1998:121).

Apparently, during this period Smith and Arthur C. Parker, whom we discuss later, learned from Putnam a bit of functionalist interpretation of archaeological materials. Bruce Trigger (1989:270–75) argued that the earliest display of functionalist interpretation could be seen in the published version of Smith's work at the Fox Farm site in Kentucky (Smith 1910). Arthur Parker continued this functionalism in his work on Iroquois sites in New York, and later it can be seen in the work of Smith's colleague William J. Wintemberg in Canada, as well as that of William S. Webb in the southeastern United States. Gordon Willey and Jeremy Sabloff (1993:58, 93 n. 17) argued that these studies were trendsetting, pioneer works and that such functionalism did not enter American archaeology as a general practice until the late 1930s and 1940s.

Harlan Smith continued serving on committees in the profession while he was at the AMNH. For example, the AAA appointed the New York contingent of Boas, Saville, and Smith to be the organization's auditing committee in 1909–10 (MacCurdy 1909:103). In 1911 Smith resigned from the AMNH to take a position as head of the newly created Archaeology Section at the Geological Survey of Canada's Victoria Memorial Museum. Nels Nelson was hired to replace him at the AMNH (Dyck 1998:115; Snead 2001:106). The Anthropology Division of the Geological Survey of Canada, of which the Archaeology Section was a part, had been founded in 1910, with Edward Sapir as its first chief. He hired Smith, who by then had 20 years of archaeological experience in British Columbia and several U.S. states, as senior archaeologist. Smith later hired William Wintemberg and Diamond Jenness as members of his staff. He began a countrywide archaeological exploration, but only three years into the new program, World War I dealt the museum a setback. Operational funds were cut, fieldwork ceased, and publications were curtailed. In the 1920s, museum programming resumed, but funding remained tight, and archaeology was downgraded to give greater priority to ethnology (Dyck 1998:116). In 1921 the division was reorganized as part of the National Museum of Canada, and Smith remained working under this new division as chief archaeologist until he retired in 1937 (Dyck 1998:119; Marquis Who's Who 1950:1143). In 1930 he finally received a university degree, being awarded an honorary A.M. from the University of Michigan (Cattell and Cattell 1938:1316).

Another of Putnam's early New York students was **George Hubbard Pepper** (1873–1924), who was born in Tottenville, on Staten Island, New York. When Pepper was only a teenager, "under his direction . . . several grave mounds of his native town were excavated. His resulting discoveries then aroused the interest of Professor Frederic W. Putnam" (Spiegelberg 1924:193–94). After graduating from high school in 1895, Pepper, with Putnam's encouragement, enrolled at Harvard for the 1895–96 school year, with the intent of becoming involved in the Peabody Museum's Honduras expedition (Heye 1924:105; Snead 2001:37). Pepper conducted some excavations on Long Island for the AMNH while waiting to go to Honduras (Snead 2001:37). But his plan to do degree work at Harvard changed when Putnam recruited him, along with Harlan Smith and Marshall Saville, to work with him at his new position with the AMNH in New York.

Putnam had been approached by brothers Talbot Hyde and Frederick Hyde Jr. to find someone to direct the Hyde Exploring Expedition, an archaeological expedition to Chaco Canyon, New Mexico, then under AMNH contract, and he suggested Pepper. According to James Snead (2001:35, 175 n. 16), Fred Hyde had attended Harvard and had spoken with Putnam there of the difficulties surrounding the first year's work of the Hyde Expedition. In 1895 Putnam agreed to take over direction of the project and appointed Pepper assistant curator for the Southwest at the AMNH, with the charge of conducting this investigation (Anonymous 1924:566; Heye 1924:106). Under the aegis of the AMNH, Pepper directed the expedition's work at the ruins of Pueblo Bonito from 1896 to 1901. During this period, other Harvard students joined Pepper as excavation assistants, including John Swanton in 1898 and William Farabee and Alfred Tozzer in 1901.

Pepper never wrote much about excavation methodology, presumably because he was simply employing techniques taught to him by Putnam. According to Jonathan E. Reyman (personal communication, 1995), the archives of the AMNH hold substantial evidence in unpublished notes that Pepper indeed used Putnam's Peabody Museum method of stratigraphic excavation, including exceedingly careful recording of artifact contexts in three dimensions. Even today, one would have difficulty matching the exquisite detail of the Pueblo Bonito room burial excavation he submitted as part of the Putnam Festschrift (Pepper 1909). Although Pepper's tenure at Harvard was short, his continued contact with Putnam through the AMNH apparently resulted in his carefully internalizing the advanced excavation methods Putnam was teaching and using.

In 1904 Pepper began working part-time for George G. Heye, who later founded the Museum of the American Indian–Heye Foundation. Pepper excavated first at Tierra Caliente, Michoacán, Mexico, and in 1907 he and Saville, with continued Heye funding, dug in Manabi, Ecuador (Anonymous 1924:567; Heye 1924:106; Kidwell 1999:236–37).

Pepper officially left the AMNH in 1909 to take the position of assistant curator at the University Museum in Philadelphia. He stayed there for a year, conducting some excavations in Michigan for the museum (Kidwell 1999:238), and in 1910 took a permanent position with the Museum of the American Indian, although he did not sever all connections with Pennsylvania until 1914 (Cattell and Brimhall 1921:537; Heye 1924:107). Although most of his work at the Museum of the American Indian was in Latin America, he conducted some excavations in the eastern United States as well. Pepper worked with George Heye at an Indian cemetery in New Jersey, and later he worked with Heye and Frederick Hodge at the Nacoochee mound in Georgia. At the latter site, under Pepper's guidance, the team cut a stratigraphic cross section of the mound, which was the major part of the documentation of the mound (Heye, Hodge, and Pepper 1918). Like George Dorsey (chapter 7), Pepper was one of Putnam's early students who moved between science and commerce (Snead 2001:59).

Frederic Putnam was active in recruiting American Indians for his program. With respect to contributions to anthropology, the Fox tribesman William Jones was the most important American Indian whom Putnam recruited at Harvard, and he was extensively involved with the cohort we are detailing at the AMNH. But Putnam had recruited two other American Indians before Jones—Cornelius C. Cusick and Antonio Apache—although there is some question about the latter's real name and ancestry. Because these two men have previously been overlooked in disciplinary histories, we discuss them at some length and then return to William Jones for a summary of his career.

Antonio Apache (1872?–1938) claimed to be a Chiricahua Apache, born in the Sierra Madre of Arizona, either the son or grandson of Cochise's brother Juan (R. Jackson 1896:5). If this was true, then he was captured during General George Crook's campaigns of 1877 against his relative Chief Geronimo (Bancroft 1893, 2:663). After his capture, Apache told Putnam, he had been taken to Fort Monroe, a coastal artillery post in southeastern Virginia. "He afterward went to Europe on a yacht, becoming proficient in various trades and receiving his education at the night schools of New York and Boston" (Dexter 1966c:328, quoting a November 1, 1893, statement by Putnam in *Inter Ocean*).

At some point before 1892, Apache came to Cambridge and met Putnam at the Peabody Museum (Bancroft 1893, 2:663; Pardue 1996:107). His early correspondence was signed "Antonio, an Apache" (Antonio Apache letters to Putnam, cited in Howard 2002:169–70). Putnam was sufficiently impressed with the young man that he hired him, among others such as Cornelius Cusick, Marshall Saville, and Harlan Smith, to serve as one of his official assistants and to collect materials from the Southwest for the Columbian Exposition. Putnam also had Boas give Antonio Apache training in how to make proper somatological measurements for the database they were collecting for the exposition (Howard 2002:170). According to Hubert Howe Bancroft (1893, 1:329–30), Apache

> was quite useful in making contacts with natives in arranging the ethnological living exhibits. He was employed in spring of 1892 to collect ethnological materials and take measurements from Apache and Navajo, and to get some SW Indians to come to the fair as part of the living exhibits. He got two silversmiths and their families, whose wives were good basketmakers and pottery makers. These Navajo and Apache were funded by the Colorado Commission. Acting as an agent for the State Commission from Colorado, Antonio accompanied a group of Navajo Indians to the fair.

Putnam subsequently arranged for the Colorado commissioners to pay Antonio Apache $50 a month to look after these Indians.

After the exposition was over Bancroft (1893, 2:663) reported, "At last accounts, Antonio's ambition was to visit the Antwerp exposition, as the employee of some American exhibitor, and eventually to complete his education at Harvard university." Apparently at Putnam's urging, Antonio Apache entered Phillips Exeter Academy in 1896, in preparation for attending Harvard. However, according to Edouard L. Desrochers, archives librarian at Phillips Exeter (personal communication to Edwin Sweeney, 1997), he did not continue class work after the first year because of poor academic performance.

In some sources of the late 1890s, Antonio Apache is linked with the Carlisle Indian Industrial School in Carlisle, Pennsylvania. Our first assumption was that he was a student at the school, in preparation for entering Exeter. Subsequent research suggested that he was not a student but that his association with Carlisle was owing to his having already embarked on his career as a promoter by the mid-1890s. A search of several investigations of the approximately 8,500 to 9,000 Indian students who attended Carlisle (Bell 1998; Ryan 1962; Witmer 1993; Barbara Landis, personal communication, 2003; also see www.epix.net/~landis/antapache.html) failed to identify Antonio Apache as a student there. They identify him only as a visitor, in one case explicitly as an agent recruiting students for the school.

In the spring of 1896 he was asked to give a graduation exercise speech, and the Carlisle school newspaper (originally *The Indian Helper*, later renamed *The Red Man*) reported, "When Antonio Apache, tall, graceful and altogether the gentleman arose from the rear of the platform and advanced to the front, he was greeted with loud and enthusiastic applause, and when General [Oliver O.] Howard arose and stepped to the side of the Indian the audience cheered" (R. Jackson 1896:5). In his introduction, Howard said that he first met Juan, brother of Cochise, in 1872, and he had learned from Antonio Apache when they met on the stage that graduation day that he was Juan's son. The following fall, when Antonio Apache returned to Carlisle and took part in the orientation ceremonies for new students, the weekly student newspaper reported: "On last Thursday [September 23, 1897], at the opening exercises of school, Antonio Apache gave an account of his trip through the British Colonies" (Anonymous 1897). In 1897, Richard Henry Pratt, then director of Carlisle, was impressed enough with Apache that he hired him to go to the Southwest to recruit Navajo and Apache children for the school (Howard 2002:177).

Other comments in the Carlisle newspaper about Apache's relationship with Carlisle over the next few years (courtesy of Barbara Landis, personal communication, 2003) seem to reinforce this image of him as agent and promoter. The issue of January 14, 1898, said,

> Mr. Antonio Apache, the inventor of "Lakota" has spared no pains to make his game, which is something like "Fox and Geese," attractive to children. There are pictures of warriors on the buffalo chase, tepees and other curious Indian pictures. The Indians on horseback that are used by the players are made of metal. It is an Apache game, adapted to white children, and it is a very easy game to learn. One dollar is the price, postage paid, to any part of the United States.

The following week's edition announced: "Miss Underwood, of Carlisle, has presented one of Antonio Apache's games, 'Lakota, or the Buffalo Chase,' to our hospital. The uniqueness of the game makes it interesting. Highly colored pictures and toy natives astride tin horses make it attractive. It is a good game for children and especially 'shut-ins.' Every hospital in the land should have a half dozen. $1 postpaid is the price."

Although Apache dropped out of Phillips Exeter after less than a year, he did follow up on his ambition to earn a living collecting materials for expositions and museums. He had a few successful ventures with expositions, but more typical was the situation at Buffalo, New York, in 1899. That year both Apache and Frederick Cummins, manager of the Indian Congress at the Greater America Exposition in Omaha, Nebraska, in 1899, competed to run the Indian concessions and exhibits at the Buffalo Pan-American Exposition of 1901. Cummins won because of stronger financial backing (Rydell 1984:130).

Thus Apache shifted to working for museums and private collectors. He secured collections for the Columbian Museum for George Dorsey; he started working for the Atchison, Topeka and Santa Fe Railroad in 1899 and for the Fred Harvey Company by 1900, until he quit in 1905. He accompanied parties of Eastern visitors through Indian country, acting as a goodwill advisor and marketing the Santa Fe Railroad. In this latter pattern he followed the trajectory of several graduates of Carlisle. Many of the alumni worked for the railroads, either in Pennsylvania or closer to home. The Atchison, Topeka, and Santa Fe Railroad employed many former Carlisle Indian students (Bell 1998:349).

The first question about Apache's identity was raised in January 1901, when the Carlisle school publication ran the disclaimer: "We are credibly informed that the man calling himself Antonio Apache is not Indian; that he wears a wig of straight stiff, black hair; that the real hair when permitted to grow is curly; that the Apache Indians where he claims origin disclaim all knowledge of him. We believe him to be an imposter, but are willing to admit a mistake whenever we have evidence" (quoted in Howard 2002:182).

This publication, with its small circulation, had little effect on the people around Antonio Apache. He went to California in 1905, borrowed $50,000 from Pacific Electric Railway Company magnate Henry E. Huntington the following year, and created an Indian village, modeled in part after the one at the 1893 Chicago exposition, at East Lake Park (now Lincoln Park) in Los Angeles. Apache had just returned from a collecting trip to Alaska and British Columbia, and over the next few years he sold artifacts to

Stewart Culin and Cyrus Gordon, then at the University of Pennsylvania Museum. He had Sioux and Navajo Indians working at the Indian village as demonstrators as well (Howard 2002:161–63). After closing this venture in 1914 (Anonymous 1938), he went on to other ventures, apparently none of them for long, and died at the Los Angeles County poor farm in 1938.

Antonio Apache seems to have been accepted by period anthropologists—Boas, Culin, Dorsey, Gordon, and Putnam, for example, are explicitly named in sources—as an Apache Indian. It has also been assumed that he was the "Antonio Apache" whom Morris Opler used as an "aging informant" in 1937 in his study of Apache peyote use. Opler (1938:271) wrote that "only one Lipan man who lived under aboriginal conditions could be found at the time of the field researches. Lipan women were barred from most activities concerning peyote, so the entire account had to be recorded from this man, Antonio Apache."

More recent assessments, however, suggest that Apache might have been a consummate con artist. The Western artists William M. Cary and Edwin W. Deming claimed in 1907 that he was of biracial African and Caucasian heritage, had been born in the deep South, and was legally named Tony Simpson (Howard 2002:182). Like the contention in 1901 by the Carlisle Indian school paper that he was not an Indian, this allegation seems to have had no effect on Antonio Apache, who was flourishing just then at his Indian village in Los Angeles. It did have ramifications later.

In 1919 Apache married a woman of American Indian origin, Mary Cota Weed. Less than a year after their marriage she asked for an annulment on grounds of fraud. The annulment was granted. The basis for the decree was that Apache had fraudulently represented himself. His name was not Antonio Apache but Tony Simpson, he was not an Indian but rather of biracial African and Caucasian heritage, and he kept an assortment of wigs, wearing them over a closely shaved head, to fool people (Summary of Annulment Decree, cited in Howard 2002:184). Kathleen Howard (2002:186) found a handwritten note in the Frederick W. Hodge papers at the Southwest Museum in Los Angeles, appended to a clipping of Apache's obituary from the *Los Angeles Times* in 1938, which stated, "Antonio Apache was a Negro faker who posed as an Indian. He wore a wig of straight black hair plastered close to the scalp. Edwin W. Deming artist of N.Y. once saw him with his wig off." Although Putnam recruited and trained a man he thought was an Apache Indian and was pleased with Antonio Apache's contributions over the next decade, it now appears that he, Boas, and their colleagues may have been taken in by an "Indian wannabe," a character common in the American West of today.

The story of **Cornelius C. Cusick** (1835–1904) is quite different from that of Antonio Apache. Initially he was an enigma to us. Putnam made a point of referring to the help of two dozen persons at the Columbian Exposition, including "Capt. C. C. Cusick," an assistant in archaeology and ethnology. Other names on this short list were well known to us, but in the beginning we could not identify Cusick or find any reason he was included on the list for special acknowledgment.

Gradually, however, the picture of an interesting person emerged. Cusick was a Tuscarora Indian who had been born on the Tuscarora, or Lewiston, reservation, just east of Niagara Falls in Niagara County, New York. His father, James Nicholas Cusick, was a Baptist minister who had been an associate and friend of James Audubon, George Catlin, and Henry Schoolcraft; he contributed to Catlin and Schoolcraft's study of American Indian mythology (Cusick 1900:1; Forsythe 2002:4). Cornelius's uncle David Cusick had also been interested in the cultural history of their people and published the book *Sketches of Ancient History of the Six Nations* in 1828.

Cornelius Cusick apparently continued his father's and paternal uncle's anthropological interests, to judge from his own first publication, a short article on Tuscarora marriage customs, which appeared in a regional anthology (Cusick 1859). After the death of his maternal uncle, William Chew, Cusick was installed to replace him as a peace chief (sachem) of the Turtle clan on September 6, 1860 (Cusick 1900:2).

In the Civil War, American Indians were initially excluded as participants in most state militias. For example, whereas Seneca Indians were allowed into troops in Pennsylvania, they at first were not permitted to enroll in New York units (Hauptman 1995:166–67). Several important Iroquois leaders, such as Cornelius Cusick, Isaac Newton Parker, and Ely Samuel Parker (aided by Lewis Henry Morgan), lobbied hard to change this ban, flooding congressional offices in March 1862 with protests against restricting Iroquois from war service (Hauptman 1993:18, 1995:166–67). The two Parker brothers were the great-uncles of Arthur C. Parker, one of Putnam's "boys" at the AMNH whom we detail later. Ely Parker was Morgan's principal informant and even, some argue, a significant second, unacknowledged author of Morgan's works on the Iroquois.

After New York Iroquois were officially allowed to enlist in the military, Cornelius Cusick became an important recruiter—so important that the unit he was associated with became known as the Tuscarora Company. Cusick was known as War Eagle among the Iroquois nations and was able to recruit because of his ability to speak eight Indian languages, as well as his prestigious lineage, long associated with success on the warpath. His grandfather Nicholas, for example, had been bodyguard and interpreter for Lafayette during the American Revolution, and his father, too, had been an important warrior (Hauptman 1993:39, 1995:167).

The most famous of the Iroquois units that served in the Civil War was D Company of the 132nd Regiment, New York Volunteer Infantry, popularly referred to as the Tuscarora Company, because part of the unit had been recruited by Lt. Cornelius C. Cusick. Between May and August 1862, Cusick and Chauncey C. Jemison, a Seneca, who was helped by Ely and Isaac Parker, recruited 25 Iroquois for this company from the Allegany, Cattaraugus, Cornplanter, and Tonawanda Indian reservations. Of the 25 Iroquois in the company (including Cook and Jemison), 16 were recruited by Cusick and 7 by Jemison. Cusick's stature or perhaps charisma can be seen in the fact that although Company D became known as the Tuscarora Company, in reality there were four times more Senecas than Tuscaroras among the 25, and Company D itself had four times more German immigrant farmers than Iroquois, so the Tuscaroras actually made up only a small percentage of the entire company (Hauptman 1993:28–41).

The company served for three years in North Carolina, almost continually on outpost duty, until just before it mustered out of service in June 1865. Lt. Cusick "was the most important Iroquois commander of Indian troops" during the Civil War (Hauptman 1993:39). Although Ely Parker was made a brigadier general and thus outranked Cusick, he never led Iroquois soldiers into combat. Cusick's Iroquois Company D troops of the 132nd excelled in the battle of Bachelor's Creek in 1864 and in subsequent engagements in North Carolina that year (www.dmna.state.ny.us/historic/btlflags/132d.html). Cusick and the members of Company D were singled out, for example, in the dispatch on the battle of New Berne as some of the heroes of the day for the Union Army (C. Smith 1891:76).

Cusick mustered out of the army in May 1865, but he petitioned to be accepted as part of the troops fighting in the trans-Mississippi West and was recommissioned as a second lieutenant in the 13th U.S. Infantry in June 1866. At that point he felt it necessary to resign his position as sachem of the Tuscarora, which he did on June 20 (Cusick 1900:2). He was stationed on the trans-Mississippi frontier for the next quarter century, serving in the Dakotas, Montana, Colorado, Utah, Oklahoma, and Texas. He transferred in 1867 to the 31st U.S. Infantry and was sent with his regiment to fight Red Cloud's Lakota warriors in Dakota Territory. When the 31st Infantry was eliminated in the downsizing of the army in 1869, he was transferred to the 22nd Infantry, where he remained until he retired on January 14, 1892. Cusick had been promoted to first lieutenant in August 1872, in charge of Company F, and then to captain of Company E in January 1888. His promotion to first lieutenant was particularly quick, considering that the army was cut in half by congressional action in 1869 and downsized again in 1870 (Forsythe 2002:9).

According to his service résumé, Cusick spent part of his 26 years in military service in the East. From September 1874 to May 1875 he did reconstruction duty in Louisiana and engaged in suppressing insurrection against the Kellogg government in New Orleans. He went to Chicago to quell strikes and riots by railroad workers in July and August 1877. Shortly thereafter he was sent to put down a strike among coal miners in Wilkes-Barre, Pennsylvania.

But for 17 of the 26 years, Cusick was stationed on the Great Plains, where he was involved in several conflicts with other American Indian peoples (Cusick 1900). He appears to have been fully accepted by his fellow officers, even though his Indian ancestry was widely known (Forsythe 2002:1). On multiple occasions he participated in armed engagements against Plains Indians, being wounded as well as receiving commendations. For example, he was wounded with a stone war club in a victorious confrontation with a Sioux chief in a battle with a detachment under Sitting Bull in August 1868. In February 1879 he reported being in charge of the transfer of Sioux Indian prisoners from Fort Buford, North Dakota, to Stillwater Penitentiary,

Minnesota, 700 miles away. The snow was two and a half feet deep and the temperature 20 to 40 degrees below zero Fahrenheit, and the group passed other parties that had frozen to death.

With General Nelson A. Miles, Cusick fought against Crazy Horse's band in the Lakota Sioux conflict of 1876–77 in Montana and the Dakotas. He and nine other officers were commended in the battle of Lame Deer in May 1877 and subsequently received brevet promotions for their performance of that battle (Greene 1991:293 n. 13). Cusick also fought in the Ute campaign in Colorado from October 1879 to January 1880. Later in his career, he taught the nineteenth-century equivalent of ROTC in the late 1880s in Georgia and gave occasional lectures at Carlisle Indian Industrial School, before retiring from the army in January 1892 (Hauptman 1993:37, 45; Pearson 2001).

Although other American Indians served as scouts and irregulars for the U.S. Army, Cusick seems to have been the only one to serve in the regular army as an officer on the western frontier except for first lieutenant Donald McIntosh of the 7th Cavalry, the first Indian graduate of West Point. The Canadian-born McIntosh, who was killed in the battle of Little Big Horn on June 25, 1876, is said to have been related, through his mother, to the Seneca orator Red Jacket (Forsythe 2002:3). Thus both Cusick and McIntosh were members of the Iroquois League.

These facts alone make Cusick an intriguing character, but for our purposes it is his anthropological connections that lend him special interest. At the time he accepted his commission in the regular army in 1866, Cusick, like all other officers, submitted a résumé of his previous activities. According to Scott Forsythe, archivist of the National Archives and Records Administration office in Chicago (personal communication, 2002), Cusick mentioned an interest in aboriginal mounds in his early résumés, an interest he apparently maintained throughout much of his life. In an update of this résumé in 1900, Cusick (1900:23–24) wrote of himself: "He is now engaged in the examination of Indian mounds, including those of most venerable antiquity in the state of Ohio." In 1875 Cusick joined the American Association for the Advancement of Science, where he met Frederic Putnam, the permanent secretary, and he remained a member of the anthropology section until 1880, using his war department address in Washington, D.C., as his home location.

At his first meeting as a member of the AAAS, Cusick presented a paper in the anthropology section, which in the 1875 proceedings is referred to only by its title, "American Antiquities" (Cusick 1876). The paper, however, was interesting enough to one of the attendees at the session, John Church, that although he reported that several papers on prehistoric archaeology had been given under the new chairmanship of Edward S. Morse of Salem, he devoted almost his entire summary of the meeting to Cusick's paper:

> Among the papers on this subject was one by Lieutenant Cornelius C. Cusick, chief of the Tuscarora Indians of New York, whose origin and position may be supposed to be obvious advantages in the pursuit of a study in which he is also deeply interested.

He discussed the mounds of Newark, Ohio. These works were supposed by Squier and Davis to be military, and to form part of a general line that extended east and west of the southern border of the great lakes. But Lieutenant Cusick disputed this position. He thinks the structures at Newark are too large, and not properly shaped for defense, and supposes they were used for herding game. He exhibited a number of objects dating from the time of the mound builders, among them a copper awl which had been handed down among the modern Indians for an unknown period, and regarded with great veneration. (Church 1875:561)

This was an active period in Cusick's life, during which he was involved in more than simply military activities. In addition to participating in the meetings of the AAAS, he had a show of several oil paintings at a Detroit gallery, according to a report in the *Detroit Free Press* of July 10, 1878 (cited in Gibson 1975:83). Scott Forsythe (personal communication, 2002) indicated that there are also references in the archives to Cusick's making paintings of western military posts, although Forsythe had been unable to locate any of them. Cusick himself reported (1900:22) that he had great interest in free-hand and map drawing, in work-drawing plans of buildings, and in the construction of field works from these plans.

Cusick made several plat maps or plans of military posts. For example, he made a plan of Fort Randall, Dakota Territory, and a survey of its immediate grounds for Army Medical Circular number 8, in February 1874. He was sent on special duty to draft plans of the public buildings at Fort Wayne, Michigan, from July to September 1875. He was again on special duty at Fort Gibson, Oklahoma, where he was engaged in surveying and grading the range in August 1879 and in drawing a plan of the fort itself in September 1879. And he was engaged in drawing plans of public buildings at Fort Clark, Texas, in the summer of 1881 (Cusick 1900:15, 16, 18, 19).

During this period as well, Cusick became a bit player in the well-known nineteenth-century "Bone Wars" between Edward Cope and Othniel Marsh. Cusick found an *Ichthyosaurus* skeleton while on duty at Fort Randall, South Dakota, in 1873, and after consultation presented it to Marsh (Cusick 1900:23).

Cusick was not the only Tuscarora Indian who contributed to anthropology in the last quarter of the nineteenth century. John Napoleon Brinton Hewitt (1859–1937), a former public school teacher, was recruited from his job as a New Jersey streetcar conductor in 1880 to assist Erminnie Adele Smith (1836–86), a cousin of Putnam's, in her study of Tuscarora grammar (Judd 1967:50; Noelke 1974:77). Smith had begun working on the Tuscarora reservation in 1875. When she died in 1886, John Wesley Powell hired Hewitt to complete her manuscript, and he continued working for the BAE on these Iroquois materials until 1912. Hewitt stayed with the BAE for 51 years, writing perhaps 100 of the articles for the *Handbook of American Indians* but leaving behind 250 unpublished manuscripts in the BAE archives (Browman 2002a:220; Noelke 1974:77–78). It might have been nothing more than coincidence (although we think not) that Smith was a cousin of Putnam's and got entry to work with the Tuscaroras the very same year the Tuscarora chief Cusick met Putnam at the AAAS meetings. We know it was no coincidence that Cusick began working for Putnam at the 1893 exposition.

Putnam had known Cusick from the six years at the AAAS and from Cusick's interest in the Ohio mounds. Putnam asked the U.S. Army to second Cusick to him for the duration of the Columbian Exposition, to assist in collecting materials, and Cusick (1900:22) reported that he had been appointed by Director-General Davis of the World's Columbian Exposition as honorary and special assistant in the Department of American Archaeology and Ethnology on September 25, 1891. After checking with the judge advocate general, however, the army decided it could not legally grant Cusick leave to work on a commercial exposition. Cusick retired from the army in January 1892 in order to continue working for Putnam.

Cusick established a branch office for relics (prehistoric and ethnographic) shortly after that in Cleveland, Ohio, home of the family of his wife, Lizzie Barnes, whom he had married in 1879. A quick search of the collections of the Peabody Museum turned up only one artifact from Cusick's work: "Babyboard; probably 125 years old; exhibited by Capt. C. C. Cusick, U.S. Army of New York" (Peabody Museum Director Records, 1870–1923: 38–22, 41–47, unaccessioned artifacts, no. 220, Peabody Museum Archives). After the exposition, Cusick continued living in Ohio. His son, Alton B. Cusick, followed in his father's military footsteps, becoming a first sergeant with the 10th Ohio Volunteer Infantry in 1898. The following year he was commissioned a lieutenant in the 44th U.S. Volunteers and went to the Philippine Islands to fight in Spanish-American War campaigns (Cusick 1900:24).

Putnam's most important Indian recruit, however, was not Cusick but **William Jones** (1871–1909), who was linked to Putnam through Harvard, the AMNH, and the meetings of the students known as Putnam's boys. Jones was born on the Sauk and Fox reservation in Oklahoma, in what was then Indian Territory. His grandfather was a Sauk and Fox chief, his father was half Fox, and his mother was an English woman, so Jones, known on the reservation as Megasiawa, or Black Eagle, was officially one-quarter Fox by blood (F. Peabody 1926:169; Rideout 1912:8, 10). Jones spent three years, from 1886 to 1889, working as a cowboy, an occupation about which he later wrote short stories for the Harvard College literary magazine.

Jones was recruited from the reservation to enter the Hampton Normal and Agricultural Institute in Virginia in the fall of 1889 by Cora Mae Folsom (1855–1943), a Hampton teacher who was searching for new students (Peabody 1926:170; Rideout 1912:28). Hampton had been founded in 1868 as a school for freed slaves, and in 1877 it added a program for Indians, which lasted until 1923 (Lindsey 1995:xi). Folsom had in fact gone out to Oklahoma to pick up Jones and several other students in 1889 (Folsom 1893). She played multiple roles at Hampton, serving as a teacher, director of pageants and exhibitions, head curator of Hampton's Blake Museum (which, after its founding in 1878, developed an extensive collection of African and Indian materials), and advisor for the school publications. For a while she apparently even shared duties between Carlisle and Hampton (Hultgren and Molin 1989:45; Lindsey 1995:90–91; Ruffins 1992:519; Walker-McNeil 1979). After graduating from Hampton, Jones next attended Phillips Andover Academy, beginning in 1892. There he met Henry Milner Rideout, who later published Jones's biography on the basis of letters Jones wrote to him, first at Andover and later at Harvard and the AMNH (Rideout 1912:29). Because Jones was a minor far from his home on the reservation, he was legally required to have a guardian at Andover, to act in lieu of his parents. Cora Folsom, at Hampton, served as his guardian not only at Andover but also afterward at Harvard (Rideout 1912:28).

After graduating from Andover, Jones applied to and was accepted at Harvard. He was encouraged by Andover headmaster Cecil F. P. Bancroft and faculty member Charles H. Forbes, whose letters of recommendation are still to be found in Jones's Harvard file (Harvard University, Pusey Library Archives, Harvard College applicant file for William Jones). Although Walter Hough (1933:205) wrote that "through advice of Prof. F. W. Putnam he entered Harvard in 1896," it appears from several sources that Jones did not meet Putnam until after he arrived at Harvard (Calhoun 1991b:329; Rideout 1912:41–42).

Jones had, in fact, originally been directed toward going to Harvard for a medical career. He wrote in his journal of February 1896, "I am going to pass my final examinations for Harvard. But whether I go to the Medical School or anywhere else is a question. If I could earn a scholarship or earn anything at Harvard I would not hesitate, but there seems no chance. I will not pose as an Indian. I will not take a cent on that score. It isn't fair, besides it would be uncomfortable" (Rideout 1912:32). Later, in an April 1896 entry, he wrote that Dr. Cecil Bancroft

> strongly urges me to go to Harvard, spend three years there for an A.B. degree, and then go to the Medical School.... I can see the general wisdom of his plan, but my case is so peculiar, so different from most others. Shall I go to college three years and then perhaps to the Medical? The one sure and strong argument for going to college first is that I am not at all sure that I am going to like medicine, and that perhaps my ethnology work in Indian may suit me better. (Rideout 1912:34)

Thus we see that Jones had already developed a incipient interest in ethnology before he reached Harvard, an interest that, it seems, awaited encouragement. The documents are relatively mute on the roots of this interest, but we do find that in his last year at Andover, Jones discovered an Algonkin Bible in the Boston Public Library and, to his surprise, found that the language's similarities to Sauk-Fox were such that he could read it. Jones had also become aware of the Horsford collection of Indian documents at Wellesley during his Andover days, and these materials contributed as well to his developing linguistic interest (Rideout 1912:33).

Even after being admitted to Harvard, with Cora Folsom again serving as his sponsor because he was an Indian, Jones was uncertain whether he could afford the expense.

But right after commencement from Andover, he received a note from Harvard, granting him $250 from the Price Greenleaf Aid Fund, and he entered Harvard in the fall of 1896 (Rideout 1912:35).

Jones's first meeting with Putnam took place during the spring semester of his freshman year. He wrote in his diary on March 6, 1897:

> My meeting with Professor Putnam was the very nicest talk I believe I ever had with an elderly man, excepting perhaps one or two with Dr. Bancroft. He took me right in, and told me just exactly what I wanted to know without the least possible questioning of my part except one or two times. I am afraid my dreams of ever becoming a doctor are all thrown aside. The field he opened out to me is certainly wide, with room enough for hundreds of intelligent workers. (Rideout 1912:41)

Jones further recorded a typical Putnam remark that day: "My boy, make yourself at home and come over to the house and see us there" (Rideout 1912:42). Putnam's openness to a host of amateurs, collectors, students, and colleagues was referred to repeatedly by such people. He was accessible to and eager to recruit all potential researchers.

Jones accordingly shifted his major to anthropology (Calhoun 1991b:329). He became a member of the Boston Folk-Lore Society in 1897 and wrote a few articles for the *Journal of American Folk-Lore* while an undergraduate. His association with that society provided him with a grant from W. W. Newell of $110 toward expenses to spend the summer of 1897 doing linguistic studies with Sauk and Fox Indians near Tama, Iowa, a branch of his Oklahoma tribal group (Rideout 1912:44–45).

Jones took the two anthropology courses offered the next academic year, Anthropology 1 and Anthropology 4, and received his highest grade yet at Harvard, a B in Anthropology 1, in the spring semester of his sophomore year (Harvard University, Pusey Library Archives, William Jones folder). He was not interested in all aspects of anthropology. He wrote in his journal in the fall of 1897 about his first semester's course (Rideout 1912:51): "Anthropology now is decidedly slow and stupid. I can't tell whether it is hard or easy, because I am not sure what it is driving at. I devote two or three hours a week to working up the notes of my summer's work, with [Roland] Dixon. He is more than interested, and thinks the material in every way good." From this it is evident that Dixon, in addition to Putnam, was much engaged in the training of Jones during his Harvard undergraduate years.

In his junior year Jones became a writer for the student publication *Harvard Monthly*, where his friend Henry Rideout was editor-in-chief, and in his senior year he was named one of the magazine's half-dozen editors. During his tenure he wrote five articles on cowboy themes, harking back to his teenage years, and four on Indian themes (*Harvard Monthly* 27 [1898] through 30 [1900]). During both his junior and senior years, Putnam awarded Jones the Winthrop Scholarship, a fellowship used primarily to support graduate students. Jones also received the Harvard Advocate Scholarship, "for excellence in English Composition," during this time (Rideout 1912:61).

For his senior honors thesis Jones opted to work up some of the Algonkin materials from New England. Putnam wrote in his annual report to the Peabody Museum trustees (1900a:272) that "Mr. William Jones, Winthrop Scholar, has made a special study to determine the language and customs of the former Indians of Massachusetts, in connection with his researches upon the Algonkins, to which Indian stock he belongs." Jones's importance to the anthropology program at the time has been poorly appreciated. The Harvard catalogue for 1899–1900 listed three Peabody Museum officers appointed by the corporation: Frank Russell, Roland Dixon, and William Jones. To put it another way, a student looking to see who in the Peabody Museum might be involved with anthropology would have seen those three names. Why Jones was listed as an "officer" is unclear, but it underlines his significance to the anthropology program.

Jones graduated from Harvard with an A.B. in anthropology, with honors, in 1900. He was the first Indian to graduate from Harvard in 235 years, since Caleb Cheeshahteamuck in 1665 (Lindsey 1995:174 n. 30). Harvard had established a short-lived Indian College in 1655, but only four or five Indians ever entered, and Cheeshahteamuck was the only one to live to obtain an A.B. Sadly, he died of tuberculosis only a year later (Morison 1936:38). Perhaps other American Indians enrolled as Jones did, simply as regular students, but we have been unable to identify any other Indian degree recipients.

After Jones graduated, Putnam sent him to work with Franz Boas at Columbia University. Putnam noted in his letter to Columbia of July 12, 1900, recommending a scholarship, that Jones "has taken courses in American Archaeology and Ethnology during the past three years, including one year's work in my Research Course, when he made a study of and wrote a thesis on the Massachusetts Indians" (Rideout 1912:70). Jones was awarded the President's University Scholarship for his first year at Columbia and received his A.M. at the end of that year (Rideout 1912:71). He was then appointed University Fellow and assistant in anthropology at Columbia for 1901–2 and was reappointed for 1902–3. Boas sent him to work with the Sauk and Fox Indians of Tama, Iowa, to conduct his Ph.D. work during the summers of 1901 and again in 1902 (Boas 1909b:137; Rideout 1912:72; Wissler 1909:123).

Jones wrote Putnam a letter on July 3, 1902, telling him of his new fiancée, Caroline Andrus (1875–1961), a teacher at Hampton School. Andrus had come to Hampton from New York at the age of 10 to help care for her ailing older sister, a teacher there (*American Missionary* 32, no. 2 [1878]:44). After her sister's death, Caroline stayed on to become part of the staff. She was Cora Folsom's assistant and succeeded Folsom as head of the Indian Department in 1911 (Hultgren and Molin 1989:46; Lindsey 1995:90–91, 110, 165, 249). In part Jones sought Putnam's blessing of the union, but he also promised Putnam that he was still pursuing his goal of earning a Ph.D. in anthropology (Peabody Museum of American Archaeology and Ethnology, Catalog Room, William Jones Biographical File). Jones thus clearly felt close to Putnam, treating him essentially as a surrogate father in this situation. Because of obligations to their respective institutions, Jones and Andrus put off their wedding date to the indefinite future.

Jones finished his Ph.D. with the dissertation "Some Principles of Algonkin Word Formation" and received his degree from Columbia in June 1904. The dissertation work was published in *American Anthropologist* that year (Jones 1904), and part of it was later included in the *Handbook of American Indian Languages* for the BAE (Boas 1909b:138). After receiving his degree, Jones served part-time as an associate curator for the AMNH and worked with BAE and AMNH funds to collect additional Sauk and Fox texts (Boas 1909c:338). After this fieldwork, he served as a research assistant for the Carnegie Institution of Washington to continue his work on Central Algonkin, spending two field seasons, in 1905 and 1906, with the Ojibwa near Lake Superior (Boas 1909b:138). He was offered an extension of his grant for the Carnegie Institution in 1906, but he also received an offer from George Dorsey to work for the Field Museum on an expedition to the Philippines (Rideout 1912:125). He accepted the job in June 1906 and after a year of preparation left for the Philippines in 1907.

In the Philippines Jones worked in the fall of 1907 with Fay-Cooper Cole, who was conducting fieldwork for his dissertation at Columbia University. Jones described Cole's collecting procedure as going "after a collection with pretty much the eye of a [Mark Raymond] Harrington, the taste of a [Stephen C.] Simms, and the care of an H. I. [Harlan] Smith" (Rideout 1912:133). He kept in touch with his former colleagues at the AMNH, writing to Harlan Smith on July 12, 1908: "Tell me about yourself, what you are doing, about the New York Museum of Natural History, and other things in general. How is Wissler? Remember me kindly to him. Say to him that I will write him one of these days. Say howdy to [Charles W.] Mead and [William C.] Orchard."

Jones, regrettably, was not to return from this trip. On March 29, 1909, he was murdered by Ilongot tribesmen in the Philippines (Rideout 1912:202). During his short professional career he had published nearly three dozen articles, and according to Franz Boas (1909b:139), "in possession of a fund of knowledge, he was modest and averse to display."

Jones's estate apparently went to Caroline Andrus, even though they had not married. Although Andrus subsequently ended up owning most of the ethnographic and archaeological materials Jones had collected, she had to fight with the Field Museum after Jones's death to get it to turn his materials over to her (C. Davis 2001). She began donating ethnographic and archaeological specimens to the Peabody Museum at Harvard beginning in 1947, until the remaining few items passed to the Peabody from her estate at her death in 1961 (Peabody Museum accession catalogue entries, 1947–61). Stephen Williams helped in cataloguing these specimens. William Jones has not been forgotten.

A major meeting place for the students working with Putnam at the AMNH was the parlor of **Harriet Arnot Maxwell Converse** (1836–1903) in New York City.

Converse kept track of 50 to 100 New England Indians who lived or temporarily worked in New York City (Parker 1908:21). She was also the hostess for a group of scholars interested in American Indians, many of whom themselves had some Indian ancestry. Her father, Thomas Maxwell, had been a good friend of the Indians at their home in Elmira, New York, and had been adopted into the Wolf clan of the Senecas (Parker 1908:15). Her second husband, Frank Buchanan Converse, whom she married after being widowed, was also originally from Elmira and had been adopted into the Senecas. In his early days Frank Converse had lived with Indians in the West, where he had become a skilled bowman.

Harriet Converse started out penning poetry, but after a meeting with General Ely S. Parker, a Seneca and the great-uncle of Arthur Parker, on the Cattaraugus reservation in 1881, she became interested in the Iroquois and changed the direction of her writing toward the myths and legends of the New York Iroquois (Parker 1908:17). In 1884 Harriet Converse herself was formally adopted as a sister to a Seneca Indian, an adoption finalized on June 15, 1885, when she was received into the Snipe clan and given the name Ga-ya-nes-ha-oh, "Bearer of the Law" (Parker 1908:19). Soon after her naming, Harriet Converse was initiated into the Pleasant Valley Lodge of the Guards of the Little Water, popularly known as a secret medicine society. Arthur Parker, one of "Putnam's boys" of the AMNH, was himself a member of this order and lodge (Parker 1908:22). In light of her services to the Seneca people, in 1891 the Name Holders of the Snipe clan decided to change her name to Ya-ie-wa-noh, "She Who Watches Over Us", once the name of the Seneca chief Cornplanter's wife. On September 18, 1891, the entire Iroquois group adopted her as a member and named her a chief, presenting her with the certificate of this action on March 25, 1892, so that Harriet Converse became the first white woman to be named a chief of the Six Nations (Browman 2002a:239; Parker 1908:24, 26).

Converse made large Iroquois collections for the State Museum of New York, the AMNH, and the Peabody Museum. She had extensive correspondence with Putnam at both the AMNH and the Peabody about Iroquois materials and ethnography. But it was the use of her salon as the regular meeting place for Putnam's AMNH students that is most important for our story. As Joy Porter (2001:48 n. 3) wrote, Putnam's "disciples liked to get together and enjoy the genial atmosphere at the Converses' salon. Young anthropologists like Mark R. Harrington, Alanson B. Skinner, and Frank G. Speck all met [Arthur] Parker for the first time there, as did the artist and teacher John W. Fenton and Parker's great friend Joseph Keppler." Who were these "disciples"?

Mark Raymond Harrington (1882–1971) seems to have begun to attend the salon at Harriet Converse's house before Arthur Parker, Alanson Skinner, Frank Speck, or the others of the so-called Putnam's boys of the AMNH. Harrington was born in Ann Arbor, Michigan, where his father was a curator at the university museum. When he was a teenager, Harrington's family moved to Mount Vernon, New York, where he began digging up pottery and arrowheads. He took these items to be identified by Putnam at the anthropology department of the AMNH (K. Evans 2001), and Putnam became his mentor and lifelong friend. When his father's illness forced Harrington to quit high school, Putnam hired him as an apprentice field archaeologist and trained him on the job (K. Evans 2001). Harrington spent the next four years, 1889 to 1902, as an assistant in anthropology at the AMNH, excavating several sites in New York and New Jersey for the museum. By 1902 he apparently had saved enough money to be able to enter the University of Michigan (Anonymous 1971:85–86). He did not end his work for Putnam, however, but continued excavating New York sites, this time as an employee of the Peabody Museum, during the summers between 1903 and 1906 (Cattell 1927:411).

During this period Harrington worked with a number of people of interest to us. Putnam sent him students to train, so that in 1901 he began working with Arthur C. Parker, who later became his brother-in-law, on the Erie site in upstate New York, supported by funds from the Peabody Museum (Putnam 1904:281, 1905:303). In 1902 he worked with Parker (whose second field season it was) and Alanson Skinner (his first season) at the Erie site, supported again by the Peabody (Putnam 1904:303). Brief results of this work were published in the June 1903 issue of *Southern Workman.* In 1905 Harrington trained the Winthrop Scholar from Harvard for that year, Irwin Hayden, who served as his assistant at excavations at sites in the Mohawk Valley—work supported by the Peabody Museum's Henry C. Warren Fund and a donation from Clarence B. Moore of the Peabody Museum Visiting Committee (Anonymous 1906b:95; Putnam 1905:301–2).

Putnam imparted to Harrington the Peabody Museum method of excavation. Harrington later reported (1924:235) that his method was first to put in a series of test pits, 18–20 inches in diameter, to determine the depth and richness of the deposits. Then he put in a trench, excavating it 3–4 inches "into the undisturbed sand below, and wide enough to allow six feet to each worker. A trench of this kind was carried forward by carefully digging down the front with a trowel, searching the soil for relics, then, with a shovel, throwing the loose earth thus accumulated back out of the way into the part already dug over, so as to expose a new front."

After attending the University of Michigan for a short while, Harrington transferred to Columbia University, where he studied with Adolph Bandelier, as well as Boas and others, earning his A.B. in 1907 and his A.M. in 1908 (Anonymous 1971:86; Cattell 1927:411). After graduating from Columbia, Harrington initially stayed in the Northeast, working for the Heye Foundation from 1908 to 1910 and from 1915 to 1928, with a brief interlude at the University Museum at Pennsylvania from 1911 to 1914 (Cattell 1927:411). While at Columbia he met Frank Covert and secured a job working as a field collector for Covert's Indian Store in New York City (Dockstader 1972:26); their field operations were officially known as Covert & Harrington, Commercial Ethnologists (K. Evans 2001).

It was through his work with Covert that Harrington met George Heye, who hired him in 1908 to acquire Indian artifacts from the eastern United States and the Caribbean for the Heye Foundation museum (Kidwell 1999:240; K. Evans 2001). Harrington's temporary move to Pennsylvania happened through his old AMNH links and his connection with the Heye Foundation. In 1907, George Heye had shifted his power base temporarily to the University Museum, where he served on the board of directors and later as vice president (Witthoft 1991:6). George Pepper, Heye's assistant at the time, was appointed assistant curator in the American Section at the museum. In 1911, Heye also brought with him the personnel of the Heye Foundation for that period, including Harrington. When Heye withdrew from Pennsylvania to found the Museum of the American Indian, Harrington moved with him (Witthoft 1991:6). Harrington had first been hired by the Heye Foundation to collect among the Iroquois and other groups, but later, using Heye's money, he made extensive collecting trips to Cuba, the Caribbean, Mexico, Canada, the Ozarks, and the U.S. Southwest, visiting and living with 43 tribes in all (Anonymous 1971:85; K. Evans 2001).

In the mid-1920s Harrington shifted from ethnographic collecting back to archaeology. He began excavations in the Southwest for the Heye Foundation, starting at Lovelock Cave in 1924 and then working at "El Pueblo Grande de Nevada" in 1925 and 1926. He was hired away from the Heye Foundation in 1928 by the Southwest Museum in Los Angeles, which offered him the position of curator. There he renewed his association with Irwin Hayden, the Harvard student he had trained two decades earlier, who was by then living in Riverside, California, although no longer practicing archaeology (see chapter 10). In 1929 Harrington hired Hayden to dig for the Southwest Museum at Mesa House in the Moapa Valley of Nevada while Harrington conducted a survey of the valley. In 1930 Harrington began work at Gypsum Cave; in 1933 he conducted excavations at Tule Springs; and from 1933 to 1935 he conducted the salvage archaeology of the Lake Mead reservoir project (K. Evans 2001), all again in Nevada. Harrington spent the rest of his career, until his retirement in 1964, exploring the antiquities of southern California, becoming involved in Paleoindian studies with work at Pinto Basin, Little Lake, Tule Springs, Borax Lake, and Calico Mountain sites. He was a prolific writer, not only publishing more than 325 items but also penning ethnographically accurate adventure stories set among pre-Columbian Indians, under the pen name Ramon de la Cuevas (Dockstader 1971:27; K. Evans 2001).

For our theme, Harrington is most important for the training he did of several people associated with Putnam in New York, such as Parker and Skinner, and of students from Harvard such as Hayden, and for his spreading of the Peabody Museum excavation method. The linkage between Harrington and Parker was particularly close, for Harrington was married to Parker's sister Edna from 1927 until her death in 1948 (Porter 2001:17, 48, 245 n. 30).

Arthur Caswell Parker (1881–1995), a "quarter-blood" Seneca and the first president of the Society for American Archaeology, was another of the anthropological members of Harriet Converse's salon group. Parker had been born on the Cattaraugus Seneca reservation, 30 miles south of Buffalo, New York, with an illustrious family heritage. Far back in his ancestry he was related to the eighteenth-century Seneca prophet

Handsome Lake and to the chiefs Cornplanter and Red Jacket, who had been awarded silver medals by George Washington for their assistance in the American Revolutionary War (Hertzberg 1979:50; Porter 2001:18; Thomas 1955:2).

Parker's grandfather Nicholson Henry Parker (1819–92) had been a civil engineer. Nicholson Parker's younger brother, Ely Samuel Parker (1822/28?–1895), had briefly attended Rensselaer Polytechnic Institute, taking coursework in civil engineering. He had joined the Union Army in 1863, making brigadier general in 1867, and resigned in 1869 to become President Ulysses S. Grant's Indian commissioner, a post he held until 1871 (Tooker 1978:15–16). More important for our theme, Ely Parker had been Lewis Henry Morgan's principal Iroquois informant, as well as silent co-author, for Morgan's 1851 *League of the Ho-dé-no-sau-nee, or Iroquois* (Hertzberg 1979:50). In addition to their interaction with Morgan, Nicholson and Ely Parker were in frequent contact with Harriet Maxwell Converse.

The Parker family moved from the Cattaraugus reservation to White Plains, a suburb of New York City, when Arthur was 11 years old (Hertzberg 1979:11; Thomas 1955:3). He enrolled in high school there, graduating in 1897. For the next few years his career trajectory was uncertain. He entered the co-educational Centenary Collegiate Institute in Hackettstown, New Jersey, in 1899 but left before the year was out. He enrolled later in 1899 at Dickinson Seminary in Williamsport, Pennsylvania, to study for the ministry. After three years of off-and-on studies, he left Dickinson as well, without completing a degree (Porter 2001:23; W. Ritchie 1977:53).

According to his own recollection, Parker had begun to frequent the AMNH in the late 1890s, while he was still in high school. During visits to the museum he met Frederic Putnam, Franz Boas, and the natural scientist Frank M. Chapman, among others (Porter 2001:22, 48). After finishing high school he also began to spend more and more time at "Uncle Frank and Aunt Hattie's salon"—referring to Frank and Harriet Converse—with the group known as "Putnam's boys of the AMNH" (Porter 2001:22). Parker had known "Aunt Hattie" Converse since childhood, as she was a close friend of his great-uncle Ely's. As he grew older, Harriet Converse served as his mentor and friend and helped him with the cost of his education (Porter 2001:45; Siegel 1993:17).

By the early 1900s, wrote Joy Porter, Arthur Parker "was in regular correspondence with Dr. Putnam at the Museum of Natural History, who was subsidizing his school attendance and encouraging his efforts to produce an article on archaeology" (Porter 2001: 23, 48, 249 n. 2). While Parker was at Dickinson, Putnam had provided him with a little financial aid, clearly encouraging Parker to continue his education (Siegel 1993:19).

Parker (1910) once wrote that he took special courses from Putnam in the period from 1901 to 1903, which has led some researchers to suppose that Parker went to school at Harvard. More careful analysis suggests that these "courses" were instead a series of informal tutorials that Putnam held at the AMNH for Parker and the rest of his "boys" (Hertzberg 1978:131). Parker himself wrote to a friend, Elaine Goodale Eastman, in 1911: "My academic schooling never went much beyond the high school, supplemented by three years' study under the direction of professor Frederick (*sic*) W. Putnam" (Hertzberg 1979:61).

Parker was appointed "Special Assistant in Archaeology" at the AMNH for 1901–2 and began his first ethnographic collecting as well as assisting in excavation projects. In the summer of 1903 he served as field assistant to Mark Harrington on an archaeological survey of the Cattaraugus reservation, which Putnam directed and arranged to have sponsored jointly by the AMNH and the Peabody Museum. It was apparently Harrington who talked Parker into finally dropping out of the seminary for good in 1903 and working with him (Porter 2001:50; Thomas 1955:4). Parker and Harrington did several excavation projects for the AMNH and Peabody Museum together in 1903–4. John Robert Siegel (1993:9 n. 10, n. 12) wrote that "under Putnam's direction, Parker developed his scholarly interests," and "it was his association with Putnam that propelled him into an archaeological career." Hazel Whitman Hertzberg (1979:52) similarly observed: "While at the seminary he continued to frequent the American Museum of Natural History, where he came under the influence of the eminent archaeologist, Professor Frederick [*sic*] W. Putnam. . . . If Parker's grandfather Nicholson served as a model of man living in and between two cultures, Putnam became Parker's model of the scientist; and there can be little question that his career profoundly influenced Parker's own."

It was at the Converse house that Parker became friends with Harrington, John Fenton, Joseph Keppler, Alanson Skinner, and Frank Speck, men with whom he kept in contact throughout his career. He was particularly closely linked to Harrington, who married Parker's younger sister Edna. Hertzberg (1979:52) noted:

> This talented group include the future anthropologist and museologist Mark R. Harrington, who introduced Parker to archaeology by taking him digging on Long Island; Alanson B. Skinner, a budding anthropologist who was involved briefly in Parker's later Pan-Indian reform efforts; John W. Fenton, teacher and painter, whose son William became a distinguished Iroquois anthropologist who republished Parker's major ethnological works; and Parker himself. Often "Putnam's boys" repaired to the home of Frank and Harriet Maxwell Converse where in Mrs. Converse's salon they found a lively group of Indians and their friends, including Joseph Keppler, the cartoonist for *Puck*. Years earlier Ely Parker himself had been a visitor at the salon.

When Frank and Harriet Converse died in 1903, Parker and Joseph Keppler became the two executors of the estate (Siegel 1993:17). Parker took over the editing of Harriet Converse's massive folklore notes and was responsible for publishing them in 1908. He also was later responsible for the analysis of much of the Converse Iroquois artifact collection in the New York Science Museum. During his work with Harriet Converse's materials, he became more interested in his own Iroquois heritage. He was officially adopted into the Bear clan and given the name Gawasowaneh, or Big Snow Snake. Parker had to be officially adopted because, although he was of Seneca ancestry, Iroquois status is reckoned through the mother's line, and Parker's mother was a non-Indian (Siegel 1993:11, 22 n. 20, Parker to Keppler, January 22, 1906).

In April 1904 Parker married, and needing to support his wife, he took a job as an ethnographic fieldworker for the New York State Library and State Museum, to collect ethnographic materials on the Iroquois for those institutions. He had previously tried briefly to support himself through journalism, acting on a suggestion from Keppler, but had not done well (Hertzberg 1979:56; Porter 2001:49). Frank Speck had taken him to talk with Boas to discuss further schooling at Columbia in 1904, and Putnam had encouraged him to enroll there. Parker opted not to enroll, although his friends Harrington and Speck did so (Hertzberg 1979:54; Porter 2001:53).

In 1905 Parker took the Civil Service examination and in 1906 was promoted to the newly established position in archaeology in the Science Division of the New York State Museum. Putnam wrote him a letter of congratulations, commenting that "in realizing your own ambitions you have brought about the consummation of my hopes for you" (Hertzberg 1979:52 n. 53). Shortly after being promoted to archaeologist, Parker began work at the Ripley site, from June 1 to October 1, 1906. The Ripley site was an Iroquois village and burial site west of Lake Erie in Chautauqua County, and its excavation is remembered as Parker's single most respected archaeological study (Parker 1907). Apparently it was John Fenton who first suggested to Parker that he should dig the Ripley site (Porter 2001:249 n. 3). Fenton had reported the site to Putnam in 1901, and Parker and Harrington had later visited it during their 1903 survey (Siegel 1993:23).

Parker's work was the first systematic excavation of an Iroquois village, but it is perhaps more important from a methodological point of view. In 1923 the Committee on State Archaeological Surveys of the National Research Council recommended in a brochure to all state societies and archaeologists that "one of the best published statements of detailed procedure will be found in Arthur C. Parker's 'An Erie Indian Village and Burial Site'" (Wissler et al. 1923:17). It went on to quote in detail the methodology described in his report. It should come as no surprise that the excavation method advocated by Parker (1907:478–79) was Putnam's Peabody Museum method. Parker credited Putnam with teaching him these techniques, writing to Putnam in 1907: "The character of my work has been the result of carrying out the methods which you have taught and which I have gleaned from your papers and addresses and from the advice and criticism which you gave me in New York" (Hertzberg 1979:250 n. 27). Parker continued to employ the Peabody Museum method, and as a keynote speaker on May 18, 1929, at the Conference on Midwestern Archaeology, held in St. Louis, Missouri, he again argued for the adoption of this methodology by both amateurs and professionals (Parker 1929).

Parker also took from Putnam a focus on functionalism in archaeological explanation. As we noted earlier, Willey and Sabloff (1993:58) and Trigger (1989:270–75) identified Putnam's students Parker and Harlan Smith as among the groundbreakers in the use of functional explanations in American archaeology. For the most part, however, Parker followed the direct historical approach in linking the archaeological sites he excavated to known Iroquois villages. This allowed him and his student William Ritchie to be among the first to employ explicit chronologies in their new regional syntheses (Willey and Sabloff 1993:126, 134).

In the first two years of his new job, Parker made both philosophical and physical restructuring changes to the museum. He brought in new methodologies, reorganized the department into several subsections—archaeology, ethnology, folklore, philology—reorganized the collections according to artifact function, began the first adequate cataloguing, and began the first comprehensive field expeditions as part of the collecting mechanism, copying methods he had learned from Putnam (Porter 2001:29, 34).

Parker also organized the New York State Archaeological Association in 1916, the same year he won the Cornplanter Award for his work in Iroquois ethnography. He was a founding member of the Society of American Indians on October 12, 1911, serving as its organizing secretary from 1911 to 1915 and as its president from 1915 to 1917. He was founder and editor of the Society of American Indians' *Quarterly Journal,* later renamed *American Indian Magazine* (Hertzberg 1979:59; Siegel 1993:2; Thomas 1955:8). He served in 1923 as chair of the "Committee of One Hundred," which had been established to deal with a new Bureau of Indian Affairs initiative. His nomination was initiated by Warren K. Moorehead, and the agenda for the committee was introduced by Herbert Spinden (Siegel 1993:174–77).

In 1924 Parker left the New York State Museum because he had been skipped over for promotion and because of problems in securing funding for his work. He accepted the directorship of the Rochester Museum of Arts and Sciences, a job he kept until his retirement in 1945 (Hertzberg 1979:68; W. Ritchie 1956:293; Siegel 1993:53). It was there that Parker trained and worked with William A. Ritchie for 21 years (Thomas 1955:12). While at Rochester he founded the journal *Museum Science* and became increasingly involved in the museum management side of affairs. But Parker also retained his interest in archaeology and indeed became the first president of the Society for American Archaeology in 1935. During his career he collected more than 100,000 ethnological specimens for the New York State Museum, published 14 books, including his *Manual for History Museums* (1935), the bible of the museum profession, and more than 300 articles. The richest period of his creativity was while he was at the New York State Museum, where he wrote eight books and 132 articles (Thomas 1955:6). He contributed to three of the major changes of the period from the 1890s to the 1920s: the redefinition of the meaning of American nationality, the professionalization of American anthropology, and the reforming of the concerns of Indian affairs (Hertzberg 1979:47). In 1997 the Society for American Archaeology established the Arthur C. Parker Scholarship for Native Americans and Native Hawaiians, in his memory. Parker, even more than William Jones, is a sterling success story of Putnam's attempts to involve American Indians in the study of their own heritage.

Alanson Buck Skinner (1886–1925) was a close friend of Mark Harrington and Arthur Parker, being a native New Yorker as well. Born in Buffalo, he moved to Staten

Island when young. As Harrington and Smith had done, Skinner began collecting Indian relics in the neighborhood of his home and brought them for identification to the AMNH, where he had a job during his summer vacation (Harrington 1926:275; Hough 1935). There he not only met Putnam but also became friends with Harlan Smith and George Pepper in the late 1890s (Harrington 1929:248). Shortly thereafter, Skinner met Harrington in 1900 and Parker in 1902, during summer school vacations, while volunteering for work with the AMNH.

In 1902 Skinner excavated shell heaps at Shinnecock Hills, Long Island, for the AMNH, working with Parker and Harrington. He published short articles on his finds there in the journal of the local history society (Skinner 1903a, 1903b). He was officially hired by the Peabody Museum in 1904, when he was 18, to work with Harrington and Parker doing excavations on the Cattaraugus reservation in western New York (Cattell 1910:430; Harrington 1929:249). In 1906, when Parker was named to the new position of state archaeologist, but with a minimal budget, Skinner volunteered for an extended period at Parker's excavations at the Ripley village site in Chautauqua County (Porter 2001:61).

After high school, Skinner tried business for a while but then drifted back to the AMNH, where he was hired as an assistant in anthropology from 1906 to 1913; he maintained less specific linkages with the museum until 1916 (Cattell 1910:430; Harrington 1935:197). In 1908 Skinner led an AMNH expedition to Hudson Bay to study the Cree Indians. The following year he led a second AMNH expedition to Hudson Bay, and in 1910 he went to Wisconsin to study the Menomini (Harrington 1929:250).

During his time at the AMNH Skinner took courses at both Harvard and Columbia, but he never finished a degree at either school. At Columbia he took coursework with Boas, Saville, and Bandelier, and at Harvard he had a fellowship in anthropology during the 1911–12 term and took courses with Dixon, Tozzer, and Farabee (Harrington 1926:275, 1929:249; Hough 1935). A short note that Skinner penned to Clark Wissler at the AMNH on November 1, 1910, gives the flavor of his activities at the Peabody: "Last night was the first meeting of the Anthropology Club. About 30 present—Barbour spoke on New Guinea. Putnam, Dixon, Tozzer, Farabee, Willoughby, Peabody and Bowditch were present. Boas speaks on "Relativism between type, language and culture" at Lowell Institute tomorrow night, and the Boston Branch of the Folklore Society meets at Peabody's Thursday night" (reproduced in Reed 1980:88).

In 1916 Skinner was hired by the Heye Foundation and, along with Edward Sapir, Frank Speck, Frederick Webb Hodge, and Louis Shotridge, was integrated into Heye's inner circle (Witthoft 1991:6). Skinner's major work for the Heye Foundation was a 1916 excavation project in Costa Rica. In 1918 he moved on to the Milwaukee Public Museum, where he became curator until 1924, when he returned to Heye's Museum of the American Indian (Harrington 1926:275; Hough 1935). He worked for that museum until his death in 1926.

Although Skinner had no direct American Indian ancestry, he was proud that his wife and daughter had Wyandot blood (Harrington 1926:276). He wrote extensively on New York state archaeology, the Wisconsin Menomini, and the ethnology of other Plains Indian groups. He thus had the American Indian linkage of "Putnam's boys of the AMNH," as well as direct contact and training with several of the notables of concern to us: Putnam, Pepper, Smith, Harrington, Parker, Speck, and Sapir, among others.

Yet another of Putnam's boys was **Frank Gouldsmith Speck** (1881–1950). Speck's father was a merchant who lived in Brooklyn. Because of poor health, Frank was sent at the age of eight to live with a Mrs. Fidelia Fielding at Mohegan, Connecticut. He lived there until he was 15, when he returned to Hackensack, New Jersey, to finish high school (Mason 1950:4; Witthoft 1991:1). While with Mrs. Fielding, he learned the Mohegan dialect of Pequot. There is evidence to suggest that the reason he had been sent there was that he was of American Indian ancestry—mixed Mahican and Dutch heritage (Beck 1951:415; Fenton 1991:17; Witthoft 1974:761, 1991:2). During this time Speck developed a considerable interest in natural history—an interest shared by many of the students Putnam recruited—and he apparently first came to Putnam's attention in this manner.

Speck entered Columbia, where he initially kept up his natural science interest, publishing a paper on snakes and toads while a freshman (Fenton 1991:16). Through his participation in Harriet Converse's salon group, he also got drawn into anthropology. He took some informal anthropological training with Putnam but was educated mainly by the faculty at Columbia, where he began anthropological coursework in his junior year, taking comparative philology with John Dyneley Prince (Witthoft 1991:3). Because of Speck's competence in Mohegan, he and Prince began work together on Algonkin. Speck had three co-authored articles (for example, Price and Speck 1903, 1904) and one article of his own in the *American Anthropologist*, all published before he received his A.B. in linguistics in 1904 (Hallowell 1951:69). He then entered graduate school, continuing his studies in anthropological linguistics with Boas, and received his A.M. at Columbia in 1905 (Cattell 1910:443; Mason 1950:4).

Speck then went to study the Yuchi of the Southeast, who had been resettled in Oklahoma, for his dissertation work. He had lost most of his material on the Pequots when John Prince's house burned in 1906 (Witthoft 1991:5). Speck accepted the George Leib Harrison Research Fellowship from the University of Pennsylvania in 1907–8 and spent the year working up his Yuchi materials for his Ph.D. Hence he received his Ph.D. in 1908 from Pennsylvania instead of Columbia (Blankenship 1991:ix; Witthoft 1991:6). After receiving his doctorate, Speck was appointed an instructor in the University Museum at Pennsylvania in 1908 and began to assist its director, George B. Gordon, in teaching and museum work (Mason 1950:3). What anthropology there was at Pennsylvania was taught only in the museum; there was still no anthropology department in the university.

Speck, however, continued his association with the old AMNH crowd, as well as making new linkages. When Speck came to the University of Pennsylvania on the fellowship in 1907, George Heye had just brought his staff there, including George Pepper and Mark Harrington, Speck's old friend from the Converse salon. In 1908 Edward Sapir, Speck's closest friend at Columbia, was appointed to succeed Speck as the Harrison Fellowship holder at the University of Pennsylvania. Sapir, Speck, and their wives rented a house together in Philadelphia (Wittoft 1991:6). Sapir, Speck, Harrington, Skinner, Frederick Hodge, Louis Shotridge, and others were all part of Heye's circle at the time. In 1910 Sapir left for the National Museum of Canada, and subsequently, in his position as "Chief of Anthropological Division of National Museum of Canada," Sapir hired Speck to conduct contract research projects on Iroquois materials (Fenton 1991:9).

Gordon and Speck had a falling out in 1911, and Gordon fired Speck. The university immediately rehired him in a new academic appointment, separate from the museum, as an assistant professor in anthropology. Thus, an official Department of Anthropology came into being (Mason 1950:3; Wittoft 1991:8). From 1886 to 1899, Daniel G. Brinton had given occasional courses in anthropology, sponsored by various departments around the university but open only to graduate students. Stewart Culin also gave a few courses in anthropology through the museum from 1900 to 1902, but they, too, were open only to graduate students. George Gordon gave some courses from 1904 to 1907 but turned over the teaching duties to Speck in 1908 (Mason 1950:3). Frank Speck, then, is "considered the real founder of the Department of Anthropology at the University of Pennsylvania" (Hallowell 1951:70).

Speck was appointed acting chair of the department in 1913 and became a full professor and chair in 1925 (Blankenship 1991:x; Mason 1950:3). His naturalist origins continued to be evidenced in his work in ethnoherpetology, ethnobotany, and ethnohistory (Beck 1951:416), and together with his interest in arts and crafts, his naturalist background sometimes drew him back into archaeology. Examples of his later archaeological publications are papers on tidewater Virginia pottery and on a small site he excavated in Labrador in 1916. He served on the editorial board of the *American Journal of Archaeology* in the 1920s (Hallowell 1951:71), was for many years an associate editor of *American Anthropologist,* and started the *Publications in Anthropology* series of the University of Pennsylvania Museum. He was a prolific writer, producing more than 400 publications. Throughout his career, Speck "identified strongly with American Indians" (Wittoft 1974:763). In the well-known 1919 case in which the AAA censured Franz Boas for condemning the alleged spying by anthropologists in Central America during World War I (see chapter 10), Speck voted on the losing side, trying to prevent the censure of his old advisor (Tozzer 1920:94).

Udo Joseph Keppler (1872–1956), yet another of the young men who met at the Converse house, was apparently first attracted to the salon through Frank Converse's musical interests but then became a lifelong friend of Arthur Parker's. Some rare sources try to distinguish Joseph Ferdinand Keppler (1838–94), cartoonist and founder of the satirical magazine *Puck* (1887–1916), from his son, Udo Joseph Keppler, but many sources conflate the two, and the situation is made more complex because Udo Joseph Keppler (sometimes referred to as Joseph Keppler Jr.) took over *Puck* after his father's death. The senior Keppler had arrived in St. Louis from Vienna in 1868, spent the next two years traveling around the country in a theatrical troupe originating from St. Louis, where he began his cartooning, and moved to New York in 1873, where his cartooning matured (Bishop 1892:229).

The younger Keppler was a newspaper writer and political cartoonist who became entranced with the Iroquois (Porter 2001:48). His anthropological interests were more than this, however. During his life, Udo Joseph Keppler collected many ethnographic documents, now at the Huntington Free Library in the Bronx, the National Museum of the American Indian, and the Smithsonian Institution. From 1904 to 1906, Parker assisted Keppler in making several purchases of Iroquois ethnographic materials, particularly wampum belts, for George Heye (Porter 2001:58). In addition, he published a few anthropological papers on Iroquois artifacts and folklore for the Museum of the American Indian–Heye Foundation (Keppler 1926, 1929a, 1929b, 1941).

The Heye Foundation connection was particularly important, for Keppler may have held some small responsibility for the founding of the Museum of the American Indian. George Heye had accompanied Keppler on visits to the Cattaraugus and Tonawanda reservations to collect Iroquois artifacts in 1899. He became enamored of the materials and made several more collecting trips with Keppler (Kidwell 1999:235). Even after Heye became a founding partner in the investment banking firm of Battles, Heye and Harrison in 1901, he continued to collect. He later used funds derived from his success as a banker to establish his research foundation and develop his museum. Keppler, along with Marshall Saville and George Pepper, encouraged him to do so (Kidwell 1999:235) and thus had a hand in the founding of the museum.

Keppler, like some of his friends, had been adopted by the Senecas, who gave him the clan name Gy-ant-wa-ka, a name once held by the famous Iroquois Cornplanter. In this position he was one of the principal speakers for the Senecas at Harriet Converse's funeral on November 22, 1903 (Converse 1905, 1:241). Mrs. Converse's chieftain emblem, a string of purple wampum, was handed over to Keppler after her funeral as a symbol of his election as her successor to chieftainship (Parker 1908:29).

Many of the Iroquois documents that were donated to the Heye Foundation in Keppler's name came not only from his own Iroquois society connections but also from Harriet Converse and later her estate, sometimes by circuitous routes. For example, the Little Water secret medicine society document in the Museum of the American Indian ("Ganoda, Chant of the Little Water Medicine Society of the Seneca," ca. 1849), detailing the medicine songs of the society on the Cattaraugus reservation, was transcribed by John Jacket and collected sometime between 1849 and 1870. It then came into the hands of Harriet Converse, also a member of this society, who had it between 1892 and 1903. She gave it to Arthur C. Parker, another member of the Seneca society. Parker gave it to anthropologist William N. Fenton, and Fenton gave it to Joseph Keppler, who donated it to the Heye museum in 1951 (Converse 1905, 1:241; Parker 1908).

John William Fenton (1875–1939), the last of "Putnam's boys" whom we mention, is in some ways the least known, which is somewhat strange considering that his son, William N. Fenton, is extremely well-known as having been an Iroquois expert. John Fenton was an artist who was born in Westport, Connecticut, and lived most of his life in neighboring New York state. He studied at the New York School of Fine and Applied Art (later part of Parsons School of Design), Fredonia Normal School in New York, and Yale. He worked as a painter, primarily of still life scenes, and a teacher (Falk 1985:199). Fenton became entranced with the Iroquois and thus became part of the Converse salon group, in which he seems to have been particularly linked with Arthur Parker. Because he was not an anthropologist, historians of anthropology have written little about him other than to note his membership in this group. He did apparently participate in some of the archaeological excavations of Harrington and Parker, and according to his son, William Fenton, it was John Fenton who pointed Arthur Parker toward the Ripley site as an ideal place for excavation.

John W. Fenton is much better known in the anthropological literature as the father of William Nelson Fenton (1908–2005). William N. Fenton (Dartmouth A.B. 1931, Yale Ph.D. 1937) worked for the BAE from 1939 to 1943 and then for the Smithsonian Institution from 1943 through 1951. He worked for the National Research Council from 1951 to 1954, when he took a job with the New York State Museum. He left the museum in 1968 to join the faculty at the State University of New York–Albany, retiring from there in 1979. William Fenton was employed as an anthropologist and community worker in the 1930s on the Tonawanda reservation, where Parker was involved in two work-relief archaeological projects, and otherwise had many connections to Parker, ultimately republishing Parker's major anthropological texts as *Parker on the Iroquois* (Parker 1968).

This cluster of students, identified under the rubric of "Putnam's boys of the AMNH," had a significant set of contributions to make, especially to the ethnography and archaeology of New England, although some of them were more widely involved in Americanist studies. The years 1890 to 1905 were clearly a time of strong associations between Frederic Putnam and American Indians and members of First Nations in the development of the field. William Jones, Arthur Parker, and Frank Speck had direct Indian ancestry; Mark Harrington and Alanson Skinner married American Indians; Joseph Keppler had been adopted by an Indian tribe; and all of them interacted at one point or another through Harriet Converse's salon in New York, a focal point for American Indian activity in the city at the time. This strong indigenous-based contribution has not previously been commented upon, but we think it a critical thread in the origins of our field, one that merits further study in the future.

Putnam had effectively established a "Peabody Museum in New York City" extension center at the AMNH. But this decade of Putnam's training program at the AMNH is generally missing in disciplinary histories. Although William Jones, George Pepper, and Harlan Smith were directly associated with Putnam at the Peabody Museum, through coursework, excavations, or both, the fact that their early careers played out mainly in New York, through the AMNH, has meant that Putnam's influence on and training of them has been largely overlooked. And because Putnam did not teach formal classes while serving at the AMNH, his influence on Mark Harrington, Arthur Parker, Alanson Skinner, Frank Speck, and the others of "Putnam's boys" has also been missed. These men, however, form a significant core of the roots of anthropology at institutions such as the AMNH and the University of Pennsylvania, indicating once again the extent of the influence of Putnam and the Peabody Museum on the origins of Americanist anthropology.

9

Professionals, Benefactors, and Supporters, 1890–1910

A SHIFT TOWARD THE PROFESSIONALIZATION OF ANTHROPOLOGY took place at the Peabody Museum after 1890, when the museum was able both to develop a rigorous undergraduate and graduate program and at last to create a critical concentration of teaching and research staff. This shift was significantly promoted by the major assistance provided by benefactors and patrons. Throughout his career, Frederic Putnam worked with many people from whom he received financial and other material support. We have already summarized the contributions of an early set of donors and benefactors of the Peabody Museum, who were instrumental in its founding days. In this chapter we single out another set of supporters who were crucial during the time of Putnam's new initiatives in education and institution-building in the 1890s and early 1900s and during the transition to his successors at the Peabody Museum.

One of the important groups was the members of the so-called Faculty of the Museum. Today the term *faculty* usually connotes teaching responsibilities. In this case it refers to the new advisory group, the "museum faculty," that was established to replace the trustees as a governing body when control of the Peabody Museum passed from the board of trustees to the Harvard Corporation on January 1, 1897, and the Peabody Museum became an official part of Harvard University.

The solution selected for governance was to copy the "museum faculty" organization that was already in place for the Museum of Comparative Zoology. Hence the articles of agreement between the trustees of the Peabody Museum and the President and Fellows of Harvard University stipulated that the president of the university (then Charles Eliot) would be president of the museum faculty, and the museum curator or the Peabody Professor (then Frederic Putnam) would be a faculty member. The other three museum faculty members, drawn from the previous trustees, were Francis Cabot Lowell, Stephen Salisbury Jr., and Charles Bowditch (Harvard University 1898). Vacancies would be filled by nominations by the museum faculty and confirmed by the Harvard Corporation and Board of Overseers.

From 1897 onward, being a member of the museum faculty meant that a person was in an advisory position with respect to the operations of the Peabody Museum. It involved no teaching or other academic obligations. Rather, the Faculty of the Museum served as a sort of executive council to provide advice and assistance to the museum director in the operations of the Peabody Museum, much as the trustees had done previously.

Francis Cabot Lowell (1855–1911) was a cousin of Abbott Lawrence Lowell, who became president of Harvard in 1909. A member of the Harvard class of 1876, Francis Lowell served as a Harvard overseer from 1886 to 1891 and again in 1894, and as a Harvard fellow in 1895. He was initially appointed a trustee of the Peabody Museum in June 1885 (Putnam 1912:217). It was in this position that he and Charles Bowditch, in 1891, signed a 10-year license for the Peabody Museum to conduct excavations in Honduras (Putnam 1892:195). After the reorganization in 1897, Lowell was carried on the masthead of the Peabody Museum's annual reports as a "member of the faculty" from 1897 until his death in 1911. He had gone into law and was elected a judge in 1905, so later annual reports often refer to him as Judge Lowell.

In addition to providing considerable service to Americanist archaeology through the Peabody Museum, Lowell was involved in assisting Harvard personnel in classical archaeology. When the 13-member board of trustees was set up in 1886 for the American School of Classical Studies in Athens, another of Lowell's cousins, James Russell Lowell, was one of the founding group, along with Martin Brimmer, William Goodwin, and Charles Eliot Norton. In 1895 Francis C. Lowell was added to the board of trustees of the American School, and after Norton's death in 1908 he served as president of these trustees, from 1908 to 1911 (Lord 1947:340–41). Thus Judge Lowell had a voice in directing the growth of both classical and anthropological archaeology during the 1890s and first decade of the 1900s.

Stephen Salisbury Jr. (1835–1905) was born and lived most of his life in Worcester, Massachusetts. (Documents differ on whether he was properly Stephen Salisbury Jr. or Stephen Salisbury III. Although he seems to have been the third in his line, most period documents use "Jr.," so we follow that convention.) He was a member of the Harvard class of 1856, along with George Peabody Russell and Charles Francis Adams, who were trustees at the original founding of the Peabody Museum. After receiving his A.M. in the same year, he went to universities in Paris and Berlin for further study. Upon his return he entered Harvard Law School in 1858 and received his LL.B. in 1861, but he never practiced law (Lincoln 1906:327). Because of his father's position as president of the American Antiquarian Society and later as a trustee of the Peabody Museum when it was founded in 1866, young Stephen was introduced to archaeology through direct family connections.

This interest in archaeology was reinforced when Salisbury visited a former Harvard classmate, David Casares, at Mérida in Yucatán in the winter of 1861–62 and became enthusiastic about Maya antiquities. **David Casares** (1835–1914) had studied for three years at the Ecole Central des Arts et Manufactures in Paris after graduating from Harvard with honors in 1856. When Casares returned to Yucatán, he taught for a short while at the College of Minerva in Mérida, until he was called to manage his father's plantation. The Casares family had a history of interest in Maya ruins and had provided considerable assistance to the Abbé Charles Etienne Brasseur de Bourbourg, author of *Histoire des nations civilisés du Mexique,* when he was in Yucatán working on his book (Salisbury 1876:23–24). Salisbury became enthralled by the Maya ruins during this visit. The next year, 1863, he joined the American Antiquarian Society (Lincoln 1906:327–28), and in 1865 he made a return trip to Yucatán for further visits to Maya sites (Salisbury 1876:24).

Stephen Salisbury Jr. appears to have dedicated himself to the family businesses for much of the next decade—first real estate and later Washburn and Moen, the largest wire manufacturer of the late nineteenth century, critical in the development of barbed wire. By the mid-1870s he had time once again to get involved in the archaeology of Yucatán. Reporting to the American Antiquarian Society on a lecture given before the American Geographical Society in 1876 by the Central American scholar Carl Hermann Berendt, Salisbury quoted Berendt as saying: "We must have museums, in which the plastic remains of the ancient American civilizations, either original, or in faithful imitations, shall, in as large numbers as possible, be collected, and duly grouped and labeled, according to the place and circumstances of their discovery" (Salisbury 1876:60).

Salisbury took up Berendt's plea and suggested to the society the following research agenda: "*First,* The Study of Native Languages. *Second,* The Study of the Antiquities themselves. *Third,* The formation of Museums, where materials for archaeological research may be brought together, and made accessible and available. From the study of aboriginal American history in this practical way, the most satisfactory results can not fail to be reached" (Salisbury 1876:61). During this period Salisbury became interested in the work of Augustus and Alice Le Plongeon in Yucatán. He published a series of articles on Maya materials (Salisbury 1876, 1877, 1878, 1883, 1890) and translated works on the Mayas and Aztecs from Spanish and German into English (Valentini 1878, 1879, 1880, 1882).

In early 1880, Louis J. Ayme arrived as American consul in Mérida, having been nominated by Salisbury and the American Antiquarian Society and appointed through the support of Massachusetts senator and Peabody Museum supporter George Hoar. Ayme explored Yucatán for the next three years, sending some materials back to Salisbury, but he left after becoming involved in feuds over artifacts with the Le Plongeons, who were rather difficult souls (see, for example, Browman 2002a:227–28; S. Williams 1991:140). Salisbury then asked Senator Hoar to nominate Edward H. Thompson, a native of Worcester, Massachusetts, to fill the post of American consul, so that Thompson could carry on archaeological work on behalf of the American Antiquarian Society (see chapter 4). After the death of Salisbury's father, Stephen Salisbury Jr. became much more active in the American Antiquarian Society, becoming vice president in 1884 and president in

1887. His election to the presidency meant, in terms of the founding agreement of the Peabody Museum, that Salisbury Jr. then became a trustee of the museum. The next year he was elected treasurer of the Peabody Museum trustees (Putnam 1889:163).

Salisbury had been sponsoring Edward Thompson's work in Yucatán, and now, as a Peabody Museum trustee, he required that some of the materials be sent to the Peabody, as well as to the museum of the American Antiquarian Society. Salisbury seconded Bowditch's interest in having the Peabody Museum become more deeply involved in excavations in Mesoamerica, and the two of them underwrote a major portion of the decade-long explorations by Peabody Museum students at Copan, in Honduras, and by Thompson at Chichen Itza (Putnam 1891:88, 1893a:203, 205). They matched each other dollar for dollar. In 1891–92, for example, Salisbury and Bowditch each gave $1,593 for the Copan fund, and in 1892–93, each gave $2,000 (Putnam 1895a:223).

In 1896 Salisbury was elected to succeed Robert Winthrop as chair of the board of trustees of the Peabody Museum. On January 1, 1897, when the Peabody Museum was officially transferred to Harvard University, Salisbury was named a member of the Faculty of the Museum.

Retaining his enthusiasm for things Maya, he arranged for funds to reemploy Edward Thompson in his explorations in Yucatán, after Thompson had left the orbit of the Peabody Museum to work for some seasons for the Columbian (Field) Museum. Putnam observed (1899a:267):

> It was through his [Salisbury's] influence that Mr. Edward H. Thompson was led to his archaeological researches in that country [Mexico]. For several years Mr. Thompson's work was reported to this Museum; then he was employed as one of the assistants in the Department of Ethnology of the World's Fair; and after that he was engaged for special research by the Field Columbian Museum. Having closed his work for the Chicago Museum he is now, thanks to Mr. Salisbury, to resume his connection with this Museum.

Salisbury continued to make substantial contributions to the Peabody Museum up until his death, in ways large and small. As Putnam observed in his obituary notice:

> Mr. Salisbury was a member of the Board of Trustees from 1887 until the Trustees, by special Act of Legislature, made over their trust to Harvard College in 1897, and since that time he was a member of the Faculty of the Museum, and was seldom absent from its meetings. Mr. Salisbury was deeply interested in our archaeological researches in Yucatán, and for several years he had contributed largely to our subscription fund for research in Central America and Mexico. He also aided the Museum in other ways. His latest gift was applied to the electric lighting of the library, laboratory, and work-rooms of the Museum. (Putnam 1907:292)

Salisbury willed his personal collection of Maya materials to the Peabody Museum, which received "the whole collection from Yucatán formerly belonging to Mr. Stephen Salisbury, including the collection of pottery vessels and stone implements obtained by Dr. Le Plongeon" from excavations at Chichen Itza (Putnam 1911:222).

Like his father's gifts to Harvard, those of the younger Salisbury, were not limited to the Peabody Museum. He gave significant funds to both the Harvard College library and the Radcliffe library. He served on the Visiting Committee of the Semitic Museum and was in part instrumental in having Putnam accept and grant part of his scarce space to the Semitic Museum collections in the 1890s, while the Semitic Museum was being built (Putnam 1891:88). During the dozen years in which the Semitic collections were housed at the Peabody, from 1891 to 1903, more than the usual collaboration took place between the classical archaeologists working in Egypt, Palestine, and Mesopotamia and the anthropological archaeologists working out of the Peabody. This closeness was particularly evident in our discussions in chapter 7 regarding doctoral dissertation defenses and cross-registered classes for the graduate students.

Salisbury Jr. shared his wealth and talents in a much larger arena. He was president of Worcester National Bank from 1884 to 1905, president of Worcester County Institution for Savings from 1882 to 1905, and a director of the Worcester and Nashua Railroad. He succeeded his father as a trustee of Worcester Polytechnic Institute, becoming president of the trustees there from 1895 to 1905, and he donated $236,000 to it over his career. He also was vice president of the trustees of Clark University, where he served as acting president of the trustees after the death of Senator Hoar. He was the long-time president of the American Antiquarian Society, leaving it $200,000 at his death. He also established the Worcester Art Museum in 1896, to which he contributed lavishly (Lincoln 1906:328–29). He was a man dedicated to scholarship, public and private education, and archaeology.

Charles Pickering Bowditch (1842–1921), Harvard class of 1863, was a classmate of Putnam's and several of the other men who studied at the MCZ and contributed to the early development of anthropology, as we outlined in chapter 3. At the Lawrence Scientific School he took classes with faculty such as Bache, Horsford, Peirce, and Rogers (Bowditch 1924:421). It appears that Bowditch knew Putnam well in their student days. Not only did the two live in Zoological Hall, but Edward Morse, in his diary, named Bowditch, along with himself, Putnam, Cooke, and Foley, as part of the student alliance to run Albert Bickmore out of the dormitory in October 1860, because they found him irritating (Wayman 1942:140). Bowditch's extensive reengagement with Putnam at the Peabody two decades later was in many ways a reunion of old college friends who had held common interests for many years.

Following graduation, Bowditch immediately volunteered for the Union Army. He joined the 55th Massachusetts Volunteer Infantry, a black infantry regiment, as second lieutenant in May 1863. He was joined in this regiment by another MCZ classmate, Burt G. Wilder, who served as assistant surgeon. Bowditch rose to the rank of captain in the regiment, but he became ill and was so weak that he was transferred to the 5th Massachusetts Volunteer Cavalry so that he could get a horse to ride. He was discharged in August 1864 because of continued illness (Bowditch 1924:423, 428). Wilder stayed with the Massachusetts infantry unit until the end of the war and then returned to Harvard in 1866 to finish his M.D., while going back to work as an assistant for Agassiz at the MCZ from 1866 to 1868 (J. Comstock 1925:532).

Following his return from the war and recovery from illness, Bowditch returned to Harvard to complete an A.M. degree in 1866 (Tozzer 1921:353). He then became involved in business, serving as a trustee of estates and director of many companies. He was most notably associated with the Pepperell Manufacturing Company, a big New England cotton textile firm, where he was on the board of directors from 1879 until his death in 1921 and served as president of the company for two periods, from 1891 to 1898 and again from 1916 to 1921 (Knowlton 1948:400–401; Yorke 1945:109, 112).

During this time, Bowditch took a pleasure trip to Yucatán in 1888 with his younger cousin, Ernest William Bowditch (1850–1918). Charles Bowditch became interested in the Mayas on this trip, much like his business acquaintance and friend Stephen Salisbury Jr. (Tozzer 1921:354). In 1888, upon their return, Ernest and Charles Bowditch donated Yucatecan artifacts they had collected to the Peabody Museum, in addition to bringing back materials for the museum sent in their care by Edward H. Thompson and Teobert Maler (Putnam 1889:41). Charles Bowditch maintained his interest in the Maya area and made substantial donations to the museum to support research, as well as securing casts and artifacts, up until his death.

Because of his decision to provide financial support for the work of Edward H. Thompson, Bowditch is credited in some museum sources with having inaugurated the Peabody research program in Middle America in that first year, 1888. In 1889–90, Bowditch was appointed to serve on the Peabody Museum Visiting Committee (Putnam 1891:100; Willoughby 1922:274). It was at this time that Putnam approached Bowditch and Francis Minot Weld, another member of the committee, about providing financial support for advanced students, and the two contributed funds to award what became known as the Visiting Committee Fellowship, the first fellowship offered by the Peabody Museum.

In 1891, Bowditch and Francis Cabot Lowell, acting as representatives of the Peabody Museum, arranged for a 10-year license with the government of Honduras for Peabody Museum explorations (Putnam 1892:195). Bowditch, with Salisbury, then put up financial support for the first official Peabody Museum Expedition to Middle America, and Bowditch supported nearly annual expeditions from the Peabody Museum to Central America for the rest of his life. For the next 30 years, in doing this, Bowditch provided much of the necessary financing for Gordon, Saville, and Owens at Copan; Maler at Usumacinta and in the Petén; Thompson at Chichen Itza and in Yucatán; Merwin and Hay in British Honduras and northern Guatemala; Lothrop in Honduras; Morley in Yucatán; and Spinden in Yucatán (Tozzer 1921:354).

Bowditch also became a trustee of the Peabody Museum in 1894, filling the position reserved for the president of the Essex Institute (Putnam 1896a:236). In 1897 he became a member of the first Faculty of the Museum, along with Salisbury Jr. and Lowell. In addition to his unflagging financial support of the fieldwork in Central America, Bowditch provided the funds that were used to construct the Middle American Hall at the Peabody Museum and to initiate the *Memoir* series there (Tozzer 1921:354; Willoughby 1922:274). He sought to enhance the Maya holdings of the museum's library, purchasing and donating more than 50,000 pages of relevant manuscripts (Tozzer 1929). After his first term as president at the Pepperell textile mill ended in 1898, he found time to write on Maya hieroglyphs himself and published a series of articles and a book on Maya hieroglyphs and calendrical systems (Bowditch 1900, 1901a, 1901b, 1904, 1909, 1910). Casts of the stelae and lintels Bowditch used in his analyses were still in the Peabody Museum collections in the 1960s.

Bowditch was so actively and thoroughly involved in anthropology at this time that he also became one of the founding members of the American Anthropological Association at the national level. At the regional level, the Boston Society for Natural History was also a hotbed of anthropological activity, and Bowditch served as vice president at the same time that Goodale, Morse, Putnam, and Scudder were officers of the group (*Proceedings of the Boston Society of Natural History* 1902–3). And in 1902, Bowditch, representing the American Antiquarian Society, was on the organizing and sponsoring committee of the Thirteenth International Congress of Americanists in New York City (Chamberlain 1902:884). His broad involvement in anthropology was extraordinary.

Bowditch's period of intensive interaction with the anthropological and archaeological community came during the break between his two terms as president of the Pepperell Company, from 1898 to 1916. Early in this period he became engaged with Putnam and Boas at the Archaeological Institute of America (AIA) in another attempt to get that organization involved in Americanist archaeology, when the Standing Committee on American Archaeology was established in 1899. This committee collaborated with the AAAS Committee on the Protection and Preservation of Objects of Archaeological Interest to develop the first draft of the federal antiquities bill in 1900, which, after several modifications, was enacted in 1906. This was the most significant legislation protecting archaeological resources in the United States in the twentieth century.

During the first years of the AIA Standing Committee on American Archaeology, only Bowditch, Boas, and Putnam were members, but as we previously observed, the AIA governing officers became unhappy with the ideas Putnam and Boas were advancing and quickly moved to dilute their influence through the committee. By the time Boas and Putnam finally resigned in frustration, the committee had been enlarged to consist of Bowditch, Boas, Putnam, J. Walter Fewkes, Alice Fletcher, Francis W. Kelsey, Charles F. Lummis, and Thomas D. Seymour (Gordon 1972:307). Before they left, however, Boas and Putnam had been able to see Americanist archaeology get some additional support.

It was Bowditch himself who funded the first fellowship given by the AIA Standing Committee on American Archaeology. Bowditch had been working for several years accumulating a corpus of documents in order to try to translate the Maya glyphs, and he "entertained the belief that such a clue [for translation of hieroglyphs] might possibly be found among the little known and isolated Lacandones of Guatemala" (Putnam 1889:266). He had first provided funds to send Teobert Maler into the Lacandón area, but Maler did not find the critical clue. Putnam finally convinced Bowditch of the wisdom of training a student to work in the field, rather than relying on volunteers such as Thompson, Ayme, and Maler, and Bowditch agreed to fund a fellowship to do so. The student selected for the AIA fellowship was Alfred M. Tozzer, whom we discuss in chapter 10. Bowditch was comfortable with Tozzer because he had watched his academic progress from his teen years, when he had worked as Bowditch's yard boy in New Hampshire, through his Harvard College education. Bowditch later established an instructorship in Central American archaeology for Tozzer and endowed a Central American fellowship for graduate students to work with him (*National Cyclopedia* 1929:291; Tozzer 1921:356–57). Bowditch's memory is honored today at the Peabody with the endowed Bowditch Chair of Mexican and Central American Archaeology and Ethnology, first held by Gordon Randolph Willey (1913–2002) from 1950 to 1986.

Upon Bowditch's death, Dixon and Tozzer recruited his son, **Ingersoll Bowditch** (1875–1938), a member of the Harvard class of 1897, to replace his father as a member of the Peabody Museum faculty. Ingersoll Bowditch had gained some field experience with the Peabody Museum under Putnam, who, in June 1897, following his graduation, sent him to survey the Ferris Cemetery site at Madisonville, Ohio, along with Dixon and Swanton (Putnam 1898a:249). In spite of his interest in the museum's work and his service as a member of the museum faculty from 1921 until his death in 1938, Ingersoll Bowditch's livelihood was in business, and he was never as actively engaged with the museum as his father had been.

One of the people with whom Bowditch and Putnam communicated in Yucatán was **Adela Catherine Breton** (1849–1923). She was a skilled watercolor artist who spent her first 37 years in Bath, England (Fallaize 1923:125). Her father was a retired naval officer with strong interests in archaeology, travel, and exotic places. When he died in 1887, she inherited enough money to allow her to begin her work, and she left almost immediately for Canada. Over the next dozen years she worked her way south through the western United States to Mexico, painting and drawing as she went, particularly beginning to focus on ruins and artifacts (M. McVicker 2000:60).

Breton's first gifts of her paintings of archaeological sites to the Peabody Museum were made in 1896, and for the next 20 years she continued to send the Peabody illustrations of artifacts and sites, as well as some actual artifacts. She spent a great deal of time copying Maya murals and stelae in Yucatán in the first two decades of the twentieth century, taking more than a dozen trips to the area and writing and publishing reports on these explorations. She began recording the mural paintings at Chichen Itza for Alfred P. Maudslay in 1900 and in this venue became familiar with a number of people who worked with the Peabody Museum, including George Gordon, Alfred Tozzer, Charles Bowditch, and Edward Thompson.

Zelia Nuttall visited Breton at Chichen Itza in 1902 and convinced Putnam to have Breton make a special series of copies of the frescoes for the Peabody Museum (M. McVicker 2000:60). Breton made a presentation based on her drawings at the International Congress of Americanists in New York City in 1902, as her debut into the wider Americanist archaeology community. An insight into how quickly she was integrated into this group comes from a short description of a dinner hosted at the meetings by Frederic Putnam. Among the other dozen people present were Alice Fletcher, Juan Bautista Ambrosetti (an Argentine archaeologist), Zelia Nuttall, Alfred Tozzer, George B. Gordon, Alice E. Putnam, Stansbury Hagar (an expert in Mesoamerican archaeoastronomy), Elizabeth D. Putnam (an archaeologist from the Davenport Museum in Iowa, sister to Edward Putnam and distant cousin of Frederic), Frederick Starr (founder of the anthropology department at Chicago), Esther Orne Clarke Putnam, and Adela Breton (Frederick Starr diary, cited in M. McVicker 2005:89).

Putnam took great interest in the archaeology of Mesoamerica, so he had an obvious link with Breton in that venue. But they may well have shared another interest. In a note written to a colleague in 1914, Breton listed as one of her long-time interests "studying early man and his works in different countries" (quoted in M. McVicker 2005:180), certainly one of the themes that dominated Frederic Putnam's research career. After 1910 Breton retired from active fieldwork but continued her interest in Mesoamerica. She was very involved in the arrangements for the International Congress of Americanists in London in 1912, serving as honorary assistant secretary and treasurer and collaborating with Franz Boas in the editing of its proceedings (Fallaize 1923:126; M. McVicker 2005:151). Although Breton published on her work in various venues, Mary Frech McVicker (2005:212) observed that because she rarely offered analyses or conclusions from her empirical observations, her work had less effect than it deserved.

A better-known contributor to the Peabody Museum in this period was **Clarence Bloomfield Moore** (1852–1936), a member of the Harvard class of 1873 who may have met Putnam during his college years. Because of family assets, Moore was able to spend a good deal of time traveling after graduation, starting in Europe and returning home in 1876 by way of Peru, cutting across the Andes to travel down the Amazon to the Atlantic (Aten and Milanich 2003:115). Moore's father's successful business, the Jesup and Moore Paper Company, was located in Philadelphia, and after his father's death, Moore and his mother fought over control of the estate's assets. The new University of Pennsylvania Museum hoped to secure funding from the family fortune, but Stewart

Culin unwisely sided with the mother, Clara Moore, in 1891. Clarence Moore deeply resented Pennsylvania's intrusion into his family's affairs, and as a result, he cut ties to that university and strengthened his allegiance to Putnam at Harvard (Aten and Milanich 2003:118).

Before leaving for Europe in 1873, Moore, while out hunting in Florida, made his first exploration of a mound, scratching around on the surface while camping on it (Aten and Milanich 2003:119). Robert Murowchick (1990:64) and Stephen Williams (1991:76) have speculated that Moore may have visited Jeffries Wyman's Harvard excavations in Florida at this time, but neither has yet found any undisputed evidence for this. Moore's first documented major donations to the Peabody Museum came in 1878 (Putnam 1879a:476). After he returned from South America, he made another casual mound excavation in Florida in 1879.

It was not until the early 1880s that Moore began to correspond regularly with Putnam about archaeology. At this time he began to donate some of his collections to the Peabody Museum and started to read widely on archaeology (Aten and Milanich 2003:120). His major archaeological excavations began only in 1891, when, because of medical problems, especially an injury to his left eye received while playing tennis, Moore changed lifestyles and began inspecting archaeological shell middens. He did so partly at the suggestion of Putnam, who provided him with technical advice on how to proceed (Aten and Milanich 2003:122; Wardle 1956:9). The outcome of this first year was published in *American Naturalist,* then edited by an old Philadelphia friend of Moore's, Edward Cope, as "A Burial Mound in Florida" (Moore 1892a).

The most detailed and stratigraphically controlled work Moore did was during his initial foray into serious collecting—his excavations of shell middens and mounds in his resurvey of sites originally recorded by Jeffries Wyman along the St. Johns River drainage in Florida. James Stoltman (1973:129) discussed this as follows:

> Among his earliest and best works were his excavations in the shell middens of the St. John's between 1892 and 1894. Traveling by river and with the aid of a crew of up to eight men, Moore was able to revisit all of Wyman's sites, to record forty-three additional sites, and to excavate on a larger scale than anyone before him. His work was surprisingly meticulous ("... not one spadeful of debris has been thrown out except in his presence ... dimensions are derived from measurements, and not from estimates," Moore 1892:917), and he proved to be a careful observer. He amassed further irrefutable evidence in support of Wyman's view that the middens were of human origin, while with *stratigraphic evidence,* he demonstrated that Wyman's opinion about the relative ages of the shell middens was indeed true.

Later Moore became more interested in finding cemeteries in order to locate high-quality ceramic vessels for museum collections. He apparently found Putnam's Peabody Museum excavation method too time consuming and shifted to more rapid digging techniques. Stoltman, who otherwise expressed a high opinion of Moore's contributions, lamented that "after 1894, Moore's work can be characterized as that of a sophisticated grave-digger" (Stoltman 1973:131).

Moore's initial work indicates a good control of the literature and issues of the day. His first article contains ground plans of the eight trenches cut plus some wall profiles from his excavations in 1891. He commented on the extant stratigraphy: "Dr. Brinton in his interesting chapter on the antiquities of Florida (*The Floridian Peninsula*), states that during his investigations he met with no stratification in the formation of any of the larger burial mounds. To this the Tick Island mound is a notable exception" (Moore 1892a:131). In the first of a six-part *American Naturalist* article published between 1892 and 1894, Moore wrote: "After a personal examination of those shell heaps their construction was attributed by Dr. Brinton to the action of the River (*Floridian Peninsula*, p. 180). Just how this conclusion was reached is difficult to understand. The writer, in several hundred excavations made in upwards of sixty localities, cannot recall a single one where the agency of man was not apparent" (Moore 1892b:912). Brinton, who visited Florida in 1856–57, believed that the huge accumulations of freshwater shells along the St. John's River were natural "hillocks" used by the Indians as convenient places to bury their dead (Brinton 1859:180, 1867:357).

Moore also followed up the cannibalism issue that had interested Wyman, Morse, Putnam, and other early excavators of shell mounds, noting that "the writer, in January 1873, found in a shell heap in a swamp near Palatka, on the west bank of the St. John's, similar evidence" of cannibalism (Moore 1893:117).

By 1894, at Putnam's suggestion, Moore had been made a member of the Peabody Museum Visiting Committee and so was contributing to archaeology at the Peabody by donating collections, funds, and commentary (Putnam 1895a:219). Moore was to remain a member of the committee for the next two decades. One sign of Putnam's recruitment of Moore was his nomination of Moore to both Section H of the AAAS and the American Antiquarian Society (Casler 1976:41). As we noted earlier, Putnam drew collectors whom he saw as having potential into the orbit of the AAAS as well as the Peabody Museum. In 1895 the University of Pennsylvania offered Moore the leadership of a Penn-sponsored expedition to Florida, but Moore turned it down, in part because of his existing links with the Peabody and in part because of his previous distaste for Penn's interfering with his estate through his mother.

Moore's support for the Peabody Museum was substantial from the 1890s through the 1910s, during which period he gave an annual gift for explorations. In 1905, for example, his donations supported fieldwork in Mesoamerica, New York state, North Dakota, and Ohio (Putnam 1906:302). By 1913 his gift had reached $4,500 a year (Putnam 1914:229).

Between 1891 and 1918 Moore excavated more than 850 sites, and he made sure to donate a few significant items from each campaign to the Peabody Museum. The bulk of his collections, however, went to the Academy of Natural Sciences in Philadelphia. In 1929, because the academy wanted to modernize its zoological exhibits and needed additional space, Moore consented to the sale of his collection to the Museum of the American Indian in New York. He was planning to attend the 1936 alumni graduation ceremonies at Harvard but became ill. The Peabody Museum staff had hoped he might arrange for the transfer of more of his collections to the museum at that time, but he died that year. Moore's contributions to American archaeology were many, and his monographs have all been republished under the hand of Stephen Williams by the University of Alabama Press.

A more flamboyant contributor was the man known as **Joseph Loubat** or **Joseph Florimond, Duc de Loubat** (1831–1927). Loubat was born in Queens, New York. His family had emigrated from France, and later he returned to live in France, from 1897 until his death (MacCurdy 1927:340). He had inherited a fortune and early in his life experimented a bit in diplomacy, taking part in a U.S. mission to Russia in 1866 and serving as a U.S. legate to the International Exposition in Paris in 1867 (Loubat 1867, 1873). He gave a tremendous amount of support to the Catholic Church, because of which Pope Leo XIII named him Duc de Loubat in 1893.

It was approximately the time Loubat moved to Paris that he became involved in supporting archaeology in both the Old and New Worlds—in the New World primarily in Mesoamerica. He sponsored the work in Mexico of Central American specialist Eduard Seler (1849–1922), an old acquaintance of Putnam's and Boas's, from 1894 onward. He subsequently provided the money that in 1899 made Seler the first professor of archaeology at the University of Berlin (Rutsch 2000:139).

Because of the duke's New York roots, Frederic Putnam was able to readily convince him in the 1890s to support part of the archaeological work at the AMNH and to assist Marshall Saville both in fieldwork in Central America and at Columbia University. In 1895, thanks to Loubat's donations, Putnam was able to secure funding for Saville to continue work at Maya sites. In February 1903, with Putnam's oversight, Loubat made an arrangement with Nicholas Murray Butler, president of Columbia University, to provide $100,000 for three years for a new Loubat Professorship of American Archaeology (Loubat 1912:24). With Putnam's support, Saville was named the Loubat Professor in spite of Boas's strong opposition—Boas wanted Eduard Seler. Later Loubat provided an additional $1 million to create an endowed chair of archaeology at Columbia (MacCurdy 1927:340), a position that Saville held until his death in 1935.

At Putnam's request, the Duc de Loubat also provided the funds to create the Mexican Hall at the AMNH (Putnam 1900b:19–20). Later, when Putnam was involved in founding the anthropology department at Berkeley, he arranged for Loubat to provide facsimiles of Mesoamerican codices for the library there. Putnam also got Loubat involved in sponsoring the Thirteenth International Congress of Americanists in New York in 1902; serving as an official correspondent of the Institut de France, he was honorary president of the congress (Chamberlain 1902:884, 889). Loubat, with his combined allegiances, has been credited with being instrumental in changing the meetings of the International Congress of Americanists from solely European venues to alternating between American and European locales in its biennial schedule (M. McVicker 2005:83).

For the Peabody Museum, Loubat's assistance initially took the form of helping to secure codices and Mesoamerican resource materials, as Putnam noted in annual reports from 1896 to 1904 (Putnam 1897:245, 1899a:271, 1900a:278, 1902a:272, 1903:297, 1904:284, 1905:303). Loubat was apparently a bit too zealous in trying to get copies of the Mexican codices out to the public; he and Zelia Nuttall got into a tiff over the publication of the Magliabecchiano Codex, which Nuttall had rediscovered in 1890. Eager to get it out, Loubat published a facsimile, apparently of poor quality, in 1900. Nuttall published the "touchstone" copy in 1903 (Tozzer 1933).

Loubat also paid for the plaster casts of Copan monuments and architecture made for the 1893 Columbian Exposition by John G. Owens, the Putnam student who first ran the Peabody's Copan project before his death from yellow fever. Loubat later paid for additional casts to be made for Putnam for the AMNH, and subsequently for the duplicates that Putnam presented to the Museum of Fine Arts, Boston, the Field Museum, the Philadelphia Museum of Science and Art, and the ethnographic museums of Paris and Berlin (Putnam 1899a:273, 1900a:273). Many of these casts still adorn the Harvard Peabody Museum and the Tozzer Library.

After 1904 Loubat became more involved in funding excavations. In the Americas this help was most evident in his support for Saville. In France it was through his assistance to the French School of Archeology. This school had been responsible for exploring the site of Delos, Greece, with excavations begun in 1872. Beginning in 1904 the effort saw considerable expansion with the aid of Loubat, a new patron. He did not ignore Americanist archaeology in his donations to French institutions: at the Sorbonne he established a foundation at the Collège de France for the study of American antiquities around 1894. A bit later, when Putnam was short of funds to continue supporting Ernest Volk in his work looking for "paleoliths" in the Delaware River valley, Loubat, along with Charles Peabody, stepped forward to provide the needed funds (Putnam 1913:215). Still later, when Charles Willoughby was curator of the Peabody Museum, the Duc de Loubat provided another $5,000 to assist a variety of projects the museum wished to fund (Willoughby 1923a:219).

Loubat also established two major book prizes, the first- and second-place Loubat Prizes, of $1,000 and $400, respectively, in 1898. The prizes were to be administered by Columbia University and awarded "for the best work printed and published in the English language on history, geography, archaeology, ethnology, philology, or numismatics of North America" for the preceding five-year interval. Many of the prizes went to anthropologists. William H. Holmes won the Loubat first prize, $1,000, for his "Stone Implements of the Potomac-Chesapeake Tidewater Province" for the period of 1894–98 and the second prize for his *Handbook of Aboriginal American Antiquities* in 1923. John Swanton received the Loubat second prize for his publication in ethnology in 1913. And in 1939, Harvard University publications made a clean sweep: Samuel Morison received the first prize for his *Three Centuries of Harvard* (1936) and Samuel Lothrop Jr. won the second prize for his *Cocle: An Archaeological Study of Central Panama* (Scott 1939:410).

A scholar who was not directly associated with the Peabody Museum but whose activities during the last quarter of the nineteenth century affected the direction or content of projects in Cambridge was **Frank Hamilton Cushing** (1857–1900). Cushing is perhaps best known for his work in ethnography, but he had an early interest in archaeology as well.

Cushing was born in Erie County, Pennsylvania, and began collecting Indian artifacts in 1870, at the age of 13, when his family moved to Medina, Orleans County, New York. There he developed an early interest in archaeology and also began experimentally reconstructing Indian implements (Phillips 1973:x). At age 17 he sent a brief report of his New York arrowhead collection, "The Antiquities of Orleans County, N.Y," to Spencer Baird at the Smithsonian Institution, who published it in the Smithsonian's annual report for 1874.

After completing his A.B. degree at Cornell in 1875, Cushing became involved in doing research with the Zunis in the American Southwest and tried to interest several benefactors in supporting the work. He finally won funding from Mary Hemenway, a Harvard and Peabody Museum patron (see Browman 2002a:236), convincing her to establish the Hemenway Southwestern Archaeological Expedition (1886–94), with Cushing as its first director. During the expedition's first two years, Cushing and his crew collected ethnographic data and excavated 11 ruins between Tempe and Phoenix, Arizona.

After two years of work, with none of the proposed reports forthcoming, Mary Hemenway lost patience with Cushing. She fired him and turned to Jesse Walter Fewkes, a former Harvard classmate of her husband, Augustus Hemenway (both class of 1875), to continue leading the expedition. As Philip Phillips observed (1973:xiii):

> The archaeological phase of the Hemenway Expedition is generally regarded as less than a success. Masses of artifacts were recovered, but little information was recorded, and no report was written until 1934, when Emil Haury based his Ph.D. dissertation on the Hemenway collections, later revised and published under the title "The Excavations of Los Muertos and Neighboring Ruins in the Salt River Valley, Southern Arizona," *Papers of the Peabody Museum of American Archaeology and Ethnology, Harvard University*, Vol. 24, No. 1, 1945. It was certainly a personal failure for Cushing.

According to Frederick Webb Hodge, another member of the expedition, Cushing took few notes, "the digging was not thorough, and Cushing's interpretations of the finds were often based on his imagination" (paraphrased in Hinsley 1994:202; see also Wilcox 2003a).

Fewkes took over the expedition in the summer of 1889 and continued directing it until 1894, when Mary Hemenway died. Of note for our theme, Fewkes hired John G. Owens, one of Putnam's first official students, as his field assistant in 1890 and 1891 (see chapter 7).

Jesse Walter Fewkes (1850–1930), the second director of the Hemenway Southwestern Archaeological Expedition, began with a close association to Harvard but moved beyond its influence later. Fewkes received his A.B. from Harvard in 1875 and both an A.M. and a Ph.D. in natural history in 1877. He was hired by the MCZ and worked as the curator of marine Radiates from 1879 to 1889 (Harvard University 1937:206). He worked at Harvard's early summer biological schools and taught with Putnam during some of those summers (Dexter 1957b:23).

Fewkes had met John Owens in 1888 at the marine lab at Wood's Hole, and the two met again at the Harvard summer school in biology in 1889. Fewkes lost his job at the MCZ in 1889, but after he was hired by the Hemenway Expedition in 1889, he recruited Owens to work as his assistant in 1890 and again in 1891. After the 1891–92 expedition Owens came back to work for Putnam on the Columbian Exposition. He then received an offer from Mary Hemenway to accompany Fewkes to the Madrid Exposition as a representative of the Hemenway Southwestern Expedition, so he changed plans and went to Madrid with Fewkes (Putnam 1892:193, 1894:215). After the 1890 season, Fewkes moved the principal research focus of the project from Zuni to Hopi.

Fewkes was an officer of the Boston Society of Natural History from 1889 to 1891, along with Putnam, Scudder, Shaler, Haynes, and Morse, so he was well known to the Harvard contingent of anthropologists. Along with Augustus Hemenway, Bowditch, and Haynes, Fewkes was named to the Visiting Committee of the Peabody Museum (Putnam 1891:100), and he was still on the committee in 1912, along with Bowditch, Moore, and others (Anonymous 1912a:672). Thus he had some oversight role in the development of the Peabody Museum's program.

Although the Hemenway expedition terminated with the death of Mary Hemenway in 1894, Hodge and Fewkes returned to excavations in the Southwest for the Bureau of Ethnology in 1894. Fewkes then joined the bureau in 1895 and ultimately, in 1918, took charge of it. He remained at the BAE until his death in 1930, after shifting to an emeritus position in 1928 owing to ill health (Judd 1967:26–29). Fewkes had continued to teach Harvard students on various expeditions in the Southwest. For example, in the spring of 1908 Sylvanus Morley and Alfred Kidder worked with Fewkes at Mesa Verde (Putnam 1909:301). In the summer of 1909 Robert Fuller worked with Fewkes at Cliff Palace (Putnam 1910:271). We meet these students again in our next chapter.

Hinsley (1994:281) has implied that Fewkes was able to stay on for the early years at the BAE only because of support from William H. Holmes, its chief from 1902 to 1909, reporting that "Fewkes seems to have been widely disliked and distrusted," and "despite indefatigable labors, Fewkes lacked focus or depth." Hinsley's assessment of Fewkes seems somewhat at odds with the assessments of others at the time.

For example, Franz Boas wrote in a letter to President Nicholas Murray Butler of Columbia University on November 15, 1902, that there were only three men adequately trained to teach archaeology in the United States: William H. Holmes, Max Uhle, and J. Walter Fewkes, and because none of these likely could be recruited to teach at Columbia, it would be the best second choice for Columbia to train a man under Eduard Seler in Berlin (Browman and Givens 1996:89).

Other colleagues, too, valued Fewkes's contributions. At this same time, the AIA appointed Fewkes to its Committee on American Archaeology, along with Putnam, Bowditch, Boas, Fletcher, and others. Thus the AIA viewed him as an important archaeologist, and he was deeply involved in shaping the direction of Americanist archaeology there (Gordon 1972:307). Later the AAA appointed Fewkes to the Division of Anthropology and Psychology of the National Research Council, which was established in 1916, and Fewkes served as a member of the division's executive committee, an important position with respect to the critical issues that redefined anthropology at this time (Bingham 1920:354). Thus Fewkes was a significant actor in our historical thread here.

We should at least mention the Hyde brothers, **Dr. Frederick Erastus Hyde Jr.** (1874–1937) and **Benjamin Talbot Babbitt Hyde** (1872–1933). At some point before 1900, they "were for a time students in this department" (Putnam 1900a:275), although neither obtained a degree from Harvard. Both were active in supporting some of Putnam's projects, but primarily through the AMNH rather than the Peabody Museum. They provided the funds for the "Hyde Expedition to the Southwest," a project that Putnam used to support some of his own fieldwork, as well as to recruit and support Aleš Hrdlička at the AMNH from 1899 through 1902. This was also the expedition for which Putnam transferred George Pepper from the Peabody Museum to the AMNH to take over as field director, and on which Alfred Tozzer later joined Putnam in the field in 1901.

Fred Hyde joined with Charles Bowditch to give Putnam the funds to purchase some pottery specimens for the Peabody Museum from the Moundville excavations near Carthage, Alabama, in addition to funds to support Volk's work at the Trenton gravel site (Putnam 1897:245, 1901c:466). He was a member of the American Folk-Lore Society from 1895 onward; served as treasurer of the revived American Ethnological Society from 1899 to 1900 and was on its executive committee with Boas; and was a member of the AIA and the AAA until his death.

Talbot, or "B. T. B.," Hyde helped support the Peabody's expedition to Syria in 1900 and furnished additional support for Henry Huxley (chapter 10) after the expedition returned (Putnam 1902a:272). A life member of the AAA, he became its second treasurer in 1903, replacing Roland Dixon, and served as an officer for the next four years. He served on the executive committee of the AAA for two terms in its first two decades, fatefully as a member of the 1919 group that voted to censure Franz Boas. Talbot Hyde did some of his own collecting at New Mexico pueblos during the 1900s, and he helped Earl Morris at Aztec Ruin in 1918.

Members of the official Visiting Committee of the Peabody Museum often became important contributors to the museum. Besides the contributions from Bowditch and others already discussed, we should acknowledge assistance in the first two decades of the twentieth century from Henry Sweet, Benjamin Arnold, Hamilton Rice, John Blake, Clarence Blake, and Lombard Jones.

Henry N. Sweet (1861–1932) received his S.B. from MIT in 1881. He first became involved with the Peabody Museum through his work as a member of Edward H. Thompson's 1888–91 expeditions to Uxmal, Kabah, Sayil, and Labna in Yucatán, which were supported in part by Putnam. Sweet also was apparently a member of one of the early Peabody Museum expeditions to Copan (Scott 1934:296).

Sweet was later appointed to the Peabody Museum Visiting Committee, and one of his actions as a member was to establish the Sweet Fund in January 1920 to assist the museum in obtaining Mesoamerican materials (Willoughby 1921:244). In the 1920s Alfred Tozzer used this fund to secure artifacts from Chichen Itza and other Maya sites, models of Chichen Itza pyramids, ethnographic textiles from Mexico, and a 3,000-item collection from a private collector of Central American materials. Sweet continued his service and donations to the museum until his death in 1932, before which he arranged for additional monies to be given to the museum from his estate (Scott 1934:296).

One of Sweet's colleagues on the visiting committee was **Benjamin Arnold** (1865?–1932). Arnold's name shows up on a large list of donations of artifacts from Mexico received by the museum during his tenure on the committee, and apparently his interest in securing Mexican materials grew during the 1920s (Scott 1934:296).

Dr. Alexander Hamilton Rice (1875–1956), referred to as "Ham Rice" in some annual reports, was born in Boston, received his A.B. from Harvard in 1898, and obtained his M.D. there in 1904. He had considerable financial means and led seven expeditions to the upper Amazon between 1905 and 1925–26. For his expedition of 1916–17, he was officially named "Agent for Collecting Specimens for the Peabody Museum" (Harvard University 1930:129). Rice collected and donated specimens to the Peabody from all his Amazon trips. In 1929 he was named "Honorary Curator of South American Archaeology and Ethnology" for the museum. He became an expert on tropical medicine and was a lecturer on this topic at the Harvard Medical School from 1921 onward and at the School of Public Health from 1925 onward. He became well known to Alfred Tozzer at the Peabody Museum.

The Peabody was the fortunate recipient of significant funds from Rice in 1922:

> The largest single gift this year was from Dr. A. Hamilton Rice through the Endowment Fund Committee. This forms a substantial addition to the permanent funds of the Museum. For many years Dr. Rice has taken an active interest in the welfare of the institution. He has contributed cases for the South American room, and during his explorations of the upper Amazon regions he missed no opportunity to secure for the

Museum such ethnological material as could be obtained from the little-known tribes with which he came in contact. (Willoughby 1923a:219)

Rice's Amazon trips led to him take increasing interest in human geography. In the late 1920s he became interested in establishing his own research institute, and in 1929 he donated funds for the construction of the "Laboratory for Geographical Explorations" at 2 Divinity Avenue, just half a block from the Peabody Museum. The building was of considerable size, and it had a fine lecture hall, often used by the Peabody Museum for large events for many years.

The agreement Rice made with Harvard University was that he would be named professor and director of geographical explorations in return for donating the building. In 1930, when the building was finished, he was indeed appointed to these two positions, which he kept until he retired in 1951. Part of Harvard's receptiveness to this plan stemmed from the fact that Rice's first wife was Eleanor Elkins Widener, widow of George Dunton Widener, and the Widener family was much involved with the libraries at Harvard.

John Harrison Blake (1808–99) and **Clarence John Blake** (1843–1919), his son, were contributors of note to the early development of anthropology at the Peabody Museum. John H. Blake made one of the earliest archaeological collections from Peru and Chile, and Clarence Blake assisted in the identification of osteological materials at the museum, as well as serving on its visiting committee for nearly a quarter century.

John H. Blake was trained as a civil engineer. He had the opportunity to visit ruins near Arica and in the Atacama Valley in Chile in 1836 and made notes on the sites, taking particular interest in the Inca highway system, bridges, and wayside *tambos,* or Inca state-supported inns (D. Wilson 1862, 2:70–71). He made a collection at that time of pottery and mummy bundles from an Inca cemetery at Bahia Chacota, just south of the existing port of Arica (Blake 1878:277). Some of the crania from his collection exhibited artificial deformation, then poorly understood, which generated a good deal of discussion about the "racial" affinities of the specimens among researchers of the day such as Samuel Morton, Daniel Wilson, and Jeffries Wyman (Blake 1878:298). Putnam noted a quite different treatment in the mummification of these Chilean specimens from that of mummies collected from Ancon, Peru, and those collected by Alexander Agassiz at Pisagua, Chile (Blake 1878:278 n. 1).

The 1836 collection was exhibited for many years at the Warren Museum in Boston, but once the Peabody Museum was established, John Blake moved part of his collections, including several mummies and his field notes, to the Peabody. Over the ensuing years, his son Clarence gradually arranged for the transfer of the remaining materials from the Warren Museum to the Peabody Museum (Putnam 1878a:195). Unlike many other collectors of the day, Blake gathered more than just pottery and skulls. Rather, he kept relatively complete assemblages of associated grave materials. Thus the coca leaf offerings he collected became an important component of the analysis of archaeological coca leaf varieties in Peru (Rury and Plowman 1983).

We should note that John Harrison Blake is not to be confused with James Henry Blake, even though both men signed themselves "J. H. Blake," and both made trips to South America in the nineteenth century and donated materials to the Peabody Museum. **James Henry Blake** (1845–1941), born in Provincetown, Cape Cod, enrolled at the Lawrence Scientific School in 1864 to study with Louis Agassiz. In 1867 Agassiz hired him as an MCZ student assistant to help organize the Thayer Expedition collections from Brazil, especially to draw the soft parts of freshwater mollusks, and he served as the artist and assistant on Agassiz's second expedition to South America (the Hassler Expedition) in 1871–72. After the Thayer funding was terminated in 1875, John Henry Blake went on to serve as an artist for the U.S. Fish Commission, the U.S. Geological Survey, and the Mississippi Geological Survey (Robert Young, Special Collections librarian, MCZ, Harvard, personal communication, 2005). During the years of the Thayer Expedition, he brought back to the Peabody Museum a cranium collection made by Dr. J. C. Warren from Peru, as well as ethnographic artifacts collected in Panama and Tierra del Fuego (Putnam 1910:274; Wyman 1871:10, 1872:23). It is sometimes difficult to ascertain which item in the Peabody Museum collections came from which J. H. Blake. So far we have not discovered how, if at all, the two J. H. Blakes might have been related.

Clarence Blake, the son of John Harrison Blake, received his M.D. from Harvard in 1865 and was a professor of otology at the Harvard Medical School from 1870 to 1913. One of the first two physicians in the country to limit his practice to otology, Blake was a founding member of the American Otological Society and editor of the original *American Journal of Otology*, founded in 1879.

In addition to providing for the transfer of the remaining materials from his father's Peruvian and Chilean research from the Warren Museum to the Peabody Museum, Clarence Blake pursued his own "special study of diseases of the ear" during the 1870s and 1880s using the cranium collections at the Peabody Museum (Putnam 1885a:417, 1911:223). Blake became interested enough in the activities of the Peabody that he was appointed to the museum's visiting committee in 1897, once the museum had been fully incorporated into the university, and served in that position for the next 22 years, providing both collections and advice. He "took an active part in the development of the Museum during that period" (Willoughby 1920:200). Among other things, he was an important financial supporter of publications such as the Putnam anniversary volume.

Dr. Lombard Carter Jones (1865–1943/44?) was a member of the Harvard college class of 1887 and received his M.D. from Harvard in 1892. Although his livelihood was in medicine, he also developed an interest in anthropology and geography, being elected a member of the Royal Geographical Society in 1902. He began collecting and donating artifacts to the Peabody Museum by 1903 and continued almost yearly donations for the next three decades. He provided the library with more than 2,000 volumes and the museum with numerous specimens. He subsequently became a member of the visiting committee for the museum and assisted it for several years in that manner as well (Biographical files, Peabody Museum Collections Department).

The members of the visiting committee, along with the museum faculty and the other educated, avocational volunteers we have discussed in this chapter, were essential to the flourishing of the Peabody Museum and its increasingly professional anthropology program after 1890. Because these contributors often acted behind the scenes, they are sometimes overlooked as vital components of the Peabody's success. All of them were important in materially enhancing the collections at the museum, and several of them made significant contributions to laboratory construction, exhibit construction, library collections, and other critical resources. They are, in a sense, unsung heroes of the continuing success of Putnam's plan for the Peabody Museum.

10

Peabody Museum Students and Faculty, 1900–1919

IN THIS CHAPTER WE RETURN TO THE STUDENTS AND ACADEMIC FACULTY at the Peabody Museum, resuming the coverage left off at the end of chapter 7. Our time frame is the first two decades of the twentieth century, encompassing 1915, the year ending the first quarter century of the Peabody anthropology program and the year of Frederic Putnam's death. Because of the significant increase in the number of students during these decades, we find the most efficient way to deal with the topic is again to fashion our discussion as a sort of chronological directory. Insofar as possible, we try to identify people and their contributions to the Peabody Museum as they sequentially entered the program, portraying the context and tenor of Peabody Museum training as it slowly matured during this quarter century. Many of the persons we identify here made contributions that have slipped through the cracks over time and merit review and reminder. Previous synthesizers have tended to focus on only one or two persons, leaving the unwary with the feeling that the "big names" were the only players on the scene. Our cohort approach again includes students in all fields who did graduate training at the Peabody Museum, although as before, archaeologists continued to predominate.

Louis Wirth (1953:40), in his review of the development of the social sciences during the early half of the twentieth century, observed: "The character of the developing social science at the turn of the century was significantly shaped by the dominant philosophy of the period with its empirical and pragmatic temper, its consequent emphasis upon the actual problems of the developing American society, its revulsion from doctrinaire metaphysics and armchair speculation, and its accent upon observation and experimentation." A pragmatic focus on ethnographic observation and field excavation certainly characterized the developing program at the Peabody Museum.

This period marks the shift away from Putnam's being often the sole instructor of anthropology at the Peabody Museum and clearly the major one. By the beginning of the 1900s, with the willingness of Harvard College now to provide instructional lines or salaries to help support some of the teaching staff, the anthropology program had separate instructors in somatology, archaeology, and ethnology. Advanced degrees, both

A.M. and Ph.D., were being granted in all three areas. Alfred Tozzer, Roland Dixon, Earnest Hooton, and others began to cover all four traditional subfields of anthropology, and Putnam became essentially emeritus, providing guidance and occasionally lecturing but seeing the second generation of instructors taking over and continuing to develop the program.

Because of the help Putnam had secured from supporters such as Charles Bowditch and Clarence Moore, more money was consistently available for fieldwork in archaeology than for the other areas of anthropology. Tozzer was particularly interested in the Maya area. His interest, together with the fact that the Carnegie Institution of Washington, during its first decade, opened a program of research support for archaeology in Central America and located its offices right next to the Peabody Museum, resulted in a particular strength in Mesoamerican archaeology. But as Boas (1919b) pointed out, the Peabody was also the only American university offering any graduate training in biological anthropology during this period, and it had a respectable program in ethnology.

Putnam was a major contributor to the professionalization of American anthropology through his development of museum research programs and advanced degree granting programs. This development was part of a larger pattern in the social sciences, a shift toward the formation of separate academic departments, resulting in the rapid emergence and growth of the social science disciplines (Ross 1979:121).

Putnam's Section H of the AAAS was part of this professionalizing trend. Among the committees that Section H established was one on the teaching of anthropology, which was changed from a provisional committee of Section H to a standing committee of the AAAS in 1900. Its initial, official AAAS membership consisted of George Grant MacCurdy as chair and Franz Boas, William H. Holmes, William J. McGee, and Frank Russell as members (Baskerville 1900:6). As chair, MacCurdy (1902:211) reported tremendous growth in the development of anthropology in only a few short years. He noted that in the committee's 1899 survey, only 11 institutions in the United States offered any anthropology courses, but just two years later, by the time of its 1901 survey, the figure had mushroomed to at least 31 institutions.

The Peabody Museum program had made a pioneering start, but it also benefited from this broader rise of interest in anthropology. By the time of Putnam's death in 1915, he had been responsible for training an enormous number of the then extant professionals in American anthropology. Roland Dixon observed (1928b:278): "Directly or indirectly he was largely responsible for the growth of most of the anthropological museums, for the acceptance of anthropology as a university study, and for the spread and popularization of an interest in the subject. His students and associates held important positions in practically every institution in the United States where anthropological work was carried on." Whereas only rare graduate students had entered the Peabody program with undergraduate training in anthropology from other institutions during the first two decades, by the 1920s this was becoming increasingly common.

In this chapter we look at some of the more than two score men who did postgraduate work in anthropology at the Peabody Museum during this time frame. Some of these people, such as Homer Kidder, Irwin Hayden, Bruce Merwin, Samuel Lothrop, Lauriston Ward, and Donald Scott, initially went on to other areas after their stint at Harvard but returned two or three decades later to conduct archaeological research at the Peabody or elsewhere. A large number of the students went into teaching in anthropology departments or doing anthropological research at museums. They founded new departments and became chairmen of departments. There were, as always, those who either lost interest in anthropology or could not find jobs in their field and went into other academic programs such as classics or education or into the private business sector. A few—Howard Wilson, John Hastings, Robert Hellman, Robert Fuller, George Howe, and Oric Bates—had their promising anthropological careers cut short when they died from diseases caught during fieldwork or lost their lives in World War I.

Henry Minor Huxley (1880–1954) was a native of Massachusetts, born in Newton. He was a member of the Harvard class of 1899, graduating with a focus in anthropology. He had a particular interest in somatology and as an undergraduate senior co-authored a paper with his instructor, Frank Russell, in 1899 (Russell and Huxley 1899, 1900). In January 1900, after graduation, Huxley joined a combined Peabody Museum–AMNH research expedition to Syria led by Howard Crosby Butler. When the expedition returned to the United States that June, Putnam arranged for Huxley to get additional support from Talbot Hyde. Huxley stayed on in the Levant for a few more months, collecting information in Lebanon and Syria (Putnam 1902a:272). He returned to enroll for the fall term at Harvard to write up this research, on Hemenway Fellowship money for 1901–2. When Frank Russell suddenly had to take medical leave because of his tuberculosis, Huxley was asked to step in to teach for him and so was also appointed an assistant in anthropology for 1901–2. The instructors for Anthropology 2, Somatology, that year were listed as "Putnam and Huxley" (Putnam 1903:296).

Huxley finished his A.M at Harvard in 1902 on a physical anthropological study of Levantine populations but then apparently had second thoughts about anthropology as a career choice and left somatology in 1903. He was employed by American Steel and Wire in Worcester, Massachusetts, from 1903 to 1907. In 1911 he received an LL.B. from Kent College in Chicago, and he became a patent attorney for the rest of his life (*National Cyclopedia* 1961).

Huxley apparently gave his anthropological papers to his old friend George Pepper at the AMNH, for his field notebooks on the Syrian and Lebanese fieldwork are included with the George Hubbard Pepper Papers at the Latin American Library at Tulane. He kept a photographic record of his research in Syria and gave the photographs to his sponsor, B. T. B. Hyde. Hyde donated several hundred photos from the "Hyde-Huxley Anthropological Expedition" to the Peabody Museum in 1924 (Willoughby 1925:263).

Much later, Dr. Carl C. Seltzer became interested in Huxley's data, and in 1938 Huxley gave the museum the anthropometric series on 800 individuals that he had collected and provided funds to Seltzer and the Peabody Museum for the analysis of these materials and publication costs (Scott 1939:412). When Seltzer published these materials in the Peabody Museum Papers series in 1940, Huxley wrote a foreword to the volume summarizing his fieldwork (Huxley 1940).

Homer Huntington Kidder (1874–1950) was Alfred Vincent (A.V.) Kidder's older brother, uncle to Alfred Kidder II and great-uncle to Tristram R. Kidder—a significant archaeological dynasty. Homer and A.V.'s father, **Alfred Kidder I** (1840–1923), had been educated in Boston and after the Civil War moved to Marquette, Michigan, where he became a mining engineer. He worked for the Jackson Iron Company, the Volunteer Mining Company, and the Pittsburgh and Lake Angeline Iron Company, all of Marquette, until he retired in 1901 (Stafford 1941:422). The family had an ancestral home in Cambridge and moved back there around 1892 (Givens 1992:2). Alfred Kidder had had contacts with Alexander Agassiz and Raphael Pumpelly in the mining business in Michigan, as well as in social circumstances in Cambridge.

Alfred Kidder had an avocational interest in archaeology. He took his boys out arrowhead collecting (Wauchope 1965:149), and he gave the Peabody Museum some of the materials he collected. For example, in 1887 Putnam (1889:39) reported receiving historic artifacts from a grave on Dead River, two miles north of Marquette, along with assorted prehistoric obsidian material from Yellowstone National Park, collected by Alfred Kidder. Alfred had many books on American Indians and prehistory in his personal library, which would have been available to both Homer and A.V. Kidder. Many of these, donated by A.V. Kidder, are still to be found in the Laboratory of Anthropology in Santa Fe, New Mexico. Because considerable research has been done on A.V. Kidder (Givens 1992; Willey 1967; R. Woodbury 1973), we know that as a child he read the annual reports of the BAE, the U.S. National Museum, the Smithsonian Institution, and the Peabody Museum, as well as Catlin's *North American Indians,* Catherwood's *Views of Ancient Monuments in Central America, Chiapas, and Yucatán,* and Stephens and Catherwood's *Incidents of Travel in Central America, Chiapas, and Yucatán* and *Incidents of Travel in Yucatán*—all from his father's library. Gordon Willey (1967:294) tells us that Alfred Kidder "was a great reader and lover of books, particularly of history and exploration, and [A.V.] Kidder attributed his own later interests in archaeology to this early conditioning."

This interest in anthropology rubbed off on Homer Kidder as well. Homer entered Harvard in 1893 and developed an interest in anthropological folklore during this period, if not earlier. The Harvard Folk-Lore Club was organized on March 8, 1894, with Homer Kidder as president. Professor Francis James Child, of the English department, was the club's official college adviser, but he was assisted by the well-known folklorist William Wells Newell of Cambridge (Harvard class of 1859). Regular meetings, at which papers were read, were held twice a month (Anonymous 1894). In December 1894, at the sixth annual meeting of the American Folk-Lore Society in Washington, D.C., Kidder gave a paper titled "Origin of the Midewiwen—Ojibwa Folk-tale." That day's session also included papers by Daniel Brinton, Frank Cushing, J. W. Fewkes, Zelia Nuttall, J. Wesley Powell, and Marshall Saville—good company indeed (Anonymous 1895b:5).

But an illness forced Homer Kidder to take an academic leave of absence, and he spent two years back home in Marquette (Bourgeois 1994:18). During this period he collected additional Ojibwa folk narratives and wrote short articles for the local newspaper on Ojibwa and Chippewa myths and culture (see, for example, Bourgeois 1994; Kidder 1898). He then returned to school, where he continued as an officer in the Harvard Folk-Lore Club, which now had 13 members; Roland Dixon was the club's new secretary-treasurer. Kidder studied English with Professor Child and graduated from Harvard in 1899. He was offered a position as instructor in the Department of English at Harvard and taught there for a year, 1900–1901. After Alfred Kidder's retirement in 1901, the Kidder family traveled extensively in Europe and other regions for the next few years (Stafford 1941:423).

Homer Kidder became actively involved with archaeological excavations twice in his career. The first time was with his Cambridge neighbor and friend Raphael Welles Pumpelly. Pumpelly's father, whom we profiled in chapter 5, was about to undertake his expedition to Anau in Turkistan in 1903–4. He allowed his son, then a Harvard junior, to invite three Harvard friends to join the expedition as volunteer archaeological assistants: Hildegarde Brooks, the daughter of an old friend of the elder Pumpelly's; Langdon Warner, who later became an instructor in fine arts at Harvard, specializing in Chinese and Japanese art; and Homer Kidder.

Kidder participated in Pumpelly's excavations at Merv and Samarqand (Pumpelly 1908, 1:xxxv). At Old Merv, Kidder reported excavating a group of nine large, complete pottery vessels in a vertical shaft; these were included with other materials in Kidder's discussion of regional glazed ceramics in the project's final report (Kidder 1908:213–14). After an invasion of locusts shut down the excavation project at Anau, Kidder and young Raphael Pumpelly were sent to do geographical explorations, embarking on an independent expedition to Zerfashan glacier and over the Pamir to Kashgar (Pumpelly 1908, 2:743). Later Kidder accompanied Pumpelly to Egypt (Stafford 1941:518).

He then returned to the United States, became involved in lumbering in Minnesota and the Gulf states, and later tried his hand at ranching and apple growing along the Columbia River in Maryhill, Washington. In 1917 he enlisted in the army as a first lieutenant, mustering out as a captain. After World War I Homer Kidder worked for four years with the Red Cross in Paris and Vienna (Bourgeois 1994:18; Stafford 1941:518), during which time he also managed to study physical anthropology at Zurich. Leaving the Red Cross, he returned to archaeology a second time, doing private archaeological and anthropological work in Algeria and Tunisia from 1923 to 1925. In 1926 he picked up a contract from the Peabody Museum to continue archaeological research in Algeria for the next year (Kidder 1927).

Kidder had been married previously, in 1908, and in 1928 he remarried. His second wife, Lilia Silvia della Morena, daughter of Count Giuseppe and Rosa Maria Annunciata Campana della Morena (Bourgeois 1994:18; Stafford 1941:518), shared his interest in archaeology. Beginning in 1929, Homer and Lilia began working in south-central France, particularly on Upper Paleolithic materials in the Dordogne caves (Barnes and Kidder 1936; Kidder 1934, 1935, 1939; Peyrony, Kidder, and Noone 1949). The two were a field team and published joint reports on their French excavation work (Kidder and Kidder 1932, 1936a, 1936b).

In 1940 Kidder again became engaged in war relief activities. He settled in Berkeley, California, after World War II, but after suffering a stroke, he moved back to Cambridge to live with his brother, A.V. Kidder. Homer Kidder visited the Upper Peninsula of Michigan as semi-invalid in 1949 to collect more Ojibwa materials, but he died in Cambridge in 1950 before he could write them up (Bourgeois 1994:18).

Alfred Marston Tozzer (1877–1954) was born in Lynn, Massachusetts. As we saw in the last chapter, he came to know Charles Bowditch while a teenager and thus may have had an early introduction to Peabody Museum business. Tozzer entered Harvard in 1896. At what point he decided to focus on anthropology is unclear, but by his senior year, when he took classes with Dixon and served as secretary and treasurer for the Harvard Anthropological Society, he clearly had begun to develop his lifelong interest in anthropology (Barber 1900:95). It is often forgotten that Tozzer was trained in general field ethnography as well as in archaeology in the Peabody program. "His initial orientation was toward linguistics and cultural anthropology. . . . if Tozzer's interest later shifted toward archaeology, it was certainly not due to any lack of talent for ethnographic fieldwork" (Phillips 1955:73).

In the summer of 1900, following receipt of his A.B., Tozzer went to California as Dixon's assistant to do linguistic work among the Wintun and Maidu peoples (Anonymous 1900:240; Putnam 1901a:299). Through his work on Maidu linguistics, he got to know both Franz Boas and Alfred Kroeber well, and they remained his close friends for life. He then entered graduate school at Harvard, where he was supported during his first year by a Winthrop Scholarship, and received his A.M. in the spring of 1901.

In the late summer and early fall of 1901, thanks to funding from Bowditch, Tozzer went with Putnam to Chaco Canyon, New Mexico, where he did both archaeological and ethnographic work (Putnam 1902a:270). On the way to Chaco Canyon, Tozzer, William Farabee, and Dr. and Mrs. Putnam joined up with George Pepper, B. T. B. Hyde, and local archaeologist Richard Wetherill (A. Andrews 1970:3). During August and early September, Tozzer worked with Putnam, Farabee, and the others doing archaeological excavations and serving as expedition photographer. In September, when Putnam and Farabee returned to Cambridge, Tozzer stayed on to collect information on Navajo linguistics, lifestyles, and sand painting. He took part in the Navajo nine-day Night Chant ritual (A. Andrews 1970:4, 5, 7; Phillips 1955:73).

Tozzer returned to Cambridge in November 1901 and the next month learned that he had been awarded the first AIA fellowship in Americanist archaeology (Putnam 1903:294). The AIA committee making the award, composed of Putnam, Boas, and Bowditch, had been appointed in 1899 and had held the authority to provide a traveling fellowship in American archaeology since that time. But it found no suitable candidates until 1901, when it gave the fellowship to Tozzer for four years (C. Bowditch 1905:41). Bowditch hoped "that the problem of the hieroglyphs might be solved through contact with some as yet undiscovered Maya-speaking group, in whom memories of their ancient civilization had not been totally extinguished, and it was this quest that largely determined Tozzer's activities during the entire 4 years of his incumbency of the Institute fellowship" (Phillips 1955:73).

Tozzer's cross-disciplinary training under Putnam allowed him to move easily between archaeology and social anthropology. He went to the Maya area planning to devote his career to linguistics, in part influenced by Bowditch's long concern with deciphering Maya hieroglyphs. His dissertation work was essentially ethnographic, and his 1904 dissertation, defended before a committee composed of Putnam, Dixon, Lowell, Goodale, and Lyon, was titled "A Comparative Study of the Mayas and the Lacandones." But once Tozzer was at Chichen Itza, working with Edward H. Thompson, his interest shifted to archaeology (Lothrop 1955:614). In December 1903, with his dissertation essentially complete, Tozzer was named assistant in Central American archaeology at the Peabody Museum (Putnam 1905:302).

Tozzer's affinity for social anthropology, however, was not forgotten. He collaborated closely with Boas on several projects, and his colleagues named him a member of Harvard's Department of Sociology in 1930. From his double position in anthropology and sociology, Tozzer made a significant contribution to the later creation of the Department of Social Relations at Harvard (Brew 1956:478).

Tozzer returned to the Maya area in 1904, in his fourth year as the America Fellow of the AIA. In the fall of 1904 he studied with Franz Boas and Adolph Bandelier at Columbia (Phillips 1955:74). Back at Harvard in the spring of 1905, he was appointed instructor in Central American archaeology (Putnam 1906:301). Almost immediately he was called to serve on doctoral committees, and in the next several years he served at defenses by Raymond Merwin, Robert Fuller, Carl Guthe, William Mechling, Frederick Sterns, and Andrew Kerr, all of whom are discussed later in this chapter.

In the fall of 1905 Tozzer offered for the first time his famous Maya seminar, Anthropology 9, "which probably propelled more students into Maya archaeology than all other courses that have been given before or since. He was a gifted teacher" (Phillips 1955:74). Tozzer remained instructor in Central American archaeology until 1912, when he was promoted to assistant professor in anthropology, becoming in subsequent years associate and then full professor of anthropology. He was named curator of Middle American archaeology and ethnology in 1913, a position he kept until his retirement.

The renewal of the Harvard permit in Guatemala allowed Tozzer to go to Tikal in 1909–10, with Raymond Merwin as his chief assistant, and to appoint Merwin to continue work there in 1910–11 (Putnam 1910:272, 1911:221). In 1910 Dixon and Tozzer represented the department and the museum at the International Congress of Americanists, held that year in Mexico City. While there, they served as the official U.S. delegates at the founding of the Universidad Nacional Autónoma de México. Dixon also represented Harvard in organizing the new International School of American Archaeology and Ethnology in Mexico City, a joint project by Harvard, Columbia, Pennsylvania, and the universities of Mexico, Berlin, and Paris.

The International School, in large part the brainchild of Franz Boas, though it never had more than half a dozen participants a year, was one of Boas's major excursions into archaeology. He believed the school should encompass ethnology, archaeology, and linguistics—the latter in order to understand ancient hieroglyphics (Boas to Seler, January 28, 1910, cited in Rutsch 2000:142). In the school's first year, Eduard Seler directed excavations at Palenque with two Mexican students, a German Fellow, and a Mexican inspector of archaeological monuments of Chiapas (Rutsch 2000:143).

Directorship of the school rotated among its patron institutions. Harvard's turn came in 1913–14, when Tozzer was sent to be the director. He took with him Clarence L. Hay, who had been named the Harvard Fellow for that term (Putnam 1914:222); institutions were allowed to nominate fellows to the International School as long as they provided the funding. William H. Mechling, who had just received his A.M. in anthropology from Harvard, was the University of Pennsylvania Fellow that year, so there was a good Harvard contingent at the school.

During their term, Tozzer and Hay worked on Valley of Mexico excavations under the sponsorship of the International School. The artifacts recovered had to be shared with the financial clients of the school. At the time of Tozzer's directorship, these included Harvard, Columbia, Pennsylvania, the Hispanic Society of America, and the governments of Mexico, Prussia, Bavaria, Austria, Russia, and Sweden (Putnam 1915:237). Whereas the founding "patron" members had been only Mexico, Prussia, France, Columbia, Harvard, and Pennsylvania, a category of "protector" memberships also existed, which allowed other institutions to pay for fellowships, scientific investigations, or publication costs. For 1913–14, the protector members included the Hispanic Society of America, Austria, Bavaria, and Sweden (Ruiz 2003:342, 347–48).

Tozzer had a difficult political year for his directorship. Two members of the school's director pool got into a serious dispute. Manuel Gamio, the Mexican scholar who was Boas's first and only Ph.D. in archaeology and who was scheduled to become the International School's director following Tozzer's term, and Jorge Engerrand, the director from the previous year, had severe disagreements. The dispute degenerated to the point that they were attacking each other's work in print (de la Peña 1996:54). As well, toward the end of 1913 the internal political situation in Mexico grew progressively more tense. Tozzer wrote to Boas, alarmed about the implications that the deteriorating

Mexican political condition and the conflict between Gamio and Engerrand held for the future of the school (de la Peña 1996:56). Rebellions in Mexico led by Francisco (Pancho) Villa and Emiliano Zapata made the situation so risky that Tozzer was forced to leave the country precipitously in April 1914.

Returning to Cambridge, Tozzer became more involved in training students and in synthesizing data on the Mayas, but his work was interrupted by World War I. He was commissioned a captain in the Aviation Section of the Signal Corps and served in Cambridge, Denver, and San Francisco (Spinden 1957:386; Willoughby 1919:240). During World War II he would again interrupt his teaching, to serve as director of the Honolulu office of the Office of Strategic Services (OSS) from 1943 to 1945 (Phillips 1955:75).

In addition to becoming chair of the Department of Anthropology at Harvard in 1921, Tozzer became a member of the Academic Board of Radcliffe in 1922 and its secretary in 1932. He was named a permanent member of the Administrative Board of Harvard College from 1928 until he retired in 1947; chair of the Tercentenary Committee in 1932; a representative to the Division of Anthropology and Psychology of the National Research Council from 1919 to 1921; and president of the AAA in 1928, being reelected in 1929. He became Harvard's John E. Hudson Professor of Archaeology in 1946, for the year just before his retirement in 1947 (Keller and Keller 2001:3; Phillips 1955:75; Spinden 1957:386; Tozzer 1920:86).

Gordon Willey (1975:3) reported that Tozzer "was also the recognized 'dean' of the field. It is no undue praise to say that he was the greatest all-time teacher of Maya archaeology." Evon Vogt (1975:23) commented that Tozzer's Lacandón work was the beginning of comparative ethnographic work among the Mayas, and "in a very genuine sense, Alfred Marston Tozzer was not only the 'dean' of Maya studies at Harvard, but he was also the 'grandfather' of most of the current social anthropological work among the Maya."

Next among the faculty is **William Curtis Farabee** (1865–1925). Farabee received his A.B. and A.M. from Waynesburg College, in Waynesburg, Pennsylvania, in 1894 and 1895, respectively, and then took a teaching job at Burgettstown, Pennsylvania, from 1896 to 1900. He entered Harvard in 1900 and was the recipient of the Hemenway Fellowship for 1900–1901 and the Austin Teaching Fellowship for 1901–3. Farabee completed his Ph.D. in 1903 with the dissertation "Hereditary and Sexual Influences in Meristic Variation: A Study of Digital Malformations in Man."

Having received his Harvard A.M. after his first year in residence at the Peabody Museum, Farabee embarked on four months of field excavation in the summer of 1901. He spent the first two months with Charles Peabody at the Oliver site in Mississippi—his first field experience—and the next two months with Putnam and Pepper in New Mexico (Putnam 1902a:270). Anthony P. Andrews (1970) wrote up the field notes from that New Mexico season, offering a glimpse of Putnam's fieldwork as well as Farabee's. Thus we know that Putnam brought Farabee and Tozzer with him from Harvard, along with his wife, and that he integrated into his crew George Pepper from the AMNH and B. T. B. Hyde, who was putting up a good part of the field funding for the AMNH side. (Putnam was still head of anthropology at the AMNH at this time.) When they arrived at Chaco Canyon, the team joined up with Richard Wetherill. Putnam went into the field the first week to dig with Farabee and Tozzer, assuring that they understood the basics of the Peabody Museum method of excavation.

The next year, funded by the Austin Teaching Fellowship, Farabee assisted in the general anthropology course, Anthropology 1. He was sent by Putnam to work with Charles Peabody in Mississippi again in 1902. Later that summer Farabee went with David Bushnell to excavate in Missouri, supported by funds from Clarence B. Moore and some of the Hearst money that Putnam controlled from the University of California–Berkeley department (Putnam 1903:294). Roland Dixon took some students to work in North Dakota in 1903, and Farabee served as the backup expert on the zooarchaeology and human osteology for the Double Ditch excavations carried out there later, primarily by George Will and Herbert Spinden (profiled later in this chapter), under Dixon's sponsorship.

After Farabee received his Ph.D. in 1903, Putnam suggested him for a curatorship at the University of Pennsylvania Museum, but when Harvard was also able to offer him an instructorship, Farabee withdrew his application at Penn to take the Peabody job. Farabee retained an interest in Pennsylvania, however, and finally left Harvard in 1913 to take the position of curator of American archaeology at the University Museum, working there until his death in 1925.

Farabee was active in fieldwork while at Harvard. In the summer of 1904 he took 15 students, including John Hastings, whom we discuss later, on an ethnographic and archaeological excursion to New Mexico, Arizona, and California, to visit sites (Putnam 1905:302). In the summer of 1905, funded by the Henry C. Warren Fund and donations by Clarence B. Moore of the visiting committee, Farabee took Vilhjalmar Stefansson, John Hastings, Louis de Milhau, and other Harvard students to Iceland to do somatological research, exploring old Icelandic burial places, collecting skeletons, and taking measurements on contemporary populations (Putnam 1906:302). In 1906 de Milhau, following his graduation, put up funds for a three-year project in Peru, a project on which he and his friend Hastings served as ethnologists. Farabee accepted the directorship of the project, taking a leave of absence from teaching from 1906 through 1909 (Putnam 1907:294, 1910:270). Without knowing it, Farabee came close to fabled Machu Picchu during this work. Hiram Bingham, who subsequently relocated and excavated Machu Picchu and whom we discuss shortly, decided to conduct research in the area in 1911 on the basis of finds Farabee made during the Harvard expedition (W. Bingham 1989:141). After returning from leave, Farabee resumed his teaching duties and set about analyzing and writing up the materials from the Peruvian project. He did not finish the write-up until 1923, and the work was published, with de Milhau's aid, as a Peabody Museum paper in 1924 (Farabee 1924).

David Ives Bushnell Jr. (1875–1941) was one of the last young men without previous academic training that Putnam recruited to work in the Peabody Museum, where Bushnell served as an assistant in archaeology from 1901 to 1904. His father was on the advisory committee of the Missouri Historical Society in St. Louis for many years, and Bushnell apparently first got interested in American Indians through his father's work (Swanton 1942:104).

In the fall of 1899 Bushnell took a canoe trip in northern Minnesota, witnessed some Chippewa ceremonies, and made notes on them that he later published in *American Anthropologist*. In the late spring and summer of 1900 he accompanied Jacob V. Brower, a good friend of Putnam's, to explore mound groups and village sites on the shores of Mille Lac, which the two wrote up almost immediately (Brower and Bushnell 1900).

The next year Putnam appointed Bushnell an assistant in archaeology at the Peabody, which seems mainly to have provided him with a base of operations. For 1902 Putnam (1903:294) reported, "I was able, however, to send Mr. D. I. Bushnell Jr., and Mr. W. C. Farabee to make an exploration of an important site in Missouri"—the Kimmswick salt works—funded jointly by a gift from Clarence Moore to the Peabody Museum and the funds given by Phoebe Hearst to the Department of Anthropology at Berkeley. For 1903 Putnam (1903:295) reported that "Mr. Bushnell, who has joined our corps of workers, has for several years been engaged in explorations in Missouri as well as farther north." In addition, Bushnell had just made an accurate model of the Cahokia mounds and given the museum collections of artifacts he had made from Cahokia and elsewhere in Illinois, Missouri, and Arkansas. In 1904–5 Bushnell went to Italy on Peabody money to study American Indian collections there (Putnam 1906:302). He stayed in Europe until 1907, visiting museums and excavations in France, Switzerland, and elsewhere.

Bushnell then returned to Charlottesville, Virginia, where he began work at the BAE on the *Handbook of American Indians* for Frederick Hodge. Bushnell apparently conducted the basic research for many of the articles, although only one of them bears his initials (Swanton 1942:104). In 1911 Bushnell began working on the book's proposed sequel, the *Handbook of North American Antiquities East of the Rocky Mountains*. He spent much of his time until 1920 working on this volume, although it was never published.

Bushnell conducted some fieldwork in 1914 at Cape Fear, North Carolina, and in 1917–18 in Louisiana. In 1921 he flew out of Scott Field (now Scott Air Force Base), near Belleville, Illinois, to take some of the first known aerial photographs of Cahokia (Swanton 1942:105). He continued working for the BAE until his death, doing work at mounds in Florida in 1925 and spending a good deal of time in the late 1920s and throughout the 1930s doing archaeology in the James and Rappahannock Valleys in Virginia. He remains a relatively unknown scholar.

Howard Barrett Wilson (1881–1903) was born in Connecticut and was a member of the Harvard class of 1903. He graduated with honors in anthropology and was supported by the Winthrop Scholarship from 1901 to 1903 (Putnam 1904:286). After being accepted into the graduate program in anthropology, Wilson went for the summer with Dixon, Kroeber, and Boas on the Huntington Expedition of the AMNH to do linguistic work among the Winton and Yana tribes. He collected some texts and myths, but after 10 days of fieldwork he was stricken with typhoid malaria and died within two weeks, on August 4 (Dixon 1903a, 103b; Jacknis 2002:530 n. 21). As we have seen before, being an anthropologist in the field carried risks. It was not infrequent in the 1890s and early 1900s that students went into the field and did not return.

Vilhjalmar Stefansson (1879–1962) was born in Arnes, Manitoba, of Icelandic descent. He became a well-known popularizer and lecturer on the ethnographic peoples of the Arctic, writing 26 books and several hundred articles (Sullivan 1963:287). Because of a flood loss, his family emigrated from Canada to North Dakota when he was an infant. His parents anglicized his name to William Stephenson, but when he was a junior at the University of North Dakota, he changed his name back to its original Icelandic spelling (Lonergan 1991d:666). That junior year was one of turbulence for Stefansson; he cut classes to take a job as a school principal, and he served as a ringleader of a campus student protest movement. Officially he was suspended for cutting class, but unofficially he was expelled because of his political activities (Hunt 1986:11; Lonergan 1991d:666). He transferred to the University of Iowa, where he finished his senior year in 1903.

The Harvard Divinity School offered Stefansson a graduate scholarship sponsored by the Unitarian Church, so his initial graduate work was in religion, not anthropology. During his first year at Harvard, however, his interest in anthropology was such that Putnam offered him a fellowship in anthropology, and Stefansson transferred to studies at the Peabody (Hunt 1986:13). In the fall of 1905 Putnam appointed him a teaching fellow in anthropology. He was supported by the Hemenway Fellowship for 1904 to 1906 and was appointed to the graduate teaching position, "Assistant in Anthropology," from 1905 to 1907.

Apparently, Stefansson was a dynamic instructor, for both Gordon Willey (1967:295) and Douglas Givens (1992:9) have credited him with helping to get A.V. Kidder interested in archaeology during Kidder's sophomore year, in 1906. Stefansson, as assistant in anthropology, was serving as teaching assistant in Farabee's Anthropology 1, General Anthropology, and Dixon's Anthropology 5, American Archaeology and Ethnology, that year, courses that Kidder took.

During the summers of 1904 and 1905 Stefansson conducted ethnographic studies in Iceland. For the 1905 season, he and Farabee, supported by Henry C. Warren Fund money and donations from Clarence Moore, took George Howe, John Hastings, and Louis de Milhau with them to Iceland, where they explored old Icelandic burial places. In this setting the three undergraduate students became interested in archaeology and somatology (Putnam 1906:302).

In 1906 Ejnar Mikkelsen, a young Danish naval adventurer, and his American partner, geologist Ernest de Koven Leffingwell, who were veterans of the 1902–4 Ziegler-Baldwin North Pole Expedition, began organizing their own Anglo-American Polar Expedition. One financial backer insisted that a qualified ethnologist accompany the group to study any natives who might be met. Mikkelsen and Leffingwell contacted Putnam, and he recommended Stefansson. He was granted a leave of absence in April 1906 to accompany the Anglo-American Expedition to the Arctic, which ended his graduate studies at the Peabody (Putnam 1907:295, 1908:300).

Because the expedition could not pay all of Stefansson's travel costs, Putnam arranged for him to go overland with funds from the Peabody Museum and the University of Toronto, in order for him study Mackenzie River Indians and collect artifacts for the Peabody and the Royal Ontario Museum (Hunt 1986:18). Stefansson left in April 1906 and joined up with the Anglo-American Expedition a year later.

Stefansson did not return to finish his degree at Harvard but continued to work in Greenland and Ellesmere Island from 1908 to 1912. From 1913 to 1918 he lived north of the Arctic Circle for more than five years. He finally received his A.M. from Harvard in 1923, and from 1928 through 1932 he was listed as an official "Associate in Anthropology" at the Peabody Museum (Harvard University 1937:418). In this position he assisted some of the graduate students in their research. For example, in 1928–29, Carl Seltzer and Martin Luther conducted a physical anthropology project on the Inuit, with aid from Stefansson (Reynolds 1930:274).

Stefansson stayed in contact with many of the people he had met at the Peabody over the years. After Herbert Spinden retired from fieldwork in the Maya area, he and Stefansson shared an apartment in New York for many years (Lonergan 1991d:667). Stefansson's interest in the Arctic took him into Canadian, Scandinavian, and Russian territorial areas, which led to his being hauled in front of the U.S. House Un-American Activities Committee (HUAC) in 1949 as a suspected communist. In the early 1950s Stefansson moved to Dartmouth and became good friends with Owen Lattimore, another Harvard graduate student, whom we discuss in chapter 12. In 1955, because Senator Joseph McCarthy had called Lattimore the Soviet Union's chief spy in the United States, Stefansson was again called before HUAC (Hunt 1986:262). He died in 1962 after making many contributions to the Peabody Museum.

David Hutton Webster (1875–1955) seems to have received some of his training at Harvard from Roland Dixon, although he received his Harvard Ph.D. in economics. Webster was born in Malone, New York, and earned both his A.B., in 1896, and his A.M., in 1897, from Stanford University. He entered the Harvard graduate program in economics in 1902, received a second A.M. at the end of that academic year, and was awarded a Ph.D. in economics in 1904. His dissertation title, "Primitive Social Control: A Study of Initiation Ceremonies and Secret Societies," appears much more anthropologically than economically oriented. Webster taught at Williams College from 1904 to 1907 and then was hired as a professor of social anthropology at the University of

Nebraska from 1907 to 1932. He left Nebraska to go to Stanford, where he again taught anthropology until he retired in 1940. During his career, he focused his research and writing on ethnology and folklore (Herskovits and Ames 1950:193).

Hiram Bingham Jr. (1875–1956) was born in Honolulu, the son of a missionary. He received his A.B. from Yale in 1898. His father wanted him to go into a seminary, but Bingham decided on sociology and enrolled in the Department of History, Sociology, and Political Economy at the University of California–Berkeley in 1899. There, the head of the department, Bernard Moses, brought him to the attention of Benjamin Ide Wheeler, a classical archaeologist as well as president of the university (A. Bingham 1989:49–53). In the spring of 1900, when Wheeler went to attend a conference in Washington, D.C., he put Bingham in charge of his class on ancient Greek institutions, on Moses's recommendation (W. Bingham 1989:32).

After receiving his A.M. from Berkeley in 1900, Bingham enrolled at Harvard. While an undergraduate at Yale, he had met Alfreda Mitchell, whose father also was a missionary. The two were married in 1900, and money from Alfreda's mother, a Tiffany heiress, became available to Bingham (A. Bingham 1989:44, 57). The Mitchells paid all his and Alfreda's living costs while he was at Harvard (A. Bingham 1989:63).

Bingham focused his graduate work on Latin American history, receiving his A.M. in that field in 1901 and his Ph.D., with the dissertation "The Scots Darien Company," in 1905. While at Harvard, Bingham's principal concern was with books on the history of South America. He made several suggestions for purchases of books, and his interest led to his being named curator of South American history and literature for the library, a position he held from 1905 to 1915 (Harvard University 1937:122). He used this curator title during his first expedition to South America in 1906–7, after his interest had begun to shift toward prehistory, because one of its ostensible objectives was to buy books for the Harvard Widener Library (A. Bingham 1989:60).

After receiving his Ph.D., Bingham was awarded a three-year contract to teach as a preceptor at Princeton, but he fell ill the first year, took sick leave, and never taught the remaining two years (A. Bingham 1989:70). While recovering, he decided to get more information from South America in order to turn his Ph.D. into a book, and he spent most of the remainder of that first year planning a trip to Venezuela and Colombia—the beginning of a series of trips to South America over the next decade. In 1909 an old Harvard acquaintance with anthropological interests, Clarence Hay, joined Bingham as a companion in his travels to the Andes (A. Bingham 1989:92). While still under contract to Princeton, Bingham accepted an appointment as university lecturer in history at Yale in June 1907.

During his third trip to South America, in 1911, Bingham relocated the old Inca citadel of Machu Picchu, a site for which he has since become famous. His succeeding 1912 expedition ran into an inter-institutional political problem. The Peruvian government, in 1908, had granted the Peabody Museum's William C. Farabee a concession to work in the Urubamba Valley. The Peabody personnel viewed Bingham as an interloper and had Harvard president A. Lawrence Lowell issue a formal protest to Lima. Bingham was actually in Peru at that point, and he talked the new Peruvian president into ignoring the concession given to Harvard and granting Bingham a special permit for Machu Picchu (A. Bingham 1989:286). He continued his work at the site until 1915. In 1914 the work there was substantially subsidized by a young Harvard undergraduate, Philip A. Means, who later helped Bingham write up the final report on Machu Picchu, as we discuss elsewhere in this chapter.

The year 1915 was both an up and a down year for Bingham. He was finally promoted to full professor in the Yale graduate school, but authorities in Cuzco accused him of smuggling gold artifacts out of Machu Picchu. He fled for home with a lawsuit pending (W. Bingham 1989:172). Nevertheless, he was recognized as an archaeological authority. When the trustees of Phillips Academy, Andover, wanted to set up an archaeological field station in the U.S. Southwest, they asked the advice of Dixon at Harvard and Bingham at Yale about candidates to fill the position. A.V. Kidder of Harvard was the nominee (Givens 1992:38–39).

Bingham continued to be listed as a member of the Yale graduate school until 1924–25, but his last teaching took place in the fall term of 1916–17. During World War I he served as an aviator, heading an allied flying school in France. He became lieutenant governor of Connecticut in 1922, serving in that position until 1924, when he was elected governor. When one of Connecticut's U.S. senators died, he then named himself to replace the senator (A. Bingham 1989:328) and served in the U.S. Senate from 1925 to 1932.

Irwin Hayden (1881–1969) was born in Winthrop, Massachusetts, and did his undergraduate work at the Bussey Institute of Harvard University, receiving a B.S. in agricultural science in 1905. For his last two years at Bussey he was student assistant to Professor Elisha Wilson Morse (Steve Hayden, personal communication, 2003). Hayden then applied to the Peabody Museum for graduate work in anthropology. He was funded for 1905–7 by the Winthrop Scholarship and for 1907–8 by the Hemenway Fellowship, and he received his anthropology A.M. in 1908.

Putnam sent Hayden to work with Mark Harrington in the Mohawk Valley on New York Iroquois sites in the summer of 1906, and the following summer Hayden worked with Raymond Merwin at Madisonville, Ohio (Putnam 1906:301, 1908:300). Hayden apparently had high hopes for a position at the Peabody Museum after receiving his A.M. In a note to his son, Julian Hayden, on his fiftieth birthday, Irwin Hayden indicated that "in 1909 Professor Putnam told me that upon his retirement, he had planned that I should undertake to carry on with his work" (Steve Hayden, personal communication, 2003).

When the hoped-for job did not transpire, Hayden quit anthropology for nearly two decades. He left Harvard to take a job in Hamilton, Montana, and stayed in that area for some time. His son, **Julian Dodge Hayden** (1911–98), was born in Missoula, Montana, in 1911, but the family soon moved to Riverside, California. After many years, Irwin Hayden returned to archaeology. In 1928 his old Harvard friend Mark Harrington became curator of the Southwest Museum in Los Angeles. When Harrington began a survey of the Moapa Valley, in southern Nevada, in 1929, he contacted Hayden, offering him the job of conducting excavations at Mesa House. Hayden accepted and brought his son Julian along (Steve Hayden, personal communication, 2003).

After finishing at Mesa House, Irwin and Julian worked at Casa Grande, Arizona, and the nearby Grewe site, where Irwin was foreman for Arthur Woodard. In 1930, father and son worked for the "Van Bergen–Los Angeles Museum Field Expeditions" in Cornfield Canyon near Navajo Mountain. That fall they went to work for Harold Colton, of the Museum of Northern Arizona, at Keet Seel, Arizona. From 1933 to 1935 Irwin Hayden took charge of the work at Keet Seel and Turkey Cave, working for the Museum of Northern Arizona on a project funded through the Civil Works Administration. He also worked on Harold Gladwin's Gila Pueblo project and then at Snaketown, Arizona, with Emil Haury. Hayden got into a brouhaha with Lyndon Hargrave of the Rainbow Bridge–Monument Valley Expedition, alleging that Hargrave was conducting a "sophomoric sawing spree" at Keet Seel to get dendrochronological samples, and quit the project. Julian Hayden replaced his father at Keet Seel as excavation director (Hayden 1934; Steve Hayden, personal communication, 2003).

Irwin Hayden then tried to establish a weekly archaeological journal for the Southwest from his home in Riverside. He had a little journalism experience, having written columns for the *Arizona Republican* and the *Coolidge Examiner* in 1930 on the excavation work at Casa Grande. Individual issues of his weekly cost him 5 cents to put out, and he set the subscription cost per issue at 10 cents. Just before he quit publishing because of lack of funds in 1936, the weekly had slightly more than 200 subscribers. Hayden subsequently wrote a column as a "political commentator" for the *Riverside News* for many years. His son, Julian, for many years ran a weekly advertising paragraph in the *Tucson Citizen*, which he also used for social commentary, no doubt having gotten the idea from his father. Irwin Hayden died at Riverside in January 1969 (Steve Hayden, personal communication, 2003).

John Walter Hastings (1883–1908) and Louis J. de G. de Milhau were an interesting pair of Harvard undergraduates. Their interjection into the Peabody research program was in some ways typical of the kinds of events that took place in the 1890s and early 1900s but would be unusual today. Both young men were apparently interested in ethnology and somatology. Hastings had been recruited by Farabee as a Harvard undergraduate to work on the Peabody Museum's expedition to the Southwest in 1904. He received his A.B. in 1905 and entered the graduate program. In the summer of 1905, he and de Milhau were members of the party of students that Farabee took to Iceland. The anthropometric measurements Hastings made of Icelandic people became the basis of his 1906 A.M. thesis (Anonymous 1906a:477; Putnam 1906:302). Hastings and de Milhau also collected 30 bird species for the MCZ during this expedition (*Annual Report of the Museum of Comparative Zoology for 1906*, 1907:264).

Hastings and de Milhau then dreamed up the idea of an expedition to South America and sold the concept to Putnam. They saw to it that their professor, Farabee, became director, and they themselves enlisted as members for the first year of the 1906–1909 Peabody Museum South American expedition. Hastings resigned his position as the expedition's ethnologist after the first six-month season in the field, to turn to literary work. He had paid his own salary costs, anonymously, for the time he was on the expedition, for a total donation of $700 (Putnam 1909:297). When he died only a year later, Putnam wrote (1909:298–99):

> It is my painful duty to record the death on April 26 of Mr. John Walter Hastings, Harvard 1905, who took a great interest in the South American Expedition and accompanied it as one of the ethnologists in the first year. It was Mr. Hastings who was the anonymous contributor towards the salary of a member of the Expedition. He and Mr. de Milhau also paid their own traveling expenses. After his return to this country, Mr. Hastings established himself in New York, where he was engaged in literary work, including the preparation of magazine articles on his South American trip, several of which were accepted for publication and will soon appear. It was his intention to elaborate these articles to be published in book form. . . . While on the Peabody Museum Expedition to Iceland in 1905, he not only made anthropological observations and collections for the Peabody Museum, but he also, in connection with Mr. de Milhau, who was a member of the Expedition, arranged for a complete series of the birds of Iceland to be sent as their joint gift to the Zoological Museum of the University.

Louis John de Grenon de Milhau (1884–1967) received his A.B. in 1906 and was apparently the more affluent member of the pair. He gave $15,000 ($5,000 a year), nearly the entire funding, for the Peabody Museum South American Expedition of 1906–9 (Putnam 1909:297). Besides serving as a project ethnologist, de Milhau "devised a cephalometer which allowed one to take measurements from the center of the auricular passage to any desired position on the head or face," which was used to good advantage in the Peruvian fieldwork (MacCurdy 1912:674).

Like Hastings, de Milhau resigned after the first season of the expedition, in his case because he had contracted malaria (de Milhau 1931). Rather than continuing in graduate school, de Milhau was made a member of the Peabody Museum Visiting Committee, serving from 1907 to 1921, and later acted as its chair (Anonymous 1912a:672; Brew 1966b:4). He entered law school at New York University in 1909, received his LL.B. there in 1911, and went on to a career in law.

Louis de Milhau kept his ties to Harvard active, also serving as a member of the visiting committee for the MCZ, to which in 1910 he donated additional bird specimens from Iceland. When Farabee finished his analyses for the 1906–9 expedition to Peru, de Milhau provided $2,500 for publication costs in 1922 and wrote the introduction to the

Peabody Museum volume *Indian Tribes of Eastern Peru*. Charles Willoughby recognized de Milhau's contributions by referring to the expedition as the "De Milhau–Peabody Expedition to Peru" (Willoughby 1923a:219).

Thomas Barbour (1884–1946), the son of a well-to-do New England textile businessman, grew up in New York City (Shor 1998:144) and was a member of the Harvard class of 1906. Like his classmates John Hastings and Louis de Milhau, Barbour used his interest in natural history and his deep pockets to help the Peabody Museum and the MCZ. He began making collecting trips for specimens in 1903 and 1904, with trips to Bermuda and the Bahamas. On his honeymoon in 1906 he went to India, Burma, China, Japan, and the East Indies, focusing especially on Dutch New Guinea. When he returned, he donated a major collection of ethnographic materials from there to the Peabody, the largest collection the museum received that year (Putnam 1908:295). He also used his honeymoon fieldwork for graduate requirements at Harvard, initially as part of his 1908 A.M. and then as the basis of his 1911 Ph.D. dissertation, "A Contribution to the Zoogeography of the East Indian Islands."

Shortly before completing his dissertation, Barbour made another long collecting trip, to the Caribbean, Peru, and Bolivia, and brought back additional anthropological specimens for the Peabody from Cuba, Peru, and Lake Titicaca (Putnam 1910:273). By this time Barbour was a strong supporter of the museum, serving in the capacity of trustee and thus as a member of the Faculty of the Museum (Haskins 1912:95). He had also begun to work with Samuel Garman, the associate curator of amphibians, reptiles, and fishes at the MCZ, who was a friend of Putnam's and the Peabody's (Romer 1964:228).

Although Barbour continued to devote the majority of his time to the MCZ, he maintained a lifelong interest in the Peabody and its students. Putnam (1915:237), reporting on the progress of construction on the final wing of the museum in the annual report for 1913–14, noted that "Dr. Barbour and Mr. Burke [Walter Safford Burke, Harvard's inspector of grounds and buildings] of the building committee deserve great credit for the way in which the plans of the new part of the building have been carried out. Willoughby is designing and superintending many of the details."

The respect and admiration that Putnam and Barbour had for each other is perhaps clearest in events two years later, when the pallbearers at Putnam's funeral were his former students and Peabody museum staff members Willoughby, Tozzer, Dixon, Spinden, and Bates—whom we might expect to have been involved—and Thomas Barbour, a surprise to those who do not know about his previous involvement with Putnam.

During World War I, as we describe later in this chapter, Barbour and several archaeologists from the Peabody served as "spies" for U.S. military intelligence in the Caribbean and Central America. Barbour worked in Cuba at the time, where he had earlier collected for the Peabody and the MCZ (Romer 1964:232).

While Barbour was collecting specimens in Florida for the MCZ in 1920, he also made a large collection of Seminole Indian artifacts for the Peabody (Willoughby

1921:243). Barbour went on to reinstitute graduate teaching at the MCZ, which had been stopped for lack of funding after Alexander Agassiz died in 1910. In 1927 Barbour became director of the MCZ. He also helped establish what is now the Smithsonian Tropical Institute in Panama. When the Peabody began running short of space in the 1930s, Barbour provided nearly 4,500 feet of space in the MCZ for the Peabody collections (Scott 1933:297). Barbour's closeness to the Peabody is also indicated by the marriage of Alfred Kidder II, son of A.V. Kidder, to Mary Bigelow Barbour (1914–78), Thomas Barbour's daughter, in 1934. Barbour was still well known and much appreciated at the Peabody Museum when Stephen Williams arrived there just eight years after his death.

Herbert Joseph Spinden (1879–1967) was born in Huron, South Dakota. He worked for the railroad in Montana, Idaho, and Washington and then went to Alaska during one of the gold rushes (*National Cyclopedia* 1938). It was only after this experience that he enrolled in Harvard as an undergraduate in 1902, at the age of 23. He obtained his A.B. in 1906 and went on to get his A.M. in 1908 and his Ph.D. in 1909, all in anthropology.

Spinden took Tozzer's course Anthropology 9, on Mexican archaeology, in its first year, 1905. He was then the teaching fellow in Anthropology 1 for the first three years Tozzer taught it. Spinden got interested in anthropology, however, from taking Anthropology 5, on North American Indians. He and his friend George Will took the course with Dixon in 1904, not because of the content, at first, but "mostly because we needed free afternoons for canoeing up the Charles." They soon got hooked by Dixon's enthusiasm (Spinden 1957:387).

In the summer of 1905, Spinden was one of four undergraduates whom Dixon recruited to go out to an excavation at a site called Double Ditch, in the Mandan area of North Dakota, near Bismarck. It was on this dig that he and George Will conducted what has been called the first modern, systematic excavation of a Plains Indian village site (McLaughlin 1998:21). Spinden and Will subsequently collaborated on field surveys and excavations in North Dakota in 1911 and 1919. Spinden also assisted Will with the illustrations and analyses of the sites and artifacts for Will's 1924 "Archaeology of the Missouri Valley" (Picha 2002; Will 1924b:291–92).

When Spinden entered graduate school, he was initially appointed Hemenway Fellow and assistant in anthropology for 1906–7, but the situation changed, and he was appointed the Austin Teaching Fellow instead (Putnam 1907:295). He held the Austin Teaching Fellowship for two years, during which he helped Dixon in teaching Anthropology 5 as part of his duties.

In the summer of 1907, Spinden and Richard R. Hellman, a colleague from the 1905 North Dakota excavations, made an expedition to the Nez Perce country to conduct linguistic, general ethnological, and archaeological research under Dixon's guidance. Hellman became sick and was unable to complete his work, but Spinden was successful (Putnam 1908:300). Consequently, the next summer he was sent back to continue archaeological and ethnological research among the Nez Perce and other Sahaptin tribes, this time under the auspices of the AMNH (Putnam 1909:300). As with so many of the early Peabody Museum students, Spinden's was a broad approach to anthropology.

A list of officers from the annual meeting of the American Folk-Lore Society in 1908 shows Spinden as a member of the nominating committee. The other names show how thoroughly Peabody Museum anthropologists and archaeologists dominated that society at the time. On the nominating committee with Spinden were Tozzer and another Peabody archaeology student, Robert Fuller. Dixon was president; Edward Putnam, second vice president; and Tozzer, permanent secretary. The first vice president, H. M. Belden, of the University of Missouri, and the treasurer, Eliot W. Remick, from Boston, had no direct Peabody linkages, but Remick had been a member of the Harvard class of 1899 (Anonymous 1908:75).

Although Spinden's fieldwork had been on peoples of the northern Great Plains and the Columbia Plateau, his dissertation took off in another direction. He had become interested in the Mayas through Tozzer's course and wrote his dissertation on of their art (Spinden 1957:387). He defended his 1909 dissertation, "Maya Art," before a committee composed of Putnam, Tozzer, Dixon, Chase, Toy, Goodale, and Denman Waldo Ross, a lecturer in the theory of design. That summer he taught one of the first anthropology summer school courses at Harvard, the Anthropology 1, General Anthropology, course (Putnam 1910:276). The published version of Spinden's dissertation was awarded the prize from the Angrand Foundation of the Bibliothèque Nationale of Paris for the best work in American anthropology for 1913–18 (Willoughby 1919:241).

It was during his Ph.D. work, which was subsidized by Bowditch, that Spinden began to study a possible correlation between the Maya calendrical system and the modern Western calendrical system. He reported his first correlation, later known as the Spinden-Morley correlation, at the 1909 AIA meetings. He apparently failed to credit Bowditch for his financial support and for the years of work Bowditch had devoted to this problem—work that Spinden had used. Robert Brunhouse (1971:160) speculated that Bowditch's having been a member of the Peabody "museum faculty" at the time might have been an unacknowledged reason for Spinden's soon leaving the Peabody for the AMNH. We think Brunhouse's idea seems unlikely.

In any case, Spinden left the employ of Harvard for a dozen years, joined the American Museum of Natural History, which had supported his 1908 fieldwork, and remained a curator there from 1909 to 1921. During World War I, Spinden, along with Peabody Museum colleagues Sylvanus Morley and Samuel Lothrop, was recruited to serve as an agent for the Office of Naval Intelligence (ONI), assisting with naval coast defense in Central America—something we discuss at length later in this chapter. In 1920–21 he returned to Harvard, where he was named an associate in anthropology of the Peabody Museum, and led the Peabody Museum Expedition to Middle America (Willoughby 1922:274). He was then named curator of Mexican archaeology at the Peabody from 1921 to 1926 and an instructor in anthropology at Harvard for the 1922–23 academic year. After 1923 he spent the bulk of his time in the field. He worked with Tozzer at Chichen Itza in 1923–24, was listed as in the field "most of the year" for 1924–25, and was absent for most of 1925–26 on the Spinden-Mason Archaeological Expedition to Middle America (Willoughby 1924:259, 1925:261, 1927:263).

Spinden took a research position as curator of the Buffalo Museum from 1926 to 1929 and then a similar position with the Brooklyn Museum from 1929 to 1951 (Lonergan 1991c:659). He served as president of the AAA in 1936–37. After his retirement, he continued to work on Maya issues. He occasionally sent documentary materials to the Peabody Museum collections, until his death in 1967. After his death, additional materials were sent to the Peabody and were dealt with while Stephen Williams was director there.

George Francis Will (1884–1955), born in Bismarck, North Dakota, was another member of the Harvard class of 1906. He had taken Dixon's Anthropology 5 in 1904 along with Spinden, and in the summer of 1905, under Dixon's guidance, he went out to work on the Mandan Indian site of Double Ditch with Spinden, Robert Hellman, and Harold Nye. The crew employed the Peabody Museum method of excavating, which was soon to sweep the Midwest (Browman 2002b). Dixon set up the project and then set the four undergraduates loose until he came back at the end of the season to check on them. Will and Spinden returned to Harvard with some exciting stories of their project. Sylvanus Morley reported that two of his favorite speakers in the Harvard Anthropological Society the next year were Will and Spinden reporting on their Mandan work (Brunhouse 1971:31).

Will majored in archaeology and ethnology at Harvard, besides taking a generous amount of botany. Upon graduation he went back to Bismarck to work in the seed business—the oldest seed firm in North Dakota—owned by his father, Oscar H. Will. Will knew Arikara, Hidatsa, and Mandan people from their visits to his father's seed store. From the beginning, Oscar Will had collected Indian corn from local tribes, as well as local seed varieties. Oscar, and subsequently George Will, found the Indian races of maize to be characterized by extreme earliness, hardiness, and drought resistance. George developed them into a series of now classic races of maize, which the two sold (McLaughlin 1998:20; Walster 1956:6–10). In 1917 George Will took over the family business, heading the firm for the next 38 years, until his death (Wedel 1956:74). George Will expanded the company's interest in native cultigens and agricultural practices, collecting information, seeds, and objects directly from Indian people and from other anthropologists (McLaughlin 1998:21).

Will went with Spinden, Hellman, and Dixon on a five-week camping trip in the Olympic Mountains of Washington in the summer of 1906 (Will 1916). In the summer of 1911 he spent a month with his friend Spinden, then of the AMNH, along the Missouri River in the Dakotas doing site surveys. Later, in the fall of 1919, the two spent 10 days there, continuing to survey sites. Spinden helped Will prepare his fieldwork reports by making all the site maps, contributing to the artifact analysis, and doing much of the writing, although he insisted that Will take credit (Will 1924b:291–92).

Will had been bitten by the archaeology bug, and as the list of his publications in the bibliography shows, he began to get involved in the archaeology of the Mandan and Arikara as well as in their agriculture. One of the major problems he had in his work was dating the sites, so when dendrochronology proved useful in the Southwest, he started trying to employ it on the northern plains (Will 1949, 1950a). He began this work in 1946, and by the time of his death in 1955 he had developed a 534-year master tree-ring sequence (McLaughlin 1998:12).

Robert Richard Hellman (1883–1911), Harvard A.B. 1906, was a good friend of Will's and one of the three students of Dixon's who participated in the Mandan excavation near Bismarck and continued an interest in archaeology. (The fourth crew member, Harold Allen Nye, Harvard A.B. 1906, did not continue in anthropology.) According to Nye and Spinden, Will was the excavation boss and identified the roots and seeds, and Hellman, who was bound for medical school, identified the bones (Walster 1956:5). Farabee later reviewed and verified the animal and human bone identifications (2002). The results of this work were published in the Peabody Museum Papers series in 1906 (Will and Spinden 1906).

Hellman and Spinden went with Dixon the next summer to the Nez Perce area to conduct linguistic, ethnological, and archaeological research. Hellman became disabled by sickness, but he recovered at the end of the season and joined Will, Spinden, and Dixon on the camping trip mentioned earlier. Hellman went on to get his M.D. from Harvard in 1910, but the following year he died from septicemia at Massachusetts General Hospital.

Herbert Eustis Winlock (1884–1950) was a member of the Harvard class of 1906. With his good friend and classmate Oric Bates, Winlock wrote a joint senior thesis on the artifact collections of Arlo Bates, Oric's father, from Maine (Bates and Winlock 1912). Winlock, whose father was a secretary of the Smithsonian Institution, majored in archaeology and anthropology at Harvard and joined the Metropolitan Museum of Art when he graduated in 1906. He conducted a series of excavations in Egypt and became the director of the Metropolitan Museum in 1932. Although he clearly followed up on his archaeological background, his trajectory takes him outside of our Americanist focus.

Two Merwin brothers received training at the Peabody: **Raymond Edwin Merwin** (1881–1928) and **Bruce Welch Merwin** (1889–1983). They had grown up in Iola, Kansas, and attended the University of Kansas, where Raymond received his A.B. in 1902 and an A.M. in 1904, and where Bruce later took training in the 1920s. In terms of Peabody Museum history, Raymond is the more important of the two.

Raymond Merwin entered Harvard in 1906. He was supported by the Hemenway Fellowship in 1907–8, the Winthrop Scholarship in 1908–9, and an appointment as associate in Central American research in 1910–11. In 1907–8 he went to work at Madisonville, where he was assisted by Irwin Hayden. Merwin was enthused by the results and initially planned to conduct his Ph.D. research there in 1908–9 (Putnam

1908:300–301). He did return to work on the Ferris Cemetery at Madisonville during the summer of 1908, supported by the Henry C. Warren Fund, but in the summer of 1909 he worked with Volk at Trenton (Putnam 1909:299, 1910:271).

By then, Tozzer had succeeded in getting the Peabody's permit for work in Guatemala renewed—it had lapsed in 1901. The Peabody had expected to contract with Teobert Maler, who had done fieldwork in the Maya area for the Peabody Museum since the 1890s, to conduct its Guatemalan research. But with Maler's sudden resignation, Tozzer had to take an academic leave of absence to become director of the 1910 expedition. He took Merwin with him as his assistant to work on the Maya ruins of Tikal, Nakum, and Holmul (Lothrop 1955:615; Putnam 1910:272, 1911:221).

The next year Raymond Merwin was appointed Fellow in Central American Archaeology and directed work at Holmul, supported by funds provided by Bowditch (Putnam 1911:221, 1912:219; Tozzer 1921:354). He defended his Ph.D. dissertation, "The Ruins of the Southern Part of the Peninsula of Yucatán, with Special Reference to Their Place in the Maya Area," in front of a committee composed of Tozzer, Chase, and Charles Rockwell Lanman, a Harvard Sanskrit professor, in 1913.

After receiving his Ph.D., Merwin continued to be employed by the Peabody Museum. With Tozzer in Mexico City in 1913–14 holding the rotating directorship of the International School of American Archaeology and Ethnology, Merwin served as field director for the Central American Expedition that season, working with Clarence L. Hay as his chief assistant and with Carl W. Bishop, the newly appointed Fellow in Central American Archaeology (Putnam 1913:214, 1914:222). In 1914–15 Merwin was again in charge of the Central American Expedition (Dixon 1916b:257). He left the museum after that year, apparently because of World War I military obligations. The work from the 1913 season at Holmul was written up two decades later by George Vaillant (Merwin and Vaillant 1932); the work from the 1914 season in Quintana Roo was transcribed by Jens Yde (Yde 1938) but is still not in published form.

Raymond's brother, Bruce Merwin, was at the Peabody Museum for a much shorter period. In the summer of 1912 he worked on the Ferris Cemetery at Madisonville, Ohio, in a sense taking over the project from Raymond, who had worked there three years earlier (Putnam 1912:222). In the summer of 1913 Bruce Merwin worked on Peabody Museum excavations at sites along the Obion River in Henry County, Tennessee (see Baldwin 1967). He used these excavations to train Carl Bishop, before Bishop went south to join Raymond Merwin in Guatemala (Anonymous 1914:369; Putnam 1914:223). Bruce Merwin did not stay at the Peabody after that year.

In 1915 he took a job at the University Museum in Philadelphia, working with ethnographic materials (see Merwin 1915 to 1919). In 1918 he served as acting secretary of the AAA, replacing first Neil Judd and then William Farabee after each in turn was called to serve in the intelligence corps (Merwin 1919b:104). Merwin left the University Museum after 1919 and went back to the University of Kansas to work on a degree in education during the early 1920s. He obtained his A.M. there in 1924—his thesis was titled

"A Study in Curriculum Building Centered about a Social Science Course Based on the American Indian"—and his Ph.D. in 1929. He then secured a job at Southern Illinois University at Carbondale, where he taught during the 1930s and 1940s, even serving a stint as acting president in 1944. Bruce Merwin continued his interest in archaeology, however, and wrote occasional publications on archaeological research as well as the place of archaeology in the educational curriculum (Merwin 1933, 1935, 1937), until his death in 1983.

Sylvanus Griswold Morley (1883–1948) was an important Maya archaeologist. The search for his early roots is complicated by the fact that one of his older cousins changed his name to Sylvanus Griswold Morley as well and attended Harvard at the same time (Harvard University 1937:667). The non-archaeologist cousin was born in Baldwinville, Massachusetts, as Sylvanus Griswold Small (1878–1970), and as a child he was called Griswold Small (T. Morley 1997, pt. 1, p. 1). In his autobiographical notes, he wrote that in 1898 his father legally changed the family name in order to relieve his sons of the cheap puns made on the name "Small" (T. Morley 1997, pt. 2, p. 4). Thus, although he graduated from Tufts with an A.B. in 1898 as "Small," he entered Harvard with a new name, Sylvanus Griswold Morley. He later wrote, "The person with the most right to complain was my cousin Sylvanus Griswold Morley, the celebrated archaeologist. The move made us homonyms, and gave rise to endless confusion. . . . Sylvanus, a most good-natured soul, never protested. He was an undergraduate at Harvard while I was in Grad. School. I sometimes received his Univ. bills, and less often billets doux from his lights of love" (T. Morley 1997, pt. 2, p. 4).

This "second" Morley (formerly "Small") received an A.M from Harvard in 1899 and a Ph.D. in philology in 1902. After teaching Spanish in the Department of Romance Languages at Harvard from 1901 to 1906, he taught briefly at the University of Colorado and the University of New Mexico and then, for most of his academic career, taught Spanish literature at the University of California–Berkeley (T. Morley 1997).

The archaeologist Sylvanus Griswold Morley (1883–1948) was born in Chester, Pennsylvania, where his father was a graduate of Pennsylvania Military Academy and later a professor of chemistry and a vice president of that school. His mother was a language teacher there (Brunhouse 1971:14; J. E. S. Thompson 1949:293). When Morley was 10 the family moved to Buena Vista, Colorado, where he "developed a deep interest in archaeology, although it was Egypt that drew him" (J. E. S. Thompson 1949:293). In 1898 a family friend put Morley in touch with Frederic Putnam. By the time Morley had completed high school, he was devoted to archaeology and wanted to make it his career. His father, however, was concerned that there were no jobs in the field and sent him to Pennsylvania Military Academy to become an engineer (Brunhouse 1971:14). The elder Morley died in 1903, so when Morley graduated with his civil engineering degree in 1904, he again looked at archaeology and entered Harvard.

Morley enrolled at Harvard to study Egyptian hieroglyphics under Albert Lythgoe, but he found Lythgoe's course unchallenging and soon shifted to Maya hieroglyphs (Brunhouse 1971:27). (A.V. Kidder [1948:267] thought Morley came to study hieroglyphs under George Reisner, but Reisner did not join the Harvard faculty until a year later.) Morley took four courses with Roland Dixon and did some of his earliest work on Maya culture with Dixon in December 1904 (Brunhouse 1971:28). But it was Tozzer and Putnam who really turned him on to the Mayas. Kidder, in his unpublished 1957 "Reminiscences" (quoted in Givens 1992:133), wrote:

> When he arrived in Cambridge he consulted Professor Putnam, then head of the Department of Anthropology, who, always anxious to stimulate research in the New World, and finding that hieroglyphs were Morley's principal concern told him that the Egyptian systems were well understood and that great progress had been made on cuneiform, but that the meaning of the Maya glyphs of Mexico and Central America was almost entirely unknown. Then and there was recruited the most ardent of all students of the Maya. He elected Tozzer's inspiring Anthropology 9, ending at midyear, and his keenness was so evident that Tozzer advised him to spend the remaining winter months of 1907 in Yucatán. He did, and it drove from his head all thought of becoming anything but a Mayanist.

Money became available in the form of the Nichols Scholarship, $200 for some fieldwork in Yucatán in the spring of 1907. Two days after Morley received the scholarship, Charles Bowditch invited him to his Peabody office to discuss Maya hieroglyphs (Brunhouse 1971:29). Morley received his A.B. in absentia on February 27, 1907, having already left for Yucatán, where he spent four months. There he met with the well-known Mesoamerican scholars Eduard Seler, Teobert Maler, and Edward H. Thompson. As an undergraduate, Morley had written that his two favorite sessions at the Harvard Anthropological Society had been the talk by his classmates Will and Spinden about their work with the Mandans and Thompson's presentation on the Mayas. When Morley returned from Yucatán, he brought artifacts from Thompson for the Peabody Museum (Brunhouse 1971:31–38).

Morley was accepted in the graduate program at Harvard in the fall of 1907. Because Tozzer and Putnam required a certain amount of fieldwork, Morley was recruited for the AIA expedition to the Southwest that summer, under the guidance of the New Mexico investigator Edgar Lee Hewett. Morley was joined by his housemate, John Gould (J. G.) Fletcher, and another neophyte, A.V. (Ted) Kidder. That fascinating story has been told from various viewpoints by J. G. Fletcher (1937), Brunhouse (1971), Woodbury (1973), Givens (1992), and others.

When Morley returned after that field season, he dedicated himself to Maya studies. At Putnam's suggestion, Bowditch contributed $600 for a brand new fellowship in Central American research for the 1907–8 term, and Morley was named to the position (Putnam 1908:301).

In the spring of 1908, as part of the graduate training program, Putnam sent Morley and A.V. Kidder back to the Southwest to obtain more field experience. They first worked with Jesse Walter Fewkes at his excavations at Mesa Verde. In June, Morley and Kidder split up, to work on different AIA-funded field projects. Morley took a party consisting of two Harvard juniors, Paul Stanwood and Warner McLaughlin, to Colorado (Putnam 1909:301). Kidder met up with Byron Cummings, of the University of Utah (later dean at the University of Arizona and director of the Arizona State Museum), and the two took a crew up Montezuma Creek and Alkali Ridge in Utah. The team included two undergraduates from the University of Utah, Neil Merton Judd (Cummings's nephew) and Clifford Lockhart, and two undergraduates from Harvard, Hugo Gilbert de Fritsch and Leavitt Cooley Parsons (Kidder 1910:337).

In August, the two AIA-funded field crews, with Morley and Kidder, joined up and met Tozzer and Dixon. They all then worked at Hewett's Rito de los Frijoles excavations in New Mexico (Putnam 1909:300). None of the four Harvard undergraduates who worked with Morley and Kidder that summer continued in anthropology, although Parsons retained an avocational interest and later donated some lithics and ceramics from a site near Macon, Georgia, to the Peabody Museum (Putnam 1910:274).

Morley finished his A.M. in 1908 and continued his graduate work at Harvard through 1909. He spent little further time in Cambridge, however, but worked during the summers in the Southwest with Hewett and during the winters in the Maya area. He collaborated with Spinden on deciphering calendrical glyphs, and his name is associated with the "Spinden-Morley" correlation, linking the Western and Maya calendrical systems, described in the paper Spinden gave at the AIA meetings in 1909 (see S.G. Morley 1910).

Morley seems to have finished most of the requirements for his Ph.D. at Harvard, if not all of them, but the degree was never granted. One speculative reason proffered by Morley's biographers is that because Morley failed to properly credit Bowditch with ideas he had "borrowed" from him, Morley was terminated in the Peabody Museum graduate program. Robert Brunhouse (1971:159) reported that Morley wrote up and published Teobert Maler's Naranjo inscriptions without Bowditch's permission, and Morley "indicated that the article represented research in partial fulfillment of the requirements for the doctorate at Harvard"—implying that this was his doctoral work. However, when Morley began the Maler report, he held the Peabody Museum fellowship in Central American archaeology, wholly subsidized by Bowditch. Brunhouse's interpretation of these facts was that the department judged Morley to have violated the ethics of scholarship. Shortly after the volume was published, Morley's official relationship with the Peabody Museum ended.

Morley was named the AIA Fellow in American Archaeology in 1908. After he left Harvard, he was hired by the AIA's School of American Archaeology in Santa Fe, New Mexico, where his title was Fellow in Central American Archaeology, with Hewett as his boss (Brunhouse 1971:48). From 1908 to 1913 Morley spent his summers working with

Hewett on AIA programs in the Southwest, and in the winters he went on AIA projects to Central America.

In 1911, one of the trustees of the Carnegie Institution of Washington (CIW), William Barclay Parsons, had strongly pushed that institution to enter the field of Central American archaeology (Reingold 1979:319). The result was that in 1913 the CIW was looking for someone to direct its new program. Frederick Hodge and William Holmes strongly supported Morley's request to join the Carnegie's new Department of Central American Archaeology, but Bowditch, Putnam, and Clark Wissler were pushing Tozzer. The Carnegie settled on Morley in 1914, and he spent the next four decades working for that organization in various positions. During World War I he worked for the Office of Naval Intelligence and was so successful that, as we discuss later, he has been called "arguably the finest American spy of World War I" (Harris and Sadler 2003:xiii).

The CIW program in Central America lasted from 1914 to 1952. Morley was involved in it for most of that time, from 1914 until his death in 1948. He appears to have had a love-hate relationship with fieldwork. On one hand, beginning in 1908 he had 40 consecutive seasons in the field; on the other, he wrote that "anyone who says he likes the bush is either a bloody fool or a bloody liar" (J. E. S. Thompson 1949:194). He seems also to have been one of the rare scientists we all would like to emulate in terms of sharing data. A.V. Kidder (1948:274) wrote with awe of "his remarkable generosity in the matter of supplying his own hard-earned, unpublished data to anyone he believed capable of using them. That, in a scientist, is the ultimate generosity."

The Carnegie Institution of Washington program in archaeology was much more closely tied to the Peabody Museum than many recognize. According to J. O. Brew (1966b:23):

> The inauguration by the Carnegie Institution of an extensive research program in Yucatán under Sylvanus G. Morley in 1914 changed the emphasis in Middle American archaeology for the next 40 years. For much of that time their headquarters were next door to us [the Peabody Museum] on Frisbie Place. Most of the Carnegie archaeologists were trained by Professor Tozzer and a very close relationship was maintained throughout. With their much greater financial resources, the Carnegie Institution was able to mount extensive excavations and carry out, more thoroughly than we could at the time, the research program inaugurated by Mr. Bowditch in 1888. The Carnegie work is not listed here but the Museum was, in fact, an integral part of it.

Alfred Vincent (A.V. or Ted) Kidder (1885–1963) was a younger brother of Homer Kidder. He had exposure to archaeology not only through his father's library and his childhood arrowhead collecting but also by means of Homer's archaeological explorations in 1904 with Pumpelly at Anau. Although A.V. had been born in Marquette, Michigan, the family moved back to Cambridge when he was seven.

A.V. Kidder entered Harvard in the fall of 1904 with an interest in natural history, thinking vaguely of medicine as a career. His first publication had been at age 15—

"A Bittern at Close Range," in *Bird Lore*, 1901—and he joined the Nuttall Ornithological Club of Cambridge around that time (Wauchope 1965:149; Woodbury 1973:7). In his sophomore year he took Anthropology 5, the North American anthropology course taught by Dixon, with Stefansson as the teaching assistant, and became interested in the field (Givens 1992:9). In the summer between his junior and senior years, after responding to a notice posted by Tozzer, he was selected to attend an AIA field school in New Mexico and Colorado. As we described earlier, he went there with two of his classmates, Morley and Fletcher, and he thereafter focused on Southwestern archaeology as his career objective.

According to Kidder, one of the most important courses he took as an undergraduate was in the fall term after he returned from this first field season in the Southwest: George Chase's Classical Philology 49, History of Greek Vase Painting. Chase's ideas on ceramic analysis were later to see inclusion in Kidder's Ph.D. dissertation. During his senior year Kidder took courses primarily with Dixon, Farabee, and Tozzer. He also took a half-course with Putnam, who commissioned him to dig a shell mound near Carpinteria, California, for the course, although it is unclear whether Kidder ever did this work (Wauchope 1965:151).

Kidder received his A.B. from Harvard in 1908. Late in the spring of that year he and Morley worked at Mesa Verde under J. Walter Fewkes, and that summer they were back in the Southwest with the two AIA crews supervised by Hewett, working in Utah and New Mexico. In the late fall Kidder was given leave of absence to travel with his family to Egypt that winter, but when he returned, Harvard expected him to resume his American studies, doing his Ph.D. research on the Southwest (Putnam 1909:300–301).

In 1910, at Putnam's request and funded by Henry C. Warren money, Kidder went to Newfoundland and Labrador to check on Merritt Fernald's theory regarding the location of Vinland, but the site turned out to be a sixteenth-century Breton settlement (Putnam 1911:222; Wauchope 1965:151). In 1911 George Reisner returned to Harvard from Egypt to begin offering courses in Egyptology. Kidder had heard about Reisner's work when he visited Egypt and Greece with his family in 1908–9, so he decided to take Reisner's course in field methods when it was offered that fall. He received his only A+ grade for this course, Egyptology 6, "Archaeological Fieldwork: Theory and Practice of Archaeological Fieldwork as a Branch of Historical Research," which was taken by three graduate students and one senior (Harvard University, Graduate School of Arts and Sciences Record Cards, Alfred Vincent Kidder). Even many years later he lauded the course as "a dandy, well thought out and very logical. I never enjoyed a course so much" (quoted in Wauchope 1965:151).

In terms of Kidder's contributions to the development of Americanist archaeology, Reisner's course was probably the most important one he took as a graduate student at Harvard. Part of the material from the course, in conjunction with Putnam's Peabody method, seems to have been key to a new discipline-wide emphasis on stratigraphic excavation led by Kidder, Nels Nelson, and Manuel Gamio after 1915 (Browman and Givens 1996). John H. Rowe wrote that "one of the things that Kidder is important for in the history of archaeology is that he introduced Reisner's standards and Reisner's methods to the New World. The documentation of this fact is probably the most important result of my long and of course very pleasant interview with him in 1955" (quoted in Wauchope 1965:151). As we have seen, these standards and methods were likely Reisner's remake of Putnam's methodology.

Kidder received his A.M. in 1912 and his Ph.D. in 1914, supported along the way with an Austin Teaching Fellowship from 1910 to 1913. His dissertation, "Southwestern Ceramics: Their Value in Reconstructing the History of the Ancient Cliff Dwelling and Pueblo Tribes. An Exposition from the Point of View of Type Distinction," was defended in front of a committee composed of Dixon, Putnam, Chase, and Lanman.

Kidder was then appointed curator of North American archaeology at the Peabody Museum in 1913, and in 1920, curator of Southwestern American archaeology. He continued working for the museum until 1929. In the summer of 1914 he went into the Kayenta area of Arizona with Samuel Guernsey; the two of them spent three summers there. Their report on the Basketmaker culture is a classic of Southwestern archaeology.

In 1915 the trustees of the Phillips Academy, Andover, on the advice of the academy's advisory committee (Roland Dixon of Harvard and Hiram Bingham of Yale), decided to fund a long-term excavation in the Pueblo area. At the suggestion of Dixon and Bingham, Kidder was offered the job. Pondering possible sites, he decided to change his research area to Pecos Pueblo and its vicinity in New Mexico, because he wanted long-term chronology and wanted to interlink other areas by cross-finds. He thought the Rio Grande and Pecos River drainages might disclose traces of early migrations of farming and pottery-making peoples from the centers of Mesoamerica (Willey 1967:293). Kidder took official leave from the Peabody Museum in June 1915 to begin the Pecos project, using Phillips Academy funds (Dixon 1916b:256).

Some Southwestern historians of archaeology have mistakenly credited Edgar Hewett with providing Kidder access to Pecos Pueblo, on the basis of Hewett's having written a paper in 1904 titled "Studies on the Extinct Pueblo of Pecos." This error has been ossified on a brass plate at the site. Actually it was Kidder's undergraduate classmate Daniel Thomas Kelly (also Harvard class of 1908) and his family who invited Kidder to work at Pecos. Pecos Pueblo and its mission church were part of the Kelly family's 30,000 acres of ranch land at that point (Daniel [Bud] Kelly II, personal communication, 2004; Williams has seen the Kelly documents). Kidder went on to direct work at the Pecos site from 1915 through 1929, making it the first large-scale and thoroughly systematic stratigraphic operation in Americanist archaeology.

During World War I, Kidder went into the Army infantry as a first lieutenant in June 1918 and mustered out in April 1919 as a captain, receiving the Cross of the Legion of Honor, Grade of Chevalier, from France. While he was in the armed forces, Carl Guthe served as director of the Pecos project (Stafford 1941:520; Willoughby 1919:240).

After the Pecos work, Kidder's career shifted toward the Mayas. His interest in the Mayas can be traced back to Tozzer's course, Anthropology 9, Maya Archaeology and Hieroglyphics, which Kidder took as an undergraduate. His first visit to Mexican archaeological sites was in 1922, with his Harvard colleague Clarence Hay (Givens 1992:87). In 1929 he oversaw some early aerial photography with Charles Lindbergh in the Maya area, in British Honduras and Yucatán. He had become an advisor to the Carnegie Institution of Washington in 1925, making suggestions on the work Morley was doing in Yucatán. In 1929 he became head of the newly created Division of Historical Research at the CIW, a position he held for the next 21 years. It was there that he introduced his "pan-scientific" approach, employing multidisciplinary investigations of archaeological sites.

Kidder served in a number of important offices in anthropology, through them exerting his influence over the evolution of the discipline. He was secretary of the AAA from 1920 to 1927, succeeding Tozzer, and concurrently treasurer from 1922 to 1926; in 1942 he was AAA president. He served as vice chair of the Division of Anthropology and Psychology of the National Research Council in 1924–25 and as its chair in 1926–27. He worked with A. L. Kroeber and Frank H. H. Roberts Jr. to draw up the constitution and bylaws of the Society for American Archaeology in 1934, and in 1937–38 he served as its third president. Along with Roberts, of the Smithsonian, and Barnum Brown, of the AMNH, he was a member of the "blue ribbon" panel of experts that confirmed the first associations of Paleoindian artifacts with extinct fauna at the Folsom site in New Mexico in 1926. He was chair of the board of the Laboratory of Anthropology in Santa Fe, and he initiated the famous Pecos Conference in 1927. In 1936 he was one of the founders of the Institute of Andean Research, a group of Andeanist scholars who joined forces as a nominal institution in order to solicit and channel funds for research (Stafford 1941:520; Wauchope 1965:154–63; Willey 1967:306–7; Woodbury 1973:48–49).

Most of Kidder's career was spent in museum and field research, beginning with his appointment as assistant curator of North American archaeology at the Peabody Museum in 1913. Although he was appointed a member of the Peabody "museum faculty" in 1939 and served in that capacity until 1951, the position, as we saw earlier, did not involve teaching. He taught one year at the University of California–Berkeley after he retired from the CIW, saying that it was the first teaching he had done since he worked as a teaching assistant for Farabee at Harvard four decades earlier (Woodbury 1973:81).

To honor his work, Kidder's colleagues established the Alfred Vincent Kidder award for excellence in Maya or Southwestern archaeology at the AAA in 1950. Kidder was another of the Harvard scholars who let his science speak for him, rather than engaging in self-promotion. As Robert Wauchope wrote (1965:166), "no one ever heard Kidder boast, however subtly. Emil Haury believes that it was Kidder's humility in his own accomplishments that, as well as any other factor, made the first Pecos conferences so productive."

The third Harvard undergraduate who went to the Southwest in the summer of 1907, together with Kidder and Morley, was **John Gould Fletcher** (1886–1950), class of 1907. Fletcher and Morley were best friends, and both lived in Branford Hall at Harvard. In his autobiography, Fletcher indicated that he had developed an interest in archaeology thanks to Morley's enthusiasm and had begun to read all the archaeology he could that year (Fletcher 1937:26). He was eager to join Morley on the venture to the Southwest: "I might come along, if I would be ready to pay my own expenses, and I might there decide whether I really wanted to be an archaeologist" (Fletcher 1937:27). Fletcher soon found the work monotonous and boring, and he began to develop a resentment against Hewett, Morley, and Kidder for their good humor. He recalled that he "began again furtively scribbling down my impressions, in the form of verses" (Fletcher 1937:30). Fletcher dropped out of archaeology after this summer experience and went on to become a well-known American poet.

Robert Gorham Fuller (1882–1919) was an undergraduate from Dover, Maine, who received his S.B. from Harvard in 1904. He had a particular interest in coin collecting, as evidenced by his first publication, a sales catalogue of his and other coin collections, in 1905 (Adams and Fuller 1905). Fuller had donated 1,798 coins from his collection to the Harvard library in 1904 (Harvard University 1905:214). After receiving his A.B., he studied law for two years and then enrolled in the Harvard Graduate School of Arts and Sciences to work on a degree in anthropology (Fuller 1919). He held the Winthrop Scholarship for 1907–8 and 1909–10 and was an "Assistant in Anthropology" for 1908–9 (Putnam 1909:306, 1911:226). Fuller apparently had skill in drawing (see Fuller n.d.a, n.d.b) and did a number of drawings of lithic specimens for the museum. And thanks to his note-taking, in two volumes of notes we have one of the few records of the contents of Dixon's North American Indian course (Fuller 1911).

Fuller received his A.M. in anthropology in 1907, but over the next few years he seems to have been of two minds about whether to continue with graduate work. His attendance was irregular, and it took him the next eight years to finish his Ph.D. For example, Putnam (1911:226) noted that for the 1909–10 year, Fuller held the Winthrop Scholarship for the first half-year but then resigned the scholarship and his assistant position in the museum to pursue a business career. He soon returned and resumed work on his Ph.D. He was appointed "Assistant in Somatology" in his final year, 1914–15. Fuller seems to have come from a well-to-do family, for he is one of the only students listed as a contributor to the 1909 Putnam Festschrift volume, which Boas edited. He was also appointed to the Peabody Museum Visiting Committee, along with Bowditch, Hemenway, Blake, Moore, de Milhau, and other generous donors to the Peabody, in 1909, keeping the position until at least 1915 (Anonymous 1912:672; Fuller 1919).

Fuller participated in various excavations in the Southwest. In 1909 he spent the summer working on a BAE-sponsored excavation under Fewkes at Spruce Tree House at Mesa Verde (Putnam 1910:271). In 1913 Mary Hemenway's son Augustus funded another Hemenway Southwestern Expedition to Arizona for 1913–14, with Willoughby and Fuller directing the project. The two conducted explorations in the Chinle Valley in northeastern Arizona and also at Mesa Verde (Anonymous 1914:369; Putnam 1914:223). In 1916 Samuel G. Guernsey, John Winthrop Edwards (class of 1918), and Fuller conducted excavations at Marsh Pass, in northwestern Arizona (Anonymous 1917b:779; Dixon 1916b:255).

Fuller's four-volume dissertation, defended in 1915 before a committee of Hooton, Dixon, and Tozzer, was titled "Observations on a Collection of Crania from the Prehistoric Stone Graves of Tennessee" and was based in part on collections that Frederic Putnam and Lucien Carr had made years before. Fuller entered the army in World War I and was promoted to captain. After returning to the United States from Europe, he died in St. Petersburg, Florida, in February 1919, either from war injuries or in the influenza epidemic (Boas, MacCurdy, and Bean 1919:113). Tozzer seems to have known him well; he wrote Fuller's obituary for the *Boston Transcript* on February 16, 1919, and announced his death, among those of seven anthropologists who died in the war, at the AAA meetings that December (Tozzer 1920:87). The largest individual gift made to the Peabody Museum library in 1919 was from Mrs. Robert G. Fuller, who contributed the books relating to anthropology that had belonged to her late husband (Willoughby 1920:200).

George Plummer Howe (1878–1917) was born in Lawrence, Massachusetts, and received his A.B. from Harvard in 1900. He then entered Harvard Medical School, where he received his M.D. in 1904. He became interested in anthropology after that time. He joined Peabody Museum students Stefansson, Hastings, and de Milhau on the 1905 expedition to Iceland. He was later recruited by Stefansson to be the surgeon for the Anglo-American Polar Expedition from 1906 to 1908 (Howe 1909). When Howe returned, he was awarded the Hemenway Fellowship at the Peabody Museum for 1908–9 and the Austin Teaching Fellowship for 1909–10. He was a member of one of the Peabody Museum expeditions to Central America, going with Robert Merwin to Tulum in 1910 (Howe 1911). But Howe ended up completing no additional degree requirements in anthropology. He subsequently was a member of the group of 20 physicians that Harvard sent to the war front in 1917. Howe was commissioned a lieutenant and had the dubious distinction of being the first American officer to die in action during the war (Harvard University 1918:142).

Henry Otley Beyer (1883–1966), born in Edgewood, Iowa, received his A.B. from the University of Iowa in 1904 and an A.M. in chemistry from the University of Denver in 1905 (Dutton 1991:56). He had become interested in the Philippines after viewing the 50-acre Philippines exhibit at the Louisiana Purchase Exposition in St. Louis in 1904, and he took a job with the Ethnological Survey Office of the Philippines Civil Service in 1905. His boss, David P. Barrows, commissioned Beyer to work among the Ifugao from 1905 to 1908 (Zamora 1974:361).

Beyer and William Jones had met in the Philippines. We do not know why Beyer left his job there to go to Harvard in 1908 to begin additional training in ethnology, but Jones's previous connection with Harvard is one possibility. Beyer entered Harvard with Winthrop Scholarship funding to work in ethnology with Dixon for the 1908–9 term (Putnam 1909:306). The following summer, 1909, Dixon sent Beyer back to the Philippines with support from the Huntington-Frothingham-Wolcott Fund to collect ethnographic specimens (Putnam 1910:275). Beyer was expected to return in the fall of 1909 to complete his studies for an advanced degree in anthropology, and he was carried on the Peabody Museum books as a graduate student for the 1909–10 school year. But in the fall of 1909 he was appointed an ethnologist for the Bureau of Science of the U.S. colonial government in the Philippines, and he conducted extensive fieldwork for it from 1910 to 1914. In October Beyer was appointed to the newly created chair of anthropology at the University of the Philippines, where he taught until his retirement in 1947. His entire formal training in the discipline was his short term doing graduate work at the Peabody Museum in 1908 and 1909 (Zamora 1974:361).

Beyer described the material he amassed during his nearly five decades of research as five sets of collections: a library on archaeology, cultural history, ethnography, folklore, and linguistics of the Philippines and neighboring countries; numerous archaeological and ethnographic specimens gathered during fieldwork; an extensive collection of Philippine pottery and glazed porcelain wares from China and Southeast Asia; a collection of tektites (glassy objects from outer space); and a major set of newspaper clippings and extracts from publications (Gosling 1997:7). At his retirement, the National Library of the Philippines received 160 bound volumes of his typescript manuscripts, indexed and mostly unpublished. This collection, known as the Philippine Ethnographic Series, was Beyer's major work, compiled between 1906 and 1918, with a few later additions (Gosling 1997:8). Beyer was the first of many people in the first quarter of the twentieth century who came to Harvard to get some training under, mainly, Dixon and Tozzer and who spent the rest of their careers in foreign countries, teaching courses at universities and conducting field research.

Clarence Leonard Hay (1884–1941), Harvard class of 1908, was the son of John Milton Hay, who had been a private secretary to President Abraham Lincoln and served later administrations as assistant secretary of state and ambassador (Hellman 1968:92). Clarence Hay entered the Harvard graduate school in 1909, pursuing an interest in Latin American archaeology, and secured his A.M. in 1911. He continued in graduate school until 1914 in anthropology but completed no additional degree work. In 1909 Hay joined Hiram Bingham on his first trip to Peru, down the Urubamba Valley, looking at Inca ruins (A. Bingham 1989:92). From January to June 1911 he was chief assistant to Raymond Merwin, who was directing the Peabody's Central American expedition, working at Holmul, and he also worked with Tozzer in Central America that year (Putnam 1913:214). In 1913–14 Hay went with Tozzer to the International School of American Archaeology and Ethnology in Mexico City, enrolling as the funded Fellow from Harvard University. While there, Hay and Tozzer excavated the site of Santiago Ahuitzotla, which was published in Bulletin 74 of the BAE in 1921 (Phillips 1955:75; Putnam 1914:222). Hay and Tozzer remained close friends all their lives.

Hay was a New Yorker, and from Mexico he returned to his hometown, where he began a 50-year association with the AMNH as a research associate in anthropology (1920–69) and a trustee (1924–54) (Hellman 1968:225). When the AMNH hired George Vaillant (see chapter 11) in 1927, he and Hay became close friends. Hay is credited with getting Vaillant interested in Archaic-period manifestations in Mexico and helping him obtain access permits (Kidder 1945:592; Strong 1945:115). Hay went back to the field in 1927 and 1932 and worked with Vaillant on restoring some of the temples at Teotihuacan. Vaillant later pulled together the work Hay and Merwin had done for the Peabody at Holmul (Merwin and Vaillant 1932).

Samuel James Guernsey (1868–1936) was born in Dover, Maine, and was interested from boyhood in Indians and artifacts. He studied at the Cowles Art School in Boston and for many years supported himself by design decoration. Subsequently, he worked from 1906 to 1910 at the Newton and Watertown Electric Light Company, a subsidiary of Edison Electric Company (*National Cyclopedia* 1943:212). In his profession as an artist, he met Putnam and Willoughby, who contracted with him to prepare figures for the Peabody Museum's models illustrating Indian life. Guernsey had first written to Putnam in 1897 to see whether he could obtain funding from the Peabody to work on models in Maine, and he was contracted to make a Haida model for the museum (Putnam 1907:294; Scott 1937:337). After he moved to Boston, he was hired to prepare figures and later complete groups for the museum, and he eventually held a full-time appointment (Kidder 1937:135)

Guernsey was named Hemenway Assistant at the Peabody Museum in 1910, assistant curator in 1914, assistant director from 1921 to 1929, and curator from 1929 until his retirement in 1936. He also served as an instructor in anthropology for the 1928–29 year. Guernsey took medical leave in 1923–24 and because of continuing ill health resigned his position as assistant director in 1929 (Reynolds 1931a:279; Willoughby 1925:262).

Guernsey initially began excavating and collecting specimens in New England (Guernsey 1916; Putnam 1913:215, 1914:224). He made his first trip to the Southwest—to Monument Valley, Arizona—in 1914, with Kidder, and continued working in Arizona for the next several seasons, exploring the Kayenta district in northeastern Arizona through 1931. Kidder (1937:136) noted that Guernsey had a remarkable flair for the implications of technological and stratigraphic evidence and was a key player in the shift from the haphazard hunt for museum specimens to purposeful research on the history of a culture: "Trained in the exacting Putnam-Willoughby school, with its strong emphasis upon detailed knowledge of specimens, he became intimately acquainted with the collections under his charge; and he had an unusual gift for the effective and instructive installation of cases. His greatest contribution, however, lay in the preparation and utilization of models. In this outstandingly important branch of museum technique he was preeminent" (Kidder 1937:136).

During his later years he also was a member, with Theodore B. Pitman, of the firm Guernsey and Pitman, a company that produced models for many institutions (Kidder 1937:135). According to Hooton (1943:236), Guernsey had polished his skills in making small-scale ethnographic models when he and Willoughby made all the exhibits for the new wing of the Peabody Museum in 1913, and it was this kind of exhibit that was later developed and made famous by Guernsey and Pitman. Many of these models were still on display when Stephen Williams first arrived at the Peabody Museum in 1954.

Oric Bates (1883–1918) entered Harvard with the class of 1905 and was a good friend of Herbert Eustis Winlock, whom we profiled earlier in this chapter. Bates did not complete his college work in 1905. He was appointed temporary assistant in charge of the Department of Egyptian Art at the Museum of Fine Arts, Boston, and went to Berlin to study for part of the 1906 year (Anonymous 1919a). He completed his A.B. in 1908 and continued employment with the Museum of Fine Arts (Coolidge 1918:vii). In the summer of 1908 he went with George Reisner to work in Nubia and Egypt; in 1909 he worked with Reisner in Samaria; and in 1910 he worked as Reisner's assistant in Libya (Bates 1915:30; Lyon 1911:227; Reisner 1930:242).

Oric Bates and his father, Arlo, an English professor at MIT, spent large portions of several summer vacations identifying and collecting materials from shell mounds along the New England coast, especially in Maine, during the first decade of the twentieth century (Willoughby 1920:199). One summer before 1911, Bates was joined by his friend Winlock, and the two wrote up an extensive manuscript report of the work and presented a well-catalogued collection to the Peabody Museum (Bourque 2002:160–61). Both Bates and Winlock had been employed as Egyptologists since 1906, Bates at the Museum of Fine Arts, Boston, and Winlock at the Metropolitan Museum of Art. It is unclear whether the two made the collections while they were undergraduates before 1906 or during vacations between 1906 and 1911, but Bruce Bourque (2002) commented that their work constituted a remarkable record of most of the important coastal sites in central Maine.

In 1911 Bates was named curator of North African literature at the Harvard library. This period also marked the beginning of his donations of Egyptian art to the Peabody Museum. For 1912–13 Bates taught a Harvard extension course on Egyptian art at the Museum of Fine Arts. In 1914 he was named curator of African archaeology and ethnology at the Peabody Museum, as well as a John Harvard Fellow, and he continued fieldwork in Egypt that season (Putnam 1915:237–38). Bates's strong linkage to the Peabody is emphasized, we think, by the fact that he served as a pallbearer at Putnam's funeral the next year, along with Barbour, Dixon, Spinden, Tozzer, and Willoughby.

On the basis of his Egyptian work, Bates became a member of the Visiting Committee of the Semitic Museum, and he made significant donations of materials to the Museum of Comparative Zoology from his African work. He also convinced the Peabody Museum to create a journal, *Harvard African Studies (Varia Africana),* and he set about editing it, assisted by graduate student Frederick H. Sterns. The first volume of the series came out in 1917 with Bates as editor and Sterns as assistant editor.

In July 1914 Bates began to copy, systematically and verbatim, ethnographic observations made by travelers and missionaries in Africa, carefully cross-referencing them, to create a master research database (Bates 1917:480). This clearly was the antecedent to the materials later continued by Roland Dixon and still later brought into the Human Relations Area Files of George Peter Murdock. By the time of his death, Bates had completed more than 4,000 such entries.

In 1915 Bates continued working up African materials, including some from his Sudan expedition that were more suitable for exhibition at the Peabody Museum than at the Museum of Fine Arts, Boston. He and Sterns expected to leave for Egypt to work in the El Faiyûm region that fall term (Dixon 1916b:256), but the outbreak of tensions in Europe meant that Bates spent only a limited time in Africa and could not carry out the work planned. Sterns was forced to remain in Boston (Willoughby 1917:253).

Bates was soon directly involved in the war. He had been appointed an instructor in navigation but wanted to play a more active role, so he went to artillery officers' training at Camp Zachary Taylor in Louisville, Kentucky, to prepare for fighting in France. At Camp Taylor, however, he caught pneumonia and died in October 1918 (Willoughby 1919:240, 1920:197). His widow, Natica Inches Bates (1887–1981), carried on his interest in Africa, generously providing funds for fieldwork in Africa through 1939 and helping in the publication of *Harvard African Studies* through 1932, when the series ended (Dixon 1930:207; Willoughby 1923a:219). Daniel F. McCall (1967:25) wrote that Bates can rightfully "be called the first American Africanist anthropologist."

Aberdeen Orlando Bowden (1881–1946) was born in Fulton, Kentucky, and received an A.B. in 1908 and an A.M. in 1910 from University of Kentucky. He served a year as principal in a Tennessee high school and then applied to Harvard in anthropology. There he was funded for 1911–12 by the Winthrop Scholarship, receiving his A.M. in 1912. After completing his degree, he left Harvard to serve as principal of high schools in Montana and South Dakota. In 1920 he became chair of the Department of Education and Philosophy at Baylor College in Waco, Texas, and in 1922 he became president of New Mexico Normal School in Silver City, a position he held until 1933 (University of Kentucky 2001). During this period he was able to secure his Ph.D. in mathematics in 1929 from Teachers College at Columbia University. In 1933 he left Silver City to become chair of the Department of Anthropology at the University of Southern California, a position he held until his death. His one-year stint at Harvard in anthropology was apparently the entirety of his formal training in the subject, which he then parlayed into a departmental chairmanship. His anthropological publications were all on Southwest and California archaeology.

Frederick Henderson Sterns (1887–1951) was born in Brooklyn but raised in Omaha, Nebraska. He received an A.B. from Oberlin College in 1909 and then taught geology and psychology at the University of Omaha for two years (Gradwohl 1978:181).

He resigned his teaching job at Omaha and, with some help from Putnam, entered the graduate program at Harvard in December 1911.

Sterns almost immediately began an extensive archaeological investigation in the Missouri River valley in Nebraska, starting work in January 1912 (Gradwohl 1978:185). In July 1912 Putnam got Sterns the Hemenway Fellowship (Gradwohl 1978:188), which he kept over the next three years. During this period he spent the summers in the field and the winters at Harvard, taking courses and doing lab analysis. The fieldwork in Nebraska was supported in part through funds given to the Peabody by Clarence B. Moore (Putnam 1914:223). Sterns's publication on the Walker Gilmore site, using the Peabody Museum method of excavation, is one of the first papers describing the use of stratigraphic principles in the Great Plains (Sterns 1915b). His Ph.D. work was supervised by Dixon, and he defended his dissertation, "The Archaeology of Eastern Nebraska, with Special Reference to the Culture of the Rectangular Earth Lodges," in 1915 before a committee composed of Dixon, Hooton, Tozzer, Lanman, and Chase.

While at Harvard, Sterns spent most of his time working on his Nebraska materials. He also aided Oric Bates with African materials for the first issues of *Harvard African Studies,* serving as assistant editor for volume 1, published in 1917. One of the interesting documents that Sterns created while at Harvard, well ahead of its time, was a manuscript on the contributions of "Women of Scientific Expeditions (1918)," a draft of which is still in the collections of the Tozzer Library at the Peabody Museum.

After completing his Ph.D., Sterns had difficulty finding academic employment. In the summer of 1916 he took Carl Guthe with him for another excavation season in Nebraska (Anonymous 1917b:779). In September Bates left for Africa, and Sterns expected to join him for the project in Egypt, but when the outbreak of hostilities in Europe shut the program down, Sterns stayed stateside (Dixon 1916b:257; Willoughby 1917:253). In 1919, after the end of World War I, because there were no appropriate jobs in academia, Sterns joined AT&T as a statistician specializing in demography. He continued excavating as an avocational archaeologist later in life (Gradwohl 1978:202).

William Hubbs Mechling (1888–1953) was born in Germantown, Pennsylvania, and received his S.B. and A.M. from the University of Pennsylvania in 1910 as one of Frank Speck's students. After earning his A.M. he assisted Dixon, who was making an Indian census for the federal government (Anonymous 1910). Mechling went to the International School in Mexico in its second year, 1911–12, when Boas was director, as the Hispanic Society of America Fellow (Anonymous 1912b:192). There he worked on linguistic issues and employed the map of Indian stocks in Mesoamerica that Frank Gerrodette had made for Putnam nearly two decades earlier (Mechling 1912). In the summer of 1912, when he left Mexico, Mechling went to New Brunswick and Quebec to do work on Maliseet (Wolastoqiyik) Indian ethnography, supported by the Geological Survey of Canada (Anonymous 1913a).

Mechling then entered Harvard, supported by a Hemenway Fellowship, where he received a second A.M. in 1913. During the winter of 1912–13 he again spent some time in the field collecting Maliseet mythology. In 1913–14 he was back at the International School in Mexico, while Tozzer was its director, this time as the University of Pennsylvania Fellow. Mechling continued the studies on Nahuatl he had begun under Boas in 1911–12, and he conducted an archaeological reconnaissance of the area covered by his linguistic studies (Tozzer 1915:392–93).

Mechling defended his Ph.D dissertation, "The Social and Religious Life of the Malecites and Micmacs," in 1917 in front of a small committee composed of Tozzer and Dixon. Along the way he picked up a Litt.B. from Oxford in 1916. Immediately following receipt of his Ph.D. he went back to Ottawa to begin working up his materials on the Maliseets and Micmacs for publication. He soon received an appointment as associate curator of North American ethnology at the Field Museum, which was to begin on July 1, 1917 (Anonymous 1917a).

Before he could assume that position, however, Mechling went on leave without pay, transferring in April to serve as an assistant in the War Trade Board in Washington, D.C. (Haskins 1918:87). When he reported there, he was commissioned as Agent 52 of the Office of Naval Intelligence (Harris and Sadler 2003:50). As we discuss later in this chapter, Mechling's spying was soon exposed, and the ONI quickly disenrolled him as an agent. Returning to the United States, he spent a few years first with the Field Museum and then with the University of Pennsylvania Museum, before leaving anthropology altogether. He spent the rest of his career as vice president of the Atlantic Elevator Company of Newark, New Jersey.

Carl Eugen Guthe (1893–1974) was born in Kearney, Nebraska, but the family moved almost immediately to Ann Arbor, Michigan (Griffin 1976:168). After receiving his S.B. from the University of Michigan, he entered Harvard in 1914 and received his A.M. in 1915. He was made teaching assistant in Anthropology 1 with Hooton and Tozzer in 1915, and the position was renewed yearly through 1917. In 1916 he was trained in Great Plains archaeology by Frederick Sterns during a season in Nebraska, and he and George Vaillant worked during the second season at Pecos with A.V. Kidder (Anonymous 1917b:779; Givens 1992:56). Guthe's dissertation, "The Lunar Count of the Mayas: A Possible Solution to the Number Series on Pages 51 to 58 of the Dresden Codex," was defended in 1917 in front of a committee composed of Tozzer and Robert Wheeler Willson of Harvard's Department of Astronomy.

Following completion of his Ph.D., Guthe was named acting director of the Phillips Academy's Pecos archaeological expedition when Kidder was called to serve in the war. He then worked with Sylvanus Morley in Central America in the early 1920 season, when he helped Morley copyedit the manuscript for his book *The Inscriptions at Copan* (Morley 1920), and again in 1921 (Brunhouse 1971:149, 151, 165). Guthe also continued working at Pecos after Kidder returned in 1920. During the fifth and sixth seasons at Pecos, Kidder sent Guthe to study ethnographic pottery-making at the Tewa pueblo of

San Ildefonso (Givens 1992:62, 143). Doing ethnoarchaeology was a relatively new concept to archaeologists at the time.

In 1922 Guthe accepted a position at the University of Michigan Museum of Anthropology, then the locus of anthropology at Michigan; the Department of Anthropology was not officially founded there until 1928–29 (Griffin 1976:169). While at the museum he became chair of the National Research Council's Committee on State Archaeological Surveys in 1927, succeeding Kidder, Dixon, and Clark Wissler. Guthe held that position until 1937. He used it to help create the Ceramic Repository for the Eastern United States in 1927 and the first institutional-level ethnobotanical lab in 1929.

During the 1930s Guthe worked tirelessly, through Section H of the AAAS, the AAA, and the Committee on State Archaeological Surveys, to found what became the Society for American Archaeology (SAA). The SAA was officially signed into being at the winter meeting of Section H on December 28, 1934. Guthe became its first secretary-treasurer, from 1935 to 1940, and was elected its eleventh president, for the 1945–46 term (Herr 1999:205). James Griffin (1976:168) credited Guthe with being the "primary person who founded" the SAA. Guthe became director of the Museum of Anthropology at Michigan in 1936, a position he held until 1944, when he resigned to become director of the New York State Museum in Albany. He held that directorship until he retired in 1953.

Earnest Albert Hooton (1887–1954) was the first faculty member hired in the Department of Anthropology, Peabody Museum, who had no previous linkage with the college. Hooton started out in archaeology but in his postdoctoral years shifted to physical anthropology, of which he was a founding father. He was born in Clemansville, Wisconsin, and received his A.B. at Lawrence College in Wisconsin. He then entered the University of Wisconsin and in 1911 received his Ph.D in classics, with a dissertation titled "The Evolution of Literary Art in Pre-Hellenic Rome" (Garn and Giles 1997:167). He was awarded a Rhodes scholarship to Oxford, where he initially continued studying classical archaeology, but he soon shifted to Iron Age and Viking archaeology. He worked on the excavation of Viking boat burials and received a diploma in general anthropology from Oxford in 1912. He stayed on at Oxford and began studying human paleoanthropology and Paleolithic archaeology with (Sir) Arthur Keith and Robert Runulph Marett (Garn and Giles 1997:168).

In 1913 William Farabee resigned in midyear and left for Pennsylvania, and Boas came up from Columbia to teach during the second term at Harvard. The anthropology department looked for a replacement for Farabee and offered Hooton the position of instructor in anthropology and associate curator of somatology beginning in the fall term (Putnam 1914:225). Accepting the position, Hooton immediately was put to work not only teaching in his new area, somatology, or biological anthropology, but also serving on every Ph.D. committee for the next decade, including those of Robert Fuller, Frederick Sterns, Edward Handy, Andrew Kerr, and Samuel Lothrop, the last three of whom we profile later in this chapter.

While studying at Oxford in 1912–13, Hooton met O. G. S. (Osbert Guy Stanhope) Crawford, who became a major figure in British archaeology. In 1914, when Hooton returned to England leading a Peabody Museum project to excavate barrows in Wiltshire, he worked with Crawford and a Harvard graduate student in archaeology, Arthur Wiltsee Carpenter, who acted as photographer and surveyor (Putnam 1915:238). Crawford (1955:107) wrote, "Later on Hooton and I did a dig on Wecombe Down, not far from Oxenwood.... Hooton was anxious to obtain some specimens of British prehistoric pottery for the Peabody Museum." This relationship was to stand Crawford in good stead. Later, with World War II approaching, Crawford began sending copies of archaeological publications to Hooton at Harvard for safekeeping during the war (Crawford 1955:267).

Peabody Museum personnel brought Hooton out to several archaeological sites to do the human osteology, as well as sending him materials from excavated sites. Hooton set about analyzing the skeletal collections Sterns had made in Nebraska (Dixon 1916b:255), and he and Willoughby (1921) worked up the burials collected from Madisonville by Metz, Swanton, and the Merwin brothers during past museum projects. In 1920, during the fourth season at Pecos, Kidder brought Hooton out to look at the burials excavated up to that point. Hooton and T. Wingate Todd conducted the analysis and wrote up the results (Givens 1992:61). Hooton's last major "stand-alone" excavation project, in which he did more archaeology than somatology, was apparently his excavations in the Canary Islands in the summer of 1915 (Willoughby 1917:255).

Hooton was the major source of Ph.D.s in physical anthropology in the United States from 1920 to 1950. Most of the doctoral-level students Hooton produced went on to professional positions in physical anthropology, thereby changing the composition of the American Association of Physical Anthropologists (AAPA), which at the time of its inception had been made up largely of anatomists and clinicians. Hooton had been a founding member of the AAPA and its president in 1936–38. His students came to dominate the AAPA as well as physical-biological anthropology for decades (Garn and Giles 1997:173–75). Hooton died in the spring of 1954, while Stephen Williams was first at Harvard; Mrs. Hooton welcomed Williams at a tea, as she had every other newcomer at the Peabody.

Philip Ainsworth Means (1892–1944) was born in Dorchester, Massachusetts, and entered Harvard with the class of 1915. His father, James Means, had made a comfortable fortune as head of James Means and Company shoes from 1878 to 1904. James Means had long been a history buff. He had also been interested in manned flight and served as editor of *Aeronautical Annual* from 1895 to 1897. In the summer of 1912, at the end of Philip's sophomore year at Harvard, he went with his father to Europe to sell some patents connected with flying (Means 1964:123, 126). It was during this trip that Philip became interested in archaeology. He wrote to his brother that while in England he purchased, on August 2, 1912, his "first serious book about ancient America," Bernal Diaz del Castillo's *The True History of the Conquest of New Spain* (quoted in Means 1964:127).

James Means offered Philip encouragement and support in his progress in archaeology (Means 1964:132). He gave Hiram Bingham a substantial contribution for the 1914 Machu Picchu expedition, with the tacit understanding that Philip would be involved. Philip Means was appointed "Assistant, Archaeology" for the expedition and spent the next eight months in Peru at Machu Picchu (A. Bingham 1989:361; Lothrop 1945:109). The fieldwork meant that Means did not complete his A.B. degree work until 1916, but it launched his career. He stayed on at the Peabody Museum to complete his A.M. thesis in 1916, receiving his degree in 1917 on the basis of his work at Machu Picchu.

Means then served as an "honorary collaborator" in archaeology for the U.S. National Museum, being sent by the Smithsonian to do some work with Ojibwa and Chippewa Indians: "In August, 1916, on the advice of Dr. Hrdlička, I visited La Point Island (now commonly called Madeline) with the intention of conducting archaeological investigations on the site of the Ojibwa village on that island" (Means 1917:1). From 1917 to 1919 he collected materials in Peru and Bolivia for the Smithsonian, the Museum of the American Indian, and the American Geographical Society (Bennett 1946:235).

In 1920 Means was appointed director of the Museo Nacional, Sección de Arqueología, in Lima, but in 1921 he resigned the job and returned to Harvard to finish his Ph.D. work (Lothrop 1945:109). He was named an associate in anthropology at the Peabody from 1921 through 1927 and again in 1931–32. He served as "Curator, Andean History and Literature," for the university library from 1920 to 1923 (Harvard University 1937:334), but he never completed his Ph.D.

Bingham had turned to Means in 1923 to help write up the work at Machu Picchu. Early in 1924 Means sent Bingham a book-length manuscript titled "Machu Picchu, a Citadel of the Incas, by Hiram Bingham and Philip Ainsworth Means." Bingham accepted Means's title and adopted his organization, text, and chapter headings, but he did not want Means listed as co-author. When the book finally appeared in print in 1930, Means's name appeared neither on the title page nor in the acknowledgments—not even in the lists of expedition members (A. Bingham 1989:324–25).

Means did not return to prehistoric field archaeology after this but spent his time studying archives in Europe and Latin America. His interest had shifted from field investigations to colonial contact history, and he was the first to translate many of the major works of Spanish conquistadors into English (Lothrop 1945:110).

Just before World War I there were several students who trained at Harvard for short periods but then left and pursued anthropological interests elsewhere. **Charles Avery Amsden** (1899–1941) was one of these. He was born in Forest City, Iowa, but the next year his family moved to Farmington, New Mexico, where his father, Avery Monroe Amsden, became a banker. Charles Amsden's interest in archaeology was encouraged as a result of the needs of a young visitor to Farmington in the summer of 1912. A.V. Kidder came there while finishing work on his degree at Harvard, "to outfit for a pack-trip to the cliff-dwelling country of the lower San Juan [River]" (Kidder 1949:xii). Kidder's traveler's checks were refused at the first bank he tried in the small town, so he crossed the street to the only other bank, where its president, Avery Amsden, was happy to help him get the needed cash. Kidder discovered that Avery Amsden had a collection of local prehistoric pottery, which Kidder carefully photographed with the aid of Amsden's young son. This action shows that Kidder received good advice from some archaeological mentor at Harvard, either Tozzer or Dixon.

Two years later Kidder returned to Farmington, with Samuel Guernsey, to outfit an expedition to the Kayenta region. This time when Kidder went to the Amsden bank, Avery Amsden, feeling that he had gotten a good take on the young archaeologist, broached a question: might Kidder use a young "hand" on this expedition on horseback into the San Juan Basin? Kidder, remembering the small boy he had seen at the Amsden house two years before, was doubtful, but he agreed. Later he admitted it had worked out well. Charles Amsden took "to the work like a duck to water and from that summer on his interest in archaeology never waned" (Kidder 1949:xii).

Amsden entered the University of New Mexico for a short time but transferred to Harvard in 1916. The First World War interrupted his schooling for three years. He served first as an ambulance driver for the French, receiving the Croix de Guerre for his actions, and later went into the U.S. Army Air Corps as a pilot. Amsden returned to Harvard to take more class work in 1919–20 but then took a year off to return to France, where he received a LL.B. from Toulouse in 1921. He resumed his Harvard studies in 1921 and received his A.B. in 1923. He went back to France for graduate work and spent the next five years as American vice consul in France, Switzerland, and Mexico (Anonymous 1941a:350).

After becoming ill while serving as consul in Mexico, Amsden resigned from the State Department (Wauchope 1965:151, 153; Woodbury 1993:21) and joined Kidder again, this time at Pecos. Although Amsden conducted one important stratigraphic excavation on his own for Kidder's project, he devoted most of his time to working on the classification of pottery for the first volume of the final project report (Kidder and Amsden 1931). In 1927 he began work in archaeology for the Southwest Museum in Los Angeles, where he was employed for the rest of his life. There he turned out a series of pamphlets on important archaeological topics such as Pinto Basin, Lake Mohave, and the Basketmakers. He still worked occasionally on Harvard projects, assisting J. O. Brew with excavations at the Hopi site of Awatovi in the late 1930s (Scott 1940:452). He was serving as vice president of the SAA at the time of his death in 1941 (Anonymous 1941a:349). Amsden's best-known work is probably the posthumously published volume *Prehistoric Southwesterners from Basketmaker to Pueblo*, an edited collection of his pamphlets put out by the Southwest Museum (Amsden 1949). The volume was completed by his friends, and many of the illustrations came from the Peabody Museum. Stephen Williams used this book in teaching his first course in Southwest archaeology at Harvard in the 1950s.

Carl Whiting Bishop (1881–1942) was born in Tokyo into a missionary family. He received his B.A. from DePauw in 1912 and went to Columbia for his A.M. in 1913. He was then appointed the newly named Fellow in Central American Research at the Peabody for 1913–14. Before he accompanied Raymond Merwin on the Central American Expedition for that year, he was sent out for field training with Bruce Merwin on excavations in Henry County, Tennessee (Putnam 1914:222–23).

Bishop's training at Harvard did not last long. Upon his return from the Maya fieldwork he was offered, and accepted, a position at the University Museum at Pennsylvania as assistant curator of Oriental art (Putnam 1915:238). He went on an archaeological expedition with that museum to China from 1915 to 1917 (Luce 1943). He was assistant naval attaché in China during the war, from 1918 to 1920. He then taught anthropology at Columbia during the 1921–22 term, and from 1922 until his death he worked as a Sinological field archaeologist for the Freer Gallery of the Smithsonian (Luce 1943; Wilbur 1943:204).

Arthur Wiltse(e) Carpenter (1890–1954) received his B.S. in 1913 and his M.S. in chemistry in 1914, both from MIT. He then was named to replace Carl Bishop as the Fellow in Central American Research at the Peabody from 1914 to 1916. In the summer of 1914 he went with Hooton to excavate English barrows, acting as photographer and surveyor (Putnam 1915:238). The next summer he spent some time excavating an Ojibwa village in Michigan (Dixon 1916b:258), before being appointed field director of the Peabody's annual Central American Expedition, leaving in December for Guatemala (Anonymous 1917b:779).

The war intervened, however, and the museum did not send its regular expedition to Central America, although Carpenter did make a short reconnaissance trip there (Willoughby 1917:252). Robert Brunhouse (1971:113) wrote that Carpenter helped spy for the United States at this time, but his name does not appear on the official list of agents recruited by the ONI in World War I (Harris and Sadler 2003:370–80). Moreover, Charles Harris and Louis Sadler (2003:113) wrote that Carpenter was deliberately not recruited because he was known to have pro-German leanings. In any case, after leaving the Peabody Museum in 1917, he went into business, working for a New York dyewood firm that had military contracts during the war (Harris and Sadler 2003:112). Carpenter continued in business in Latin America during the 1920s, occasionally sending the Peabody Museum artifacts from Colombia and other countries where he had business dealings (Willoughby 1929:297).

Andrew Affleck Kerr (1877–1929), born in Ogden, Utah, obtained his A.B. from the University of Utah in 1907. He taught high school in Utah from 1907 to 1916 and then entered the graduate program at the Peabody in 1916, just as the conflict in Europe began. He received his A.M. in 1917 and was sent that summer to explore cliff dwellings in Utah. For the 1918–19 year he received the Hemenway Fellowship to support his studies. He defended his Ph.D. dissertation, "Similarities in Material Culture between the Old and the New World," before Tozzer, Hooton, and Dixon in 1921. He then went to teach archaeology and anthropology at his alma mater, the University of Utah, where he became chair of the department in 1926. In field expeditions for the school between 1921 and his death in 1929, he collected more than 10,000 artifacts for his institution (*National Cyclopedia* 1940).

Edward Smith Craighill Handy III (1892–1980) was a member of the Harvard class of 1915. He continued graduate work at the Peabody, receiving his A.M. in 1916, and then took a short break for war service. He returned as the teaching assistant in Anthropology 1 for 1919–20 and finished his Ph.D. in 1920 with the dissertation "Polynesian Religion: An Analysis and Correlation of its Elements, with Preliminary Investigation of Their Origin," defended before Dixon, Hooton, and Lanman. He went on to a distinguished career in Pacific area social anthropology at the Bernice P. Bishop Museum in Hawaii, often working with his wife, Willowdean Chatterson Handy.

Willowdean Chatterson Handy (1889–1965) spent her anthropological career working in Polynesia. She was born in Louisville, Kentucky, and obtained her Ph.B. in 1909 from the University of Chicago. She entered the graduate program at Radcliffe in 1915, the same year her soon-to-be husband Edward Handy joined the graduate program at the Peabody Museum. She continued her graduate work at Radcliffe through 1917, presumably finishing with an A.M., although the Radcliffe records are mute on this point. Willowdean Handy and her husband moved to Hawaii in 1920 to take positions at the Bishop Museum, where she conducted research in the Marquesas and other Polynesian Islands (Herskovits and Ames 1950:65; Mann 1991b).

There were some students who received degrees in the 1900s who did not return to make contributions in anthropology at Harvard for several decades after their initial association with the university. Among those were Lauriston Ward and Donald Scott.

Lauriston Ward (1883–1960) was a member of the class of 1903, receiving an A.B. in English. He did not turn to anthropology for another three decades. In 1932 he entered graduate school in anthropology at Harvard, and in 1934 he completed his A.M. there. He was then appointed assistant curator of Asiatic archaeology. When Roland Dixon died in December 1934, Ward took over Dixon's course in Asiatic archaeology and ethnology, and he was also named assistant to the director (Scott 1936:317). He then initiated a series of excavation projects focusing on the Neolithic period in Syria and Iraq and continued these projects and teaching until the 1947–48 term, when he retired. Stephen Williams knew Ward from 1954 to 1960, and even though Ward was no longer teaching, he was still involved with Middle Eastern archaeology and the American School of Prehistoric Research (Brew 1960:50–53). He remained active at the Peabody Museum until his death.

Donald Scott (1879–1967) was a member of the Harvard class of 1900. He had a successful career as a cotton commission merchant and as a book and newspaper publisher before he returned to Harvard in the late 1920s to do graduate work in anthropology (Pusey 1968:42). In 1928 he became involved in the Peabody Museum's Utah Archaeological Survey along the Colorado River, and he received his A.M. on the basis of that research in 1930. When Samuel Guernsey resigned as assistant director of the Peabody in 1929 because of poor health, Scott was appointed to replace him, serving half-time as assistant director, with the rest of his time to be devoted to working on his Ph.D. in Southwestern archaeology (Reynolds 1930:272, 1931a:279). When

Plate 33

Sylvanus Griswold Morley in Yucatan with local crew, 1908.

S. G. Morley and Frances Rhoads Morley, Chichen Itza, ca. 1930.

Plate 34

Alfred Vincent Kidder in Arizona, 1912.

Carl Eugen Guthe, left, with A.V. Kidder, Cristino Varela, Martin Varela, and Mariano Quintana, Pecos, New Mexico, 1916.

Plate 35

A.V. Kidder in the Southwest, 1912.

Herbert J. Spinden, far left, and Frans Blom, far right, standing in front of the SS *Saramaca,* 1926, before their departure to Yucatan. (Between Spinden and Blom, left to right: Gregory Mason and F. Whiting of the New York Times; Ludlow Griscom of the American Museum of Natural History, later of the MCZ at Harvard; Capt. DuChane of the *Saramaca;* and O. T. McClurg, publisher from Chicago.)

Plate 36

Thomas Barbour and two indigenous men off the coast of New Guinea, 1906.

Samuel J. Guernsey and two Navajos in the Southwest, ca. 1920s.

Members of the Carnegie Institution of Washington (CIW) field group at Chichen Itza, ca. 1920. Left to right: Earl H. Morris, Anne Axtell Morris, Oliver Ricketson, Sylvanus G. Morley, Edith Ricketson, Karl Ruppert, and Jean Charlot.

Plate 37

Senior members of the Harvard Faculty of Anthropology in 1928–29. Standing, left to right: Earnest A. Hooton, Carleton S. Coon, Herbert J. Spinden, A.V. Kidder, Fredrick R. Wulsin, and Samuel J. Guernsey. Sitting: Alfred M. Tozzer, Charles C. Willoughby, Edward Reynolds, and Roland B. Dixon.

Archaeological Club meeting at Mr. Dixon's home, 1921. Left to right: Earnest A. Hooton, Andrew Affleck Kerr, Charles C. Willoughby, Alfred M. Tozzer, Li Chi, Biraha Sankar Guha, Samuel J. Guernsey, and Gerald Paul Lestrade.

Plate 38

Caroline Stewart Bond (Day), 1919.

Bond Day in her 1932 publication, *Some Negro-White Families in the United States.*

Ellen Sewall Collier (Spinden), 1919.

William Leo Hansberry.

Plate 39

George Schwab with his wife, Jewell Schwab, on the Nyong River, Cameroon, ca. 1920.

Schwab with drum in King Njoya's palace, Cameroon, 1929–30.

Plate 40

Julio Caesar Tello excavating in Peru.

George Way Harley, Monrovia, Liberia, 1925.

Frans Ferdinand Blom and Stela 2, Uaxactun, Guatemala, ca. 1920.

Plate 41

Oliver Garrison Ricketson Jr. examining an artifact in Belize, ca. 1922–23.

Ricketson napping, Belize, ca. 1922–23.

Plate 42

George Clapp Vaillant, 1945.

Ralph Linton, at right, after landing at Puerto Barrios, Guatemala, with two companions, 1914–15.

Left to right: Unidentified (Wiggins?), John Savage Bolles, Karl Ruppert, A.V. Kidder, Harry Pollock, and Gustav Strømsvik, Chichen Itza, 1931.

Plate 43

Harriet "Hattie" Cosgrove (second from left) and Burton C. "Burt" Cosgrove (far right) with A.V. Kidder (second from right) in Lordsburg, New Mexico, 1933, when they were working together at the Pendleton Ruin. Also pictured are Madeleine Kidder at left, Burt Cosgrove Jr. to Hattie's left, and one of the Kidder children.

Plate 44

John Otis Brew on expedition in Utah, 1931.

William Henry Claflin Jr., Muley Twist, Water Pocket Fold, Utah, 1929.

Donald Scott during the Peabody's Utah Archaeological Survey along the Colorado River, 1930.

Plate 45

Coon and his assistant, Mustapha, excavating in Morocco, 1947.

Carleton Steven Coon in the
Radcliffe College yearbook of 1948.

Martin Luther (1899–1950) in
"Greenland costume," 1930.

Plate 46

Earnest Albert Hooton, a founder of the discipline of physical anthropology, in the classroom, 1940.

Hooton holding a hominid skull.

Plate 47

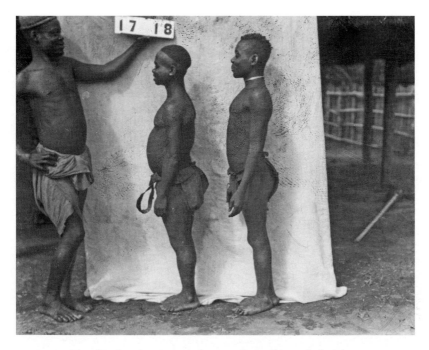

Two Gombari Pygmy men photographed in front of a backdrop by Patrick Tracy Lowell Putnam, 1929.

Lauriston Ward, ca. 1930s.

Samuel K. Lothrop, Eleanor Lothrop, and Julio C. Tello, Pachacamac, Peru, ca. 1944–47.

Plate 48

William White Howells's statistics lab, 1931–32.

Edward Reynolds resigned as director of the Peabody Museum in February 1932, Scott was named to replace him (Scott 1933:296). Scott served in that post until he retired in June 1948 and J. O. Brew became director of the museum. Although Scott worked intermittently in Southwestern archaeology during vacations for the rest of the 1930s, particularly at the site of Awatovi in the late 1930s, he never completed his Ph.D. Nevertheless, he was named Peabody Professor of American Archaeology and Ethnology in 1941, a position he kept until his retirement in 1948.

Equally important for Harvard was Scott's service in founding the Harvard University Press and helping it grow, an interest that benefited the Peabody Museum in its own publication ventures. As a member of Century Company Publishers of New York, Scott was named to a new committee on providing assistance to students in printing and publishing at the Harvard Business School beginning in 1909. From 1913 to 1915 he gave several lectures on publishing in the course Business 20C, An Introduction to the Technique of Printing. The prospectus in 1912 calling for the establishment of Harvard University Press was signed by President A. Lawrence Lowell, Donald Scott, and four others (T. J. Wilson 1964:556). Scott "was one of the prime movers in the establishment of the press and a member of the first Board of Syndics" (T. J. Wilson 1964:553). He served on various committees of the university press from 1913 until he became director of the Peabody in 1932. He then took a dozen years off from helping the press but returned to serve as a member of its board of directors in 1944, a position he held until his death in 1967 (Pusey 1968:42).

Samuel Kirkland Lothrop Jr. (1892–1965), like A.V. Kidder, no doubt became interested in archaeology because of family ties to the Peabody. His great-grandfather, Samuel Kirkland Lothrop Sr. (1804–86), had been good friends with the Peabody Museum trustee and benefactor Robert Charles Winthrop. Samuel K. Lothrop Sr. was also a good friend of Alpheus S. Packard and of the Rev. James Means, grandfather of Philip Means.

Samuel Lothrop Jr. was born in Milton, Massachusetts. As a child he alternated between living in Massachusetts and Puerto Rico, where his father had business interests in the sugar industry (Willey 1976:253). Lothrop was a member of the Harvard class of 1915. When he entered graduate school, he and his wife, Rachel Warren, a student at Radcliffe, worked as Kidder's assistants at Pecos for the first season, in 1915; this was Lothrop's first fieldwork (Anonymous 1917b:779). He did some additional fieldwork in Mesoamerica in 1916 and 1917 and was named research associate for Central America at the Peabody Museum from 1915 to 1917. During World War I he became involved with the Office of Naval Intelligence, conducting surveillance in Latin America under the guise of doing archaeology, as we soon discuss further. He returned to graduate school in 1919, where he was named an associate in anthropology for 1919–20 and a John Harvard Fellow for 1920–21. He finished his Ph.D. dissertation, "The Ceramics of Northern

Costa Rica and Western Nicaragua," which he defended in front of a committee consisting of Tozzer, Dixon, and Hooton in 1921.

Lothrop then took a job with the Carnegie Institution of Washington, continuing to focus on archaeology in Mesoamerica, until 1924, when he shifted to the Museum of the American Indian. He left the latter in 1930, after the 1929 stock market crash resulted in the sudden dissolution of the Heye Foundation's research staff (Willey 1976:255). Lothrop rejoined the Peabody Museum in 1931 as a research associate in anthropology (Scott 1933:300), later becoming curator of Andean archaeology. He kept his museum association, working mainly on sites in Panama and Costa Rica, until he retired in 1957 (Lonergan 1991b:424). His Peabody Museum publication *Coclé: An Archaeological Study of Central Panama* won the second-place Loubat Prize in 1938.

Lothrop also helped supervise the Robert Woods Bliss pre-Columbian collections. Bliss had begun collecting materials in 1912, installed them at Dumbarton Oaks in Washington, D.C., in 1920, and donated the continually enlarging collections to Harvard in 1940. Alfred Tozzer had been a classmate of Bliss's (both class of 1900) and was an early advisor on the collections. Lothrop took over this role from Tozzer when he returned to the Peabody.

The Peabody Museum was to benefit in another fashion from the association between Bliss and Lothrop. Both men were interested in Latin American archaeology, and both were men of independent means. Thus the two became the original financial "angels" for work done through the Institute of Andean Research, founded in 1936 (Willey 1976:258). This organization would support the Latin American field research of many of the Peabody Museum archaeologists in the late 1930s, as we describe in chapter 12.

Lothrop and Julio Tello, a former Harvard graduate student who was by then director of the Department of Archaeology at the Museo Histórico Nacional in Lima, Peru, spent part of 1941 working up textiles of the prehistoric Peruvian Paracas culture at the Peabody Museum (Scott 1942:430). When the Second World War expanded to include the United States, Lothrop returned to Peru to collect intelligence for the military, as he had done in World War I. He served as one of about 350 agents of the Special Intelligence Service under the FBI, from December 1940 through 1944. He used positions at the Institute of Andean Research, the Peabody Museum, and the Carnegie Institution of Washington as cover. Officially he was conducting archaeological investigations for these groups. In practice he did almost no actual fieldwork during this period but spent his time gathering military intelligence (Harris and Sadler 2003:312; Willey 1976:257).

Lothrop was only one of many anthropologists who were caught up in World War I, and the Peabody Museum, with which he was affiliated at the time, was only one of many anthropological institutions affected by it. The anthropological community as a whole expressed a good deal of patriotism. At the Peabody Museum, the top floor was taken over by a radio school once the United States joined the war, and part of the first floor became classrooms for the Army Training Corps. Most of the department played some part in the war effort. Alfred Tozzer, as we have seen, was commissioned a captain in the Signal Corps, and Roland Dixon worked on special investigations for the State Department. Homer Kidder served as a first lieutenant in the infantry in France; Charles Peabody was commissioned a first lieutenant to teach military science to college recruits; and Oric Bates died while in training as an artillery officer (Willoughby 1919:238–40). The situation was the same at other university and museum anthropology departments.

Nor was Lothrop alone in using anthropological research as a cover while working for military intelligence during the First World War. The British employed British archaeologists—T. E. Lawrence and Leonard Wooley in Syria and Gertrude Bell in Egypt and Iraq—as agents to gather intelligence of German activities (Price 2003:32). In the United States, at least seven men with anthropological connections, in addition to academics from other fields, served with the Office of Naval Intelligence in Latin America during the First World War. Not all of them had Harvard affiliations. For example, Agent 141, Theodoor de Booy (1881–1919), after conducting archaeological explorations in the Caribbean, held a position at the Museum of the American Indian–Heye Foundation from 1912 through 1917. In 1918 he began archaeological work in Venezuela, supported partially as an associate curator at the University Museum at Pennsylvania. But he soon shifted to work for the ONI, using his credentials as an archaeologist as cover.

Four of the agents, however—Samuel Lothrop, Sylvanus Morley, Herbert Spinden, and William Mechling—did have Harvard associations, and Morley was responsible for recruiting two others. Soon after the war, their spying would lead to one of the unhappier controversies in the history of American anthropology, resulting in the censure of Franz Boas, who objected to the agents' activities as unethical, by his peers.

Sylvanus Morley was perhaps the most important of the archaeologist spies for the ONI in Latin America. The ONI deployed nearly 30 agents in Mexico and Central America during World War I, and Morley apparently was responsible for recruiting a significant number of them. He ultimately ran a team of 10 subagents (Harris and Sadler 2003:37, 162). Morley had been approached by a fellow member of the Cosmos Club in Washington, D.C., Charles Alexander Sheldon, chief of naval operations, to provide a "list of available anthropologists" who might be recruited as agents. Bringing the list with him, Morley was commissioned as Agent 53 in April 1917, with the rank of ensign in the Naval Coastal Defense Reserves, for a four-year tour of duty. He was to search for German submarine bases, combat pro-German activities, and organize an intelligence network to cover the coast of Central America (Harris and Sadler 2003:46, 48). Morley recruited other agents from among his Harvard Peabody and CIW associates, his Cosmos Club friends, and his other anthropological acquaintances.

Although Morley traveled in uniform when in the United States, while in Central America he "conspicuously maintained his archaeological cover" (Harris and Sadler

2003:240). The Carnegie Institution of Washington even paid Morley the difference between his monthly naval salary and his CIW salary of $2,640 a year (Brunhouse 1971:115; Harris and Sadler 2003:54). It apparently was Morley's field cover and his recruitment of so many fellow anthropologists to work with him that led Charles Harris and Louis Sadler (2003:xiii, 315) to declare that "Morley was arguably the finest American spy of World War I" and that his anthropological agents were "arguably the best American intelligence network in World War I." Morley continued to provide the Military Information Division with maps and reports from 1919 to 1922, apparently to fulfill the requirements of his four-year commission (Harris and Sadler 2003:291).

Samuel Lothrop knew Sylvanus Morley from the Cosmos Club as well as from Lothrop's fieldwork while a graduate student. In April 1917 Morley sent Lothrop a telegram in Honduras, asking him to leave his field project and meet with Morley in Washington the next month. Lothrop was commissioned as civilian Agent 173 in May 1917 (Harris and Sadler 2003:60, 63). In April 1918, when Central America was divided into five sections, Section 2, the east coast of Nicaragua, fell under Lothrop's supervision. Soon he was transferred to Section 1, Costa Rica. Later that year he resigned as a civilian agent and officially joined the ONI (Harris and Sadler 2003:180–81, 201).

Contrary to the argument of Harris and Sadler (2003:54) that the archaeologists did no archaeology and collected no materials while working for the ONI, Lothrop continued to collect and send artifacts to the Peabody during this time. In 1917 he ran the Peabody's Central American Expedition in Honduras and Guatemala, and when his ONI responsibilities were shifted to Costa Rica, the Central American Expedition went there with him (Willoughby 1919:238). He is said to have used Maya hieroglyphs to encode his notes (Harris and Sadler 2003:212).

Herbert Spinden, as we saw earlier, was a good friend of Morley's and several of the other people involved in the "spying scandal." In April 1917, just as Morley was recruiting Lothrop, he also wrote to the AMNH, for which Spinden was leading a five-year survey in Central America, asking the museum to send Spinden to work with him as a spy. It did so, and Spinden was commissioned that month as Agent 56 (Harris and Sadler 2003:49).

Spinden, too, continued his archaeological activities while working for the ONI. The AMNH was pleased with his collecting and in March 1918 asked him to continue working with Morley and the ONI for another year, at the same $2,200 salary the AMNH had paid him for 1917 (Harris and Sadler 2003:109). When Central America was divided into five sections in 1918, Spinden was assigned Section 3, El Salvador and the Pacific coast of Honduras and Nicaragua. In November his area was expanded to cover Panama and Colombia as well (Harris and Sadler 2003:270), suggesting that he was an effective agent.

Another agent whom Morley recruited was Thomas Francis William Gann (1867–1938), Agent 242. A doctor who served as a district medical officer in Belize from 1894 to 1923, Gann established a reputation as an amateur archaeologist and became friends with Morley, accompanying him on several expeditions. During the war, besides working as an agent for the British, he became one of Morley's most important ONI subagents, gathering intelligence under cover of being an archaeologist. Later, from 1919 to 1938, Gann became a lecturer in Central American archaeology at the University of Liverpool (Harris and Sadler 2003:37, 162, 240, 297). He caused an uproar when he smuggled a Maya jade plaque out of Mexico in order to donate it to Harvard. Morley, who had hired Gann for the CIW's Chichen Itza project, had to drop his appointment.

Morley also recruited John Held Jr. (1889–1958), an artist who had become friends with Spinden through the AMNH. In 1916 Held visited New Mexico, where he met Morley at the American School of Archaeology in Santa Fe. The next year Morley offered him a position as archaeological artist on the CIW's expedition to Central America, and when Morley went to work for the ONI, he brought Held with him as a paid civilian subagent, Agent 154 (Harris and Sadler 2003:51, 62). He purportedly was to study Maya art forms, but his real job was to sketch the coastline and scout for sites for military operations. By 1918 Held and Morley were responsible for Section 4 of Central America, the north coast of Honduras (Harris and Sadler 2003:180). Held worked again for intelligence during the Second World War, in the Army Signal Corps (Harris and Sadler 2003:294).

One Harvard-associated ONI agent, William Mechling, was conspicuously unsuccessful as a spy. Mechling, having worked with Boas at the International School in Mexico City and having received his Ph.D. from Harvard in 1917, was hired by the Field Museum in Chicago in March of that year. Because of his reserve officer status, he was called to war service before he could begin the job. The ONI commissioned him Agent 52 in April 1917, and he quickly recruited his friend John Alden Mason to serve with him. Mason had received his Ph.D. in anthropology under Kroeber at Berkeley in 1911 and from then until 1913 had been the University of Pennsylvania Fellow at the International School in Mexico City. There he had worked with Boas and become friends with Mechling and Manuel Gamio. In April 1917, while Mason was working as curator of Mexican and South American archaeology at the Field Museum, Mechling telegraphed him, asking him come to Washington, D.C. Granted permission by Berthold Laufer at the Field Museum, Mason did so and was commissioned Agent 157 (Harris and Sadler 2003:50).

After being commissioned, Mechling and Mason departed for Mexico, requesting permits to work in Yucatán, ostensibly to collect for the Field Museum. Mechling, however, was apparently not cut out for the spying business. He immediately ran into trouble and was arrested and thrown in jail. Mason had to appeal to Manuel Gamio to help get him released. Their cover was blown. The ONI recalled the two in August and decommissioned them in September. Their career as spies had lasted less than six months (Harris and Sadler 2003:50–53). As we saw earlier, Mechling did not remain in anthropology for much longer. Mason, on the other hand, had a long career in Americanist anthropology and archaeology, returning to the Field Museum until 1924 and then holding a curatorship at the University Museum at Pennsylvania until his retirement in 1955.

It appears to have been Mechling and Mason's attempt to work for the ONI that precipitated the events resulting in Franz Boas's later censure by the American Anthropological Association. From correspondence included in several sources (Harris and Sadler 2003; Rutsch 1997; Stocking 1968, 1974), we can make the following reconstruction.

In July 1917 Manuel Gamio wrote to his friend and old Ph.D. advisor, Boas, that Mason and Mechling had applied for permission to conduct archaeological work in Yucatán—for the Peabody Museum, he thought. Boas wrote to Alfred Tozzer, asking how the Peabody was involved, but Tozzer answered that because of confidentiality, he could not comment on Mason and Mechling's project. At the same time, Boas wrote to Berthold Laufer at the Field Museum, asking him what Mason was doing. Laufer replied that Mason had been granted indefinite leave from the Field Museum in April to work on a political mission for the War Department. Laufer clearly indicated that the archaeological project was a cover and asked Boas not to tell Gamio about the political aspect of the work.

But Boas did write to Gamio, indicating that Mason and Mechling were not working for the Field Museum but acting as government agents. Gamio was surprised, responding to Boas that when Mechling had come in April, he had offered him a job as an ethnologist working for the national museum. Mechling had declined, and he and Mason had then gone to Yucatán.

What seems particularly to have upset Boas was that Mechling and Mason were widely known to have worked with him while he was director of the International School in Mexico. He saw a need to try to distance himself from their activities. Therefore, in addition to replying to Gamio, Boas wrote in early August to Ezequiel Chávez, another old Mexican colleague involved with the International School, to denounce Mechling and Mason's activities. Chávez wrote back in September, asking Boas to return to Mexico to help stop that kind of activity (Rutsch 1997:160–61). Boas did not go, but he continued monitoring American anthropological work in Mesoamerica. In December 1917 he wrote to Robert H. Lowie that he had found that Mason, Mechling, Morley, and Spinden were all spying for the United States (Harris and Sadler 2003:285–87). Boas must also have been well acquainted with the activities of Theodoor de Booy, who was a friend of Boas's and a fellow in Boas's American Ethnological Society. Indeed, Boas surely knew about the activities of all the anthropologists who were involved one way or another in the alleged spying.

Despite having clearly known about the spying for two years, it was not until 1919 that Boas wrote the public letter "Scientists as Spies," which finally sparked controversy. He first sent the letter to *Science,* where his old friend and former Columbia colleague John McKeen Cattell was editor, but Cattell had refused to publish it because of its contents (Lesser 1981:18). Disregarding this warning, Boas sent the piece to *The Nation,* which published it in October (Boas 1919a). Among other things, Boas wrote:

A person, however, who uses science as a cover for political spying, who demeans himself to pose before a foreign government as an investigator and asks for assistance in his alleged researches in order to carry on, under this cloak, his political machinations, prostitutes science in an unpardonable way and forfeits the right to be classed as a scientist.

By accident, incontrovertible proof has come to my hands that at least four men, who carry on anthropological work, while employed as government agents, introduced themselves to foreign governments as representatives of scientific institutions in the United States, and as sent out for the purpose of carrying on scientific researches. They have not only shaken the belief in the truthfulness of science, but they have also done the greatest possible disservice to scientific inquiry. In consequence of their acts every nation will look with distrust upon the visiting foreign investigator who wants to do honest work, suspecting sinister designs.

The anthropological community, even if individual members did not know precisely which four men Boas meant, already knew about the activities he was castigating. All the institutions involved knew of their personnel's work for military intelligence and in some cases even helped pay their salaries. Morley and Spinden, both navy ensigns, were publicly recorded as such in the Navy Registers for 1917 and 1918 (Harris and Sadler 2003:63); their intelligence-gathering roles were a matter of public record early in the war. Many of these agents, including Morley and Spinden, wore uniforms when in the United States and talked about their activities openly with their anthropological colleagues.

Moreover, the Allies had just won the war a month before Boas's letter appeared, and the accused anthropologists were seen as having contributed to the successful war effort. Many of their peers considered them patriots and even heroes for having helped end the war. They were colleagues, friends, and acquaintances. Their accuser, on the other hand, had made no secret of his pro-German stance during the war (for example, see Boas 1916). He had been an active participant in pro-German groups such as the Germanistic Society of America. Harris and Sadler (2003:287) commented that "Franz Boas did everything he could to blow Mason and Mechling's cover, which, along with their own indiscretion, helps to explain why their mission failed so miserably."

Boas's broadside might have been unpopular for those reasons alone, but political contests for control of power bases within anthropology were involved, too. These contests were far too complex for us to discuss closely here, and much has been written about them elsewhere (see Lesser 1981; Price 2000, 2001, 2002, 2003; Stocking 1968). Briefly, they revolved around control of the American Anthropological Association and the National Research Council (NRC), the latter, established in 1916, being an important new source of funding. Boas and other sociocultural anthropologists were viewed as attempting to take control of the AAA from archaeologists and physical anthropologists, many of them associated with the government institutions in Washington, D.C.— the Smithsonian, the U.S. National Museum, and the Bureau of American Ethnology.

Boas had indeed conducted some complex maneuvering through the AAA to get himself named to the council of the new NRC Division of Anthropology and Psychology. As David Price (2000:24) noted, Boas's opponents viewed the ethical questions he raised in his letter as merely a smoke screen for his political agenda.

The issue was further complicated by the fact that Boas was involved in a U.S. federal court case at the time, supporting a Dutch (or perhaps Austrian) émigré ethnographer, Herman Marie Bernelot Moens (1875–1938), who in 1918 had been accused by the Department of Justice of being a German spy (Anonymous 1919b). Convicted, Moens was appealing his case in 1919. On November 25 that year, barely two weeks before Boas's own hearing at the AAA, Boas was in contact with Moens about setting up a meeting to consult with him on the appeal, in which Boas was going to testify for the defense (Boas 1919c). One of the people testifying for the prosecution in the Moens case was the Washington, D.C., physical anthropologist Aleš Hrdlička. The prominence of Hrdlička versus Boas in the Moens case makes it evident that this case must be considered another component of the political battle for control of anthropology between Boas and the "Washington anthropologists."

In any case, the executive council of the AAA discussed the letter at its 1919 meeting in Cambridge. Board member Neil M. Judd introduced a resolution to censure Boas, and it passed by 20 votes to 10. The effective result of the censure was that Boas was removed from the AAA board and the NRC committee, although these actions turned out scarcely to impede the ultimate influence he and his students would exert over the discipline in the next quarter century. The broader philosophical issue—the ethics of collaboration between anthropologists and intelligence-gathering agencies—was swamped by the disciplinary infighting, and exactly such cooperation between academia and military agencies would continue during World War II and later. Indeed, a majority of the U.S. anthropologists whom we cover in chapter 12 seem to have worked happily in one component or another of military intelligence during the Second World War.

By the time World War I had ended and the spying controversy had begun to fade, anthropology at Harvard had matured, passing its quarter-century mark. The Peabody Museum's anthropology program was a leader in developing curriculum. Many departments around the country were being founded by the archaeologists, ethnologists, and biological anthropologists who were receiving Ph.D.s from the Peabody. The fortuity of the Carnegie Institution of Washington's situating its archaeological headquarters adjacent to the Peabody Museum aided the growth and dominance of archaeology at the museum, which took over the reins from the government archaeologists of the Smithsonian Institution, Bureau of American Ethnology, and U.S. National Museum.

The training of graduate students at the Peabody Museum was now being influenced heavily by the "cohort effect." One can easily define clusters of nascent scholars that formed, burgeoned, and were replaced by other clusters. We see Herbert Spinden,

George Will, and Robert Hellman, for example, doing fieldwork together under Roland Dixon and becoming friends. We see Spinden later working with Sylvanus Morley on Maya calendrics and serving with him in naval intelligence during the war. Morley himself received his field training in the U.S. Southwest together with A.V. Kidder, who later worked for three seasons in Arizona with Samuel Guernsey and at Pecos Pueblo with Charles Amsden, Carl Guthe, George Vaillant, Earnest Hooton, and Samuel Lothrop. The interconnections are myriad. The intellectual development of the apprentice anthropologists was clearly affected as much by their colleagues as by their instructors. As illustrated by events associated with the "spy scandal" of 1919, the discipline had also grown to encompass strong, competing intellectual schools, vying for political control of anthropological research and training.

11

Growth and Professionalism in the Twenties

THE PERIOD FROM AFTER WORLD WAR I TO THE GREAT DEPRESSION, roughly 1919 to 1929, saw significant growth in anthropology at Harvard. In addition to an increase in the size of the program, it was marked by a continued shift toward more professionalism in research related to museum collections, so that contributions by non-anthropologists were of increasingly less importance. Initially, Alfred Tozzer and archaeology tended to dominate the graduate program. In part this was because the offices of the Carnegie Institution of Washington (CIW) were next door to the Peabody Museum, at 10 Frisbie Place, in a late-nineteenth-century home turned into a research facility. Close ties formed between the two research staffs, and many students were able to secure employment on CIW archaeological projects. (Strangely, only two of the students working for the CIW during this period completed their Ph.D.s.) But as the 1920s continued, Roland Dixon and, especially, Earnest Hooton recruited and trained more advanced students in sociocultural and biological anthropology.

The graduate anthropology program at Harvard had obtained sufficient international renown by the end of its first quarter century (1890–1915) that it began to attract foreign students. This was a significant change, for until then it had been European institutions that tended to attract this audience. Although we focus here on graduate students, we should note that this was also the period when European scholars began occasionally coming to social sciences at Harvard on exchange programs. For example, Lucien Levy-Bruhl served as an exchange professor from France for the 1919–20 term (Harvard University 1937:298).

With respect to graduate students, Julio Tello and Eduardo Noguera entered the program from Latin America. From East Asia came Li Chi, Ssu-Yung Liang, Nenozo Utsurikawa, Marcelo Tangco, and Biraja Guha. And unlike some of its sister institutions, the Harvard program encouraged African American students, with Caroline Day and William Hansberry receiving degrees. We look first at the students from abroad.

Julio César Tello (1880–1947) was a Quechua Indian born in Huarochiri, Peru. On his mother's side he was descended from one of the Inca rulers of Huarochiri (Cleland

1991:686). He received his S.B. in medicine at the Universidad Nacional de San Marcos in Lima in 1908 and his M.D. in 1909. He won a national scholarship to study abroad and decided to enroll at Harvard when Harvard offered him a tuition scholarship. Tello had provided the Peabody Museum with artifacts as early as 1909 and had sent examples of trephined skulls to the medical school in 1910–11, so he had some previous contact with Harvard (Putnam 1911:225). He at first had some language trouble at Harvard, but Dixon tutored him in the evenings, "a kindness of which he often spoke with gratitude. As a result, he soon could follow lectures intelligently" (Lothrop 1948:51).

Tello received his A.M. from Harvard in 1911. Because of this success, he was awarded another scholarship from Peru for 1912. He decided to go to Europe to continue his studies but ran out of money there. He asked Tozzer for a new connection with the Peabody Museum in a letter of September 29, 1912. Frederic Putnam replied to him on November 13, 1912, informing Tello that he had been appointed an "Associate in Anthropological Research in Peru," with a stipend of $300 for 1912–13 (Peabody Museum, Biographical Files). In order to return to Peru after he finished that year, Tello had to borrow funds from Putnam for the trip (Lothrop 1948:51).

Back in Lima in 1913, Tello became director of the Department of Archaeology at the Museo Histórico Nacional. He also became the first Peruvian archaeologist to apply scientific methods to excavations, employing in part procedures he had learned at the Peabody Museum (Cleland 1991:686). He remained in touch with Putnam, Tozzer, and Charles Willoughby and occasionally sent artifacts to the museum. In 1936 he was appointed honorary curator of Andean archaeology for the Peabody Museum (Scott 1938:353), a position he held until his death (Harvard University 1937:353).

In 1941, in order to gain some additional wartime intelligence sources, the Department of State made a grant to the Institute of Andean Research to conduct archaeological work in Peru. William D. Strong, of Columbia University, was selected to run the project, and Gordon Willey, who later had a long and distinguished career at the Peabody Museum, came along as his assistant. They needed a field project as official cover, and Tello arranged for them to work at Pachacamac (Gorenstein 2002:1255). Samuel Lothrop also returned to Peru because of the war, again acting as an agent gathering military intelligence. Thus in 1941–42, Tello and Lothrop worked together on Paracas textiles (Scott 1942:430). Although Tello also rendered assistance to Alfred Kidder II, John Rowe, and Harry and Marion Tschopik (see chapter 12) in their work in Peru in the early 1940s, it was mainly as a facilitator of paperwork for their Andean projects. The Paracas textile work was his last major research project for the Peabody Museum.

Eduardo Guadalupe Noguera Auza (1896–1977) was born in Mexico City. He studied in Europe from 1911 to 1914, when war broke out. He was a good friend of Manuel Gamio's, and when Noguera returned to Mexico, Gamio recommended that he continue his work at Harvard (Berlin 1978:618). Noguera entered Harvard as a "special student," and for the next three years the Peabody Museum supported his studies through the Winthrop Scholarship and the Hemenway Fellowship. He did not complete his degree requirements and returned to Mexico in 1920. After a period working there, Noguera went abroad in 1923–24 to take part in the excavation program of the American School of Prehistoric Research (later incorporated as part of the Peabody Museum research agenda) and also to study at the Ecole d'Anthropologie in Paris, but he completed no degree work there either.

Noguera had begun excavations in Mexico in 1920, when he returned from Harvard, and he continued excavating there over the next half century. He was named head of archaeology for the Dirección de Antropología from 1925, when he returned from France, until 1941 (Berlin 1978:618). From 1941 to 1946 he was director of the Museo Nacional de Arqueología e Historia, and from 1946 to 1956, director of pre-Hispanic monuments for the Instituto Nacional de Antropología e Historia (Berlin 1978:619).

Noguera also taught archaeological ceramics and stratigraphic culture history part-time at the Escuela Nacional de Antropología e Historia and in the anthropology section of the Instituto de Investigaciones Históricas of the Universidad Nacional Autónoma de México (which was later transformed into the Instituto de Investigaciones Antropológicas) from 1937 to 1961, when he retired. He then continued research in Mexico until his death. He is probably best known to archaeologists in the United States for his work at Casas Grandes in Chihuahua, although he also conducted excavations at Tlatilco, Cuicuilco, Tizatlan, Tenayuca, Labna, Sayil, Teotihuacan, Cholula, Monte Alban, Xochicalco, and several other sites. On the basis of this fieldwork, he wrote four books and more than 150 articles.

Nenozo Utsurikawa/Utsushikawa (1884–1947) was born in Japan with the family name Utsushikawa. When he came to the United States to enter school, his official documents became garbled, and the name was incorrectly rendered Utsurikawa. Deciding not to fight this spelling error, he remained Utsurikawa while in the United States, and most publication sources in English translate his name as Utsurikawa.

Utsurikawa was first sent to preparatory school for the University of Illinois in 1909 to learn English. From there he went to the University of Chicago, where he received his Ph.B. in 1914 (Ko 2003:81). He left Chicago for Harvard, to study with Dixon, and was supported in his first year by Winthrop funds and the next two years by Hemenway funds. His dissertation, "Some Aspects of the Decorative Art of Indonesia: A Study in Ethnographic Relations," was defended in 1917 before Dixon and Hooton. Dixon thought highly enough of his work that he helped arrange for Utsurikawa to receive the Frederick Sheldon Traveling Fellowship from Harvard, which supported him in further work the next year, 1918, in Indonesia (Harvard University 1937:1071).

Utsurikawa returned to Japan in 1919. He taught first at Keio Gijuku University and then at Tokyo Shoka University. Political rhetoric heated up in Japan, and because of Utsurikawa's U.S. training, he was edged out of positions on the main islands. In 1928 he became a professor of ethnology at Taihoku Imperial University on Taiwan, a newly established colonial institution, where he created and chaired the Department of

Ethnology and Anthropology. Utsurikawa focused on ethnological and archaeological research among the tribal peoples of Taiwan for the next two decades. Even though relegated to the periphery by political enemies, "he played a significant role in theoretical development" in anthropology in Japan from 1930 through 1945 (Ko 2003:82).

Utsurikawa stayed in touch with Dixon and the Peabody Museum, sending back ethnographic materials from time to time from Taiwan and other Asian locales (Reynolds 1931a:292; Willoughby 1919:241). When the Japanese left Taiwan at the end of World War II, Utsurikawa's Harvard compatriot, Li Chi, took over as his successor at the university in Taipei. Unfortunately, Li Chi found that the ethnological and archaeological materials Utsurikawa had collected had been damaged by U.S. Air Force bombing at the end of the war (Ko 2003:111, 365 n. 4). When he returned to Japan, Utsurikawa remained active in the field, helping to establish the postwar Archaeological Society shortly before he died (Groot 1948:169).

Li Chi (1896–1979), also found in the literature as Li Ji and Chi Li, was born in Chung-hsiang, Hupeh, China. When he came to the United States, he went first to Clark University to study sociology and psychology. There he received his A.B. in 1919 and his A.M. in 1920 (Chang 1991:407). He then transferred to Harvard to study anthropology and was supported for his first two years there by Winthrop Scholarship funds. In 1923 he received his Ph.D. with the dissertation "The Formation of the Chinese People: An Anthropological Inquiry," defended before Dixon, Hooton, Chase, and William Zebina Ripley of the Department of Political Economy. He returned to China to take a job at Nankai College, Tientsin, from 1923 to 1925 and then taught at Tsinghua Research Institute in Beijing from 1925 to 1928 (Hsu 1980:217; National Research Council 1938:258).

Li Chi assumed responsibility for organizing the first archaeological section at the Institute of History and Philology, Academia Sinica, Taipei, in 1928. Through this institute he ran 15 projects at Anyang and Lungshan from 1928 to 1937 (Hsu 1980:217). In those places he "was able for the first time to apply modern archaeological concepts and methods"—including stratigraphy and context—"to an important Chinese site on a continuing basis, which enabled these concepts and methods to take root in the Chinese scholarly community" (Chang 1980:218). There he also recruited and trained the first generation of Chinese archaeologists. After the war, Li Chi moved to Taiwan, where he took over the museum and department established by Utsurikawa. He reestablished the Department of Archaeology and Anthropology at National Taiwan University, the first Chinese program to train professional archaeologists (Chang 1991:408). Li Chi provided inspiration and guidance to **Kwang-Chih Chang** (1931–2001), who wrote his B.A. thesis on the Lungshan culture at National Taiwan University in 1954. Chang came to the United States in 1955, received his Ph.D. from Harvard in 1960, and later taught Chinese archaeology at Harvard and Yale for many years.

Ssu-Yung Liang or **Siyong Liang** (1904–54) was a junior colleague of Li Chi's. He was born while his family was in political exile in Yokohama, Japan, but spent most of his youth in Beijing. When he came to the United States, he first attended Dartmouth, where he received his A.B. in 1926. He apparently entered the graduate school at Harvard before completing his degree requirements at Dartmouth, for he is listed as having worked on his 1927 A.M. degree at Harvard from 1925 to 1927 (Harvard University 1930:1346). He then continued his association with Harvard, first from 1927 through 1929 working in Cambridge. For the summer of 1929, Liang and his Harvard classmate William B. Bowers received two of six scholarships in archaeology awarded by the Laboratory of Anthropology in Santa Fe, New Mexico, to work with A.V. Kidder at Pecos (Cole, Dixon, and Kidder 1929:571). From 1930 through 1932 Liang was a fellow at the Harvard-Yenching Institute in Beijing. Although he was ostensibly working on his Ph.D. during this time, he never completed the degree. He helped Li Chi run the excavations at Anyang during fields seasons from 1928 through 1937, and through their program they were responsible for training all of China's archaeological leaders for the next four decades (Chang 1981:158). Liang wrote English summaries of Li Chi's and his own work (Liang 1930, 1931), which for many years were key references on the Chinese Neolithic. He continued working with his old Harvard classmates from time to time, supplying Gabriel Lasker, for example, with a series of teeth for his study of Chinese people born and reared in China and North America (Lasker 1945).

Marcelo V. Tangco (1893–1987) came to Harvard from the Philippines to work with Dixon and Hooton. Born in Manila, he received his A.B. from the University of the Philippines in 1916 and his S.B. in education there in 1918. He was then hired by H. Otley Beyer as his assistant to teach anthropology at the university (Zamora 1978:591).

Beyer recognized the need for Tangco to get more background in anthropology, so he helped arrange for Tangco to be sent as a fellow from the University of the Philippines for training in the United States from 1921 to 1925. Tangco went to Beyer's alma mater, Harvard, to work with Dixon beginning in 1921. He received his A.M. in 1922 at Harvard and stayed for another year of coursework with Dixon and Hooton (Zamora 1978:595). Dixon then sent Tangco on to Berkeley to work with A. L. Kroeber. Tangco took courses at Berkeley from 1923 to 1925 but received no further degree. He then returned to the University of the Philippines to continue as Beyer's assistant, handling most of the undergraduate and graduate teaching in anthropology there from 1925 to 1941 and, after the war, from 1946 to 1954, while Beyer conducted research (Zamora 1978:592).

Tangco was the first Filipino trained as an anthropologist who taught in the Philippines and thus is the native founding father of anthropology there, in contrast to foreign founders such as Beyer. Tangco was the first person to teach physical anthropology in the country. When Beyer retired in 1954, Tangco became chair of the department and thus was the first Filipino to be a full professor and a chair of an anthropology department (Zamora 1978:589). He continued in these positions until he himself retired in 1958.

Biraja Sankar Guha (1894–1961) was born of high-caste status in Assam, in British-ruled India. At college he majored in philosophy, receiving his A.B. in 1912 and his A.M. in 1915 in that field from the University of Calcutta. After earning his A.M., he joined the staff of Bangabasi College as a lecturer in philosophy (Biwas 1961:120). Guha had met Roland Dixon when Dixon carried out an anthropological survey in India in 1912. His contacts with Dixon "helped him in making the decision to switch over to anthropology, and especially to come to Harvard for his professional training" (Sinha 1963:384).

Guha entered Harvard in 1920 and was supported for 1921–23 as a graduate assistant by Hemenway Fund money. Before coming to Harvard, he had done some ethnographic work with tribes in Assam and Bengal. His first field investigation in the United States under Dixon consisted of work with the Utes and Navajos of Colorado and New Mexico as a "Special Research Officer" of the Smithsonian Institution (Sinha 1963:384). He received a second A.M. in anthropology from Harvard in 1922 and his Ph.D. in 1924. He defended his dissertation, "The Racial Basis of the Caste System in India," before Dixon and Hooton.

Guha returned to India, where in 1926 he joined the anthropology faculty at the only institution where the subject was taught then, the newly opened department at the University of Calcutta. In 1927 he became the "Superintending Anthropologist" at the Zoological Survey of India, a position he held until 1945. He began massive works on the ethnology of India under the aegis of that institution. In 1936, while still at the Zoological Survey, he helped establish the Indian Anthropological Institute at Calcutta (Sinha 1963:382). He helped establish the Anthropological Survey of India in 1945 and became its first director in 1946, holding the job until he retired in 1954 (Biwas 1961:120). At Calcutta, Guha was a colleague of Panchanan Mitra, whose 1930 Yale Ph.D. dissertation, "A History of American Anthropology" (Mitra 1933), is an important but little-known document.

Although Harvard College had admitted students of African American ancestry as early as the 1790s, such students faced a rough period right after the First World War, with increasing racism, xenophobia, and immigration quotas. As we described in chapter 6, Harvard had started the century "color-blind," but by the 1920s President Lowell had overridden the faculty and put racial, religious, and ethnic quotas in place. Acting on his own, Lowell in 1922 barred blacks from living in the freshman dormitories, although freshman dorm living was compulsory for whites. Whereas previously the university had provided living quarters for all students, now blacks were left on their own (Titcomb 1993:6). Against this background we see, in contrast, that anthropologists at the Peabody were still working comfortably with the African American students who came their way.

Caroline Stewart Bond Day (1889–1948) was born in Montgomery, Alabama. She was born Caroline Fagan Stewart but later changed her name to Caroline Stewart Bond and then married Aaron Day in 1920 (Ross, Adams, and Williams 1999:39, 41). She received her A.B. from Atlanta University in Georgia in 1912 and then taught and worked for four years. She entered Radcliffe in 1916 and received her second A.B. there in 1919. While pursuing studies through Radcliffe, she was introduced to anthropology in a class taught by Earnest Hooton and began research for her senior honors thesis with him. The project developed into a research interest on which she continued to work sporadically for the next dozen years.

From 1920 to 1927 Caroline Bond Day worked in academia, teaching English and drama and writing essays and short stories (Caroline Bond Day Papers, Harvard University). She returned as a graduate student to work with Hooton at the Peabody Museum in 1927. She received her A.M. there in 1929, on the basis of research she had done with some 300 mixed-ancestry African American families (Willoughby 1928:273). Her thesis, "A Study of Some Negro-White Families in the United States," was published in 1932. She continued teaching in anthropology for two years after receiving her A.M. and then went into social work. She had planned to return to Harvard to complete her Ph.D. but was never able to accomplish this.

William Leo Hansberry (1894–1965) was another Southern student of African ancestry, born in Gloster, Mississippi. His father, Elden, had taught history there at Alcorn College, a segregated school for black students. Hansberry enrolled in Atlanta University in 1915 but found little in the curriculum to support his interests. After reading several works by W. E. B. Dubois, who had done his undergraduate work at Harvard, Hansberry transferred to Harvard as a special student in the spring of 1917. He was accepted into the college as a regular student for the 1918 term. Hansberry was called to war duties but returned and received a special "war degree" S.B. in 1921.

Hansberry began graduate work in anthropology in 1921–22, working particularly with Hooton. But apparently he was short of funds, for he took a one-year teaching job at Straight College in New Orleans. In 1922 he accepted an offer to teach in the Department of History at Howard University in Washington, D.C., and that year he taught the first course on African civilization offered at any American university. In 1925 he established the African Studies program at Howard.

Hansberry returned to the Peabody to continue work on his degree part-time in 1929, on partial leave from Howard University, and was supported in part by a Winthrop Scholarship for 1929–30. After he completed his A.M. in 1932, he went back to teaching African studies at Howard. He did some fieldwork in East and West Africa but did not publish widely; his single major contribution, on Ethiopian history, was published posthumously. He continued teaching at Howard until he retired in 1959 (Harvard University 1937:297). If his name seems familiar, perhaps it is because his niece, Lorraine Hansberry, wrote the famous novel *A Raisin in the Sun*.

Two contemporaries of Hansberry's at Harvard, George Schwab and George Harley, though not themselves of African ancestry, also worked in Africa and had long associations with the Peabody Museum through their African studies. **George Schwab** (1876–1955) was born in Clinton, Massachusetts, and graduated from Amherst in 1905. His early association with Harvard was through gifts of ethnological and zoological specimens to the Peabody Museum and the MCZ, beginning as early as 1910. He began his occasional studies of African folklore in 1914 (Schwab 1914), sending additional anthropological source materials to the Peabody from time to time.

Schwab entered the anthropology program at the Peabody in 1918. One of his first projects was to construct a linguistic and tribal map of Africa for the U.S. Peace Commission at the end of World War I, a project he worked on with Hooton (Mark 1995:114; Willoughby 1920:198). Schwab received his A.M. from Harvard in 1919 and continued in graduate work in anthropology. He was supported as an "Associate in Anthropology in Cameroon" from 1919 to 1922 and with a Hemenway Fellowship in 1918–19 and 1921–22, but he did not complete his Ph.D. work (Willoughby 1921:243).

Schwab was named a museum "Research Associate in Anthropology for Liberian Ethnology" in 1924 and kept this affiliation until 1949 (Brew 1950:333), when he retired. When Harvey Firestone offered to support an anthropological expedition to Liberia in 1928, Hooton remembered his previous work with Schwab a decade before and connected Firestone with Schwab. Schwab went to Liberia that year and there met George W. Harley, M.D., worked with him and produced some joint publications with him. Schwab also worked in Cameroon, Kenya, and elsewhere in Africa, writing other anthropological papers on those areas (Reynolds 1932:296; Scott 1933:300).

George Way Harley (1894–1966), born in Asheville, North Carolina, was a physician who became a medical missionary and was thus interested in medical anthropology. At George Schwab's suggestion (Mark 1995:115), after the two met in Liberia in 1928, Harley took leave from his missionary duties to study at the Peabody with Thaw Fellowship support in 1930–31, but he completed no degree work. He was, however, appointed a second Peabody Museum research associate in anthropology for Liberia in 1931—joining Schwab, who had been appointed in 1924—and was initially stationed with Schwab in that country (Harvard University 1937:243). Harley finished his Ph.D. in 1938 with the dissertation "Native African Medicine" at the Hartford Seminary Foundation, Kennedy School of Missions. He published the dissertation in 1941 through Harvard and some of his other work through the Peabody Museum (Harley 1941a, 1941b).

Harley's position allowed him to take leave every seven years, and indeed we find him returning to Harvard to study and consult every seven years after his initial studies—that is, in 1937–38 and 1945–46. Thus he happened to be at Harvard when Patrick Putnam, whom we discuss later in this chapter, returned from equatorial Africa in the fall of 1945 and was able to provide Putnam with some advice on his work on his Pygmy data (Mark 1995:114). Harley's best-known work is the publication he wrote jointly with Schwab in 1947 on Liberian tribes (Schwab and Harley 1947). He maintained his association with Harvard through the late 1950s.

We know little of the women graduate students in anthropology during the 1920s, because of the traditional division between all-male Harvard and all-female Radcliffe. Although the records available for Harvard students in these early years are relatively abundant, those for Radcliffe women are scarce. In addition to Caroline Bond Day, we have found small amounts of information about four other women—Ellen Collier, Ruth Sawtell, Mary Butler, and Laura Thompson—who successfully pursued graduate work in anthropology in the 1920s. There were others, as the statistics in the next chapter show, but because of the paucity of records, we have yet to identify their contributions.

Ellen Sewall Collier (Spinden) (1897–1985) was born in Cohasset, Massachusetts. She graduated with "special distinction in history" from Radcliffe in 1919. Whether the "history" was actually Mesoamerican prehistory, we do not know, for Radcliffe students could not major in anthropology until 1925. In 1927 Collier entered graduate school at Radcliffe, receiving the $500 Augustus Anson Whitney and Benjamin White Whitney Fellowship in anthropology and specializing in archaeology (B. Brown 1929:14). While she was studying at the Peabody Museum, Alfred Tozzer recruited her to work on the massive project begun and funded by Charles Bowditch, involving the translation of the collected works of Eduard Seler. Her contribution was the 202-page translation from German to English of some of Seler's papers on Chichen Itza (version in the unpublished master file, Tozzer Library, vol. 5, pt. 2, no. 3, pp. 197–388).

In the fall of 1928 Ellen Collier married Herbert Spinden, the well-known Mayanist (chapter 10). She completed her A.M. in Mexican archaeology at Radcliffe in 1929 and left the Peabody Museum graduate program, but she found work on the staff of the Brooklyn Museum. Ellen Spinden sustained her anthropological interests. In 1930 she was elected to the AAA executive council for a three-year term (1930–33), at the same time her husband was elected first vice president of the AAA.

In 1929 and again in 1931, Herbert and Ellen Spinden made extended research visits to the Totonac site of El Tajin in Mexico. Ellen Spinden wrote up the work, which was the definitive study of this site in English for many years (E. Spinden 1933). She also went with her husband on Maya excavation projects in 1934, 1935, and 1936, but like many other wives, although she worked diligently in the field, she was essentially invisible except for rare footnotes barely acknowledging her presence. Of particular note, however, is that in December 1934 she was one of the 31 scholars who signed the papers founding the Society for American Archaeology (Guthe 1935:146). Although we have no definite divorce date for the couple, information from the Radcliffe Schlesinger Library archives indicates that her husband left in 1938, that Ellen then moved to Springfield, Massachusetts, where she took courses at the Springfield Business Institute in 1938–39, and that she then moved back to her family home in Cohasset. Herbert Spinden remarried in 1948, so the divorce must have been finalized by then. Except for the period of around 1927–38, we have so far found no other mention of archaeological or anthropological work by Ellen C. Spinden.

Ruth Otis Sawtell (Wallis) (1895–1978) was born in Springfield, Massachusetts, and also graduated with the Radcliffe class of 1919, with a major in English. She worked for an area newspaper after graduation, from 1919 to 1920, but then was influenced by Hooton to return to graduate school (Collins 1979:85). She received her A.M. in anthropology from Radcliffe in 1923. While she was at the Peabody, the staff put her English skills to use by making her assistant editor of the journal *Harvard African Studies,* and she worked with Hooton and Natica I. Bates on volume 3, for 1922. She also worked for A.V. Kidder, serving as a research assistant for the Pecos expedition from 1920 to 1923 (Collins 1979:85).

For 1923–25 Sawtell received the Radcliffe Traveling Fellowship in Science to conduct research in physical anthropology and archaeology in England, Germany, and France (Collins 1979:85). When she returned, she presented to the Peabody materials from her 1924–25 explorations in the Dordogne and Ariege, France, where she excavated two Azilian graves in the French Pyrenees at Montardit. She wrote up her work as a report for *Papers of the Peabody Museum,* "Azilian Skeletal Remains from Montardit (Ariege), France," in 1930 (Wallis 1931; Reynolds 1931a:288; Willoughby 1927:265).

Sawtell then transferred to Columbia in 1926 to work with Franz Boas on children's growth studies. She became the physical anthropologist for the Bureau of Education Experiments in New York City, collecting data there for her Ph.D., which she received in 1929 from Columbia. In 1930 she accepted the position of assistant professor at the University of Iowa, but her stay in Iowa was brief. She married **Wilson Dallam Wallis** (1886–1970) in 1931 and moved to Minneapolis, where he was teaching at the University of Minnesota. Wilson Wallis had been trained in ethnology at Oxford, came to the University of Pennsylvania in 1911, and obtained his Ph.D. there in 1915 (Kidwell 1999:238). While at Penn, Wallis became friends with William Mechling, one of the reputed spies during World War I whom we discussed in chapter 10, while Mechling was back there briefly after a year at the International School in Mexico. In the winter of 1913, Wallis went to Canada with Mechling, assisting him in his Geological Survey of Canada–sponsored ethnographic work with the Micmac and Maliseet Indians. The two also had Heye Foundation money to purchase artifacts for the University of Pennsylvania Museum.

Wilson Wallis is credited with founding the Department of Anthropology at Minnesota and was department chair there from 1938 to 1954. Because of the tenor of the times, particularly nepotism rules, it was difficult for Ruth Sawtell Wallis to obtain a job as a spouse. She secured a job at Hamline University in St. Paul from 1931 to 1935, but between 1935 and 1956 she was employed only intermittently. After her husband retired, she again found a reliable teaching position, at Annhurst College in Connecticut, from 1956 to 1966. After she married Wallis, the two carried out some joint ethnographic work among the Micmacs. She repaid Radcliffe for its support by supporting Elizabeth Colson's first year of graduate work there in 1940–41. Ruth Sawtell

Wallis maintained her writing skills: her first novel, *Too Many Bones,* published in 1943, won the Red Badge Prize for best first mystery (Collins 1979:86).

Mary Butler (Lewis) (1903–70), who was born in Media, Pennsylvania, appears to have been another of the first Radcliffe students to take advantage of the newly liberalized links between the Radcliffe and Harvard graduate programs. Butler received her A.B. from Vassar College in 1925. She then went to the Sorbonne in Paris for a year before returning to enter the graduate program at Radcliffe. She received her A.M. from Radcliffe in 1930, apparently based on the archaeology of Adena sites in West Virginia, although she also took coursework on the Mayas with Tozzer. On his recommendation, she transferred to the University of Pennsylvania in 1930, where she worked for the 1932 field season with John Alden Mason and Linton Satterthwaite at Piedras Negras in Guatemala. That work was the basis of her 1936 Ph.D. from the University of Pennsylvania, with the dissertation "Piedras Negras Pottery."

After receiving her degree, Butler continued doing fieldwork, as well as some teaching. She conducted excavations in western Pennsylvania in 1936 for the University of Pennsylvania Museum and a survey of the Hudson Valley in 1939–40 for Vassar. She continued work in Guatemala, with three additional field seasons at Alta Verapas and Quiche between 1939 and 1941, funded by her own grants. She taught briefly at Hunter College in 1937–38, at Vassar in 1939–40, and at Bryn Mawr in 1942–43. She was named an assistant at the University of Pennsylvania Museum from 1930 to 1939 and a research associate from 1940 through 1970. Most of her active fieldwork was limited to the period before she married Clifford Lewis III in 1942. During her career, Butler's early publications were mainly on the Mayas, and her later ones, mainly on Pennsylvania archaeology (Herskovits and Ames 1950:25; Keur 1971:255).

Laura Maud Thompson (Duker) (1905–2000) was another female graduate student who pops up briefly on our screen at Harvard in the late 1920s. She was born in Honolulu and received her A.B. from Mills College in Oakland, California, in 1927 (Parezo and Stephenson 2001:510). She moved to Boston, where she spent a short time as a social worker, and then went to the Peabody for the 1927–28 year with a $350 Radcliffe Anthropology Graduate Scholarship. After a year, however, feeling that the approach taken at the Peabody in her area was less than promising, she left to complete her Ph.D. work with Kroeber at Berkeley, where she received her Ph.D. in 1933. While working on her degree, she was employed from 1929 to 1933 as the assistant ethnologist at the Bernice P. Bishop Museum in Hawaii, a job apparently based on her Harvard training.

Laura Maud Thompson became well known for her applied anthropology studies, first in Guam with the Chamorro people, later in Fiji, and later still with American Indians in the U.S. Southwest and with Icelandic groups (Parezo and Stephenson 2001:511). In 1941 she was appointed director of research at the U.S. Bureau of Indian Affairs, and she worked with John Collier there from 1941 to 1947 (Warner 1988:129). Among her subsequent work was collaboration on the Hutterite project run by John W.

Bennett of Washington University in St. Louis. Bennett later founded the Department of Anthropology at Washington University.

A significant number of the students who entered the graduate program at the Peabody Museum in the early 1920s were attracted to it because of Tozzer's ongoing research in the Maya area. Many of these students went on to work for the Carnegie Institution of Washington. The number of students going into Maya studies tapered off in the late 1920s, perhaps as the available positions at the CIW, in particular, were filled by people who spent the rest of their careers there. During the decade from 1919 to 1929, Tozzer recruited nearly a dozen students into his Mesoamerican research program.

Oliver Hazard Perry La Farge (1901–63) was one of the students influenced by Tozzer to become a Mayanist. He was born in New York, the son of Christopher Grant La Farge (1862–1938), an artist who later did work on Navajo art for Elsie Clews Parsons at the AMNH. C. Grant La Farge was also secretary of the School of Fine Arts at the American Academy in Rome during the 1910s, so Oliver was exposed to both classical and Americanist archaeology while growing up.

Oliver La Farge went to prep school at Groton, where, according to Douglas Byers (1966b:408), "a copy of [Osborn's 1916] *Men of the Old Stone Age* in the Groton Library excited his imagination, and led him into archaeology. He went to Harvard with the avowed purpose of studying anthropology and solving the problems of the European Paleolithic." He entered Harvard in the fall of 1920. In the summer after the 1921–22 term, he investigated a Narragansett burial ground in Rhode Island (Willoughby 1923a:220). What finally changed La Farge's mind to favor work in the Americas was the next season's excavations with Samuel Guernsey at sites on the upper Chinle Wash of northeastern Arizona (Byers 1966b:408). He subsequently led another party on this project between his senior year, in 1924, and his first year of graduate work (Willoughby 1925:262).

It was during the 1924–25 year that La Farge met the Mayanist Frans Blom, which led to another change in his research direction. La Farge had been given the Hemenway Fellowship for his first year of graduate work, to continue his project on Chinle Wash. But Blom had just secured a position at the Middle America Research Institute at Tulane University, and he offered La Farge a chance to work with him in the Maya area on the First Tulane University Expedition, to collect linguistic and ethnographic data (Byers 1966a:406).

With Tozzer's blessing, La Farge resigned the second half-year of his Hemenway Fellowship and left for Tulane to take part in the expedition. Returning from the field, he stayed on at Tulane, taking an assistantship in ethnology there from the spring of 1926 through 1928. In 1927 he led the Third Tulane Expedition, to Jacaltenango, Guatemala, devoting his time mainly to ethnography. Thus La Farge's interest shifted from archaeology to ethnology early in his career. In 1928, however, when he came up for promotion at Tulane, he was fired, because he had apparently insulted the family of one of the university's trustees during a Mardi Gras ball.

La Farge returned to Harvard for the 1928–29 academic year, serving as a teaching assistant for Tozzer and writing up his 1927 field season to complete the work for his A.M. degree, which he received in 1929. He was a talented writer, and soon after he completed his A.M. he wrote the novel *Laughing Boy*, for which he received the Pulitzer Prize in 1930. La Farge continued doing Maya ethnography, working for much of the rest of his career in association with museums in Santa Fe, New Mexico, but returning to Harvard to serve on the Peabody Museum Visiting Committee when called.

Frans Ferdinand Blom (1893–1963) was born in Copenhagen to a wealthy family; later in life he was able to support his work in part from family fortunes (Brunhouse 1971:192). Blom received his Ph.B. from the University of Copenhagen in 1916, in fine and applied arts (Byers 1966a:406). He went to work from 1919 to 1922 for the Compañía Petrolera El Águila in Mexico (Grollig 1991:64), where he served as a guide and began to explore Maya ruins. He left the oil company for a job with the Mexican Dirección de Antropología in 1922 and was sent to do drawings for Sylvanus Morley, who was working on CIW excavations. Morley decided to add Blom to his field staff. Morley then wrote to Tozzer at Harvard requesting scholarship money for Blom, with the plan that Blom would complete his A.M. in two fall semesters, spending the intervening spring and summer in the field with Morley (Brunhouse 1971:193).

Blom thus enrolled at Harvard for the fall semester of 1923 and again in the fall of 1924, supported by Winthrop Scholarship money, and received his A.M. in 1925. It was at Harvard that he met Oliver La Farge. Blom apparently disliked the academic life (Brunhouse 1971:198), so when William E. Gates, whom Blom had known in Guatemala, became head of the new Institute of Middle American Research at Tulane and invited Blom to join his staff in late 1924, Blom lost no time accepting the offer (Brunhouse 1971:201). Gates had trained with Morley at the CIW in 1921 and later (Brunhouse 1971:151). In the early 1930s Blom began work at Uxmal, in Yucatán, but when money ran out during the Great Depression, he slipped into poor physical and mental health. He took many years to recover, but when he did, he continued ethnographic work in Chiapas among the Lacandones (Byers 1966a:407).

Harry Evelyn Dorr Pollock (1900–1982), born in Salt Lake City, received his undergraduate degree from Harvard in 1924, along with La Farge. Like several other students, he had been recruited into anthropology through Tozzer's class on the Mayas (Pollock 1948). After graduation Pollock worked for a New York City bond brokerage firm for the next five years.

But Pollock became disenchanted with brokerage work. According to one story, recollected by Robert Brunhouse (1971:229), Pollock met Morley at the Harvard Club in New York City in November 1927 and, at Morley's invitation, joined the CIW staff in 1928. According to a story Pollock told Gordon Willey (Willey 1983:783), Pollock met his old college classmate Ledyard Smith at the Harvard Club, fresh from his first season at Uaxactun, Guatemala, and it was Smith who lured him back into archaeology. Either way, whether through Morley's influence or Smith's, it was Pollock's connections with his former classmates from Tozzer's courses that led him to leave the bond brokerage business in 1928 and join the Carnegie Institution's field program in Central America.

Morley, as the Carnegie's field director, thought Pollock needed additional training and sent him to Harvard to begin graduate studies in 1928. He received his A.M. in 1930 and his Ph.D. in 1936, with the dissertation "Round Structures in Aboriginal Middle America." Earning his Ph.D. took a relatively long time because Pollock was simultaneously working for the CIW and had to fit his graduate studies around his job. To expedite matters, the Peabody Museum offered Pollock, Ledyard Smith, and Oliver Ricketson Jr., all of whom were working on degrees in the early 1930s, office space and facilities in the museum, even though they were also CIW employees at the time (Reynolds 1932:297).

After completing his Ph.D., Pollock continued working for the CIW's Department of Archaeology, based partly in the Peabody but working mainly out of the CIW offices, adjacent to the museum. Pollock was one of the few Ph.D.s who were part of the Carnegie program; most of the people there whom we profile in this section completed only A.M. training.

During World War II Pollock served as a major in the U.S. Army Air Corps. He returned to the CIW archaeology division after the war and became its director in 1950 when Kidder retired. Pollock became widely known for his work with the late Maya Puuc architectural style and for his excavations at Coba and Mayapan. When the CIW Department of Archaeology began to wind down, Pollock was appointed a Peabody Museum research fellow in Middle American archaeology in 1952 (Brew 1954:373), while keeping the position of director of archaeology at the CIW. He maintained the joint title until July 1, 1958, when the Division of Archaeology of the CIW closed. Pollock then transferred completely to the Peabody, becoming curator of Middle American archaeology in 1962 and honorary curator in 1968, when he retired.

Oliver Garrison Ricketson Jr. (1894–1952), born in Pittsburgh, was another CIW archaeologist initially recruited by Tozzer. Ricketson was a great-nephew of Andrew Carnegie, a member of the Harvard class of 1916, and one of the first four students to take physical anthropology from Earnest Hooton (Lothrop 1953:69). Ricketson entered Harvard Medical School in 1916 but left the following year to join the navy for World War I. In 1919, after the war's end, he returned to finish one year of medical school but then left again and went to live with the Wetherill family in the Chaco Canyon archaeological area of New Mexico (Lothrop 1953:69). While there, he was recruited by Samuel Guernsey to work on Harvard excavations in 1920. In 1921 he went to work with Morley on CIW excavations in Yucatán (Lothrop 1953:69).

In 1922 Morley sent Ricketson back to Harvard for more training. Ricketson entered graduate school in 1922, spent a season working in the Southwest in 1923, and received his A.M. in 1924. He took over the Uaxactun excavations for the CIW in 1926 and, as

Pollock had done, split his time between the Peabody and the CIW for the next several years. He wrote up his Uaxactun material for his Ph.D. dissertation, "Stratigraphy and Its Interpretation at Uaxactun, Guatemala," in 1933. After receiving his Ph.D., he continued working for the CIW. Throughout his career he collected and donated Maya materials from his projects to the Peabody Museum. Ricketson resigned from the CIW in 1941 to join the war effort. Among his activities was searching for rubber trees in Amazonia with the ethnobotanist Hugh Cutler in 1943 (Lothrop 1953:70). After the war he retired from active research.

Karl Ruppert (1895–1960) was another of the Mayanists who began graduate work but, having secured a position at the CIW, did not complete his Ph.D. Ruppert was born in Phoenix, Arizona, and did his undergraduate work at the University of Arizona, receiving his A.B. in 1920. He met Byron Cummings (1843–1954) at the university and became his assistant on the Kayenta project in 1920. From 1922 through 1925 Ruppert worked part-time as Cummings's assistant at the Arizona State Museum, taking care of the museum when Cummings was on leave excavating at Cuicuilco, Mexico, in 1922 and again in 1924–25 (Bostwick 2006:82). After receiving his A.B., Ruppert also worked with Neil Judd at Chaco Canyon during each summer season from 1921 through 1926 (Gifford and Morris 1985:398; Lambert 1961:101). He returned to school to get his first A.M. at George Washington University in 1924, but he was then called back to work at the Arizona State Museum for the rest of 1924 and early 1925.

Ruppert was offered a job with the CIW in 1925 and worked with that organization for the next 32 years (Lambert 1961:102). Like other CIW personnel who earned degrees from Harvard, Ruppert entered the Peabody graduate program in 1925, supported by the Winthrop Scholarship for the 1925–26 year. He finished his second A.M., in Maya studies, at Harvard in 1928. Although he continued in the graduate program for Ph.D. work for another few years, he ultimately dropped out to spend full time on projects at Chichen Itza and elsewhere for the CIW (Lambert 1961:102).

Augustus Ledyard Smith (1901–85) and **Robert Eliot Smith** (1899–1983) were brothers recruited by Tozzer to work in the Maya area. The Smith family had moved back and forth between Europe and the United States at the turn of the century because of the family business. Robert E. Smith was born in France, and Ledyard Smith, in Milwaukee, but both boys were educated for some years in Switzerland (Willey 1988:684). The family later moved back to Boston, and both sons attended Harvard. Robert graduated in 1922 with a degree in history and romance languages. Ledyard received his degree in 1925 and worked in the family business in Milwaukee for the next two years.

An old Harvard friend, Oliver Ricketson Jr., recruited Ledyard Smith to work for the CIW. He started work at Uaxactun, first assisting Ricketson and then serving as field director for the project. Ledyard Smith obviously thrived in this field, and he soon helped Morley recruit one of his old classmates, Harry Pollock, in 1928, as well as his brother, Robert, in 1929, to come work for the CIW (Willey 1983:783).

Tozzer arranged for CIW personnel doing research and write-up to have office space and facilities in the nearby Peabody Museum. Hence Ledyard Smith, Oliver Ricketson, and Harry Pollock all were working in the Peabody during the off seasons in the early 1930s (Reynolds 1932:298).

After finishing the excavations at Uaxactun, Ledyard Smith worked with A.V. Kidder, first on site survey and then on excavations in the Guatemala highlands along the Motagua drainage. After serving in World War II as an information specialist, Smith returned to excavating in the Guatemalan highlands until 1950, when he began work at Mayapan with Karl Ruppert and, for a short time, his brother, Robert. Ledyard Smith continued excavating in Mesoamerica for the CIW until 1958, when the CIW's Division of Archaeology was disbanded (Willey 1988:684). He then joined the Peabody Museum as assistant curator of Middle American archaeology (Brew 1959:512). He worked as Gordon Willey's assistant at Altar de Sacrificios and then at Seibal before retiring in 1970 (Brew 1961:607; Willey 1988:684).

Robert Smith returned to Harvard after his first season working with his brother at Uaxactun, in 1929, and began taking graduate courses in archaeology. He, too, completed no degree work. Instead, he accepted a permanent position with the CIW in 1932 and served as the CIW's representative in Guatemala City for the next 20 years, helping to establish the National Museum of Anthropology there. He worked for the CIW with Ricketson and Ledyard Smith at Uaxactun (Scott 1935:312) and later at Mayapan, as well as other sites. Later he developed a ceramic sequence for the Pyramid of the Sun at Teotihuacan (Brew 1963:613; Scott 1935:312). After the CIW closed in 1958, he served as an associate archaeologist for the Instituto Nacional de Antropología e Historia de Mexico from 1960 to 1962. He ended his career as a research associate in Middle American ceramics at the Peabody Museum from 1965 to 1968 and as an honorary research associate of that institution until his death in 1983.

George Clapp Vaillant (1901–45) was born in Boston and entered Harvard with the class of 1922. During his sophomore year he joined **Singleton Peabody Moorehead** (1900–64), also class of 1922, on a trip to Maine, where Moorehead's father, Warren K. Moorehead, of the Robert S. Peabody Foundation in Andover, was excavating a Red Paint culture cemetery at Waterville. There Vaillant got hooked on archaeology (Kidder 1945:589). In his junior year Vaillant went with Guernsey to work in northeastern Arizona. In his senior year he excavated with Kidder at Pecos early in the season, and later in the season with Guernsey again in Arizona (Kidder 1945:589, 591).

Vaillant worked with Kidder for more seasons than any other Harvard student except Carl Guthe, learning much of his craft from Kidder (Givens 1992:56). Kidder's influence was such that throughout his career Vaillant gave priority to the study of chronology and cultural history (Tolstoy 1991:717). He returned the favor to his old classmate Singleton Moorehead, helping to recruit him as an assistant on Kidder's 1922 Pecos excavation. Moorehead put his architectural skills to work doing site drawings at Pecos (Givens 1992:56, 64), and he later had a long career as the historical architect at Colonial Williamsburg in Virginia.

Vaillant entered graduate school in the fall of 1922 to study with Tozzer. In 1923–24 he was sent to work with George Reisner in Egypt and at Carthage (Strong 1945:115). In the summers of 1924 and 1925 he worked with Kidder at Pecos. After the 1925 season, Kidder, Vaillant, and Earl H. Morris did a small project together for the AMNH in Canyon de Chelly, Arizona, which launched Vaillant's association with the AMNH. After that project the three joined Samuel Guernsey for a survey in Chihuahua, Vaillant's first official archaeological work in Mexico. In 1926 Vaillant went with Morley to Chichen Itza (Kidder 1945:591). He was supported by Winthrop Scholarship money in 1926–27 and completed his dissertation, "The Chronological Significance of Maya Ceramics," in 1927. After receiving his Ph.D. he was appointed assistant curator of Mexican archaeology at the AMNH and put in charge of AMNH work in Mexico, where he began eight years of excavations in the Valley of Mexico, at Zacatenco, Ticoman, El Arbolillo, Teotihuacan, Gualupita, Azcapotzalco, Chiconauhtla, and Nonoalco (Kidder 1945:597).

Vaillant's work at the AMNH began his close association with Clarence L. Hay, a trustee of the AMNH, who later supported much of Vaillant's work financially. Hay, as we noted in chapter 10, had worked in Mexico with Tozzer and Gamio and got Vaillant interested in the Archaic period (Kidder 1945:592). Vaillant soon became an expert on the Archaic, as well as the Aztecs, returning to Harvard to install the Aztec exhibit at the Peabody in 1933 (Scott 1934:302). While Vaillant was at the AMNH, Clark Wissler made it possible for him to give courses on Mesoamerica at Yale, New York University, and Columbia between 1938 and 1942 (Kidder 1945:597).

In 1936 Vaillant helped establish the Institute of Andean Research, whose first funding came from the Department of State. The institute was established ostensibly for purely intellectual reasons, but the persisting rumor in the Andean republics was that it had an underlying information-gathering component. In 1941 he became director of the University Museum at Pennsylvania, but he soon became involved in the war effort. From 1943 to 1945 Vaillant was the first cultural attaché to Peru and, according to Thomas Patterson (1995:78), contributed to Office of Strategic Services (OSS) activities in Latin America along with Ledyard Smith, Carleton Coon (whom we profile later), and others. After the war Vaillant returned to the directorship of the University Museum, but sadly, he committed suicide later in 1945.

Both Alfred Tozzer and A.V. Kidder could be viewed as senior archaeologists at the Peabody Museum, although Tozzer's primary appointment was through the Department of Anthropology, and Kidder's was as a nominal staff member of the museum. Tozzer had been around longer and thus had secured greater visibility, but Kidder, too, began recruiting graduate students for the program. Kidder's arrangement at the Peabody Museum limited him mainly to doing museum activities and conducting fieldwork, so he had less direct contact with students. Likely as a result, he initially was less able to attract students into Southwestern archaeology; not being a professor in the department, he could not be directly involved in their degree programs. Nevertheless, several archaeology students who ended up in Mesoamerica and elsewhere did receive part of their field training with Kidder at Pecos. Kidder also sat on a number of Ph.D. defenses. Emil Haury (1995), for example, has written on this aspect of Kidder's work.

We have already covered several of the students in whose training Tozzer was primarily involved. We turn now to some of the students whom Kidder mentored: Ralph Linton, the brothers Frank H. H. Roberts and Henry Roberts, Douglas Byers, Frederick Johnson, and J. O. Brew. Kidder also continued recruiting skilled avocational amateurs as museum contributors, as Putnam had done, even though this activity was gradually phased out as a popular practice during the first quarter of the twentieth century. Kidder was particularly involved with contributors C. Burton Cosgrove, Harriet Cosgrove, William Claflin Jr., and Raymond Emerson.

Ralph Linton (1893–1953) was one of the first students attracted to Harvard because of Kidder's Southwestern work. Linton was born in Philadelphia and received his A.B. from Swarthmore in 1915. He had become interested in archaeology as a youngster, collecting arrowheads and going on archaeological exploration trips with his father, Prof. Edwin Linton, who collected stone tools in Massachusetts and later donated them to the Peabody Museum (Kluckhohn 1958:236; Putnam 1914:229). As an undergraduate, Linton spent the summer of 1912 excavating sites in New Mexico and Colorado, and the following summer he went on the Archaeological Institute of America (AIA) project in Quirigua, Guatemala (McKern 1954:382).

Linton did his A.M. work at the University of Pennsylvania, receiving his degree there in 1916. While at Penn he trained with Ernest Williams Hawkes, with whom he co-authored an important paper, "A Pre-Lenape Site in New Jersey," published first in the University Museum series in 1916 and later, as a shorter summary, in *American Anthropologist* (Hawkes and Linton 1916, 1921). This was one of the first published works on a Late Archaic site south of New England (Gillin 1954:275). In the summer of 1916 Linton went out to excavate at Aztec, New Mexico, as a crew member for the AMNH project there (Kluckhohn 1958:237).

Linton then enrolled in the graduate program at Columbia in 1916–17 to study with Boas, before being called to the war, where he served in field artillery as a corporal. After returning from military service, he apparently tried to reenter classes at Columbia, but he attended his first classes in 1919 in uniform. As we described in the previous chapter, the war was a sore point for Boas. Clyde Kluckhohn (1958:238) reported that Boas took offense at Linton's attending class in uniform and threw him out of the program, whereupon Linton enrolled at Harvard.

He spent the summer of 1919 working with Jesse Walter Fewkes for the National Park Service at Mesa Verde, where he excavated one of the first known Basketmaker III pithouses (Givens 1992:33). After his first term of classes at Harvard he became involved in a two-year anthropological expedition to the Marquesas Islands for the Bernice P. Bishop Museum of Hawaii (McKern 1954:382). He completed his Harvard Ph.D. with the dissertation "The Material Culture and Archaeology of the Marquesas Islands" in 1925, a key point in his shift from archaeology to ethnology.

In 1922, while conducting his dissertation research, Linton had also taken a job as assistant curator of ethnology with the Field Museum, a position he kept until 1928, and he supervised archaeological excavations at the Hopewell site in Ohio for the Field Museum in 1924. After completing his Ph.D., he carried out ethnographic fieldwork for the Field Museum in Madagascar from 1925 to 1927 (Kluckhohn 1958:238).

In 1928–29 Linton took a teaching job at the University of Wisconsin, a position he kept until 1937. While there, he supervised several summers of archaeological field excavations for the Milwaukee Public Museum and the University of Wisconsin (Gillin 1954:236; Kluckhohn 1958:238). By the time he moved to Columbia in 1937, he had shifted more or less completely out of archaeology. He taught at Columbia from 1937 to 1946 and then moved to Yale to finish his career, from 1946 to 1953. He served as president of the AAA in 1946 and as vice president of Section H of the AAAS in 1947. Because of works such as *The Study of Man* (1936), Linton is often thought of as an ethnologist, but the early part of his career was in archaeology. He was an anthropologist in the best sense of the word. (Stephen Williams, during his graduate student days at Yale, from 1950 to 1953, lived in the attic of Linton's home and got to know Linton and his wife well.)

Frank Harold Hanna Roberts Jr. (1897–1966) was born in Centerburg, Ohio, but moved with his family in 1900 to Wyoming, where his father taught history and civics. In 1904 his father took a position at the University of Denver, where Frank's brother Henry, also later a Harvard graduate student, was born (Stephenson 1967:84). In 1910 Roberts's father was named president of Las Vegas Normal University at Las Vegas, New Mexico (where Edgar Hewett had been), and Frank Roberts received part of his undergraduate education there (Judd 1966:1226; Stephenson 1967:84). After serving in the army in World War I, he finished his degree in history and English at the University of Denver in 1919.

After a short stint as a reporter and city editor for his hometown *Las Vegas Daily Optic* in 1919–20, Frank Roberts returned to Denver and received his A.M. in political science in 1921 (Stephenson 1967:84). He then began teaching Spanish and anthropology at the University of Denver with Abel Etienne Bernardeau Renaud, the founder of the Department of Anthropology there. Roberts also took the position of assistant curator of archaeology at the Colorado Historical and Natural History Society, under Jean Allard Jeançon, with whom he conducted archaeological excavations during the summers (Stephenson 1967:84). Between 1921 and 1924, Jeançon and Renaud, along with Frank and Henry Roberts, worked at a site near Chimney Rock in Archuleta County, Colorado. Frank Roberts later took some of these materials to donate to the Peabody Museum.

Now hooked on archaeology, Roberts decided to secure further training with the best Southwestern archaeologist of the day, and he entered Harvard with Kidder's support in 1924. He was funded in his first year by a Hemenway Fellowship and in his second year served as Hooton's teaching assistant, receiving his second A.M., now in anthropology, in 1926. At Kidder's suggestion, that summer he worked on Neil Judd's National Geographic Society–funded excavations at Pueblo Bonito in Chaco Canyon. He wrote up his portion of the season's work as his dissertation, "The Ceramic Sequence in the Chaco Canyon, New Mexico, and Its Relation to the Cultures of the San Juan Basin." His Ph.D. was granted in 1927.

While working with Judd in 1926, Roberts was offered a position at the AMNH, but he turned it down to accept an offer from the BAE. After receiving a dispensation to return to Harvard and finish his Ph.D., he worked for the BAE for the next 36 years, until 1964 (Judd 1966:1226). Roberts's peers recognized him early on as a first-rate field archaeologist. For example, in 1927 he was one of the three-member "blue-ribbon" panel that went out to investigate the association of extinct bison with stone spear points at Folsom, New Mexico, in conjunction with Barnum Brown, of the AMNH, and A.V. Kidder. In the early 1930s Roberts worked briefly in Yucatán on a CIW project, taking Harvard graduate student Frederick Johnson with him (MacNeish 1996:270). He worked at Shiloh National Military Park for the Civil Works Administration (CWA) in 1933, but the work came to an end with the demise of the CWA in 1934 (Haag 1985:274). He conducted the first Paleoindian excavations at Lindenmeier, Colorado, in 1934–35, and with his brother Henry, he worked at the Agate Basin site in 1942. He then joined the war effort to work for the Office of Naval Intelligence (Stephenson 1967:87).

In 1933–34, along with A.V. Kidder and Alfred Kroeber, Frank Roberts helped draw up the constitution and bylaws of the Society for American Archaeology, and he served as its president in 1950 (Woodbury 1973:49). He became the director of the River Basins Surveys of the Inter-Agency Archaeological Salvage Programs set up by the SAA, the AAA, and the American Council of Learned Societies in 1946, and he held the position until 1957. In 1958 he became the last director of the BAE. When he retired in 1964, the BAE was abolished and merged with the Department of Anthropology of the U.S. National Museum to form the new Smithsonian Office of Anthropology (Judd 1966:1228). Throughout his career, Roberts was considered a major Paleoindian scholar.

Henry Buchtel Roberts (1910–79) was born in Denver and, like his brother, did his undergraduate work at the university there, in addition to working seasonally at the site in Archuleta County with Jeançon and Renaud between 1921 and 1924. Henry Roberts entered Harvard as a graduate student in 1927, three years after his brother. He was supported by a Hemenway Fellowship in the first year and as a teaching assistant to Tozzer in the second.

Henry Roberts, J. O. Brew, and Donald Scott (see chapter 10) were the principal Peabody Museum researchers who began working in the Fremont archaeological culture area in Utah. They conducted surveys and excavations there between 1927 and 1930, supported by funds from William Claflin Jr. and Raymond Emerson, after whom the project, the Claflin-Emerson Expedition, was named (Reynolds 1930:272, 1931a:285). Claflin and Emerson participated in the first year; during the second year Scott and Roberts shared control; and in the third season, 1929, Henry Roberts was in charge. The work was written up in 1930 by Roberts and scheduled to be published in the Papers of the Peabody Museum of American Archaeology and Ethnology, vol. 12, no. 4, in 1931 as "Peripheral Cultures of the Southwest with Special Reference to the Archaeology of Utah," but the Great Depression prevented it from being issued.

During the excavation season of 1931 Henry Roberts was in charge of the Peabody Museum's expedition at Sitio Conte, Panama, with a field crew consisting of Louis Wedlock, Douglas Byers, and Frederick Johnson. The Sitio Conte project was another one supported partly with funds from William Claflin Jr. (Reynolds 1932:295). In the winter season of 1932 Roberts was responsible for working up more of the Fremont materials from the Claflin-Emerson Expedition, and in the winter of 1933 he worked for the CIW, analyzing Maya ceramics (Scott 1933:301, 1934:301). After several years of fieldwork, Henry Roberts had not completed a degree. He clearly liked fieldwork more than he did the subsequent write-up and analysis. He gradually picked up more excavation work with federal projects over the next few years, working, for example, with his brother Frank at the Agate Basin site in 1942 (Stephenson 1967:88). In 1956 he shifted to full-time work with the Smithsonian Institution, but he worked primarily with the Marine Invertebrate Division until he retired in 1973.

Douglas Swain Byers (1903–78) was born in Newton Center, Massachusetts, and was a member of the Harvard graduating class of 1925. He considered taking graduate training in anthropology, having become interested in the field while working as a cook for Guernsey in Arizona in 1924 (Byers 1966b:408). But he opted first to go after a business degree and spent the 1925–26 year taking classes at Harvard Business School. The next year he shifted to graduate work in anthropology and received his A.M. in that discipline in 1928.

Byers continued to pursue coursework for his Ph.D., but he was diverted by other obligations and never received the degree. He was named assistant dean in charge of records for Harvard College in 1929, keeping the position until 1931. He kept his foot in the door at the Peabody, managing to participate in summer excavation projects. The director of the Peabody Museum then, Edward Reynolds, was spending a good deal of time putting the museum on a sound financial footing, and he needed help in the day-to-day operations. Thus Byers was named assistant to the director at the Peabody from 1931 to 1933.

During the time he was at the Peabody, Byers participated in excavations at Pecos with Kidder, in the Chinle, Arizona, area with Brew, and at Sitio Conte in Panama with Henry Roberts. He also conducted ethnographic work under Kidder on the Navajo reservation and with Oliver La Farge in Guatemala (MacNeish 1979:708; Reynolds 1932:295; Scott 1933:296, 301). In 1933, with Donald Scott the new director at the Peabody, Byers looked for another position. Kidder helped get him hired as assistant director of the Robert S. Peabody Foundation for Archaeology, in Andover, Massachusetts, in 1933. He became director there in 1936 and held the job until he retired in 1966. Over the years he served as the editor of *American Antiquity* (1938–47) and as the thirteenth president of the SAA (1947–48).

Frederick Johnson (1904–94) was a frequent colleague of and collaborator with Douglas Byers in archaeology. Johnson was born in Everett, Massachusetts, and began doing ethnographic fieldwork with Frank Speck in 1917 as a young teenager (MacNeish 1996:269). He graduated from Tufts with an A.B. in 1929 and immediately entered graduate school at Harvard, where, after the first year, he was supported by the Hemenway Fellowship for the subsequent three years. In 1931 he became the assistant to Samuel Lothrop at Sitio Conte in Panama. During Johnson's first season, he worked with fellow students Byers, Louis Wedlock, and Henry Roberts. For the next two years Johnson continued excavating at the site in the summers and writing up the Panamanian materials under Lothrop's supervision during the academic terms (Reynolds 1932:295; Scott 1933:299–300, 1934:299).

In 1933 Johnson left the graduate program without obtaining a degree. He went with Frank Roberts to Yucatán, where he was hired as an archaeologist by the CIW (MacNeish 1996:270). He worked for the CIW for the next few years, but in 1936, when Byers was promoted to director of the Robert S. Peabody Foundation, he offered his old Harvard friend Johnson a job as curator. The two of them worked together at the Peabody Foundation for many years thereafter, jointly involved in a series of archaeological excavation projects. From 1939 to 1942 Johnson was in charge of one of the larger salvage excavation projects at the Boylston Street Fish Weir in Boston, and in 1944 and 1948 he was head of the Andover-Harvard Yukon Expedition.

Frederick Johnson served as the twelfth president of the SAA, from 1946 to 1947, a year before Byers succeeded him in the presidency. In the late 1940s Johnson served as an advisor to Willard Libby, helping to select the first experimental radiocarbon samples to be dated. He was also a significant player on the "Committee for the Recovery of Archaeological Remains," which helped advise the Smithsonian Institution's River Basins Surveys. When Byers retired as director of the Robert S. Peabody Foundation in 1967, Johnson served as director for one year, a period dedicated mainly to selecting Richard S. MacNeish as the next long-term director of the foundation, beginning in 1969. Johnson had previously been instrumental in providing MacNeish with support for his Tehuacan archaeobotanical project in Mexico (MacNeish 1996:271).

John Otis Brew (1906–88), usually known as J. O. or "Jo" Brew, was born in Malden, Massachusetts. He earned his A.B. at Dartmouth, developing an interest in classical archaeology and getting a degree in fine arts there in 1928, before entering the graduate program at Harvard later that year (Woodbury 1990:452). Brew evidently had an important sponsor at the Peabody: he holds the record for the longest period of Peabody Museum fellowship aid for the twentieth century, more than 13 years. He was the recipient of the Thaw Fellowship from 1930 to 1936 and from 1942 to 1943, the Hemenway Fellowship from 1936 to 1937, and the Winthrop Scholarship from 1937 to 1941.

Brew first did some fieldwork for the museum in Fulton County, Illinois, in 1930, under the direction of Fay-Cooper Cole who had founded a department of anthropology at the University of Chicago in 1929. He was then sent on the Claflin-Emerson Expedition to Utah from 1931 to 1933. He took part in the Harvard Irish Expedition with Hugh Hencken and Hallam Movius (discussed in the next chapter) in 1934 and then returned to the Southwest to conduct archaeological work at Alkali Ridge in Utah. He next directed the Peabody Museum's Awatovi Expedition in northeastern Arizona from 1935 to 1939 (H. Davis 2008; Scott 1933:299–300, 1934:299; Woodbury 1990:452–53). Brew was involved in Claflin-Emerson funding for research in the Southwest long enough that William H. Claflin III entered Harvard as an undergraduate and worked with Brew in 1939 on a survey of the Mogollon area (Scott 1941:429).

In 1941 Brew finished his Ph.D. with the dissertation "The Archaeology of Southeastern Utah and Its Place in the History of the Southwest." At the Peabody Museum he was the Chester Hastings Arnold Fellow and assistant curator, Southwest, for 1940–41, and after receiving his degree he was promoted to curator of Southwestern archaeology. He became curator of North American archaeology in 1945 and director of the museum from 1948 to 1967. Fred Johnson named Brew, Kidder, and William S. Webb to form the Committee for the Recovery of Archaeological Remains, which subsequently developed the River Basins Surveys program with the Smithsonian Institution in May 1945 (Wendorf and Thompson 2002:317). Brew served as SAA president in 1949–50 and as AAA president in 1954. After resigning the directorship of the Peabody in 1967, he continued to hold the position of Peabody Professor of American Archaeology and Ethnology until he retired in 1972, although he did no teaching (Woodbury 1990:456).

Besides recruiting students, Kidder enlisted outside personnel to assist in Peabody Museum activities. Particularly important in this regard were C. Burton Cosgrove, Harriet Cosgrove, William Claflin Jr., and Raymond Emerson.

Kidder recruited **Cornelius Burton "Burt" Cosgrove Jr.** (1875–1936) and **Harriet "Hattie" Lovejoy Silliman Cosgrove** (1877–1970) in 1924 to begin working with him in the Southwest. Hattie Cosgrove had been born in Atkinson, Kansas, and Burt Cosgrove in Santa Fe, New Mexico. In 1909 they settled in Silver City, New Mexico, where Burt ran a hardware store (Kidder 1957:52–53). Like many other New Mexico residents, they developed an interest in local archaeology and began to collect artifacts of the prehistoric Mimbres culture. In 1919 they purchased a Mimbres site and began excavating it. But unlike most other local collectors, they kept notes, made plans, took photographs, saved every potsherd and bone, and carefully labeled all the artifacts (Kidder 1957:53). In the summer of 1920 the Cosgroves decided they needed to learn additional archaeological field skills and visited the excavations of Frederick

Hodge at Hawikku, Neil Judd at Pueblo Bonito, and A.V. Kidder at Pecos. It was there that Kidder first made their acquaintance, and he later indicated that he had been impressed with their self-taught techniques (Kidder 1957:53).

Hattie and Burt Cosgrove began their work for Kidder at the Mimbres site of Swarts Ruin in 1924, finishing the excavations in 1927 (Cosgrove and Cosgrove 1932). They sold their hardware store in 1925 and moved to Cambridge, where they joined the Peabody Museum staff as research assistants to work up their materials (Woodbury 1993:25). This was one of the rare times in the Peabody Museum's twentieth-century history when amateur archaeologists were given such status (see Brew 1968:7). The Cosgroves completed their analyses only a few years later (Cosgrove and Cosgrove 1932).

Kidder had a good deal of confidence in the Cosgroves. When Samuel Guernsey was unable to return to the field because of poor health, Kidder sent them on a survey of the Mimbres Valley for the museum, the beginning of a four-year excavation project (Willoughby 1925:262, 1928:272, 1929:295). During their fieldwork the Cosgroves discovered that the nearby caves had excellent preservation. Hence the museum shifted its activities to the dry caves of southern New Mexico and southwestern Texas in 1928–29, following the completion of the Mimbres project (Kidder 1957:54).

Hattie and Burt Cosgrove helped with a number of other projects. When William H. Claflin Jr. needed some help with excavations he was conducting at Stallings Island, Georgia, in 1929, they assisted him. They worked with Kidder at the Pendleton ruins in New Mexico in 1933. And in 1935, when J. O. Brew began his work at Awatovi, they joined his team as his principal assistants (Kidder 1957:54; Reynolds 1931a:285).

Sadly, Burt Cosgrove was taken ill and died while working for the project in 1936. In spite of his death, Hattie stayed with the project, supervising the processing of the pottery that year and in the succeeding years at Awatovi. In the 1938 season alone, she and her assistants processed 243,871 potsherds. Altogether she oversaw the stabilization of some 8,500 whole vessels and is said to have processed more than half a million potsherds for the project (H. Davis 2008:47; M. Elliott 1995:174). Hattie Cosgrove continued as an active research associate in the museum for several more years. She planned to retire in 1942, but because of a shortage of personnel during the war, she continued for another two years. She finally retired in 1944, at the age of 67, but then stayed on for four more years as a volunteer (Kidder 1957:55).

William Henry Claflin Jr. (1893–1982) was born in Swampscott, Massachusetts. He had a strong interest in archaeology from childhood. Family influence no doubt was important in this pursuit. For example, his parents, William Sr. and Mary B. Claflin, had been signers—along people we discussed earlier, such as Oliver Wendell Holmes, Mary Hemenway, and Francis Parkman—of the successful petition in February 1889 asking Congress to make the Casa Grande ruin in Arizona a national monument (Lee 1970:19). In addition, the family owned a home near Augusta, Georgia, adjacent to the property of the Charles C. Jones family, who had excavated test units on Stallings

Island back in the 1870s. Young Claflin had become a collector of arrowheads by the age of seven and had begun to do some poking around in the Stallings Island mounds by 1906–8 (Webster 2003:4; S. Williams 1994:10).

Claflin made his first trip to the Southwest in 1912. He traveled extensively in the Hopi area, visited ruins in the Jeddito drainage, and saw Awatovi (Elliott 1995:164). He received his A.B. from Harvard in 1915 and immediately took a job in the banking business. Later he worked for Lampson and Hubbard Corporation, a hat manufacturer, and at the investment firm Tucker, Anthony, and Company. After 1923 he became involved in his wife's family's sugar business, Soledad Sugar, taking over when his father-in-law died in 1926 and spending winters in Cuba (Webster 2003:4).

Over the years, Claflin and his wife, Helen, developed close ties to the Peabody Museum. Claflin had maintained an active presence on the Harvard campus after graduation, serving first as varsity hockey coach from 1922 to 1924. He helped support Guernsey's work in northeastern Arizona from 1920 to 1923, and in 1923 he went out to spend two weeks excavating Basketmaker sites with Kidder on Guernsey's project (Webster 2003:5). He provided the major financial support for the Cosgroves' work in the Mimbres Valley from 1924 to 1927.

Claflin and his good friend Raymond Emerson visited southern Utah in 1924 and became the financial sponsors of the Peabody Museum's survey and excavation work there by Donald Scott, J. O. Brew, Henry Roberts, and Noel Morss (whom we profile later in this chapter) from 1928 to 1931. This was the project that became known as the Claflin-Emerson Expedition. Some of the materials from the project became the basis for the definition of the Fremont culture, as written up by Morss. The remaining materials were published years later by James Gunnerson (1969).

Claflin came to know Burt and Hattie Cosgrove through his support of their Mimbres work. In 1929 he and his wife, Helen, hired the Cosgroves to help them in their excavations at Stallings Island, Georgia. Claflin got right into the analysis of the materials and published *The Stallings Island Mound, Columbia County, Georgia* in the Papers of the Peabody Museum series in 1931. The museum named him curator of Southeastern archaeology in 1928. Ten years later he resigned that title to become treasurer of Harvard Corporation, a job he held through 1948.

Although the Southeast was perhaps Claflin's first love, the Southwest was the area in which he had the greatest effect on Peabody Museum archaeology. He helped Kidder there, and he funded a significant portion of the Fremont culture work in the Claflin-Emerson Expedition of 1928–31. J. O. Brew first saw the Alkali Ridge site during the Claflin-Emerson work, and Claflin went on to help fund part of Brew's excavations at Alkali Ridge from 1931 to 1934 (Scott 1936:321).

Claflin was key in establishing the Awatovi project. According to Brew, its director (1949b:vii): "The Awatovi Expedition grew out of Mr. Claflin's interest in the prehistory of the Hopi country. During various trips to northern Arizona he had acquired a thorough knowledge of the Reservation which has been of inestimable value to the

Expedition. Faith in the archaeological possibilities of the Jeddito Valley led Mr. Claflin to instigate an extensive reconnaissance trip in 1935, which was followed by four seasons of intensive excavations." Claflin was again joined by Raymond Emerson as a financial angel, and Henry S. Morgan and Philip R. Allen made significant contributions as well. But for most of the Awatovi project, Claflin was the major backer.

Claflin's contributions at Awatovi were not only financial. He and his family were part of the field crew. Brew (1939:114), while detailing the baskets, cloth bags, cloth, rope, twine, and wood objects collected from more than 100 burials excavated in the 1937 season, reported: "Much of our success in preserving this extremely fragile material was due to the careful work of Mr. William H. Claflin Jr., who was in charge of this part of the excavation." Helen Claflin and daughters Helen and Katherine were listed as "general assistants" for the first three field seasons, and son William Claflin III, a Harvard undergraduate at the time, was in charge of reconnaissance, during which he recorded and collected ceramic samples from 296 sites (Brew 1949:viii; Scott 1941:429). Once Bill Claflin became treasurer of Harvard Corporation in 1938, his ability to participate in the fieldwork was severely limited, and he was unable to join the crew for the final season in 1939. After he resigned that position in 1948, he again became active with the Peabody Museum. After his death in 1982, the majority of his collection of 33,000 archaeological and 2,000 ethnographic artifacts was donated to the Peabody (Webster 2003:8).

Raymond A. Emerson (1886–1977) received his S.B. from Harvard in 1911, so he likely had just graduated when Bill Claflin entered Harvard as a freshman. His grandfather was the poet Ralph Waldo Emerson (Harvard class of 1821). Raymond Emerson went into business after receiving his degree. He and Claflin had become good friends because of shared interests, and the two of them funded the Peabody expedition to the Fremont area from 1928 to 1931. In 1938 the museum named Emerson to replace Ingersoll Bowditch, who had just died, as a member of the nonteaching "museum faculty" (Scott 1939:405), a position Bowditch had held since 1921. Emerson, too, had a long tenure as a member of this oversight body, serving until he retired in 1956, with a short break during World War II while he served as a major in the armed forces from 1941 to 1944.

Not every archaeology graduate student at the Peabody Museum ended up being channeled into the Maya area or the U.S. Southwest. A few, such as Philip Phillips, Arthur Kelly, and Walter Cline, specialized in other areas, out of either interest or job necessity. And as in any other graduate program, there were of course students who started out in the degree program, made contributions through their fieldwork and other activities, but dropped out to follow other careers. Among such people at the Peabody were Louis Wedlock, Paul Scott, Robert Franks, and Noel Morss. Several of them kept alive their avocational interest in anthropology and made later contributions to the field.

Philip Phillips (1900–1994) was a student who did the opposite: he embarked on another career but returned later to archaeology. He was born in Buffalo, New York, and attended Williams College as an undergraduate, receiving his A.B. in 1922. He then went to Harvard's School of Design for an architecture degree. He earned his M.Arch. in 1927 with the thesis project "A Small Villa on a Lake." While at Harvard, Phillips became good friends with a fellow architectural student, Singleton Peabody Moorehead, who also received his M.Arch. in 1927, and with George Vaillant, then an anthropology graduate student.

Phillips set up his own architectural firm in Buffalo in 1927, but after a few good years it collapsed with the onset of the Great Depression. At the urging of his college friends Moorehead and Vaillant, Phillips returned to Harvard in 1930 to work with Roland Dixon (Willey 1996:39). His first fieldwork at the Peabody was on an Iroquois site in New York. When Dixon died in 1934, Phillips shifted to Tozzer as his advisor. Tozzer wanted him to work in the Maya area, but for family reasons, Phillips decided on the U.S. Southeast. He continued his Ph.D. work on lower Mississippi Valley ceramics in collections at the Peabody and other museums, including the AMNH (Willey 1996:39; S. Williams 2003).

Phillips was appointed assistant curator of Southeast archaeology at the Peabody in 1937 (Scott 1939:405), three years before completing his Ph.D. with the dissertation "An Introduction to the Archaeology of the Mississippi Valley" in 1940. This extraordinary volume—some 768 pages of densely packed information—remains to be published.

Phillips began excavations in the Ouachita Valley, Arkansas, in 1939, conducting stratigraphic tests at two sites near Arkadelphia. The following year the work expanded into a new project, an archaeological survey of the lower Mississippi Valley, with James A. Ford and James B. Griffin (Scott 1940:453, 1941:430). The results of this 1940–47 project were published in 1951 as *Archaeological Survey in the Lower Mississippi Alluvial Valley, 1940–1947*, written with Ford and Griffin. Phillips continued doing archaeology in the Southeast until he retired in 1970. Others of his better-known works are *Method and Theory in American Archaeology* (1958), written with Gordon Willey, and *Pre-Columbian Shell Engravings from the Craig Mound at Spiro, Oklahoma*, written with James A. Brown and others and published in six volumes from 1975 to 1982. Phillips's long-term Lower Mississippi Valley Survey was later turned over to his friend Stephen Williams, who continued its activities until his retirement in 1993. He used it as a training ground for a number of his Ph.D. students. The survey still functions today, now under the leadership of T. R. Kidder.

Arthur Randolph Kelly (1900–1979) was a graduate student who started out in physical anthropology but shifted to archaeology owing to the job market in the 1930s. A Texas native, Kelly obtained his A.B. from the University of Texas in 1921. After serving as curator of anthropology at its museum from 1921 to 1923, he entered Harvard in 1924 and was supported during his first two years by Hemenway Fellowship funds. He received his A.M. in 1926 and from 1927 to 1929 conducted an anthropomorphic study of 9,000 subjects, trying to correlate race and crime. He completed his Ph.D. dissertation, "The Physical Anthropology of the Mexican Population in Texas: A Study of Race Mixture," in 1929.

After graduation he taught for the University of Illinois and conducted archaeological work at Starved Rock and Cahokia over the next two years. He maintained some links with Harvard, working on Cherokee-white relations in the Carolinas in 1930 as a Harvard research fellow on a National Research Council (NRC) grant (Reynolds 1931a:285). When the Civil Works Administration was established in 1933, Kelly was named supervisor of the archaeological excavations at Ocmulgee mounds in Georgia, with James Ford as his assistant. With the demise of the CWA act in 1934, leading to the end of CWA-sponsored projects, Kelly managed to continue excavations at Ocmulgee, now using Federal Emergency Relief Administration funds (Haag 1985:274). Later in the 1930s he became chief archaeologist in the Archaeological Site Division of the National Park Service for a time. He then, like Phillips, went on to a lengthy career in archaeology in the Southeast, among other activities excavating at Etowah and teaching at the University of Georgia. Kelly had a reputation as a "character" and was well known at the Southeastern Archaeological Conferences for his lengthy commentaries.

Walter Buchanan Cline (1904–52) was born in Los Angeles. He was a member of the Harvard class of 1926, graduating with a degree in anthropology. In both the summer of his sophomore year and the summer between his senior year and first year of graduate school, he was sent out to survey and map earthworks along the Sudbury River in Massachusetts (Willoughby 1924:260, 1927:264). During his junior year he worked on the Thebes project for the Egyptian staff of the Metropolitan Museum of New York, and in his senior year he worked under Earnest Hooton's direction on some materials from Libya, which sealed his interest in Africa (Coon 1953:x).

Cline was partially supported during his graduate years at Harvard by serving as tutor at Dunster House from 1926 to 1936. He spent his summers doing research in Morocco, Libya, Egypt, Ethiopia, Saudi Arabia, and Syria (Coon 1953:x; Reynolds 1930:273; Willoughby 1928:273). After 1930 his fieldwork was supported by the Frederick Sheldon Traveling Fellowship for North Africa and by funds provided by Natica I. Bates, the widow of Oric Bates. Cline received his A.M. in anthropology in 1933 and secured his Ph.D. with the dissertation "The Sources of Metals and Techniques of Metal Working in Negro Africa" in 1936. In 1927–28 he served as a teaching assistant to Tozzer in the introductory General Anthropology course, and after 1929 he supported his graduate work also by serving as an instructor in anthropology for the department.

For the rest of his career, however, Cline focused on ethnography rather than archaeology. Following the receipt of his Ph.D., he accepted a position at the University of Minnesota, where he organized the African division of the Department of Anthropology and taught from 1936 to 1942. During World War II he served in the OSS in Morocco. He returned to Minnesota and taught for one year, from 1946 to 1947. Then, because of an ailment he had picked up during the war, he took sick leave and returned to his family home in California (Coon 1953:x). During the early 1950s, until his death, Cline taught occasional courses at the University of California–Los Angeles.

Louis Lorne Wedlock (1903–73) received his A.B. in anthropology in 1928 and completed his A.M. in 1929. He was funded for his Ph.D. work in 1930–32 with a Winthrop Scholarship and joined Henry Roberts, Doug Byers, and Fred Johnson in working on Lothrop's project in Panama in 1931 (Reynolds 1932:295). Afterward he shifted into agriculture and disappears from our view.

Paul F. Scott was an artifact collector from Pennsylvania who was recruited into the graduate program in the 1920–21 year. In the summer of 1921 he was sent to excavate the prehistoric village site of Ulster, near Athens, Pennsylvania, which had been discovered by workmen digging a gas pipeline trench (Willoughby 1922:276). In addition to midden deposits, he excavated two Late Woodland–Owasco burials there and subsequently brought the excavated materials to the museum. He then dropped out of the program.

Robert Augustus Franks Jr. was born in Pittsburgh. His father had been in the steel industry and served as Andrew Carnegie's financial secretary. Robert A. Franks Sr. had also been a trustee of the Carnegie Institution of Washington and a member of its incorporation in 1905. No doubt because of his father's work with the CIW, Robert Jr. became interested in anthropology and enrolled in the Peabody Museum graduate program from 1926 to 1928. During this period he went on one of the summer field school excavations in France sponsored by the American School of Prehistoric Research (ASPR) (Bricker 2002:283). The academic approach was unsuited to his ends, however, and he left without a degree, beginning a career in business. Nevertheless, he became a trustee of the ASPR in 1929 and served archaeology through that venue.

Noel Morss (1904–81) was born in Boston and apparently was encouraged to participate in archaeological projects by his neighbor, Hugh Hencken (Demb 1992). As a Harvard undergraduate Morss was a member of the Peabody Museum expedition to the Chinle Valley in 1923–24 and the expedition in 1925 with Kidder and Guernsey (Willoughby 1926:252). He received his A.B. in economics in 1926.

Morss began graduate work in the anthropology department in that academic year. He participated in Peabody Museum expeditions in northeastern Arizona in 1927 and then along the upper Fremont River, with funds provided by Raymond Emerson and William Claflin, in 1928 and 1929 (Brew 1982:345; Willoughby 1929:295; Reynolds 1930:272). He wrote up this work, which became the defining work on the Fremont culture, as *The Ancient Culture of the Fremont River in Utah* (Morss 1932), published in the Papers of the Peabody Museum series. At the same time, he was taking coursework in the law school, and he obtained his LL.B from Harvard in 1929.

Morss then went into law practice and spent most his career as an attorney, but he kept an avocational hand in archaeology. He served as a trustee of the American School of Prehistoric Research from 1926 to 1953. When the ASPR became part of the Peabody Museum in 1953, with Hencken as its director, Morss served as its secretary-treasurer from 1954 to 1980. He was also a founding member of the Council of Old World Archaeology in 1953 and chair of the Peabody Museum Visiting Committee in 1954 (Demb 1992).

In a rather different category is a scholar who started out at Harvard, but not in anthropology, and who many years later became important in the development of archaeology in Iowa. **Charles Reuben Keyes** (1871–1951) was born and died in Mount Vernon, Iowa, and spent most of his career in that town. As a boy of 14 he became interested in archaeology by collecting Indian relics from rock shelters along the Cedar River (Gillette 1952). He received his Ph.B. from Cornell College in Mount Vernon in 1894. In 1897 he went to Harvard, where he received his A.M. in German literature in 1898. He continued in graduate work there until 1900 but did not complete his doctorate.

Keyes was hired at his alma mater, Cornell College, and taught German language and literature there for 38 years. He studied German literature in Berlin and Munich in 1912–13, at which time he received the only formal training in archaeology that we have been able to discover, when he took a seminar titled "Archaeology of Western Europe" (Isaac 2001). His publications, however, reflect a wide range of interests, including several contributions in ornithology, studies of Iowa geology, some works in Germanic studies, and later some on Iowa archaeology. In 1923 Keyes finally finished his Harvard Ph.D. work in German philology.

In 1922 Keyes's career took a turn back toward archaeology, his boyhood interest. That year he met with the superintendent and the Board of Curators of the Iowa State Historical Society to present a plea for preserving the rapidly disappearing mounds in the state. Following this meeting, the state hired Keyes as the newly created director of the Iowa Archaeological Survey. The part-time position paid a salary of $500 per year, and Keyes initially carried out his duties during the summer breaks from his teaching at Cornell College. In this position, he served as a member of the National Research Council's Committee on State Archaeological Surveys for many years, and he was instrumental in founding the Plains Conference for Archaeology and the Central States Anthropological Society. He kept the position of director of the Iowa Survey for 26 years, until 1948, then being emeritus until his death in 1951.

Considering his three decades in that position, there are relatively few publications on archaeology by Keyes. Charles Gillette (1952) explained:

> And yet his attic laboratory was filled with the fruits of twenty-nine years of diligent research as Director of the Iowa Archeological Survey. Dr. Keyes' modest publications give only a clue to the magnitude of this study. He felt that whether he published results of his work or not was a little consequence. What was important was that the knowledge that he had gained must be accurately and adequately recorded. Each site he investigated was meticulously located and numbered on county and township maps. Each artifact he collected or received for the Survey was carefully catalogued and fully described.

Keyes is the kind of scholar with Harvard roots who is easy to miss in working on the history of the discipline. He does not show up in the Peabody Museum annual reports, not having been a student there, and his relative paucity of publications means he is little known outside his native state. Nevertheless, his Midwestern colleagues of the time, such as James B. Griffin, John W. Bennett, and Henry C. Shetrone, were aware of his work and in their publications cited his contributions to developing the archaeological landscape.

In a somewhat similar vein are the contributions of **Kenneth Roscoe Macgowan** (1888–1963), who was born in Winthrop, Massachusetts, and received his S.B. from Harvard in 1911. Macgowan became chairman of the Department of Theater Arts at UCLA. He had, however, developed an interest in "early man in the Americas" during his undergraduate days at Harvard (Herskovits 1950:117). He had become a good friend of George Vaillant's, and in the 1940s, Macgowan, Vaillant and William Duncan Strong (of Columbia University) planned to write a trilogy dealing with American archaeology. Macgowan was to cover North America; Vaillant, Middle America; and Strong, South America (Hester 1964:376). Although Vaillant died in 1945, before the trilogy could be completed, Macgowan published his part, *Early Man in the New World*, in 1950. The volume went through several original and revised editions and for many years was one of the standard textbooks in the field.

Frederic Putnam had recruited and trained students in all the major areas of anthropology and by the turn of the century had staff teaching in three of them—archaeology, sociocultural anthropology, and physical anthropology. For the first few decades of the twentieth century, Roland Dixon was the prime source in ethnology and sociocultural anthropology, and Earnest Hooton became the prime physical anthropologist. Dixon, however, did not start turning out Ph.D. students until the late teens, and Hooton not until the late 1920s, so graduate education at the Peabody Museum in the first quarter of the twentieth century was dominated by students in archaeology. This changed in the 1920s, with a new contingent of Dixon's and Hooton's students. Once again, as had been the case in Putnam's time, the mix of the three major fields was fairly equal.

In biological anthropology, Earnest Hooton recruited or trained at least a dozen people in the 1920s. They included colleagues and collaborators such as Laurance Redway and Edward Reynolds and graduate students such as Harry Shapiro, Carleton Coon, George D. Williams, Richard Post, Fred Hulse, Gordon Bowles, C. Wesley Dupertuis, Carl Seltzer, Martin Luther, William Lessa, and W. W. Howells.

Laurance David Redway (1890–1960) was a longtime "Associate in Physical Anthropology" at the Peabody Museum, beginning in the late 1920s. He was born in Cincinnati, Ohio, and was a member of the Harvard class of 1912. He went on to obtain his M.D. from Harvard in 1916 and continued research in ophthalmology after his graduation (*National Cyclopedia* 1962:418). During the 1920s he worked with a number of Hooton's students at the Peabody Museum, including W. W. Howells and Richard Post, whom we cover shortly. In the 1930s he worked with H. T. E. Hertzberg, as discussed in the next chapter.

Edward Reynolds (1860–1936) was born in Boston and received his A.B. from Harvard in 1881. He earned his M.D. there in 1885 and from then until 1901 was an instructor in obstetrics and gynecology. He subsequently went into a successful private practice. In the 1920s he became a member of the Visiting Committee of the Peabody Museum. After his retirement from clinical practice, he began conducting research at the Peabody on prehistoric human pelves with Hooton, and in 1927 he was named "Associate Curator of Somatology," a title he kept for the next decade (Willoughby 1928:273). His research on prehistoric pelves was written up and published as one of the Peabody Museum Papers in 1931 (Reynolds 1931b).

In 1925 Reynolds began working on the skeletal collection from the well-known Pecos Pueblo site in New Mexico with Hooton, George Williams, Habib Yusuf Rihan of the Harvard Dental School, and others (Hooton, Rihan, and Reynolds 1930). Reynolds helped in other areas of the museum at the time as well. For example, in 1926 he obtained for the museum a collection of eoliths and paleoliths from England from the British archaeologist J. Reid Moir (Willoughby 1928:274–75).

When Charles Willoughby retired in 1928, Reynolds was tapped to replace him as director of the museum. In large part this appointment seems to have been made because of Reynolds's financial acumen. He had been chair of a highly successful fund drive in 1906 for the twenty-fifth anniversary of the class of 1881, reaching the then commendable sum of $113,775. Reynolds served as director of the Peabody Museum for three and a half years, from 1928 to 1932, stepping down in February 1932 because of failing health (Scott 1933:296). Reporting his death in 1936, Donald Scott (1937:338) remarked that "Dr. Reynolds's efforts to ensure for the Museum some measure of financial stability were unsparing." Later, in reporting the work of the museum for the years 1928–39, Scott observed that the number of workers at the museum had more than tripled and that the Peabody was able annually to send expeditions to a dozen foreign countries, besides supporting some two score research projects in Cambridge. "This rapid growth," he wrote, was "set in motion through the efforts of our late director, Dr. Edward Reynolds" (Scott 1945:349).

Turning next to the students who trained under Hooton, we begin with **Harry Lionel Shapiro** (1902–90), Hooton's first Ph.D. Shapiro was born in Boston, entered Harvard in 1919, and completed his undergraduate work with the class of 1923. Hooton recruited him into anthropology as an undergraduate (Howells 1990:499), but when he entered the graduate program, he was sent, like all anthropology students at the time, to secure some archaeological field experience. He excavated an Indian burial place in Dartmouth, Massachusetts, in 1924 (Willoughby 1925:262). He was supported by the Thaw Fellowship for 1924–25 and received his A.M. in 1925. During his next and last year at Harvard, he was named a tutor in anthropology. He received his Ph.D., with the dissertation "A Study of Race Mixture as Exemplified in the Descendants of Tahitians and English Mutineers of the *Bounty*," in 1926.

Shapiro was 24 when he came to the AMNH in the summer of 1926, following receipt of his degree, looking for a job. Louis R. Sullivan had established physical anthropology at the AMNH by 1916, and Henry F. Osborn and Pliny E. Goddard interviewed and hired Shapiro as a replacement for Sullivan (Hellman 1968:202; Nelson 1948:246). One might suppose that Osborn later regretted this decision, for it was Shapiro who made it widely known that Nels C. Nelson had ghostwritten most of Osborn's *Men of the Stone Age* (Hellman 1968:202).

Shapiro spent his entire career at the AMNH, serving as the chair of anthropology there from 1942 to 1970. His position allowed him to teach courses at Columbia University as well, and he taught there from 1939 to 1973 (Howells 1990:499). When he served as president of the AAA in 1948, he set up the committee of archaeologists who selected the samples for the initial radiocarbon dating trials by Libby in the late 1940s, naming Hallam Movius from the Peabody to select the Old World samples. Shapiro did not forget his alma mater or his colleagues in archaeology; in 1967, at the request of the new Peabody Museum director, Stephen Williams, he served on the Ad Hoc Committee to evaluate the museum's needs for the next century.

Carleton Stevens Coon (1904–81) was born in Wakefield, Massachusetts. He entered Harvard with the class of 1925, intending to study classics and Egyptology, but in his sophomore year he took an introductory course from Hooton and changed his major to anthropology (Hunt 1982:239). He continued with graduate work after receiving his A.B. and began focusing on North Africa. In his second year of graduate work he received the Frederick Sheldon Traveling Fellowship and spent the year in Morocco (Willoughby 1927:264). For 1927–28 he was a tutor in anthropology, and he completed additional work on the physical anthropology of the Berbers in Morocco under the guidance of Hooton (Willoughby 1928:273). Thus Coon seems at this point to have been on track to be a physical anthropologist. In 1928 he received both his A.M. and his Ph.D., completing a dissertation titled "A Study of the Fundamental Racial and Cultural Characteristics of the Berbers of North Africa as Exemplified by the Riffians." Coon conducted several seasons of fieldwork in Morocco and Albania over the next two decades (Hunt 1982:240; Reynolds 1930:275, 1931a:287; Scott 1940:450).

Coon was also hired as an instructor in anthropology at Harvard after receiving his Ph.D. and then advanced to professorial positions, teaching there until 1948. His introduction to teaching ethnology was rather abrupt. In his autobiography, he described being called in to take over Dixon's general ethnography course in midstream when Dixon died in 1934 (Coon 1981:136). Coon recalled that he had no resource help from Dixon's research files, because Dixon had ordered that his papers be destroyed. Dixon's teaching notes, at least, were not destroyed, although Coon found them only after finishing the course. He remarked that the notes were meager in content, because Dixon had an encyclopedic ethnography of everywhere in his head and lectured with few notes in front of him.

Coon then was named curator of Old World ethnology at the Peabody Museum in 1935 (Scott 1937:336). He continued to be responsible for teaching part of the sociocultural anthropology curriculum at Harvard, along with Clyde Kluckhohn, who had been hired to replace Lloyd Warner (see chapter 12).

Coon was given leave in World War II to work as a military attaché in Latin America for the OSS, joining other anthropologists who worked there for the OSS or other intelligence-related services during the war (Patterson 1995:78). Late in life Coon recounted his war experiences in the book *A North Africa Story: The Anthropologist as OSS Agent, 1941–43* (Coon 1980).

When Coon retired from Harvard in 1948 and Kluckhohn took over sole responsibility for the sociocultural courses, Harvard social anthropology became more "mainstream" (Keller and Keller 2001:89). Upon Coon's "retirement," the University of Pennsylvania made him an offer, and he moved there to teach for another 15 years, from 1948 to 1963. While at Penn he wrote the volumes for which he is perhaps still best known, *Caravan: The Story of the Middle East* (1951) and *The Origin of Races* (1962), still splitting himself between ethnography and biological anthropology. In this he was much like Ralph Linton in taking a broad view of the field. In addition to his anthropological contributions, Coon wrote poetry and novels and is known in comparative literature circles for those works. Coon's ability as a storyteller was exhibited not only in his publications but also when he showed up at the Harvard Faculty Club for lunch and, as he often did, regaled his Harvard friends (including Stephen Williams) with tales.

George Dee Williams (1898–1961) was born in Sarahsville, Ohio. He received his A.B. from Ohio State in 1919 and then entered medical school there, receiving his M.D. in 1922 (G. Williams 1963). He interned at City Hospital in Youngstown, Ohio, from 1922 to 1923 and then practiced medicine another two years before coming to Harvard to study with Hooton. He received his A.M. in 1926, supported first by a Thaw Fellowship and the next year by Winthrop funding (Harvard University 1937:773). For his A.M. he worked on the pathology of Kidder's Pecos skeletal materials. This material was ultimately published as part of the skeletal studies of Pecos Pueblo (Hooton, Rihan, and Reynolds 1930).

After his A.M. work Hooton had Williams shift to doing blood work on the Mayas of Yucatán for his dissertation research. He spent eight months in Yucatán collecting materials from more than 2,500 Maya residents (Willoughby 1927:264–65, 1928:273–75). While at Harvard, he also spent a season in Europe with George MacCurdy working on the American School of Prehistoric Research excavations. Williams received his Ph.D. in 1929 with the dissertation "Race Mixture in Yucatan," which was published in 1931 as *Maya-Spanish Crosses in Yucatan*.

In 1928, just before completing his degree, Williams took a job as assistant professor of anatomy at the medical school of Washington University in St. Louis. By 1935 he had established the Department of Physical Anthropology and Anatomy there, together with

Mildred Trotter (1899–1991), who also started out in medicine but went back to obtain graduate training in physical anthropology in the 1920s, and Robert James Terry (1871–1966). This marked the beginning of professional anthropology at Washington University.

Williams kept up his Maya research interests for several years. He continued working on a project for the Peabody Museum on mestizos in Yucatán through 1930 (Reynolds 1931a:287). He became interested in the differential effects of infectious diseases on different populations, publishing the paper "TB in the Negroes of Georgia" in 1939 and that year getting a government grant to study mixed-race populations in Brazil. He left Washington University in 1941 to work for the U.S. Army in the war effort, mustering out in 1945 (G. Williams 1963:1011). After the war he worked in Veterans Administration hospitals in Chamblee, Georgia; Buffalo, New York; Philadelphia; and Martinsburg, West Virginia, until his death in 1961.

Frederick Seymour Hulse (1906–90), who was born in New York City, was another of Hooton's students. His father was a missionary and went to Cuba in 1915. Hulse lived there until 1918, when he was sent back to the United States to boarding school. After two years at Williams College, he transferred to Harvard and graduated in 1927. He had decided to major in anthropology because of Dixon's book *Racial History of Man* (Giles 1996:175).

Hulse went straight into graduate work, supported for the first two years by the Thaw Fellowship, and received his A.M. in 1928. The following year he had Hemenway funding, and Hooton sent him to Cuba to begin his dissertation research. Hooton provided Hulse with employment on a variety of projects at Harvard to help support him. Between 1928 and 1930 Hulse took 17 traditional anthropometric measurements and 40 morphological measurements on 200 Cubans and 500 Andalusians (Scott 1930:275), which formed the basis of his 1934 Ph.D. dissertation, "The Comparative Physical Anthropology of Andalusians and Cubans."

While working on his dissertation, Hulse worked at the AMNH for Harry Shapiro, taking anthropomorphic measurements in Hawaii in 1931. He then went to work for Alfred Kroeber in California, taking the same sets of measurements on Japanese Americans. Kroeber sent him on an expedition to Mexico in 1935 to take additional measurements on Mexican populations (Giles 1996:177). His first teaching position was at the University of Washington, where he taught in 1936–37, but the position disappeared because of lack of funding during the Great Depression. In 1938 Hulse joined Arthur Kelly as part of a team excavating Irene Mound, five miles from Savannah, Georgia. He continued working for the Works Progress Administration for the next few years, until the war intervened. After the war he taught at Colgate from 1946 to 1948, returned to the University of Washington from 1948 to 1958, and finally took a position at the University of Arizona, where he stayed until his retirement. He died in Tucson in 1990. Along the way he became well known for training students in forensic anthropology.

Richard Howell Post (1904–93) was born in New York City and received his S.B. from Princeton in 1926. He entered Harvard to train with Hooton in 1927. Among his early work at the Peabody was the statistical analysis of Caroline Bond Day's materials, which he wrote up in a museum document, "A Study of Facial Traits in Negro-White Crosses," in June 1928. In the summer of 1930 he joined fellow Harvard graduate student Walter Cline and other graduate students from Berkeley, Chicago, Columbia, and Washington, under the supervision of Leslie Spier, to make ethnographic observations of the Okanogan in Washington state, for which he collected and wrote up the physical anthropology (Spier 1938:3). While finishing his degree, he served as an instructor in zoology at Smith College from 1930 to 1936.

After obtaining his Harvard Ph.D., with the dissertation "Anthropometric Studies in Bilateral Asymmetry," in 1936, Post took a job as a research fellow in public health at Johns Hopkins University, and then as a statistician for the Department of Agriculture (National Research Council 1938:78). During World War II he was called to serve as U.S. vice consul in Uruguay in 1943, and he continued working for the State Department for a time after the war. Most of his research was conducted in the public health arena, but in the 1960s he contributed several papers on social biology and racial variants of vision, nasal features, hearing, and lactation in *Eugenics Quarterly*, which brought him back into discussions with biological anthropologists.

Gordon Townsend Bowles (1904–91), who was born in Tokyo, was the son of a Quaker missionary who worked in Hawaii and Asia. He received his A.B. from Earlham College in Indiana in 1925 but did not enter graduate school at the Peabody until 1928. During his first year he collected physical anthropometry data on some 2,000 pairs of Harvard fathers and sons (Reynolds 1930:274), a study he enlarged slightly and published in 1932 as *New Types of Old Americans at Harvard and Eastern Women's Colleges*. In 1929–30 he was Hooton's teaching and research assistant.

Bowles became a fellow of the Harvard-Yenching Institute in China from 1930 to 1932 and pursued his doctorate research in Tibet, China, and northern India (Reynolds 1932:299). He returned to Harvard, was named an "Assistant in Anthropology" at the Peabody, and finished his doctorate in 1935 with the dissertation "Racial Origins of the Peoples of the Central Chinese-Tibetan Border." After receiving his Ph.D. he was named "Research Associate in Anthropology for Ethnology and Physical Anthropology of Central Asia," a position he held until 1938. He then took a one-year position teaching at the University of Honolulu, and from 1939 to 1940 he excavated a burial site on Oahu for the Bishop Museum. During World War II he worked for the Far Eastern Section of the State Department, specializing in Japan. After the war he was a research associate at the Peabody Museum from 1946 to 1947 and then took a job teaching anthropology at Syracuse University. There he continued his interest in anthropometry and Asia, summarizing much of his research in his 1977 book, *The People of Asia*.

Clarence Wesley Dupertuis (1907–92) was born in Yacolt, Washington, and entered Harvard in 1925 as a member of the class of 1929. After receiving his S.B., he took a year off before entering graduate school in 1930. There he was supported by a Thaw Fellowship for the first year and a Winthrop Scholarship for the second. He received his A.M. in anthropology in 1931. In 1933 he was a member of the Peabody Museum project "Survey of the Irish Free State," directed by Hooton (see chapter 12). Hugh Hencken and Hallam Movius were charged with doing the archaeology; Conrad Arensberg and Solon Kimball, the social anthropology; and Dupertuis, the physical anthropology (Scott 1936:318). Dupertuis took anthropometric measurements on some 10,000 Irish males (Scott 1937:340). During this period he was listed as an assistant in anthropology for the Peabody, the equivalent of a teaching assistant today.

Hooton set Dupertuis to work developing exhibits for the upcoming Chicago World's Fair in 1933–34 (Scott 1934:301). In 1936 he took a job at the Columbia-Presbyterian Medical Center in clinical anthropology. Dupertuis finished his Ph.D. dissertation, "An Anthropological Study of Midgets," in 1940 and spent the rest of his career in clinical anthropology in a number of medical schools.

Carl Coleman Seltzer (1908–2003), born in Boston, was also a member of the Harvard class of 1929 and continued at the Peabody to earn his graduate degrees under Hooton. In the year after he received his A.B., he and Martin Luther worked on taking measurements from Inuit groups in southern Greenland, with aid from Vilhjalmar Stefansson, then an associate in anthropology at the Peabody, and they continued this work into the 1930 field season. The 1931 field season was cancelled because of the shortfall of funds owing to the onset of the depression (Reynolds 1930:274, 1931:286, 1932:297). Seltzer wrote up the material the team had collected for his 1933 Ph.D. dissertation, "The Physical Anthropology of the Mediaeval Icelanders with Special Reference to the Question of Their Racial Origin."

After receiving his degree, Seltzer won a two-year NRC fellowship for 1933–35 and studied the Hopis, Yaquis, and Navajos, continuing his anthropometric studies. With jobs scarce, he shifted into medical anthropology, with an appointment at the Harvard School of Public Health from 1937 until he retired in 1976. During those four decades, his research focused primarily on the adverse effects of smoking.

Initially, however, he was able to continue his interest in physical anthropology, with the analysis in 1938 of the anthropomorphic measurements taken by Henry Huxley (see chapter 10) during his expedition to Lebanon and Syria in 1900. Huxley provided the financial support for the research, and the analysis was published as volume 16, number 2, of the Papers of the Peabody Museum (Seltzer 1940). During the 1950s Seltzer was named "Research Fellow, Physical Anthropology," continuing his ties with the Peabody while working at the Harvard School of Public Health.

Martin M. Luther (1899–1950) enrolled at Harvard in 1920 and took undergraduate classes there through 1924, although he is listed as having received his A.B. from Wake Forest University in 1924 (Anonymous 1950). He then entered the graduate program at Harvard in 1924, where he worked with Hooton for the next several years. In 1926–27 he collected anthropometric and sociological data on Finnish immigrants in Massachusetts. He went to Finland in June 1927 to collect comparative materials for this study. In 1928 he worked with Carl Seltzer and Vilhjalmar Stefansson, collecting data in Iceland and Greenland, and he collected more information during fieldwork in Greenland in 1929. He returned to Harvard and, using the statistical laboratory Hooton was developing, analyzed the anthropometric data he had collected on Inuits and Europeans, finishing in 1931 (Reynolds 1930:274, 1931a:286, 1932:297). Apparently, Luther was an excellent field-worker. Hooton (1930:553) wrote, "Give me [George] Schwab and Luther and a few other men whom I could name, and enough to keep them traveling up and down the far places of the earth," and with them, he opined, one could complete worldwide anthropological investigations in record time.

During his tenure in graduate school Luther was involved in a balancing act between involvement in a textbook publishing business in Boston (later moved to Magnolia, a suburb of Gloucester, Massachusetts) and taking care of family business on an ancestral cotton plantation near Fayetteville, North Carolina (Anonymous 1930). But he continued his research during the early years of the depression. He returned to graduate school at Harvard in 1934–35, working in Hooton's Statistical and Anthropometric Laboratory on sociological data from an industrial physiology project in Gloucester, Massachusetts, one of the applied sociocultural projects in which museum personnel became involved during the depression (Scott 1935:312). In 1935, however, he became president of the Excelsior Company (Anonymous 1950) and apparently left anthropological research permanently in order to manage this textbook printing company.

William Armand Lessa (1908–97) was recruited into the graduate program by Hooton but did not stay to complete his degree. Lessa, who was born in Newark, New Jersey, received his A.B. from Harvard in 1928 in chemistry. He had taken a course in human evolution from Hooton, was intrigued, and decided to enter the graduate program at the Peabody in 1928. For 1928–29, Hooton had Lessa do anthropometric research on a series of 12,000 criminals. He then sent Lessa to do work with his old student Harry Shapiro at the Columbia-Presbyterian Medical Center in 1929–30. Shapiro helped Lessa get a job at the University of Hawaii, as a research associate doing physical anthropology, from 1930 to 1933, but the funding dried up in 1933, and Lessa ended up doing a series of odd jobs for the next few years.

Lessa entered the graduate program at the University of Chicago in 1939 and received his A.M. there in 1941. For 1941–42 he taught physical anthropology at Brooklyn College, before being called into the war. He completed his Ph.D. in 1947 at the University of Chicago, on the basis of his war experiences, with the dissertation "Disintegration and Reintegration of the Italian Community as the Result of War and Military Occupation." Following receipt of his degree, he obtained a position at the University of California–Los Angeles, where he focused on the ethnology and physical anthropology of Polynesia and Micronesia for the rest of his career (Herskovits and Ames 1950:108).

William White Howells (1908–2005) was born in New York City. Along with Wesley Dupertuis and Carl Seltzer, he entered Harvard with the class of 1929.

Like his classmates, he became attracted to physical anthropology after taking classes with Hooton (Giles 1979:328). He continued for graduate work at Harvard, paying his way part of the time by working as an associate in anthropology at the Peabody Museum, helping Laurance Redway with his studies of eye pigmentation (Reynolds 1932:297). He received his Ph.D., with the dissertation "The Peopling of Melanesia as Indicated by Cranial Evidence from the Bismarck Archipelago," in 1934. Much of his later field research also focused on Oceania. After receiving his degree, he went to work for the AMNH, staying there through 1939.

Howells accepted a job at the University of Wisconsin in 1939 and was there until 1954, except for a few years during World War II, when he worked for the Office of Naval Intelligence (Giles 1979:328). He served as president of the AAA in 1951. In 1954 he returned to Harvard to teach, having been called back to replace his old mentor, Hooton, who had just died, and stayed there the next two decades. Howells retired in 1974 and died at his Maine home in 2005. He pioneered multivariate statistical quantitative methods for the study of morphological problems and population relationships in paleoanthropology, and he was regarded as an expert in human evolution. In 1998 Howells provided the funds for an endowed directorship of the Peabody Museum. He was a well-known leader in the field, a great teacher, and a wonderful colleague, requiring little commentary from us.

We look next at graduate students in sociocultural anthropology from 1919 through 1929. Before this decade the Peabody Museum had relied on some outside scholars, such as Charles Newcombe, to fill weak areas in the ethnographic collections, and it had begun sending out its own students to underrepresented areas of the world for the same purpose. But the anthropology program had produced few Ph.D.s in ethnology and sociocultural anthropology. Throughout his career, Roland Dixon, the main instructor in cultural anthropology before Carleton Coon came on the scene, was a very private person, seemingly more interested in doing his own field research and trying to answer the "big questions" of the day than in trying to "reproduce" himself by recruiting and training students for their degrees. Nevertheless, the number of advanced degrees for students interested in sociocultural anthropology began to increase during the 1920s, particularly after Coon finished his degree and joined the faculty, with students such as Mischa Titiev, Kenneth Emory, Gordon MacGregor, Scudder Mekeel, Robert McKennan, Fred Wulsin, Pat Putnam, and Milton Katz.

Charles Frederic Newcombe (1851–1924) was a medical doctor who practiced in England and then Canada for several years before becoming interested, in 1889, in the archaeology, ethnology, and natural history of Victoria, British Columbia, where he lived (Goddard 1925:352). The early collections of Northwest Coast ethnography in the Provincial Museum at Victoria were for the most part made by Newcombe. In 1901 he joined John Swanton in working with the Jesup Expedition of the AMNH in the Queen

Charlotte Islands. In 1902 Newcombe began working for George Dorsey and the Field Museum as a field ethnologist, making collections in British Columbia and later writing up a report on his work and installing the collections at the Field Museum in 1905. He took a company of Nootka Indians to the Louisiana Purchase Exposition in St. Louis in 1904, receiving a gold medal from the fair (Goddard 1925:352).

After finishing work for the Field Museum, Newcombe solicited and completed many commissions to acquire ethnographic materials for museums in the United States and Europe. Between 1916 and 1922 he was appointed "Researcher, Northwest Coast," for the Peabody Museum and secured a good portion of the Kwakiutl and Haida materials, including totem poles, that are in the museum's collections (Willoughby 1918:241, 1919:239, 1922:275, 1923a:220). At least one of these poles has since been repatriated to its tribe. Newcombe retired in 1922 and in his last few years limited himself to writing up previous work. Not yet having a significant graduate student group in sociocultural anthropology, the Peabody Museum was still dependent on recruiting outside help such as Newcombe's. This was soon to change.

Morris or **Mischa Titiev** (1901–78) was born in Russia and came to Boston with his family in 1907. He entered Harvard with the class of 1923, graduating in English literature and going on to secure his A.M. in that field in 1924. Later, during his Ph.D. work in English literature, he "discovered" anthropology and shifted into that department. He completed his Ph.D. dissertation, "The Social Organization of the Hopi Indians," in 1935 (Jorgensen 1979:342). Although the official records at Harvard carried him as Morris (Mischa) Titiev, throughout the rest of his professional life he used only the name Mischa. His Ph.D. work is of particular note because he included ethnographic perspectives at the Hopi pueblos from both men and women, having been assisted by Radcliffe student Charis Dennison in collecting ethnographic data from Hopi women (Scott 1934:300).

The first job Titiev took following receipt of his Ph.D. was as "junior archaeologist" with the Historic Sites and Buildings unit of the National Park Service. In 1936 he was hired at the University of Michigan, where he spent the rest of his career as a social anthropologist. During World War II he served with the OSS, working in East Asia. He was handicapped during much of his professional career by a severely disabling disease, which resulted in his death in 1978 (Jorgensen 1979:342–43).

Kenneth Pike Emory (1897–1992) seems to have been another student attracted to Harvard because of Dixon's work in the Pacific Rim. Emory was born in Fitchburg, Massachusetts, and received his S.B. from Dartmouth in 1920. Through family connections (his family had moved to Hawaii in 1900), he secured a position as assistant ethnologist at the Bernice P. Bishop Museum after his graduation. That year he was sent to Maui to assist Robert T. Aitken in an archaeological survey of the ruins in Haleakala Crater (Kirch 1922:1).

Recognizing the need for additional training, Emory went to work with Kroeber at Berkeley in 1921. But after a semester there, he was given another field assignment for the Bishop Museum—an archaeological survey of the island of Lanai—which he carried out from July 1921 through January 1922 (Kirch 1992:3). He was then sent to study with Dixon at Harvard for 1922–23 and received his A.M. at Harvard in 1923.

Emory then returned to the Bishop Museum, where he was a junior staffer working with Edward Handy, Willowdean Handy, and John F. G. Stokes. He continued to do archaeological survey work for the Bishop Museum during the 1920s and 1930s. In 1940 he was sent to Yale to work on his Ph.D., but the war soon intervened. After the war he returned to Yale, working on the lexicostatistics of Polynesian cultural relationships and completing his Ph.D. dissertation, "Eastern Polynesia: Its Cultural Relationships," in 1947. He spent the rest of his career working for the Bishop Museum, focusing his research mainly on ethnological rather than archaeological topics (Mann 1991a:182).

Gordon MacGregor (1902–83) was born in Haverhill, Massachusetts, and attended Yale, where he received his A.B. in 1925. In the 1928–29 academic year he began graduate work at Harvard, supported at first by Hemenway Fellowship money. Once he had fixed his research topic on the Pacific, he obtained funds from the Bishop Museum in Hawaii and completed his Ph.D. dissertation, "The Western Diffusion of Polynesian Culture as Seen in the Tokelau Islands," in 1935. But jobs were scarce because of the depression, and his first postdoctorate position was that of an archaeologist with the Egyptian Exploration Society.

Although his early experience was in Oceanic ethnology and Old World archaeology, MacGregor devoted most of his career to applied anthropology in government agencies. From 1936 to 1945 he was an anthropologist with the Bureau of Indian Affairs (BIA). From 1945 to 1947 he was superintendent of the Northern Cheyenne Agency, and from 1947 to 1949 he was with the BIA again, working to remove the Fort Berthold Indians along the Missouri River during federal dam construction. In the 1950s he shifted back to overseas work. From 1949 to 1951 he was the Pacific specialist for the Office of Territories; from 1951 to 1953, applied anthropologist with the Technical Cooperation Administration; from 1953 to 1956, associated with the Committee on International Exchange under Fulbright-Hays; and from 1957 to 1966, an anthropologist with the Public Health Service.

Haviland Scudder Mekeel (1902–47) was an undergraduate recruited into sociocultural anthropology by Dixon. Born in St. Louis, he started college at Princeton in 1921 but ran into academic difficulties and dropped out for two years. He then entered Harvard in 1926 (MacGregor 1948:95). After receiving his A.B. in 1928, he was offered the Winthrop Scholarship for graduate work but opted to go to Chicago in 1928–29 for his A.M. instead. He attended Kroeber's summer field school in New Mexico in 1929 and the next academic year transferred to Yale. While there he worked with the Pine Ridge Lakota Sioux, the basis of his 1932 Ph.D. from Yale. He served as director of applied anthropology for John Collier and the BIA from 1935 to 1937, when he shifted to working for the Laboratory of Anthropology at Santa Fe until 1940. He then went to the University of Wisconsin at Madison, where he got involved in psychological anthropology until his death in 1947.

Robert Addison McKennan (1903–82) was born in Helena, Montana, earned a Harvard doctorate, but spent most of his academic career at Dartmouth. He received his A.B. from Dartmouth in 1925 and the next academic year served as an instructor in citizenship for Dartmouth. In 1927 he entered graduate school at Harvard. He decided on doing ethnography in Alaska for his doctorate research and secured the Frederick Sheldon Traveling Fellowship for 1929–30 to conduct research on the upper Tanana River there. The bulk of his fieldwork was ethnographic, although he did conduct a small archaeological excavation at Tetlin Village, Alaska. When he returned, he supported himself by taking a part-time instructorship in sociology at Dartmouth while he wrote up his field research.

McKennan received his Ph.D. from Harvard in 1933 with the dissertation "Indians of the Upper Tanana, Alaska." With degree in hand, he became a full-time instructor in sociology at Dartmouth, where he taught until he retired in 1969. McKennan's career research focus was the ethnography of Arctic peoples. He developed the Northern Studies Program, with its special "Arctic Seminar," at Dartmouth in 1953–54. He officially taught in sociology, because although the first instructor in archaeology, Charles Hawes, was hired in 1909, Dartmouth offered no degree in anthropology until enough anthropologists were hired to create a joint Department of Anthropology and Sociology in 1961. Anthropology became a separate department there in 1967.

Frederick Roelker Wulsin (1891–1961), born in Cincinnati, received his A.B. from Harvard, majoring in philosophy, in 1912. He went on for graduate work and received his master's in civil engineering in 1915. That year he also collected briefly in Madagascar for the Museum of Comparative Zoology. During World War I Wulsin served as a first lieutenant in the navy aboard the U.S.S. *Leviathan*. After the war he went into business in China and Mongolia for about a decade. In 1921–22 he made major collections for the MCZ in China and Tibet, which seems to have influenced his decision to return to enter the graduate program at the Peabody Museum in 1925.

Receiving an A.M. in anthropology in 1926, Wulsin was named a tutor in anthropology for 1926–27, an associate in anthropology for 1927–28, and an instructor in anthropology and assistant curator in African archaeology and ethnology for 1928–29 (Harvard University 1937:475). In 1927–28 he led a major expedition to the Ubangi-Shari basin in the Congo, financed by the Bureau of International Research of Harvard and Radcliffe Colleges. The expedition also included Peabody anthropology graduate students Patrick Putnam and Milton Katz. In 1929, when Wulsin had to return to the Peabody, he hired Patrick Putnam to continue working in the Congo, paying him out of his own pocket. Wulsin wrote up the previous season's work as his Ph.D. dissertation, "Cultural Development in the Shari Basin: A Study in African Archaeology," defended in 1929 (Reynolds 1930:273; Willoughby 1929:296).

After receiving his degree, Wulsin continued teaching at the Peabody Museum for a year, serving also as assistant to the director, and participated in some explorations in Morocco and Iran with Carleton Coon (Brew 1966b:13; Reynolds 1930:275).

The Coon-Wulsin linkage was strengthened when Coon's son later married Wulsin's daughter. For the 1930–31 year, Wulsin worked in Iran for the University Museum at Pennsylvania. He lectured at Boston University from 1933 to 1936 and then, like many others during the depression, had to seek other employment. After serving in World War II, he returned to teach social anthropology at Tufts University from 1945 until he retired in 1958. He kept in touch with his Peabody friends until his death.

Patrick Tracy Lowell Putnam (1904–53), a native of New York City, received his A.B. in anthropology from Harvard in 1925. He then traveled a while (Willoughby 1928:273) before joining Wulsin's Harvard-Radcliffe Bureau of International Research expedition to the Congo in 1927–28 to collect linguistic and ethnological data (Reynolds 1930:273). Putnam became enthralled with the Bambuti Pygmies of the Ituri forest and returned in 1928–29 to continue research there, financed by a private grant from Wulsin. He lived with the Bambutis for the next quarter century, returning to Harvard to collaborate with Coon in working up what he expected to be the definitive ethnography of the Congo Pygmies (Scott 1947:267; see also Mark 1995). While living, he was the foremost anthropological expert on Pygmies, and he helped Colin Turnbull, author of the well-known *The Forest People*, do his research. Unfortunately, Putnam did not complete his definitive work before he died in 1953 of a virulent lung disease brought home with him from Africa. (Patrick Putnam had no connection to Frederic W. Putnam that we can identify.)

Milton Katz (1907–95) graduated summa cum laude in anthropology from Harvard in 1927. He had been an undergraduate friend of Fred Hulse's and initially entered graduate work in anthropology at the Peabody following receipt of his A.B. (Giles 1996:177). He received a fellowship to study African languages and went to Europe to study, but he wanted to get into the field, so when he met Wulsin and Putnam on their way to Africa, he went with them (Mark 1995:3). He and Wulsin spent two months doing the archaeological work for the project, but Katz contracted malaria during the fieldwork, which apparently caused him to lose enthusiasm for anthropology (Mark 1995:8).

Katz shifted to law, received his J.D. from Harvard in 1931, and went into a career in law, government, and international relations. He first went to Washington, D.C., where he worked with the Securities and Exchange Commission and the U.S. Attorney General's office. He returned to Harvard in 1938 to take a position in its law school. After World War II he was head of European operations for the Marshall Plan. He became Byrne Professor of Administrative Law at Harvard in 1949, and after a leave to serve as an ambassador, he returned in 1954 to become Henry L. Stimson Professor of Law and director of international legal studies at Harvard.

The 1920s marked the "modernization" of the anthropology department at the Peabody Museum, such that by the end of the decade Harvard was clearly a mainstream leader of American anthropology. The department had 24 graduate students in 1929–30, most of them working for their Ph.D.s, but it still lacked funds to support more than five of them in the field (Reynolds 1930:271). This financial problem was to be changed significantly by museum director Edward Reynolds in the next few years.

The Peabody Museum was now clearly involved in training not just students with interests in North America but students with global interests. And the shift was not just in area of interest but also in the ethnicity of the students themselves. African American scholars such as Day and Hansberry were now getting degrees. Latin American scholars such as Tello and Noguera came for training. Women, who had been relegated to the minority position during the professionalization in the 1890s, were reappearing, with scholars such as Ruth Sawtell and Laura Thompson. As we show in the next chapter, this shift would accelerate markedly after 1925.

In view of the xenophobia and "Yellow Peril" propaganda sweeping the nation in the 1920s, it is perhaps especially significant to see the inclusion at the Peabody of Southeast and East Asian students, from places such as India, Japan, and China. Although Chi, Guha, and Utsurikawa were the first Ph.D. students from these countries in the Peabody Museum program, they were part of a broader trend at Harvard: Chi was the twelfth Chinese Ph.D. at Harvard (the first being Minfu Tah Hu in 1917); Guha, the sixth Indian Ph.D. (the first being Subharama Swaminadhan in 1900); and Utsurikawa, the fifth Japanese Ph.D. (the first being Kingo Miyabe in 1889). Enrollment of Southeast and East Asian students had been sporadic from 1890 to 1910, but beginning in 1910, at least a half dozen secured their A.M. or Ph.D. degree (Harvard University 1930), although only about half that number did so in Harvard College itself, where quotas were in place.

By the 1929 academic year, the Peabody had strong programs in place in archaeology, physical anthropology, and sociocultural anthropology. Hooton had developed his program in physical anthropology into a powerhouse, training most of the physical anthropologists in the country for many years. As Eugene Giles noted (1991:304), "until after World War II there was essentially no place for graduate work in physical anthropology other than Harvard; consequently most senior physical anthropology positions have been held by his students."

Alfred Tozzer had been able to take advantage of projects in Central America fielded by the Carnegie Institution of Washington, with its offices next door to the Peabody, to recruit a large number of students interested in the region. CIW staff were sent to the Peabody to obtain advanced degrees—primarily master's degrees but on rare occasions Ph.D.s. Tozzer, the "dean" of Central American archaeological studies, was able to exploit CIW funds to send students out for training and to provide positions for some of his graduate students. CIW research support was such that A.V. Kidder shifted from the Southwest to take over the new position of director of research at the CIW in 1929.

In addition to strengths in Southwestern and Maya archaeology, a new emphasis on Old World archaeology was being developed at the Peabody Museum. In sociocultural anthropology, Dixon was recruiting more students from his research areas, students such as Guha, Chi, and Utsurikawa, rather than attracting American students, and by the end of the decade a new emphasis on applied anthropology was developing. Sociocultural anthropology was strengthened by new instructors such as Carleton Coon and, in 1929, W. Lloyd Warner, whom we discuss in the next chapter.

12

An Explosion of Scholars, 1929–1939

Dealing with students who were trained at Harvard's Peabody Museum and Department of Anthropology between 1929 and 1939 is difficult for a variety of reasons. One is proximity: because some of these people are still alive or only recently deceased, few retrospectives have yet appeared that might put their contributions into a synthetic perspective. In addition, we studied or worked with some of these people, which makes it more difficult to view their contributions from a scholarly distance. Yet another issue is the burgeoning number of persons involved. Although a mere handful of names from this period shows up in typical histories of anthropology, we have identified more than 160 persons who trained or did research at the Peabody at this time, at least five dozen of whom could be said to have influenced the directions of growth of the discipline. We believe each of them merits at least several pages of discussion, yet space often limits us to a few paragraphs. Sometimes we devote the least discussion to the best known of these people, in the hope that their names and contributions are already familiar to readers and therefore less needs to be said about them.

The 1930s was the period when women graduate students, in addition to women researchers, became a continuing, significant presence in Harvard anthropology. Prior to the professionalization of the discipline, when there were no degree-granting institutions in anthropology, both serious female and male avocational researchers made major contributions to anthropology. When university training began, the historical accident that the first success of degree programs came at places like Harvard and Columbia—restricted male domains at the undergraduate level even at the beginning of the twentieth century—meant that anthropology became almost exclusively the province of men for many years. Women only slowly reemerged as serious contributors.

At Harvard, the pattern of male exclusivity changed in about 1925 at the graduate level. From the beginning of the anthropology program in the 1890s, Putnam and his staff had offered a limited range of undergraduate courses to female students. But initially there was a perceived "glass ceiling" in terms of women majoring in the discipline, much less going on to graduate work and professional positions. This was to change.

As can be seen in the table on page 391, the years 1925–28 seem to reflect a critical shift in graduate education in anthropology at Harvard. For the first time there were consistent numbers of women graduate students, although they still made up perhaps no more than 20 to 25 percent of the total. At the same time, the number of male graduate students doubled. No longer was there a mere handful of graduate students, most of whose names became familiar to all students of the history of the discipline. Now the graduate degree program at the Peabody, combining enrollments from both Harvard and Radcliffe, totaled 25 to 30 students each year.

This shift seemed so dramatic that we suspected some change had taken place in the admissions process or in the financing available to anthropology students during this decade. Neither seems to have been the case. We looked at the annual reports for Harvard University, carefully perusing the president's reports, the graduate dean's reports, the Radcliffe reports, and the Peabody Museum reports, for the years 1921 through 1930, as well as the composite summaries of graduate school policy shifts up to 1930 (Haskins 1930), expecting to find the smoking gun—for example, mention of the success of a new graduate student initiative or of a new initiative in anthropology. But the documents were mute. The fact that Alfred Tozzer was appointed a member of the Academic Board of Radcliffe beginning in 1922–23 might help explain the increase of women in the anthropology graduate program, but it does not address the increasing enrollment of men in the same time frame.

For the women of Radcliffe, although their access to instruction significantly improved, taking courses in anthropology was still no easy matter before 1925. Doris Zemurray Stone (1980:20) recollected that as an undergraduate in the 1920s, she was "required to obtain permission from the president of Harvard to attend classes at the Peabody Museum, and with that permission came the warning that if my deportment was not entirely proper, my association with that austere building would be ended."

This might hardly seem like progress, but when the anthropology program began in the 1890s and early 1900s, Harvard College did not permit Radcliffe undergraduates in classes with Harvard students at all; rather, the anthropology staff had to teach separate sections to the women in Radcliffe buildings. Thus the ability of female undergraduates actually to take classes with male students in the Peabody Museum was a significant policy shift. Only a limited number of dual sections of anthropology classes had been made available to Radcliffe students earlier; now they had potential access to all anthropology classes. The notable increase in the numbers of Radcliffe students going on to take graduate work in anthropology in the 1920s may reflect this changed status.

For 1923–25, the Harvard graduate school documents refer first to a concern that the university's increase in graduate fees to the highest level in the country will have a negative effect on enrollment. Then they express a verbal sigh of relief when it does not. The number of graduate students increased inexorably from 1919 to 1929. In the 1919–20 academic year, there were 564 graduate students at Harvard; by 1928–29, the number had nearly doubled, to 1,003, with the growth rate relatively constant from year to year.

Numbers of Graduate Students in Anthropology Enrolled at Harvard and Radcliffe, 1890–1940

Academic Year	Harvard	Radcliffe
1890–91	2	—
1891–92	3	—
1892–93	2	—
1893–94	2	—
1894–95	1	—
1895–96	1	—
1896–97	2	—
1897–98	4	—
1898–99	1	—
1899–1900	3	—
1900–01	3	—
1901–02	2	—
1902–03	2	—
1903–04	0	—
1904–05	5	—
1905–06	3	—
1906–07	5	—
1907–08	5	—
1908–09	5	—
1909–10	9	—
1910–11	5	—
1911–12	4	—
1912–13	8	—
1913–14	4	—
1914–15	5	—
1915–16	3	—
1916–17	8	—
1917–18	2	—
1918–19	1	—
1919–20	5	—
1920–21	5	—
1921–22	6	—
1922–23	3	—
1923–24	9	—
1924–25	9	0
1925–26	12	4
1926–27	10	5
1927–28	15	5
1928–29	24	5
1929–30	22	6
1930–31	22	4
1931–32	26	4
1932–33	27	10
1933–34	26	8
1934–35	21	6
1935–36	20	4
1936–37	25	2
1937–38	21	6
1938–39	20	6
1939–40	25	5

In anthropology, Peabody Museum director Charles Willoughby (1928:272) noted a large increase of both undergraduate and graduate students for 1926–27 and a still larger one the following year, with 450 undergraduates and 18 graduate students, the largest enrollments in the department to that date (Willoughby 1929:297). When Edward Reynolds took over as director the next year, he noted the good news of a continuing enrollment increase to 24 graduate students but the worrisome news that the museum had funds to send only five of them into the field that season (Reynolds 1930:271). In contrast, Harry Shapiro (1981:432) reported that when he graduated with his A.B. in 1923, there were only four undergraduate majors and three graduate students in the department. There is no question that something caused an almost tsunami-like shift in the interest in anthropology at Harvard in the 1925–27 period.

To address the issue of funding graduate student research, Reynolds launched the Peabody Museum Association in the late spring of 1929 and otherwise managed to secure major new funding for research (Reynolds 1930:270). The result was that by 1933–34 Donald Scott reported that the museum had 44 field projects that season—18 in archaeology, 18 in physical anthropology, and 11 in ethnology (summing to more than 44 because three encompassed more than one subfield). This growth spurt allowed Scott (1936:315) to observe further that the Peabody Museum staff and graduate students had participated in 432 expeditions since the museum was founded in 1866—348 on its own funds, 19 with Harvard College funds, and 85 under other auspices. The funding totals suggest 452 projects, but Scott's area-by-area project count comes to only 432; presumably the totals do not match because some projects had more than one funding source. (The Peabody Museum Association had a checkered trajectory. It disappeared when J. O. Brew was museum director but was reactivated in the 1960s by Stephen Williams. It disappeared again in 1977 but was restored once more in the 2000s under William Fash.)

The growth of the department in the 1930s is reflected in changes in the graduate curriculum. Reviewing the annual reports of the university for courses taught each year throughout the 1930s, we found that during the early part of the decade, the course Anthropology 15, Field Methods in Anthropology, was taught only at intervals of roughly every two to three years. The teaching faculty was listed as the entire departmental staff, and the course never had an enrollment of more than eight students.

With the 1937–38 school year, however, the departmental curriculum began to be reorganized. Among the changes was the division of the former methods course into three new courses along subdisciplinary lines. Thus, in 1938–39 a new course, Anthropology 15a, Field Methods in Archaeology, was offered. The instructors were listed as Alfred Tozzer assisted by J. O. Brew, and the course drew 11 students: 5 graduates, 2 juniors, 1 sophomore, 1 special student, and 2 Radcliffe students. The next year, 1939–40, saw the introduction of Anthropology 15b, Field Methods in Ethnography, taught by visiting professor Leslie Spier from Yale, with 10 students. In 1940–41, Anthropology 15c, Field Methods in Physical Anthropology, was offered for the first time, taught by Earnest Hooton and Carleton Coon, with eight students, and Anthropology 15a, Field Methods in Archaeology, was given a second time, taught again by Tozzer and Brew, with an enrollment of eight.

The archaeology field methods course had both a classroom instruction component and hands-on laboratory training exercises. According to a description of the course in the *Harvard Crimson* (Anonymous 1941b), one part of the laboratory portion of the course consisted of learning how to excavate bones and artifacts buried in sandboxes in the basement lab by the teaching assistant. Another part involved actual fieldwork, that year the excavation of part of a colonial cellar in Concord, Massachusetts. Although the sandboxes still existed in the Peabody Museum basement in the 1950s, apparently the class was terminated with the onset of World War II.

The research projects of most of the men doing graduate work in anthropology receive mention in the annual reports of the Peabody Museum more than once. The women students were under separate registration through Radcliffe, and their published annual records are much less complete. With a reorganization of the honors program at Radcliffe in the mid-1920s, anthropology for the first time became a possible honors concentration. The first Radcliffe student listed as graduating with special distinction in anthropology was Harriet Hammond in 1928, and thereafter, for the period of our research, an average of one Radcliffe student per year was listed as an anthropology honors graduate. Thus the upsurge in women entering the graduate program at the Peabody Museum was paralleled by a new availability of anthropology for undergraduate women at Radcliffe, both likely owing to Tozzer's influence in his position on the Radcliffe board.

Nevertheless, for most women students interested in anthropology, graduate education at Harvard appears to have effectively ended at the A.M. level. Although some Radcliffe students in the 1920s went on to get their Ph.D.s eventually, it was usually after two or three decades, and most often at other institutions. In part this might have been because women students were more intensely challenged by the faculty at the Peabody regarding their future plans. For example, Ruth Sawtell Wallis reported that "her professors, E. A. Hooton and A. M. Tozzer, asserted that most young women in graduate work abandoned it if they married. They added, however, if she had serious intentions to study, they would help her in every way" (Collins 1979:85).

Doris Zemurray Stone (1980:20–21) wrote about the same issue for women working toward advanced degrees in anthropology at Harvard, recollecting, "I was advised against studying for a Ph.D. Women simply weren't encouraged to go that far, particularly in anthropology. . . . And eventually, when I returned to the Peabody Museum for a visit in the 1940s, one of my former professors, who also thought little good came from educating females because they soon grew up and were married, invited me to speak at a weekly tea gathering at his home." Although Stone did not name names, Earnest Hooton was well known for holding weekly teas for anthropology graduate students at that time and until his death in 1954. Both Stone and Wallis, however, made it clear that once they made the difficult choice, the faculty at the Peabody Museum were extremely supportive of their work. As we show next, it remained for women like Marie Wormington and Alice Brues to become the first substantial cohort of female anthropology Ph.D.s at Harvard.

Regrettably, for some of the women students who undertook graduate work in anthropology, we have only passing mentions of their studies. For example, **Helen Thayer Adams** (1899–1983) received her A.B. from the University of Wisconsin in 1924. She entered Radcliffe in 1932 to study anthropology, on a Radcliffe scholarship, and received her A.M. in anthropology from Radcliffe in 1936. This is all that is recorded in the official reports or literature. We have a bit more information on a dozen other Radcliffe students who went on to graduate work.

With the heavy emphasis on archaeology at the Peabody Museum in the 1920s and 1930s, it is perhaps unsurprising that many of the Radcliffe students whom we can identify were involved in archaeological research. **Harriet Hammond (Elliston)** (1904–2002), the first official recipient of honors in anthropology from Radcliffe, in 1928, was born in Cambridge. After receiving her A.B. she was awarded the Augustus Anson Whitney and Benjamin White Whitney Fellowship, in the amount of $500, to study abroad in anthropology in 1928–29 (Brown 1929:14). With the grant, she went to England and entered graduate school at Oxford University, where she received her A.M. in anthropology in 1929.

After completing her graduate work there, she returned to Cambridge. She worked at the Fogg Art Museum from 1929 to 1930 and then shifted back to the Peabody Museum, where she worked on African archaeology, reconstructing pottery and creating South African exhibits from 1931 to 1935. She left the Peabody in 1935 to marry William Arthur Elliston, an English surgeon. Although nothing specific is detailed about her earlier area of expertise, her 1930 publication on Maya art (Hammond 1930) suggests that she had begun as a student of Tozzer's and as a Maya archaeologist.

Gretchen Froehlich Cutter (Sharp) (1909–88) graduated with honors in anthropology from Radcliffe College in 1931. She later enrolled in the graduate program at the University of Chicago, where she listed herself as having been a student from 1936 to 1938. For the next three years she worked as director for various Works Progress Administration (WPA) archaeological projects. For example, in 1940 she directed a large WPA excavation project at the Fisher site, near Channahon in Will County, Illinois, working for the University of Chicago and the Illinois State Museum (Adams 1940:82). She subsequently consulted with James Griffin (Griffin 1943:283 n. 34) on the analysis of the ceramics from this site, but the work was never published. After World War II she became an expert in early American folk art.

Others of the women students in the 1930s also worked in archaeology, but again we have only sketchy details about them. **Dorothy Newton (Inglis)** was a Peabody Museum secretary who worked with Hugh Hencken and Hallam Movius on their fifth

Harvard Archaeological Expedition to Ireland, in 1936, as we discuss later in this chapter. The next season she worked with J. O. Brew at Awatovi. **Katherine Burks Young (Hearn)** (1916–78) graduated cum laude in anthropology from Radcliffe in 1937. She went on to work with Tozzer at the Peabody Museum on Basketmaker culture materials from Durango, Colorado, in 1937–39 for her A.M. thesis (Scott 1940:457). She then worked with Hooton until 1940, when she married and moved to South Africa. **Mary Whittemore (McEvoy)** (1917–2001) graduated cum laude in anthropology from Radcliffe in 1938. She wrote her senior honors thesis on her excavation work in 1937 at the University of New Mexico's Chaco Canyon field school, and a revised version of the paper was published by Clyde Kluckhohn and Paul Reiter in 1939. In 1938 she continued graduate work at the Peabody, working with Kluckhohn on his Navajo research project. In 1941 she married Charles Dillon McEvoy Jr. and left the field.

Margaret Soutter Woods (Keith) (1910–2001) and **Janet McCleery Woods (Dickey)** (1910–2005) were twins who came into the anthropology program at the Peabody in 1932 with A.B.s from Bryn Mawr. Margaret Woods worked on the University of New Mexico excavations for five of the six seasons between 1931 and 1937. The sixth season she worked at the Hittite site of Tarsus in Turkey. She received her A.M. from Radcliffe in 1938 on the basis of her work at the site of Chetro Ketl in Chaco Canyon (Woods 1935, 1937), but then she married and became a tax specialist at the U.S. Department of Treasury. Janet Woods worked on the New Mexico projects for four seasons between 1931 and 1935, receiving her A.M. from Radcliffe in 1936 on the basis of this research. She then married, and although she did make collections of archaeological specimens for the National Museum of Bogotá in the late 1930s, while her husband conducted oil exploration in Colombia, she dropped out of academic research.

Hannah Marie Wormington (1914–94), born in Denver, Colorado, received her A.B. in 1935 from the University of Denver, where she studied Paleoindian materials from the Lindenmeier site under Etienne Renaud. Renaud had earlier recruited the Roberts brothers to anthropology and sent them on to Harvard, as we saw in chapter 11. After Wormington graduated, Renaud sent her to work on Upper Paleolithic sites in France. When she returned in 1937, she began working for the Denver Museum of Natural History with Jesse D. Figgins on Paleoindian materials. She continued working for the museum for the next 31 years, retiring in 1968 (Knudson 2004:701; Stanford 1996:275).

Before Wormington began her work at the Denver Museum, she was awarded and accepted a fellowship through Radcliffe for the 1937–38 academic year. During that time she worked on her best-known publication, *Ancient Men in North America,* the first edition of which was published in 1939. Wormington married George D. Volk in 1940. She worked intermittently on her advanced degrees over the next decade and a half, returning to Cambridge in 1940–41 for another series of studies. She received her A.M. from Radcliffe in 1951 and her Ph.D. in 1954, with the dissertation "The Archaeology of the Upper Colorado Plateau Area in the Northern Periphery of the

Southwestern United States." The fourth edition of her text *Ancient Men in North America* was published in 1957.

Dennis Stanford (1996:275) claimed that Marie Wormington was the second female student to be admitted to study at the Peabody Museum, and Ruthann Knudson (2004:702) wrote that she "was one of the first women to be allowed to participate in anthropology classes at Harvard University." Neither statement is correct. Wormington was preceded by a score or more women graduate students and by several times that many undergraduates. She was, however, a superior scholar. She went on to become the first female president of the SAA in 1968, and her work on Paleoindian materials is well known and respected.

Work by Radcliffe graduate students in archaeology was not limited to North American sites. **Ruth Sears (Chute)** (1905–86) received her A.B. from Smith College in 1927. She then participated in expeditions of the American School of Prehistoric Research (ASPR) in Palestine and Yugoslavia in the late 1920s and early 1930s. On the basis of this work she received her A.M. in anthropology from Radcliffe in 1933 and stayed on in the Ph.D. program through 1935. She continued working at the Peabody after she married Richard Chute. In 1936–37 she and Henry W. Eliot made a study of the pottery and other artifacts from the 1927–31 Semitic Museum excavations of Nuzi, near Kirkuk, Iraq, under the supervision of Lauriston Ward. These analyses were published as appendixes in the site report (Starr et al. 1939), which came out in the Harvard-Radcliffe Fine Arts series. Chute's work was listed in volume 1 of this report as "The Pottery from Pit L4 of Yorgan Tepa: Prehistoric and Ga. Sur Levels." Chute later served as a Radcliffe College overseer from 1955 to 1961.

Another Old World specialist was Radcliffe student **Elizabeth S. Eaton**, who worked on Egyptian materials after receiving her A.B. From 1936 to 1942 she worked for the Department of Egyptian Art at the Museum of Fine Arts, Boston. She wrote articles on its collections in 1937 and 1941. She also worked on Egyptian materials at the Peabody Museum in 1938–39 (Scott 1940:457). During World War II she served as an ensign in the U.S. Naval Reserves in Washington, D.C, from 1942 to 1945.

Isabel Hannah Guernsey (1907–71), the daughter of Samuel Guernsey, was placed in charge of the textile collection at the Peabody Museum at least from 1937 through 1941. In 1937 she received an Institute of Andean Research fellowship to go to Peru and unwrap several Paracas culture mummies (Scott 1938:359); she published the preliminary work in 1938 (Guernsey 1938). She brought back one mummy to the Peabody Museum, where each stage of the unwrapping was carefully recorded in photographs and drawings. Nearly 100 separate pieces of textiles were removed, one of which was 47 feet long and 12 feet wide. Objects of gold, shell, and bone, together with food offerings, were included in the mummy bundle. This work was subsequently written up by Guernsey, Alfred Kidder II, and Harry Tschopik Jr. (Scott 1940:454). For the 1940–41 year, Guernsey went to work at Pucara, Peru, with Kidder (Scott 1941:450). During the war, the museum staff was dramatically reduced, and Isabel Guernsey does not appear on the roster after 1941–42.

Isabel Guernsey worked during the 1940–41 season in Peru with **Marion Hutchinson Tschopik** (1910–91) and Harry Tschopik Jr. (whom we profile later). Marion Hutchinson was a graduate student in the Peabody anthropology program and received her A.M. from Radcliffe in 1933. In 1937 she served as a Peabody Museum secretary for J. O. Brew and accompanied Brew to excavate at Awatovi that field season. She married Harry Tschopik in 1939, and that year she assisted him, Isabel Guernsey, and Alfred Kidder II in analyzing the Paracas mummy bundle (J. Rowe 1958:133). The Tschopiks then left for two and a half years of research in Puno, Peru, with Institute of Andean Research funding. While Harry Tschopik became involved in ethnographic work, Marion conducted some test excavations, investigated pre-Columbian tombs, and studied the ceramic assemblages of the Late Intermediate period and Late Horizon cultures in the northern Titicaca basin, work that was published a few years later (Tschopik 1946). Today, her work is still the single most important published source on late period ceramics in the region.

Doris Zemurray Stone (1909–94) had the longest association with Harvard of any of this cadre of women in archaeology, from the receipt of her A.B. degree at Radcliffe in 1930 through 1980. She served as a Radcliffe trustee from 1941 to 1952 and again from 1968 to 1980, as well as being long associated with the Peabody Museum.

Doris Stone was the daughter of Samuel Zemurray, president of the United Fruit Company until his retirement in 1951. Samuel Zemurray established the Samuel Zemurray Jr. and Doris Zemurray Stone Radcliffe Professorship in 1947, in memory of his son, a major in the army who was killed in 1943 in North Africa, and in honor of his daughter, with an endowment of a quarter million dollars. Several prominent women scholars have held this professorship at Radcliffe. In addition, Samuel Zemurray endowed the Middle American Research Institute (MARI) at Tulane University in 1924. After Doris Stone graduated from Tulane, she and her husband, Roger Thayer Stone, worked with MARI from 1931 until 1939, when they moved to Costa Rica, where Roger ran a coffee plantation, and later to Honduras. Doris kept her ties as an associate at MARI for the next two decades. Since their deaths, Tulane has honored them with buildings on its campus: the Roger Thayer Stone Center for Latin American Studies and a dormitory named for Doris Stone at Newcomb College.

Doris Zemurray Stone was officially appointed a research fellow in Central American archaeology at the Peabody Museum in 1942, with a focus on Costa Rica and Honduras (Scott 1944:335). Her first formal paper for the museum, "Archaeology of the North Coast of Honduras," had been published in the Memoirs series in 1941 (Scott 1943:456). She later served as a member of the Visiting Committee of the Peabody Museum. By mid-century she had become president of the board of directors of the National Museum of Costa Rica. She was the well-known author of several books on Central American archaeology and a significant supporter of many museum projects (for more on Stone, see S. Williams 1986b).

Some women students went into physical anthropology rather than archaeology, although only one woman actually completed a Ph.D. in that subfield in the Radcliffe graduate program. More typical was **Charlotte Elizabeth Davis (Grubb)** (1912–89), an anthropology honors graduate at Radcliffe in 1933 who went on to earn an M.S. at Boston University on the basis of a longitudinal study, "A Ten Year Follow-up Study of Fifty-eight Rheumatic Fever Patients." Sometimes Earnest Hooton also recruited professional women from other institutions temporarily into his research programs. **Helen Lucerne Dawson** (1904–82) received a Ph.D. in physiology in 1932 from Washington University in St. Louis and worked in the Department of Anatomy of the University of Iowa College of Medicine for most of the rest of her career. In 1935–36, however, with an NRC fellowship in physical anthropology and some funds from the Peabody Museum, Dawson conducted an anthropometric survey of 2,000 women in western Ireland as part of the Peabody Museum's Ireland research group. Together with the survey by the Peabody's Wesley Dupertuis of 10,000 men in Ireland, Dawson's project formed the first good, countrywide anthropometric survey (Scott 1937:340). In the summer of 1936 Dawson received funding to work in Hooton's Statistical and Anthropometric Laboratory, doing the statistical analyses of her Irish anthropometric data (Scott 1938:355), before returning to the University of Iowa.

The sole female physical anthropologist trained by Hooton during this period who went on to secure a Ph.D. was **Alice Mossie Brues** (1913–2007). Brues, born in Boston, had close ties to Harvard because her father, Charles Thomas Brues, taught entomology and zoology at the MCZ for many years. After receiving her A.B. from Bryn Mawr in philosophy and psychology in 1933, Brues entered Radcliffe to continue graduate work in 1936. She intended to do her doctoral research in comparative religion, but after she took an anthropology course in the summer after her graduation, Hooton persuaded her to shift into physical anthropology (Dufour 1988:23). In the 1938–39 year she was listed as conducting genetic studies on American siblings with Hooton (Scott 1940:458). She wrote this material up for her dissertation, "Study of Family Resemblances in Metrical and Morphological Characteristics: Sibling Resemblances as Evidence for the Genetic Determination of Traits of the Eye, Skin, and Hair in Man." She received her Ph.D. in anthropology from Radcliffe in 1940.

Brues then took a position as research associate and director of Hooton's statistical lab in the Peabody Museum and during World War II did applied anthropometry for the Army Air Corps there (Scott 1943:452, 1944:336). In 1946 she accepted a position teaching anatomy at the University of Oklahoma School of Medicine. In 1965 she moved to the University of Colorado, where she continued research focused on morphology, evolution, and forensics, until she retired in 1984. She served as president of the American Association of Physical Anthropologists from 1971 to 1973.

Some Radcliffe students went into sociocultural anthropology, although according to one source (Parezo and Stephenson 2001:510), they were not particularly encouraged to do so. One of the first we have identified is **Anne Hutchinson Fuller** (1910–83), who was born in Brookline, Massachusetts. After beginning her undergraduate work at Smith College, she received her A.B. from Radcliffe in 1932, with an honors thesis titled

"Animal Ornamentation on Near East and Mediterranean Pottery." She received graduate fellowships in anthropology at Harvard for the next three years, which funded her work at the American School of Oriental Research in Jerusalem and allowed her to complete her A.M. from Cambridge University in 1935 (Allen 1984:4).

Fuller entered the University of Chicago graduate program and in 1935–36 was listed as a participant in Robert Redfield's University of Chicago seminar series on race and cultural contacts, where she reported on work she had done under Harvard/Radcliffe auspices at an Arab village in Lebanon. In 1937–38 she completed additional fieldwork in Lebanon with sponsorship from Harvard's Center for Middle Eastern Studies. Her ethnography *Buarij: Portrait of a Lebanese Muslim Village* was published in the Harvard Middle Eastern Monographs Series in 1961. During the war, Fuller enlisted in the Women's Army Corps and served in both the European and Pacific theaters. She was transferred to the OSS because of her knowledge of the Near East and worked for that agency in Cairo and Italy (Price 2008:222). After the war she stayed in the CIA until 1950, when she resigned and moved to Greece. There she worked with the Red Cross on rehabilitation of refugee populations and, from 1953 to 1963, taught anthropology in the College Year in Athens program (Allen 1984:4).

Charis Denison (Crockett) (1905–64) was a Phi Beta Kappa, magna cum laude graduate in anthropology from Radcliffe in 1934. In the 1932–33 field season she conducted ethnological work at the Hopi pueblos for Mischa Titiev, providing him with essential cultural information from female informants (Scott 1934:300). In 1935–36 she conducted research in Guatemala. She then married Harvard graduate Frederick Eugene Crockett (1907–78), who had traveled with Admiral Byrd to the South Pole in 1930 and later worked with the OSS and the CIA in Southeast Asia.

In 1936–38 Charis Crockett traveled with her husband by schooner to the South Pacific, collecting materials and continuing her anthropological research. In 1939 she returned from an expedition to Dutch New Guinea, where she had collected anthropometric data on 843 adult males, as well as considerable ethnological information (Scott 1940:450). She spent 1940–41 at the Peabody Museum, conducting statistical analyses of her anthropometric data and writing up the ethnographic materials (Scott 1942:433). Earnest Hooton, who, as we have seen, had reservations about training women students for graduate work, was extremely impressed by her research. In the introduction to Crockett's *The House in the Rain Forest* (1942), her popular book on her Dutch New Guinea research, Hooton wrote the following backhanded acclamation: "Actually, she measured nearly 900 greasy, smelly, filthy cannibals—a remarkable achievement for any tough, male anthropologist and a miracle for a fragile, blond female. On each savage she did a total of about 120 measurements or observations" (Hooton 1942:ix–x). After 1941 we lose track of Charis Crockett's trajectory, perhaps because of the secrecy associated with her husband's job as an OSS-CIA employee.

Alice Dukes Blyth (Child) (1918–97) was born in New York and was the sister of the much better known psychological anthropologist Beatrice Blyth Whiting (1914–2003), a long-time Harvard professor. Alice Blyth graduated with honors from Radcliffe in 1939, writing a 93-page thesis on Navajo ethnography, "The Possible Significance of Life History Material to the Ethnographer as Demonstrated by a Study of Son of Old Man Hat," under the direction of Clyde Kluckhohn. She married Irvin Long Child, whom she had met through her sister, then a student at Yale. Irvin Child had just received his Ph.D. from Yale in 1939 and took a two-year position in psychology at Harvard from 1939 to 1941. Alice Child continued in graduate studies in anthropology at Harvard, and Irvin accompanied her to Costa Rica for a year's fieldwork during this period. After 1941 Irvin Child returned to Yale, where he taught for the rest of his life. Although no advanced degree is listed for Alice, she and her husband later collaborated on various research projects, culminating in their book nearly 50 years later, *Religion and Magic in the Life of Traditional Peoples* (Child and Child 1993).

Hsien Chin Hu (1910–?), known as Lottie, received her A.B. from the National University of Peking in 1932 and entered the graduate program at the Peabody Museum in 1936. She received a Radcliffe fellowship to study anthropology in 1938–39, continued work under the direction of Eliot Chapple for the 1939–40 term, and completed her A.M. in anthropology from Radcliffe in 1940 (Scott 1940:447). She was then sent for further training to Columbia University, where she received her Ph.D. in 1949 with a dissertation titled "The Common Descent Group in China and Its Function." Her area of particular interest was the ethnology of China and Southeast Asia.

In general, female students of the earlier part of the twentieth century have been stereotyped as most likely ending up in sociocultural anthropology. Archaeology, given the awkwardness of the field situation in terms of the mores of the day, as well as the perception that females were not up to the physical labor required, has been assumed to have been a less typical career choice for female graduate students. But because of the transitions going on in the Harvard program at the time, a preference for sociocultural anthropology turns out not to have been the case at the Peabody Museum. There, at least in terms of the records we have recovered, archaeology seems to have been the focus selected most often. Still, one should not read too much into the preliminary pattern we have developed. We simply do not have access to enough information on the choices of the other female graduate students to make any didactic statements.

Reviewing the men in the anthropology program at the Peabody Museum in 1929–39, we again start with the archaeologists, although developments in sociocultural anthropology and physical anthropology were perhaps even more important. Whereas the 1920s had been dominated by Maya research, a substantial emphasis was now being placed on Old World archaeological research at Harvard, and the areas of interest of the burgeoning number of graduate (and staff) researchers was diversifying.

Alfred Tozzer continued to have an active program training students in Maya archaeology, including Robert Wauchope, Bill Andrews, Gordon Ekholm, Stanley Boggs,

John Longyear, Drexel Paul, John Denison, and Frank Cresson. Carnegie Institution of Washington (CIW) funding was winding down, and depression-era Civil Works Administration (CWA) and WPA jobs were opening up. Thus this cohort of Mayanists came into a different job market.

Robert Wauchope (1909–79) was the first of this batch of Tozzer's students. He was born in Columbia, South Carolina, and earned a merit badge collecting arrowheads as an Eagle Boy Scout (E. W. Andrews 1981:113). His father, an academic, wrote to a friend, Vernon Kellogg, then permanent secretary of the National Research Council (NRC), to see if he could find a summer archaeological expedition for his 17-year-old son. A.V. Kidder has just advanced from vice chair of the Division of Anthropology and Psychology at the NRC in 1925–26 to serve as chair for 1926–27. Kellogg approached him to see whether he knew of any such projects, and Kidder invited Wauchope to join him at Pecos the next season (Wauchope 1965:156). Thus Wauchope worked as a field assistant at Pecos in 1927, the first summer after he entered the University of South Carolina. There he met Harriet and Burt Cosgrove, who invited him to work with them and William Claflin the next season, 1928–29, at Stallings Island, Georgia (E. W. Andrews 1981:113).

Wauchope's early archaeological training thus took place with Harvard-associated people, so it seems foreordained that he entered graduate school at the Peabody after receiving his A.B. from South Carolina in 1931. In the 1932 season he was sent to Uaxactun to work, receiving his A.M. in 1933 on the basis of his preliminary work there. He continued working in Guatemala the next two seasons, studying Maya house types with CIW funding (Scott 1935:312).

Wauchope's Ph.D. was delayed until 1943 because the first time he took his orals, he failed them (E. W. Andrews 1981:116). Getting a Ph.D. at Harvard was no walk in the park. Many of the people whom we mention as having begun but not completed their graduate work at the Peabody left for this reason. Wauchope then took a job with the University of Georgia, serving as director of the WPA Archaeological Survey for Georgia. In 1940 he began teaching anthropology at the University of North Carolina–Chapel Hill. He then moved to Tulane. Frans Blom had left the Middle American Research Institute there in 1940, and the center was in disarray. In 1942 Wauchope was offered the position of director of MARI and professor of anthropology, and he accepted. In the meantime, he had successfully retaken his exams at Harvard and completed his dissertation, "Archaeological Excavations at Zacualpa, Department of Quiche, Guatemala: A Study of Interrelations of Environment, Technology, and Human Society." He received his Ph.D. in 1943.

Like a great number of his colleagues, Wauchope worked for the OSS as an intelligence officer during World War II (Andrews 1981:113). The executive secretary of the AAA, Frederick Johnson, had provided the OSS with a list of anthropologists and their areas of geographical expertise, so that they could efficiently be recruited to help the Allies gather military intelligence in the proper foreign theaters (Price 2003:34). Wauchope served in the Mediterranean department from 1943 to 1945. He then returned to Tulane and became exceptionally well known for his Maya studies, a renown recognized in part by his election to the presidency of the SAA in 1954–55.

Edward Wyllys Andrews IV (1916–71), informally known as Bill, began his archaeological career as a junior in high school. Andrews had contacted Hooton, who got him a position on the field crew at Mesa Verde with Byron Cummings in 1932. There he met Sylvanus Morley, who invited him to come to Chichen Itza for the spring 1934 excavations (Wauchope 1972:394). Andrews, a Chicago native, started at the University of Chicago after graduating from high school in 1933 but transferred to Harvard in 1934 to pursue his growing interest in Maya studies, (Wauchope 1972:394).

Andrews continued working on Maya projects under CIW funds and received his A.B. in 1938. He then continued to work on CIW projects for his doctoral dissertation, "The Archaeology of Southwestern Campeche and Its Position in Maya History," and completed his Ph.D. in 1942 (Scott 1940:459). He continued employment with the CIW but almost immediately, in 1943, was called to work as an intelligence agent for the OSS in the European and African theaters. He remained with the OSS and CIA for several years after the war, working in Africa and the Middle East, finally leaving the CIA in 1955 to accept a position at MARI at Tulane (Wauchope 1972:398). He spent the rest of his career working in the northern lowland Maya area, in Yucatán, Quintana Roo, and Campeche. His son, E. Wyllys Andrews V, is also a Harvard graduate who has made a notable career in Maya archaeology.

Gordon Frederick Ekholm (1909–87), a native of St. Paul, Minnesota, received his A.B. in 1933 from the University of Minnesota, where he participated in Lloyd Wilford's field schools in North Dakota and Minnesota (National Research Council 1938:25). He entered the graduate program at Harvard in 1934, beginning work in the archaeology of northern Mesoamerica. After finishing his A.M. at Harvard in 1937, he was hired part-time at the AMNH. He earned his Ph.D. with the dissertation "Cultural Patterns in the Archaeology of Northwestern Mexico" and then received funding from the Institute of Andean Research to continue work in Mexico City. He subsequently continued work at the AMNH, initially serving as special field assistant in northwestern Mexican archaeology under the direction of George Vaillant. He was curator of Mexican and Central American archaeology at the AMNH from 1942 until he retired in 1974.

Ekholm's position at the AMNH allowed him time off to teach Mexican archaeology, and he was a part-time lecturer in this area at Columbia University from 1943 to 1971. He served as a member of Harvard's Dumbarton Oaks Advisory Committee on Pre-Columbian Art from 1961 until 1974 and was president of the SAA for the 1953–54 term. He was a quiet, self-effacing person. Although he wrote widely on Mexican art and sculpture, in his later years he dedicated himself particularly to the issue of trans-Pacific contact.

Stanley Harding Boggs (1914–91) received his A.B. at Northwestern University in 1935 and his A.M. from the University of Arizona in 1936. He then came to Harvard for

Ph.D. work, studying there from 1936 to 1940. In 1938 he worked on the archaeology of Haiti, under the guidance of Samuel E. Morison of Harvard's history department. Then, with CIW funding, he worked at Copan and at Maya sites in El Salvador, on the recommendation of Alfred Kidder (E. W. Andrews 1996:57; Scott 1940:458–59).

After deciding not to finish his dissertation at Harvard, Boggs continued working with the CIW until 1948, when he took the job as head of the Department of Archaeology in El Salvador. He left that job in 1954, returned to the United States from 1954 to 1963, and in 1963 returned to El Salvador. He worked and wrote broadly on El Salvador during his nearly 50-year career.

John Munro Longyear III (1914–2011) received his A.B. from Cornell in 1936 and then entered the Peabody program. In 1937 he went out to Utah for training with John Gillin, visiting a total of 37 sites that season (Scott 1938:358). He then spent the rest of the season excavating at Awatovi in Arizona. In 1938 he went to work at Copan in Honduras, with CIW funding, and he completed his Ph.D. dissertation, "Copan Ceramics: Their Chronological and Historical Significance," in 1940 (Scott 1940:458).

Longyear was then named a research associate in Middle American archaeology at the Peabody. In 1941 he worked in the Chiriquí area of Panama for Samuel Lothrop (Scott 1942:430). He moved on to El Salvador for the 1941–42 field season, being directed by Kidder under Institute of Andean Research funding (Wauchope 1995:162), before taking leave to fight in the war. Afterward, he returned to work on Maya issues at the Peabody, holding the John G. Owens Fellowship in Central American and Mexican Archaeology. He resigned that position in 1948 to take a job at Colgate University, where he taught for the next 30 years, until he retired in 1978 (Brew 1949a:305).

Anthony Joseph Drexel Paul Jr. (1914–99) began his archaeological work as a Harvard undergraduate, participating in an excavation in the Ulua Valley, Honduras, directed by Alfred Kidder II and William Duncan Strong, of the Smithsonian Institution, with financial assistance from William Popenoe, of the United Fruit Company (Scott 1937:341). Paul explored in Panama later that season for the Philadelphia Academy of Natural Sciences. He received his A.B. at Harvard in 1937 and then worked with Kidder to complete the report on their Honduras work (Strong, Kidder, and Paul 1938).

Drexel Paul was the great-grandson of the founder of Drexel University in Philadelphia, and his family apparently saw archaeology as an improper career. Thus Paul turned to law, receiving his law degree from the University of Virginia in 1941 and becoming principal partner of a Philadelphia law firm from 1956 to 1985. He served as board chair of Drexel University from 1970 to 1974. Drexel Paul was a friend and classmate at Harvard of Franklin Delano Roosevelt Jr. (1914–88), so it is no surprise to see both his wealth and his political connections used on behalf of a few Harvard enterprises over the years.

Other Peabody graduate students also started out in Maya archaeology but did not continue. **John Hopkins Denison Jr.** (1906–43) entered the graduate program in 1930 and apparently got his first exposure to archaeology in the Fremont area of Utah with Scott, Brew, and Kidder on the Emerson-Claflin Expedition (Scott 1933:300). After receiving his A.M. in 1933 on the basis of this work, he went to the Maya area on a CIW project in 1934–35 for his Ph.D. research, but he left the project in 1935, taking an excavation position with the Oriental Institute at the University of Chicago. He died in the North Africa campaign of 1943.

Frank Macomb Cresson Jr. (1911–94), who was born in Philadelphia, graduated from Williams College in 1933 and took a position with the University of Pennsylvania Museum that year. After field trips to Chaco Canyon in 1933 and the Mimbres area of New Mexico in 1934, he went to the Maya site of Piedras Negras in 1935 and worked there the next three seasons. He then wrote up the Piedras Negras ceramics, publishing his analysis in 1937 in the twenty-fifth anniversary volume of the Philadelphia Anthropology Society, and entered the University of Pennsylvania graduate program to pursue his Maya interests. He reportedly received his A.M. from Pennsylvania that year (National Research Council 1940:32). He transferred to the Harvard graduate program in 1938 to study with Tozzer, worked on Maya and Mexican sweat houses while there, but dropped out in 1940, with no further degree. In 1941 Cresson was hired to write up the WPA excavations in Somerset County, Pennsylvania, but the document, "Hilltop and Valley Sites of Southwestern Pennsylvania," was never published. In 1942 Cresson published in the *Pennsylvania Archaeologist* a report on archaeological village sites in southwestern Pennsylvania that he had excavated for the Pennsylvania Historical Commission, but then he seems to have left the field.

Although Alfred Tozzer had left active fieldwork in Mesoamerica by the 1930s, he was still not only training students but also providing an attractive venue for research scholars to work on shared interests. For the 1933 year, **Alfredo Barrera-Vásquez** (1900–80) came to work with Tozzer on Maya linguistics at the Peabody Museum. Barrera-Vásquez, who was born in Yucatán, was a professor at the Universidad de Yucatán and also worked for the Museo Nacional. He published extensively on Maya linguistics during his life (Herskovits and Ames 1950:10).

The Peabody Museum had a number of donors, too, who continued to supply it with materials from Middle America. One of the more important was **Francis Russell Hart** (1868–1938), a colleague of Samuel Zemurray, Doris Zemurray Stone's father. Hart became president of the Cartagena-Magdalena Railway Company of Colombia, with headquarters in Boston, in 1895. In 1901 he became a member of the board of United Fruit Company, and from 1908 to 1919 he was also named consul for Colombia in Boston. Hart's two main interests were the history of the Caribbean and MIT. He had studied electrical engineering at MIT but left in his senior year, in 1889. In addition to his contributions and service to MIT, Hart was a member of the Peabody Museum Visiting Committee for many years, until his death in 1938, and a regular, generous donor to the Peabody Museum's work in Middle and South America from 1923 onward.

Starting with George Dorsey (chapter 7), the Peabody had had occasional scholars, such as Philip Means and Samuel Lothrop, working in South America, but it had no major program or commitment to the southern hemisphere. This low level of activity continued through the 1930s, with a few students such as Alfred Kidder II and John Rowe.

Alfred Kidder II (1911–84), known as Alfie to his friends, was the third generation of the Kidder family to have ties with and to contribute to the Peabody Museum. Born in Nantucket, Kidder II entered Harvard in 1929 and graduated in 1933. In the summer of 1931 he joined Brew, Scott, and others on the Claflin-Emerson project in Utah, although he had earlier been on many field projects with his father in the Southwest (Scott 1933:300). He continued into graduate work at the Peabody Museum, receiving his A.M. in 1933. He married Mary Barbour, daughter of Thomas Barbour, director of the MCZ and a major contributor to the Peabody's collections, in 1934. The day after their wedding, the couple left for Venezuela, where Kidder conducted his doctoral fieldwork (Scott 1935:310). While finishing his Ph.D., he spent one season working in Honduras in 1936. He completed his dissertation, "Archaeological Investigations in Venezuela," in 1937.

Kidder was appointed instructor in anthropology for one year immediately after receiving his Ph.D., and he left that summer for his first season of fieldwork in Peru. In 1940 he was appointed assistant curator of Andean archaeology at the Peabody Museum, and he retained a research interest in the Andes for the rest of his life. During the war he was recruited to collect intelligence information during his operations in the Andes (Scott 1942:427). He is best known for his work at the Formative period sites of Chiripa (Bolivia) and Pucara (Peru) in the Titicaca basin. Kidder kept up his association with the Peabody Museum until 1950, when he resigned to accept the position of associate director of the University Museum at Pennsylvania. He spent the rest of his academic career there but occasionally came back to the Peabody while visiting his parents in Cambridge.

John Howland Rowe (1918–2004) was born in Sorrento, Maine. He was exposed early on to archaeological stylistic analysis. His father, Louis Earle Rowe, had gone to Egypt with George Reisner in the summer of 1911, after receiving his A.M. from Brown University. Because of poor job prospects in archaeology, the elder Rowe took the position of director of the Museum of Art at the Rhode Island School of Design when he returned. Not only was Earle Rowe interested in art and archaeology, but he also married Margaret Talbot Jackson, who was then assistant director of the Minneapolis Institute of Arts. Reisner remained a friend of the family and was a visitor to the household when John Rowe was a child. In 1928, when John was 10, his parents traveled to Egypt, leaving him in Rome, and he became fascinated with classical ruins (Burger 2007:34).

John Rowe enrolled at Brown University, where he majored in classical archaeology. He used the undergraduate prize he received with his 1939 A.B. to travel to Peru and visit Inca ruins. He then planned to study at Berkeley with A. L. Kroeber, but because of his father's death, he instead enrolled at Harvard. Rowe's first fieldwork was in Maine in 1938, while he was at Brown. Philip Means recommended that he take the Philips Andover Academy's field school in Maine, and Rowe worked under Douglas Byers and Frederick Johnson in excavating the Richards shell heap in Blue Hill (A. Rowe 2007:224). Then he discovered the Waterside shell heap on his mother's property in Sorrento, and after a month of the Andover field school, he switched to conducting an excavation at Waterside. He followed up with a second season at Sorrento during the first year he was at the Peabody, in 1940, a project he wrote up as a paper for the first volume of the Peabody Museum Excavators' Club (J. Rowe 1940). In 1941, after receiving his Harvard A.M., Rowe began Ph.D. work in Cuzco, Peru, under Kidder's direction (Scott 1942:429). He continued work in Peru through 1943, funded partly by some minor teaching and research jobs in Cuzco. After spending 1944–45 as a sergeant in the 280th Engineer Combat Battalion in central Europe, he completed his Harvard Ph.D. dissertation, "An Introduction to the Archaeology of Cuzco," in 1947 (Schreiber 2007:197).

Rowe took a position with the Smithsonian Institution, doing research in Peru and Colombia, from 1946 to 1948. In 1948 he was hired at the University of California–Berkeley, where he spent the rest of his academic career, retiring in 1988. He kept some ties to Harvard, working with Gordon Willey and Donald Collier on a Huari, Peru, survey in 1950 and serving for at least two decades on the board of directors of Harvard's Dumbarton Oaks pre-Columbian collections in Washington, D.C. For many years Rowe was the sole North American researcher training students in Peruvian archaeology.

One new pattern to emerge among the archaeology students in the 1930s was that some of them came not to work with Tozzer in the Maya area, A.V. Kidder in the Southwest, or Coon in the Middle East but to get the credentials to conduct archaeology in their own states. Most of them came to Harvard, secured their degree, and went home to do archaeology. Among these students were Thomas Campbell, Frank Hibben, Lloyd Wilford, Elmer Harp, Ivar Skarland, Paul Gebhard, Gene Stirling, Kenneth Disher, and Sidney Thomas.

Thomas Nolan Campbell (1908–2003) was a Texas boy, born in the town of Munday, who received his A.B. in 1930 and his A.M. in 1936 from the University of Texas before going east to Harvard. He conducted his fieldwork—the basis for his Harvard A.M. in 1940—in southwestern Texas in 1937 and 1938. He worked in the field at that time with **John Charles Kelley** (1913–97) who later came to Harvard and got his Ph.D. in 1948 (Scott 1939:410, 1940:457). Campbell finished his doctoral work with the dissertation "The Archaeology of the Texas Coast and Its Relation to That of Mexico and the Lower Mississippi Valley." He received his Ph.D. in 1947 and returned to the University of Texas, where he taught until he retired in 1992.

Frank Cummings Hibben (1910–2002) was born in Lakewood, Ohio. He worked for the Ohio State Museum as a high school student from 1926 to 1930 before going to Princeton, where he received his A.B. in 1933. He then attended the University of New Mexico, earning his S.M. in 1936 (National Research Council 1938:44). Needing more training than was available at New Mexico, Hibben enrolled at Harvard in 1936. Although he was officially a member of the graduate program, we find surprisingly little evidence of his interactions with any of the Peabody Museum staff. He began excavations at Sandia Cave, near Albuquerque, New Mexico, in 1937, working there through 1941. He completed his Ph.D. at Harvard in 1941, defending a dissertation titled "The Gallina Culture of North Central New Mexico." Returning to the University of New Mexico, he took the position of assistant professor of anthropology there. He became the founding director of the university's Maxwell Museum of Anthropology and spent much of the rest of his rather controversial career in New Mexico. His work at Sandia Cave, which produced allegedly "very early" cultural remains, was challenged. The controversy was not limited to his archaeological findings. For example, David H. Price (2002:16) referred to "adventurer and purported archaeologist Frank Hibben" being chased and shot at by Chinese troops in the 1950s when he employed archaeology as a cover to plant secret devices to monitor Chinese nuclear tests in Outer Mongolia for the CIA.

Lloyd Alden Wilford (1894–1982) was born in Baldwin, Wisconsin, but spent his archaeological career mainly in Minnesota. After getting his first A.B., he served in the U.S. Navy in China in World War I. After the war he took a law degree at Minnesota in 1920, practiced law for a while, and then returned to school at the University of Minnesota from 1927 to 1929, receiving an A.B. in 1928 and an A.M. in 1929 in anthropology. He worked with Albert Ernest Jenks at Mimbres sites in New Mexico during the 1928–31 seasons (Johnson 1983:779). He then entered Harvard in 1929 and was sent for training on an ASPR project in Algeria in 1930. While enrolled at Harvard, Wilford also had a civil service appointment, doing archaeology with Jenks in Minnesota between 1932 and 1935 (National Research Council 1938:106). This research was the basis for his dissertation, "Minnesota Archaeology, with Special Reference to the Mound Area." He received his Ph.D. from Harvard in 1937.

Wilford then returned to his civil service appointment, working at this job until called to serve in World War II. After the war he obtained an academic appointment to teach archaeology and physical anthropology at the university. He made it a practice to move to several sites each season. He ran training projects for 23 field seasons before retiring in 1959, and he conducted test excavations at 130 sites during this period (Johnson 1983:780). Among the later well-known archaeologists whose first experiences in field archaeology were with Wilford were Gordon Ekholm, Stephen Williams, and Williams's twin brother, Philip.

Elmer Harp Jr. (1912–2009) was born in Cleveland, Ohio. He entered Harvard in 1931 but took three years off for financial reasons and so did not receive his B.S., cum laude in anthropology, until 1938. Following his graduation, he took classes in industrial engineering at Case Western School of Applied Sciences in Cleveland and obtained employment as an engineer in a local electrical company. He joined the U.S. Navy in 1943 and was a line officer in motor torpedo boats in the Mediterranean and the Pacific until 1946.

Harp then entered graduate school at Harvard and secured an A.M. in anthropology in 1947. That year he was also appointed curator of the Dartmouth College Museum, the base from which he began his fieldwork, studying Canadian Dorset Eskimo ruins (Brew 1951:364). He earned his Ph.D. in 1953 with the dissertation "The Cultural Affinities of the Newfoundland Dorset Eskimo."

Harp continued employment at Dartmouth College, where he is credited with founding the Department of Anthropology. He served as director of the Dartmouth College Museum from 1961 to 1968 and was chair of the Department of Anthropology from 1960 to 1972 and from 1975 to 1976, before retiring in 1977. He trained several generations of students at his excavations at Port Au Choix in Newfoundland. He is best known for his work on the Canadian Atlantic coast, in Newfoundland and Labrador, and around Hudson Bay, but he was also a pioneer in the use of photography in archaeological site surveys. As recently as 2005, at the age of 93, he continued to write and publish, and he himself provided information for our summary.

Ivar Skarland (1899–1965) was born in Hoylandet, Norway, earned a degree in forestry in Norway in 1921, and came to work in the lumber industry in British Columbia in 1927. He moved to Alaska in 1928 and entered the university in Fairbanks in 1931. During his studies there, he met Otto William Geist, who had been excavating at the site of Kukulik, St. Lawrence Island. Geist recruited Skarland as a field assistant on excavations at the site in 1934 and again in 1935, and Skarland shifted his interest to archaeology (Irving 1965:147).

After receiving his A.B. in 1935, Skarland entered Harvard in 1937, received his A.M. in 1942, and returned briefly to teaching at Fairbanks before being call to serve in the army in World War II. After the war, in 1945, he was named chair of the Department of Anthropology at Alaska, but he also reenrolled in the graduate program at Harvard to complete his Ph.D. He did so in 1949, with the dissertation "The Geography of Alaska in Pleistocene and Early Post-glacial Times: A Study of the Environment from an Anthropological Viewpoint." He then continued as chair at the University of Alaska until his death in 1965.

Paul Henry Gebhard (1917–) was born in Rocky Ford, Colorado, and began working on Colorado archaeology with Etienne B. Renaud in 1934–35, while still in high school (Cassells 1983:227). As he had done with the Roberts brothers and Marie Wormington, Renaud sent Gebhard to Harvard for further training. As an undergraduate, Gebhard went to the Middle East and the Indus Valley with Walter Taylor and John Bodel in 1939 (Scott 1940:456). He received his S.B. at Harvard in 1940 and then entered graduate school at the Peabody Museum, spending his summer field seasons in Colorado working on Yuma and Folsom culture materials (Scott 1941:431). He finished his Harvard A.M. in 1942 and continued his doctoral research on stone tools from Colorado. During this time he also worked with Philip Phillips, James A. Ford, and James B. Griffin on their Lower Mississippi Valley Survey in 1946 (S. Williams 2003:xx). He finished his dissertation, "Stone Objects from Prehistoric North America with Respect to Distribution, Type and Significance," and received his Ph.D. in 1948.

Gebhard had a radical change of research interests after his degree work. While waiting for his degree to be conferred, he joined Alfred Kinsey in the zoology department at the University of Indiana–Bloomington in 1947 and quickly became deeply involved in the Kinsey Institute's sexual research studies. He was the second director of the institute, from 1956 until he retired in 1982. (We were in touch with him for this section.)

Some Peabody Museum graduate students worked in the U.S. Southeast, perhaps mainly through WPA and CWA programs. **Gene McNaughton Stirling** (1905–77), brother of the much better known Mesoamerican archaeologist Matthew William Stirling (1896–1975), was one such person. Gene Stirling received his A.B. from Berkeley in 1928 and was a graduate student at Harvard from 1930 to 1934, during which time he was employed at least part-time for the Bureau of American Ethnology (Anonymous 1977). When Matthew Stirling assumed direction of the WPA and CWA excavations in Florida in 1931, he hired Gene Stirling as one of his field supervisors. Gene Stirling later supervised the Belle Glade project in Dade and Broward Counties in 1933–34 (Scott 1935:311) and went on to conduct a six-month acculturation study of the Seminoles, which he wrote up for the Applied Anthropology Unit of the Office of Indian Affairs (Scott 1936:319).

In the summer of 1931 Stirling directed the excavations at Powell Mound 2, just south of the main Powell Mound at Cahokia, working for the University of Illinois under the aegis of Arthur R. Kelly. Stirling named the premound materials the "Old Village" culture and the mound materials the "Bean Pot" culture. In 1947 James Griffin renamed the two groups the "Old Village" and "Trappist" phases, and those terms were used until 1971. At that point, the Old Village phase at Cahokia was renamed the Stirling culture phase, in honor of Gene Stirling's work.

In 1938 and 1939 Stirling served as director of archaeology for the state of Wyoming. He moved to California, where, except for one short term as a visiting professor of anthropology at Stanford, he shifted out of anthropology into a successful real estate business.

Both Stirling and his wife, Rebecca, had done graduate training in anthropology, so he retained a lifelong interest in the field. For example, he remembered his days at Harvard by giving generous donations as needed: $1,000 to unrestricted research in 1946 to help postwar graduate students get into the field, and later a generous gift to the Hooton Research Fund in 1955. In 1968 Gene and Rebecca Stirling provided the AAA with endowment funds for the Stirling Award in "cultural and personality studies," in memory of their daughter, an award still given every other year by the association.

Kenneth Buchtel Disher (1905–62) was born in St. Edward, Nebraska, and received his A.B. from Pomona College in California in 1930. He was a graduate student at the Peabody Museum during 1933 and 1934 (Scott 1935:311) but left in 1934 to take archaeological positions first with the Tennessee Valley Authority (TVA) and then the National Park Service (NPS). In 1946 he took the position of director of the Cleveland Museum of Natural History, but he resigned in 1948 to take on museum jobs with UNESCO and also in New York and Pennsylvania. He dedicated his career to museum management but never completed his advanced degree work.

Sidney Johnston Thomas (1904–82?) was born in Comanche, Texas, and received his A.B. and his A.M. from the University of Texas, with a thesis on Basketmaker materials from a Val Verde, Texas, rock shelter. He became a fellow graduate student of Disher's at the Peabody in 1933–34 and left with Disher to serve as an archaeological supervisor with the TVA in 1934. He took a position with the Bureau of Indian Affairs in 1935 (National Research Council 1938:98). Thomas seems to have been interested in material culture studies. While at Harvard he did a project on prehistoric sandals from the Southwest (Scott 1935:310–11), and he later wrote a paper for *American Anthropologist* on Sioux medicine bundles, before he went into the war and left anthropology, later becoming a businessman in Albuquerque, New Mexico.

Once Philip Phillips began doing archaeology in the Southeast at the Peabody Museum in the mid-1930s, the museum began a long-term commitment to training researchers in that area. Phillips had a museum position, not a departmental one, so he did no classroom teaching. Rather, he took students from the graduate program into the field with him. The earliest students to work with Phillips, however, although they became well-known Americanist archaeologists, did not maintain a focus in the Southeast. Because their work began at the very end of the time frame for this chapter, we touch briefly on only two of them, Chester Chard and Mott Davis.

Chester Stevens Chard (1915–2002) received his A.B. from Harvard in 1937 and continued with graduate work until he left for the war in 1942. He served as editor for the Excavators' Club, made up of Harvard archaeology students, which we discuss later in this chapter. He and his wife, along with Mott Davis, worked on the Lower Mississippi Valley Survey for Phillips in 1940–41 (Scott 1942:431). After the war, Chard left Harvard in 1947 and went to Berkeley to work on his doctorate. He finished his Ph.D., writing a dissertation on the Kamchadal tribe of eastern Siberia, as one of Robert Lowie's last students. He taught at the University of Wisconsin–Madison throughout his whole career, 1958 to 1974, with a focus on Arctic studies.

Edward Mott Davis Jr. (1918–98), the great-grandson of Lucretia Mott, was born in Shirley, Massachusetts. He entered Harvard as an undergraduate in 1937, received his S.B. in 1940, and went on to graduate work, receiving his A.M. in anthropology in 1942. His sister, Penrose ("Penny"), married Eugene Worman, a fellow Peabody Museum graduate student whom we profile later, at about this time. Davis served with the Air Transport Command during the war.

Mott Davis was a charter member of the Harvard–Peabody Museum Excavators' Club, which was made up of Harvard and Radcliffe students and was particularly active just before World War II. He reported that while he was at Harvard, the group conducted excavations at Blue Hills, Massachusetts; Nantucket Island; the Palmer-Taylor shell mound on the St. John's River in Florida; and Plimouth Plantation (Anonymous 1999). Davis apparently turned his senior honors thesis into the club's first official publication—*The Archaeology of Northeastern Asia, with an Introduction by Lauriston Ward* (E. M. Davis 1940; Hester Davis, personal communication, 2006).

Davis began his fieldwork in the Southwest, working during the last season of the Awatovi excavations in 1939, and then worked with Phillips on the Lower Mississippi Valley Survey in 1940. After his tour of military duty, he took over the family farm in Shirley, Massachusetts, for a few years but then returned to graduate school at Harvard. Not long after the birth of his first son, Jonathan Ogden Davis (who later became a well-known Great Basin archaeologist), in 1948, he took a position at the University of Nebraska. There his excavations were mainly at the Lime Creek and Red Smoke sites in western Nebraska, and these were the basis of his 1954 Ph.D. dissertation at Harvard, "The Culture History of the Central Great Plains prior to the Introduction of Pottery." In 1956 Davis moved from Nebraska to the University of Texas–Austin, where he taught for 32 years (Anonymous 1999; S. Williams 2003:xx).

With A.V. Kidder's work in the teens, the Peabody Museum had established a strong archaeological presence in the U.S. Southwest, and the program continued to attract students interested in that area. After 1929, however, when Kidder became research director for the Carnegie Institution of Washington, with its focus on Central America, he no longer conducted projects in the Southwest. Southwestern research at the Peabody then changed direction. Some students focusing on that region, such as Emil Haury, already had research projects in hand before entering the graduate program and came just to secure from Harvard the additional professional training they needed for a Ph.D. Others were recruited to work on J. O. Brew's Awatovi project, one of the major excavations of a Pueblo Indian site the Southwest (H. Davis 2008), on the dating of archaeological tree-ring samples, or on other projects as part of their graduate training.

Because Brew was still working on his own Ph.D. while he directed the project, it was not one in which large numbers of graduate students were trained at the Ph.D. level. Nevertheless, a significant number of people who already were or who became archaeology students at the Peabody worked at Awatovi. Brew also recruited many professionals associated with other institutions to work on the project, sometimes naming them research associates of the Peabody, but we cannot include them all here. We profile Emil Haury first and then offer a quick rundown of Awatovi participants with Harvard student associations, a few people whom Brew recruited to work on tree-ring dating at

Harvard, and a handful of Harvard students who did work in the Southwest that was unaffiliated with the Awatovi project.

Emil Walter Haury (1904–92) had started at Bethel College in Newton, Kansas, where his father had been one of the five Mennonite founders of the college. Byron Cummings, then of the Arizona State Museum, visited the college during Haury's second year there, in 1924, and young Haury asked to go with Cummings on his next summer field trip (Bostwick 2006:115). Thus, in 1925 Haury took a job as Cummings's assistant at the museum, going with him to excavate at Cuicuilco, Mexico. Haury entered the University of Arizona that fall, received his A.B. in 1927, and continued for an A.M. in 1928 (Haury 1995:713).

In 1927–28 Haury provided assistance to Cummings, who temporarily had been named ninth president of the University of Arizona while the university searched for a permanent replacement. The following year Haury went to teach at what is now Northern Arizona University, continuing to do fieldwork in the pueblos (R. Thompson 1995:644–45). It was during his research in 1929 that he and Lyndon Lane Hargrave found the sizable charcoal fragment that allowed A. E. Douglass to link his two floating tree-ring chronologies and put dendrochronology on a firm basis in the Southwest (R. Thompson 1995:646).

In 1930, Harold S. Gladwin offered Haury the position of assistant director of the Gila Pueblo Archaeological Foundation, with the understanding that for the first three years Haury would have to work only half-time so that he could enroll at Harvard and take graduate coursework the rest of the time (Haury 1995:711).

For his doctoral research, Haury took on the project of working up the Mary Hemenway collections from Los Muertos and other Hohokam sites in Arizona, made during the 1880s and 1890s, which had never been thoroughly analyzed (Scott 1933:301, 1934:301). This research formed the basis of his 1934 dissertation, "The Archaeology of the Salt River Valley, Arizona: A Study of the Interrelations of Two Ethnic Groups." Haury's doctoral committee was chaired by Roland Dixon and had as members A.V. Kidder, Alfred Tozzer, and Earnest Hooton (R. Thompson 1995:647).

Haury's notes show how intimate the department at Harvard still was in the early 1930s. He mentioned that he and his wife stayed with Dixon when they first arrived in Cambridge, later finding that it was unheard of for Dixon, a bachelor, to have a woman stay in his house (Haury 1995:725). In 1932 Haury assisted Hallam Movius with an experiment in which they calcined modern human femurs in order to check for shrinkage from burning; they reported observing none (Haury 1995:727). And after his successful Ph.D. defense, Haury reported, Kidder and Tozzer walked over to his apartment to congratulate him. He was out at dinner celebrating, so they left a note letting him know they had come by (Haury 1995:730). Hardly the picture of an austere and coldly proper department that some pundits have painted.

After his receiving his Ph.D., Haury helped set up a small tree-ring lab at the Peabody and subsequently helped Brew with tree-ring studies at Awatovi (Scott

1935:314, 1939:407). In 1937 Haury left Gladwin's institute, because Byron Cummings was retiring and a job was opening up at the University of Arizona. Haury became head of the Department of Anthropology at Arizona and director of the Arizona State Museum (R. Thompson 1995:648). He went on to develop an important doctoral program at the university, professionalized the museum, and conducted his own research at Ventana Cave and the Hohokam site of Snaketown. He also ran an important field school at Point of Pines, where Stephen Williams spent the summer of 1949, after finishing his A.B. at Yale.

Turning to the Awatovi participants who were students at Harvard in one capacity or another, we look first at **Erik Kellerman Reed** (1914–90). Reed was born in Quincy, Massachusetts, and received his A.B. in anthropology from George Washington University in 1932, before entering the Harvard graduate program. He received his A.M. from Harvard in 1933, and that summer he excavated with Frank Roberts in Arizona. The next year he worked with Emil Haury at the Harris Mimbres site in New Mexico (Steen 1981:1). Because WPA projects needed qualified archaeologists, he worked in 1934–35 for the Civil Works Administration, doing archaeology in Florida and the Southeast (Scott 1935:311). He continued doing a series of small projects for the government in the Southwest, was hired by the National Park Service in 1937, and continued employment with them until he retired in 1969 (Steen 1981:2).

Thus, although Reed worked at Awatovi with Brew and the Harvard crews, he did so as an NPS regional archaeologist (Scott 1940:452). In 1942 he excavated the Mancos Canyon site in Colorado, but the following year, like so many of his Peabody Museum peers, he was called into the armed services in military intelligence. Reed continued to work in military intelligence in Europe until 1946, but apparently he had nearly finished his Ph.D. work before going into the service, for he received his Harvard Ph.D. in 1944, with the dissertation "An Archaeological Study of Mancos Valley, Southwestern Colorado, and Its Position in the Prehistory of the American Southwest." After the war Reed continued in his position with the NPS. Although he did some work for NPS in Guam, most of his research was focused on the U.S. Southwest, from the Santa Fe office. The broad training that graduate students received at Harvard was also evident in Reed's career as he wrote up anthropometry and analyses of human skeletal materials from the Southwest, in addition to its archaeology.

Richard Page Wheeler (1909–97) was another member of the Awatovi Expedition. Wheeler was born in Chicago but grew up in Ohio. He attended Philips Exeter Academy before entering Harvard in 1929. After a two-year lacuna following graduation, he went to work with Paul Martin at Lowry Ruin in Colorado in 1934. The following year he was hired as a summer fellow at the Museum of Northern Arizona, working at Sunset Crater, Grand Falls, and Wupatki. He returned to Harvard for a year of graduate work in 1935–36, and in the summers of 1936 and 1937 he worked at Awatovi, where he was charged with the study of stone, bone, and antler artifacts. After meeting his future wife, Wheeler dropped out of archaeology for 10 years and worked on his father-in-law's farm in Michigan. In 1948 he returned to archaeology, according to Hester Davis (2008:1956), receiving his A.M. from Harvard then. He secured a job working for the Missouri River Basin Survey from 1948 until 1959 and then transferred to the National Park Service, where he worked on the Wetherill Mesa project until 1965. He then shifted to Washington, D.C., to serve as a technical publications editor, retiring in 1974 (Davis with Wheeler 1998). He finally published the Awatovi bone and antler materials in 1978.

John Christian Fisher Motz III (1908–91) was born in Monessen, Pennsylvania, near Pittsburgh, and was trained as an engineer at the Carnegie Institute of Technology, graduating in 1933. He became involved in archaeology by doing cartographic surveying work for archaeologists in the Southwest. He worked at Wupatki, Arizona, in 1933–34, and the next year he worked for Julian and Irwin Hayden, Harold Gladwin, and Emil Haury at Snaketown. His cousin later married Julian Hayden (Hester Davis, personal communication, 2002).

Intrigued by archaeology, Motz entered Harvard in 1936, because that was where Emil Haury and Irwin Hayden had trained. The first year, Tozzer set him to carrying out a statistical analysis of Maya pottery for his master's work (Scott 1938:361). Brew then recruited him to do cartographic work during the next season at Awatovi. Motz's last year at the Peabody was 1940, when he was the only field assistant for the first season of Phillips's Lower Mississippi Valley Survey (S. Williams 2003:xix).

Motz then returned home to Pittsburgh and married the daughter of the mayor. During World War II he worked for the Pittsburgh Housing Authority. At Harvard he had been known as Fisher Motz, but in Pittsburgh, because of anti-Semitic bias, he began using the name Chris Motz. He dropped out of anthropology entirely and continued working in municipal government after the war (Hester Davis, personal communication, 2002).

John Tilton Hack (1913–91) was a geology major at Harvard. He received his A.B. in 1935, A.M. in 1938, and Ph.D. in 1940, all in geological sciences. For the Awatovi project, Brew recruited Hack to study the physiography of the Jeddito basin, the water resources potentially used by the people of Awatovi Pueblo, and prehistoric coal working in the Hopi region (Scott 1939:407, 1941:429, 1942:432, 1943:455–56). Hack's dissertation, "Geography and Geology of the Hopi Country, Arizona," reflected this focus. After obtaining his Ph.D., Hack first took a job at Hofstra College, from 1941 to 1943, and then went to work for the U.S. Geological Survey.

Richard Benjamin Woodbury (1917–2009), originally from West Lafayette, Indiana, was involved in the Awatovi project from 1938 onward, replacing Richard Wheeler in charge of stone and bone artifacts. Woodbury received his S.B. from Harvard in 1939 and his A.M. in 1942. After serving in the U.S. Army Air Corps during the war, he finished his Harvard Ph.D. in 1948, with a dissertation based on his analysis of the Awatovi artifacts: "Prehistoric Stone Implements of Northeastern Arizona: A Study of the Origin, Distribution and Function of the Stone Tools, Ornaments, and Weapons of the Jeddito District." It was later published in the Peabody Museum papers

(R. Woodbury 1954). From 1947 to 1950 Woodbury worked for the museum on the United Fruit Company's Zaculeu Project in Guatemala (N. Woodbury 1991:767).

Woodbury retained his interest in the Southwest. In the late 1940s, he and Watson Smith began working up the early volumes of analyses for the Awatovi project (Brew 1949a:299). Smith, Woodbury, and Woodbury's wife, Nathalie Ferris Sampson Woodbury, also jointly worked up Frederick Hodge's Hawikku site materials in the early 1960s (Brew 1963:609).

Over his career Woodbury taught at the University of Kentucky (1950–52), Columbia University (1952–58), the University of Arizona (1959–63), and the University of Massachusetts–Amherst (1969–81), where he was the founding chair. He served on the curatorial staff of the Smithsonian Institution from 1963 to 1969. In addition to writing research publications in Mesoamerican and Southwestern archaeology, Woodbury served as editor of both *American Anthropologist* (1954–58) and *American Antiquity* (1975–78) (N. Woodbury 1991).

Samuel Watson Smith (1897–1993) was one of the most important scholars recruited to the Peabody Museum through participation in the Awatovi project. Smith was born and raised in the Cincinnati, Ohio, area. As a youngster in 1907, he visited the Peabody Museum's operations at Madisonville, directed by the Merwin brothers, which introduced him to archaeology (Smith 1992:109). Smith received Ph.B. from Brown in 1919 and took several jobs in industry over the next few years. He then came to get his LL.B. from Harvard in 1924 and worked in a law firm in Providence from then until the early 1930s (R. Woodbury 1995:665).

In 1933 Smith took the opportunity to go with Paul S. Martin to excavate for the Field Museum at Chaco Canyon, a career-changing event. During that field season, Smith met J. O. Brew in Colorado. After a semester at Berkeley in 1934, studying anthropology with Lowie and Kroeber, Smith returned to the Southwest and joined Ansel Hall's Rainbow Bridge–Monument Valley Expedition, also visiting Brew at Alkali Ridge that summer (Smith 1992:115, 121, 126). In the fall of 1935 Smith was invited by Lyndon Hargrave to work at the Museum of Northern Arizona. There, he and Brew met again in 1935–36, and Brew invited Smith to join the Awatovi Expedition. Smith ended up working for the Rainbow Bridge–Monument Valley Expedition for the first half season and then moved to Awatovi for the second half season in 1936 and 1937. In 1938 and 1939 he worked the full seasons at Awatovi (Smith 1992:147).

Between 1939 and 1942 Smith worked on writing up the painted kiva materials from Awatovi with Penny Davis (Worman) and Marjorie Vasey (R. Thompson 1996:322). After the excavations were completed at Awatovi, Smith was added as a research associate in anthropology at the Peabody Museum in 1941, but he soon left to serve in the war, first as a major in the U.S. Army Air Force as a photo interpreter and then for the Office of Naval Intelligence and Office of Strategic Services in the Pacific theater (Scott 1942:428; R. Thompson 1996:322). He met and married Lucy Cranwell in New Zealand in 1943.

At Awatovi, Smith had supervised the reconstructions of 200 kiva paintings, as well as the church murals of the Franciscan mission. After the war he returned to the Peabody to work up these materials, later publishing the church murals jointly with J. O. Brew and Ross Montgomery, an expert on historical religious architecture whom Brew had enlisted as a consultant (Montgomery, Smith, and Brew 1949), and the kiva paintings by himself (W. Smith 1952). During this period he spent the summers working on the Upper Gila Expedition for the Peabody Museum.

Smith had residences in Maine, Massachusetts, and Arizona. From 1948 onward, his house in Tucson, Arizona, became the focal point for the museum's archaeological program in the Southwest. Smith ended his seasonal pilgrimage between Tucson and Cambridge in 1954, and by 1955 he had converted a six-room guest house into a private laboratory and research library, dedicated to the completion of the Awatovi analyses and other projects (Brew 1956:660, 670). This building served until 1974 as the "Peabody Museum West of the Pecos."

Smith spent most of his postwar career working up Awatovi and Hawikku excavation materials, although he did serve on the managing board of the School of American Research—the renamed School of American Archaeology—in Santa Fe in the 1950s. In the postwar period he also provided other services for the Peabody Museum, among them working with Philip Phillips on surveying and rearranging the North American archaeological holdings in the Peabody's collections for J. O. Brew. This was an extraordinary operation that has gone unnoticed except by those who used the collections in the decades that followed. Both Phillips and Smith considered this effort a "reviving" activity after their wartime experiences. The two had side-by-side offices at the Peabody, and Stephen Williams shared Smith's office when he first came to the Peabody in January 1954.

At the time of the Awatovi project, tree-ring dating was the new technology sweeping the archaeological scene. Through J. O. Brew, Harvard apparently made several attempts to set up a dendrochronological lab. Among the people recruited in this attempt were Edmund Schulman, Donovan Senter, and W. S. Stallings.

Edmund Schulman (1908–58) received his A.B. in 1933 and his A.M in 1935 from the University of Arizona before coming to Harvard, where he was recruited to continue working on tree-ring data. He was never in the anthropology program proper but spent a good deal of his time at Harvard's Blue Meteorological Observatory. He received his A.M. in 1935 and his Ph.D. in 1944, writing a dissertation titled "The History of Precipitation and Run-off in the Colorado Basin as Indicated by Tree-Rings." Schulman's was the first degree in climatology at Harvard since 1918. He helped Brew and Donovan Senter with tree-ring dates for Awatovi.

Donovan Cowgill Senter (1909–81) received his A.B. in 1934 and his A.M. in 1936 from the University of New Mexico. He seems initially to have been interested in physical anthropology, for his A.M. thesis was titled "The Calcanea of Kuaua Pueblo." In 1936, at the old Quarai Pueblo mission, where Senter had been working since 1934, he married Florence May Hawley (1906–91), who had received a Ph.D. in anthropology from Chicago in 1934. Their first joint publication, for *American Anthropologist* in 1937, was on Hopi and Navajo child burials, again showing a biological anthropological focus.

Senter held a Hemenway Fellowship at the Peabody Museum for the 1936–37 year, and while there he worked on tree-ring dating of materials from the Southwest, perhaps those excavated earlier by A.V. Kidder. But he did not return to Harvard, and later he went into applied anthropology. He and Florence Hawley divorced in 1947, and she married Bruce T. Ellis in 1950. Florence Hawley Ellis taught at the University of New Mexico for 37 years and became well known in Southwestern archaeology in her own right.

William Sidney Stallings Jr. (1910–89), born in Mexico City, received his A.B. in 1931 and his A.M. ("Pueblo Architecture in the Rio Grande Drainage") in 1932 at the University of Arizona. He was then hired as a dendrochronologist at the Laboratory of Anthropology in Santa Fe, New Mexico, but was apparently given release time later to pursue graduate studies. He did graduate work at Yale from 1936 to 1937 and at Harvard from 1939 to 1941. Stallings's work at Harvard, too, revolved around Harvard's attempt to set up and sustain some kind of tree-ring dating expertise, in this case for the Awatovi project. In 1941 Stallings left Harvard without a degree, accepting a job as assistant director of the Taylor Museum in Colorado Springs, an association he continued until 1947. He then became a high-ranking member of the CIA's photo intelligence division; it was his group that first identified Russian missiles in Cuba (Brugioni 1991:21).

Other people from Harvard who were not directly connected with the Awatovi project also worked in the greater Southwest. Some, such as Walter W. Taylor, had linkages with Clyde Kluckhohn and his Navajo project; others harked back to the Claflin-Emerson Expedition, on which Brew had also worked.

Walter Willard Taylor Jr. (1913–97), born in Chicago but raised in Connecticut, received his A.B. in geology from Yale in 1935 and then took a job doing excavations for the Museum of Northern Arizona. He also ran the University of New Mexico archaeological field schools for the next three summers. He met Clyde Kluckhohn while doing some Navajo work in 1937 and, with Kluckhohn's encouragement, enrolled in Harvard. Kluckhohn was very important in Taylor's subsequent theoretical focus, an influence that some archaeologists have found strange, because Kluckhohn was a sociocultural anthropologist, not an archaeologist. It was their shared Southwestern interest that brought the two together and resulted in Kluckhohn's oversight of Taylor's work.

Taylor was assigned the project of analyzing the cordage from Southwestern sites in the Peabody collections (Scott 1940:457), and from this project apparently grew his interest in studying perishable artifacts in the greater Southwest. Taylor began his studies in dry caves in Coahuila, Mexico, in 1939 and continued working there in the winters for the next three years, his research funded primarily by the Smithsonian Institution–U.S. National Museum (Scott 1940:456, 1943:456).

Taylor was called to work for the OSS in 1942, but he had finished his Ph.D. work before going into intelligence and received his degree in 1943 (Euler 1997).

His dissertation, "The Study of Archaeology: A Dialectic, Practical, and Critical Discussion with Special Reference to American Archaeology and the Conjunctive Approach," was published in 1948 in the memoirs series of the AAA. With Kluckhohn's encouragement, Taylor had lobbied for a new approach to Americanist archaeology, feeling that too many archaeologists at the time were simply creating sterile space-time cultural sequences. He harshly criticized many of his peers and professors by name, creating considerable ill will. Although his work on "conjunctive archaeology" is seen by many as one of the first statements of what later became known as "processual archaeology," Taylor was never able to actualize his theoretical model. This problem, together with the personal ill will he created, no doubt contributed to the fact that processual archaeology did not reappear as a major trend for another decade.

Taylor mustered out of the service in 1945 but kept a reserve association with military intelligence, not resigning his commission as captain of intelligence until 1955. He was at the Peabody for a short time in 1945 and then went to teach at the University of Washington from 1946 to 1948. Subsequently, he held teaching and research positions at the University of Texas, in Santa Fe, and in Mexico (Escuela Nacional de Antropología e Historia, 1955–58), until he accepted the chairmanship of the anthropology department at Southern Illinois University–Carbondale in 1958. He stayed there as chair until 1963 and then as research professor until he retired in 1974. Taylor donated a number of books to the Tozzer Library at the Peabody Museum after his retirement, so he seems still to have had positive feelings about his time at Harvard.

William Benton Bowers II (1906–86) graduated cum laude in anthropology as a member of the Harvard class of 1928, with his degree delayed until 1929. He went into the Peabody Museum graduate program and was among the students given scholarships in archaeology in 1929 by the Laboratory of Anthropology in New Mexico to work at Pecos Pueblo under A.V. Kidder's guidance, along with Ssu-yung Liang (see chapter 11) and others. Bowers received his A.M. in 1931 on the basis of this work. He was also a member, along with Brew, Kidder II, Denison, and Waldo Forbes, on the 1931 Claflin-Emerson Expedition to Utah (Scott 1933:300). He continued working on his Ph.D. until he dropped out of the program in 1937 and went into a career in real estate. Bowers and his wife were frequent lenders of art objects to Harvard's Fogg Art Museum in the 1930s, suggesting that perhaps, like several of his contemporaries, his interest lay more in collecting artifacts than in the anthropological exegesis of cultures.

Waldo Emerson Forbes Jr. (1908–74) born in Newton, Massachusetts, was a member of the Harvard class of 1934, receiving his degree in 1935. He then entered the graduate program at the Peabody. His interest in archaeology may have stemmed from the fact that his uncle, Edward Waldo Forbes, was director of the Fogg Art Museum on campus from 1909 to 1944. Waldo Forbes Jr. participated in the Claflin-Emerson Expedition to Utah in 1931 as an undergraduate, working with Bowers, Brew, Denison, and Kidder II (Scott 1933:300). During the summer before his senior year, he went with Hugh Hencken, Hallam Movius, and Amory Goddard to do archaeological work on the second Harvard Archaeological Expedition to Ireland (Scott 1934:298). The next year he accompanied Carleton Coon to Abyssinia, and then he shifted to southern Arabia because of political unrest (Scott 1935:308). He remained a research associate in anthropology at the Peabody for another year (Scott 1936:317) and then left the program, later becoming a successful rancher in Wyoming.

Old World archaeological exploration increased significantly at the Peabody Museum in the 1930s with the addition to the archaeological staff first of Carleton Coon, as discussed in the last chapter, and then of Hugh Hencken and Hallam Movius.

Hugh O'Neill Hencken (1902–81), who had been born in Boston, was named a Peabody research associate and subsequently curator in European archaeology for 1929–30, with a Ph.D. fresh in hand from Cambridge University (Reynolds 1931a:288). In the summer of 1931 he visited Ireland with Lloyd Warner and set up a field project there, which included Movius in the summer of 1932, the first official year of the "Harvard Archaeological Expedition to Ireland" in County West Meath (Reynolds 1932:298). During the five years of the project, from 1932 through 1936, Hencken and Movius were assisted by Amory Goddard, F. L. W. Richardson, and Waldo E. Forbes, among others.

Hencken continued working in European and North African archaeology, specializing in the European Bronze and Iron Ages, during his tenure at the Peabody. He was responsible for keeping together and acquiring for the Peabody a collection of more than 13,000 items from central European Iron Age burials made by the Duchess of Mecklenberg before the First World War. When George MacCurdy died in 1947, Hencken became the new head of the American School of Prehistoric Research, a position he kept for the next three decades. As director of the ASPR he ran excavations in Morocco from 1947 to 1949. In 1949–51 he served as president of the Archaeological Institute of America. As requested, he regularly taught a few courses for the Department of Anthropology at Harvard, which were well received. After Hencken retired in 1972, the ASPR became the Peabody Museum's "department" of Old World prehistory. Hencken was a gentleman of the "old school," a true colleague, and a well-known figure in his field.

Hallam Leonard Movius Jr. (1907–87) was born in Newton, Massachusetts, and entered Harvard in 1926. After receiving his S.B. in 1930, he continued in graduate school at the Peabody. He excavated in central Europe during the 1930 and 1931 seasons with Robert Ehrich and Vladimir Fewkes, and he trained with the American School of Prehistoric Research in France. After a short project in Palestine in 1932, he joined Hencken on the first Harvard Archaeological Expedition to Ireland, and he participated in the next three years of the project as well. He completed his Ph.D., with the dissertation "The Late-Glacial and Early Post-Glacial Cultures of Ireland: A Study in Palaeolithic Survivals," in 1937 (Scott 1933:298, 1934:298, 1936:318).

After receiving his doctorate, Movius continued working for the Peabody Museum, initially as a research associate. In 1937 he began working in the Irrawaddy Valley of southern Burma, first with Helmut de Terra, of the CIW, and Père Teillard de Chardin, and later adding Edwin H. Colbert, of the AMNH (Scott 1938:358). It was on the basis of this fieldwork, between 1937 and 1940, that he defined the famous "Movius line," dividing hand ax from chopper–chopping tool traditions in Asia. From 1942 to 1946 he served in the intelligence group of the U.S. Army Air Corps, later the U.S. Air Force, starting out as a lieutenant and mustering out as a lieutenant colonel (Scott 1945:348).

Following the war, Movius carried out work on the Russian Paleolithic from 1946 to 1948. In the summer of 1948 he shifted to work in southwestern France (Brew 1950:321). He was granted tenure at Harvard in 1950 and began his seminal work at Abri Pataud, France, in 1953, continuing that project through 1964. The project was one of the most important French Paleolithic excavations done by an American scholar. His program at Abri Pataud was a "school" for cave excavations, and he trained a large number of students, men and women, from the United States and elsewhere. Movius supervised several Ph.D. dissertations from this project and other Old World Paleolithic venues. Something of a taskmaster in the field, he was nevertheless acclaimed by his "cave workers." Movius was still working on analyses of the Abri Pataud materials in 1970 when a stroke caught up with him, after a career teaching Old World archaeology at the Peabody Museum for more than four decades. He retired from teaching at Harvard in 1974 and from the museum in 1976, after having taught several generations of Old World archaeologists, who carry on his tradition throughout the country.

Amory Goddard (1900–1987) was a member of the Harvard class of 1923 but left in 1922, before finishing his degree. He spent the winter season of 1923 in Egypt assisting at George Reisner's Meroe excavations, which apparently led to his returning to the Peabody nearly a decade later to take up archaeology as a special student in 1931. He went on the second expedition to Ireland with Hencken and Movius (Scott 1934:298), working there with fellow students Frederick L. W. Richardson and Waldo E. Forbes. Goddard apparently decided archaeology was not his career after all; he left the graduate program in 1933 and went into business.

James Harvey Gaul (1911–45) received his S.B. from Harvard in 1932 and continued in graduate work at the Peabody, with a focus on central Europe. His work toward his degree was materially slowed because he both accepted a teaching job in anthropology at Brooklyn College at the same time and held a research position with the Oriental Institute of the University of Chicago. Thus he did not finish his Harvard A.M. work until 1938. In the summer of that year, Gaul and Bruce Howe worked with Dorothy Garrod for the ASPR in the Middle East. Gaul then spent the winter in Bulgaria doing work on the Neolithic period and the Bronze Age (Scott 1940:449). He finished his Ph.D. dissertation, "The Neolithic Period in Bulgaria," in 1940. He was recruited by the ONI in 1941 and transferred from it to the OSS in 1945. Captured, he was shot by a firing squad at the Mauthausen concentration camp in Linz, Austria, in 1945 (Luce 1945).

Bruce Howe (1912–2012) received his A.B. from Yale in 1935 and then came to Harvard to do graduate work with Coon and Hencken. He worked with Dorothy Garrod in Turkey and Bulgaria in the summer of 1938. When James Harvey Gaul stayed on to work in Bulgaria, Howe went to work on Paleolithic sites in Greece that winter (Scott 1940:449). He finished his A.M in 1939 and then went to conduct research on Upper Paleolithic sites in France in 1940 (Scott 1941:433). After the war he began working at a Paleolithic site in Tangier with Movius, Coon, and two other graduate students, under the guidance of Hencken, who had just taken over the reins of the ASPR (Scott 1948:310, 314).

Howe continued working in Tangier for the next few seasons. In 1947 he excavated the Caves of Hercules in Tangier with Coon, Hencken, and Charlene Croft, and in 1948 and 1949 he and Cabot Briggs continued work in Morocco (Brew 1949a:297). Howe completed his Ph.D. in 1952, defending a dissertation titled "The Paleolithic of the Tangier Zone in Morocco." He was then appointed a research fellow in Paleolithic archaeology at the Peabody and became one of the founding members of the Council of Old World Archaeology, acting as the ASPR representative. He also accepted a part-time position at the Oriental Institute at the University of Chicago, where he began working on some materials from Jarmo for Robert Braidwood. For the next decade he split his time, working and lecturing at the Oriental Institute in the winter term and conducting research for the ASPR during the summers (Brew 1953:383, 1954:366, 1961:606). In 1970 Howe retired and was appointed honorary associate of Palaeolithic archaeology at the Peabody. He moved to Newport, Rhode Island, and for many years after his retirement was a member of the Prehistory Department of the University of Istanbul, teaching there well into the 1990s.

Derwood "Ted" W. Lockard (1906–76), who was born in Oak Park, Illinois, received his A.B. from the University of Chicago in 1929 but did not enter the graduate program at Harvard until 1935. Because of his interest in the Middle East, he participated in expeditions to Turkey in 1929 and to Iran in 1930–33 with the Oriental Institute. After he entered Harvard, he carried out research on the Sir Aurel Stein collection from southern Iran at the Fogg Art Museum in 1937–38, research that formed the basis for his 1939 A.M. degree (Scott 1939:413). The following season, Lockard, his wife, and Lauriston Ward went to Egypt, Syria, and Iraq. They made surface collections from 120 mounds in Iraq and Syria, in order to define Neolithic cultural assemblages in the region (Scott 1940:447, 1941:432).

Shortly after Lockard was appointed a Peabody Museum research associate in Middle Eastern archaeology in 1941, he was called to the war, during which he worked for the ONI (Price 2008:222). He continued working for the CIA after the war, not returning to Harvard until 1954, by which time his interests had shifted from archaeology to Middle Eastern ethnography. Appointed a research fellow and lecturer in Middle Eastern ethnography, he taught courses in that area through the mid-1960s. In 1967 he was appointed associate director of the Center of Middle Eastern Studies at Harvard, and he continued in that position and as a lecturer until he retired in 1973.

Robert William Ehrich (1908–92) entered Harvard in 1926 and received his A.B. in 1931. Ehrich and Vladimir Fewkes, later a Peabody Museum research associate, met in the summer of 1927, when both were students of George MacCurdy's at the ASPR field project in Europe (Ehrich and Pleslová-Stiková 1968:11). The next summer Fewkes recruited Ehrich to join him in archaeological explorations in Czechoslovakia (Reynolds 1930:273). Later that year Ehrich also worked at the site of Nuzi, Kirkuk, Iraq, for the Fogg Museum, on behalf of the Peabody Museum (Reynolds 1930:273).

Ehrich and Fewkes continued fieldwork in central Europe in the summer of 1929, when Ehrich, representing the Peabody Museum, and Fewkes, representing the University Museum at Pennsylvania, signed a multiyear agreement with the Czech government for explorations of Neolithic sites in Czechoslovakia (Reynolds 1931a:283). The Harvard-Pennsylvania Czechoslovakian Expedition then went into the field for the next several seasons. Ehrich continued in the graduate program at Harvard after he received his A.B., studying particularly with Hooton and Coon. He wrote up the first part of his Czechoslovakian research as his A.M. thesis and received his degree in 1933 (Reynolds 1930:273, 1931a:283, 1932:294; Scott 1933:297).

In 1932 Ehrich was named a John Harvard Fellow, a position he used to fund his doctoral research in anthropometry in Montenegro, where he collected 852 anthropometric samples (Scott 1933:299). For the next few years Ehrich returned to excavate each summer in central Europe with Fewkes and worked on analyzing the Montenegro samples while he was back at Harvard. In 1939, the 1927–31 excavations at Nuzi were published in the Harvard-Radcliffe Fine Arts Series for the Semitic Museum, with Ehrich writing up the physical anthropology of the burials. In 1946 Ehrich completed his Ph.D. dissertation, "A Racial Analysis of Montenegro." Publication of the findings of the Harvard-Pennsylvania Czechoslovakian Expedition (Ehrich and Pleslová-Stiková 1968) was delayed because of Fewkes's death in 1941. After receiving his Ph.D., Ehrich taught at Brooklyn College, where his interest at first remained split between archaeology and physical anthropology. Later he focused primarily on archaeology. In 1972 Ehrich returned to serve as a research associate in European archaeology at the Peabody, working on his anuscript "Contributions to the Archaeology of Czechoslovakia" with co-author Evzen Plesl. That unpublished material resides in the archives of the Peabody. (Ehrich and Plesl n.d.).

Vladimir Jaroslav Fewkes (1901–41)—not to be confused with Jesse Walter Fewkes, who worked in the U.S. Southwest (see chapter 9)—was born in Nymburk, Czechoslovakia, but came to the United States in 1920. He received his S.B. in 1926, his A.M. in 1928, and his Ph.D. in 1931 from the University of Pennsylvania (Speck 1942:476). Vladimir Fewkes and Robert Ehrich had begun working together in Czechoslovakia in the summer of 1928 and continued doing so for the next several years (Reynolds 1930:273). In 1930 Fewkes, representing Pennsylvania, and Ehrich, representing the Peabody, signed the agreement with the Czech government for the joint Harvard-Penn expedition and began excavating at Homolka, Czechoslovakia (Reynolds

1931a:283). Fewkes was associate director of the ASPR from 1929 to 1934 and acting director in 1938 (Bricker 2002:281). He and Ehrich directed ASPR students at sites in Yugoslavia and Czechoslovakia during this period. Because of the ASPR's and the Peabody's shared interests, Fewkes was also named a research associate at the Peabody Museum from 1932 through 1937. In 1938 he was recruited to do some New World archaeology, working at Irene Mound near Savannah, Georgia, but after one season of work for the WPA he returned to Pennsylvania and his central European archaeological interests (Mason 1942:115), until his death in 1941.

Henry Ware Eliot Jr. (1879–1947) was the older brother of the poet T. S. Eliot. The family was related to both Charles William Eliot, the long-time Harvard University president, and William Greenleaf Eliot, who founded Washington University in St. Louis. Eliot's father was CEO of a brick company in St. Louis, and after graduating from Harvard in 1902, Henry Eliot seems to have gone into this family business. From 1937 until his death in 1947, however, he was a research fellow in Middle Eastern archaeology at the Peabody Museum. He worked with Robert Ehrich on the Nuzi materials from Iraq (Eliot 1939a, 1939b). For the last 15 years of his life he worked on collating the diagnostic traits and ceramic sequences for late Neolithic and Bronze Age sites in Iraq and Iran, from items that had been published piecemeal in journals, site reports, obscure newspaper articles, and other occasional venues. This collation was published posthumously as a Peabody Museum volume in 1950 (Brew 1951:367).

Besides the people we have already covered in this chapter and in chapter 11 who attended the American School of Prehistoric Research field schools, there were other Harvard graduate students for whom we have less information. One such person included in the ASPR list of students (Bricker 2002:282–83) was **Curtice M. Clay Aldridge** (1910–2003), also known as Henry to his undergraduate classmates. Aldridge received his A.B. in anthropology from Cornell in 1933. He was enrolled at Harvard in the anthropology graduate program from 1932 to 1935 but is not listed as having received a degree in Harvard summaries for as late as 1947. However, *Who Was Who in American Art* lists him as having received an A.M. from Harvard, so perhaps he did receive one in anthropology that failed to get listed in our documents. He embarked on a 50-year career working in art museums, serving as director of five different museums during that time.

Dwight Whitney Morrow Jr. (1908–76) received his A.B. from Amherst in 1931. He was a graduate student at Harvard, taking some anthropology courses, from 1934 through 1936 and received an A.M. there in 1935. Like Stanley Boggs, Morrow spent a summer working with Samuel Eliot Morison on questions of Columbus's voyage in the Caribbean. Morrow eventually became interested in agricultural history and received his Ph.D. from Harvard in 1957 in that area. He went on to teach at Lincoln University (Pennsylvania), Temple University, and the Monterey Institute of Foreign Studies in California. Dwight Morrow Jr. was the brother of Anne Spencer Morrow and thus the brother-in-law of Charles Lindbergh.

Beyond Europe and the Middle East, the countries of Asia beckoned to a few of the anthropology students in the 1930s. **Eugene Clark Worman Jr.** (1915–69) was born in Madras, India, and retained an interest in his expatriate homeland throughout his life. He was a member of the Harvard class of 1937 and directly entered the anthropology graduate program. For his first field season he received an ASPR fellowship and worked on Peabody projects in central Europe, learning excavation methods. He then received a Sheldon Traveling Fellowship in 1939 to study lithic assemblages in India and Ceylon (Scott 1940:448). On returning from India, he served as a teaching assistant for Carleton Coon in Anthropology 1 while working on his A.M. In the summer of 1941 he was employed by Frank H. H. Roberts on excavations near San Jon, New Mexico. Worman earned his A.M. in 1942 and in that same year married Penrose "Penny" Davis, Mott Davis's sister. During the war, from 1942 to 1945, Worman worked as a civilian for the U.S. Navy, and afterward he returned to Harvard to complete his Ph.D., in 1946. His dissertation was titled "The Problem of a Neolithic Culture in India." Following receipt of his doctorate, he was awarded an NRC grant through the Peabody Museum to continue his work in India, on a project titled "Survey of Indian Prehistory and Early History," from 1946 to 1949. Subsequently he went into a career in the CIA (Price 2002:17).

Cheng Te-k'un (Zheng Dekun) (1907–2001) received his A.B. in 1930 and his A.M. in 1931 at Yenching University in China. Later in the 1930s he became associated with West China Union University, where Rev. David Graham and Dr. William Morse were also on the staff. As we describe shortly, Morse and Graham became research associates of the Peabody Museum in the early 1930s. Apparently impressed by this bright young Chinese archaeologist, Morse and Graham helped arrange for him to come to the Peabody. The linkage was no doubt aided by the previously established Harvard-Yenching Institute, the venue in which many Harvard researchers visited to study Chinese issues during the early twentieth century.

Cheng enrolled in the graduate program at Harvard in 1938, researching the formative civilizations of China for his Ph.D. dissertation, "Prehistoric Archaeology of Szechuan." He received his degree in 1941. The annual reports of the Peabody Museum list Cheng as having a continuing job at West China Union University. But with the Japanese invasion of China and the expanding Pacific war, it is unclear whether he actually returned there. After the war he was still in the West, and from 1951 to 1966 he taught as a lecturer in the Department of Eastern Art and Archaeology at Cambridge University in England. He then returned to teach in Taiwan but retired from the principal university there in 1974. He spent the three decades after receiving his Ph.D. researching and writing on the first civilizations of China, particularly the Shang.

While working on his Ph.D. in the summer of 1940, Cheng took Harvard students Mott Davis (reviewed earlier in this chapter), John Pelzel, Earle Carleton, John Cox, Melvin Pollard, Charles Shop, and Harold Winchester with him on explorations in Siberia, Manchuria, China, Japan, and Southeast Asia (Scott 1941:432). This fieldwork experience seems to have influenced the careers of several of these students, whom we mention briefly here (John Pelzel is profiled later in this chapter). **Earle Joseph Carleton Jr.** (1919–96) was a member of the Harvard class of 1941. He entered graduate school in anthropology at Harvard with a Thaw Fellowship in 1941–42 but was soon called to the war and served in the OSS in the Pacific theater. **John Hadley Cox** (1917–2005) received his A.B. from Yale in 1935 and taught in China from then until 1937. He was enrolled in the anthropology graduate program at Harvard from 1938 to 1942, when he, too, was called to war. From 1943 to 1947 he served in the OSS. After the war he taught Eastern art and archaeology at the University of Michigan, and later history at Georgetown.

Melvin Pollard (1922–93) was a member of the Harvard class of 1941 and entered the anthropology program at the Peabody in 1941–42, before being called to military service. After the war he worked in Japan, doing geological surveys for the Allied Supreme Command. **Charles Henry Bedford Sutton Shop** was a graduate student at the Peabody from 1939 to 1941, when he left to serve in the war. He apparently decided not to continue in anthropology after the war but instead took a position teaching at Manumit Prep School in Pawling, New York. **Harold Purcell Winchester Jr.** (1918–2001) was a member of the Harvard class of 1939. He had participated in the Awatovi excavations in 1938 and after graduation entered the Peabody graduate program, working on a degree until he left for war duties in 1941. In 1944 he went to the University of Chicago to finish his Ph.D., completing his degree in 1947. He then taught the ethnology of Northeast Asia in the anthropology program at the University of Minnesota.

One last student who was interested in Asia was **Harold Medill Sarkisian** (1909–93), a graduate student at the Peabody Museum from 1938 until 1943. Sarkisian's family had a rug business in Denver, specializing in products from Iran and China, and he was particularly interested in the development of textiles. He began thesis work on the development of early looms and loomed textiles in East Asia and the Pacific in 1939 and continued it until being called to the war (Scott 1940:456, 1941:432). Afterward he worked briefly for the British government before returning to Denver to take over the family business. Through the Denver Art Museum, he continued work on textiles from Iran and China after he retired in the 1970s, and throughout his life he sent materials to the collections of the Fogg and Peabody Museums.

Archaeology was not the only area of growth at the Peabody Museum in the 1930s. Major new initiatives in physical anthropology and sociocultural anthropology got under way as well. The chief focus in physical anthropology was anthropometry, and Hooton established a separate Statistical and Anthropometric Laboratory specializing in statistical analyses of anthropometric data. In 1933–34 the Peabody Museum had 44 field research projects and another 18 projects being carried out in the statistics lab. By 1936–37 the volume had increased such that more than 5 million separate items were run through the lab's system that year (Scott 1935:309, 1938:363). Hooton was processing data for

Aleš Hrdlička at the U.S. National Museum (UNSM), Harry Shapiro at the AMNH, and other colleagues at the Field Museum, Boston College, and Cornell University. The anthropometry lab had an early card-run sorting machine (not a computer) for this work, which was still in the lab as late as 1954, when Stephen Williams saw it.

Hooton recruited a variety of professionals to work in his lab and to provide additional expertise for his students. Indeed, we were surprised by the number of visiting scholars Hooton apparently attracted to his lab, although the Peabody Museum annual reports give no precise figures. But these researchers obviously enriched the resources available to the physical anthropology students. **Clarence Raymond Carpenter** (1905–75), for example, was American anthropology's first field primatologist. During his career he taught mainly at Stanford and at Pennsylvania State University. In 1936–37, because of his association with an MCZ project for which he was studying the social behavior of gibbons in Borneo and Siam, he was appointed a research associate at the Peabody Museum (Scott 1938:354). In this capacity, he helped Sherwood Washburn, whom we profile shortly, on the same project.

William Washington Graves (1865–1949) was a participant in the many links between the Peabody Museum and Washington University in St. Louis. A physician who had joined the St. Louis University School of Medicine in 1914, Graves was strongly interested in anthropometry and came to work in Hooton's lab in 1933–34. The lab gave him statistical help in his project to classify criminals by scapular types (National Research Council 1938:35; Scott 1935:312).

William Reginald Morse (1874–1939), another medical doctor, was the dean of medicine at the West China Union College medical school (later the West China Center of Medicine, Sichuan University), which he had helped to found in 1914. He was first appointed a Peabody Museum research associate in 1930–31 (Reynolds 1932:297) and spent that year in residence, writing up his nine field seasons of anthropomorphic studies of Tibetans, of Chinese in Szechwan, and of some "non-Chinese" tribes of western China (Scott 1933:302). He maintained these studies through the Peabody for the rest of the decade. During much of this period he also collaborated with the Reverend David Crockett Graham in China, who then was museum director for the West China Union University there. Their collaboration resulted in Graham's occasional donation of Chinese and Tibetan materials and contributions to medical anthropology at the Peabody.

A third physician was **Dr. William Herbert Sheldon** (1899–1977), who held an M.D. and a Ph.D. in psychology, both from Chicago. He was teaching at the University of Wisconsin in 1937–38 when the Peabody Museum appointed him a research associate in physical anthropology. Sheldon had been recruited and introduced to Hooton by Wesley Dupertuis, whom Sheldon had met through their common medical interests. Sheldon was interested in studying somatotypes and became involved in analyzing the large body of data on the constitutional types of Harvard freshmen that Hooton had collected over the years (Scott 1940:458–59). He continued working on this project in association with the museum until he was called into the army in 1942.

A final example of the researchers attracted to Hooton's lab is anthropologist **Henry Field** (1902–86), who had received an A.B. from Oxford University in 1925 and an A.M. there in 1929. Born in Chicago, a nephew of Marshall Field and Stanley Field—the founder and president, respectively, of the Field Museum of Natural History—Henry Field started his career as assistant curator of physical anthropology at the Field Museum in 1925. From 1928 through 1934 he participated in the excavation of Kish, the Sumerian-Akaddian capital in Iran, meanwhile collecting more than 2,000 sets of anthropometric measurements of people in Iraq and Iran. Field was a "research guest" of the Peabody Museum for 1936–37 while he processed these measurements in Hooton's lab, work that resulted in his D.Sc. from Oxford in 1937 (National Research Council 1938:29; Scott 1938:363). Field renewed his association with the Peabody in 1950 as a research associate in physical anthropology, a title he held through 1969. Consequently, several of his publications on the Mesopotamian region were based on research completed at Harvard.

Besides drawing other professionals to carry out projects in his lab, Hooton attracted a large number of students throughout the 1930s, especially in the later years of the decade. These students made a permanent mark on the Peabody Museum and dramatically enhanced the ambiance for their peers in archaeology and sociocultural anthropology.

James Madison Andrews IV (1905–88) was born in Schenectady, New York. He received his A.B. from Harvard in 1929 and his A.M. in 1933, the latter on the basis of anthropometric fieldwork on Indian groups in Quebec and Massachusetts (National Research Council 1938:4). He was then sent for two years to study economic, anthropometrical, and medical practices in Thailand, under the direction of Carle Zimmerman, of the Harvard sociology department. Zimmerman had previously worked in Thailand, and he helped Andrews secure the research permits he needed (Scott 1936:320). Andrews collected more than 4,000 anthropometric records and spent the next three years doing statistical analyses in Hooton's lab. He received his Ph.D. in 1939, with the dissertation "An Anthropological Survey of Siam."

Andrews then was appointed assistant curator of somatology for the Peabody Museum, his primary responsibility being to run the anthropometric statistical lab. He occasionally participated in archaeological salvage excavations. For example, in 1940 he and Janet W. Raymond excavated a set of late prehistoric burials at Chathamport, Massachusetts. In 1943 Andrews left for a stint with the ONI in the war. He returned to the Peabody after the war, again as assistant curator of somatology, taking over the supervision of anthropometric studies for the U.S. Army Quartermaster Corps from Hooton and helping to train Stanley Garn, whom we discuss later. In January 1948 he left the museum to take the job of chief statistician for the CIA. Ultimately he rose to become the assistant director of the CIA, serving in that position until he retired in 1957 (Price 2003:34; Scott 1948:311).

Lloyd Cabot Briggs (1909–75), Boston-born, entered Harvard in 1927 and received his A.B. in 1931. His succeeding graduate career was less timely. He went to the American School of Prehistoric Research for one season as a graduate student, and he worked with Homer Kidder in the early 1930s in France. He also went to Oxford to study, before returning to Harvard to finish his A.M. in 1938. Briggs then went to work in a brokerage house, and when the United States entered World War II, he was recruited into the OSS and served in North Africa until 1947 (Price 2008:222). After the war he returned to Harvard to work on his Ph.D. Hooton served as his doctoral advisor and sent Briggs to Algeria to work on an ASPR project with Hugh Hencken and Bruce Howe (Brew 1950:327)—the basis of his 1952 dissertation, "The Pre-Neolithic Inhabitants of Northwest Africa."

After receiving his Ph.D., Briggs was named a research associate in North African archaeology at the Peabody Museum, a position he kept until his death in 1975. He was hired at Franklin Pierce College in Rindge, New Hampshire, where he founded the Department of Anthropology and served as its chair until he died. While there, he worked mainly in physical anthropology and community studies. Because Briggs lived in Boston and commuted to Franklin Pierce College, he was also frequently at the Peabody Museum during this period.

Hans Theodore Edward Hertzberg (1905–2000), a native of San Antonio, Texas, received his A.B. from Rice University in 1928 and began graduate work at the University of Texas in 1931. In 1933 he transferred to Harvard, where he finished his A.M. in 1936. He supported himself during the 1930s by working on archaeological projects in Texas and Kentucky in the summers. Hertzberg's association with anthropometry arose from his working on the research into eye pigmentation that Peabody Museum research associate Laurance Redway had begun in the late 1920s. By 1937 Hertzberg had organized more than 500 color plates of human eye pigment and begun statistical analyses of this data set in Hooton's lab for his dissertation (Scott 1936:321, 1937:345, 1938:361, 1939:413). Apparently he was called to the war before he completed his degree. After the war he continued working for the biophysics branch of the Aerospace Medical Research Lab at Wright-Patterson Air Force Base, in Dayton, Ohio, from 1946 until he retired in 1972. There he worked mainly on the anthropometrics of cockpit design.

Sherwood Larned Washburn (1911–2000) was born and grew up in Cambridge, Massachusetts. He had been an unpaid volunteer at the MCZ while still in college prep school, working for Thomas Barbour, who was a family friend. Thus, when he entered Harvard, he intended to major in zoology. But "an introductory general anthropology course, taught there by a close family friend and stimulating lecturer, Alfred Tozzer, served to reveal its cross-disciplinary roots and to capture permanently his interest in its breadth of scope and scientific relevance for the human condition" (Howell 2003:4–5).

Washburn received his A.B. from Harvard in 1935. His first postgraduate work in anthropology was essentially a zooarchaeological project, in which he studied animal bones recovered from Neolithic sites to see what light they shed on human diet and behavior (Scott 1937:336). Although Washburn began his graduate career as a teaching assistant for Lloyd Warner and Walter Cline, he faithfully attended the tea Earnest

Plate 49

W. W. Howells in China, 1975.

Frederick Roelker Wulsin and
Janet Wulsin in Shansi, China, 1921.

F. R. Wulsin with hunters in Tibet, 1921.

Plate 50

Philip Phillips was named assistant curator of Southeast archaeology at the Peabody in 1937. Below, Phillips excavating at the Mayersville site, Lower Mississippi Survey, 1950s.

Plate 51

Harriet Hammond (Ellis).

Katherine Burks Young (Hearn).

Doris Zemurray (Stone).

Alice Dukes Blyth (Child).

Plate 52

Hannah Marie Wormington.

Doris Zemurray Stone visiting Sam Lothrop's excavations at Pachacamac, Peru, 1940s.

Plate 53

Robert Wauchope (far left) with members of the Peabody's expedition team at the Pendleton Ruin, New Mexico, 1933. Also pictured (among others) are A.V. Kidder (third from left) and Hattie and Burt Cosgrove (fourth from right and far right).

Edward Wyllys Andrews IV, 1938.

Plate 54

The Peabody Museum expedition to Awatovi in 1935–1939 brought together dozens of Harvard students, alumni, faculty, and staff from all branches of anthropology and archaeology. This group photo from 1939 includes (standing, left to right) Donald Scott, E. Mott Davis, Carlos Garcia-Robiou, Charles "Happy" Foote, Al Lancaster, Watson Smith, John T. Hack, Richard B. Woodbury, Haych Claflin, and Lindsay Thompson; seated: Peter Blos, Evelyn Brew, Alfred V. Kidder, Madeleine (Mrs. Charles) Amsden, Louise (Mrs. Donald) Scott, Joe Brew, and Earl Morris.

Plate 55

Thomas Nolan Campbell.

Dorothy Newton (Inglis).

John Christian Fisher Motz III.

Richard Page Wheeler.

Plate 56

Marion Hutchinson (Tschopik).

Erik Kellerman Reed.

Kenneth D. MacLeish.

Harold P. Winchester Jr.

Plate 57

Social anthropology students Conrad Arensberg (far left) and Solon Kimball (third from right) visited the Awatovi excavations in 1939. (Also pictured, left to right: Arensberg, John Hack, Dick Woodbury, Kent Bryant, Kimball, Mott Davis, Al Lancaster.)

Samuel Watson (Wat) Smith preserving the kiva murals at Awatovi, 1938.

Plate 58

Hugh O'Neill Hencken (third from left) was presented with an honorary degree from the National University of Ireland by Eamon de Valera (center), president of Ireland, in 1937.

Hencken at the excavations of the Ashakar cave sites in Tangier, 1947.

Plate 59

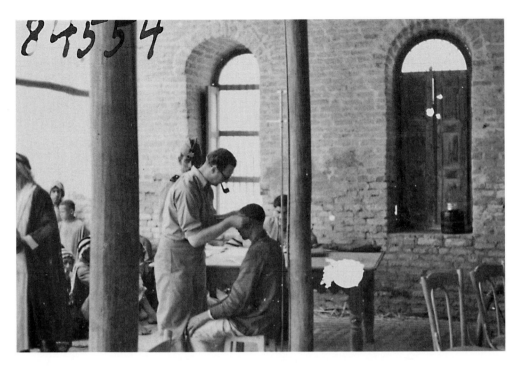

Henry Field taking cranial measurements in Iraq, 1934.

Vladimir Jaroslav Fewkes, Yugoslavia, 1930s.

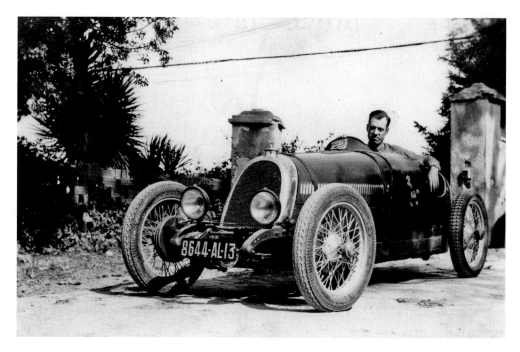

Lloyd Cabot Briggs in his Bugatti, 1947.

Owen Lattimore, Inner Mongolia, 1932.

Plate 61

Hallam Leonard Movius Jr. excavating at Abri Pataud, France, 1963.

Plate 62

Many Harvard students and faculty interrupted their work to serve in WWII. Bruce Howe in uniform, 1940s, and in Gabes, Tunisia, as chief archaeologist of the ASPR investigations of Oued Akarit, 1951.

Plate 63

Harry D. Pollock in uniform, 1940s.

Pollock and Olmec head, Tabasco, Mexico, 1957.

Henry Ware Eliot Jr.

Sherwood Larned Washburn, 1935.

Plate 64

Conrad Maynadier Arensberg, 1931.

Clyde Kay Maben Kluckhohn, 1940.

Arthur K. Loveridge paying his porters, Sabei, Uganda, 1933.

Hooton gave every afternoon at his home, which all graduate students were expected to attend (DeVore 1992:414).

As a graduate student, Washburn took little training in anthropology, mainly focusing on courses in comparative anatomy and vertebrate paleontology, particularly because of his developing interest in primatology. In 1937 he went on Harold J. Coolidge's "Asiatic Primate Expedition," supported by a Sheldon Traveling Fellowship, studying the social aspects of primates in Southeast Asia (Scott 1938:345). Washburn was guided in fieldwork procedures by primatologist Clarence R. Carpenter, who was then a research associate at the Peabody Museum. This research was the basis of his 1940 Ph.D. dissertation, "A Preliminary Metrical Study of the Skeletons of Langurs and Macaques."

While finishing his Ph.D., Washburn took a job at the medical school at Columbia University, where he taught from 1939 to 1947. He then moved to the University of Chicago, holding a joint position in anthropology and anatomy from 1947 to 1958. In 1958 he moved to the University of California–Berkeley and taught there until his retirement in 1979 (Howell 2003:6–9). After retirement Washburn returned to live in Cambridge, where he served as a science advisor to the Science Museum of Boston. Throughout his career, Washburn was interested in functionalist explanations in primate studies.

Byron Oroville Hughes (1906–80), a native of Newport, Idaho, received an A.B. in 1933 and an A.M. in 1934 from the University of Michigan, before coming to Harvard. For his Harvard research, Hooton assigned him an anthropometric study of Armenian children in Boston and Detroit, which formed the basis of his second A.M., this time from Harvard, in 1936 (Scott 1936:321). He continued this project, completing during the next year an anthropometric study of 1,700 adult Armenian males in Boston, Detroit, New York City, and Troy, New York, for his Ph.D. research (Scott 1937:345). He received his doctorate in 1938 with a dissertation titled "The Physical Anthropology of Native-Born Armenians." Because jobs were scarce, he took a position with the University Elementary School at the University of Michigan following his graduation, and he seems not to have returned to anthropology.

Marshall Thornton Newman (1911–94) was another of Hooton's students in the early 1930s who focused primarily on issues of anthropometrics. He was born in New Bedford, Massachusetts, and did his undergraduate work at the University of Chicago, receiving a B.Phil. in 1933. While at Chicago he spent three summers excavating Indian burial sites in central and southern Illinois, and after graduation he spent a further eight months excavating Indian skeletal remains in Florida for the Smithsonian Institution. He received an A.M. from Chicago in 1935 and then worked as the Bolton Fellow in Anatomy and Physical Anthropology at Case Western Reserve University from 1935 to 1936 (M. Crawford 1995:683). Thus, when he entered Harvard to work with Hooton in 1936, he had considerable experience in archaeology and physical anthropology. Newman continued this trajectory of field research while he was at the Peabody Museum, including working on some TVA projects in Tennessee. He received his Ph.D. in 1941; his dissertation was called "An Analysis of Indian Skeletal Material from Northern Alabama and Its Bearing upon the Peopling of the Southeastern United States."

Right after receiving his degree, Newman worked with Samuel Lothrop and Julio Tello at the Institute of Andean Research, analyzing Paracas mummies from Peru. (He replaced **Harold Laurence Oppenheimer** [1919–85; Harvard A.B. 1939], who worked on the Paracas project in 1940 as a first-year Peabody graduate student in physical anthropology but who, after the war, did not resume a career in anthropology.) After that year's work, Newman took a position in 1942 with the U.S. National Museum, where he worked for the next two decades. He then moved into a more academic position at Portland State University from 1962 to 1966, serving as chair of the anthropology department during the last two years. He concluded his academic career at the University of Washington in Seattle, remaining there from 1966 until his retirement in 1979 (Crawford 1995:684). He was particularly interested in dermatoglyphics and in the effects of environmental factors on populations.

Yet another student working in anthropometrics was **Charles Ernest Snow** (1910–67). Snow received his A.B. in geology from the University of Colorado and then came to the Peabody to study with Hooton. He began working on an anthropometric study of two groups of Jewish children, 1,500 individuals in all, the initial evaluations of which he completed for his A.M. in 1935. Further analyses of this group in contrast to non-Jewish students resulted in his Ph.D. dissertation, "Comparative Growth of Jewish and Non-Jewish Pupils in a Greater Boston Public School" (Scott 1936:321). After receiving his degree in 1938, Snow took a position in physical anthropology with the Alabama Museum of Natural History, working under the museum's contract with the WPA on TVA excavations. When the contract ended in 1949, Snow took a position teaching at the University of Kentucky, where he stayed for the next 26 years. There he published burial analyses for Archaic sites such as Indian Knoll and for various Adena and Techefuncte sites and on Pickwick Basin anthropometry in general (Bass 1968:369). He was well known by Southeastern archaeologists for his good research.

For the later 1930s, we start with **John Lawrence Angel** (1915–86). Angel was born in London. His mother, Elizabeth Day Seymour, was the daughter of the American classical archaeologist Thomas Day Seymour (Ortner and Kelley 1988:145), several of whose activities helped shaped his grandson's career. Seymour had been on the administrative committee of the American School of Classical Research (ASCR) in Athens from 1887 to 1901, which exposed J. Lawrence Angel to archaeological excavations, and he was president of the AIA from 1903 to 1907, during which time the 1906 Antiquities Act was passed, with the AIA's help. Lawrence Angel's family stayed in London until 1928 and then returned to the Seymour family home in Connecticut.

After Angel entered Harvard as an undergraduate, he participated in archaeological excavations in New Mexico and Arizona during the summers of 1934 and 1935. He received his A.B. from Harvard in 1936 and spent the summer in Santa Fe that year. He then went for some additional fieldwork on WPA projects in Macon, Georgia.

With this Americanist field experience in hand, he received money from Harvard to go to the ASCR to study human skeletal remains from past digs that were curated at the school. He had completed the analysis of 421 "Classical Geometric" period skeletons by 1939, when illness forced him to return to the United States (Scott 1938:359, 1939:409, 1940:449). The statistical analysis of these materials in Hooton's lab formed the basis of Angel's 1942 Ph.D. dissertation, "A Preliminary Study of the Relations of Race to Culture, Based on Ancient Greek Skeletal Material."

Angel was a teaching assistant at Harvard from 1939 to 1941, an instructor at Berkeley from 1941 to 1942, and, immediately after finishing his degree, an instructor at the University of Minnesota from 1942 to 1943. In 1944 he was offered a position in anatomy at Jefferson Medical College in Philadelphia, and he worked there from 1944 through 1962, when he moved to become a curator of physical anthropology at the U.S. National Museum. That job allowed him also to teach physical anthropology courses for one semester each year at George Washington University. He worked in both places until his death in 1986 (Ubelaker 1989:6). Throughout his life, Angel kept a focus on the eastern Mediterranean, beginning mainly with anthropometry and paleodemography but later adding forensic anthropology.

Joseph Benjamin Birdsell (1908–94) was trained at Harvard when Hooton's statistical lab was running at full bore. Hooton sent him to work with Norman Barnett Tindale (1900–93), who was associated with the Museum of South Australia and the University of Adelaide. Tindale was working on the social anthropology of Australian Aborigines, and Birdsell joined him to do the physical anthropology. During a 15-month project, Birdsell collected anthropometric data on 2,458 "full and mixed blood aborigines," and Tindale collected the associated ethnographic details (Scott 1939:408). While completing his analyses, Birdsell supported himself by teaching sociology at Washington State University from 1941 through 1943. After receiving his Ph.D. in 1942 ("The Trihybrid Origin of the Australian Aborigine"), Birdsell no doubt planned to continue at Pullman, but like the majority of his peers, he served in the war instead. Afterward he returned briefly to the Peabody. In 1947 he obtained a job at the University of California–Los Angeles, with which he was associated for several decades, focusing his research on founding populations and demographic units.

Gabriel Ward Lasker (1912–2002), like Lawrence Angel, was born in England. The family moved to the United States in 1914 in order to avoid internment as German aliens during World War I (Little 2003:890). Lasker entered the University of Wisconsin in 1930 but after two years transferred to Michigan and received his A.B. there in 1934. In 1935–37 he went to China with his family and became interested in "Peking man" and other hominid fossils. Consequently, he entered Harvard to study with Hooton when the family returned to the United States in 1937 (Little 2003:890). Hooton directed him into Chinese anthropometric work.

Lasker received his A.M. at Harvard in 1940. He was a teaching fellow in anatomy at the Harvard Medical School from 1942 to 1943, when he was called for war duties.

Because of his strong German ties, Lasker was granted conscientious objector status and worked for the U.S. Forest Service to fulfill his government obligations (Little 2003:890). He completed his Ph.D. ("Physical Characteristics of Chinese: A Study of Physical Differences and Development among Chinese at Home and Abroad") in 1945. The next year he obtained a position teaching anatomy at Wayne State University, where he remained until he retired in 1982. He continued his research in demography and anatomy there but is perhaps best known because of his position as editor of *Human Biology* from 1953 to 1988, the last 17 years of which he served as chief editor.

Muzaffer Süleyman Senyürek (1915–61), along with Hsien Chin Hu, was one of the few foreign students who came through Hooton's program. Senyürek had received the equivalent of an A.B. from the Lyceum of Smyrna, Turkey, in 1933. Attracted by Hooton's reputation, he later came to Harvard. There he received his A.M. in anthropology in 1939 and his Ph.D. in 1940, writing a dissertation titled "A Metric Approach to the Study of the Evolution of Human Dentition: A Metrical Study of the Teeth of Primates." Senyürek assisted Carleton Coon with work on fossils of Tangiers (Senyürek 1941). Following the receipt of his degree, he returned to Turkey, where he taught at the University of Ankara from 1939 to 1959 and then served as dean from 1959 until his death. He produced multiple publications on analyses of fossil hominid teeth and bones.

Stanley Marion Garn (1922–2007) entered Harvard as a freshman in the fall of 1939, the end of our time frame, and in some ways he marks the end of a generation of Hooton's students in anthropometry. Garn finished his A.B. in 1943 and then continued as a graduate student, doing work for the U.S. Army Quartermaster Corps under the supervision of Hooton and John M. Andrews. After the war he conducted studies of hair, nutrition, coronary disease, and dental malocclusions for the Peabody Museum and the Forsyth Dental Infirmary for Children, in Boston (Scott 1948:308, 311, 312), receiving his A.M. in 1947 and his Ph.D. in 1948 ("Human Hair: Its Composition, Anatomy and Distribution"). He continued working for the anthropology department and the Forsyth Dental Infirmary until 1952, when he took a job with the Fels Research Institute in Yellow Springs, Ohio, doing studies of human growth. There he became one of the principal founders of the field of dental anthropology. He moved to the University of Michigan's Center for Human Growth and Development in 1968 and taught there for much of his career. Garn was a prolific researcher, with more than 350 publications on his résumé.

Some of Hooton's students, as happens with every professor, went in other directions after completing their academic training. **John Knox Bodel Jr.** (1906–86) entered graduate school in 1938, spent the summer of 1939 working on "Problems in the Archaeology of Palestine, Syria, Mesopotamia, and the Indus Valley" with Gabriel Lasker, Walter Taylor, Paul Gebhard, and Frances Hammond, and afterward worked up a paper on the basis of the research titled "Condylo-diaphysial Angle of the Humerus" (Scott 1940:456, 458). Bodel finished his A.M. in 1940 and seemingly took a break to recoup financially, going to teach at the Hotchkiss School in Lakeville, Connecticut. After a break for his war duties, he came back to Harvard to complete his Ph.D. in 1951, with the dissertation "Distribution and Permanence of Body Build in Adolescent Boys," but he then returned to Hotchkiss School to teach for the next two decades.

Norman Emil Gabel (1903–97?) was a Michigan undergraduate, a member of the class of 1928. He entered graduate school at the University of Arizona, received his A.M. there in 1933, and then came to Harvard, where he earned his Ph.D. in 1941 ("A Comparative Racial Study of the Papago"). In 1938 Emil Haury recruited him to teach in the anthropology department at Arizona, which he did for a few years, carrying out comparative racial studies of Papago and Apache Indians. After the war Gabel took a job at the University of California–Santa Barbara. While there he worked on anthropometric studies of Fiji Islanders well into the 1960s, but he seems to have published little in anthropology after the 1940s.

The late 1930s were a high point in Hooton's research and his production of new Ph.D.s. His lab attracted numerous students and visiting professionals, and he conducted anthropometric analyses for American institutions such as the AMNH and the USNM and for foreign institutions as well. For example, in 1934 the lab generated the analysis "Anthropometric Data on Tribes of Asiatic Russia" for Boris N. Vishniefsky of the Museum of Archaeology and Ethnography in Leningrad (Scott 1935:312).

Apparently, the Statistical and Anthropometric Laboratory was also generating access to enough funds for Hooton to support his students in collecting anthropometric data around the world. One of his financial angels was **John Charles Phillips** (1875–1938), a member of the Peabody's "museum faculty" from 1931 to 1938 (and no relation to Philip Phillips). John Phillips had received his S.B. from Harvard in 1899 and his M.D. in 1904. His travels allowed him to secure ethnographic materials from Mexico and Central America, the Great Plains, the Arctic, and North Africa, with his first donations to the Peabody Museum coming in 1907 (Putnam 1909:302). He also made numerous donations to the MCZ, where he was associate curator of birds for many years, beginning in 1912. He taught at the Harvard Medical School and was named chief surgeon there in 1916.

Phillips's most important contributions to the Peabody Museum came later in his life, after he was named a member of the Peabody Museum Visiting Committee. In that position he was responsible in 1924 for raising a good part of the money needed to finish the fourth floor of the museum, including what was to become Hooton's statistical lab, and for increasing the research funding for fieldwork (Willoughby 1926:251, 253). In 1929–30 he provided the funds for Gordon Bowles to collect anthropometry data on Harvard fathers and sons (Reynolds 1930:274). Edward Reynolds had Phillips named to the museum faculty in 1931, a position he held until his death in 1938, when he was replaced by A.V. Kidder (Scott 1940:447). Phillips maintained an active interest in Hooton's anthropometric studies while he served as a museum faculty member.

In the third field, sociocultural anthropology or ethnography, although some students were being trained at Harvard three decades earlier, the real expansion came in the 1930s. Earlier, Roland Dixon had held the primary responsibility for sociocultural anthropology, after his appointment to the Department of Anthropology faculty in 1900. But over the years he became increasingly focused on his own research and less engaged in training graduate students. It was not until Harvard hired Lloyd Warner, in 1929, and then Clyde Kluckhohn, in 1935, that graduate training in sociocultural anthropology flourished. In some ways it may be seen as having developed around two research centers—Warner's industrial physiology research at Newburyport, Massachusetts—part of the applied sociocultural anthropology training curriculum—and Kluckhohn's Navajo ethnographic research, which we detail shortly.

Although Warner began teaching at the Peabody in the 1929–30 academic year, he was still working on his Ph.D.—something he apparently never acquired—which may initially have handicapped his ability to recruit students. Antecedent to or contemporary with Warner were some occasional researchers in sociocultural anthropology who went out on solitary research projects under Dixon's guidance rather than working as part of larger research programs. We look at these people first, before turning to Warner, Kluckhohn, and their students.

John Berdan Charlesworth (1888–1932), a graduate of Cambridge University, was named a research associate in African ethnology at the Peabody Museum in 1930, with funding for fieldwork, analysis, and publication of his work on Bantu people in Tanganyika (Reynolds 1931a:284, 1932:295). After two years studying the Basukuma Bantus in the field, however, he contracted blackwater fever and died of the disease at sea on his way back to the United States for treatment (Anonymous 1932).

John Philip Gillin (1907–73) did his initial training in sociology at the University of Wisconsin, where he received an A.B. in 1927. After a short period of training in Europe, he returned to Wisconsin to work on an A.M. But after taking anthropology courses from Ralph Linton there, he switched to anthropology, completing his A.M. in 1930 (Reina 1976:80). During the summer before he received his degree, he also took some archaeological training with Alonso Pond, from Beloit, and worked in the Laboratory of Anthropology's summer field training program in Santa Fe, New Mexico (R. Woodbury 1993:117).

Gillin then came to Harvard, where he received his second A.M. in 1932. That summer he was sent for an eight-month project working with Caribs in British Guiana. The Peabody had been contacted by Sir Edward Durham, governor of the then colony, inviting the museum to send some researchers to work there (Scott 1933:300, 1934:298). Gillin finished his Ph.D. dissertation, "The Barama River Caribs of British Guiana," in 1936, teaching at Sarah Lawrence that year to support his writing. He continued working for the Peabody Museum as well, and after receiving his degree, he and his wife undertook a trip to Ecuador on behalf of the museum, to collect ethnographic and anthropomorphic data (Scott 1936:318, 1937:346).

Following this research, Gillin was hired at the University of Utah, where he became involved in doing archaeological excavations at 37 sites, assisted by John Longyear from the Peabody (Scott 1938:358). The summaries of this project were published in two reports (Gillin and Anderson 1938; Gillin and Allen 1941), one co-authored with Gillin's colleague Robert Anderson (1914–?) at the University of Utah and the other with **Glover Morrill Allen** (1879–1942), a member of the Harvard class of 1901 who held a Ph.D. in biology from Harvard. Allen was a curator at the MCZ, taught zoology at Harvard College, and had a longtime peripheral interest in zooarchaeology. He helped Alfred Tozzer identify animal figures in Maya codices (Tozzer and Glover 1910), served as Sherwood Washburn's senior honors advisor in 1934–35 (Howell 2003:4), and analyzed the canid remains from Pueblo Bonito for Neil Judd. He also did the analysis of the animal bones for Gillin on his Utah project.

Clearly, Gillin continued his earlier archaeological interest during the time he was at Utah. In 1942 he returned to the field of his doctoral work, ethnography, when he moved from the University of Utah to Duke University. Almost immediately, however, he was enrolled in work for the war effort, assigned to the Board of Economic Welfare, working in Peru. In 1944 he was shifted to the Institute of Social Anthropology of the Smithsonian Institution and did an excellent ethnography of Pueblo Moche, near Trujillo, Peru. After the war, in 1946, Gillin left Duke to take a job at the University of North Carolina–Chapel Hill. He left there in 1959 to become dean of social sciences at the University of Pittsburgh, a position he kept until 1972, when he retired because of ill health (Reina 1976:81–83, 86). Gillin was a well-known specialist in Latin American ethnography and served terms as president of the Society for Applied Anthropology as well as the AAA.

Owen Lattimore (1900–1989) was another of the "lone scholars," as it were. He was born in Washington, D.C., but raised in China, where his parents were expatriate workers. He spoke fluent Chinese and was deeply familiar with the country; Chiang Kai Shek was a personal acquaintance. After secondary school, Lattimore worked in China for five years as a businessman and journalist before turning to exploration and field research (Kahin 1989:945). He came to study at Harvard for one year. The Peabody then named him a fellow at the Harvard-Yenching Institute in 1930–31 and sent him to China to collect materials for the museum (Scott 1931:283).

Lattimore finished no graduate work beyond this one year. He was named director of the Johns Hopkins Page School of International Relations from 1939 until 1950, when, because of his linkages with China, Senator Joseph McCarthy accused him of being a Communist spy, which caused him to lose his job.

Anthropology at Harvard was consistently linked to Chinese studies. The linkage involved not only Euro-American students studying in China but also Chinese students themselves. In archaeology, we have already mentioned Cheng Te-k'un, and in discussing female students, we identified the work of Hsien Chin Hu in sociocultural anthropology. There were also male students in sociocultural anthropology, such as Han Yi Feng and Yueh-Hwa Lin.

Han Yi (Han-chi) Feng (1899–1977) was born in I-chang, China, and attended West China Union University in Szechuan. Feng likely was influenced to come to Harvard by David Graham and William Morse of that university, who were just being engaged as research associates at the Peabody Museum in the early 1930s. Feng was in the graduate program at Harvard from 1931 to 1933 (National Research Council 1938:257). He then shifted his enrollment to the University of Pennsylvania, where he received his A.M. in 1934 and his Ph.D. in 1936, with a dissertation titled "The Chinese Kinship System." Between 1935 and 1937 Feng was also a fellow of the Harvard-Yenching Institute. In 1936 he returned to West China Union University, where his research focused primarily on the ethnology and secondarily on the archaeology of Northeast Asia (Herskovits and Ames 1950:54).

Yueh-Hwa (Yaohua) Lin (1910–2000) was born in Gutian, Fukien (Fuijan) Province, China. He attended Yenching (Yanjing) University in Peking, where he received his A.B. in 1932 and his A.M. in 1935. He entered the graduate program at the Peabody Museum in 1937 and continued his studies there, receiving his Ph.D. ("The Miao-Man Peoples of Kweichow") in 1940. He returned to Yenching University in 1941 and became chair of the Department of Sociology until 1952. That year he moved to Central Nationalities University in Beijing and established the first department of anthropology there. Lin's focus was on general ethnology and applied anthropology in Yunnan, Sichuan, and Tibet (Reshetov 1991).

The arrival of W. Lloyd Warner brought to the Harvard anthropology department the first major, multiperson research projects in applied sociocultural anthropology. These projects were developed in conjunction with Elton Mayo (1880–1949), of the Harvard Graduate School of Business Administration, and its Committee on Industrial Physiology. One was a study of the town of Newburyport, Massachusetts, and its shoe factory (Patterson 2001:73–74). Officially called the "Social Anthropological Survey of Newburyport," it was conducted from 1931 to 1934 and became known as the Yankee City project. The second was a study of Penn Craft, a cooperative community developed by the American Friends Service Committee for unemployed coal miners in a depressed area of western Pennsylvania. The third, begun in 1934 and continued until Warner moved to the University of Chicago in 1935, was titled "Class in the Deep South: Anthropo-Social Studies of a Mississippi Community." Conducted in Natchez, Mississippi, it was popularly known just as "Deep South." A significant number of Harvard students received their graduate training partly through these research projects.

William Lloyd Warner (1898–1970) received his A.B. from the University of California–Berkeley in 1925 and began graduate work there with A. L. Kroeber, conducting field research in Arnhem Land, Australia, from 1926 to 1929. He came to Harvard in 1929 with an instructorship in the Department of Anthropology, intending to write up his Arnhem Land research for his dissertation, a goal he apparently never realized (Warner 1988:49). He was initially funded by a Laura Spelman Rockefeller Memorial Fellowship through Harvard's Graduate School of Business Administration, because the business school's Elton Mayo (1880–1949) enlisted Warner to help him with a project called the Western Electric Hawthorne study. Mayo was cofounder of Harvard's Committee on Industrial Physiology, which was funded by Laura Spelman Rockefeller Memorial monies.

After the Western Electric Hawthorne concluded, Warner was involved during the rest of his six years at Harvard with three major team research projects: the Newburyport–Yankee City, Penn Craft, and Deep South projects. For the Yankee City study, Warner helped set up Eliot Chapple as the field director. Among the other graduate students in social anthropology who worked on this project were Conrad Arensberg, Allison Davis, Burleigh Gardner, Solon Kimball, Josiah Low, and Leo Srole. J. O. Brew and Paul Sanborn Lunt were also employed on the project for short periods (Patterson 2001:99; Warner 1998:50). Warner oversaw the completion of the doctoral work by Chapple, Arensberg, Gardner, and Kimball.

In 1932 Warner took Arensberg and Kimball with him to Ireland to join the Irish project of Hallam Movius and Hugh Hencken, doing the social anthropology. Both Arensberg and Kimball had received training through the Newburyport project, and they ran a similar set of observations in Ireland from 1932 until 1934, aided by Amory Goddard and Frederick Richardson. In 1933 Warner sent Burleigh Gardner and Allison Davis to work on the Deep South project in Natchez, Mississippi (Scott 1934:300).

In 1935 it became apparent that because of his lack of a doctoral degree, Warner could not stay at Harvard. The department began searching for a social anthropologist with a Ph.D. in hand, and after it hired Clyde Kluckhohn, Earnest Hooton helped convince Warner to move to the University of Chicago (Warner 1988:113). Warner was then at Chicago from 1935 until 1959 and subsequently at Michigan State until his death in 1970. When he moved to Chicago in 1935, he took with him two students, Eliot Davis and Leo Srole, who had begun their work at Harvard and finished it with him at Chicago. There Warner co-founded the university's Committee on Industrial Relations, the aegis under which Davis and Srole finished their degrees.

The young man whom Warner put in charge of the Newburyport fieldwork, **Eliot Dismore Chapple** (1909–2000), had received his A.B. from Harvard in 1931. He became Warner's first Ph.D. student at Harvard, finishing his degree in 1933 with the dissertation "The Theory of Association as Applied to Primitive and Civilized Communities, with Special Emphasis upon the Functional Approach," derived from his Newburyport research. Chapple was associated primarily with Harvard's Graduate School of Business Administration, where he was an instructor in social anthropology and research assistant for the Committee on Industrial Physiology from 1931 until 1939. He also co-taught courses at the Peabody Museum with instructors including Arensberg, Coon, Hooton, Kluckhohn, and Ward. He then shifted to the Harvard Medical School from

1940 to 1945, and in 1946 he set up his own consulting firm, E. D. Chapple Company (Herskovits and Ames 1950:30).

Eliot Chapple had been assigned the field directorship of the Newburyport project partly because his family lived in Salem, Massachusetts, so he had some personal knowledge of the area (Warner 1988:50). Later, using the Newburyport model, Chapple helped Frederick Richardson set up his research at the Penn Craft resettlement program in western Pennsylvania through the social anthropology program of the Graduate School of Business Administration at Harvard (Harvard University 1940:273). When Chapple moved on to the medical school, he arranged for Richardson to take over his position at the business school.

Warner's second Ph.D. was **Conrad Maynadier Arensberg** (1910–97). Arensberg had become interested in anthropology through family connections in Pittsburgh. The poet and art collector Walter Conrad Arensberg, Harvard class of 1900, a brother or cousin of our Arensberg's father, Charles F. C. Arensberg, had been one of the first members of the Harvard anthropology club (see chapter 7), and Conrad followed this family interest.

Conrad Arensberg, like Eliot Chapple, was a member of the Harvard class of 1931 and continued in graduate work at the Peabody. During his senior year and his first year of graduate school, 1931–32, Arensberg worked on the Newburyport project with Chapple, under Warner's direction. The next summer Warner took Arensberg and Solon Kimball to County Clare, Ireland, to conduct sociological research for the ongoing project run by Hencken and Movius. Arensberg continued research there in 1932 and 1933, writing it up as his 1934 Ph.D. dissertation, "A Study of Rural Life in Ireland as Determined by the Functions and Morphology of the Family."

Arensberg was then appointed a junior fellow at Harvard, from 1934 to 1938. During that time he taught social anthropology courses with Kluckhohn and Chapple and continued his research in Ireland with Kimball (Harvard University 1938; Scott 1937:340). In 1938 he secured a position in the Department of Social Sciences and Economics at MIT. In 1941 he became chair of the Department of Sociology and Anthropology at Brooklyn College, a job he held until 1943, when he left to become a military intelligence officer in the war. After the war, in 1946, he secured the position of chair of the Department of Sociology at Barnard College, Columbia University, moving to the Department of Anthropology at Columbia in 1952. He taught social anthropology there until his retirement in 1979.

Warner's third and fourth Ph.D.s at Harvard were Burleigh Gardner and Solon Kimball, both of whom received their degrees just after Warner moved to Chicago. **Burleigh Bradford Gardner** (1902–88) received both his 1930 A.B. and his 1931 A.M. from the University of Texas before coming to Harvard. He was recruited by Warner to work with William Davis on the Deep South project in Mississippi (Scott 1934:300), which became the basis of his 1936 dissertation, "Race Relationships in a Mississippi Community." After receiving his Ph.D., Warner took a position as social anthropologist for the Soil Conservation Service in New Mexico. He subsequently published the results of the Deep South project with Davis and Warner (Davis et al. 1941) and went on to a successful career in industrial sociology.

Solon Toothaker Kimball (1909–82) was born in Manhattan, Kansas, and received his A.B. from Kansas State Agricultural College (now Kansas State University) in 1930. He then went to Harvard and was sent to the Laboratory of Anthropology's summer field training program in Santa Fe (R. Woodbury 1993:117). When he returned to Harvard, he worked under Chapple at Newburyport. After receiving his A.M. in 1933, he began field research with Arensberg in County Clare, Ireland, under Warner's guidance (Scott 1934:298). This work formed the basis of his dissertation, "The Tradesman and His Family in the Economic Structure of an Irish Town."

After receiving his Ph.D. in 1936, Kimball secured the position of chief of the Sociology Survey for the Navaho Service, U.S. Department of Agriculture, in Gallup, New Mexico, and worked on applied anthropological studies of the Navajo tribe from 1938 to 1942 with the Bureau of Indian Affairs. From 1942 to 1945 he worked for the federal government in the Community Organization section of the War Relocation Authority program, with 14 other anthropologists and 8 sociologists, under the direction of Edward H. Spicer (A. Moore 1984:386). He taught at Michigan State University from 1945 to 1948, the University of Alabama (where he was chair of the Department of Sociology) from 1948 until 1953, Columbia University from 1953 to 1966, and the University of Florida from 1966 to 1980, when he retired.

William Allison Davis (1902–83) was born in Virginia of ex-slave ancestors. He received his A.B. from Williams College in Massachusetts in 1924. He first entered graduate school at Harvard in the English department, receiving his A.M. in English and comparative literature in 1925. He taught English at Hampton College in Virginia for the next six years, from 1925 to 1931, but found the work unsatisfying (Browne 1999:171).

Davis decided to return to Harvard to study with Warner at the Peabody Museum, where he received his second A.M., in anthropology, in 1932. The following year Warner sent Davis to get some hands-on training in sociocultural anthropology on the Newburyport project with Eliot Chapple. Then, in 1934, Warner initiated his well-known Deep South project with funding from the Harvard Business School's Committee for Industrial Physiology. Warner sent Davis and Burleigh Gardner to Natchez to work on the project (Scott 1934:300, 1935:311).

Davis had not yet finished his degree work when Warner moved to the University of Chicago, and he decided to follow his dissertation advisor to Chicago to complete his Ph.D. Apparently, the anthropology department there lacked funds to support him, so Davis taught social anthropology at Dillard University in New Orleans from 1935 to 1939 while doing his graduate work. Then, from 1939 to 1942, he worked at Atlanta University, first at its Center for Child Development and later as head of the Department of Education.

Davis finally received his Ph.D., with a dissertation titled "The Relation between Color Caste and Economic Stratification in Two 'Black' Plantation Counties," from the University of Chicago in 1942. A good portion of his dissertation had been published the year before, with Gardner and Warner, as *Deep South: A Social Anthropological Study of Caste and Class* (Davis et al. 1941). After receiving his degree, Davis immediately accepted an appointment in the Department of Education at the University of Chicago, where he taught until he retired. In 1948 he became the first African American tenured professor at Chicago (Browne 1999:172). While there, he developed the well-known "Davis-Ellis intelligence test" for children. His accomplishments in education were of such significance to his field that they were recognized in a commemorative 29-cent U.S. postage stamp bearing his image in 1994.

Leo Srole (1908–93) received his S.B. from Harvard in 1933, and he, too, entered the graduate program at the Peabody to study with Warner. Under Warner's supervision, he went to work with Chapple at Newburyport (Scott 1935:311), and in 1935 he transferred to Chicago to finish his dissertation work with Warner. Srole received his Ph.D. from Chicago in 1940, after defending a dissertation titled "Ethnic Groups and American Society: A Study of Dynamics of Social Stratification." He continued working along the lines of Warner's research, later conducting a major team project on social psychiatry, the Midtown Manhattan project.

Josiah Orne Low (1879–1956) was another person whom Warner recruited to work on the Newburyport project. He had received his S.B. from Harvard in 1902, gone into the securities business, and sold out before the 1929 crash. He then returned to Harvard, and although he did not officially enroll in the graduate program, he joined the Newburyport project in 1931 (Warner 1988:109). When Warner moved to the University of Chicago, Low moved with him. Low, near retirement age, apparently had no desire to complete a degree, but while he was at Chicago, he and Warner published the 1947 volume *The Social Systems of the Modern Factory: The Strike—A Social Analysis*.

Frederick Leopold William Richardson Jr. (1908–98) received his S.B. in geology from Harvard in 1931 and entered the anthropology graduate program in 1933. After obtaining his S.B., he excavated at the site of Ur from 1931 to 1933 with the University of Pennsylvania Museum, conducting a study of irrigation systems of southern Iraq in 1933. This apparently piqued his interest in social anthropology, and he entered Harvard in that field rather than archaeology. Warner then sent him to work in Ireland in 1934 with Kimball and Arensberg.

After Warner left Harvard, Richardson became Chapple's student. Through the social anthropology program of the Graduate School of Business Administration, Richardson began studying the Penn Craft resettlement program in western Pennsylvania in 1938 (Harvard University 1940:273). This work culminated in his 1941 Ph.D. dissertation, "An Anthropological and Geographical Approach to a Resettlement Problem in the Pennsylvania Coal Region."

Immediately upon finishing his Ph.D., Richardson was appointed a research associate of the Department of Industrial Research of the Harvard Business School. From 1942 to 1945 he was granted academic leave to serve in the war effort, and he worked on the Lend-Lease program. After the war he taught at Yale from 1946 to 1949 and then returned to Harvard, to the School of Public Health, from 1949 to 1954. He later worked in joint business school–anthropology programs, first at the University of Pittsburgh from 1962 to 1966 and then at the University of Virginia from 1966 to 1980. The bulk of his research was in applied anthropology.

Another of Chapple's students was **Charles Ford Harding III** (1915–94), who received his A.B. in 1938. He completed his Ph.D. dissertation, "Simultaneous Measures of Human Relations and Emotional Response," in 1940 and then published it with Chapple in *Proceedings of the National Academy of Sciences*. After he finished his dissertation, Harding assisted Chapple in a brain wave study (Scott 1941:433) but then, finding no job, went home to Winnetka, Illinois. He completed a law degree at the University of Chicago in 1943 but maintained an interest in anthropology and continued to publish occasionally on the social anthropology and applied anthropology of North American Indians.

The replacement of Lloyd Warner by Clyde Kluckhohn signaled a major change in the direction of sociocultural anthropology at Harvard. The emphasis now shifted away from Warner's interests in urban sociology and applied anthropology and returned to indigenous ethnography and anthropological theory.

Clyde Kay Maben Kluckhohn (1905–60) had been born in Le Mars, Iowa. He started college at Princeton, but because of an illness during his freshman year, he left Princeton and went to recuperate at a ranch near Ramah, New Mexico. There he began to study the Navajos' culture and language (Parsons and Vogt 1962:141). After regaining his health, he finished his A.B. at Wisconsin in 1928. He then went to study at Vienna in 1931–32 and at Oxford, as a Rhodes Scholar, in 1932. At Oxford he received a second A.B. Later in 1932 he accepted the position of assistant professor of anthropology at the University of New Mexico, where he taught until 1934. While at New Mexico, he also finished up the work required for his A.M. at Oxford, and he received that degree in 1934.

Kluckhohn applied to Harvard in 1935 and both entered graduate school and was appointed an instructor in the Department of Anthropology that year. He completed his Ph.D. dissertation, "Some Aspects of Contemporary Theory in Social Anthropology," at Harvard in 1936 and was immediately appointed an assistant professor and curator of Southwestern ethnology at the Peabody. He served in World War II, helping to set up the Office of War Information in Washington, D.C., in 1943–44. Upon his return to Harvard, he was promoted to full professor in 1946. He served as chair of the Department of Anthropology from 1957 to 1960 (Parsons and Vogt 1962:146).

In 1936, as soon as he completed his Ph.D., Kluckhohn initiated a multiyear project with the Navajos at Ramah, an interest that consumed 37 years of his life as an anthropologist. This program also began his long-term interest in a theory of culture and his focus on values. His research took him in an "anti-Boasian" direction. Kluckhohn wrote of the dangers of unbounded cultural relativism and looked, rather, for universals in human culture. Although he is generally thought of as a social anthropologist, he was in fact an old-fashioned general anthropologist. That is, he was interested in all of anthropology, including archaeology and physical anthropology.

Although the Navajos were his first interest, he also was much interested in Central and East Asian cultures. He served as an advisor to General MacArthur's headquarters in Japan, where he worked with John Pelzel, and he helped found the Russian Research Center at Harvard and served as its director in 1947–48 (during which time he was also serving as president of the AAA).

The work of the new sociocultural students in the department reflected Kluckhohn's interests—the Navajo people and a return to ethnography. But Kluckhohn encouraged solid field research anywhere and had students also working in areas such as Peru, Oceania, and East Asia. And his interest in theory cut across disciplinary lines. History of science scholars studying the work of Walter Taylor, one of Kluckhohn's advisees, have all remarked on Kluckhohn's influence on Taylor's conjunctive approach and his critical assessment of the lack of theory in the archaeology of his day.

Because Kluckhohn began his program with the Navajos near the end of the time frame for our discussion, some of the students we mention in what follows had barely begun their research with him in the late 1930s; their most significant anthropological training and contributions came later. We offer brief commentaries on these people but have curtailed the description of their careers.

David Friend Aberle (1918–2004) entered Harvard in 1936 and received his A.B. in 1940. He spent the next year in graduate studies at Columbia but returned to collect Navajo recreational information for Kluckhohn the next field season (Scott 1943:455). After serving in the war, he returned to Harvard as a graduate student in 1946–47 and was named an instructor in "social relations" in 1947, at the same time reactivating his graduate status at Columbia, where he received his Ph.D. in 1950. After various positions at Harvard, Johns Hopkins, Michigan, Manchester University, Brandeis, and Oregon, Aberle moved to the University of British Columbia in 1967, retiring from teaching in 1983. He is best known for his Navajo and Southwestern work, research that began with Kluckhohn and continued throughout his life.

John Leslie Landgraf (1914–84) was a fellow graduate student of Aberle's at Columbia. His association with Kluckhohn is a bit late for our time frame, but we include him as a part of the general picture. He worked in the summer of 1941 mapping the physical environment of the Ramah Navajos in New Mexico, and for the academic year of 1941–42 he was Kluckhohn's research assistant on the Navajo project.

He completed his Ph.D. at Columbia in 1951 on land use by the Ramah Navajos. He then changed careers, moving from anthropology to become a director of the GRE testing service.

Kenneth D. MacLeish (1917–77) received his A.B. from Harvard in 1938. He had spent the summer of 1937 excavating at Awatovi with J. O. Brew and then entered the graduate program in 1938, spending the next season working for Kluckhohn on the linguistics and ethnology of the Moenkopi Hopis, the basis of his 1940 A.M. thesis (Scott 1940:455). MacLeish then went to work doing applied anthropology for the Bureau of Agricultural Economics of the U.S. Department of Agriculture. Following the war, he worked for a period as a journalist before becoming an editor at *National Geographic* in 1956, a position he kept until his death.

Roy Lynden Malcolm (1913–91) was one of Kluckhohn's early graduate students, registered in the graduate program from 1936 to 1938. He did research on pottery and housing types among the contemporary Navajo residents of Chaco Canyon, New Mexico (Scott 1939:410), publishing an article on the topic in *American Antiquity* (Malcolm 1939). After leaving the graduate program at Harvard without receiving a degree, he went to work for the Southwest Museum in Los Angeles. He served in naval intelligence during World War II and after the war worked in the reconstruction in Japan with some of his Harvard classmates.

Yet another graduate student of Kluckhohn's with a Southwestern focus was **William Henderson Kelly** (1902–1980). Kelly received his A.B. from the University of Arizona in 1936 before entering Harvard. He became a research fellow in Southwestern ethnology, working with Kluckhohn, in 1941 (Scott 1943:453), received his A.M. from Harvard in 1942, and continued work in northern Mexico, receiving his Ph.D. in 1944 ("A Preliminary Study of the Cocopa Indians of Mexico with an Analysis of the Influence of Geographic Position and Physical Environment on Certain Aspects of Their Culture"). Kelly stayed on for the next few years as an instructor in anthropology at Harvard, but in 1947 he returned to the University of Arizona, where he continued a career dealing with applied anthropology in the Southwest. He retired in 1966.

Leland Clifton Wyman (1897–1988), born in Livermore Falls, Maine, was another Harvard graduate who, after a career elsewhere, returned to anthropology. Wyman received his A.B. from Bowdoin College in 1918. He then volunteered for service in World War I, spending 1918–19 serving at Walter Reed Hospital. Released from war duties, he entered graduate school at Harvard in 1919 and completed his Ph.D. in zoology ("The Physiology of Vertebrate Melanosphores") in 1923. He was hired as a professor of physiology at the Boston University School of Medicine and Massachusetts General Hospital in 1922 and kept that job until his retirement in 1962.

Leland Wyman became interested in ethnoentomology and ethnobotany in the U.S. Southwest and developed a "second career in Navajo studies" in the late 1920s (McAllester 1989). He met with Charles Amsden to secure help with some of the prehistoric Navajo textile samples he had collected. Wyman began offering a course on Southwestern Indian cultures at Boston University in the early 1930s, when he could do so outside his duties at the medical school (McAllester 1982:7).

In 1932, Clyde Kluckhohn, then director of the University of New Mexico summer field school, asked Wyman to teach physiological anthropology there, which he did for three seasons. Later in the 1930s, after Kluckhohn moved to Harvard, Wyman and Kluckhohn collaborated on a series of reports on Navajo ceremonies and rituals. After his retirement in 1962, Wyman worked for the University of New Mexico, continuing his research on the Navajos, and amassed one of the major extant collections of Navajo sand paintings, with a catalogue of 1,469 items (McAllester 1989).

Harry Schlessinger Tschopik Jr. (1915–56) was another of Kluckhohn's graduate students recruited initially for the Navajo project. He later pursued an interest in Andean ethnography. Tschopik was born in New Orleans and had become interested in archaeology during his high school years (Rowe 1958:132). He began college at Tulane in 1932 but transferred to Berkeley in 1934. He continued his archaeological interests there, doing fieldwork in the Sacramento Valley with Waldo Wedel, and received his A.B. from Berkeley in 1936.

Tschopik entered Harvard intending to pursue archaeological research in the eastern United States or Central America, but during his first summer Kluckhohn recruited him to do Navajo ethnographic work at Ramah. Tschopik found this much more fulfilling and shifted his concentration from archaeology to ethnography. During the next two seasons he focused on Navajo material culture, particularly pottery and basketry (Scott 1939:410, 1940:457), and on the basis of this work received his A.M. in 1940.

With his degree in hand, Harry Tschopik and his new wife, Marion, whom we profiled earlier in this chapter, received a two-and-a-half-year grant from the Institute of Andean Research to conduct work in the central Andes. Because Alfred Kidder II was working in Pucara at the time, the Tschopiks went to Peru with him and focused on the Aymara peoples in the Puno region, near Pucara (Scott 1941:429, 1942:427).

In 1942 Tschopik joined the war effort and was stationed in Peru with the OSS (J. Rowe 1958:135). Following the war he took a position for the 1945–46 year with the Institute of Social Anthropology of the Smithsonian Institution, working in Peru. He conducted ethnographic studies at Sicaya and Huancayo, Junin, and also, returning to his former interest in archaeology, excavated two caves near Chupaca, Junin (J. Rowe 1958:134). He returned to Harvard in late 1946 to begin writing up his dissertation, "The Function of Magic in an Aymara Indian Community," under Kluckhohn. In March 1947 he was offered a curator's job at the AMNH, replacing Clark Wissler, who had just retired. Tschopik served as curator of North and South American ethnology at the AMNH from 1947 until he died in 1956, also teaching part-time at Columbia University from 1949 until 1951. He finished his Harvard Ph.D. in 1951, while working at the AMNH. Tschopik had a series of ethnographic projects in progress when he unexpectedly died.

Clyde Kluckhohn had graduate students carrying out research not only in the Americas but also in Oceania and Asia. A few students had begun ethnographic research in Asia or Oceania in the 1930s even before Kluckhohn arrived, most likely under Roland Dixon's influence. Moreover, Kluckhohn had a peer and colleague, Douglas Oliver, on the Peabody staff who specialized in Pacific Island ethnology.

Douglas Llewellyn Oliver (1913–2009), a native of Rushton, Louisiana, was likely recruited into anthropology when he was one of three Boy Scouts selected in 1923 to go on a safari in Kenya and what was then Rhodesia, now Zimbabwe, funded by George Palmer Putnam's *Boys' Books by Boys* series. While on this safari, Oliver took pictures of African natives and their daily life settings, handing out Boy Scout buttons on one occasion as payment for permission to take photographs (Douglas, Martin, and Oliver 1928:16, 50).

Oliver entered Harvard, where he received his A.B. in 1934, and then went to Vienna for graduate work, eventually receiving his Ph.D. there in 1941. In the meantime, he returned to the Peabody just as Clyde Kluckhohn arrived, in 1935. But whereas Kluckhohn was immediately cycled into teaching responsibilities, Oliver had a museum appointment and so had the luxury of doing full-time research until he assumed teaching responsibilities 12 years later. The Peabody Museum had received a generous grant from Cornelius Crane to fund research in New Guinea, and Oliver began preparing for that project (Scott 1938:354). Because of political problems, the expedition was unable to enter New Guinea, so Oliver and his wife transferred the project to the village of Siwai in Bougainville, where they arrived in the fall of 1937. They stayed there doing research until returning to Harvard in the spring of 1940 (Scott 1940:449).

During the war Oliver worked for the "United States Commercial Company," an OSS cover entity, in the Pacific, as did Philip Phillips (Munro 2006:33). When he returned to Harvard in 1948 he had a teaching post and taught in the anthropology department for the next quarter century. During this time he was also curator of Oceanic ethnology for the Peabody Museum. Oliver initially maintained some linkages with the U.S. government, serving as special assistant for Far Eastern affairs for the Department of State in 1948–49.

During his last few years at Harvard, from 1969 to 1973, Oliver served half-time for Harvard and half-time as the newly appointed Pacific Islands chair in anthropology at the University of Hawaii. He shifted to full-time teaching at Hawaii after he left Harvard in 1973, until he retired in 1978. Oliver was extremely well respected for his expertise in Oceania and continued to write on Pacific Island ethnology into the early twenty-first century.

Richard Lauriston Sharp (1907–93), born in Madison, Wisconsin, was a student who entered the Ph.D. program at Harvard in 1931, no doubt to study with Dixon. The son of a University of Wisconsin philosophy professor, Sharp completed his own A.B. in philosophy there in 1929. But as an undergraduate he made several summer trips to archaeological sites in the Southwest (Kirsch 1994:1358), and from 1929 to 1931 he studied Southeast Asian ethnology in Vienna, before enrolling at Harvard. Through the Australian National Research Council, the Peabody Museum received a three-year grant for Sharp to conduct fieldwork in the ethnology of Australian tribes in Queensland. He left for Australia after completing his A.M. in 1932 and returned in January 1936. With a dissertation titled "The Social Anthropology of a Totemic System in North Queensland, Australia," he received his Ph.D in 1937 (Scott 1935:312, 1937:345).

Sharp then accepted a position teaching anthropology at Cornell and remained there until 1956, when he moved to the University of Washington. During World War II he was granted leave and worked for the State Department in its Southeast Asian Affairs section. This work influenced Sharp to shift his area of research from Australia to Thailand after the war.

John Campbell Pelzel (1914–99) was born in Philadelphia but moved with his family to Korea in 1918 and did not return to the United States until 1931. He entered the University of Chicago, received his A.B. in 1935, and then enrolled at Harvard for graduate work. He may initially have had an interest in Mexico, for he conducted an "exhaustive" study of Mexican manuscripts in 1936 (Scott 1937:345). But he then pursued an interest in Asia. He was one of a half dozen students who went with Cheng Te-k'un to conduct archaeological work in Siberia, Manchuria, China, Japan, and Southeast Asia in 1940 (Scott 1941:432), and he completed his A.M. at Harvard in 1941.

Pelzel then was called to military service and rose to the rank of major in the U.S. Marine Corps by the end of the war. He was at Harvard briefly after the war, to begin work on problems of stratification and association in modern Japanese society, but soon he was recalled to Japan to help General MacArthur with reconstruction efforts there, becoming chief of the Public Opinion and Sociological Research Division (Ko 2003:193; Scott 1948:311, 317). Pelzel completed his Ph.D. dissertation, "Social Stratification in Japanese Urban Economic Life," in 1950 and began his teaching career at Harvard, in linguistics and cultural anthropology. He also served as curator of Far Eastern ethnology for the Peabody Museum. Between 1964 and 1977 he apparently returned to Japan and Korea to conduct applied anthropology projects, and he also served as director of the Harvard-Yenching Institute during the 1970s. In 1977 he returned to Harvard as a professor of "assistance and experimentation," and for a decade after he retired in 1979 he served as a consultant to the American military on Japanese affairs. He moved to Arizona at that time.

Paul King Benedict (1912–77) was born in Poughkeepsie, New York. He received his A.B. in 1934 from the University of New Mexico, where he had become involved in both archaeology and cultural anthropology. While at New Mexico, he had met Clyde Kluckhohn in 1932. When Kluckhohn took his new teaching position at Harvard in 1935, Benedict followed him, enrolling in the graduate program that fall (Blust 1998:2). He received his A.M. at Harvard in 1936 and went for a year of fieldwork in Southeast Asia in 1937–38 for his Ph.D. research. When he returned, A. L. Kroeber hired him to supervise his "Sino-Tibetan Philology Project" at Berkeley, funded by the Works

Progress Administration, and Benedict spent 1938 to 1940 working there. He returned to Harvard in 1940 and completed his Ph.D. ("Kinship of Southeast Asia") in 1941.

Benedict then decided he was interested in psychiatry and entered the New York Medical School at Columbia University in 1941. The war soon intervened, and he worked for the OSS in East Asia from 1942 through 1944 (Blust 1998:4). Following the war he worked for the U.S. Public Health Service while completing his medical training, and he received his M.D. from New York Medical College in 1948. He was a practicing psychiatrist in New York from 1949 through 1966, when he returned to his interests in Oceanic and Asian anthropological linguistics. Most of his contributions in the field thus came in the later part of his life (Blust 1998).

Schuyler van Renesselaer Cammann (1912–91) entered the Peabody Museum graduate program in 1938 and received his A.M. in 1941 on the basis of research on the ethnology and Buddhist iconography of Tibet (Scott 1940:456). He continued in the graduate program through 1942, when he was called to the war. Afterward he was at the University of Pennsylvania for a time, before receiving his Ph.D. in the modern history of Tibet from Johns Hopkins in 1951. His career was mainly in history, but he did return to the Peabody to help found the Council of Old World Archaeology there in 1953.

Gordon MacGregor (1902–83) was born in Haverhill, Massachusetts, and went to Yale, where he received his A.B. in 1925. After a few years he decided to return to school and enrolled at Harvard in 1928 for his doctoral work. The first year he was supported by Hemenway Fellowship money. He worked during his first summer of graduate school on the Harvard-Penn Czech archaeological project, under the direction of Vladimir Fewkes and Robert Ehrich.

Once MacGregor fixed his research topic on Pacific-area ethnography, he obtained funds from the Bishop Museum in Hawaii for his work. He completed his Ph.D. dissertation, "The Western Diffusion of Polynesian Culture as Seen in the Tokelau Islands," in 1935. Jobs were scarce because of the Great Depression, and his first postdoctoral position was that of an archaeologist with the Egyptian Exploration Society. Although his early experience was in Old World archaeology and Oceanic ethnology, MacGregor devoted most of his career to applied anthropology in government agencies. From 1936 to 1949 he was an anthropologist with the Bureau of Indian Affairs, and he worked as an applied anthropologist for other federal agencies from then until he retired in 1966.

Not all the contributors to the anthropology program and the museum were students or anthropology faculty. Here we mention a few others—a curator, a collector, a financial supporter, and a member of the sociology faculty—who also made major contributions.

Frederick Rhodes Pleasants (1906–76) was a vital cog in keeping the Peabody Museum functioning smoothly during the 1930s and 1940s, although he has been little recognized. Born in Montclair, New Jersey, Pleasants received his A.B. from Princeton in 1930. He then studied at the Sorbonne before entering the Harvard graduate program in 1933, eventually receiving his A.M. in primitive art and museum studies in 1938. In 1933–34 he helped arrange an exhibit at the Fogg Art Museum of African and Oceanic materials lent by the Peabody. In 1936 he arranged a special Tercenary Exhibit of Peabody materials, including a map showing the locations of the 430 expeditions sent out by the Peabody Museum until that time (Scott 1937:339). In 1939 Pleasants began working with the archaeology of the Totonac culture of Mexico, on the basis of a 1935 collecting trip he had taken. But in 1940 he was hired as an assistant to the museum director and given the charge of reorganizing old exhibits and putting up new ones for the museum (Scott 1941:427, 1942:428). He left for war service in 1942 and returned to museum work after the war. While at the Peabody, Pleasants began writing a major paper, "Anthropological Museums: Their History and Functions" (Scott 1948:308, 311), apparently the basis of a Ph.D. dissertation that he never finished. He later worked at the Brooklyn Museum in the 1950s and taught at the University of Arizona in the 1960s.

Arthur Loveridge (1891–1980) was trained in England and worked in Kenya and Tanganyika (Tanzania) from 1914 to 1923 as a naturalist and museum curator. He came to the MCZ as a curator of herpetology in 1923 and worked there for the next three decades, until he retired in 1957. He provided assistance and collections to the Peabody Museum over much of that time as well. In 1930 he assisted his British compatriot and new Peabody Museum associate John Charlesworth with ethnological work in Tanganyika for the Peabody (Reynolds 1931a:283). In 1934, at the suggestion of Thomas Barbour (see chapter 10), Loveridge began officially collecting specimens for the Peabody Museum as well as the MCZ during his field expeditions in East Africa (Scott 1935:314). Over his lifetime, he made no fewer than five major collecting trips to Africa, bringing back significant ethnographic materials for the Peabody Museum each time.

Cornelius Crane (1905–62) was an important donor to the Peabody and other museums in the 1930s. He had become interested in Oceania while taking his friend Sidney Shurcliff and various Field Museum associates on a trip to the South Seas on his 148-foot yacht in 1928–29. He provided the funding for, among other things, Douglas Oliver's long-term work in Bougainville.

One other person involved in the training of social anthropologists at Harvard during this decade was **Carle Clark Zimmerman** (1897–1983), an associate professor of sociology at Harvard from 1934 to 1963. Not only did a number of students take Zimmerman's courses, but he also aided in some of their research projects. For example, he obtained the funds necessary for James Andrews to conduct a two-year research project in Thailand on economic, social, and medical issues (Scott 1936:320), and he materially assisted other students in similar ways.

By the decade from 1929 to 1939, the anthropology program at Harvard had reached a first phase of maturity. It encompassed approximately 30 graduate students each year, at least a quarter of whom were women. Female students regularly secured A.M. degrees, and members of the pioneering cohort were now beginning to obtain Ph.D.s. as well. Anthropology clearly had become a coeducational domain, and the number of female students was inexorably increasing.

A growing number of gifted foreign students was also coming to Harvard—from Europe, Asia, Africa, and Latin America—because of its developing reputation as one of the world's premier graduate training schools in anthropology. The scope of research by faculty and students had expanded to include ethnic groups from around the world: Australia, Japan, China, Oceania, Thailand, and India in the Pacific Rim; northern and sub-Saharan Africa; the Middle East; several European and Latin American countries; and the United States and Canada. Large, multiyear projects increased in frequency, including archaeological work in Ireland, Czechoslovakia, the U.S. Southwest, and the Maya area. In sociocultural anthropology the period started out with the big industrial sociology projects—Yankee City, Penn Craft, and Deep South—and ended with the long-term focus on the Navajos and other tribes of the Southwest by Kluckhohn and his students. In physical anthropology, Hooton's Statistical and Anthropometric Laboratory had become *the* place to conduct one's analyses in anthropometric studies. With the exception of anthropological linguistics, Harvard offered one of the strongest programs in the country and continued to train a new generation of innovative scholars.

By this time, too, the graduate student cohort had become a critical component of the educational experience. We have tried to show throughout this book that in order to understand the educational forces that affected students, one must look not just at lists of courses and professors but also at the peers with whom students interacted. Although the greatest numbers of graduate students at Harvard in the 1930s still concentrated in archaeology, they did not operate in a vacuum. A substantial number of graduate students now concentrated in biological and sociocultural anthropology, and they all influenced one another. A member of the entering graduate class of 1931 formed intellectual linkages and sometimes close friendships with his or her classmates, who might be involved in any combination of archaeological, ethnographic, and anthropometric research. All contemporaneous anthropology graduate students, along with the classes they took and the research projects available for them to participate in, were part of the educational process that shaped and informed the cohort of neophyte anthropologists developing at the Peabody Museum. For the most part, they were anthropologists first; their specialties came second. The well-trained Ph.D. of the time was expected to be knowledgeable and at least minimally capable in all fields of anthropology.

As an example of what we call the cohort effect, during Emil Haury's three years at Harvard, he overlapped with some 60 staff members and fellow graduate students. Half of them were focusing on archaeology, and a quarter each on physical anthropology and sociocultural anthropology. How many of these people participated with Haury in seminars, field research projects, or simply late-night arguments about the discipline? To do a thorough assessment of the effects of the Harvard experience on Haury, one would have to investigate the intellectual trajectories of all five dozen. Which fellow students had major effects on Haury's thinking? Which ones had only minor influence, and which ones apparently made no contribution to his thinking? Our research opens the door, but the major analyses remain to be done.

The graduate students discussed in this chapter became founders and leaders of many of the departments of anthropology that continued to be established around the country. Many of them were among the first students to have had the luxury of taking both undergraduate and graduate training in anthropology. Standing on the shoulders of the first generation of Americanist anthropological researchers, they were in a position to develop more coherent theoretical approaches—to begin to flesh out and pursue the necessary methodological and theoretical structure of the discipline. They merit a complete study of their own, a book-length disquisition into their influence on the development and growth of Americanist anthropology. That task we leave to others.

Bibliography

ABBREVIATIONS

AAAS American Association for the Advancement of Science
AMNH American Museum of Natural History
BSNH Boston Society of Natural History
PMAAE Peabody Museum of American Archaeology and Ethnology
PMAE Peabody Museum of Archaeology and Ethnology

ARCHIVAL SOURCES

Archives of the Carnegie Museum of Natural History, Pittsburgh: Clippings, Indian Mounds, Accession 17719.

Harvard University Archives: Graduate School of Arts and Sciences (GSAS) Record Cards, UAV 161.272.5, Box 8, Alfred Vincent Kidder 1901–1914; UAV 161.201.10, Andrew McLane.

Peabody Museum Archives and Collections Department, Harvard University: Biographical Files (loose-leaf file folder); Ephraim George Squier to Jeffries Wyman, April 14, 1868, De Mortillet correspondence, Accession File 68-13; Inventory of the Papers of Caroline Bond Day, 1996; Patrick T. Jackson, Chairman, American Reenforced Paper Company, Boston, to Donald Scott, Director of the Peabody Museum, December 23, 1946; Notes by an anonymous student on a lecture given on November 5, 1902, in Frank Russell's course "Anth 4 Prehistoric Archaeology—European Ethnology"; Putnam Papers, Accession File 999-24.

Pusey Library Archives, Harvard University: Board of Overseers Records.

WORKS ATTRIBUTABLE TO AUTHORS

Abbott, Charles C.

1872 "The Stone Age in New Jersey." *American Naturalist* 6(3):144–16, 6(4): 199–299.

1873 "Occurrence of Implements in the River Drift at Trenton, New Jersey." *American Naturalist* 7(4):204–9.

1877 "Report on the Discovery of Supposed Palaeolithic Implements from the Glacial Drift, in the Valley of the Delaware River, near Trenton, New Jersey." *Annual Reports of the PMAAE* 2(1):30–43.

1878 "Second Report on the Palaeolithic Implements from the Glacial Drift in the Valley of the Delaware River, near Trenton, New Jersey." *Annual Reports of the PMAAE* 2(2):225–57.

1881 "Historical Sketch of the Discoveries of Palaeolithic Implements in the Delaware Valley." *Proceedings of the BSNH* 21:124–32.

1882 "A Recent Find in the Trenton Gravels." *Proceedings of the BSNH* 22:96–104.

1886 "Sketch of Frederick Ward Putnam." *Popular Science Monthly* 29(5):693–96.

1887 "On the Antiquity of Man in the Valley of the Delaware." *Proceedings of the BSNH* 23:424–26.

1888a "Remarks upon Paleolithic Implements." *Proceedings of the BSNH* 24:157.

1888b "Evidences of the Antiquity of Man in Eastern North America." *Science* 12(291):103–5.

Adams, Geoffrey Charlton, and Robert Gorham Fuller

1905 *Catalogue of the Collections of Geoffrey C. Adams, Robert G. Fuller and Others, Consisting of a Fine Collection of "Elephant" Coins in Various Metals ... Which Will Be Sold at Public Auction ... June 1906.* New York: Geoffrey Charlton Adams.

Adams, Robert McCormick

1940 "Northern Mississippi Area." *American Antiquity* 6(1):82–84.

Agassiz, Alexander, and Leon S. Griswold

1896 "The Florida Elevated Reef." *Bulletin of the Museum of Comparative Zoology* 28(2):1–62.

Agassiz, George Russell

1913 (ed.) *Letters and Recollections of Alexander Agassiz, with a Sketch of His Life and Work.* Boston: Houghton Mifflin.

1927 "Theodore Lyman," in *Later Years of the Saturday Club, 1870–1920,* M. A. De Wolfe Howe, ed., pp. 149–53. Boston: Houghton Mifflin.

1930 "The Museum of Comparative Zoology, 1858–1928," in *The Development of Harvard University since the Inauguration of President Eliot, 1869–1929,* S. E. Morison, ed., pp. 400–412. Cambridge, Mass.: Harvard University Press.

Agassiz, Louis

1859 "On the Best Arrangement of a Zoological Museum." *Proceedings of the BSNH* 7:191.

Allen, Peter S.

1984 "Anne Hutchinson Fuller." *Anthropology Newsletter* 25(6):4.

Allen, Susan Heuck

2002 "The Archaeology of the AIA: An Introduction," in *Excavating Our Past: Perspectives on the History of the Archaeological Institute of America*, S. H. Allen, ed., pp. 1–28. Boston: Archaeological Institute of America.

Almazan, Tristan, and Sarah Coleman

2003 "George Amos Dorsey: A Curator and His Comrades," in *Curators, Collections, and Contexts: Anthropology at the Field Museum, 1893–2002*, S. E. Nash and G. M. Feinman, eds., pp. 87–97. Chicago: Field Museum of Natural History.

Amsden, Charles Avery

1949 *Prehistoric Southwesterners from Basketmaker to Pueblo*. Los Angeles: Southwest Museum.

Andrews, Anthony P.

1970 "The Chaco Canyon Project: The Tozzer-Farabee Expedition, 1901." Independent study project paper for Dr. Stephen Williams, Harvard University. Tozzer Library, Harvard University, accession 976-58.

Andrews, Ebenezer Baldwin

1877a "Report on Exploration of Ash Cave in Benton Township, Hocking County, Ohio." *Annual Reports of the PMAAE* 2(1):48–50.

1877b "Report on Explorations of a Cave and Mounds in Southeastern Ohio." *Annual Reports of the PMAAE* 2(1):51–74.

1878 *An Elementary Geology, Designed Especially for the Interior States*. Cincinnati: Van Antwerp, Bragg and Co.

Andrews, E. Wyllys, V

1981 "Robert Wauchope, 1909–1979." *American Antiquity* 46(1):113–24.

1996 "Stanley Harding Boggs, 1914–1991." *American Antiquity* 61(1):57–61.

Anonymous

1871 "Notes." *American Naturalist* 5(7):448–50.

1883a "Notes and News." *Science* 1(8):235–38.

1883b "Papers Read Before Section H." *Science* 2(32):365–71.

1883c "Proceedings of the Section of Anthropology." *Science* 4(87):343–46.

1884a "The Origin of the Ohio Mounds" (review of Lucien Carr's 1883 *The Mounds of the Mississippi Valley Historically Considered*). *Science* 4(81):151–52.

1884b "Proceedings of the Section of Anthropology." *Science* 5(87):342–46.

1885a "Proceedings of the Section of Anthropology." *Science* 6(136):230–34.

1885b "Notes and News." *Science* 6(143):382.

1886 "The Fall Meeting of the National Academy." *Science* 8(198):448–51.

1887   "Proceedings of Scientific Societies." *American Naturalist* 21(9):869–74.

1889   "Post-Pliocene Footprints." *Living Age* 181(2341):384.

1893   "An Aboriginal Soapstone Quarry." *Manufacturer and Builder* 25(2):38.

1894   "Harvard Folk-Lore Club." *Journal of American Folk-Lore* 7(27):323.

1895a   "Anthropology in Harvard University." *Science* 2(29):72–73.

1895b   "Sixth Annual Meeting of the American Folk-Lore Society." *Journal of American Folk-Lore* 8(28):1–6.

1896a   "A Lecture on Bones." *Pittsburgh Dispatch,* September 3, 1896.

1896b   "Record of Geographical Progress." *Journal of the American Geographical Society of New York* 28(1):54–69.

1897   *The Indian Helper* (Carlisle Indian Industrial School weekly student paper), vol. 12, no. 51, October 1.

1900   "Peabody Museum." *Harvard Graduates' Magazine* 9(34):239–40.

1904   "Robert Singleton Peabody." *American Anthropologist* 6(5):745–46.

1906a   "Scientific Notes and News." *Science* 23(586):477–80.

1906b   "Scientific Notes and News." *Science* 24(603):94–96.

1906c   "Recent Progress in American Anthropology: A Review of the Activities of Institutions and Individuals from 1902 to 1906." *American Anthropologist* 8(3):441–558.

1908   "Nineteenth Annual Meeting of the American Folk-Lore Society." *Journal of American Folk-Lore* 21(80):74–81.

1910   "Anthropologic Miscellanea." *American Anthropologist* 12(4):733.

1911   "Dr. Wills DeHass." *American Anthropologist* 11(4):815.

1912a   "University and Educational News." *Science* 36(933):671–72.

1912b   "International School of American Archaeology and Ethnology in Mexico." *American Anthropologist* 14(1):192–94.

1913a   "Anthropological Work by the Geological Survey of Canada." *American Anthropologist* 15(1):144.

1913b   "Death of Ernest Jackson: Graduated from Harvard with the Class of 1878." *Boston Globe,* February 27, 1913.

1914   "Anthropologic Miscellanea." *American Anthropologist* 16(2):369–74.

1915   "Frederic Ward Putnam." *Science* 42(1088):638–39.

1917a   "William Hubbs Mechling." *American Anthropologist* 19(1):153.

1917b   "Anthropologic Miscellanea." *American Anthropologist* 19(4):776–80.

1919a   "Oric Bates." *American Journal of Archaeology* 23(1):76.

1919b   "Moens, Mystery Man. Agent, Named in Bruce Case, Trailed by Secret Service. Suspected as German Spy." *Washington Post,* May 30, p. 9.

| 1924 | "George Hubbard Pepper." *American Anthropologist* 26(4):566–67.
| 1927 | "George Byron Gordon." *American Anthropologist* 29(3):366.
| 1930 | "Harvard Man Reports Eskimos Intelligent and Skilled in Arts." *Christian Science Monitor,* February 8, 1930.
| 1932 | "John Berdan Charlesworth." *Science* 75(1952):555.
| 1938 | "Antonio Apache." *Phillips Exeter Academy Bulletin,* October, p. 27.
| 1941a | "Charles Avery Amsden." *American Antiquity* 6(4):349–50.
| 1941b | "Course in Ditch Digging Offered by the University." *Harvard Crimson,* March 4.
| 1942 | "Notes and News." *American Antiquity* 8(2):179–86.
| 1950 | "Martin Luther, Boston Publisher, 50, Kin of Churchman." *Boston Daily Globe,* April 13, p. 33.
| 1971 | "Mark Raymond Harrington: 1882–1971." *Masterkey for Indian Lore and History* 45(3):84–88.
| 1977 | "Gene McNaughton Stirling." *Anthropology Newsletter* 18(3):3.
| 1999 | "E. Mott Davis." *Austin (Texas) American-Statesman,* January 2.

Appel, Toby A.

| 1988 | "Jeffries Wyman, Philosophical Anatomy, and the Scientific Reception of Darwin in America." *Journal of the History of Biology* 21(1):69–94.
| 1992 | "A Scientific Career in the Age of Character: Jeffries Wyman and Natural History at Harvard," in *Science at Harvard University: Historical Perspectives,* C. A. Elliott and M. W. Rossiter, eds., pp. 96–120. Bethlehem, Pa.: Lehigh University Press.

Aten, Lawrence E., and Jerald T. Milanich

| 2003 | "Clarence Bloomfield Moore: A Philadelphia Archaeologist in the Southeastern United States," in D. D. Fowler and D. R. Wilcox, eds., *Philadelphia and the Development of Americanist Archaeology,* pp. 113–33. Tuscaloosa: University of Alabama Press.

Augney, William M.

| 1892 | "The De Laincel Fund for the Study of the Maya Language and Its Graphic System." *Science* 20(491):6.

Bache, Alexander D.

| 1839 | *Report on Education in Europe to the Trustees of the Girard College for Orphans.* Philadelphia: Lydia R. Bailey.

Badger, Reid

| 1979 | *The Great American Fair: The World's Columbian Exposition and American Culture.* Chicago: Nelson Hall.

Baker, Lee D.

1998 *From Savage to Negro: Anthropology and the Construction of Race, 1896–1954.* Berkeley: University of California Press.

Baldwin, Elizabeth Ellen

1967 "The Obion Site: An Early Mississippian Center in Western Tennessee." Ph.D. dissertation, Department of Anthropology, Harvard University.

Bancroft, Hubert Howe

1893 *The Book of the Fair: An Historical and Descriptive Presentation of the World's Science, Art, and Industry, as Viewed through the Columbian Exposition in Chicago in 1893.* 2 vols. Chicago: Bancroft.

Barber, M. W., ed.

1900 *The Harvard University Register of Organizations and Athletic Events and Directory of Officers and Students 1899–1900,* vol. 26. Cambridge, Mass.: Caustic and Chaflin.

Barnes, Alfred S., and Homer H. Kidder

1936 "Différentes techniques de débitage a la Ferrassie." *Bulletin de la Société Préhistorique Française* 33:272–88.

Barnhart, Terry A.

1986 "Curious Antiquity: The Grave Creek Controversy Revisited." *West Virginia History* 46:103–24.

2004 "In His Own Right: Dr. Edwin Hamilton Davis and the Davis Collection of American Antiquities." *Journal of the History of Collections* 16(1):59–87.

2005 *Ephraim George Squier and the Development of American Archaeology.* Lincoln: University of Nebraska Press.

Bartlett, K. S.

1939 "Dr. Reisner Solved Crime Mystery of Egypt Thousands of Years Ago." *Boston Globe,* June 11.

Bartsch, Paul, Harald Alfred Rehder, and Beulah E. Shields

1947 "A Bibliography and Short Biographical Sketch of William Healey Dall." *Smithsonian Miscellaneous Collections* 104(15):1–96.

Baskerville, Charles

1900 "Report of the Secretary." *Proceedings of the AAAS* 49:6.

Bass, William M.

1968 "Charles Ernest Snow, 1910–1967." *American Journal of Physical Anthropology* 28(3):369–72.

Bates, Oric

1915 "Archaic Burials at Marsa Matruh." *Ancient Egypt* 2:158–65. London: Macmillan.

1917 "The African Department of the Peabody Museum." *Harvard Graduate Magazine* 25(100):479–85.

Bates, Oric, and Herbert Eustis Winlock

1912 "Archaeological Material from the Maine Littoral, with Especial Reference to the Bates Collection." Senior thesis, Anthropology 20, Harvard University.

Beck, Horace P.

1951 "Frank G. Speck, 1881–1950." *Journal of American Folklore* 64(254):415–18.

Beckham, Stephen Dow

1969 "George Gibbs, 1815–1873: Historian and Ethnologist." Ph.D. dissertation, Department of History, University of California–Los Angeles.

Bell, Genevieve

1998 "Telling Stories Out of School: Remembering the Carlisle Indian Industrial School, 1879–1918." Ph.D. dissertation, Stanford University.

Bender, Thomas

1987 *New York Intellect: A History of Intellectual Life in New York City, from 1750 to the Beginnings of Our Own Time.* New York: Knopf.

1993 *Intellect and Public Life: Essays on the Social History of Academic Intellectuals in the United States.* Baltimore, Md.: Johns Hopkins University Press.

Bennett, Wendell C.

1946 "Philip Ainsworth Means, 1892–1944." *American Anthropologist* 48(2):234–37.

Berlin, Heinrich.

1978 "Eduardo Noguera, 1896–1977." *American Antiquity* 43(4):618–21.

Bernstein, Bruce

1993 "Roland Dixon and the Maidu." *Museum Anthropology* 17(2):20–26.

Bickmore, Albert S.

1868 *Travels in the East Indian Archipelago.* London: J. Murray.

Billings, John S.

1889 "Memoir of Spencer Fullerton Baird, 1823–1887." *National Academy of Sciences, Biographical Memoirs* 3(7):141–69.

Bingham, Alfred Mitchell

1989 *Portrait of an Explorer: Hiram Bingham, Discoverer of Machu Picchu.* Ames: Iowa State University Press.

Bingham, Walter V.

1920 "The Division of Anthropology and Psychology of the National Research Council." *Science* 51(1319):353–57.

Bingham, Woodbridge

1989 *Hiram Bingham: A Personal History.* Boulder, Colo.: Bin Lan Zhen/Desktop Publishing Services.

Bishop, Joseph B.

1892 "Early Political Caricature in America." *The Century* 44(2):219–31.

Biwas, Praphulla Chandra

1961 "Dr. B. S. Guha." *Mankind Quarterly* 2(2):120–21.

Blake, John Harrison

1878 "Notes on a Collection from the Ancient Cemetery at the Bay of Chacota, Peru." *Annual Reports of the PMAAE* 2(2):277–304.

Blankenship, Roy, ed.

1991 *The Life and Times of Frank G. Speck, 1881–1950.* Publications in Anthropology 4. Philadelphia: University of Pennsylvania.

Blust, Robert Andrew

1998 "In Memoriam: Paul King Benedict, 1912–1997." *Oceanic Linguistics* 37(1):1–11.

Boas, Franz

1887a "The Study of Geography." *Science* 9:137–41.

1887b "The Occurrence of Similar Inventions in Areas Widely Separated." *Science* 9(224):485–86.

1887c "Museums of Ethnology and Their Classification: Letters from William H. Dall and Franz Boas." *Science* 9(228):587–89.

1887d "Museums of Ethnology and Their Classification: Letters from J. W. Powell and Franz Boas." *Science* 9(229):614.

1891 "Anthropological Investigations in Schools." *Pedagogical Seminary* 1:225–28.

1902 "The Foundation of a National Anthropological Society." *Science* 15(386):804–9.

1904 "The History of Anthropology." *Science* 20(512):513–24.

1909a "Race Problems in America." *Science* 29(752):839–49.

1909b "William Jones." *American Anthropologist* 11(1):137–39.

1909c "William Jones." *Southern Workman* 38(6):337–39.

1912 "International School of American Archaeology and Ethnology in Mexico." *American Anthropologist* 14:192–94.

1913 "Archaeological Investigations in the Valley of Mexico by the International School, 1911–1912," in *Proceedings of the 18th Session of the International Congress of Americanists,* pp. 176–79. London.

1915a   "Frederic Ward Putnam." *Science* 42(1080):330–32.

1915b   "Summary of the Work of the International School of American Archaeology and Ethnology in Mexico, 1910–1914." *American Anthropologist* 17(2):384–91.

1916   "Why German-Americans Blame America." *New York Times,* January 8, p. 8.

1919a   "Scientists as Spies." *The Nation* 109:797.

1919b   "Report on the Academic Teaching of Anthropology." *American Anthropologist* 21(1):41–48.

1919c   Franz Boas to Herman M. Bernelot Moens, Nov. 25, 1919 (copy), American Philosophical Library Archives, Philadelphia, Pa., Franz Boas Collections, 1862–1942, item 635.

Boas, Franz, Roland B. Dixon, Frederick W. Hodge, Alfred L. Kroeber, and Harlan I. Smith, eds.

1909   *Putnam Anniversary Volume: Anthropological Essays Presented to Frederic Ward Putnam in Honor of His Seventieth Birthday, April 16, 1909, by His Friends and Associates.* New York: G. E. Stechert.

Boas, Franz, George G. MacCurdy, and Robert Bennett Bean

1919   "Captain Robert G. Fuller." *American Anthropologist* 21(1):113–14.

Boas, Franz, Alfred M. Tozzer, and Aleš Hrdlička

1919   "Report on Anthropology and Its Relations to the National Research Council by a Committee of the American Anthropological Association." *American Journal of Physical Anthropology* 2(1):109–11.

Bostwick, Todd W.

2006   *Byron Cummings: Dean of Southwest Archaeology.* Tucson: University of Arizona Press.

Bourgeois, Arthur P.

1994   "Introduction," in *Ojibwa Narratives of Charles and Charlotte Kawbawgam and Jacques LePique, 1893–1895,* recorded with notes by Homer H. Kidder, edited by Arthur P. Bourgeois, pp. 3–20. Detroit, Mich.: Wayne State University Press.

Bourque, Bruce

2002   "Maine Shell Midden Archaeology (1860–1910) and the Influence of Adolphe von Morlot," in *New Perspectives on the Origins of Americanist Archaeology,* D. L. Browman and S. Williams, eds., pp. 148–63. Tuscaloosa: University of Alabama Press.

Bowditch, Charles Pickering

1900   "The Lords of the Night and the Tonalamatl of the Codex Borbonicus." *American Anthropologist* 2(1):145–54.

1901a   "Memoranda on the Maya Calendars Used in the Books of Chilam Balam." *American Anthropologist* 3(1):129–38.

1901b   "On the Age of Maya Ruins." *American Anthropologist* 3(4):697–700.

1904   (ed.) *Mexican and Central American Antiquities, Calendar Systems, and History: Twenty-four Papers by Seler, Forstemann, Schellhas, Sapper, and Dieseldorff.* Bulletin of the Bureau of American Ethnology, no. 28. Washington, D.C.: Government Printing Office.

1905   "Report of the Committee on American Archaeology." *American Journal of Archaeology* 9:41–44.

1909   "The Dates and Numbers of Pages 24 and 46 to 50 of the Dresden Codex," in *Putnam Anniversary Volume: Anthropological Essays Presented to Frederic Ward Putnam in Honor of His Seventieth Birthday, April 16, 1909, by His Friends and Associates,* F. Boas et al., eds., pp. 268–98. New York: G. E. Stechert.

1910   *The Numeration, Calendar Systems, and Astronomical Knowledge of the Mayas.* Cambridge, Mass.: Harvard University Press.

1924   "War Letters of Charles P. Bowditch." *Proceedings of the Massachusetts Historical Society* 57(7):414–93.

Bowditch, Henry I.

1855   "Plan of an Ancient Fortification at Marietta, Ohio (1787), by Winthrop Sargent." *Memoirs of the American Academy of Arts and Sciences* 5:25–28.

Bowles, Gordon Townsend

1932   *New Types of Old Americans at Harvard and Eastern Women's Colleges.* Cambridge, Mass.: Harvard University Press.

1977   *The People of Asia.* New York: Charles Scribner's Sons.

Brew, John Otis

1939   "Preliminary Report of the Peabody Museum Awatovi Expedition of 1937." *American Antiquity* 5(2):103–14.

1949a   "82nd Annual Report of the PMAAE," in *Report of the President of Harvard College and of the Departments, 1947–1948,* pp. 293–305.

1949b   "Preface," in *Franciscan Awatovi: The Excavation and Conjectural Reconstruction of a 17th-Century Spanish Mission Establishment at a Hopi Indian Town in Northeastern Arizona,* by R. G. Montgomery, W. Smith, and J. O. Brew, pp. vii–viii. Papers of the PMAAE, vol. 36. Cambridge, Mass.: Harvard University.

1950   "83rd Annual Report of the PMAAE," in *Report of the President of Harvard College and of the Departments, 1948–1949,* pp. 316–33.

1951   "84th Annual Report of the PMAAE," in *Report of the President of Harvard College and of the Departments, 1949–1950,* pp. 349–73.

1953   "86th Annual Report of the PMAAE," in *Report of the President of Harvard College and of the Departments, 1951–1952,* pp. 367–402.

1954 "87th Annual Report of the PMAAE," in *Report of the President of Harvard College and of the Departments, 1952–1953*, pp. 349–73.

1956 "90th Annual Report of the PMAAE," in *Report of the President of Harvard College and of the Departments, 1955–1956*, pp. 349–73.

1959 "92nd Annual Report of the PMAAE," in *Report of the President of Harvard College and of the Departments, 1957–1958*, pp. 511–16.

1961 "94th Annual Report of the PMAAE," in *Report of the President of Harvard College and of the Departments, 1959–1960*, pp. 605–11.

1963 "96th Annual Report of the PMAAE," in *Report of the President of Harvard College and of the Departments, 1961–1962*, pp. 598–615.

1966a *Early Days of the Peabody Museum at Harvard University*. Cambridge, Mass.: Peabody Museum.

1966b *People and Projects in the Peabody Museum 1866–1966*. Cambridge, Mass.: Peabody Museum.

1968 "Introduction," in *One Hundred Years of Anthropology*, J. O. Brew, ed., pp. 3–25. Cambridge, Mass.: Harvard University Press.

1982 "Noel Morss, 1904–1981." *American Antiquity* 47(2):344–45.

Bricker, Harvey M.

2002 "George Grant MacCurdy: An American Pioneer of Palaeoanthropology," in *New Perspectives on the Origins of Americanist Archaeology*, D. L. Browman and S. Williams, eds., pp. 265–85. Tuscaloosa: University of Alabama Press.

Brimmer, Martin, and Minna Timmins Chapman (Mrs. John Jay Chapman)

1892 *Egypt: Three Essays on the History, Religion, and Art of Ancient Egypt*. Boston: Houghton Mifflin.

Brinton, Daniel G.

1859 *Notes on the Floridean Peninsula*. Philadelphia: Joseph Sabin.

1867 "Artificial Shell Deposits of the United States," in *Annual Report of the Smithsonian Institution for 1866*, pp. 356–58. Washington, D.C.

1884 "Memoir of Dr. C. H. Berendt." *Proceedings of the American Antiquarian Society* 3:205–10.

1889 "Post-Pliocene Footprints." *Living Age* 181(2341):384.

1895 "*The Hill Caves of Yucatan*, by Henry C. Mercer." *Science* 2(52):900–901.

Brower, Jacob Vradenberg, and David Ives Bushnell Jr.

1900 *Mille Lac*. Memoirs of Explorations in the Basin of the Mississippi, vol. 3. St. Paul, Minn.: H. L. Collins.

Browman, David L.

2002a "Frederic Ward Putnam: Contributions to the Development of Archaeological Institutions and Encouragement of Women Practitioners," in

New Perspectives on the Origins of American Archaeology, D. L. Browman and S. Williams, eds., pp. 209–41. Tuscaloosa: University of Alabama Press.

2002b "Origins of Americanist Stratigraphic Excavation: The Peabody Museum Method and the Chicago Method," in *New Perspectives on the Origins of American Archaeology,* D. L. Browman and S. Williams, eds., pp. 242–64. Tuscaloosa: University of Alabama Press.

2002c "Henry Chapman Mercer: Archaeologist and Cultural Historian," in *New Perspectives on the Origins of American Archaeology,* D. L. Browman and S. Williams, eds., pp. 185–208. Tuscaloosa: University of Alabama Press.

2002d "The Peabody Museum, Frederic W. Putnam, and the Rise of U.S. Anthropology, 1866–1903." *American Anthropologist* 104(2):508–19.

Browman, David L., and Douglas R. Givens

1996 "Stratigraphic Excavation: The First 'New Archaeology.'" *American Anthropologist* 98(1):80–95.

Browman, David L., and Stephen Williams, eds.

2002 *New Perspectives on the Origins of American Archaeology.* Tuscaloosa: University of Alabama Press.

Brown, Bernice V.

1929 "Report of the Dean," in *Annual Report of Radcliffe College, 1927–1928,* pp. 9–23. Cambridge, Mass.: Radcliffe College.

Brown, Edward Hoagland

1949 "Harvard and the Ohio Mounds." *New England Quarterly* 22(2):205–28.

Browne, Dallas L.

1999 "Across Class and Culture: Allison Davis and His Works," in *African-American Pioneers in Anthropology,* I. E. Harrison and F. V. Harrison, eds., pp. 168–90. Urbana: University of Illinois Press.

Bruce, Robert V.

1987 *The Launching of Modern American Science, 1846–1876.* New York: Knopf.

Brugioni, Dino A.

1991 *Eyeball to Eyeball: The Inside Story of the Cuban Missile Crisis.* Edited by R. F. McCort. New York: Random House.

Brunhouse, Robert L.

1971 *Sylvanus G. Morley and the World of the Ancient Mayas.* Norman: University of Oklahoma Press.

Bryan, Alan K.

1973 "New Light on Ancient Nicaraguan Foot Prints." *Archaeology* 26(2):146–47.

Burger, Richard L.

2007 "John Howland Rowe (June 10, 1918–May 1, 2004)." *Andean Past* 8:33–44.

Butterfield, Herbert

1950 *The Whig Interpretation of History.* London: G. Bell and Sons.

Byers, Douglas S.

1966a "Frans Blom, 1893–1963." *American Antiquity* 31(3):406–7.

1966b "Oliver La Farge, 1901–1963." *American Antiquity* 31(3):408–9.

Calhoun, Michele

1991a "George Amos Dorsey," in *International Dictionary of Anthropologists,* C. Winters, ed., pp. 153–54. New York: Garland.

1991b "William Jones," in *International Dictionary of Anthropologists,* C. Winters, ed., pp. 329–30. New York: Garland.

Carr, Lucien

1877 "Report on the Exploration of a Mound in Lee County, Virginia, Conducted for the Peabody Museum." *Annual Reports of the PMAAE* 2(1):75–94.

1878 "Observations on the Crania from the Stone Graves in Tennessee." *Annual Reports of the PMAAE* 2(2):361–84.

1879a "Measurements of Crania from California." *Annual Reports of the PMAAE* 2(3):497–505. Cambridge, Mass.: Harvard University.

1879b "Observations on the Crania from the Santa Barbara Islands, California," in *Reports upon Archaeological and Ethnological Collections from Vicinity of Santa Barbara, California, and from Ruined Pueblos of Arizona and New Mexico, and Certain Interior Tribes,* by F. W. Putnam et al., pp. 277–92. Geographical Surveys West of the One Hundredth Meridian, vol. 7, Archaeology. Washington, D.C.: U.S. Army Engineer Department.

1880 "Notes on the Crania of New England Indians." *Anniversary Memoirs of the BSNH, 1830–1880,* pp. 1–11.

1883a "The Mounds of the Mississippi Valley, Historically Considered." *Memoirs of the Geological Survey of Kentucky,* series 2, vol. 2, pt. 2, pp. 1–107.

1883b "On the Social and Political Position of Women among the Huron-Iroquois Tribes." *Annual Reports of the PMAAE* 3(3):207–32.

1885 "Review: *Prehistoric America.*" *Science* 5(108):176–78.

1888 *Missouri: A Bone of Contention.* Boston: Houghton Mifflin.

1896 "The Food of Certain American Indians and Their Method of Preparing It." *Proceedings of the American Antiquarian Society* 10:155–89.

1897 "Dress and Ornaments of Certain American Indians." *Proceedings of the American Antiquarian Society* 11:381–454.

1900a "An Error in the Resolution of Congress Admitting Missouri into the Union." *Proceedings of the Massachusetts Historical Society,* Feb., pp. 448–54.

1900b "The Mascoutins." *Proceedings of the American Antiquarian Society* 13:448–62.

Carr, Lucien, and Nathaniel Southgate Shaler

1876 *On the Prehistoric Remains of Kentucky.* Memoirs of the Kentucky Geological Survey, vol. 1, pt. 4. Frankfort, Ky.: Yeoman Press.

Casler, Patricia Joanne

1976 "Personalities, Politics, and Patrons of the Peabody Museum of American Archaeology and Ethnology, 1866–1896." Senior thesis, Department of History, Harvard College.

Cassells, E. Steve

1983 *The Archaeology of Colorado.* Boulder, Colo.: Johnson Books.

Cattell, Jaques, ed.

1927 *American Men of Science: A Biographical Directory.* New York: Science Press.

Cattell, J. McKeen, ed.

1910 *American Men of Science: A Biographical Directory.* 2nd ed. New York: Science Press.

Cattell, J. McKeen, and Dean R. Brimhall, eds.

1921 *American Men of Science: A Biographical Directory.* 3rd ed. New York: Science Press.

Cattell, J. McKeen, and Jaques Cattell, eds.

1938 *American Men of Science: A Biographical Directory.* 6th ed. New York: Science Press.

Caullery, Maurice Jules Gaston Corneille

1922 *Universities and Scientific Life in the United States.* J. H. Woods and E. Russell, translators. Cambridge, Mass.: Harvard University Press.

Chamberlain, Alexander Francis

1887 "The Relationship of the American Languages." *Science* 10(252):57–76.

1889 "The Archaeology of Scugog Island." *Proceedings of the Canadian Institute,* 3rd series, 7:14–15.

1894 "Anthropology in Universities and Colleges." *Pedagogical Seminary* 3(1):48–60.

1902 "International Congress of Americanists at New York." *Science* 16(414):884–99.

Champlin, Peggy

1994 *Raphael Pumpelly: Gentleman Geologist of the Gilded Age.* Tuscaloosa: University of Alabama Press.

Chang, Kwang-Chih

1980 "Li Chi (1896–1979)." *Journal of Asian Studies* 40(1):218–19.

1981 "Archaeology and Chinese Historiography." *World Archaeology* 13(2):156–69.

1991 "Li Ji (Li Chi)," in *International Dictionary of Anthropologists*, C. Winters, ed., pp. 407–8. New York: Garland.

Chase, George H.

1930 "The Fine Arts, 1874–1929," in *The Development of Harvard University since the Inauguration of President Eliot 1869–1929*, S. E. Morison, ed., pp. 130–45. Cambridge, Mass.: Harvard University Press.

Chester, Hilary Lynn

2002 "Frances Eliza Babbitt and the Growth of Professionalism of Women in Archaeology," in *New Perspectives on the Origins of Americanist Archaeology*, D. L. Browman and S. Williams, eds., pp. 164–84. Tuscaloosa: University of Alabama Press.

Child, Alice Blyth, and Irvin L. Child

1993 *Religion and Magic in the Life of Traditional Peoples.* Englewood Cliffs, N.J.: Prentice Hall.

Chinas, Beverly Newbold

1999 "Zelia Maria Magdalena Nuttall," in *American National Biography*, J. A. Garrity and M. C. Carnes, eds., vol. 16, pp. 559–60. New York: Oxford University Press.

Christenson, Andrew L.

1985 "The Identification and Study of Indian Shell Middens in Eastern North America, 1643–1861." *North American Archaeologist* 6(3):227–43.

Church, John A.

1875 "Scientific Miscellany." *Galaxy* 20(4):561–69.

Claflin, William H., Jr.

1931 *The Stalling's Island Mound, Columbia County, Georgia.* Papers of the PMAAE, vol. 14, no. 1. Cambridge, Mass.: Harvard University.

Clark, Hubert Lyman

1931 "Samuel Garman," in *Dictionary of American Biography*, vol. 7, p. 154. New York: Charles Scribner's Sons.

Cleland, Kathryn M.

1991 "Julio Cesar Tello," in *International Dictionary of Anthropologists*, C. Winters, ed., pp. 686–87. New York: Garland.

Cockerell, Theodore D. A.

1920 "Biographical Memoir of Alpheus Spring Packard, 1839–1905." *National Academy of Sciences, Biographical Memoirs* 9(6):181–236.

Cole, Douglas

1999 *Franz Boas: The Early Years, 1858–1906.* Seattle: University of Washington Press.

Cole, Fay-Cooper

1931 "George A. Dorsey." *American Anthropologist* 33(3):413–14.

Cole, Fay-Cooper, Roland B. Dixon, and Alfred V. Kidder

1929 "Anthropological Scholarships." *American Anthropologist* 31(3):571–72.

Collins, June M.

1979 "Ruth Sawtell Wallis, 1895–1978." *American Anthropologist* 81(1):85–87.

Comstock, Ada Louise

1943 "Twenty Years at Radcliffe." *Radcliffe Quarterly* 26(August):15–18.

Comstock, John Henry

1925 "Burt Green Wilder." *Science* 61(1586):531–33.

Conklin, Edwin G.

1944 "The Early History of the *American Naturalist*." *American Naturalist* 78(774):29–37.

Conn, Steven

1998 *Museums and American Intellectual Life, 1876–1926.* Chicago: University of Chicago Press.

Converse, Charles Allen

1905 *Some of the Ancestors and Descendants of Samuel Converse, Jr., of Thompson Parish, Killingly, Connecticut, Major James Converse, of Woburn, Massachusetts, Hon. Heman Allen, M.C., of Milton and Burlington, Vermont, Captain John Bixby, Sr. of Killingly, Connecticut.* 2 vols. Boston: E. Putnam.

Coolidge, Archibald Cary

1918 "Oric Bates." *Harvard African Studies (Varia Africana)*, vol. 2, pp. vii–viii. Cambridge, Mass.

Coon, Carleton

1951 *Caravan: The Story of the Middle East.* New York: Holt, Rinehart.

1953 "Walter Buchanan Cline: A Memoir." *Kroeber Anthropological Society Papers* 8–9:ix–xxx. Berkeley: University of California.

1962 *The Origin of Races.* New York: Knopf.

1980 *A North Africa Story: The Anthropologist as OSS Agent, 1941–43.* Ipswich, Mass.: Gambit.

1981 *Adventures and Discoveries: The Autobiography of Carleton S. Coon.* Englewood Cliffs, N.J.: Prentice Hall.

Cosgrove, Harriet Silliman, and Cornelius Burton Cosgrove

1932 *The Swarts Ruin: A Typical Mimbres Site in Southwestern New Mexico. Report of the Mimbres Valley Expedition, Seasons of 1924–1927.* Papers of the PMAAE, vol. 15. Cambridge, Mass.: Harvard University.

Crawford, John

1890 "Finds in Nicaragua." *American Antiquarian* 12(2):108–12.

1891a "Notes on Central American Archaeology and Ethnology." *Proceedings of the BSNH* 25:247–53.

1891b "Neolithic Man in Nicaragua." *American Antiquarian* 13(5):293–96.

1892 "The Geology of Nicaragua." *Proceedings of the AAAS* 40:261–70.

1893a "Hydrographic Area of the Rio Wanque or Coco in Nicaragua." *Science* 21(530):174–77.

1893b "Recent Discoveries in Northeastern Nicaragua: Granite Hills, Moutonned Ridges and Gold-Containing Lodes or Reefs, and Leads or Placer Mines." *Science* 22(563):269–72.

1893c "Evidence of Man in Nicaragua during the Early Neolithic Age, and the Probable Present Tribal Name and Locality of His Descendants." *Proceedings of the BSNH* 26:49–59.

1895a "A List of Words from the Sumo Indian Language." *Archaeologist* 3(5):157–60.

1895b "The Archaeology of Nicaragua." *Archaeologist* 3(7):219–23.

1895c "Evidence of Aborigines in Nicaragua." *Proceedings of the AAAS* 43:370.

1895d "Shell-Mounds in Nicaragua." *Proceedings of the AAAS* 43:370.

1896 "A Story of the Amerique Indians of Nicaragua." *American Antiquarian* 18(5):269–73.

1897a "Names and Statues of the Amerique People." *American Antiquarian* 19(1):21–25.

1897b "The Pre-historic Route from Asia and the Oceania Islands to the Western Coast of America." *American Antiquarian* 19:135–37.

Crawford, Michael H.

1995 "Marshall T. Newman (1911–1994)." *Human Biology* 67(5):683–87.

Crawford, O. G. S. (Osbert Guy Stanhope)

1955 *Said and Done: The Autobiography of an Archaeologist.* London: Weidenfeld and Nicolson.

Cresson, Hilborne T.

1887 "River Dwelling on the Mud Flats of the Delaware River." *American Antiquarian* 9(6):363–65.

1888a "Early Man in the Delaware Valley." *Proceedings of the BSNH* 24:141–50.

1888b "Remarks upon a Chipped Implement Found in Modified Drift, on the East Fork of the White River, Jackson County, Indiana." *Proceedings of the BSNH* 24:150–52.

1889a "Palaeolithic Implements from Ancient Terraces on the Delaware River near Naaman's Creek." *Proceedings of the AAAS* 37:329.

1889b "Chipped Implement from the Drift on the East Fork of the White River, Jackson County, Indiana." *Proceedings of the AAAS* 37:329.

1890 "Supposed Aboriginal Fish-Weirs in Naaman's Creek, near Claymont, Del." *Science* 15(367):116–17, 15(371):181, and 15(376):251–52.

1892a "Remarks upon the Graphic System of the Ancient Mayas." *Science* 20(492):25–26.

1892b "Palaeolithic Man in the Southern Portion of the Delaware Valley." *Science* 20(512):304–5.

1893a "Minor Phonetic Elements of Maya Hieroglyphs." *Science* 21(541):325–26.

1893b "Brief Remarks upon the Alphabet of Landa." *Proceedings of the AAAS* 41:281–83.

1893c "Interpretation of Maya Glyphs by Their Phonetic Elements, Part 1." *Science* 22(567):325–28.

1894 "Interpretation of Maya Glyphs by Their Phonetic Elements, Part 2." *Science* 23(575):76–78.

Crockett, Charis Denison

1942 *The House in the Rain Forest.* Boston: Houghton Mifflin.

Croissant, Jennifer L.

2000 "Narrating Archaeology: A Historiography and Notes toward a Sociology of Archaeological Knowledge," in *It's About Time: A History of Archaeological Dating in North America,* S. E. Nash, ed., pp. 186–206. Salt Lake City: University of Utah Press.

Crowfoot, John W.

1943 "George Reisner: An Impression." *Antiquity* 17:122–28.

Cusick, Cornelius C.

1859 "Marriage Ceremony of the Pagan," in *Poems of the Mohawk Valley, and on Scenes in Palestine, Together with an Essay on the Origin of Poetry, with Miscellaneous Poems and Sketches,* by P. Camp, C. Cusick, and W. N. Duane, p. 125. Utica, N.Y.: Curtiss and White.

1876 "American Antiquities." *Proceedings of the AAAS* 24:333.

1900 *Military History of Captain C. C. Cusick, U.S. Army: Extracts from* Biographical Cyclopedia of Niagara County, New York, *by Wiley and Garner, 1892, and from the Work Entitled* Officers of the Army and Navy Who Served in the Civil War, *by Major William H. Powell, U.S. Army, and Medical Director Edward Shippen, U.S. Navy, and from* The History of the State of New York in the Civil War, *by Hugh Hastings, N.Y. State Historian, with an Addendum by Cornelius C. Cusick*. Chicago: National Archives and Records Administration, Great Lakes Region.

Cutler, Manasseh

1888 [1798] "Note to Dr. Cutler's Charge at the Ordination of Rev. Daniel Slay, Pastor, of the Church of Marietta, Ohio, Given at Hamilton, Massachusetts, August 15, 1798," in *Life, Journals, and Correspondence of Rev. Manasseh Cutler, LL.D.*, W. P. Cutler and J. P. Cutler, compilers, vol. 2, pp. 14–17. Cincinnati: Robert Clarke.

Dall, William Healey

1870 "On the Distribution of the Native Tribes of Alaska, and the Adjacent Territory." *Proceedings of the AAAS* 18:263–73.

1872 "Prehistoric Remains: Interesting Explorations in the Aleutian Islands." *San Francisco Bulletin*, November 6, p. 1.

1873 "Notes on Pre-historic Remains in the Aleutian Islands." *Proceedings of the California Academy of Sciences* 4, pt. 5, pp. 283–87.

1874 "Notes on Some Aleut Mummies." *Proceedings of the California Academy of Sciences* 5:399–400.

1875 "Alaskan Mummies." *American Naturalist* 9(8):433–40.

1876 "On the Remains of Later Pre-historic Man, Obtained from Caves in the Catherina Archipelago, Alaska Territory." *Smithsonian Contributions to Knowledge* 22:1–40.

1877a "On Succession in the Shell-Heaps of the Aleutian Islands," in *Contributions to North American Ethnology*, vol. 1, *Tribes of the Extreme Northwest*, pt. 1, pp. 41–91. Washington, D.C.: U.S. Geological and Geographical Survey, Department of the Interior.

1877b "On the Origin of the Innuit," in *Contributions to North American Ethnology*, vol. 1, *Tribes of the Extreme Northwest*, pt. 1, pp. 93–106. Washington, D.C.: U.S. Geological and Geographical Survey, Department of the Interior.

1878 "Social Life among Our Aborigines." *American Naturalist* 12(1):1–10.

1881 "The Succession of Strata of Shell-Heaps of the Aleutian Islands." *Bulletin of the Philosophical Society of Washington* 2:65–66.

1885 "Memorandum on the Mounds at Satsuma and Enterprise, Florida." *American Journal of Archaeology* 1:184–89.

1912 "On the Geological Aspects of the Possible Human Immigration between Asia and America." *American Anthropologist* 14(1):12–18.

1926 "Edward Sylvester Morse." *Science* 63:157–58.

Daniel, Glyn

1981 *A Short History of Archaeology.* London: Thames and Hudson.

Danien, Elin

1999 "George Byron Gordon," in *American National Biography,* J. A. Garraty and M. C. Carnes, eds., vol. 9, pp. 286–87. New York: Oxford University Press.

Darnell, Regna

1998 *And Along Came Boas: Continuity and Revolution in Americanist Anthropology.* Philadelphia: John Benjamins.

2001 *Invisible Genealogies: A History of Americanist Anthropology.* Lincoln: University of Nebraska Press.

Davis, Allison, Burleigh B. Gardner, Mary R. Gardner, and W. Lloyd Warner

1941 *Deep South: A Social Anthropological Study of Caste and Class.* Chicago: University of Chicago Press.

Davis, Collis H.

2001 *Headhunting William Jones.* Text of 58-minute video documentary. Electronic document, www.okara.com/portfolio/html/wmjones.html.

Davis, E. Mott, Jr.

1940 *The Archaeology of Northeastern Asia, with an Introduction by Lauriston Ward.* Papers of the Excavators' Club, vol. 1, no. 1. Cambridge, Mass.: Harvard University.

Davis, Hester A.

2008 *Remembering Awatovi: The Story of an Archaeological Expedition in Northern Arizona, 1935–1939.* Cambridge, Mass.: Peabody Museum Press.

Davis, Hester A., with Valerie Wheeler

1998 "Richard P. Wheeler." *Anthropology Newsletter* 39(3):32.

DeHass, Wills

1851 *History of the Early Settlement and Indian Wars of Western Virginia: Embracing an Account of the Various Expeditions in the West, Previous to 1795.* Wheeling, W. Va.: H. Hobitzell.

1868a "Archaeological Researches in the West." *Scientific American* 19(1):6.

1868b "Western Archaeology." *Scientific American* 19(6):83.

1869a "Archaeology of the Mississippi Valley." *Proceedings of the AAAS* 17:288–302.

1869b "Report on Archaeology and Ethnology." *Proceedings of the AAAS* 17:303–4.

1881a "The Mound-Builders: An Inquiry into Their Assumed Southern Origin." *Smithsonian Miscellaneous Collections* 25:55–57.

1881b "Antiquity of Man in America." *Proceedings of the AAAS* 30:363.

1881c   "Progress of Archaeological Research." *Proceedings of the AAAS* 30:363.

1881d   "The Mound Builders: An Inquiry into Their Assumed Southern Origin." *Proceedings of the AAAS* 30:363.

1882a   "Monumental and Art Remains in the Lake Regions of Ohio, Pennsylvania, and New York." *Proceedings of the AAAS* 31:594.

1882b   "Mountain Antiquities." *Proceedings of the AAAS* 31:594.

1882c   "Geological Testimony to the Antiquity of Man in America." *Proceedings of the AAAS* 31:594.

1886a   "Effigy Mounds of Wisconsin." *Proceedings of the AAAS* 34:421.

1886b   "American Archaeology: Progress of Discovery." *Proceedings of the AAAS* 34:421.

1888   "Systems of Symbols Adapted for American Prehistoric Archaeology." *Proceedings of the AAAS* 36:318.

de Laguna, Frederica

1960   "Ethnography," in *Selected Papers from the American Anthropologist, 1888–1920*, F. de Laguna, ed., pp. 451–56. Evanston, Ill.: Row, Peterson.

de la Peña, Guillermo

1996   "Nacionales y extranjeros en la historia de la antropología mexicana," in *La historia de la antropología en México: Fuentes y transmisión*, M. Rutsch, compiler, pp. 41–82. Mexico City: Universidad Iberoamericana and Instituto Nacional Indigenista.

Demb, Sarah R.

1992   "Historical Note," in *Noel Morss (1904–1981) Papers, 1927–1980: A Finding Aid.* Peabody Museum of Archaeology and Ethnology, Harvard University. Electronic document, www.oasis.lib.harvard.edu/oasis/deliver/~pea00007.

de Milhau, Louis John de Grenon

1931   "Louis John de Grenon de Milhau," in *Class of 1906, 25th Anniversary*, p. 355. Cambridge, Mass.: Harvard University.

DeVore, Irven

1992   "An Interview with Sherwood Washburn." *Current Anthropology* 33(4):411–23.

Dexter, Ralph W.

1956   "The Early *American Naturalist* as Revealed by Letters to the Founders." *American Naturalist* 90(853):209–25.

1957a   "The Salem Meeting of the AAAS (1869)." *Essex Institute Historical Collections* 93(4):260–66.

1957b   "The Summer School at the Peabody Academy of Science 1876–1881." *American Institute of Biological Sciences Bulletin* 7(1):21–23.

1965 "The 'Salem Secession' of Agassiz Zoologists." *Essex Institute Historical Collections* 101(1):27–39.

1966a "Frederic Ward Putnam and the Development of Museums of Natural History and Anthropology in the United States." *Curator* 9(2):151–55.

1966b "Contributions of Frederic Ward Putnam to the Development of Anthropology in California." *Science Education* 50(4):314–18.

1966c "Putnam's Problems Popularizing Anthropology." *American Scientist* 54(3):315–32.

1970 "Peabody Academy's Caleb Cooke, the Devoted." *Biologist* 52(3):112–19.

1974 "From Penikese to the Marine Biological Laboratory at Woods Hole: The Role of Agassiz's Students." *Essex Institute Historical Collections* 110(2):151–61.

1976 "The Role of F. W. Putnam in Developing Anthropology at the American Museum of Natural History." *Curator* 19(4):303–10.

1979 "The Impact of Evolutionary Theories on the Salem Group of Agassiz Zoologists (Morse, Hyatt, Packard, Putnam)." *Essex Institute Historical Collections* 115(3):144–72.

1980 "F. W. Putnam's Role in Developing the Peabody Museum of American Archaeology and Ethnology." *Curator* 23(3):183–93.

1982a "The Putnam–Metz Correspondence on Mound Explorations in Ohio." *Ohio Archaeologist* 32(4):24–28.

1982b "F. W. Putnam as Secretary of the AAAS (1873–1898)." *Essex Institute Historical Collections* 118(2):106–18.

1984 "'Dear Alice': Letters of F. W. Putnam to His Daughter (1874–1914)." *Essex Institute Historical Collections* 120(2):110–31.

Dinnerstein, Leonard

1994 *Antisemitism in America.* New York: Oxford University Press.

Dixon, Roland Burrage

1903a "Howard B. Wilson." *American Anthropologist* 5(4):739.

1903b "Howard Barrett Wilson." *Journal of American Folk-Lore* 16(63):274.

1913 "Some Aspects of North American Archaeology, with Discussion by W. H. Holmes, George Grant MacCurdy, and Berthold Laufer." *American Anthropologist* 15(4):549–77.

1914 "The Early Migrations of the Indians of New England and the Maritime Provinces." *Proceedings of the American Antiquarian Society* 24:65–76.

1916a *Oceanic Mythology.* Boston: Marshall Jones.

1916b "Annual Report of the Acting Curator for 1914–1915, PMAAE," in *Annual Report of the President and Treasurer of Harvard College for 1914–1915,* pp. 254–61.

1923 *The Racial History of Man.* New York: Charles Scribner's Sons.

1928a *The Building of Cultures.* New York: Charles Scribner's Sons.

1928b "Frederic W. Putnam," in *Dictionary of American Biography*, vol. 15, pp. 276–78. New York: Charles Scribner's Sons.

1930 "Anthropology, 1866–1929," in *The Development of Harvard University since the Inauguration of President Eliot, 1869–1929*, S. E. Morison, ed., pp. 202–15. Cambridge, Mass.: Harvard University Press.

Dixon, Roland B., and Charles D. Drew

1897 "Observations on the Physiography of Western Massachusetts." *Science* 6(153):847.

Dockstader, Frederick J.

1972 "Mark Raymond Harrington, 1882–1971." *Indian Notes* 8:26–27.

Donohue, Alice A.

1985 "One Hundred Years of the *American Journal of Archaeology:* An Archival History." *American Journal of Archaeology* 89(1):3–30.

Dorsey, George Amos

1893 "South American Archaeology at the World's Fair." *American Antiquarian* 15(6):373–76.

1894 "The Study of Anthropology in American Colleges." *Archaeologist* 2(12):368–73.

1896 "The History of the Study of Anthropology at Harvard University." *Denison Quarterly* 4(2):77–97.

1900 "The Department of Anthropology of the Field Columbian Museum: A Review of Six Years." *American Anthropologist* 2:247–65.

1903 "The American Anthropological Association." *American Anthropologist* 5(1):178–92.

Dorson, Richard M.

1980 "John Reed Swanton," in *Dictionary of American Biography, Supplement 6*, pp. 611–13. New York: Charles Scribner's Sons.

Dort, Anne V.

1954 "The Archaeological Institute of America: Early Days." *Archaeology* 7(4):195–201.

Doughty, Howard

1962 *Francis Parkman*. New York: Macmillan.

Douglas, Robert Dick, Jr., David R. Martin Jr., and Douglas L. Oliver

1928 *Three Boy Scouts in Africa, on Safari with Martin Johnson*. New York: G. P. Putnam's Sons.

Drooker, Penelope Ballard

1997 *The View from Madisonville: Protohistoric Western Fort Ancient Interaction Patterns*. Ann Arbor: Museum of Anthropology, University of Michigan.

Dufour, Darna L.

1988 "Alice Mossie Brues (1913–)," in *Women Anthropologists: A Biographical Dictionary*, U. Gacs et al., eds., pp. 23–28. New York: Greenwood.

Dunham, Dows

1942 "George Andrew Reisner." *American Journal of Archaeology* 46(3):410–12.

Dunning, Rev. Edward O.

1872 "Account of Antiquities in Tennessee," in *Annual Report of the Smithsonian Institution for 1870*, pp. 376–80. Washington, D.C.

Dupree, A. Hunter

1959 *Asa Gray, 1810–1888*. Cambridge, Mass.: Belknap Press.

Dutton, Lee S.

1991 "Henry Otley Beyer," in *International Dictionary of Anthropologists*, C. Winters, ed., pp. 56–57. New York: Garland.

Dyck, Ian

1998 "Toward a History of Archaeology in the National Museum of Canada: The Contributions of Harlan I. Smith and Douglas Leechman, 1911–1950," in *Bringing Back the Past: Historical Perspectives on Canadian Archaeology*, P. J. Smith and D. Mitchell, eds., pp. 115–33. Hull: Canadian Museum of Civilization.

Edwards, Amelia B.

1892 "Pharaohs, Fellahs, and Explorers." *Atlantic Monthly* 69(415):682–84.

Ehrich, Robert W.

1939 "Late Cemetery Crania," in *Nuzi: Report on the Excavation at Yorgan Tepa near Kirkuk, Iraq, Conducted by Harvard University in Conjunction with the American Schools of Oriental Research and the University Museum of Philadelphia, 1927–1931*, R. F. S. Starr, ed., vol. 1, pp. 570–90. Cambridge, Mass.: Harvard-Radcliffe Fine Arts Series.

Ehrich, Robert W., and Emilie Pleslová-Stiková

1968 *Homolka: An Eneolithic Site in Bohemia*. Cambridge, Mass.: Peabody Museum, Harvard University.

Ehrich, Robert W., and Evzen Plesl

n.d. "Contributions to the Archaeology of Czechoslovakia," Manuscripts (2012.1.20). Peabody Museum Archives, Harvard University.

Eliot, Charles William

1924 "Fiftieth Anniversary." *Proceedings of the Massachusetts Historical Society* 57(1):5–13.

1969 "Inaugural Address [1869]," in *A Turning Point in Higher Education: The Inaugural Address of Charles William Eliot as President of Harvard College, October 19, 1869*, N. M. Pusey, ed., pp. 1–30. Cambridge, Mass.: Harvard University Press.

Eliot, Henry Ware, Jr.

1939a "Chronology," in *Nuzi: Report on the Excavation at Yorgan Tepa near Kirkuk, Iraq, Conducted by Harvard University in Conjunction with the American Schools of Oriental Research and the University Museum of Philadelphia, 1927–1931*, R. F. S. Starr, ed., vol. 1, pp. 507–22. Cambridge, Mass.: Harvard-Radcliffe Fine Arts Series.

1939b "The Pottery from Kudish Saghir," in *Nuzi: Report on the Excavation at Yorgan Tepa near Kirkuk, Iraq, Conducted by Harvard University in Conjunction with the American Schools of Oriental Research and the University Museum of Philadelphia, 1927–1931*, R. F. S. Starr, ed., vol. 1, pp. 608–15. Cambridge, Mass.: Harvard-Radcliffe Fine Arts Series.

Elliott, Clark A.

1992 "Appendix 2: Chronological Overview of Harvard Science (1636–1945)," in *Science at Harvard University: Historical Perspectives*, C. A. Elliott and M. W. Rossiter, eds., pp. 331–60. Bethlehem, Pa.: Lehigh University Press.

Elliott, Melinda

1995 *Great Excavations: Tales of Early Southwestern Archaeology, 1888–1939*. Santa Fe, N.M.: School of American Research Press.

Elman, Robert

1977 *First in the Field: America's Pioneering Naturalists*. New York: Mason/Charter.

Emerson, Edward Waldo

1918 *The Early Years of the Saturday Club*. Boston: Houghton Mifflin.

Emmert, John W.

1891 "Ancient Cemeteries in Tennessee." *American Anthropologist* 4(1):94–95.

Euler, Robert C.

1969 "The Archaeology of the Canyon Country," in *John Wesley Powell and the Anthropology of the Canyon Country*, D. D. Fowler, R. C. Euler, and C. S. Fowler, eds., pp. 8–20. Geological Survey Professional Paper 670. Washington, D.C.: Department of the Interior.

1997 "Walter Willard Taylor, 1913–1997." *SAA Bulletin* 15(4):23.

Evans, Kenneth J.

2001 "Mark Harrington (1882–1971): Raymond of the Caves." *Las Vegas Review-Journal*. Electronic document, www.1st100.com/part1/harrington.html.

Evans, Nancy L.

1987 "Frederick Starr: Missionary for Anthropology." M.A. thesis, Department of Anthropology, Indiana University, Bloomington.

Evelyn, Douglas E.

1985 "The National Gallery at the Patent Office," in *Magnificent Voyagers: The United States Exploring Expedition, 1838–1842,* H. J. Viola and C. Margolis, eds., pp. 227–42. Washington, D.C.: Smithsonian Institution.

Eyde, Richard H.

1985 "Expedition Botany: The Making of a New Profession," in *Magnificent Voyagers: The United States Exploring Expedition, 1838–1842,* H. J. Viola and C. Margolis, eds., pp. 25–42. Washington, D.C.: Smithsonian Institution.

Fahnestock, Polly J.

1984 "History and Theoretical Development: The Importance of a Critical Historiography in Archaeology." *Archaeological Review from Cambridge* 3(1):7–18.

Falk, Peter H.

1985 *Who Was Who in American Art, 1898–1947.* Madison, Conn.: Sound View Press.

Fallaize, Edward Nichol

1923 "Adela C. Breton." *Man* 33:125–26.

Farabee, William Curtis

1924 *Indian Tribes of Eastern Peru.* Papers of the PMAAE, vol. 10. Cambridge, Mass.: Harvard University.

Farlow, William Gilson

1889 "Memoir of Asa Gray, 1810–1888." *National Academy of Sciences, Biographical Memoirs* 3(8):161–75.

Fenton, William Nelson

1959 "John Reed Swanton, 1873–1958." *American Anthropologist* 61(4):663–68.

1991 "Frank G. Speck's Anthropology, 1881–1950," in *The Life and Times of Frank G. Speck, 1881–1950,* R. Blankenship, ed., pp. 9–31. University of Pennsylvania Publications in Anthropology 4. Philadelphia.

Fewkes, Jesse Walter

1891 "A Few Summer Ceremonials at Zuni Pueblo." *Journal of American Ethnology and Archaeology (Hemenway Southwestern Archaeological Expedition)* 1:1–62.

1892a "A Few Summer Ceremonials at the Tusayan Pueblos." *Journal of American Ethnology and Archaeology (Hemenway Southwestern Archaeological Expedition)* 2:1–160.

1892b "A Report on the Present Condition of a Ruin in Arizona called Casa Grande." *Journal of American Ethnology and Archaeology (Hemenway Southwestern Archaeological Expedition)* 2:177–93.

1912   "The Problems of Unity or Plurality and the Probable Place of Origin of the American Aborigines." *American Anthropologist* 14(1):1–4.

Fewkes, Jesse Walter, and John G. Owens

1892   "The La-la-kon-ta: A Tusayan Dance." *American Anthropologist* 5(2):105–29.

Fewkes, Jesse Walter, Alexander M. Stephen, and John G. Owens

1894   "The Snake Ceremonials at Walpi." *Journal of American Ethnology and Archaeology (Hemenway Southwestern Archaeological Expedition)* 4:1–126.

Fleming, Donald

1986a   "Eliot's New Broom," in *Glimpses of the Harvard Past*, B. Bailyn et al., eds., pp. 63–76. Cambridge, Mass.: Harvard University Press.

1986b   "Harvard's Golden Age?" in *Glimpses of the Harvard Past*, B. Bailyn et al., eds., pp. 77–95. Cambridge, Mass.: Harvard University Press.

Fletcher, Alice C.

1882   "The Sun Dance of the Ogallala Sioux." *Proceedings of the AAAS* 31:580–84.

1894   "The Shadow or Ghost Lodge: A Ceremony of the Ogallala Sioux." *Annual Reports of the Peabody Museum* 3(4):296–307.

1895   "The Sacred Pole of the Omaha Tribe." *American Antiquarian* 17(5):257–68.

1898   "A Study from the Omaha Tribe: The Import of the Totem," in *Annual Report of the Smithsonian Institution for 1897*, pp. 577–86. Washington, D.C.

1909   "Tribal Structure: A Study of the Omaha and Cognate Tribes," in *Putnam Anniversary Volume: Anthropological Essays Presented to Frederic Ward Putnam in Honor of His Seventieth Birthday, April 16, 1909, by His Friends and Associates*, F. Boas et al., eds., pp. 256–67. New York: G. E. Stechert.

1915   "The Study of Indian Music." *Proceedings of the National Academy of Sciences* 1:231–35.

Fletcher, Alice C., Francis La Flesche, and John C. Fillmore

1893   *A Study of Omaha Indian Music.* Papers of the PMAAE, vol. 1, no. 5. Cambridge, Mass.: Harvard University.

Fletcher, Alice, and Tilly [Matilda] C. Stevenson

1889   "Report of the Committee on the Preservation of Archaeological Remains on the Public Lands." *Proceedings of the AAAS* 37:35–37.

Fletcher, John Gould

1937   *Life Is My Song: The Autobiography of John Gould Fletcher.* New York: Farrar and Rinehart.

Flint, Earl

1882   "Antiquities of Nicaragua: Origin of the Palenque Builders." *American Antiquarian* 4(4):289–302.

1883 "Rock Inscriptions in Peru," in *Annual Report of the Smithsonian Institution for 1881*, pp. 681–82. Washington, D.C.

1884 "Human Footprints in Nicaragua." *American Antiquarian* 6:112–14.

1886a "Pre-Adamite Foot-prints." *American Antiquarian* 8:230–33.

1886b "Nicaraguan Foot Prints Again." *American Antiquarian* 8:373–74.

1888a "Human Foot Prints in the Eocene." *American Antiquarian* 10:252–54.

1888b "Paleolithics in Nicaragua." *American Antiquarian* 10:381–82.

1889a "The Age of the Nicaraguan Foot Prints." *American Antiquarian* 11:120–21.

1889b "Nicaraguan Foot-prints." *American Antiquarian* 11(5):306–11.

1890 "What Dr. Flint Has to Say about the Nicaragua Footprints (Extracts from a letter of Dr. Earl Flint of Revas, Nicaragua, to Hilborne T. Cresson of Philadelphia)." *Science* 15(362):30–32.

Flint, Timothy

1826 *Recollections of the Last Ten Years, Passed in Occasional Residences and Journeyings in the Valley of the Mississippi, from Pittsburgh and the Missouri to the Gulf of Mexico, and from Florida to the Spanish Frontier, in a Series of Letters to the Rev. James Flint of Salem, Massachusetts.* Boston: Cummings, Hilliard and Co.

1828 *The Condensed History and Geography of the Western States, or the Mississippi Valley.* Cincinnati: E. H. Flint.

1833 *Indian Wars of the West: Containing Biographical Sketches of Those Pioneers Who Headed the Western Settlers in Repelling the Attacks of the Savages, Together with a View of the Character, Manners, Monuments, and Antiquities of the Western Indians.* Cincinnati, Ohio: E. H. Flint.

Florimond, Joseph (Le Duc de Loubat)

1912 *Joseph Florimond, Le Duc de Loubat, 1894–1912.* Paris: Typographie Philippe Renouard.

Folsom, Cora M.

1893 "Record of Returned Indian Students," in *Twenty-two Years' Work of the Hampton Normal and Agricultural Institute at Hampton, Virginia*, pp. 317–493. Hampton, Va.: Normal School Press.

Ford, Henry A., and Kate B. Ford, compilers

1881 *History of Cincinnati, Ohio.* Cleveland, Ohio: L. A. Williams.

Forsythe, Scott M.

2002 "Cornelius C. Cusick: An Indian Officer in the Frontier Army." Paper presented at the annual meeting of the Western History Association, San Diego, October.

Fowler, Don D.

1986 "Conserving American Archaeological Resources," in *American Archaeology Past and Future: A Celebration of the Society for American Archaeology 1935–1985*, D. J. Meltzer, D. D. Fowler, and J. A. Sabloff, eds., pp. 135–62. Washington, D.C.: Smithsonian Institution Press.

2000 *A Laboratory for Anthropology: Science and Romanticism in the American Southwest, 1846–1930.* Albuquerque: University of New Mexico Press.

Fowler, Don D., and Catherine S. Fowler

1969a "John Wesley Powell's Anthropological Fieldwork," in *John Wesley Powell and the Anthropology of the Canyon Country*, D. D. Fowler, R. C. Euler, and C. S. Fowler, eds., pp. 2–7. Geological Survey Professional Paper 670. Washington, D.C.: Department of the Interior.

1969b "The Ethnography of the Canyon Country," in *John Wesley Powell and the Anthropology of the Canyon Country*, D. D. Fowler, R. C. Euler, and C. S. Fowler, eds., pp. 20–28. Geological Survey Professional Paper 670. Washington, D.C.: Department of the Interior.

Fritz, Gayle J., and Bruce D. Smith

1988 "Old Collections and New Technology: Documenting the Domestication of *Chenopodium* in Eastern North America." *Midcontinental Journal of Archaeology* 13(1):3–27.

Fry, C. George, and Jon Paul Fry

1989 *Congregationalists and Evolution: Asa Gray and Louis Agassiz.* Lanham, Md.: University Press of America.

Fuller, Anne Hutchinson

1961 *Buarij: Portrait of a Lebanese Muslim Village.* Harvard Middle Eastern Monographs, no. 6. Cambridge, Mass.: Harvard University Press.

Fuller, Robert Gorham

1911 "Anthropology V: Notes on Dr. Dixon's Lectures." Typescript, 2 vols. Harvard University Archives.

1919 "Robert Gorham Fuller," in *Harvard College Class of 1904, Secretary's 15th Annual Report*, p. 166. Cambridge, Mass.: Riverside Press.

n.d.a "Drawings of Types of Stone Implements in the Peabody Museum." Unpublished paper, PMAAE. Harvard University Archives.

n.d.b "Types of Stone Implements in North America." Unpublished paper, PMAAE. Harvard University Archives.

Gallatin, Albert

1836 *A Synopsis of the Indian Tribes within the United States East of the Rocky Mountains, and in the British and Russian Possessions in North America.*

Transactions and Collections of the American Antiquarian Society, vol. 2, pp. 1–422. Worcester, Mass. Reprint, 2008, Merchantville, N.J.: Evolution.

Gamio, Manuel

1942 "Franz Boas en Mexico." *Boletín Bibliográfico de Antropología Americana* 6(1–3):35–42.

Garman, Samuel W.

1882 "Remarks on Indian Medicine." *Proceedings of the BSNH* 22:95.

1888 "An Andean Medal." *Bulletin of the Essex Institute* 20:1–4.

1889 "On the Age of the Andean Medal." *Bulletin of the Essex Institute* 21:94–98.

Garn, Stanley M., and Eugene Giles

1997 "Earnest Albert Hooton (November 20, 1887–May 3, 1954)." *National Academy of Sciences, Biographical Memoirs* 71:166–79.

Gerrodette, Frank Honore

1892 "Linguistic Stocks of the Indians of Mexico and Central America." Unpublished paper in the Tozzer Library, Harvard University.

Gibbs, George

1855 "No Antiquities in Oregon," in *Information Respecting the History, Conditions and Prospects of the Indian Tribes of the United States,* H. R. Schoolcraft, ed., vol. 5, pp. 662–65. Philadelphia: Lippincott.

1862 "Instructions for Archaeological Investigations in the United States," in *Annual Report of the Smithsonian Institution for 1861,* pp. 292–96. Washington, D.C.

1867 [1863] *Instruction for Research Relative to the Ethnology and Philology of America.* Smithsonian Miscellaneous Collections 7, no. 11. Washington, D.C.

Gibson, Arthur Hopkin, compiler

1975 *Artists of Early Michigan: A Biographical Dictionary of Artists Native to or Active in Michigan, 1701–1900.* Detroit, Mich.: Wayne State University Press.

Gifford, Carol A., and Elizabeth A. Morris

1985 "Digging for Credit: Early Archaeological Field Schools in the American Southwest." *American Antiquity* 50(2):395–411.

Gilbertson, Albert N.

1914 "In Memoriam: Alexander Francis Chamberlain." *American Anthropologist* 16(2):337–48.

Giles, Eugene

1979 "William W. Howells," in *International Encyclopedia of the Social Sciences,* D. L. Sills, ed., vol. 18, pp. 328–30. New York: Free Press.

1991 "Earnest Albert Hooton," in *International Dictionary of Anthropologists*, C. Winters, ed., pp. 303–4. New York: Garland.

1996 "Frederick Seymour Hulse, February 11, 1906–May 16, 1990." *National Academy of Sciences, Biographical Memoirs* 70:174–89.

Gillette, Charles E.

1952 "Charles Reuben Keyes." *American Antiquity* 18(2):155.

Gillin, John P.

1954 "Ralph Linton, 1893–1953." *American Anthropologist* 56(2):274–81.

Gillin, John P., and Glover Morrill Allen

1941 *Archaeological Investigations in Central Utah: Report of the Joint Expedition of the University of Utah and the Peabody Museum, Harvard University, 1937*. Papers of the PMAAE, vol. 17, no. 2. Cambridge, Mass.: Harvard University.

Gillin John P., and Robert Anderson

1938 *Archaeological Investigations in Nine Mile Canyon, Utah, during the Year 1936*. Bulletin of the University of Utah, vol. 28, no. 11. Salt Lake City.

Gillman, Henry

1870 "Lake Superior Plants Compared with Eastern Specimens." *American Naturalist* 3(3):155–56.

1871 "The Flattest Tibia on Record." *American Naturalist* 5(10):663.

1874 "The Mound-Builders and Platycnemism in Michigan," in *Annual Report of the Smithsonian Institution for 1873*, pp. 364–90. Washington, D.C.

1875a "Perforation of the Humerus Conjoined with Platycnemism." *American Naturalist* 9(7):427–28.

1875b "Artificial Perforation of the Cranium." *American Naturalist* 9(8):473–77.

1876a "Certain Characteristics Pertaining to Ancient Man in Michigan," in *Annual Report of the Smithsonian Institution for 1875*, pp. 234–45. Washington, D.C.

1876b "The Ancient Men of the Great Lakes." *Proceedings of the AAAS* 24:316–31.

1877a "Peculiarities of the Femora from Tumuli in Michigan." *Proceedings of the AAAS* 25:300–307.

1877b "Some Observations on the Orbits of Mound Crania." *Proceedings of the AAAS* 25:307–11.

1877c "Investigations of the Burial Mound at Fort Wayne, on the Detroit River, Michigan." *Proceedings of the AAAS* 25:311–25.

1878a "Additional Facts concerning Artificial Perforation of the Crania in Ancient Mounds in Michigan." *Proceedings of the AAAS* 26:335–40.

1878b "Crania Utilized as Cinerary Urns in a Burial Mound in Florida." *American Naturalist* 12(11):752–54.

1879 "Remarkable Burials Custom from a Mound in Florida: The Cranium Utilized as a Cinerary Urn." *Proceedings of the AAAS* 27:309–11.

1898 *Hassan, a Fellah: A Romance of Palestine.* Boston: Little, Brown.

Givens, Douglas R.

1992 *Alfred Vincent Kidder and the Development of Americanist Archaeology.* Albuquerque: University of New Mexico Press.

Goddard, Pliny Earle

1925 "Dr. Charles F. Newcombe." *American Anthropologist* 27(2):352–53.

Goodale, George Lincoln

1889 "Sketch of the Life and Works of Dr. Asa Gray." *Proceedings of the BSNH* 24:191–98.

1913 "Alexander Agassiz." *National Academy of Sciences, Bibliographical Memoirs* 7(12):389–405.

Gordon, Dudley

1972 *Charles F. Lummis: Crusader in Corduroy.* Los Angeles: Cultural Assets Press.

Gorenstein, Shirley

2002 "Gordon Randolph Willey (1913–2002)." *American Anthropologist* 104(4):1254–56.

Gosling, Andrew

1997 "An American in Manila: Otley Beyer and His Collection at the National Library of Australia." *National Library of Australia News* 7(10):6–8.

Gradwohl, David M.

1978 "Fred H. Sterns: A Pioneer in the Pursuit of Plains Prehistory." *Nebraska History* 59(2):180–209.

Grandgent, Charles H.

1927 "William Watson Goodwin (1831–1912)," in *Later Years of the Saturday Club, 1870–1920,* M. Howe, ed., pp. 214–22. Boston: Houghton Mifflin.

Gray, Asa

1875a "Address of Professor Asa Gray: Memorial of the Late Professor Jeffries Wyman." *Proceedings of the BSNH* 17:96–124.

1875b "Report of the Curator." *Annual Reports of the PMAAE* 1(8):7–12.

Green, Martin

1966 *The Problem of Boston: Some Readings in Cultural History.* New York: W. W. Norton.

Greene, Jerome A.

1991 *Yellowstone Command: Colonel Nelson A. Miles and the Great Sioux War, 1876–1877.* Lincoln: University of Nebraska Press.

Greene, John C.

1984 *American Science in the Age of Jefferson.* Ames: Iowa State University Press.

Griffin, James B.

1943 *The Fort Ancient Aspect: Its Cultural and Chronological Position in Mississippi Valley Archaeology.* Ann Arbor: University of Michigan.

1976 "Carl Eugen Guthe (1893–1974)." *American Antiquity* 41(2):168–72.

Griffin, James B., David J. Meltzer, Bruce D. Smith, and William C. Sturtevant

1988 "A Mammoth Fraud in Science." *American Antiquity* 53(3):578–82.

Grinnell, George Bird

1910 "Othniel Charles Marsh, Paleontologist, 1831–1899," in *Leading American Men of Science,* D. S. Jordan, ed., pp. 283–312. New York: Henry Holt.

Griswold, Leon Stacy

1891 *Whetstones and the Noviculites of Arkansas.* Annual Report of the Geological Society of Arkansas for 1890, vol. 3.

1892 "The Purchase of Whetstones." *Manufacturer and Builder* 24(8):182.

1893a "Indian Quarries in Arkansas." *Proceedings of the BSNH* 26:25–26.

1893b "A Basic Dike in the Connecticut Triassic." *Bulletin of the Museum of Comparative Zoology,* 2nd series, 16(4):239–42.

1896 "Notes on the Geology of Southern Florida." *Bulletin of the Museum of Comparative Zoology,* 2nd series, 28(2):27–62.

1898 "The Geology of Helena, Montana, and Vicinity." *Journal of the Association of Engineering Societies* 20(1):1–18.

Grollig, Francis X.

1991 "Frans F. Blom," in *International Dictionary of Anthropologists,* C. Winters, ed., pp. 64–65. New York: Garland.

Groot, Gerard

1948 "Archaeological Activities in Japan since August 15, 1945." *American Anthropologist* 50(1):166–71.

Gruber, Jacob W.

1967 "Horatio Hale and the Development of American Anthropology." *Proceedings of the American Philosophical Society* 111(1):5–37.

1981 "American Archaeology and Physical Anthropology in Historical Perspective." *American Journal of Physical Anthropology* 56(4):473–82.

Guernsey, Isabel Hannah

1938 "A Study of Ancient Peruvian Textiles." *Report for the Institute of Andean Research 1937–38,* pp. 7–8.

Guernsey, Samuel James

1916 "Notes on Explorations of Martha's Vineyard." *American Anthropologist* 18:81–97.

Gunnerson, James H. (with appendixes by Walton C. Galinat and Margaret A. Towle)

1969 *The Fremont Culture: A Study in Culture Dynamics on the Northern Anasazi Frontier, including the Report of the Claflin-Emerson Expedition of the Peabody Museum.* Papers of the PMAE, vol. 59, no. 2. Cambridge, Mass.: Harvard University. Reprint, 2009, Salt Lake City: University of Utah Press.

Guthe, Carl E.

1935 "The Society for American Archaeology: Organization Meeting." *American Antiquity* 1(2):141–46.

Guyot, Arnold

1878 "Memoir of Louis Agassiz, 1807–1873." *National Academy of Sciences, Biographical Memoirs* 2(3):39–73.

Haag, William G.

1985 "Federal Aid to Archaeology in the Southeast, 1933–1942." *American Antiquity* 50(2):272–80.

Hale, Horatio E.

1846 *Narrative of the United States Exploring Expedition, 1838 to 1842,* vol. 6, *Ethnography and Philology.* Philadelphia: Lea and Blanchard.

1893 "Sketch of Sir Daniel Wilson." *Popular Science Monthly* 44(12):256–65.

Hallowell, A. Irving

1951 "Frank Gouldsmith Speck, 1881–1950." *American Anthropologist* 53(1):47–75.

1960 "The Beginnings of Anthropology in America," in *Selected Papers from the American Anthropologist, 1888–1920,* F. de Laguna, ed., pp. 1–90. Evanston, Ill.: Row, Peterson.

Hammond, Harriet

1930 "Maya Art." *Fogg Art Museum Notes* 2:203–21.

Hanaford, Phebe A.

1870 *The Life of George Peabody; Containing a Record of Those Princely Acts of Benevolence which Entitle Him to the Esteem and Gratitude of All Friends of Education and the Destitute, both in America, the Land of His Birth, and in England, the Place of His Death.* Boston: B. B. Russell.

Handlin, Oscar

1986a "Making Men of the Boys," in *Glimpses of the Harvard Past,* B. Bailyn et al., eds., pp. 45–63. Cambridge, Mass.: Harvard University Press.

1986b "A Small Community," in *Glimpses of the Harvard Past,* B. Bailyn et al., eds., pp. 97–113. Cambridge, Mass.: Harvard University Press.

Harley, George Way

1938 "Native African Medicine." Ph.D. dissertation, Hartford Seminary Foundation, Kennedy School of Missions.

1941a *Notes on the Poro in Liberia.* Papers of the PMAE, vol. 19, no. 2. Cambridge, Mass.: Harvard University.

1941b *Native African Medicine, with Special Reference to Its Practice in the Mano Tribe of Liberia.* Cambridge, Mass.: Harvard University Press.

Harrington, Mark Raymond

1901 "An Abenaki 'Witch–Story.'" *Journal of American Folk-Lore* 14:160.

1903a "Notes on Indian Camp Sites near Silver Lake." *Proceedings of the Natural History Association of Staten Island,* vol. 8, January 10.

1903b "Recent Excavations in Indian Camp Sites at Mariner's Harbor." *Proceedings of the Natural History Association of Staten Island,* vol. 8, March 14.

1903c "Shinnecock Notes." *Journal of American Folk-Lore* 16:37–39.

1906 "Da-ra-sa-kwa: A Caughnawaga Legend." *Journal of American Folk-Lore* 19:127–29.

1908a "Iroquois Silverwork." *Anthropological Papers of the AMNH* 1:351–69.

1908b "The Last of the Iroquois Potters." *New York State Museum Bulletin* 133:222–27.

1908c "Catawba Potters and Their Work." *American Anthropologist* 10(3):398–407.

1908d "Vestiges of Material Culture among the Canadian Delaware." *American Anthropologist* 10(3):408–18.

1908e "Some Seneca Corn-Foods and Their Preparation." *American Anthropologist* 10(4):575–90.

1909a "Some Unusual Iroquois Specimens." *American Anthropologist* 11(1):85–91.

1909b "The Rock-Shelters of Armonk, New York." *Anthropological Papers of the AMNH* 3:128–38.

1909c "Ancient Shell Heaps near New York City." *Anthropological Papers of the AMNH* 3:167–79.

1924 "An Ancient Village Site of the Shinnecock Indians." *Anthropological Papers of the AMNH* 22(5):227–83.

1926 "Alanson Skinner." *American Anthropologist* 28(1):275–80.

1929 "Alanson Skinner." *Indian Notes* (Museum of the American Indian) 2(4):246–57.

Harris, Charles H., III, and Louis R. Sadler

2003 *The Archaeologist Was a Spy: Sylvanus G. Morley and the Office of Naval Intelligence.* Albuquerque: University of New Mexico Press.

Harrison, Charles Custis

1927 "Dr. George Byron Gordon." *Museum Journal* 18(1):5–8.

Hartt, Charles Frederick

1871a "Brazilian Rock Inscriptions." *American Naturalist* 5(3):139–47.

1871b "The Ancient Indian Pottery of Marajo, Brazil." *American Naturalist* 5(5):259–71.

1872a "On the Occurrence of Face Urns in Brazil." *American Naturalist* 6(10):607–10.

1872b "Notes on the Lingoa Geral, or Modern Tupi of the Amazonas." Boston: n.p.

1875a "On the Manufacture of Pottery among Savage Races." *American Naturalist* 9(2):78–93.

1875b "The Indian Cemetery of the Gruta das Momia, Southern Minas Gerais, Brazil." *American Naturalist* 9(4):205–17.

1875c *Amazonian Tortoise Myths.* Rio de Janeiro: W. Scully.

Harvard University

1879 *Annual Report of the President and Treasurer of Harvard College for 1878–1879.*

1886 "President's Report for 1885–1886," in *Annual Report of the President and Treasurer of Harvard College for 1885–1886,* pp. 3–24.

1895 *The Harvard University Catalogue, 1895–96.*

1898 "Appendix: The Transfer of the Peabody Museum," in *Annual Report of the President and Treasurer of Harvard College for 1896–1897,* pp. 278–80.

1899 "President's Report for 1898–1899," in *Annual Report of the President and Treasurer of Harvard College for 1898–1899,* pp. 5–54.

1905 "The Library," in *Reports of the President and Treasurer of Harvard College, 1903–1904,* pp. 209–35.

1918 "The Faculty of Medicine," in *Reports of the President and Treasurer of Harvard College, 1916–1917,* pp. 142–46.

1930 *Quinquennial Catalogue of the Officers and Graduates, 1636–1930.*

1937 *Historical Register of Harvard University, 1636–1936.*

1938 *Official Register of Harvard University,* vol. 35, no. 4.

1940 "Report of the President of Harvard College and Report of Departments." *Official Register of Harvard University,* vol. 37, no. 12.

Haskins, Charles H.

1912 "The Graduate School of Arts and Sciences," in *Reports of the President and Treasurer of Harvard College, 1911,* pp. 88–105.

1918 "The Graduate School of Arts and Sciences," in *Reports of the President and Treasurer of Harvard College for 1916–1917,* pp. 77–95.

1930   "The Graduate School of Arts and Sciences, 1872–1929," in *The Development of Harvard University since the Inauguration of President Eliot, 1869–1929*, S. E. Morison, ed., pp. 451–62. Cambridge, Mass.: Harvard University Press.

Hauptman, Laurence M.

1993   *The Iroquois in the Civil War: From Battlefield to Reservation.* Syracuse, N.Y.: Syracuse University Press.

1995   *Between Two Fires: American Indians in the Civil War.* New York: Free Press.

Haury, Emil Walter

1995   "Wherefore a Harvard Ph.D.?" *Journal of the Southwest* 37(4):710–33.

Haven, Samuel Foster

1856   *Archaeology of the United States, or, Sketches, Historical and Bibliographical, of the Progress of Information and Opinion respecting Vestiges of Antiquity in the United States.* Washington, D.C.: Smithsonian Institution.

Hawkes, Ernest William, and Ralph Linton

1916   "A Pre-Lenape Site in New Jersey." *University Museum Anthropological Publications* 6(3):45–77. Philadelphia.

1921   "A Pre-Lenape Site in New Jersey." *American Anthropologist* 19(4):487–94.

Hawkins, Hugh

1972   *Between Harvard and America: The Educational Leadership of Charles W. Eliot.* New York: Oxford University Press.

1979   "University Identity: The Teaching and Research Functions," in *The Organization of Knowledge in Modern America, 1860–1920*, A. Oleson and J. Voss, eds., pp. 285–312. Baltimore, Md.: Johns Hopkins University Press.

Hayden, Irwin

1934   *An Archaeologist Afield: Keet Seel Ruins.* Riverside, Calif.

Haynes, Henry Williamson

1881a   "Discovery of Palaeolithic Flint Implements in Upper Egypt." *Memoirs of the American Academy of Arts and Sciences* 10:357–61.

1881b   "The Argillite Implements Found in the Gravels of the Delaware River, at Trenton, N.J., Compared with the Palaeolithic Implements of Europe." *Proceedings of the BSNH* 21:132–37.

1882a   "Some Indications of an Early Race of Men in New England." *Proceedings of the BSNH* 21:382–91.

1882b   "Some New Evidences of Cannibalism among the Indians of New England from the Island of Mt. Desert, Me." *Proceedings of the BSNH* 22:60–63.

1882c   "What Is the True Site of 'the Seven Cities of Cibola' Visited by Coronado in 1540?" *Proceedings of the American Antiquarian Society* 1:421–35.

1883a   "Notes upon Ancient Soap-stone Quarries, Worked for the Manufacture of Cooking Utensils." *Proceedings of the American Antiquarian Society* 2:364–65.

1883b   "Agricultural Implements of the New England Indians." *Proceedings of the BSNH* 22:437–43.

1885   "Notes on Copper Implements of America." *Proceedings of the American Antiquarian Society* 3:335–38.

1886a   "The Bow and Arrow Unknown to Palaeolithic Man." *Proceedings of the BSNH* 23:269–74.

1886b   "Localities of Quarries Worked by Indians for Material for Their Stone Implements." *Proceedings of the BSNH* 23:333–36.

1886c   "Early Explorations in Mexico," in *Narrative and Critical History of America*, J. Winsor, ed., vol. 2, pp. 473–504. Boston: Houghton Mifflin.

1888   "Indian Wrist-Guard." *Science* 11(266):121–22.

1889a   "The Prehistoric Archaeology of North America," in *Narrative and Critical History of America*, J. Winsor, ed., vol. 1, pp. 329–68. Boston: Houghton Mifflin.

1889b   "Recent Progress in American Archaeology," in *Tenth Annual Report of the Archaeological Institute of America*, pp. 95–105. Cambridge, Mass.

1890a   "Prehistoric Man in America." *American Anthropologist* 3(2):198–200.

1890b   "Supposed Aboriginal Fish-Weirs in Naaman's Creek, near Claymont, Del." (Letter.) *Science* 15(369):151.

1890c   "A Paleolithic Implement from the Valley of Tuscarawas, Ohio." *Proceedings of the BSNH* 25:49–52.

1893a   "Further Evidence of Cannibalism among the Indians of New England." *Proceedings of the BSNH* 26:29–32.

1893b   "Paleolithic Man in North America." *Science* 21(522):66–67.

1893c   "Paleolithic Man in North America." *American Antiquarian* 15(1):37–42.

1893d   "The Palaeolithic Man Once More." *Science* 21(532):208–9.

1893e   "The Palaeolithic Man in Ohio." *Science* 21(538):291.

1893f   "Early Man in Minnesota." *Science* 21(540):318–19.

1894   "Palaeolithic Pottery." *Science* 23(581):161–62.

1895   "Shells as Implements." *Science* 2(44):593.

1900   "Progress of American Archaeology during the Past Ten Years." *Journal of the Archaeological Institute of America*, series 2, 4:17–39.

Hellman, Geoffrey

1968   *Bankers, Bones, and Beetles: The First Century of the American Museum of Natural History.* Garden City, N.Y.: Natural History Press.

Herold, Elaine A. Bluhm

1971 *The Indian Mounds at Albany, Illinois.* Anthropological Papers, no. 1. Davenport, Iowa: Davenport Museum.

Herr, Melody

1999 "Communities of American Archaeology: Identity in the Era of Professionalization." Ph.D. dissertation, History of Science, Johns Hopkins University.

Herskovits, Melville J., and Barbara Ames, eds.

1950 *Directory of Anthropologists.* 3rd ed. Ann Arbor, Mich.: Edwards Brothers.

Hertzberg, Hazel Whitman

1978 "Arthur C. Parker, Seneca, 1881–1955," in *American Indian Intellectuals,* M. Liberty, ed., pp. 128–38. St. Paul, Minn.: West Publishing.

1979 "Nationality, Anthropology, and Pan-Indianism in the Life of Arthur C. Parker (Seneca)." *Proceedings of the American Philosophical Society* 123(1):47–72.

Hester, Joseph Aaron, Jr.

1964 "Kenneth Macgowan, 1888–1963." *American Antiquity* 29(3):376–78.

Hewett, Edgar Lee

1904 "Studies on the Extinct Pueblo of Pecos." *American Anthropologist* 6(4):426–39.

Heye, George G.

1924 "George Hubbard Pepper." *Indian Notes* 1(3):105–10.

Heye, George G., Frederick W. Hodge, and George H. Pepper

1918 "The Nacoochee Mound in Georgia." *Contributions from the Museum of the American Indian, Heye Foundation* 4(3):1–103. New York.

Higginson, Thomas Wentworth

1883 "The Hundred Year's War." *Harpers New Monthly Magazine* 67(397):20–32.

Higham, John

1979 "Matrix of Specialization," in *The Organization of Knowledge in Modern America, 1860–1920,* A. Oleson and J. Voss, eds., pp. 3–18. Baltimore, Md.: Johns Hopkins University Press.

Hinsley, Curtis M., Jr.

1981 *Savages and Scientists: The Smithsonian Institution and the Development of American Anthropology, 1846–1910.* Washington, D.C.: Smithsonian Institution Press.

1983 "Ethnographic Charisma and Scientific Routine: Cushing and Fewkes in the American Southwest, 1879–1893," in *Observers Observed: Essays on Ethnographic Field Work,* G. W. Stocking Jr., ed., pp. 53–69. Madison: University of Wisconsin Press.

1984   "Wanted: One Good Man to Discover Central American History." *Harvard Magazine* (Discovery Supplement) 85(2):64A–64H.

1985   "From Shell-Heaps to Stelae: Early Anthropology at the Peabody Museum," in *Objects and Others: Essays on Museums and Material Culture,* G. W. Stocking Jr., ed., pp. 49–74. Madison: University of Wisconsin Press.

1992   "The Museum Origins of Harvard Anthropology, 1866–1915," in *Science at Harvard University: Historical Perspectives,* C. A. Elliott and M. W. Rossiter, eds., pp. 121–45. Bethlehem, Pa.: Lehigh University Press.

1993   "In Search of the New World Classical," in *Collecting the Pre-Columbian Past,* E. H. Boone, ed., pp. 105–22. Washington, D.C.: Dumbarton Oaks.

1994   *The Smithsonian and the American Indian: Making a Moral Anthropology in Victorian America.* (Paperback edition, with new title and new preface, of *Savages and Scientists* [1981]). Washington, D.C.: Smithsonian Institution Press.

1999   "Frederic Ward Putnam," in *Encyclopedia of Archaeology, Part 1: The Great Archaeologists,* T. Murray, ed., vol. 1, pp. 141–74. Santa Barbara, Calif.: ABC-Clio.

2003   "Drab Doves Take Flight: The Dilemmas of Early Americanist Archaeology in Philadelphia, 1889–1900," in *Philadelphia and the Development of Americanist Archaeology,* D. D. Fowler and D. R. Wilcox, eds., pp. 1–20. Tuscaloosa: University of Alabama Press.

Hodge, Frederick W.

1903   "Frank Russell." *American Anthropologist* 5(4):737–38.

Holder, Charles Frederick

1910   "Louis Agassiz, Zoologist, 1807–1873," in *Leading American Men of Science,* D. S. Jordan, ed., pp. 147–69. New York: Henry Holt.

Holmes, Oliver Wendell, Sr.

1874   "Professor Jeffries Wyman: A Memorial Outline." *Atlantic Monthly* 34(205):611–23.

Holmes, William H.

1893   "A Question of Evidence." *Science* 21(527):135–36.

1919   *Handbook of Aboriginal American Antiquities.* Washington, D.C.: Government Printing Office.

Hooton, Earnest A.

1930   "Finns, Lapps, Eskimos, and Martin Luther." *Harvard Alumni Bulletin* 32(19):545–53.

1942   "Introduction," in *The House in the Rain Forest,* by C. Crockett, pp. ix–x. Boston: Houghton Mifflin.

1943 "Charles Clark Willoughby, 1857–1943." *American Antiquity* 9(2):235–39.

Hooton, Earnest A., Habib Yusuf Rihan, and Edward Reynolds

1930 *The Indians of Pecos Pueblo: A Study of Their Skeletal Remains.* Papers of the Southwestern Expedition 4. Andover, Mass.: Department of Archaeology, Phillips Academy.

Hooton, Earnest A., and Charles C. Willoughby

1920 *Indian Village Site and Cemetery near Madisonville, Ohio.* Papers of the PMAAE, vol. 8, no. 1. Cambridge, Mass.: Harvard University.

Horan, Sharon

1992 "Charles Conrad Abbott: Associations with the Peabody and the Museum of Archaeology and Paleontology." *Bulletin of the Archaeological Society of New Jersey* 47:29–36.

Hough, Walter

1911 "Edward Palmer." *American Anthropologist* 9:173.

1933 "William Jones," in *Dictionary of American Biography,* vol. 10, pp. 205–6. New York: Charles Scribner's Sons.

1935 "Alanson Buck Skinner," in *Dictionary of American Biography,* vol. 17, p. 197. New York: Charles Scribner's Sons.

Howard, Kathleen L.

2002 "Creating an Enchanted Land: Curio Entrepreneurs Promote and Sell the Indian Southwest, 1880–1940." Ph.D. dissertation, Department of History, Arizona State University.

Howard, Leland O.

1937 "Biographical Memoir of Edward Sylvester Morse, 1838–1925." *National Academy of Sciences, Biographical Memoirs* 17(1):1–30.

Howe, George Plummer

1909 "Appendix III: Medical Notes on Northern Alaska," in *Conquering the Arctic Ice,* by E. Mikkelsen, pp. 451–55. London: W. Heineman.

1911 "The Ruins of Tuloom." *American Anthropologist* 13(4):539–50.

Howell, F. Clark

2003 "Sherwood Larned Washburn, 1911–2000." *National Academy of Sciences, Biographical Memoirs* 84. Washington, D.C.

Howells, William W.

1990 "Harry Lionel Shapiro, 1902–1990." *American Journal of Physical Anthropology* 83(4):499–500.

Hsu, Cho-Yun

1980 "Li Chi (1896–1979)." *Journal of Asian Studies* 40(1):217–18.

Hughes, Hector James

1930 "Engineering and Other Applied Sciences in the Harvard Engineering School and Its Predecessors, 1847–1929," in *The Development of Harvard University since the Inauguration of President Eliot, 1869–1929,* S. E. Morison, ed., pp. 413–42. Cambridge, Mass.: Harvard University Press.

Hultgren, Mary Lou, and Paulette Fairbanks Molin

1989 "To Lead and to Serve: American Indian Education at Hampton Institute, 1878–1923," in *To Lead and to Serve: American Indian Education at Hampton Institute, 1878–1923,* M. L. Hultgren and P. F. Molin, eds., pp. 15–56. Virginia Beach: Virginia Foundation for the Humanities and Public Policy in cooperation with Hampton University.

Hunt, Edward E., Jr.

1982 "Carleton Stevens Coon, 1904–1981." *American Journal of Physical Anthropology* 58(3):239–41.

Hunt, William R.

1986 *Stef: A Biography of Vilhjalmur Stefansson, Canadian Arctic Explorer.* Vancouver: University of British Columbia Press.

Hurt, R. Douglas

1996 *The Ohio Frontier: Crucible of the Old Northwest, 1720–1830.* Bloomington: Indiana University Press.

Huxley, Henry Minor

1902a "Preliminary Report of an Anthropological Expedition to Syria." *American Anthropologist* 4(1):47–51.

1902b "Syrian Songs, Proverbs, and Stories: Collected, Translated and Annotated." *Journal of the American Oriental Society* 23:175–288.

1940 "Foreword," in *Contributions to the Racial Anthropology of the Near East, Based on Data Collected by Henry M. Huxley,* by Carl C. Seltzer, pp. i–vii. Papers of the PMAAE, vol. 16, no. 2. Cambridge, Mass.: Harvard University.

Ingersoll, Ernest

1885 "The Peabody Museum of American Archaeology." *Lippincott's Magazine of Popular Literature and Science* 10:474–87.

Irving, Laurence

1965 "Ivar Skarland (1899–1965)." *Arctic* 18(2):147–48.

Isaac, Barry L.

2001 *CSAS: The Early Years.* Central States Anthropological Society. Electronic document, www.iupui.edu/~csas/csashistoryearlyyear.htm.

Jacknis, Ira

2000 "A Museum Prehistory: Phoebe Hearst and the Founding of the Museum of Anthropology, 1891–1901." *Chronicle of the University of California: Journal of University History* 4:47–77.

2002 "The First Boasian: Alfred Kroeber and Franz Boas, 1896–1905." *American Anthropologist* 104(2):520–32.

Jackson, Ernest

1901 "Ernest Jackson," in *Harvard College Class of 1878, Secretary's Report, 1901*, pp. 59–60. Cambridge, Mass.: Riverside Press.

1908 "Ernest Jackson," in *Harvard College Class of 1878, Secretary's Report, 1908*, p. 46. Cambridge, Mass.: Riverside Press.

Jackson, Robert

1896 "Our Graduating Exercises, the Eighth, and Anniversary Exercises, the Seventeenth: The Orations." *The Red Man: The Present and Future* (journal of Carlisle Indian Industrial School) 13(8):1–7.

Jacobs, Wilbur R.

1991 *Francis Parkman, Historian as Hero: The Formative Years.* Austin: University of Texas Press.

James, Janet Wilson

1971 "Fannie Pearson Hardy Eckstorm," in *Notable American Women, 1607–1950: A Biographical Dictionary,* E. T. James, J. W. James, and P. S. Boyer, eds., vol. 1, pp. 549–51. Cambridge, Mass.: Belknap Press.

James, Mary Ann

1992 "Engineering an Environment for Change: Bigelow, Peirce, and Early Nineteenth-Century Practical Education at Harvard," in *Science at Harvard University: Historical Perspectives,* C. A. Elliott and M. W. Rossiter, eds., pp. 55–75. Bethlehem, Pa.: Lehigh University Press.

Jefferson, Thomas

1784 *Notes on the State of Virginia, Written in the Year 1781, Somewhat Corrected and Enlarged in the Winter of 1782, for the Use of a Foreigner of Distinction, in Answer to Certain Queries Proposed by Him, 1782.* Paris: Privately printed.

Jefferson, Thomas, James Wilkinson, George Turner, Caspar Wistar, Adam Seybert, Charles Wilson Peale, and Jonathan Williams

1799 "Circular." *Transactions of the American Philosophical Society* 4:xxxvii–xxxix. Philadelphia.

Jeter, Marvin D., ed.

1990 *Edward Palmer's Arkansaw Mounds.* Fayetteville: University of Arkansas Press.

Johnson, Elden

1983 "Lloyd Alden Wilford, 1894–1962." *American Antiquity* 48(4):779–81.

Jones, William

1904 "Some Principles of Algonquian Word-Formation." *American Anthropologist* 6(3), Supplement.

Jordan, David Starr

1892 "Agassiz at Penikese." *Popular Science Monthly* 40(8):721–29.

Jorgensen, Joseph C.

1979 "Mischa Titiev, 1901–1978." *American Anthropologist* 81(2):342–44.

Joyce, Barry Alan

2001 *The Shaping of American Ethnography: The Wilkes Exploring Expedition, 1838–1842.* Lincoln: University of Nebraska Press.

Judd, Neil M.

1966 "Frank H. H. Roberts, Jr., 1897–1966." *American Anthropologist* 68(5):1226–32.

1967 *The Bureau of American Ethnology: A Partial History.* Norman: University of Oklahoma Press.

Kaeppler, Adrienne L.

1985 "Anthropology and the U.S. Exploring Expedition," in *Magnificent Voyagers: The United States Exploring Expedition, 1838–1842*, H. J. Viola and C. Margolis, eds., pp. 119–48. Washington, D.C.: Smithsonian Institution.

Kaeser, Marc-Antoine

2002 "On the International Roots of Prehistory." *Antiquity* 76(291):170–77.

Kahin, George McT.

1989 "Owen Lattimore (1900–1989)." *Journal of Asian Studies* 48(4):945–46.

Kehoe, Alice Beck

1998 *The Land of Prehistory: A Critical History of American Archaeology.* New York: Routledge.

Keller, Morton, and Phyllis Keller

2001 *Making Harvard Modern: The Rise of America's University.* New York: Oxford University Press.

Kennedy, John M.

1968 "Philanthropy and Science in New York City: The American Museum of Natural History, 1868–1968." Ph.D. dissertation, Department of History, Yale University.

Keppler, Udo Joseph

1926 "Cayuga Adoption Custom." *Indian Notes* 3:73–75.

| 1929a | "The Peace Tomahawk Algonkian Wampus." *Indian Notes* 6:130–38.
| 1929b | "Some Seneca Stories." *Indian Notes* 6:372–76.
| 1941 | "Comments on Certain Iroquois Masks." *Contributions from the Museum of the American Indian, Heye Foundation* 12(4):3–40.

Kerr, Andrew Affleck

| 1929 | "Archaeological Fieldwork in North America during 1928." *American Anthropologist* 31(2):357.

Kershaw, Gordon E.

| 1999 | "James Bowdoin II (1726–1790)," in *American National Biography,* J. A. Garraty and M. C. Carnes, eds., vol. 3, pp. 272–74. New York: Oxford University Press.

Keur, Dorothy Louise

| 1971 | "Mary Butler Lewis, 1903–1970." *American Anthropologist* 73(1):255–56.

Kidder, Alfred Vincent

| 1910 | "Explorations in Southeastern Utah in 1908." *American Journal of Archaeology* 14(3):337–59.
| 1937 | "Samuel James Guernsey." *American Anthropologist* 39(1):135–37.
| 1945 | "George Clapp Vaillant, 1901–1945." *American Anthropologist* 47(4):589–602.
| 1948 | "Sylvanus Griswold Morley, 1883–1948." *El Palacio* 55:267–74.
| 1949 | "Introduction," in *Prehistoric Southwesterners from Basketmaker to Pueblo,* by C. A. Amsden, pp. xi–xiv. Los Angeles: Southwest Museum.
| 1957 | "Harriet and Burton Cosgrove." *New Mexico Quarterly* 27:52–55.

Kidder, Alfred Vincent, and Charles Avery Amsden

| 1931 | *The Pottery of Pecos,* vol. 1. Papers of the Southwestern Expedition, no. 5. Andover, Mass.: Robert S. Peabody Foundation for Archaeology, Phillips Academy.

Kidder, Homer Huntington

| 1898 | "Two Local Indian Traditions." *Mining Journal,* January 1, Special St. Luke's Edition, p. 13. Marquette, Mich.
| 1908 | "Note on the Occurrence of Glazed Ware at Afrosiab, and of Large Jars at Ghiaur Kala," in *Explorations in Turkestan: Expedition of 1904: Prehistoric Civilizations of Anau,* R. Pumpelly, ed., vol. 1, pp. 211–16. Washington, D.C.: Carnegie Institution of Washington.
| 1927 | "Notes on the Pigmentation of Skin, Hair, and Eyes of the Kabyles." *Harvard African Studies* 8:225–27.
| 1929 | "The Central Ojibway," in *The Book of Huron Mountain: A Collection of Papers concerning the History of the Huron Mountain Club and the Antiquities and the*

Natural History of the Region, B. H. Christy, ed., pp. 40–55. Huron Mountain, Mich.: Huron Mountain Club.

1934 "Dimensional Characters of Upper Paleolithic Flint Industries in Corrèze and Dordogne," in *Proceedings of the First International Congress of Prehistoric and Protohistoric Sciences, 1932,* p. 76. London.

1935 "Les nucléi prismatiques," in *Compte Rendu de la XI Session du Congres Préhistorique de France, 1934,* p. 470. Paris.

1939 "Une ébauche de sculpture magdalénienne," in *Mélanges de préhistoire et d'anthropologie offerts par ses collègues, amis et disciples au professeur comte H. Begouen,* pp. 221–24. Toulouse.

Kidder, Lilia, and Homer H. Kidder

1932 *Fouilles du Puy-de-Lacan (Corrèze): Pierres avec signes et autres objets.* Paris: E. Leroux. (Reprinted from *Revue Archéologique,* 5th séries, vol. 35.)

1936a "Le Puy-de-Lacan et ses gravures Magdaléniennes." *Anthropologie* 46:17–31.

1936b "The Cave of Puy-de-Lacan: A Magdalénien Site in South-Central France." *American Anthropologist* 38(3):439–51.

Kidwell, Clara Sue

1999 "Every Last Dishcloth: The Prodigious Collecting of George Gustav Heye," in *Collecting Native America, 1870–1960,* S. Krech III and B. A. Hail, eds., pp. 232–58. Washington, D.C.: Smithsonian Institution Press.

King, Eleanor M., and Bryce P. Little

1986 "George Byron Gordon and the Early Development of the University Museum," in *Raven's Journey: The World of Alaska's Native People,* S. A. Kaplan and K. J. Barsness, eds., pp. 16–53. Philadelphia: University Museum, University of Pennsylvania.

Kirch, Patrick Vinton

1992 "In Memoriam: Kenneth Pike Emory (1897–1992)." *Asian Perspectives* 31(1):1–8.

Kirk, Lowell

2001 "The Bat Creek Stone." Tellico Plains Mountain Press. Electronic document, www.telliquah.com/Batcreek.htm.

Kirsch, A. Thomas

1994 "Lauriston Sharp (1907–1993)." *Journal of Asian Studies* 53(4):1358–59.

Kluckhohn, Clyde

1958 "Ralph Linton." *National Academy of Sciences, Biographical Memoirs* 31(10):236–53.

Knowlton, Evelyn H.

1948 *Pepperell's Progress: History of a Cotton Textile Company 1844–1945.* Cambridge, Mass.: Harvard University Press.

Knudson, Ruthann

2004 "Hannah Marie Wormington," in *Notable American Women,* vol. 5, *A Biographical Dictionary Completing the Twentieth Century,* S. Ware, ed., pp. 701–3. Cambridge, Mass.: Belknap Press.

Ko, Dong H.

2003 "The Historical Development of Japanese Cultural Anthropology from 1868 to 2002." Ph.D. dissertation, Department of Anthropology, Washington University, St. Louis.

Koelsch, William A.

1983 "'A Profound though Special Erudition': Justin Winsor as Historian of Discovery." *Proceedings of the American Antiquarian Society* 93:55–94.

1987 *Clark University, 1887–1987: A Narrative History.* Worcester, Mass.: Clark University Press.

2004 "Franz Boas, Geographer, and the Problem of Disciplinary Identity." *Journal of the History of the Behavioral Sciences* 40(1):1–22.

Kohlstedt, Sally Gregory

1986 "International Exchange and National Style: A View of Natural History Museums in the United States, 1850–1900," in *Scientific Colonialism: A Cross-Cultural Comparison,* N. Reingold and M. Rothenberg, eds., pp. 167–90. Washington, D.C.: Smithsonian Institution Press.

1999 "Creating a Forum for Science: AAAS in the Nineteenth Century," in *The Establishment of Science in America: 150 years of the American Association for the Advancement of Science,* S. G. Kohlstedt, M. M. Sokal, and B. V. Lewenstein, eds., pp. 7–49. New Brunswick, N.J.: Rutgers University Press.

Kohlstedt, Sally Gregory, Michael M. Sokal, and Bruce V. Lewenstein

1999 "Appendix B. Administrative Officers, 1848–1998," in *The Establishment of Science in America: 150 years of the American Association for the Advancement of Science,* S. G. Kohlstedt, M. M. Sokal, and B. V. Lewenstein, eds., pp. 170–72. New Brunswick, N.J.: Rutgers University Press.

Kraft, Herbert C.

1993 "Dr. Charles Conrad Abbott, New Jersey's Pioneer Archaeologist." *Bulletin of the Archaeological Society of New Jersey* 48:1–12.

Kroeber, Alfred L.

1917 "Frederic Ward Putnam." *American Anthropologist* 17(4):712–18.

1936 "Roland Burrage Dixon." *American Anthropologist* 38(2):294–97.

1940 "The Work of John R. Swanton," in *Smithsonian Miscellaneous Collections 100: Essays in Historical Anthropology of North America, Published in Honor of John*

R. *Swanton in Celebration of His Fortieth Year with the Smithsonian Institution,* pp. 1–2. Washington, D.C.: Smithsonian Institution.

1943 "Franz Boas: The Man," in *Franz Boas, 1858–1942,* by A. L. Kroeber et al., pp. 5–26. American Anthropological Association Memoir 61.

Kuklick, Bruce

1996 *Puritans in Babylon: The Ancient Near East and American Intellectual Life, 1880–1930.* Princeton, N.J.: Princeton University Press.

Lacovara, Peter

1981 "The Hearst Excavations at Deir-el-Ballas: The Eighteenth Dynasty Town," in *Studies in Ancient Egypt, the Aegean, and the Sudan: Essays in Honor of Dows Dunham on the Occasion of his 90th Birthday,* W. K. Simpson and W. M. Davis, eds., pp. 120–21. Boston: Museum of Fine Arts.

La Flesche, Francis

1923 "Alice C. Fletcher." *Science* 58(1494):115.

Lamar, Howard R.

1998 *The New Encyclopedia of the American West.* New Haven, Conn.: Yale University Press.

Lamb, Daniel S.

1906 "The Story of the Anthropological Society of Washington." *American Anthropologist* 8(3):564–79.

Lambert, Marjorie F.

1961 "Karl Ruppert, 1893–1960." *American Antiquity* 27(1):101–3.

Land, William G.

1933 *Thomas Hill: Twentieth President of Harvard.* Cambridge, Mass.: Harvard University Press.

Lasker, Gabriel W.

1945 "Observations on the Teeth of Chinese Born and Reared in China and America (including Data on Peking Prisoners Collected by Liang Ssu-Yung)." *American Journal of Physical Anthropology* 3(2):129–50.

LeBaron, John Francis

1912 "Description of Stone Ruins in Eastern Nicaragua." *Records of the Past* 11(5):217–22.

Lee, Ronald F.

1970 *The Antiquities Act of 1906.* Washington, D.C.: Office of History and Historic Architecture, Eastern Service Center, National Park Service, U.S. Department of the Interior.

Legrain, Leon

1927   "George Byron Gordon." *American Journal of Archaeology* 31:355–56.

Lesser, Alexander

1981   "Franz Boas," in *Totems and Teachers: Perspectives on the History of Anthropology,* S. Silverman, ed., pp. 1–34. New York: Columbia University Press.

Levin, Michael, Gail Avrith, and Wanda Barrett

1984   *An Historical Sketch, Showing the Contribution of Sir Daniel Wilson and Many Others to the Teaching of Anthropology at the University of Toronto.* Toronto: Department of Anthropology, University of Toronto.

Lewenstein, Bruce V.

1999   "Shifting Science from People to Programs: The AAAS in the Postwar Years," in *The Establishment of Science in America: 150 years of the American Association for the Advancement of Science,* S. G. Kohlstedt, M. M. Sokal, and B. V. Lewenstein, eds., pp. 103–66. New Brunswick, N.J.: Rutgers University Press.

Liang, Ssu-Yung [Siyong]

1930   *New Stone Age Pottery from the Site of Hsi-Yin Tsun, Shansi, China.* American Anthropological Association, Special Publication 37.

1931   "Some Problems of Far Eastern Archaeology." *American Anthropologist* 34(3):365–76.

Lincoln, Waldo

1906   "Stephen Salisbury, A.M." *New England Historical and Genealogical Register* 60(6):325–29.

Lindsey, Donal F.

1995   *Indians at Hampton Institute, 1877–1923.* Urbana: University of Illinois Press.

Linton, Ralph

1936   *The Study of Man: An Introduction.* New York: D. Appleton-Century.

Little, Michael A.

2003   "Gabriel Ward Lasker (1912–2002)." *American Anthropologist* 105(4):889–92.

Livingstone, David N.

1987   *Nathaniel Southgate Shaler and the Culture of American Science.* Tuscaloosa: University of Alabama Press.

1992   "A Geologist by Profession, a Geographer by Inclination: Nathaniel Southgate Shaler and Geography at Harvard," in *Science at Harvard University: Historical Perspectives,* C. A. Elliott and M. W. Rossiter, eds., pp. 146–66. Bethlehem, Pa.: Lehigh University Press.

Lonergan, David

1991a "Frank Hamilton Cushing," in *International Dictionary of Anthropologists*, C. Winters, ed., pp. 131–33. New York: Garland.

1991b "Samuel Kirkland Lothrop," in *International Dictionary of Anthropologists*, C. Winters, ed., pp. 424–25. New York: Garland.

1991c "Herbert Joseph Spinden," in *International Dictionary of Anthropologists*, C. Winters, ed., pp. 659–60. New York: Garland.

1991d "Vilhjalmur Stefansson," in *International Dictionary of Anthropologists*, C. Winters, ed., pp. 665–67. New York: Garland.

Lord, Louis E.

1947 *A History of the American School of Classical Studies at Athens, 1882–1942.* Cambridge, Mass.: Harvard University Press.

Lothrop, Samuel K.

1937 *Cocle: An Archaeological Study of Central Panama.* 2 vols. Cambridge, Mass.: Peabody Museum.

1945 "Philip Ainsworth Means, 1892–1944." *American Antiquity* 11(2):109–12.

1948 "Julio C. Tello, 1880–1947." *American Antiquity* 14(1):50–56.

1953 "Oliver Garrison Ricketson, Jr., 1894–1952." *American Antiquity* 19(1):69–72.

1955 "Alfred Marston Tozzer, 1876–1954." *American Anthropologist* 57(3):614–19.

Loubat, Joseph Florimond (Le Duc de Loubat)

1867 *Official Papers Relating to the Conduct of the Legation of the United States at Paris, with Regard to the Commissioners for the International Exposition of 1867.* Paris: E. Briere.

1873 *Narrative of the Mission to Russia in 1866, of the Hon. Gustavus Vasa Fox, Assistant-Secretary of the Navy,* J. D. Champlin Jr., ed. (from the journal and notes of Joseph Florimond Loubat). New York: D. Appleton.

1912 *Joseph Florimond, Le Duc de Loubat, 1894–1912.* Paris: Typographie Philippe Renouard.

Luce, Stephen B.

1942 "George Andrew Reisner." *American Journal of Archaeology* 46(3):410–12.

1943 "Carl Whiting Bishop." *American Journal of Archaeology* 47:227.

1945 "James Harvey Gaul." *American Journal of Archaeology* 49(4):582.

Lurie, Edward

1960 *Louis Agassiz: A Life in Science.* Chicago: University of Chicago Press.

Lyon, David G.

1911 "The Semitic Museum," in *Reports of the President and Treasurer of Harvard College, 1909–1910*, pp. 222–29.

1930 "Semitic Museum, 1880–1929," in *The Development of Harvard University since the Inauguration of President Eliot, 1869–1929*, S. E. Morison, ed., pp. 231–40. Cambridge, Mass.: Harvard University Press.

MacCurdy, George Grant

1902 "The Teaching of Anthropology in the United States." *Science* 15(371):211–16.

1903 "Anthropology at the Washington Meeting." *American Anthropologist* 5(1):118–25.

1905 "The American Anthropological Association." *Science* 22(567):591–93.

1909 "Anthropology at the Baltimore Meeting." *American Anthropologist* 11(1):101–19.

1912 "Anthropology at the Washington Meeting for 1911." *Science* 35(904):665–76.

1924 *Human Origins: A Manual of Prehistory.* New York: D. Appleton.

1927 "Duke de Loubat." *American Anthropologist* 29(2):340.

Macgowan, Kenneth

1950 *Early Man in the New World.* New York: Macmillan.

MacGregor, Gordon

1948 "H. Scudder Mekeel, 1902–1947." *American Anthropologist* 50(1):95–100.

MacNeish, Richard S.

1979 "Douglas Swain Byers, 1930–1978." *American Antiquity* 44(4):708–10.

1996 "Frederick Johnson, 1904–1994." *American Antiquity* 61(2):269–73.

Madeira, Percy C., Jr.

1964 *Men in Search of Man: The First Seventy-five Years of the University Museum of the University of Pennsylvania.* Philadelphia: University of Pennsylvania Press.

Mainfort, Robert C., Jr., and Sarah R. Demb

2001 "Edwin Curtiss's Archaeological Explorations along the St. Francis River, Northeast Arkansas, 1879–1880." *Arkansas Archaeologist* 41:1–27.

Mainfort, Robert C., Jr., and Mary L. Kwas

1991 "The Bat Creek Stone: Judeans in Tennessee?" *Tennessee Anthropologist* 16(1):1–19.

2004 "The Bat Creek Stone Revisited: A Fraud Exposed." *American Antiquity* 69(4):761–70.

Malcolm, Roy Lynden

1939 "Archaeological Remains, Supposedly Navaho, from Chaco Canyon, New Mexico." *American Antiquity* 5(1):4-20.

Mann, Thomas L.

1991a "Kenneth Pike Emory," in *International Dictionary of Anthropologists*, C. Winters, ed., pp. 181–82. New York: Garland.

1991b "Willowdean C. Handy," in *International Dictionary of Anthropologists*, C. Winters, ed., p. 268. New York: Garland.

Marcou, Jules

1896   *Life, Letters, and Works of Louis Agassiz.* 2 vols. New York: Macmillan.

Mark, Joan

1980   *Four Anthropologists: An American Science in Its Early Years.* New York: Science History Publications.

1988   *A Stranger in Her Native Land: Alice Fletcher and the American Indians.* Lincoln: University of Nebraska Press.

1995   *The King of the World in the Land of the Pygmies.* Lincoln: University of Nebraska Press.

Marquis Who's Who

1950   *Who Was Who in America,* vol. 3. Chicago: Marquis Who's Who.

Marsh, Othniel Charles

1866   "Description of an Ancient Sepulchral Mound." *American Journal of Science and Arts* 42(125):1–11.

1879   "Ancient Pottery from Chiriqui, Central America." *Proceedings of the AAAS* 27:339.

Mason, John Alden

1942   "Vladimir J. Fewkes." *American Antiquity* 8(1):114–17.

1943   "Franz Boas as an Archaeologist," in *Franz Boas, 1858–1942,* by A. L. Kroeber et al., pp. 58–66. American Anthropological Association Memoir 61.

1950   "Frank Gouldsmith Speck, 1881–1950." *University Museum Bulletin* 15(1):2–5. Philadelphia.

Mason, Otis T.

1877   "Anthropology." *American Naturalist* 11(10):624–27.

1880a   "Anthropology." *American Naturalist* 14(3):216–22.

1880b   "Anthropology." *American Naturalist* 14(11):813–18.

1888   "Anthropology in 1886." *Annual Report of the Smithsonian Institution for 1887,* pp. 523–70. Washington, D.C.

Mayer, Alfred Goldsborough

1910   "Alexander Agassiz." *Popular Science Monthly* 77(5):418–46.

McAllester, David P.

1982   "Leland C. Wyman: A Biography and Bibliography," in *Navajo Religion and Culture: Selected Views. Papers in Honor of Leland C. Wyman,* D. M. Brugge and C. J. Frisbie, eds., pp. 1–20. Papers in Anthropology, no. 17A. Santa Fe: Museum of New Mexico.

1989   "Leland C. Wyman (1898–1988)." *American Anthropologist* 91(2):441.

McCall, Daniel F.

1967 "American Anthropology and Africa." *African Studies Bulletin* 10(2):20–34.

McCaughey, Robert A.

1974 "The Transformation of American Academic Life: Harvard University 1821–1892." *Perspectives in American History* 8:239–334.

McCown, Theodore D.

1948 "George Grant MacCurdy, 1863–1947." *American Anthropologist* 50(3):516–24.

McGee, William John

1903 "The American Anthropological Association." *American Anthropologist* 5(1):178–92.

McKern, William C.

1954 "Ralph Linton." *American Antiquity* 19(4):382–83.

McLaughlin, Castle

1998 "The George F. Will Collection at the Peabody Museum: A Cornucopia from Native North America." *Symbols,* Spring, pp. 19–21. Cambridge, Mass.: PMAE.

McVicker, Donald A.

1989 "Prejudice and Context: The Anthropological Archaeologist as Historian," in *Tracing Archaeology's Past: The Historiography of Archaeology,* A. L. Christenson, ed., pp. 113–26. Carbondale: Southern Illinois University Press.

1992 "The Matter of Saville: Franz Boas and the Anthropological Definition of Archaeology," in *Rediscovering Our Past: Essays on the History of American Archaeology,* J. E. Reyman, ed., pp. 145–59. Aldershot, U.K.: Avebury.

McVicker, Mary Frech

2000 "Parlours to Pyramids." *Archaeology* 53(6):60–62.

2005 *Adela Breton: A Victorian Artist amid Mexico's Ruins.* Albuquerque: University of New Mexico Press.

Mead, Frances Harvey

1894 "Massachusetts in the Department of Ethnology at the World's Columbian Exposition," in *World's Columbian Exposition, 1893: Report to the Managers Massachusetts Board,* pp. 159–68. Chicago: World's Columbian Exposition.

1905 "The Peabody Museum of Harvard University." *Records of the Past* 4(3):65–79.

1914 Unsigned, 19-page typescript attributed to Mead. Peabody Museum Archives and Collections Department, Accession File 2001.7, Harvard University.

1915 "John C. Kimball" (1-page manuscript). Peabody Museum Archives and Collections Department, Accession File 2001.7, Harvard University.

1984 *Conejos County, Colorado.* Colorado Springs: Century One Press.

Means, James Howard

1964 *James Means and the Problem of Manflight, during the period 1882–1920.* Washington, D.C.: Smithsonian Institution.

Means, Philip Ainsworth

1917 "Preliminary Survey of the Remains of the Chippewa Settlements on La Pointe Island, Wisconsin." *Smithsonian Miscellaneous Collections* 66(14):1–14.

Mechling, William H.

1912 "The Indian Linguistic Stocks of Oaxaca." *American Anthropologist* 14(4):643–82.

Meltzer, David J.

2003 "In the Heat of Controversy: C. C. Abbott, the American Paleolithic, and the University Museum, 1889–1893," in *Philadelphia and the Development of Americanist Archaeology,* D. D. Fowler and D. R. Wilcox, eds., pp. 48–87. Tuscaloosa: University of Alabama Press.

Meltzer, David J., and William C. Sturtevant

1983 "The Holly Oak Shell Game: An Historic Archaeological Fraud," in *Lulu Linear Punctated: Essays in Honor of George Irving Quimby,* R. C. Dunnell and D. K. Grayson, eds., pp. 325–52. Anthropological Papers 72. Ann Arbor: Museum of Anthropology, University of Michigan.

Merriam, Clinton Hart

1927 "William Healey Dall." *Science* 65(1684):345–47.

Merwin, Bruce Welch

1915 "The Copper Eskimo." *Museum Journal* 6:163–68.

1916a "Some Ojibway Buffalo Robes." *Museum Journal* 7:93–96.

1916b "Wampum." *Museum Journal* 7:125–33.

1917a "A Voodoo Drum from Hayti." *Museum Journal* 8:123–25.

1917b "Dutch Guiana Pottery." *Museum Journal* 8:180–85.

1918a "The Art of Quillwork." *Museum Journal* 9:50–55.

1918b "The Patty Stuart Jewett Collection." *Museum Journal* 9:225–43.

1919 "Basketry of the Chitimacha Indians." *Museum Journal* 10:29–34.

1933 "Alleged Siouian Sites of Southern Illinois." *Transactions of the Illinois State Academy of Science* 25:106.

1935 "Archaeology in Southern Illinois." *Transactions of the Illinois State Academy of Science* 28:79–80.

1937 "Rock Carvings in Southern Illinois." *American Antiquity* 3(2):179–82.

Merwin, Raymond E., and George C. Vaillant

1932 *The Ruins of Holmul, Guatemala.* Memoirs of the PMAAE, vol. 3, no. 2. Cambridge, Mass.: Harvard University.

Metz, Charles L.

1878 "The Prehistoric Monuments of the Little Miami Valley." *Journal of the Cincinnati Society of Natural History* 1(3):119–28.

1879 "Sacrificial Altars Found in Ohio." *American Antiquarian* 2(2):147–49.

1881 "The Prehistoric Monuments of Anderson Township, Hamilton County, Ohio." *Journal of the Cincinnati Society of Natural History* 4(5):293–305.

Metz, Charles L., and Frederic W. Putnam

1886 "The Marriott Mound, No. 1, and Its Contents." *Annual Reports of the PMAAE* 3(5):449–66.

Miller, R. Berkeley

1978 "Anthropology and Institutionalization: Frederick Starr at the University of Chicago, 1892–1923." *Kroeber Anthropological Society Papers* 51–52:49–60. Berkeley: University of California.

Mitra, Panchanan

1933 *A History of American Anthropology.* Calcutta: University of Calcutta.

Montgomery, Ross G., Watson Smith, and John O. Brew

1949 *Franciscan Awatovi: The Excavation and Conjectural Reconstruction of a 17th-Century Spanish Mission Establishment at a Hopi Indian Town in Northeastern Arizona.* Papers of the PMAAE, vol. 36. Cambridge, Mass.: Harvard University.

Moore, Alexander

1984 "Solon Toothaker Kimball (1909–1982)." *American Anthropologist* 86(2):386–93.

Moore, Clarence Bloomfield

1892a "A Burial Mound in Florida (Tick Island)." *American Naturalist* 26(302):129–43 and 26(307):568–79.

1892b "Certain Shell Heaps of the St. John's River, Florida, Hitherto Unexplored: Part 1." *American Naturalist* 26(311):912–22.

1893 "Certain Shell Heaps of the St. John's River, Florida, Hitherto Unexplored, Part 2." *American Naturalist* 27(312):113–17.

Moorehead, Warren King

1893a "A New Science at the Fair." *North American Review* 157(443):507–9.

1893b "The Results of Search for Paleolithic Implements in the Ohio Valley." *Science* 21(531):192.

Morgan, Lewis Henry

1851 *League of the Ho-dé-no-sau-nee, or Iroquois.* New York: M. H. Newman.

Morison, Samuel Eliot

1930 "Introduction," in *The Development of Harvard University since the Inauguration of President Eliot, 1869–1929*, S. E. Morison, ed., pp. xxv–xc. Cambridge, Mass.: Harvard University Press.

1936 *Three Centuries of Harvard, 1636–1936*. Cambridge, Mass.: Harvard University Press.

Morley, Sylvanus Griswold

1908 "The Excavation of the Cannonball Ruins in Southwestern Colorado." *American Anthropologist* 10(4):596–610.

1910 "The Correlation of Maya and Christian Chronology." *American Journal of Archaeology* 14(2):193–204.

1920 *The Inscriptions at Copan*. Washington, D.C.: Carnegie Institution of Washington.

Morley, Thomas

1997 "Autobiographical Writings of Sylvanus Griswold (Small) Morley, 1878–1970" (77 pages; includes a handwritten text of 1935 and typewritten materials added in 1958 and 1965; this copy made by Thomas Morley in 1997). Electronic document, www.dcn.davis.ca.us/GO/rgf/.

Morse, Edward Sylvester

1863 "Report of Account of Excavations at Goose Island, Maine, and Occurrence of Rare Helices beneath Indian Deposits, November 17, 1862." *Portland (Maine) Society of Natural History* 1(2):98.

1867a "Shell Heaps on Goose Island." *Proceedings of the BSNH* 11:288–89.

1867b "Great Antiquity of the Shell Heaps at Goose Island." *Proceedings of the BSNH* 11:301–2.

1869 "Report on Remarks on Evidences of High Antiquity in the Kjoekkenmoedden Deposits of New England." *Canadian Naturalist* 4:329.

1877 "Remarks on Lingula, and Japanese Pottery." *Proceedings of the BSNH* 19: 266–67.

1879 *Shell Mounds of Omori*. Tokyo: Science Department, University of Tokyo.

1880 "Remarks on the Antiquities of Japan." *Proceedings of the BSNH* 20:304.

1881a "Prehistoric Man in America." *North American Review* 132 (June):602–16.

1881b "Worked Shells in New England Shell-Heaps." *Proceedings of the AAAS* 30:343–44.

1882 "The Variation of Shells of the Kjoekenmoeddings." *Proceedings of the BSNH* 21:307.

1884a "Man in the Tertiaries." *American Naturalist* 18(10):1001–12.

1884b "Method of Arrow Release." *Proceedings of the AAAS* 32:426.

1885 "Ancient and Modern Methods of Arrow-Release." *Bulletin of the Essex Institute* 17:146–47.

1889 "On Ancient Arrows and a New Method of Arrow Release." *Proceedings of the AAAS* 37:329.

1892 "On the Older Forms of Terra Cotta Roofing." *Essex Institute Historical Collections* 24:1–72.

1894 "On the So-Called Bow-Puller of Antiquity." *Essex Institute Historical Collections* 26:141–66.

1898 "Was Middle America Peopled from Asia?" *Popular Science Monthly* 54(1):1–15.

1899a "Pre-Columbian Musical Instruments in America." *Popular Science Monthly* 54(5):712–14.

1899b "The Damariscotta Shellheaps." *Popular Science Monthly* 55(1):95.

1902 "Address on Alpheus Hyatt, at Memorial Meeting, BSNH, February 5, 1902." *Proceedings of the BSNH* 30:415–20.

1907 "Jean Louis Rudolph Agassiz." *Popular Science Monthly* 71(6):542–49.

1915 "Frederick Ward Putnam, 1839–1915: An Appreciation." *Essex Institute Historical Collections* 52:3–8.

1923 "Agassiz and the School at Penikese." *Science* 58(1502):273–75.

1925 "Shell-Mounds and Changes in the Shells Composing Them." *Scientific Monthly* 21(Oct):429–40.

Morss, Noel

1932 *The Ancient Culture of the Fremont River in Utah*. Papers of the PMAAE, vol. 12, no. 3. Cambridge, Mass.: Harvard University.

Muller, Jon

2002 "Rediscovering Illinois: The Development of Archaeology in Illinois," in *Histories of Southeastern Archaeology*, S. Tushingham, J. Hill, and C. H. McNutt, eds., pp. 99–114. Tuscaloosa: University of Alabama Press.

Muller-Scheessel, Nils

2001 "Fair Prehistory: Archaeological Exhibits at French 'Expositions Universelles.'" *Antiquity* 75(288):391–401.

Munro, Douglas

2006 "On Douglas Oliver's Pacific Islands," in *Text and Contexts: Reflections on Pacific Island Historiography*, Douglas Munro and Brij V. Lal, eds., pp. 51–64. Honolulu: Univeristy of Hawaii Press.

Murowchick, Robert E.

1990 "A Curious Sort of Yankee: Personal and Professional Notes on Jeffries Wyman (1814–1874)." *Southeastern Archaeology* 9(1):55–66.

Murray, Stephen O.

1988 "W. I. Thomas, Behaviorist Ethnologist." *Journal of the History of the Behavioral Sciences* 24(4):381–91.

1991a "Roland Burrage Dixon," in *International Dictionary of Anthropologists*, C. Winters, ed., pp. 149–52. New York: Garland.

1991b "John Reed Swanton," in *International Dictionary of Anthropologists*, C. Winters, ed., p. 680. New York: Garland.

Murray, Timothy

1989 "The History, Philosophy, and Sociology of Archaeology: The Case of the Ancient Monuments Protection Act, 1882," in *Critical Traditions in Contemporary Archaeology: Essays in the Philosophy, History and Socio-politics of Archaeology,* V. Pinsky and A. Wylie, eds., pp. 55–67. New York: Cambridge University Press.

2002 "Epilogue: Why the History of Archaeology Matters." *Antiquity* 76(291):234–38.

Nadaillac, Marquis de (Jean-Francois Albert de Pouget)

1884 *Prehistoric America.* Translated by N. D'Anvers, pseudonym of Nancy R. E. Meugens Bell. Edited with notes by William H. Dall. London: J. Murray.

The National Cyclopedia of American Biography, being the History of the United States

1900 "Samuel Garman." Vol. 10, p. 294. Clifton, N.J.; James T. White.

1929 "Charles Pickering Bowditch." Vol. 20, pp. 290–91. Clifton, N.J.; James T. White.

1932 "George Amos Dorsey." Vol. 22, pp. 200–201. Clifton, N.J.; James T. White.

1938 "Herbert Joseph Spinden." Supplement, vol. 3, pp. 73–74. Clifton, N.J.; James T. White.

1940 "Andrew Affleck Kerr." Vol. 28, p. 63. Clifton, N.J.; James T. White.

1943 "Samuel James Guernsey." Vol. 30, pp. 212–13. Clifton, N.J.; James T. White.

1961 "Henry Minor Huxley." Vol. 43, pp. 55–56. Clifton, N.J.; James T. White.

1962 "Laurance David Redway." Vol. 45, pp. 418–19. Clifton, N.J.; James T. White.

National Research Council

1938 *International Directory of Anthropologists.* Washington, D.C.: National Research Council.

1940 *International Directory of Anthropologists, Section 1: Western Hemisphere.* Washington, D.C.: National Research Council.

Nelson, Nels C.

1948 "Clark Wissler, 1870–1947." *American Antiquity* 13(2):244–47.

Noelke, Virginia Hull McKimmon

1974 "The Origin and Early History of the Bureau of American Ethnology, 1879–1910." Ph.D. dissertation, Department of History, University of Texas, Austin.

Norton, Charles E.

1849 "Ancient Monuments in America." *North American Review* 68:466–96.

1903 "The Founding of the School at Athens." *American Journal of Archaeology* 7(3):351–56.

Nuttall, Zelia M.

1886 "The Terracotta Heads of Teotihuacan." *American Journal of Archaeology* 2(2):157–72.

1895 "Ancient Mexican Feather Work at the Columbian Historical Exposition at Madrid," in *Report of the Commission to the Madrid Columbian Historical Exposition, 1892: Commemoration of the Fourth Centenary of the Discovery of America*, pp. 329–37. Washington, D.C.: United States Commission.

1901 *The Fundamental Principles of Old and New World Civilizations: A Comparative Research Based on a Study of the Ancient Mexican Religious, Sociological and Calendrical Systems.* Papers of the PMAAE, vol. 2. Cambridge, Mass.: Harvard University.

1902 *Codex Nuttall: Facsimile of an Ancient Mexican Codex Belonging to Lord Zouche of Harynworth, England.* Cambridge, Mass.: PMAAE.

1904 "The Periodical Adjustments of the Ancient Mexican Calendar." *American Anthropologist* 6:486–500.

1906 "The Astronomical Methods of the Ancient Mexicans," in *Boas Anniversary Volume: Anthropological Papers Written in Honor of Franz Boas . . . Presented to Him on the Twenty-fifth Anniversary of His Doctorate . . .*, pp. 290–98. New York: G. E. Stechert.

1908 "Some Unsolved Problems in Mexican Archaeology." *American Anthropologist* 8(1):133–49.

1910 "The Island of Sacrificios." *American Anthropologist* 12(2):257–95.

1926a "The Aztecs and Their Predecessors in the Valley of Mexico." *Proceedings of the American Philosophical Society* 65(4):245–55.

1926b *Official Reports on the Towns of Tequizistlan, Tepechpan, Acolman, and San Juan Teotihuacan Sent by Francisco de Castaneda to His Majesty, Philip II, and the Council of the Indies, in 1580.* Papers of the PMAAE, vol. 11, no. 2. Cambridge, Mass.: Harvard University.

1927 "The Ancient American Civilizations and Calendars." *Science* 66:194–95.

1930 "Documentary Evidence concerning Wild Maize in Mexico: A Contribution towards the Solution of the Problem of the Origin of Cultivate Maize." *Journal of Heredity* 21:217–20.

Oleson, Alexandra, and John Voss

1979 "Introduction," in *The Organization of Knowledge in Modern America, 1860–1920*, A. Oleson and J. Voss, eds., pp. vi–xxii. Baltimore, Md.: Johns Hopkins University Press.

Opler, Morris E.

1938 "The Use of Peyote by the Carrizo and Lipan Apache Tribes." *American Anthropologist* 40(2):271–85.

Ordway, Albert

1862 "On the Supposed Identity of the *Paradoxides harlani, Green,* with the *Paradoxides spinosus, Boeck:* On the Occurrence of Other Fossil Forms at Braintree, Massachusetts." *Proceedings of the BSNH* (January 2). 6 pages.

Ortner, Donald J., and Jennifer O. Kelley

1988 "J. Lawrence Angel (1915–1986)." *American Anthropologist* 90(1):145–48.

Owens, John G.

1890 "Food Resources and Foods of the Hopi Indians." Manuscript prepared for the Hemenway Southwestern Archaeological Expedition, Harvard University. Present location unknown.

1892 "Natal Ceremonies of the Hopi Indians." *Journal of American Ethnology and Archaeology* (Hemenway Southwestern Archaeological Expedition) 2:161–75.

Packard, Alpheus Spring, Jr.

1877 "Biographical Memoir of Henry James Clark." *National Academy of Sciences, Biographical Memoirs* 1(14):312–28.

1878 "Memoir of Jeffries Wyman, 1814–1874." *National Academy of Sciences, Biographical Memoirs* 2(4):74–126.

1884 "Our Aryan Ancestors." *American Naturalist* 18(3):269–70.

1885 "Notes on the Labrador Eskimo and Their Former Range Southward." *American Naturalist* 19(5):471–81 and 19(6):553–60.

1887 "Tertiary Man." *American Naturalist* 19(11):1078–79.

1891 "Among the Prehistoric Monuments of Brittany." *American Naturalist* 23(298):870–90.

1895 "The Java 'Missing Link.'" *The Independent* (New York City) 47:992.

1903 "Alpheus Hyatt." *Proceedings of the American Academy of Arts and Sciences* 38(26):715–27.

Palmer, Edward

1871 "Food Products of the North American Indians," in *Report of the Commissioner of Agriculture for 1870*, pp. 409–28. Washington, D.C.: U.S. Department of Agriculture.

1873 "Indian Rope and Cloth." *American Naturalist* 7:755.

1874a "The Manufacture of Pottery by Indians." *American Naturalist* 8:245–47.

1874b "The Berries of *Rhamnus croceus* as Indian Food." *American Naturalist* 8:247.

1875 "Clay-Balls as Slung Shot or Cooking Stones." *American Naturalist* 9:183–84.

1878a "Cave Dwellings in Utah." *Annual Reports of the PMAAE* 2(2):269–72.

1878b "Plants Used by the Indians of the United States." *American Naturalist* 12(9):593–606 and 12(10):646–55.

1882 "Mexican Caves with Human Remains." *American Naturalist* 16(4):306–11.

Paolucci, Anne, and Henry Paolucci, eds.

1995 *Justin Winsor: Native American Antiquities and Linguistics.* New York: Council on National Literatures.

Pardue, Diana F.

1996 "Marketing Ethnography: The Fred Harvey Indian Department and George A. Dorsey," in *The Great Southwest of the Fred Harvey Company and the Santa Fe Railway,* M. Weigle and B. A. Babcock, eds., pp. 102–9. Phoenix, Ariz.: Heard Museum.

Parezo, Nancy J., and Rebecca A. Stephenson

2001 "Laura Maud Thompson, 1905–2000." *American Anthropologist* 103(2):510–14.

Parker, Arthur Caswell

1907 "Excavations in an Erie Indian Village and Burial Site at Ripley, Chautauqua Co., N.Y., Being the Record of the State Museum Archaeological Expedition of 1906." *Bulletin of the New York State Museum* 117:459–554.

1908 "Introduction," in *Myths and Legends of the New York State Iroquois,* by H. M. Converse, edited and annotated by A. C. Parker, pp. 6–30. Bulletin 125. Albany: New York State Museum, Education Department.

1910 "Arthur Caswell Parker," in *American Men of Science,* 2nd ed., J. M. Cattell, ed., p. 358. New York: Science Press.

1929 "The Value to the State of Archaeological Surveys," in *Report of the Conference on Midwestern Archaeology, Held in St. Louis, Missouri, May 18, 1929,* F-C. Cole, ed., pp. 31–41. Bulletin 74. Washington, D.C.: National Research Council.

1935 *A Manual for History Museums.* New York: Columbia University Press.

1968 *Parker on the Iroquois.* Edited with an introduction by William N. Fenton. Syracuse, N.Y.: Syracuse University Press.

Parker, Franklin

1971 *George Peabody: A Biography.* Nashville, Tenn.: Vanderbilt University Press.

Parkman, Francis, Jr.

1849 *The California and Oregon Trail: Being Sketches of Prairie and Rocky Mountain Life.* New York: G. Putnam.

1851 *History of the Conspiracy of Pontiac, and the War of the North American Tribes against the English Colonies after the Conquest of Canada.* Boston: Little and Brown.

Parmenter, Ross

1971 "Zelia Maria Magdalena Nuttall," in *Notable American Women, 1607–1950: A Biographical Dictionary,* E. T. James, J. W. James, and P. S. Boyer, eds., vol. 2, pp. 640–42. Cambridge, Mass.: Belknap Press.

Parsons, Samuel H.

1793 "Natural History Discoveries Made in the Western Country." *Memoirs of the American Academy of Arts and Sciences* 2:119–27.

Parsons, Talcott, and Evon Z. Vogt

1962 "Clyde Kay Maben Kluckhohn, 1905–1960." *American Anthropologist* 64(1):140–61.

Patterson, Thomas Carl

1995 *Toward a Social History of Archaeology in the United States.* Fort Worth, Tex.: Harcourt Brace.

2001 *A Social History of Anthropology in the United States.* Oxford: Berg.

Peabody, Charles

1903 "Notes on Negro Music." *Journal of American Folk-Lore* 16(62):148–52.

1904 *Explorations of Mounds, Coahoma County, Mississippi.* Papers of the PMAAE, vol. 3, no. 2. Cambridge, Mass.: Harvard University.

1905 "American Archaeology during the Years 1900–1905: A Summary." *American Journal of Archaeology,* 2nd series, 9(2):182–96.

1908 "The Exploration of Bushey Cavern, Maryland." *Phillips Academy Bulletin* 4, pt. 1, pp. 3–26. Andover, Mass.: Department of Archaeology, Phillips Academy.

1910 "The Exploration of Mounds in North Carolina." *American Anthropologist* 12(3):425–33.

1912 "L'etat present de la question d' homme glaciare de Trenton (Etats-Unis)," in *Proceedings of the 14th International Congress of Prehistoric Anthropology and Archaeology,* vol. 2, pp. 415–517. Geneva.

1913 "Henry Williamson Haynes." *American Anthropologist* 15(2):336–46.

Peabody, Charles C., and Warren K. Moorehead

1904 *The Exploration of Jacobs Cavern, McDonald County, Missouri.* Phillips Academy Bulletin 1. Andover, Mass.: Department of Archaeology, Phillips Academy.

Peabody, Frances Greenwood

1926   *Education for Life: The Story of Hampton Institute.* Garden City, N.Y.: Doubleday, Page.

Peabody, George

1868a   "Letter of Gift, to Robert C. Winthrop, Charles Francis Adams, Francis Peabody, Stephen Salisbury, Asa Gray, Jeffries Wyman, and George Peabody Russell, Georgetown, October 8, 1866." *Annual Reports of the PMAAE* 1 (1):25–26.

1868b   "Instrument of Trust. Georgetown, October 8, 1866." *Annual Reports of the PMAAE* 1(1):26–28.

Pearson, Jeffrey V.

2001   "Nelson A. Miles, Crazy Horse, and the Battle of Wolf Mountains." *Montana, the Magazine of Western History* 51:53–67.

Peet, Stephen D.

1890   "Supposed Aboriginal Fish-Weirs in Naaman's Creek, near Claymont, Del." (Letter.) *Science* 15(369):151.

Pepper, George H.

1909   "The Exploration of a Burial Room in Pueblo Bonito, New Mexico," in *Putnam Anniversary Volume: Anthropological Essays Presented to Frederic Ward Putnam in Honor of His Seventieth Birthday, April 16, 1909, by His Friends and Associates,* F. Boas et al., eds., pp. 196–252. New York: G. E. Stechert.

Peterson, Clarence Stewart

1958   *Known Military Dead during the Spanish American War and the Philippines Insurrection, 1898–1901.* Baltimore, Md.: Privately printed.

Peyrony, Denis, Homer H. Kidder, and H. V. V. Noone

1949   "Outils en silex émousses du Paléolithique supérieur." *Bulletin de la Société Préhistorique Française* 46:298–301.

Phillips, Philip

1955   "Alfred Marston Tozzer, 1877–1954." *American Antiquity* 21(1):72–80.

1973   "Introduction," in *Exploration of Ancient Key Dwellers' Remains on the Gulf Coast of Florida by Frank Hamilton Cushing,* pp. ix–xvii. Cambridge, Mass.: Peabody Museum Press.

Phillips, Philip, and James A. Brown, with Eliza McFadden, Barbara C. Page, and Jeffrey P. Brain

1975–82 *Pre-Columbian Shell Engravings from the Craig Mound at Spiro, Oklahoma.* 6 vols. Cambridge, Mass.: Peabody Museum Press.

Phillips, Philip, James Ford, and James Griffin

1951 *Archaeological Survey in the Lower Mississippi Alluvial Valley, 1940–1947.* Cambridge, Mass.: Peabody Museum Press. Republished 2003 with an introduction by Stephen Williams.

Phillips, Philip, and Gordon R. Willey

1958 *Method and Theory in American Archaeology.* Chicago: University of Chicago Press.

Picha, Paul

2002 "Unpacking Will and Spiden's (1906) *The Mandans:* Early 20th Century Archaeology and Culture History at Harvard University and the Middle Missouri Subarea." Abstracts of the 67th Annual Meetings, Society for American Archaeology, Denver, p. 230.

Pickering, John

1820 *An Essay on a Uniform Orthography for the Indian Languages of North America.* Cambridge, Mass.: Hilliard and Metcalf.

Pollock, Harry E. D.

1948 "Harry E. D. Pollock," in *Harvard Class of 1923, 25th Anniversary Volume,* p. 694. Cambridge, Mass.: Harvard University.

Porter, Joy

2001 *To Be Indian: The Life of Iroquois-Seneca Arthur Caswell Parker.* Norman: University of Oklahoma Press.

Potter, William Bleecker, and Edward Evers

1880 *Contributions to the Archaeology of Missouri by the Archaeological Section of the St. Louis Academy of Science,* pt. 1, *Pottery.* Salem, Mass.: Salem Press.

Powell, Arthur G.

1980 *The Uncertain Profession: Harvard and the Search for Educational Authority.* Cambridge, Mass.: Harvard University Press.

Powell, John Wesley

1881 "On Limitations to the Use of Some Anthropologic Data," in *First Annual Report of the Bureau of Ethnology,* pp. 71–86. Washington, D.C.: Government Printing Office.

1884 "Report of the Director," in *Fifth Annual Report of the Director of the United States Geological Survey,* pp. vii–xxxii. Washington, D.C.: Government Printing Office.

1890a "Prehistoric Man in America." *Forum* 8(5):489–503.

1890b   "Problems of American Archaeology." *Forum* 8(6):638–52.

1894   "Report of the Director," in *Twelfth Annual Report of the Bureau of Ethnology, 1890–1891,* pp. xxi–xlvii. Washington, D.C.: Government Printing Office.

1897   "Report of the Director," in *Sixteenth Annual Report of the Bureau of American Ethnology for 1894–95,* pp. iii–xcix. Washington, D.C.: Government Printing Office.

Price, David H.

2000   "Anthropologists as Spies." *The Nation* 271(16):24–27.

2001   "The Shameful Business: Leslie Spier on the Censure of Franz Boas." *History of Anthropology Newsletter* 27(2):9–12.

2002   "Interlopers and Invited Guests: On Anthropology's Witting and Unwitting Links to Intelligence Agencies." *Anthropology Today* 18(6):16–21.

2003   "Cloak and Trowel: Should Archaeologists Double as Spies?" *Archaeology* 56(5):30–35.

2008   *Anthropological Intelligence: The Deployment and Neglect of American Anthropology in the Second World War.* Durham: Duke University Press.

Price, John Dyneley, and Frank Gouldsmith Speck

1903   "The Modern Pequots and Their Language." *American Anthropologist* 5(2): 193–212.

1904   "Dying American Speech Echoes from Connecticut." *Proceedings of the American Philosophical Society* 42:346–52.

Pumpelly, Raphael

1869   *Across America and Asia: Notes of a Five Years' Journey Around the World and of Residence in Arizona, Japan, and China.* New York: Leypoldt and Holt.

1908   (ed.) *Explorations in Turkestan: Expedition of 1904. Prehistoric Civilizations of Anau.* 2 vols. Washington, D.C.: Carnegie Institution of Washington.

1918   *My Reminiscences.* 2 vols. New York: Henry Holt.

Pusey, Nathan M.

1968   "President's Report," in *Report of the President of Harvard College and Reports of the Departments, 1966–1967,* pp. 5–61.

1969   "Introduction," in *A Turning Point in Higher Education: The Inaugural Address of Charles William Eliot as President of Harvard College, October 19, 1869,* pp. v–xii. Cambridge, Mass.: Harvard University Press.

Putnam, Edward K.

1919   "The Davenport Collection of Nazca and Other Peruvian Pottery." *Proceedings of the Davenport (Iowa) Academy of Sciences* 13:1–46.

Putnam, Frederic Ward

1865   "On an Indian Grave Opened on Winter Island, Salem." *Proceedings of the BSNH* 10:246–47.

1868a   "On Aboriginal Utensils from Nicaragua." *Proceedings of the BSNH* 12:218.

1868b   "On Indian Remains in Essex County, 1867." *Proceedings of the Essex Institute, Salem, 1867*, pp. 186, 197–99.

1869a   "On Shellheaps, and on Certain Archaeological Specimens." *Proceedings of the Essex Institute, Salem, 1868*, p. 31.

1869b   "On Aboriginal Utensils from Nicaragua, 1868." *Proceedings of the Essex Institute, Salem, 1868*, p. 218.

1869c   "The McNeil Expedition to Central America, 1868." *American Naturalist* 2:484–86, 612–13.

1870a   "Two Rare Specimens of Indian Carving Wrought from Steatite." *Bulletin of the Essex Institute, Salem, 1869*, pp. 1, 21.

1870b   "Remarks on Stone and Copper Implements from Wakefield." *Bulletin of the Essex Institute, Salem, 1869*, p. 90.

1870c   "On Shellheaps in Essex County, Massachusetts." *Bulletin of the Essex Institute, Salem, 1869*, p. 123.

1870d   "On Skulls of Several Species of Bears, and a Molar Tooth of a Bear Found in a Shellheap on Goose Island, Massachusetts." *Bulletin of the Essex Institute, Salem, 1869*, p. 138.

1871   "On the Great Mound in St. Louis." *American Naturalist* 4:62–63.

1872a   "Description of an Ancient Fortification on the Wabash River." *Proceedings of the BSNH* 15:28–35.

1872b   "On the Skulls of Mound-Builders." *Proceedings of the BSNH* 15:228–29.

1875a   "On the Habits of the Blind Crawfish and the Reproduction of Lost Parts." *Proceedings of the BSNH* 18:16–20.

1875b   "Archaeological Explorations in Indiana and Kentucky." *American Naturalist* 9(7):410–15.

1875c   "The Pottery of the Mound Builders." *American Naturalist* 9(6):321–38.

1875d   "Report to Professor Asa Gray, Curator pro tempore of the Peabody Museum of American Ethnology and Archaeology." *Annual Reports of the PMAAE* 1(8):12–52.

1875e   "Jeffries Wyman." *Proceedings of the American Academy of Arts and Sciences* 10:496–505.

1876   "Report of the Curator." *Annual Reports of the PMAAE* 1(9):7–23.

1877   "Report of the Curator." *Annual Reports of the PMAAE* 2(1):7–12.

1878a   "Report of the Curator." *Annual Reports of the PMAAE* 2(2):191–206, 221.

1878b "Remarks on the Male of the Eel." *Proceedings of the BSNH* 19:279–81.
1879a "Report of the Curator." *Annual Reports of the PMAAE* 2(3):466–81.
1879b "Remarks on Chambered Mounds in Missouri." *Proceedings of the BSNH* 20:304–5.
1879c "Remarks on Some Bones of N.E. Indians and on Some Archaeological Explorations in Tennessee." *Proceedings of the BSNH* 20:331–33.
1879d "Remarks on the Ornamentation of Some Aboriginal American Pottery." *Proceedings of the BSNH* 20:333–34.
1880a "Report of the Curator." *Annual Reports of the PMAAE* 2(4):715–31.
1880b "On a Piece of Pottery from St. Francis River, Ark." *Proceedings of the BSNH* 21:90–91.
1880c "Nature of a Peculiar Carved Bone Found at Scarborough, Me." *Proceedings of the BSNH* 21:107–9.
1880d "Exhibition of an Archaeological Collection from Coahuila, Mexico." *Proceedings of the BSNH* 21:118–20.
1881a "Report of the Curator." *Annual Reports of the PMAAE* 3(1):7–28.
1881b "Paleolithic Implements from Wakefield, Mass." *Proceedings of the BSNH* 21:122–24.
1881c "Recent Archaeological Explorations at Madisonville, Ohio." *Proceedings of the BSNH* 21:216–22.
1882a "Report of the Curator." *Annual Reports of the PMAAE* 3(2):55–73.
1882b "Remarks on Stone Implements from Marshfield, Mass., and Sag Harbor, N.Y." *Proceedings of the BSNH* 21:405–6.
1883a "Report of the Curator." *Annual Reports of the PMAAE* 3(3):159–92.
1883b "Remarks on Earth-works in the Little Miami Valley." *Proceedings of the BSNH* 22:358.
1883c "Explorations of Emblematic Mounds in Ohio and Wisconsin." *Proceedings of the BSNH* 22:432.
1883d "Archaeological Frauds." *Science* 1(4):99.
1883e "An Indian Burial-Mound." *Science* 1(6):168.
1883f "Aztec Music." *Science* 2(37):549.
1883g "The Work of the Cambridge Archaeological Museum." *Science* 3(57):287–88.
1884a "Report of the Curator." *Annual Reports of the PMAAE* 3(4):339–76.
1884b "Account of Recent Explorations of Ohio Mounds." *Proceedings of the BSNH* 23:215–18.
1885a "Report of the Curator." *Annual Reports of the PMAAE* 3(5):400–18.
1885b "Account of His Recent Excursions in Wisconsin and Ohio (1883)." *Proceedings of the American Antiquarian Society* 3:4–20.

1886a   "Report of the Curator." *Annual Reports of the PMAAE* 3(6):477–501, 508.

1886b   "On the Methods of Archaeological Research in America." *Johns Hopkins University Circulars* 5(49):89–92.

1886c   "The Peabody Museum's Explorations in Ohio." *American Naturalist* 20(12):1017–27.

1887a   "Report of the Curator." *Annual Reports of the PMAAE* 3(7):535–70.

1887b   "A Collection of Perforated Stones from California." *Proceedings of the BSNH* 23:356.

1887c   "Obituary of Miss Cordelia A. Studley." *Proceedings of the BSNH* 23:419–20.

1887d   "Paleolithic Implements from America and Europe." *Proceedings of the BSNH* 23:421–24.

1887e   "An Appeal for Aid in the Explorations [F. W. Putnam to R. C. Winthrop, chair of trustees, August 6, 1886]." *Annual Reports of the PMAAE* 3(7):529–34.

1888a   "Report of the Curator." *Annual Reports of the PMAAE* 4(1):11–16.

1888b   "On Collections of Paleolithic Implements." *Proceedings of the BSNH* 24:157–66.

1888c   "Notes on Two Species of Wasps Observed at the Serpent Mound in Ohio." *Proceedings of the BSNH* 23:465.

1888d   "The Serpent Mound in Adams Co., Ohio." *Proceedings of the BSNH* 23:518.

1888e   "The Loss of Cordelia Adelaide Studley." *Proceedings of the BSNH* 23:419–20.

1888f   "Announcement of the Death of Professor Asa Gray." *Proceedings of the BSNH* 23:486–87.

1889   "Report of the Curator." *Annual Reports of the PMAAE* 4(2):31–52, 55, 163, 266.

1890a   "Report of the Curator." *Annual Reports of the PMAAE* 4(3):66, 73–78.

1890b   "Remarks on Early Man in America." *Proceedings of the BSNH* 24:268–69.

1890c   "Prehistoric Remains in the Ohio Valley." *Century* 39(5):698–703.

1890d   "The Serpent Mound of Ohio." *Century* 39(6):871–88.

1891   "Report of the Curator." *Annual Reports of the PMAAE* 4(4):87–100, 102, 106–7.

1892   "Report of the Curator," in *Annual Reports of the President and Treasurer of Harvard College,* pp. 188–98, 203.

1893a   "Report of the Curator," in *Annual Reports of the President and Treasurer of Harvard College,* pp. 198–210.

1893b   "Realization More than Fulfilled in the Great Departments." *Daily Inter Ocean,* November 1, p. 6.

1894   "Report of the Curator," in *Annual Reports of the President and Treasurer of Harvard College,* pp. 213–23.

1895a "Report of the Curator," in *Annual Reports of the President and Treasurer of Harvard College*, pp. 218–26.

1895b "The History, Aims, and Importance of the AAAS." *Science* 2(33):171–74.

1896a "Report of the Curator," in *Annual Reports of the President and Treasurer of Harvard College*, pp. 236–44.

1896b "Certain Sand Mounds of Florida." *Science* 3(58):205–7.

1897 "Report of the Curator," in *Annual Reports of the President and Treasurer of Harvard College*, pp. 239–49.

1898a "Report of the Curator," in *Annual Reports of the President and Treasurer of Harvard College*, pp. 4, 9, 242–51.

1898b "Editorial Note," in *Prehistoric Burial Places in Maine*, by C. C. Willoughby, pp. 387–88. Papers of the PMAAE, vol. 1, no. 6. Cambridge, Mass.: Harvard University.

1899a "Report of the Curator," in *Annual Reports of the President and Treasurer of Harvard College*, pp. 266–75.

1899b "A Problem in American Anthropology." *Science* 10(243):225–36.

1900a "Report of the Curator," in *Annual Reports of the President and Treasurer of Harvard College*, pp. 271–79.

1900b "The Mexican Hall of the American Museum of Natural History." *Science* 11(262):19–21.

1901a "Report of the Curator," in *Annual Reports of the President and Treasurer of Harvard College*, pp. 292–302.

1901b "American Archaeology and Ethnology." *Harvard Graduates Magazine* 3(36):528–29.

1901c "Archaeological and Ethnological Research in the United States." *Proceedings of the American Antiquarian Society* 14:461–70.

1902a "Report of the Curator," in *Annual Reports of the President and Treasurer of Harvard College*, pp. 267–74.

1902b "Memorial of Professor Alpheus Hyatt." *Proceedings of the BSNH* 30:413–33.

1903 "Report of the Curator," in *Annual Reports of the President and Treasurer of Harvard College*, pp. 292–300.

1904 "Report of the Curator," in *Annual Reports of the President and Treasurer of Harvard College*, pp. 278–87.

1905 "Report of the Curator," in *Annual Reports of the President and Treasurer of Harvard College*, pp. 300–306.

1906 "Report of the Curator," in *Annual Reports of the President and Treasurer of Harvard College*, pp. 301–6.

1907   "Report of the Curator," in *Annual Reports of the President and Treasurer of Harvard College,* pp. 292–300.

1908   "Report of the Curator," in *Annual Reports of the President and Treasurer of Harvard College,* pp. 292–303.

1909   "Report of the Curator," in *Annual Reports of the President and Treasurer of Harvard College,* pp. 295–306.

1910   "Report of the Curator," in *Annual Reports of the President and Treasurer of Harvard College,* pp. 270–76.

1911   "Report of the Curator," in *Annual Reports of the President and Treasurer of Harvard College,* pp. 220–26.

1912   "Report of the Curator," in *Annual Reports of the President and Treasurer of Harvard College,* pp. 217–23.

1913   "Report of the Curator," in *Annual Reports of the President and Treasurer of Harvard College,* pp. 214–20.

1914   "Report of the Curator," in *Annual Reports of the President and Treasurer of Harvard College,* pp. 221–30.

1915   "Report of the Curator," in *Annual Reports of the President and Treasurer of Harvard College,* pp. 236–46.

1973 [1898]   "Annual Report of the Peabody Museum of American Archaeology and Ethnology, 1898," in *The Selected Archaeological Papers of Frederic Ward Putnam,* S. Williams, compiler, pp. 159–69. New York: AMS Press.

Putnam, Frederic W., with Charles C. Abbott, Samuel S. Haldeman, Harry C. Yarrow, Henry W. Henshaw, Lucien Carr, Albert S. Gatchet, and Bartolome Ferrer

1879   *Reports upon Archaeological and Ethnological Collections from Vicinity of Santa Barbara, California, and from Ruined Pueblos of Arizona and New Mexico, and Certain Interior Tribes.* Geographical Surveys West of the One Hundredth Meridian, vol. 7, Archaeology. Washington, D.C.: U.S. Army Engineer Department.

Putnam, Frederic W., and Samuel Garman

1875   "On the Male and Female Organs of the Sharks and Skates, with Special Reference to the Use of Claspers," in *Proceedings of the AAAS* 17:143–44.

Putnam, Frederic W., and Charles C. Willoughby

1896   "Symbolism in Ancient American Art." *Proceedings of the AAAS* 44:302–22.

Rabineau, Phyllis

1981   "North American Anthropology at the Field Museum of Natural History." *American Indian Art* 6(4):30–37, 79.

Reed, James S.

1980   "Clark Wissler: A Forgotten Influence in American Anthropology." Ph.D. dissertation, Graduate Educational Policies Council, Ball State University, Muncie, Ind.

Reina, Ruben E.

1976   "John Phillip Gillin, 1907–1973." *American Anthropologist* 78(1):79–86.

Reingold, Nathan

1979   "National Science Policy in a Private Foundation: The Carnegie Institution of Washington," in *The Organization of Knowledge in Modern America, 1860–1920*, A. Oleson and J. Voss, eds., pp. 313–41. Baltimore, Md.: Johns Hopkins University Press.

1986   "Graduate School and Doctoral Degree: European Models and American Realities," in *Scientific Colonialism: A Cross-Cultural Comparison*, N. Reingold and M. Rothenberg, eds., pp. 129–49. Washington, D.C.: Smithsonian Institution Press.

Reisner, George Andrew

1910   "The Harvard Expedition to Samaria: Excavations of 1908." *Harvard Theological Review* 3(2):248–63.

1930   "Egyptology, 1896–1928," in *The Development of Harvard University since the Inauguration of President Eliot, 1869–1929*, S. E. Morison, ed., pp. 241–47. Cambridge, Mass.: Harvard University Press.

Reshetov, Aleksandr Mikhailovich

1991   "Lin Yuehua," in *International Dictionary of Anthropologists*, C. Winters, ed., p. 410. New York: Garland.

Reynolds, Edward

1930   "63rd Annual Report of the PMAAE," in *Report of the President of Harvard College and of the Departments, 1928–1929*, pp. 266–77.

1931a   "64th Annual Report of the PMAAE," in *Report of the President of Harvard College and of the Departments, 1929–1930*, pp. 279–92.

1931b   *The Evolution of the Human Pelvis in Relation to the Mechanics of the Erect Posture*. Papers of the PMAAE, vol. 11, no. 5. Cambridge, Mass.: Harvard University.

1932   "65th Annual Report of the PMAAE," in *Report of the President of Harvard College and of the Departments, 1932–1933*, pp. 292–99.

Rideout, Henry Milner

1912   *William Jones: Indian, Cowboy, American Scholar, and Anthropologist in the Field*. New York: Frederick A. Stokes.

Riese, Berthold

1991 "Teobert Maler," in *International Dictionary of Anthropologists,* C. Winters, ed., pp. 442–43. New York: Garland.

Ritchie, John, Jr.

1898 "The AAAS." *New England Magazine* 58(6):639–61.

Ritchie, William A.

1956 "Arthur Caswell Parker, 1881–1955." *American Antiquity* 21(3):293–95.

1977 "Arthur Caswell Parker," in *Dictionary of American Biography,* Supplement 5, pp. 533–34. New York: Charles Scribner's Sons.

Rivinus, Edward F., and Elizabeth M. Youssef

1992 *Spencer Baird of the Smithsonian.* Washington, D.C.: Smithsonian Institution Press.

Robbins, Christine C.

1968 "John Torrey (1796–1873): His Life and Times." *Bulletin of the Torrey Botanical Club* 95:561.

Rodgers, Andrew Denny, III

1942 *John Torrey: A Story of North American Botany.* Princeton, N.J.: Princeton University Press.

Romer, Alfred S.

1964 "Thomas Barbour." *Systematic Zoology* 13(4):227–34.

Ross, Dorothy

1972 *G. Stanley Hall: The Psychologist as Prophet.* Chicago: University of Chicago Press.

1979 "The Development of the Social Sciences," in *The Organization of Knowledge in Modern America, 1860–1920,* A. Oleson and J. Voss, eds., pp. 107–38. Baltimore, Md.: Johns Hopkins University Press.

Ross, Hubert B., Amelia Marie Adams, and Lynne Mallory Williams

1999 "Caroline Bond Day: Pioneer Black Physical Anthropologist," in *African-American Pioneers in Anthropology,* I. E. Harrison and F. V. Harrison, eds., pp. 37–50. Urbana: University of Illinois Press.

Rossiter, Margaret W.

1975 *The Emergence of Agricultural Science: Justus Liebig and the Americans, 1840–1880.* New Haven, Conn.: Yale University Press.

1992 "Philanthropology, Structure, and Personality; or, the Interplay of Outside Money and Inside Influence," in *Science at Harvard University: Historical Perspectives,* C. A. Elliott and M. W. Rossiter, eds., pp. 13–27. Bethlehem, Pa.: Lehigh University Press.

Rowe, Ann Pollard

2007 "Reminiscences of John Howland Rowe." *Ñawpa Pacha* 28:224–27.

Rowe, John H.

1940 *Excavations in the Waterside Shell Heap, Frenchman's Bay, Maine.* Papers of the Excavators' Club, vol. 1, no. 3. Cambridge, Mass.: Peabody Museum.

1958 "Harry Tschopik, Jr., 1915–1956." *American Anthropologist* 60(1):132–40.

Rudolph, Frederick

1977 *Curriculum: A History of the American Undergraduate Course of Study since 1636.* San Francisco: Jossey-Bass.

Ruffins, Faith Davis

1992 "Mythos, Memory and History: African American Preservation Efforts, 1820–1990," in *Museums and Communities: The Politics of Public Culture*, I. Karp, C. M. Kreamer, and S. D. Lavine, eds., pp. 506–611. Washington, D.C.: Smithsonian Institution Press.

Ruiz, Carmen

2003 "Insiders and Outsiders in Mexican Archaeology (1890–1930)." Ph.D dissertation, Department of History, University of Texas, Austin.

Rury, Phillip M., and Timothy Plowman

1983 "Morphological Studies of Archaeological and Recent Coca Leaves (*Erythroxylum* spp.)." *Botanical Museum Leaflets* 29:297–400.

Russell, Frank

1900 "Anthropology at the New York Meeting of the American Association." *Science* 12(294):265–69.

1902 "Know, Then, Thyself." (President's address, American Folk-Lore Society.) *Science* 15(380):561–71.

Russell, Frank, and Henry M. Huxley

1899 "A Comparative Study of the Physical Characteristics of the Labrador Eskimo and the New England Indians." *Proceedings of the AAAS* 48:365–79.

1900 "A Comparative Study of the Physical Structures of the Labrador Eskimos and the New England Indians." *Scientific American,* Supplement, 49(1254):20106–7. (Abridged version of the 1899 *Proceedings of the AAAS* article.)

Rutsch, Mechthild

1997 "La concepción de ciencia, ética y educación en la correspondencia de Ezequiel A. Chávez y Franz Boas," in *Ciencia en los márgenes: Ensayos de historia de las ciencias en México,* M. Rutsch and C. Serrano, eds., pp. 127–66. Mexico City: Universidad Nacional Autónoma de México.

2000 "El patrimonio arqueológico mexicano y la International School of American Archaeology and Ethnology." *Ludus Vitalis* 8(14):131–63.

Ryan, Carmelita S.

1962 "The Carlisle Indian Industrial School." Ph.D. dissertation, Department of History, Georgetown University.

Ryan, Will Carson

1939 *Studies in Early Graduate Education: The Johns Hopkins, Clark University, the University of Chicago.* New York: Carnegie Foundation for the Advancement of Teaching.

Rydell, Robert W.

1984 *All the World's a Fair.* Chicago: University of Chicago Press.

Safford, William Edwin

1911 "Edward Palmer." *Popular Science Monthly* 78(4):341–54.

Salisbury, Stephen

1876 "Comments on Central American Archaeology." *Proceedings of the American Antiquarian Society* 66:19–61.

1877 "Dr. Le Plongeon in Yucatan: The Discovery of a Statue Called Chac-Mool, and the Communications of Dr. Augustus Le Plongeon concerning Explorations in the Yucatan Peninsula." *Proceedings of the American Antiquarian Society* 68:70–119.

1878 "Remarks on a Terra-cotta Figure from Isla Mujeres, Northeast Coast of Yucatan." *Proceedings of the American Antiquarian Society* 71:71–89.

1883 "Comment on Aymé's Notes on Mitla: Francisco de Burgoa's Description." *Proceedings of the American Antiquarian Society* (n.s.) 2(1):82–100.

1890 "Copies of Maya Pottery and Implements." *Proceedings of the American Antiquarian Society* (n.s.) 6:358–59.

Sargent, Winthrop

1799 "A Letter from Colonel Winthrop Sargent to Dr. Benjamin Smith Barton Accompanying Drawings and Some Accounts of Certain Articles, Which Were Taken Out of an Ancient Tumulus, or Grave, in the Western Country (1794)." *Transactions of the American Philosophical Society* 4:177–79. Philadelphia.

Saville, Marshall H.

1890 "The Sanborn Bowlder." *Proceedings of the BSNH* 24:586–88.

1893a "Explorations on the Main Structure of Copan, Honduras." *Proceedings of the AAAS* 41:271–75.

1893b "Vandalism among the Antiquities of Yucatan and Central America." *Proceedings of the AAAS* 41:276–77.

Schmidt, Hubert

1908   "Archaeological Excavations in Anau and Old Merv," in *Explorations in Turkestan: Expedition of 1904. Prehistoric Civilizations of Anau*, R. Pumpelly, ed., vol. 1, pp. 81–216. Washington, D.C.: Carnegie Institution of Washington.

Schreiber, Katharina

2007   "In Memoriam: John Howland Rowe, 1918–2004." *Ñawpa Pacha* 28:195–201.

Schuchert, Charles

1939   "Biographical Memoir of Othniel Charles Marsh, 1831–1899." *National Academy of Sciences, Biographical Memoirs* 20(1):1–78.

Schuchert, Charles, and Clara Mae LeVene

1940   *O. C. Marsh, Pioneer in Paleontology.* New Haven, Conn.: Yale University Press.

Schumacher, Paul

1874   "Remarks on the Kjoekkenmoeddings on the Northwest Coast of America," in *Annual Report of the Smithsonian Institution for 1873*, pp. 354–62. Washington, D.C.

1875   "Ancient Graves and Shell-Heaps of California," in *Annual Report of the Smithsonian Institution for 1874*, pp. 335–50. Washington, D.C.

1877a   "Researches in the Kjoekkenmoeddings and Graves of a Former Population of the Coast of Oregon." *Bulletin of the U.S. Geological and Geographical Survey of the Territories* 3(1):27–35.

1877b   "Researches in the Kjoekkenmoeddings and Graves of a Former Population of the Santa Barbara Islands and the Adjacent Mainland." *Bulletin of the U.S. Geological and Geographical Survey of the Territories* 3(1):37–56.

1877c   "Methods of Making Stone Weapons." *Bulletin of the United States Geological and Geographical Survey of the Territories* 3(3):547–49.

1878   "The Method of Manufacturing of Several Articles by the Former Indians of Southern California." *Annual Reports of the PMAAE* 2(2):258–68.

1879a   "The Method of Manufacturing Pottery and Baskets among the Indians of Southern California." *Annual Reports of the PMAAE* 2(3):521–25.

1879b   "The Method of Manufacture of Soapstone Pots," in *Reports upon Archaeological and Ethnological Collections from the Vicinity of Santa Barbara, California, and from Ruined Pueblos of Arizona and New Mexico, and Certain Interior Tribes,* by F. W. Putnam et al., pp. 117–21. Geographical Surveys West of the One Hundredth Meridian, vol. 7, Archaeology. Washington, D.C.: U.S. Army Engineer Department.

1882   "An Ancient Fortification in Sonora, Mexico." *American Antiquarian* 4(3):227–29.

Schwab, George

1914   "Bulu Folk-tales." *Journal of American Folk-lore* 27:266–88.

Schwab, George W., and George Way Harley, eds.

1947   *Tribes of the Liberian Hinterland.* Papers of the PMAAE, vol. 31. Cambridge, Mass.: Harvard University.

Scott, Donald

1930   "63th Annual Report of the PMAAE," in *Report of the President of Harvard College and of the Departments, 1928–1929*, pp. 279–92.

1933   "66th Annual Report of the PMAAE," in *Report of the President of Harvard College and of the Departments, 1931–1932*, pp. 296–303.

1934   "67th Annual Report of the PMAAE," in *Report of the President of Harvard College and of the Departments, 1932–1933*, pp. 296–303.

1935   "68th Annual Report of the PMAAE," in *Report of the President of Harvard College and of the Departments, 1933–1934*, pp. 305–14.

1936   "69th Annual Report of the PMAAE," in *Report of the President of Harvard College and of the Departments, 1934–1935*, pp. 315–23.

1937   "70th Annual Report of the PMAAE," in *Report of the President of Harvard College and of the Departments, 1935–1936*, pp. 336–48.

1938   "71st Annual Report of the PMAAE," in *Report of the President of Harvard College and of the Departments, 1936–1937*, pp. 352–65.

1939   "72nd Annual Report of the PMAAE," in *Report of the President of Harvard College and of the Departments, 1937–1938*, pp. 402–14.

1940   "73rd Annual Report of the PMAAE," in *Report of the President of Harvard College and of the Departments, 1938–1939*, pp. 445–61.

1941   "74th Annual Report of the PMAAE," in *Report of the President of Harvard College and of the Departments, 1939–1940*, pp. 427–36.

1942   "75th Annual Report of the PMAAE," in *Report of the President of Harvard College and of the Departments, 1940–1941*, pp. 427–35.

1943   "76th Annual Report of the PMAAE," in *Report of the President of Harvard College and of the Departments, 1941–1942*, pp. 452–58.

1944   "77th Annual Report of the PMAAE," in *Report of the President of Harvard College and of the Departments, 1942–1943*, pp. 334–38.

1945   "78th Annual Report of the PMAAE," in *Report of the President of Harvard College and of the Departments, 1943–1944*, pp. 348–51.

1947   "80th Annual Report of the PMAAE," in *Report of the President of Harvard College and of the Departments, 1945–1946*, pp. 264–68.

1948   "81st Annual Report of the PMAAE," in *Report of the President of Harvard College and of the Departments, 1946–1947*, pp. 303–20.

Seitz, Don Carlos

1911 *Letters from Francis Parkman to E. G. Squier.* Cedar Rapids, Iowa: Torch Press.

Seltzer, Carl Coleman

1940 *Contributions to the Racial Anthropology of the Near East, Based on Data Collected by Henry M. Huxley, with a Foreword by Henry M. Huxley.* Papers of the PMAAE, vol. 16, no. 2. Cambridge, Mass.: Harvard University.

Senyürek, Muzaffer Süleyman

1941 *Fossil Man in Tangier.* Introduction by Carleton S. Coon. Papers of the PMAAE, vol. 16, no. 3. Cambridge, Mass.: Harvard University.

Shaler, Nathaniel Southgate

1877 "Report on the Age of the Delaware Gravel Beds Containing Chipped Pebbles." *Annual Reports of the PMAAE* 2(1):44–47.

1890 "Science and the African Problem." *Atlantic Monthly* 66(393):36–45.

1891 *Nature and Man in America.* New York. Charles Scribner's Sons.

1892 *The Story of Our Continent: A Reader in the Geography and Geology of North America.* Boston: Ginn and Co.

1909 *The Autobiography of Nathaniel Southgate Shaler, with a Supplementary Memoir by His Wife.* Boston: Houghton Mifflin.

Shapiro, Harry L.

1981 "Earnest A. Hooton, 1887–1954." *American Journal of Physical Anthropology* 56(4):431–34.

Sheftel, Phoebe Sherman

1979 "The Archaeological Institute of America, 1879–1979: A Centennial Review." *American Journal of Archaeology* 83(1):3–17.

Shils, Edward

1979 "The Order of Learning in the United States: The Ascendancy of the University," in *The Organization of Knowledge in Modern America, 1860–1920*, A. Oleson and J. Voss, eds., pp. 19–50. Baltimore, Md.: Johns Hopkins University Press.

Shor, Elizabeth Noble

1998 "Thomas Barbour," in *American National Biography*, J. A. Garraty and M. C. Carnes, eds., vol. 2, pp. 144–45.

Siegel, John Robert

1993 "Two Cultures, One Cause: Biculturalism and Native American Reform in the Career of Arthur Caswell Parker (Gawasowaneh), 1906–1925." Ph.D. dissertation, Department of History, Purdue University.

Sinclair, Bruce

1992 "Harvard, MIT, and the Ideal Technical Education," in *Science at Harvard University: Historical Perspectives,* C. A. Elliott and M. W. Rossiter, eds., pp. 76–95. Bethlehem, Pa.: Lehigh University Press.

Sinha, Dharanidhar Prasad

1963 "Biraja Sankar Guha, 1894–1961." *American Anthropologist* 65(2):382–87.

Skinner, Alanson Buck

1903a "Notes on Indian Camp Sites near Silver Lake." *Proceedings of the Natural History Association of Staten Island,* vol. 8, January 10 issue.

1903b "Recent Excavations in Indian Camp Sites at Mariner's Harbor." *Proceedings of the Natural History Association of Staten Island,* vol. 8, March 14 issue.

1908 "A Massachusetts Steatite Quarry." *American Anthropologist* 10(4):702–3.

Smith, Charles G.

1891 "Report of Capt. Charles G. Smith, 132nd New York Infantry," in *The War of the Rebellion: A Compilation of the Official Records of the Union and Confederate Armies,* series 1, vol. 33, pp. 73–76. U.S. War Records Office. Washington, D.C.: Government Printing Office.

Smith, Harlan Ingersoll

1894a "Caches of the Saginaw Valley, Michigan." *Proceedings of the AAAS* 42:300–303.

1894b "Anthropology at the University of Michigan." *University Record* 3:98–100.

1894c "Anthropological Work at the University of Michigan." *Proceedings of the AAAS* 42:308.

1895 "Anthropological Matters in Michigan." *Proceedings of the AAAS* 43:352–53.

1910 "The Prehistoric Ethnology of a Kentucky Site." *Anthropological Papers of the AMNH* 6(pt. 2):173–241.

Smith, Harriette Knight

1895 "The Lowell Institute." *New England Magazine* 17(6):713–30.

Smith, Kevin E.

1999 "Peabody Museum Expeditions: Some Preliminary Information." *Newsletter of the Middle Cumberland Archaeological Society* 24(2):3–5.

2003 "Excerpts from the *Daily American* (Nashville)." *Newsletter of the Middle Cumberland Archaeological Society* 28(2):4–5.

Smith, Watson

1952 *Kiva Mural Decorations at Awatovi and Kawaika-a, with a Survey of Other Wall Paintings in the Pueblo Southwest.* Papers of the PMAAE, vol. 37. Cambridge, Mass.: Harvard University.

1992 "One Man's Archaeology." *Kiva* 57(2):101–91.

Snead, James E.

2001 *Ruins and Rivals: The Making of Southwest Archaeology.* Tucson: University of Arizona Press.

2002 "The 'Western Idea': Local Societies and American Archaeology," in *Excavating Our Past: Perspectives on the History of the Archaeological Institute of America,* S. H. Allen, ed., pp. 123–40. Boston: Archaeological Institute of America.

Sokal, Michael M.

1999 "Promoting Science in a New Century: The Middle Years of the AAAS," in *The Establishment of Science in America: 150 Years of the American Association for the Advancement of Science,* S. G. Kohlstedt, M. M. Sokal, and B. V. Lewenstein, eds., pp. 50–102. New Brunswick, N.J.: Rutgers University Press.

Spaulding, Albert C.

1985 "Fifty Years of Theory." *American Antiquity* 50(2):301–8.

Speck, Frank G.

1942 "Vladimir Jaroslav Fewkes." *American Anthropologist* 44(3):476–77.

Spiegelberg, A. F.

1924 "In Memoriam: Death of George H. Pepper." *El Palacio* 16(12):193–94.

Spier, Leslie

1938 "Preface," in *The Sinkaietk or Southern Okanagon of Washington,* by W. Cline et al., L. Spier, ed., pp. 3–4. Contributions from the Laboratory of Anthropology, no. 6. Menasha, Wisc.: George Banta.

Spiess, Arthur E.

1985a "Charles Clark Willoughby (1859–1943) and His Plaster Models: Maine's First Archaeologist and His Records." *Bulletin of the Maine Archaeological Society* 25(2):43–53.

1985b "Wild Maine and the Rusticating Scientist: A History of Anthropological Archaeology in Maine." *Man in the Northeast* 30:101–29.

Spinden, Ellen S.

1933 "The Place of Tajin in Totonac Archaeology." *American Anthropologist* 35(2):225–70.

Spinden, Herbert Joseph

1909 "Maya Art." Ph.D. dissertation, Department of Anthropology, Harvard University.

1913 *A Study of Maya Arts.* Memoirs of the Peabody Museum, vol. 6. Cambridge, Mass.: Harvard University.

1917 "The Origin and Distribution of Agriculture in America," in *Proceedings of the 19th International Congress of Americanists*, pp. 269–76. Washington, D.C.

1925 "The Answer of Ancient America." *Forum* 74(2):162–67 and 74(3):371–79.

1927 "The Prosaic vs. the Romantic School in Anthropology," in *Culture: The Diffusion Controversy*, by G. E. Smith, B. Malinowski, H. J. Spinden, and A. Goldenweiser, pp. 47–98. New York: W. W. Norton.

1928 *Ancient Civilizations of Mexico and Central America*. Handbook Series, no. 3. New York: American Museum of Natural History.

1929 "Population of Ancient America," in *Annual Report of the Smithsonian Institution*, pp. 451–71. Washington, D.C.

1931 "Indian Symbolism," in *Introduction to American Indian Art*, F. W. Hodge, H. J. Spinden, and O. La Farge, eds., pp. 75–93. New York: Exposition of Indian Tribal Arts.

1933a "Indian Manuscripts of Southern Mexico," in *Annual Report of the Smithsonian Institution*, pp. 429–51. Washington, D.C.

1933b "Origins of Civilizations in Central America and Mexico," in *The American Aborigines: Their Origin and Antiquity*, D. Jenness, ed., pp. 217–46. Toronto: University of Toronto Press.

1935 "Archaeological Sites Today," in *Renascent Mexico*, H. C. Herring and H. Weinstock, eds., pp. 243–57. New York: Covici, Friede.

1939 "Sun Worship," in *Annual Report of the Smithsonian Institution*, pp. 447–69. Washington, D.C.

1948 "Mexican Calendars and the Solar Year, " in *Annual Report of the Smithsonian Institution*, pp. 393–405. Washington, D.C.

1957 "Alfred Marston Tozzer, 1877–1954." *National Academy of Sciences, Biographical Memoirs* 30(14):382–97.

1974 "The Sky Loom," in *Children of Light: A Collection of Five Songs, Prayers, and Chants from Native American Cultures of the Southwest*, H. J. Spinden et al., translators. Santa Fe, N.M.: Press of the Palace of the Governors Museum.

Squier, Ephraim G., and Edwin Davis

1848 *Ancient Monuments of the Mississippi Valley: Comprising the Results of Extensive Original Surveys and Explorations*. Washington, D.C.: Smithsonian Institution.

Stafford, Morgan Hewitt

1941 *A Genealogy of the Kidder Family Comprising the Descendants in the Male Line of Ensign James Kidder, 1626–1676, of Cambridge and Billerica in the Colony of Massachusetts Bay*. Rutland, Vt.: Tuttle Publishing.

Stanford, Dennis

1996   "Hannah Marie Wormington, 1914–1994." *American Antiquity* 61(2):274–78.

Stanton, William Ragan

1975   *The Great United States Exploring Expedition of 1838–1842.* Berkeley: University of California Press.

1991   *American Scientific Exploration 1803–1860: Manuscripts in Four Philadelphia Libraries.* Philadelphia: American Philosophical Society Library.

Starr, Frederick

1892   "Anthropological Work in America." *Popular Science Monthly* 41:289–307.

1893   "Anthropology at the World's Fair." *Popular Science Monthly* 43:610–21.

Starr, Richard F. S., ed.

1939   *Nuzi: Report on the Excavation at Yorgan Tepa near Kirkuk, Iraq, Conducted by Harvard University in Conjunction with the American Schools of Oriental Research and the University Museum of Philadelphia, 1927–1931.* 2 vols. Cambridge, Mass.: Harvard Radcliffe Fine Arts Series.

Steen, Charles R.

1981   "The Life and Times of Erik Kellerman Reed." *Anthropological Papers of the Archaeological Society of New Mexico* 6:1–14.

Stenger, Wallace

1954   *Beyond the Hundredth Meridian: John Wesley Powell and the Second Opening of the West.* Boston: Houghton Mifflin.

Stephenson, Robert L.

1967   "Frank H. H. Roberts, Jr., 1897–1966." *American Antiquity* 32(1):84–94.

Sterns, Frederick Henderson

1915a   "The Archaeology of Eastern Nebraska, with Special Reference to the Culture of the Rectangular Earth Lodges." Ph.D. dissertation, Department of Anthropology, Harvard University.

1915b   "A Stratification of Cultures in Eastern Nebraska." *American Anthropologist* 17(1):121–27.

1917a   "The Paleoliths of the Eastern Desert." *Harvard African Studies (Varia Africana)* 1:48–82.

1917b   "Darfur Gourds." *Harvard African Studies (Varia Africana)* 1:193–96.

1918a   "Some Bisharin Baskets in the Peabody Museum." *Harvard African Studies (Varia Africana)* 2:194–96.

1918b   "Women of Scientific Expeditions." Unpublished manuscript, 10 pp. Tozzer Library, PMAAE.

Stevens, John Austin, Jr.

1874 "A Memorial of George Gibbs." *Annual Report of the Smithsonian Institution for 1873*, pp. 219–25. Washington, D.C.

Stocking, George W., Jr.

1968 "The Scientific Reaction against Cultural Anthropology, 1917–1920," in *Race, Culture, and Evolution: Essays in the History of Anthropology*, by G. W. Stocking Jr., pp. 270–307. New York: Free Press.

1974 (ed.) *A Franz Boas Reader: The Shaping of American Anthropology, 1883–1911*. Chicago: University of Chicago Press.

1989 "Romantic Motives and the History of Anthropology," in *Romantic Motives: Essays on Anthropological Sensibility*, G. W. Stocking Jr., ed., pp. 3–9. Madison: University of Wisconsin Press.

Stocking, George W., and Susan P. Montague

1979 "Interview and Department Focus: George Stocking on Fay-Cooper Cole." *Journal of Anthropology* 1(2):1–17. DeKalb: Northern Illinois University.

Stoltman, James B.

1973 "The Southeastern United States," in *The Development of North American Archaeology: Essays in the History of Regional Traditions*, J. F. Fitting, ed., pp. 117–50. Garden City, N.Y.: Anchor Books.

2004 "History of Archaeological Research," in *Handbook of North American Indians*, vol. 14, *Southeast*, R. D. Fogelson, ed., pp. 14–30. Washington, D.C.: Smithsonian Institution.

Stone, Doris Z.

1980 "A Fair Period for a Field Study." *Radcliffe Quarterly* 66(3):20–22.

Story, Ronald

1980 *The Forging of an Aristocracy: Harvard and the Boston Upper Class, 1800–1870*. Middletown, Conn.: Wesleyan University Press.

Strong, William Duncan

1945 "George Clapp Vaillant, 1901–1945." *American Antiquity* 11(2):113–16.

Strong, William Duncan, Alfred Kidder II, and A. J. Drexel Paul Jr.

1938 *Preliminary Report on the Smithsonian Institution–Harvard University Archaeological Expedition to Northwestern Honduras, 1936*. Smithsonian Miscellaneous Collections, vol. 97, no. 1. Washington, D.C.

Studley, Cordelia A.

1883 "Notes upon the Human Remains from the Caves of Coahuila, Mexico." *Annual Reports of the PMAAE* 3(3):233–59.

1885 "Description of the Human Remains Found in the 'Intrusive Pit' in the Large Mound of the Turner Group, Little Miami Valley, Ohio, during the Explorations of Messrs. Putnam and Metz." *Proceedings of the AAAS* 33:618.

Sturtevant, E. Lewis

1885 "Indian Corn and the Indians." *American Naturalist* 9(3):225–34.

1894 "Notes on Maize." *Bulletin of the Torrey Botanical Club* 21(12):503–23.

Sullivan, Walter

1963 "Vilhjalmur Stefansson, 1879–1962." *Geographical Review* 53(2):87–291.

Summers, Adams P., and Thomas J. Koob.

1997 "A Biographical Sketch of Samuel Walton Garman," in *Plagiostomia: The Sharks, Skates and Rays,* A. P. Summers, ed., pp. l–lxxii. Los Angeles: Benthic Press.

Swanton, John Reed

1937 "Biographical Memoir of William Henry Holmes, 1846–1933." *National Academy of Sciences, Biographical Memoirs* 17(10):223–53.

1938 "John Napoleon Brinton Hewitt." *American Anthropologist* 40(2):286–89.

1942 "David I. Bushnell, Jr." *American Anthropologist* 44(1):104–10.

1946 "John Reed Swanton," in *Harvard Class Record Book, 50th Class Report, Harvard College Class of 1896,* pp. 394–98. Cambridge, Mass.

Swauger, James L.

1940 "A Review of Mr. F. H. Gerrodette's Notes on the Excavation of the McKees Rocks Mound." *Pennsylvania Archaeologist* 10(1):8–10, 23–24.

Sweet, George W.

1894 "Incidents of the Threatened Outbreak of Hole-in-the-Day and Other Ojibways at Time of Sioux Massacre of 1862." *Collections of the Minnesota Historical Society* 6:401–8.

Thayer, William Roscoe

1915 "Memoir of Lucien Carr." *Proceedings of the Massachusetts Historical Society* 49:91–94.

Thomas, Cyrus

1894 *Report on the Mound Explorations of the Bureau of Ethnology.* 12th Annual Report of the Bureau of Ethnology, pp. 1–730. Washington, D.C.

Thomas, W. Stephen

1955 "Arthur Caswell Parker: 1881–1955, Anthropologist." *Rochester History* 7(2):1–30.

Thompson, Edward Herbert

1888a   "Archaeological Research in Yucatan." *Proceedings of the American Antiquarian Society* 4:248–54.

1888b   "Explorations in Labna, Yucatan." *Proceedings of the American Antiquarian Society* 4:379–85.

1890   "The Hammock–Making of Yucatan." *Littell's Living Age* 185(2391):251–52.

1893a   "The Ancient Structures of Yucatan Not Communal Dwellings." *Proceedings of the American Antiquarian Society* 8:262–69.

1893b   "Yucatan at the Time of Its Discovery." *Proceedings of the American Antiquarian Society* 8:270–73.

1896   "Ancient Tombs of Palenque." *Proceedings of the American Antiquarian Society* 10:418–21.

1897   *The Chultunes of Labna, Yucatan: Report of Explorations by the Museum, 1888–89 and 1890–91.* Memoirs of the PMAAE, vol. 1., no. 3. Cambridge, Mass.: Harvard University.

1898   "Ruins of Xkichmook, Yucatan." *Field Columbian Museum Anthropological Series* 2(3):207–29.

1904   *Archaeological Researches in Yucatan: Reports of Explorations for the Museum.* Memoirs of the PMAAE, vol. 3, no. 1. Cambridge, Mass.: Harvard University.

1911   "The Genesis of the Maya Arch." *American Anthropologist* 13(4):501–16.

1914   "The Home of a Forgotten Race: Mysterious Chichen Itza in Yucatan." *National Geographic* 25(6):585–648.

1929   "Forty Years of Research and Exploration in Yucatan." *Proceedings of the American Antiquarian Society* 39:38–48.

1932   *People of the Serpent: Life and Adventure among the Mayas.* Boston: Houghton Mifflin.

Thompson, J. Eric S.

1949   "Sylvanus Griswold Morley, 1883–1948." *American Anthropologist* 51(2):293–97.

Thompson, Raymond Harris

1995   "Emil W. Haury and the Definition of Southwestern Archaeology." *American Antiquity* 60(4):640–60.

1996   "Samuel Watson Smith, 1897–1993." *Kiva* 61(3):316–27.

Thoresen, Timothy H. H.

1975   "Paying the Piper and Calling the Tune: The Beginnings of Academic Anthropology in California." *Journal of the History of the Behavioral Sciences* 11(3):257–75.

Thwing, Charles Franklin

1881 "The Peabody Museum of Archaeology and Ethnology." *Harper's New Monthly Magazine* 63(377):670–78.

Titcomb, Caldwell

1993 "The Black Presence at Harvard: An Overview," in *Blacks at Harvard: A Documentary History of African-American Experience at Harvard and Radcliffe*, W. Sollors, C. Titcomb, and T. A. Underwood, eds., pp. 1–7. New York: New York University Press.

Tolstoy, Paul

1991 "George Clapp Vaillant," in *International Directory of Anthropologists*, C. Winters, ed., pp. 717–18. New York: Garland.

Tooker, Elizabeth

1978 "Ely S. Parker, Seneca, ca. 1828–1895," in *American Indian Intellectuals*, M. Liberty, ed., pp. 14–32. St. Paul, Minn.: West Publishing.

Tozzer, Alfred Marston

1904 "A Comparative Study of the Mayas and the Lacandones." Ph.D. dissertation, Department of Anthropology, Harvard University.

1908 "Harvard Anthropological Society." *Science* 27(697):757–58.

1909 "The Putnam Anniversary." *American Anthropologist* 11(2):285–88.

1915 "Report of the Director for 1913–1914." *American Anthropologist* 15(2):391–95.

1920 "Anthropology at the Cambridge Meeting and Proceedings of the American Anthropological Association." *American Anthropologist* 22(1):86–96.

1921 "Charles Pickering Bowditch." *American Anthropologist* 23(3):353–59.

1929 "Charles Pickering Bowditch," in *Dictionary of American Biography*, vol. 2, p. 492. New York: Charles Scribner's Sons.

1933 "Zelia Nuttall." *American Anthropologist* 35(3):475–82.

1936a "Frederic Ward Putnam, 1839–1915." *National Academy of Sciences, Biographical Memoirs* 16:125–53.

1936b "Roland Burrage Dixon." *American Anthropologist* 38(2):291–94.

Tozzer, Alfred M., and Glover M. Allen

1910 *Animal Figures in the Maya Codices*. Papers of the PMAAE, vol. 4. Cambridge, Mass.: Harvard University.

Tozzer, Alfred M., and Carleton S. Coon

1943 "Roland Burrage Dixon," in *Studies in the Anthropology of Oceania and Asia, Presented in Memory of Roland Burrage Dixon*, C. S. Coon and J. M. Andrews IV, eds., pp. ix–xi. Papers of the PMAAE, vol. 20. Cambridge, Mass.: Harvard University.

Tozzer, Alfred Marston, and Alfred L. Kroeber

1936   "Roland Burrage Dixon." *American Anthropologist* 38(2):291–300.

Trigger, Bruce G.

1966   "Sir Daniel Wilson: Canada's First Anthropologist." *Anthropologica* (Ottawa) 8(1):3–28.

1989   *A History of Archaeological Thought.* New York: Cambridge University Press.

1992   "Daniel Wilson and the Scottish Enlightenment." *Proceedings of the Society of Antiquaries of Scotland* 122:55–75.

Tschopik, Marion H.

1946   *Some Notes on the Archaeology of the Department of Puno, Peru.* Papers of the PMAAE, vol. 27, no. 3. Cambridge, Mass.: Harvard University.

Turner, James

1999   *The Liberal Education of Charles Eliot Norton.* Baltimore, Md.: Johns Hopkins University Press.

Ubelaker, Douglas H.

1989   "J. Lawrence Angel, 1915–1986." *American Antiquity* 54(1):5–8.

1999   "George Amos Dorsey," in *American National Biography,* J. A. Garraty and M. C. Carnes, eds., vol. 6, pp. 764–65. New York: Oxford University Press.

Underwood, Sarah A.

1891   "Women's Work in Science." *New England Magazine* 9(6):695–701.

University of Kentucky

2001   "University of Kentucky Alumni Association Hall of Distinguished Alumni." Electronic document, www.uky.edu/Alumni/alumnihall/bowdenAO.htm.

Utsurikawa, Nenozo

1919   "On the Ifuagos in Northern Luzon, Philippine Islands." *Journal of the Anthropological Society of Tokyo* 34:221–33.

1921   "Demon Design on the Bornean Shield: A Hermeneutic Possibility." *American Anthropologist* 23(1):138–48.

Valentini, Philipp Johann Josef

1878   "The History, Use, and Detailed Explanation of the Mexican Calendar Stone." Stephen Salisbury, translator. *Proceedings of the American Antiquarian Society* 71:91–110.

1879   "Mexican Copper Tools: The Use of Copper by the Mexicans before the Conquest." Stephen Salisbury, translator. *Proceedings of the American Antiquarian Society* 73:1–41.

1880 "The Katunes of Maya History: A Chapter in the Early History of Central America, with Special Reference to the Pio Perez Manuscript." Stephen Salisbury, translator. *Proceedings of the American Antiquarian Society* 74:71–117.

1882 "The Olmecas and the Tultecas: A Study in Early Mexican Ethnology and History." Stephen Salisbury, translator. *Proceedings of the American Antiquarian Society* (n.s.) 2(2):193–220.

Van Tassel, David D.

1960 *Recording America's Past: An Interpretation of the Development of Historical Studies in America, 1607–1884.* Chicago: University of Chicago Press.

Veysey, Laurence R.

1965 *The Emergence of the American University.* Chicago: University of Chicago Press.

Vogt, Evon Z.

1975 "Alfred Marston Tozzer and Maya Social Anthropology," in *The Maya and Their Neighbors (A Series of Events to Celebrate the Dedication of the Tozzer Library on October 21, 1974),* pp. 22–33. Cambridge, Mass.: PMAE.

Volk, Ernest

1894a "Observations on the Use of Argillite by Prehistoric People in the Delaware Valley." *Proceedings of the AAAS* 42:312–17.

1894b "Cache Finds from Ancient Village Sites in New Jersey," in *Memoirs of the International Congress of Anthropology,* C. S. Wakeland, ed., pp. 140–42. Chicago: Schulte Publishing.

1911 *The Archaeology of the Delaware Valley: Results of Excavations Made Chiefly in the Neighborhood of Trenton, N.J.* Papers of the PMAAE, vol. 5. Cambridge, Mass.: Harvard University.

1912 "Early Man in America." *American Museum Journal* 12(5):181–85.

von Morlot, Adolphe

1861 "General Views on Archaeology," in *Annual Report of the Smithsonian Institution for 1860,* pp. 284–343. Washington, D.C.

1863 "An Introductory Lecture to the Study of High Antiquity, Delivered at the Academy of Lausanne, Switzerland, on the 29th of November, 1860," in *Annual Report of the Smithsonian Institution for 1862,* pp. 303–17. Washington, D.C.

Wade, Mason

1942 *Francis Parkman: Heroic Historian.* New York: Viking Press.

Wakeland, Charles Staniland

1894 "Preface," in *Memoirs of the International Congress of Anthropology,* C. S. Wakeland, ed., pp. vii–x. Chicago: Schulte Publishing.

Walker-McNeil, Pearl Lee

1979 "The Carlisle Indian School: A Study of Acculturation." Ph.D. dissertation, American University.

Wallis, Ruth Otis Sawtell

1931 *Azilian Skeletal Remains from Montardit (Ariège) France.* Papers of the PMAAE, vol. 11, no. 4. Cambridge, Mass.: Harvard University.

1943 *Too Many Bones.* New York: Dodd, Mead.

Walster, Harlow Leslie

1956 "George Francis Will, 1884–1955: Archaeologist, Anthropologist, Ethnologist, Naturalist, Nurseryman, Seedsman, Historian. A Biography." *North Dakota History* 23(1):4–25.

Wardle, Harriet Newell

1956 "Clarence Bloomfield Moore (1852–1936)." *Bulletin of the Philadelphia Anthropological Society* 9(2):9–11.

Warner, Mildred Hall

1988 *W. Lloyd Warner, Social Anthropologist.* New York: Publishing Center for Cultural Resources.

Warren, Claude N., and Susan Rose

1994 *William Pengelly's Spits, Yards and Prisms: The Forerunners of Modern Excavation Method and Techniques in Archaeology.* Torquay, U.K.: Torquay Natural History Society.

Warren, Edward

1860 *The Life of John Collins Warren, M.D., Compiled Chiefly from His Autobiography and Journals.* 2 vols. Boston: Ticknor and Fields.

Warren, John Collins

1822 *Comparative View of the Sensorial and Nervous Systems in Men and Animals.* Boston: J. W. Ingraham.

1855 *Description of a Skeleton of the Mastodon Giganteus of North America.* Boston: John Wilson and Sons.

Watson, George E.

1985 "Vertebrate Collections: Lost Opportunities," in *Magnificent Voyagers: The United States Exploring Expedition, 1838–1842,* H. J. Viola and C. Margolis, eds., pp. 43–70. Washington, D.C.: Smithsonian Institution.

Wauchope, Robert

1965 "Alfred Vincent Kidder, 1885–1963." *American Antiquity* 31(2):149–71.

1972 "Edward Wyllys Andrews IV, 1916–1971." *American Antiquity* 37(3):394–403.

Wayman, Dorothy Godfrey

1942 *Edward Sylvester Morse: A Biography.* Cambridge, Mass.: Harvard University Press.

Webster, Laurie D.

2003 "William H. Claflin, Jr., and the Making of a Collection," in *Collecting the Weaver's Art: The William Claflin Collection of Southwestern Textiles,* L. D. Webster, compiler, pp. 2–11. Cambridge, Mass.: Peabody Museum Press.

Wedel, Waldo R.

1956 "George Francis Will, 1884–1955." *American Antiquity* 22(1):73–76.

Wendorf, Fred, and Raymond H. Thompson

2002 "The Committee for the Recovery of Archaeological Remains: Three Decades of Service to the Archaeological Profession." *American Antiquity* 67(2):317–30.

Weslager, Clinton A.

1941 "An Incised Fulgur Shell from Holly Oak, Delaware." *Bulletin of the Archaeological Society of Delaware* 3(4):10–15.

Wheeler, Richard Page

1978 "Bone and Antler Artifacts," in *Bones from Awatovi, Northeastern Arizona,* by S. J. Olsen and R. P. Wheeler, pp. 35–74. Papers of the PMAE, vol. 70, nos. 1–2. Cambridge, Mass.: Harvard University.

Whisnant, David E.

1995 *Rascally Signs in Sacred Places: The Politics of Culture in Nicaragua.* Chapel Hill: University of North Carolina Press.

Whitehill, Walter Muir

1949 *The East India Marine Society and the Peabody Museum of Salem: A Sesquicentennial History.* Salem, Mass.: Peabody Museum.

Wilbur, C. Martin

1943 "Carl Whiting Bishop." *Far Eastern Quarterly* 2:204–7.

Wilcox, David R.

2003a "Restoring Authenticity: Judging Frank Hamilton Cushing's Veracity," in *Philadelphia and the Development of Americanist Archaeology,* D. D. Fowler and D. R. Wilcox, eds., pp. 88–112. Tuscaloosa: University of Alabama Press.

2003b "Creating Field Anthropology: Why Remembering Matters," in *Curators, Collections, and Contexts: Anthropology at the Field Museum, 1893–2002,* S. E. Nash and G. M. Feinman, eds., pp. 31–47. Chicago: Field Museum of Natural History.

Wilder, Burt Green

1875 "Sketch of Dr. Jeffries Wyman." *Popular Science Monthly* 6(3):355–60.

1910a   "Jeffries Wyman, Anatomist, 1814–1874," in *Leading American Men of Science,* D. S. Jordan, ed., pp. 171–209. New York: Henry Holt.

1910b   "Burt G. Wilder," in *American Men of Science,* 2nd ed., J. McK. Cattell, ed., p. 511. New York.: Science Press.

Wilkes, Charles

1978   *Autobiography of Rear Admiral Charles Wilkes, U.S. Navy 1798–1877.* W. J. Morgan et al., eds. Washington, D.C.: Naval History Division, Department of the Navy.

Will, George Francis

1909   "Some Observations Made in Northwestern South Dakota." *American Anthropologist* 11(2):257–65.

1910a   "Some New Missouri River Valley Sites in North Dakota." *American Anthropologist* 12(1):58–60.

1910b   "The Bourgeois Village Site." *American Anthropologist* 12(3):473–76.

1911   "A New Feature in the Archaeology of the Missouri Valley in North Dakota." *American Anthropologist* 13(4):585–88.

1913   "No-Tongue, a Mandan Tale." *Journal of American Folk-Lore* 26(102):331–37.

1916   "George Will," in *Harvard College Class of 1906, Secretary's Report, 1916,* p. 307. Cambridge, Mass.: Riverside Press.

1921   "An Unusual Group of Mounds in North Dakota." *American Anthropologist* 23:175–79.

1924a   "Indian Agriculture at Its Northern Limits in the Great Plains Region of North America," in *Proceedings of the International Congress of Americanists* (1922), vol. 1, pp. 202–305. Rio de Janeiro.

1924b   "Archaeology of the Missouri Valley." *Anthropological Papers of the AMNH* 22:283–344.

1930a   "Arikara Ceremonials." *North Dakota Historical Quarterly* 4:247–65.

1930b   "The Mandan Lodge at Bismarck." *North Dakota Historical Quarterly* 5:38–48.

1933   "A Resume of North Dakota Archaeology." *North Dakota Historical Quarterly* 7:150–61.

1946   *Tree Ring Studies in North Dakota.* Bulletin 338. North Dakota Agricultural Experiment Station.

1949   "Dendrochronology in the Dakotas." *Notebook, Laboratory of Anthropology, University of Nebraska* 1:114–16 (Proceedings of the 5th Plains Conference for Archaeology, 1948).

1950a   "Dendrochronology, Climate, and Prehistory of the Upper Missouri." *Anthropological Papers of the University of Utah* 11:95–97 (Proceedings of the 6th Plains Archaeological Conference, Lincoln, 1948).

1950b   "Vegetal Remains in Northern Plains Archaeology." *Plains Archaeological Conference Newsletter* 3(2):11.

Will, George F., and Thad C. Hecker

1944   "Upper Missouri River Valley Aboriginal Culture in North Dakota." *North Dakota Historical Quarterly* 11:5–126.

Will, George F., and George E. Hyde

1917   *Corn among the Indians of the Upper Missouri.* St. Louis, Mo.: William Harvey Miner.

Will, George F., and Herbert J. Spinden

1906   *The Mandans: A Study of Their Culture, Archaeology, and Language.* Papers of the PMAAE, vol. 3, no. 4. Cambridge, Mass.: Harvard University.

Willey, Gordon R.

1967   "Alfred Vincent Kidder, October 29, 1885–June 11, 1963." *National Academy of Sciences, Biographical Memoirs* 39(8):293–322.

1973   "Introduction," in *Archaeology of the United States, or, Sketches, Historical and Bibliographical, of the Progress of Information and Opinion Respecting Vestiges of Antiquity in the United States,* by S. F. Haven (reprint of 1856 publication), pp. vii–ix. New York: AMS Press.

1975   "Alfred Marston Tozzer and Maya Archaeology," in *The Maya and Their Neighbors (A Series of Events to Celebrate the Dedication of the Tozzer Library on October 21, 1974),* pp. 3–10. Cambridge, Mass.: PMAE.

1976   "Samuel Kirkland Lothrop, July 6, 1892–January 10, 1965." *National Academy of Sciences, Biographical Memoirs* 48(10):252–73.

1983   "Harry Evelyn Dorr Pollock, 1901–1982." *American Antiquity* 48(4):782–84.

1988   "Augustus Ledyard Smith, 1901–1985." *American Antiquity* 53(4):683–85.

1996   "Philip Phillips, 1900–1994." *American Antiquity* 61(1):39–43.

Willey, Gordon R., and Jeremy A. Sabloff

1974   *A History of American Archaeology.* London: Thames and Hudson.

1980   *A History of American Archaeology.* 2nd ed. London: Thames and Hudson.

1993   *A History of American Archaeology.* 3rd ed. London: Thames and Hudson.

Williams, George Dee

1931   *Maya-Spanish Crosses in Yucatan.* Papers of the PMAAE, vol. 13, no. 1. Cambridge, Mass.: Harvard University.

1963   "George Dee Williams," in *Who's Who in the East,* 9th ed., p. 1011. New York: Marquis Publications.

Williams, Stephen

1973 "Introduction," in *Antiquities of the Southern Indians, Particularly of the Georgia Tribes,* by C. C. Jones Jr. (reprint of 1873 publication), pp. vii–ix. New York: AMS Press.

1986a "Pioneers in the Archaeology of Middle Tennessee." Paper presented at the Southeastern Archaeological Conference, Nashville, Tenn., November.

1986b "Doris Stone: The Pathways of a Middle American Scholar," in *Research and Reflections in Archaeology and History: Essays in Honor of Doris Stone,* E. W. Andrews V, ed., pp. 199–202. New Orleans, La.: Middle American Research Institute, Tulane University.

1987 "A Brief Review of Developments in the Archaeology of the Cincinnati Locality." Lecture delivered at the Cincinnati Museum of Natural History, February 19.

1991 *Fantastic Archaeology: The Wild Side of North American Prehistory.* Philadelphia: University of Pennsylvania Press.

1994 "The Ocmulgee Investigations in Historical Perspective," in *Ocmulgee Archaeology, 1936–1986,* D. J. Hally, ed., pp. 8–14. Athens: University of Georgia Press.

2000 "Reviewing Some Late 19th Century Archaeology Studies: Exploding the Myth of the 'Myth.'" Paper presented at the Mid-South Conference, Memphis, Tenn., June.

2003 "Introduction," in *Archaeological Survey in the Lower Mississippi Alluvial Valley, 1940–1947,* by P. Phillips, J. A. Ford, and J. B. Griffin [1951], S. Williams, ed., pp. xi–xxxii. Tuscaloosa: University of Alabama Press.

Willis, Bailey

1934 "Raphael Pumpelly, 1837–1923." *National Academy of Sciences, Biographical Memoirs* 16(2):23–62. (Reprinted from *Bulletin of the Geological Society of America* 36, 1925.)

Willoughby, Charles C.

1898 *Prehistoric Burial Places in Maine.* Papers of the PMAAE, vol. 1, no. 6. Cambridge, Mass.: Harvard University.

1916 "49th Annual Report of the Curator for 1914–1915, PMAAE," in *Annual Reports of the President and Treasurer of Harvard College,* pp. 254–61.

1917 "50th Annual Report of the Curator for 1915–1916, PMAAE," in *Annual Reports of the President and Treasurer of Harvard College,* pp. 251–55.

1918 "51st Annual Report of the Curator for 1916–1917, PMAAE," in *Annual Reports of the President and Treasurer of Harvard College,* pp. 240–44.

1919 "52nd Annual Report of the Curator for 1917–1918, PMAAE," in *Annual Reports of the President and Treasurer of Harvard College,* pp. 234–42.

1920   "53rd Annual Report of the Curator for 1918–1919, PMAAE," in *Annual Reports of the President and Treasurer of Harvard College*, pp. 197–200.

1921   "54th Annual Report of the Curator for 1919–1920, PMAAE," in *Annual Reports of the President and Treasurer of Harvard College*, pp. 241–45.

1922   "55th Annual Report of the Curator for 1920–1921, PMAAE," in *Annual Reports of the President and Treasurer of Harvard College*, pp. 274–78.

1923a   "56th Annual Report of the Curator for 1921–1922, PMAAE," in *Annual Reports of the President and Treasurer of Harvard College*, pp. 219–23.

1923b   "The Peabody Museum of Archaeology and Ethnology, Harvard University." *Harvard Graduates' Magazine* 31(124):495–503.

1924   "57th Annual Report of the Curator for 1922–1923, PMAAE," in *Annual Reports of the President and Treasurer of Harvard College*, pp. 259–63.

1925   "58th Annual Report of the Curator for 1923–1924, PMAAE," in *Annual Reports of the President and Treasurer of Harvard College*, pp. 261–64.

1926   "59th Annual Report of the Curator for 1924–1925, PMAAE," in *Annual Reports of the President and Treasurer of Harvard College*, pp. 251–54.

1927   "60th Annual Report of the Curator for 1925–1926, PMAAE," in *Annual Reports of the President and Treasurer of Harvard College*, pp. 263–66.

1928   "61st Annual Report of the Curator for 1926–1927, PMAAE," in *Annual Reports of the President and Treasurer of Harvard College*, pp. 272–76.

1929   "62nd Annual Report of the Curator for 1927–1928, PMAAE," in *Annual Reports of the President and Treasurer of Harvard College*, pp. 295–99.

Willoughby, Charles C., and Earnest A. Hooton

1922   *The Turner Group of Earthworks, Hamilton County, Ohio.* Papers of the PMAAE, vol. 8, no. 3. Cambridge, Mass.: Harvard University.

Wilson, Daniel

1862   *Prehistoric Man: Researches into the Origin of Civilization in the Old and the New World.* 2 vols. London: Macmillan.

Wilson, Howard B.

1903   "Notes on Syrian Folk-lore Collected in Boston." *Journal of American Folk-Lore* 16:133–47.

Wilson, Leonard G.

1998   *Lyell in America: Transatlantic Geology, 1841–1853.* Baltimore, Md.: Johns Hopkins University Press.

Wilson, Richard Guy

1979   "The Great Civilization," in *The American Renaissance, 1876–1917*, pp. 10–70. New York: Brooklyn Museum.

Wilson, Thomas J.

1964   "Harvard University Press," in *Report of the President of Harvard College and of the Departments, 1962–1963,* pp. 553–56.

Winlock, Herbert Eustis

1924   "The Tombs of the Kings of the Seventeenth Dynasty at Thebes." *Journal of Egyptian Archaeology* 10:217–77.

1928   "Tomb of Senmut Excavated." *El Palacio* 24:209–11.

1931   "Toilet Aids Four Thousand Years Old." *El Palacio* 32:192–93.

1932a   "Excavations at the Temple of Deir el Bahri, 1921–1931." *Proceedings of the American Philosophical Society* 71:321–41.

1932b   "The Museum's Excavations at Thebes." *Bulletin of the Metropolitan Museum of Art* 27(3):4–37.

1940   "The Origin of the Ancient Egyptian Calendar." *Proceedings of the American Philosophical Society* 83:447–74.

1955   *Models of Daily Life in Ancient Egypt, from the Tomb of Meket-Re at Thebes.* Cambridge, Mass.: Harvard University Press.

Winsor, Justin

1884–89   (ed.) *Narrative and Critical History of America.* 8 vols. Boston: Houghton Mifflin.

1889   "The Progress of Opinion Respecting the Origin and Antiquity of Man in America," in *Narrative and Critical History of America,* J. Winsor, ed., vol. 1, pp. 369–412. Boston: Houghton Mifflin.

Wintemberg, William J.

1940   "Harlan Ingersoll Smith." *American Antiquity* 6(1):63–64.

Winthrop, Robert Charles, Jr.

1897   *A Memoir of Robert C. Winthrop.* Boston: Little, Brown.

Winthrop, Robert Charles, Sr.

1878   "Introductory Remarks." *Annual Reports of the PMAAE* 2(2):177–84.

1894   *Reminiscences of Foreign Travel: A Fragment of Autobiography.* Boston: John Wilson and Son.

Wirt, Julia J.

1878   "Explorations of a Mound near Utah Lake, Utah." *Proceedings of the Davenport (Iowa) Academy of Natural Sciences* 2:28–29, 82.

Wirth, Louis

1953   "The Social Sciences," in *American Scholarship in the Twentieth Century,* M. Curti, ed., pp. 33–82. Cambridge, Mass.: Harvard University Press.

Wissler, Clark

1909 "Dr. William Jones." *American Museum Journal* 9:123–24.

1915 "Frederic Ward Putnam." *American Museum Journal* 15:315–17.

1942 "The American Indian and the American Philosophical Society." *Proceedings of the American Philosophical Society* 86(1):189–204.

1944 "Marshall Howard Saville," in *Dictionary of American Biography*, vol. 21, Supplement 1, pp. 647–48. New York: Charles Scribner's Sons.

Wissler, Clark, Amos W. Butler, Roland B. Dixon, Frederick W. Hodge, and Berthold Laufer

1923 "State Archaeological Surveys: Suggestions in Method and Technique." Brochure. Washington, D.C.: Committee on State Archaeological Surveys, Division of Anthropology and Psychology, National Research Council.

Witmer, Linda F.

1993 *The Indian Industrial School, Carlisle, Pennsylvania, 1879–1918*. Carlisle, Pa.: Cumberland Historical Society.

Witthoft, John

1974 "Frank Gouldsmith Speck," in *Dictionary of American Biography*, Supplement 4, pp. 761–63. New York: Charles Scribner's Son.

1991 "Frank Speck: The Formative Years," in *The Life and Times of Frank G. Speck, 1881–1950*, R. Blankenship, ed., pp. 1–8. Publications in Anthropology, no. 4. Philadelphia: University of Pennsylvania.

Wolfe, Elizabeth F.

1982 "Contributions of Karl Hermann Berendt to Central American Archaeology." *Kroeber Anthropological Society Papers* 61–62:1–19. Berkeley: University of California.

Woodbury, Nathalie F. S.

1991 "Richard B. Woodbury," in *International Dictionary of Anthropologists*, C. Winters, ed., pp. 767–68. New York: Garland.

Woodbury, Richard B.

1954 *Prehistoric Stone Implements of Northeastern Arizona*. Papers of the PMAAE, vol. 34. Cambridge, Mass.: Harvard University.

1973 *Alfred V. Kidder*. New York: Columbia University Press.

1990 "John Otis Brew, 1906–1988." *American Antiquity* 55(3):452–459.

1993 *Sixty Years of Southwestern Archaeology: A History of the Pecos Conference*. Albuquerque: University of New Mexico Press.

1995 "Samuel Watson Smith, 1897–1993." *American Antiquity* 60(4):665–67.

Woodring, Wendell Phillip

1958   "William Healey Dall." *National Academy of Sciences, Biographical Memoirs* 31(4):92–113.

Woods, James Haughton

1899   *The Value of Religious Facts: A Study of Some Aspects of the Science of Religion.* New York: E. P. Dutton.

1906   *Practice and Science of Religion: A Study of Method in Comparative Religion.* New York: Longmans, Green.

Woods, Margaret Soutter

1935   "Talus Unit No. 1, Chetro Ketl," in *U.S. National Park Service, Southwestern Monuments, Monthly Report for August,* pp. 144–46. Washington, D.C.

1937   "Talus Unit No. 1 at Chaco," in *U.S. National Park Service, Southwestern Monuments, Monthly Report for October,* pp. 321–323. Washington, D.C.

Wright, George Frederick

1881   "An Attempt to Estimate Age of the Palaeolithic Bearing Gravels in Trenton, New Jersey." *Proceedings of the BSNH* 21:137–41.

1887   "On the Age of the Ohio Gravel-Beds." *Proceedings of the BSNH* 23:427–36.

1892   *Man and the Glacial Period . . . with an Appendix on Tertiary Man by Prof. Henry W. Haynes.* New York: D. Appleton.

1893   "Some Detailed Evidence of an Ice-Age Man in Eastern America." *Science* 21(522):65–66.

1919   "Charles Conrad Abbott and Ernest Volk." *Science* 50(1298):451–53.

Wyman, Jeffries

1854   "Cranium of a Flathead Indian from the Columbia River." *Proceedings of the BSNH* 4:83–84.

1856   "Indian Cemetery, Atlantic Hill, near Nantucket Beach." *Proceedings of the BSNH* 6:20–21.

1857   "On the Cranial Capacity of a Digger Indian." *Proceedings of the BSNH* 6:127.

1864   "On Indian Mounds of Atlantic Coast." *Proceedings of the BSNH* 10:72.

1866   "On the Distorted Skull of a Child from the Hawaiian Islands." *Proceedings of the BSNH* 11:70–71.

1867a   "On Malformed Skulls." *Proceedings of the BSNH* 11:115.

1867b   "Account of the Shell Mounds of Florida." *Proceedings of the BSNH* 11:158.

1867c   "Description of the Shell Heaps at Salisbury." *Proceedings of the BSNH* 11:242–43.

1867d   "On an Esquimaux Fire Stick." *Proceedings of the BSNH* 11:285.

1867e   "Account of a Visit to an Indian Shell Heap near Mount Desert, Me." *Proceedings of the BSNH* 11:288.

1867f	"On Flint Implements from Northern Europe." *Proceedings of the BSNH* 11:301.
1867g	"Shell Heaps on Goose Island." *Proceedings of the BSNH* 11:301.
1867h	"Visit to Dighton Rock." *Proceedings of the BSNH* 11:305.
1867i	"Measurement of Some Human Crania." *Proceedings of the BSNH* 11:292.
1867j	"Examination of Animals of the New England Shell Heaps." *Proceedings of the BSNH* 11:337–38.
1868a	"Report of the Curator." *Annual Reports of the PMAAE* 1(1):5–18.
1868b	"On the Inscription on the Dighton Rock." *Proceedings of the BSNH* 12:218–19.
1868c	"An Account of Some Kjokkenmoeddings, or Shell Heaps, in Maine and Massachusetts." *American Naturalist* 1(11):561–84.
1868d	"On the Fresh-water Shell-Heaps of the St. Johns River, East Florida." *American Naturalist* 2(8):393–403 and 2(9):449–63.
1869	"Report of the Curator." *Annual Reports of the PMAAE* 1(2):5–20.
1870	"Report of the Curator." *Annual Reports of the PMAAE* 1(3):5–12.
1871	"Report of the Curator." *Annual Reports of the PMAAE* 1(4):5–24.
1872	"Report of the Curator." *Annual Reports of the PMAAE* 1(5):5–30.
1873	"Report of the Curator." *Annual Reports of the PMAAE* 1(6):5–23.
1874	"Cannibalism of the Florida Indians." *Proceedings of the BSNH* 17:14–15.
1876	"Primitive Man." *American Naturalist* 10(5):278–82.

Yde, Jens

| 1938 | "Architectural Remains along the Coast of Quintana Roo: A Report of the Peabody Museum Expedition, 1913–1914, Compiled from the Field Notes of Raymond E. Merwin." Manuscript, Tozzer Library archives, Harvard University. |

Yorke, Dane

| 1945 | *The Men and Times of Pepperell.* Boston: Pepperell Manufacturing Co. |

Zamora, Mario D.

| 1974 | "Henry Otley Beyer, 1883–1966." *American Anthropologist* 76(2):361–62. |
| 1978 | "Marcelo Tangco: Native Father of Philippine Anthropology." *Eastern Anthropology* 31(4):589–96. |

Picture Credits

Unless otherwise noted below, all images reproduced in this volume are housed in the archives of the Peabody Museum of Archaeology and Ethnology and are copyright © the President and Fellows of Harvard College. When known, photographer, artist, and original place of publication are listed in addition to the Peabody Museum number.

Cover	For cover pictures, see credits below for plates 22 (top) and 54.
Frontispiece	2004.24.29951.
Page 2	2010.1.31.

PLATES

1	Engraving attributed to John Harris after William Burgis. Courtesy of Massachusetts Historical Society.
2, top left	Harvard University Archives, HUP Agassiz, Louis (17).
2, top right	Harvard University Archives, HUP Agassiz, Louis (16).
2, bottom left	Courtesy of the Museum of Comparative Zoology, Harvard University. Peabody Museum print 2012.0.61.
2, bottom right	2004.1.324.25.
3, top left	Photo by Oliver Wendell Holmes, August 11, 1865 (detail). 2004.24.31071.
3, top right	2004.24.5463.
3, bottom	2004.24.24669.
4, top	Engraving by J. C. Buttre. 967-23-10/45261b.
4, bottom left	Photo by J. E. Purdy, Boston, 1903. Courtesy of Library of Congress Prints and Photographs Division. LC-USZ62-63651.
4, bottom right	Courtesy of Historical and Special Collections, Harvard Law School Library.
5, top	2004.1.326.3.
5, bottom	2004.1.324.1.1.
6, top left	Photo from the album of Mrs. Henry P. McLean, The Schlesinger Library, Radcliffe Institute, Harvard University.
6, top right	Bronze relief by Bela Lyon Pratt. Harvard Art Museums/Fogg Museum, Harvard University Portrait Collection. Gift of Mr. George R. Agassiz to Harvard University, 1912, B33. Photo: Imaging Department © President and Fellows of Harvard College.
6, bottom left	2003.0.17.17.1.
6, bottom right	Courtesy of Historical and Special Collections, Harvard Law School Library.
7, top left	James R. Rice and Sons Engravers. 2004.1.324.13.
7, top right	2004.1.324.12.
7, bottom left	2004.1.324.5.
7, bottom right	2004.1.324.23.
8, top left	2004.1.324.7.
8, top right	2004.1.324.6.

8, bottom	Crayon portrait by E. H. Miller, 1888. 88-56-10/84070.
9, top	2004.29.6041.
9, bottom	Photo by E. Jane Gay. Jane Gay Dodge Papers, The Schlesinger Library, Radcliffe Institute, Harvard University.
10, top left	2004.1.324.9.
10, top right	2004.1.324.16.
10, bottom left	2004.24.25826.
10, bottom right	2004.1.324.10.
11, top left	58-34-20/35732.
11, top right	2004.1.324.26.
11, bottom	2004.24.28444.
12, top	2004.24.1231.
12, bottom	2004.1.149.1
13, top	2004.24.27154.
13, bottom	2004.24.1563.
14	2004.24.1790.
15, top	2004.24.1099.
15, bottom	2004.24.1100.
16, top	2004.24.7186.
16, bottom	2004.24.1113.
17, top	2004.24.7023.
17, bottom	2004.24.1777.
18, top left	2004.1.324.8.
18, top right	2004.1.324.17.
18, bottom	2004.24.300.
19, top	2004.24.1926.2.
19, bottom	2004.24.28511.
20, top left	Photo by David L. De Harport. 2004.24.22856.
20, top right	2004.24.32585.
20, bottom left	1928 Radcliffe College yearbook. The Schlesinger Library, Radcliffe Institute, Harvard University.
20, bottom right	Photo by Frederick P. Orchard. 2004.24.21026.
21	2004.1.324.19.
22, top	2004.24.32580.
22, bottom	Courtesy Curtis M. Hinsley. Public domain.
23, top	2004.24.27155.
23, bottom	47-41-10/99955.1.1.
24, top left	2004.24.29401.1.
24, top right	2004.1.324.20.
24, bottom	2004.29.5193.
25, top	2004.24.29405.
25, bottom	2004.24.1780.
26, top left	2004.24.29497.
26, top right	2004.1.324.18.
26, bottom left	2004.1.324.11.
26, bottom right	2004.1.324.14.
27, top left	2004.24.30989.
27, bottom right	Painting by Ignace Gaugengigl. Photo by Frederick P. Orchard. 2004.24.16988.

Picture Credits | 559

28, top	2004.24.31072.
28, bottom	2004.24.6314.
29, top	2004.24.3469.
29, bottom	41-72-10/99968.911.
30, top	09-3-30/11855.2.1.
30, bottom	2004.24.28554.
31, top	2009.1.25.
31, bottom	2004.24.30990.
32	2004.1.324.2.
33, top	2004.24.30533.
33, bottom	58-34-20/29872.
34, top	2004.24.29730.
34, bottom	65-18-10/100077.1.32.
35, top	2004.24.29729.
35, bottom	2004.24.30535.
36, top left	2004.24.4462A.
36, top right	2004.24.5601D.
36, bottom	2004.24.31352.
37, top	2004.24.7355.
37, bottom	2004.24.28013.
38, top left	1919 Radcliffe College yearbook. The Schlesinger Library, Radcliffe Institute, Harvard University.
38, top right	From *A Study of Some Negro-White Families in the United States*, by Caroline Bond Day, plate 34. Copyright © 1932 by the President and Fellows of Harvard College.
38, bottom left	1919 Radcliffe College yearbook. The Schlesinger Library, Radcliffe Institute, Harvard University.
38, bottom right	Courtesy of the Moorland-Spingarn Research Center, Howard University Archives. All rights reserved.
39, top	2004.24.31427.
39, bottom	2004.24.8420.
40, top left	2004.24.34562.
40, top right	2012.0.26.
40, bottom	58-34-20/58368.
41, top	58-34-20/68096.
41, bottom	2000.25.1.144.
42, top left	2004.24.31527.
42, top right	Photo by Neil M. Judd. 2004.24.23240.
42, bottom	65-18-10/100077.1.43.
43	Photo by E. H. Thompson. © Judge Burt Cosgrove. Courtesy of the Peabody Museum of Archaeology and Ethnology, Harvard University. 2011.24.1.1.71.1.
44, top left	Photo by E. H. Thompson. 2004.24.29009.
44, top right	Photo by Dave Rust. 2005.1.110.1.130.
44, bottom	971-21-10/100162.1.2694.
45, top	2004.24.31020.
45, bottom left	1948 Radcliffe College yearbook. The Schlesinger Library, Radcliffe Institute, Harvard University.

45, bottom right	Harvard Alumni Magazine, 1930. 2004.24.25981.
46, top	1940 Radcliffe College yearbook. The Schlesinger Library, Radcliffe Institute, Harvard University.
46, bottom	2004.24.24667.
47, top	Photo by Patrick T. L. Putnam. 2004.24.7560.2.
47, bottom left	2012.0.28.
47, bottom right	49-22-30/11821.73.
48	2008.1.274.
49, top left	2004.24.26978.
49, top right	2004.24.27562.
49, bottom	56-55-60/15722.
50, top	Lower Mississippi Survey Archives, Peabody Museum.
50, bottom	993-23-10/100524.1.8.6.1.
51, top left	1928 Radcliffe College yearbook. The Schlesinger Library, Radcliffe Institute, Harvard University.
51, top right	1937 Radcliffe College yearbook. The Schlesinger Library, Radcliffe Institute, Harvard University.
51, bottom left	1930 Radcliffe College yearbook. The Schlesinger Library, Radcliffe Institute, Harvard University.
51, bottom right	1939 Radcliffe College yearbook. The Schlesinger Library, Radcliffe Institute, Harvard University.
52, top	Image Archives, Denver Museum of Nature & Science. All rights reserved.
52, bottom	49-22-30/11821.75.
53, top	Photo by Harriet S. Cosgrove. 2004.24.22002.
53, bottom	1938 Harvard College class album. Harvard University Archives, HUD 338.04.
54	© J. O. Brew. 2012.0.30.
55, top left	Photo probably by Hattie Cosgrove. 2004.1.123.1.88.
55, top right	Photo by Hattie Cosgrove. 2004.1.123.1.82.
55, bottom left	Photo by Hattie Cosgrove. 2004.1.123.1.81.
55, bottom right	995-11-10/99994.1.14.
56, top left	Photo by Hattie Cosgrove. 2004.1.123.1.79.
56, top right	Photo by Hattie Cosgrove. 2004.1.123.1.60.
56, bottom left	2004.1.123.1.714.
56, bottom right	Photo by Hattie Cosgrove. 2004.1.123.1.58.
57, top	2004.1.123.1.50.
57, bottom	Smith 1952: fig. 35b. Photo probably by J. O. Brew. 2004.1.123.1.96.
58, top	2004.24.27635.
58, bottom	2004.24.29245.
59, top	53-26-60/15921.376.
59, bottom	2004.24.22232.
60, top	2012.0.33.
60, bottom	2010.5.36050.
61, top	998-27-40/14628.1.16.
61, bottom	2007.1.25.
62, top	Courtesy of the Berry Hill Trust. All rights reserved.
62, bottom	Courtesy of the Berry Hill Trust. All rights reserved.
63, top left	2012.0.31.

| 63, top right | Photo by Philip Phillips. 2004.24.30189.1.
| 63, bottom left | 976-22-10/53082.
| 63, bottom right | 1935 Harvard College class album. Harvard University Archives, HUD 335.04. Photo by William Henry Lewis Jr.
| 64, top left | 1931 Harvard College class album. Harvard University Archives, HUD 331.04. Photo by Carl E. Pickhardt Jr. and James L. Madden.
| 64, top right | 1950 Radcliffe College yearbook. The Schlesinger Library, Radcliffe Institute, Harvard University.
| 64, bottom | Photo by Mrs. Arthur K. Loveridge. 2004.24.14600.

Index

Illustration numbers appear in **boldface**. Where relevant to the text, women are cross-referenced under both maiden and married names.

AAA. *See* American Anthropological Association
AAAS. *See* American Association for the Advancement of Science
AAPA. *See* American Association of Physical Anthropologists
Abbott, Charles Conrad, 84, 92, 111, 116, 120, 158, 236, **pl. 10**; biographical sketch of, 88–90
Aberle, David Friend: biographical sketch of, 450
Academy of Natural Sciences, 33, 37, 88, 237, 238, 241, 287
Adams, Charles Francis, 41–42, 278
Adams, Helen Thayer: biographical sketch of, 402
AES. *See* American Ethnological Society
Agassiz, Alexander Emmanuel Rudolph, 29, 47, 50, 51, 54, 57, 71, 123, 131, 148, 154, 188, 189, 294, **pl. 6**; biographical sketch of, 49; death of, 315; Garman and, 111; Griswold and, 109; Kidder and, 300; Lyman and, 49; MacCurdy and, 222; Morse and, 64; Powell and, 167; Pumpelly and, 142; Putnam and, 48, 52, 188; Shaler and, 73, 74; shell mounds and, 31
Agassiz, Elizabeth Cabot (née Cary), 27, 182, **pl. 6**; biographical sketch of, 49–50
Agassiz, Jean Louis Rodolphe ("Louis"), 3, 15, 34, 37, 40, 47, 57, 60, 62, 72, 80, 85, 149, 152, 153, 187, **pl. 2**; Andrews and, 87; apprenticeships with, 58; Baird and, 39; Bickmore and, 69; biographical sketch of, 23–27; Blake and, 29; Bowditch and, 282; Clark and, 48–49; Cooke and, 63; death of, 71; Garman and, 110; Gibbs and, 20; Gray and, 27, 38, 39, 77; Hyatt and, 61; institutional development/political activism and, 26–27; laboratory of, 55; Morse and, 64, 65; Packard and, 70, 71; Palmer and, 102; Peabody and, 45; Pickering and, 35; Pumpelly and, 141, 142; Putnam and, 23, 26, 27, 50, 51, 52, 53, 54, 58, 77, 188, 238; rebellion against, 42, 58, 188; research museum and, 26; Scudder and, 68; secession and, 63; Shaler and, 72, 74; University Lecture series and, 185; Verrill and, 63; on Winthrop, 44; Wyman and, 29, 32; Zoological Club and, 56
AIA. *See* Archaeological Institute of America
Aldridge, Curtice M. Clay: biographical sketch of, 431
Allen, Glover Morrill: biographical sketch of, 443
Allen, Joel Asaph, 49, 57, 61, 74
American Academy of Arts and Sciences, 15, 22, 38, 43, 157, 362; Bowdoin and, 12; Carr and, 93; Gallatin and, 19; Perkins and, 150; Sargent and, 13
American Anthropological Association (AAA), 5, 156, 157, 173, 193, 211, 218, 347, 450; Boas and, 248, 272, 346, 348; Bowditch and, 283; Brew and, 373; Chamberlain and, 177; Collier and, 359; Dixon and, 214; Dorsey and, 203; Fletcher and, 108; formation of, 209; Fuller and, 328; Gillin and, 443; Guthe and, 335; Howells and, 389; Hyde and, 292; Linton and, 369; MacCurdy and, 223, 224; Merwin and, 319; presidency of, 243; Putnam and, 78, 195, 239, 243, 248; Roberts and, 370; Russell and, 209; Saville and, 200; Shapiro and, 383; Spinden and, 317; Stirling and, 417; Taylor and, 426; Tozzer and, 305
American Anthropologist, 156, 211, 239, 272; Bushnell and, 307; Chamberlain and, 177; Fletcher and, 108; Jones and, 262; Linton and, 368; Senter and, 425; Speck and, 271; Thomas and, 418; Woodbury and, 423

563

American Antiquarian Society, 14, 22, 43, 174; Bowditch and, 283; Gallatin and, 19; Haven and, 19; Putnam and, 120; Salisbury and, 278, 279, 280, 281; Thompson and, 120; *American Antiquity,* 228, 372, 423, 451
American archaeology, 43, 81, 116, 157, 188, 229
American Association for the Advancement of Science (AAAS), 37, 59, 125, 126, 134, 141, 147, 154, 161, 174, 187; Bickmore and, 69; Chamberlain and, 177; Crawford and, 113; Curtiss and, 104; Cusick and, 256, 257; Dall and, 74, 75; DeHass and, 144, 145, 146; Dorsey and, 203; Fletcher and, 107, 108; founding of, 23; Garman and, 111; Gillman and, 87–88; Hale and, 36; Linton and, 369; Marsh and, 162; Moore and, 287; Morse and, 67; Nuttall and, 114; Packard and, 71; Powell and, 165; Putnam and, 60, 76, 77, 78, 82, 98, 123, 129, 133, 237, 238–39, 240, 243, 298; reorganization of, 77–78; Russell and, 209; Scudder and, 68; Smith and, 99; Thompson and, 239; Volk and, 120; Wheatland and, 53; American Association of Museums, 222
American Association of Physical Anthropologists (AAPA), 336, 406
American Ethnological Society (AES), 18, 19, 22, 292, 346
American Folk-Lore Society, 108, 309, 292, 301, 316
American Geographical Society, 279, 337
American Historical Association, 160, 173
American Journal of Archaeology, 114, 147, 177, 272
American Museum of Natural History (AMNH), 114, 206, 207, 210, 228, 243, 254, 270, 292, 326, 345, 434, 441; Bickmore and, 69; Boas and, 245; Converse and, 262; Dixon and, 212; Dorsey and, 202, 203; Ekholm and, 410; Farabee and, 306; Harrington and, 263, 264, 265; Hay and, 330; Howells and, 389; Hulse and, 385; Huxley and, 299; Jones and, 258, 259, 262; La Farge and, 362; Linton and, 368; Loubat and, 288; Movius and, 428; Newcombe and, 389; Parker and, 266, 267; Peale and, 35; Pepper and, 249; Phillips and, 377; Putnam and, 119, 195, 199, 237, 241, 242, 245, 246, 247, 249, 250, 274, 275; Roberts and, 370; Shapiro and, 383; Skinner and, 270; Smith and, 247, 248; Speck and, 271–72; Spinden and, 316; Tschopik and, 452; Vaillant and, 367; Will and, 317; Wilson and, 308
American Naturalist, 59, 70, 76, 286, 287; Abbott and, 88; Cooke and, 63, 64; Morse and, 65; Palmer and, 102; Putnam and, 79, 237; Wyman and, 30
American Philosophical Society, 13, 14, 17, 22
American School of Archaeology, 345
American School of Classical Research (ASCR), 438, 439
American School of Classical Studies, 143, 147; Brimmer and, 148–49; establishing, 153; Goodwin and, 149; Lowell and, 278; Peabody and, 216; Ware and, 153; Wheeler and, 241
American School of Prehistoric Research (ASPR), 218, 384, 415, 428; Briggs and, 436; Chute and, 404; Ehrich and, 430, 431; Eliot and, 431; Fewkes and, 431; founding of, 224; Franks and, 379; Hencken and, 427; Howe and, 429; MacCurdy and, 222, 223; Morss and, 379; Movius and, 427; Noguera and, 353; Putnam and, 222; Ward and, 340; Worman and, 432
Americanist anthropology, 3, 5, 22, 90, 147, 269, 275, 298, 393–94, 458; history of, ix, 8, 11
Americanist archaeology, 3, 4, 19, 30, 31, 43, 81, 98, 116, 141, 143, 157, 158, 166, 188, 229, 283; revolutionizing, 78
AMNH. *See* American Museum of Natural History
Amsden, Avery Monroe, 337, 349
Amsden, Charles Avery, 451; biographical sketch of, 337–38
Amsden, Madeleine, **pl. 54**
Andrews, Ebenezer Baldwin, 84, 92; biographical sketch of, 86–87
Andrews, Edward Wyllys ("Bill"), IV, 408, **pl. 53**; biographical sketch of, 410
Andrews, Edward Wyllys, V, 410
Andrews, James Madison, IV, 456; biographical sketch of, 435

Andrews, Walter Scott: biographical sketch of, 230
Andrus, Caroline, 261–62
Angel, John Lawrence: biographical sketch of, 438–39
Anthropological Society of Washington (ASW), 146, 147, 156, 239; Carr and, 93; DeHass and, 145; Fletcher and, 108; Powell and, 164, 165
anthropology, 3, 24, 58, 129, 166, 172, 173, 235, 299; American Renaissance and, 81; as coeducational domain, 457; development of, 5, 7, 168, 169, 242–43, 277; foreign students and, 457; graduate training in, 458; growth of, 7, 23, 141, 168, 169, 351; philosophy of, 216; theory/practice, 3, 449
anthropometrics, 430, 433, 434, 435, 437, 439, 457
Antiquities Act (1906), 108, 240, 438
Apache, Antonio ("Anthony"), 234, 236, **pl. 22**; biographical sketch of, 250–53
Appleton, Thomas Gold, 154; biographical sketch of, 148
Archaeological Institute of America (AIA), 29, 131, 141, 147, 149, 152, 167, 213, 218, 247; Agassiz and, 51; Bowditch and, 283; Fewkes and, 292; Fletcher and, 108; Goodwin and, 149; Gurney and, 150; Haynes and, 155, 156, 157, 158, 159, 160; Hencken and, 427; Hyde and, 292; H. P. Kidder and, 150; Kidder and, 324; Linton and, 368; MacCurdy and, 224; Morley and, 321, 322, 323; Norton and, 151, 153, 155; Nuttall and, 114; Parkman and, 152, 154, 155; Peabody and, 217; Perkins and, 150, 152; Powell and, 152, 164, 165, 166; Putnam and, 131, 152, 156, 168, 222; Spinden and, 316, 322; Tozzer and, 303
Arensberg, Charles F. C., 446
Arensberg, Conrad Maynadier, 231, 387, 445, 447, 448, **pl. 57**, **pl. 64**; biographical sketch of, 446
Arensberg, Walter Conrad, 231, 446
Arizona State Museum, 322, 365, 420, 421
Arnold, Benjamin: biographical sketch of, 293
ASCR. *See* American School of Classical Research
ASPR. *See* American School of Prehistoric Research

ASW. *See* Anthropological Society of Washington
Augustus Anson Whitney and Benjamin White Whitney Fellowship, 359, 402
Austin Teaching Fellowship, 138, 190, 220, 305, 306, 315, 328
Awatovi Expedition, 338, 403, 405, **pl. 54**, **pl. 57**; Brew and, 373, 419; Claflin and, 375, 376; Cosgroves and, 374; Hack and, 422; Haury and, 420–21; MacLeish and, 451; Motz and, 422; Reed and, 421; Schulman and, 424; Smith and, 423, 424; Wheeler and, 421, 422; Winchester and, 433; Woodbury and, 422, 423
Ayme, Louis J., 279, 284

BAAS. *See* British Association for the Advancement of Sciences
Babbitt, Frances Eliza, 123, 157
Bache, Alexander Dallas, 38, 39, 50, 281
BAE. *See* Bureau of American Ethnology
Baird, Spencer, 102, 111, 164, 167, 290
Baird, Stephen, 39, 60, 62
Bandelier, Adolph, 155, 264, 270, 303
Barbour, Mary Bigelow (Mrs. Alfred Kidder II), 315, 413
Barbour, Thomas, 270, 331, 413, 436, 456, **pl. 36**; biographical sketch of, 314–15
Barnard, James M., 47, 57
Barrera-Vásquez, Alfredo: biographical sketch of, 412
Bartlett, John Russell, 18, 19, 20
Bates, Arlo, 318, 331
Bates, Natica Inches, 332, 360, 378
Bates, Oric, 228, 299, 314, 318, 333, 343, 378; biographical sketch of, 331–32
Bell, Gertrude, 343
Bell, James MacKintosh: biographical sketch of, 231
Benedict, Paul King: biographical sketch of, 454–55
Bennett, John W., 361–62, 381
Berendt, Carl Hermann, 84, 279; biographical sketch of, 85–86
Berger, Robert, **pl. 29**
Bernice P. Bishop Museum, 455; Bowles and, 386; Emory and, 390, 391; Handy and, 340; Handy III and, 340; Linton and, 369; MacGregor and, 391; Thompson and, 361

Beyer, Henry Otley, 355; biographical sketch of, 328–29
BIA. *See* Bureau of Indian Affairs
Bickmore, Albert Smith, 29, 57, 58, 62, 281; biographical sketch of, 69–70
Bigelow, William Sturgis, 66–67, **pl. 6**
Bingham, Hiram, Jr., 306, 325, 329, 337; biographical sketch of, 310–11
Birdsell, Joseph Benjamin: biographical sketch of, 439
Bishop, Carl Whiting, 319; biographical sketch of, 338–39
Blake, Clarence John, 293; biographical sketch of, 294–95
Blake, James Henry, 327; biographical sketch of, 295
Blake, John Harrison, 293; biographical sketch of, 294–95
Blom, Frans Ferdinand, 362, 409, **pl. 35**, **pl. 40**; biographical sketch of, 363
Blos, Peter, **pl. 54**
Blyth, Alice Dukes (Mrs. Irvin Child), **pl. 51**; biographical sketch of, 407–8
Boas, Franz, 26, 68, 98, 156, 193, 202, 203, 205, 207, 210, 231, 233, 234, 237, 240, 241, 243, 245, 247, 261, 262, 266, 270, 271, 272, 283, **pl. 30**; Americanist archaeology and, 284; anthropology and, 7, 173; Apache and, 250, 253; biological anthropology and, 298; Breton and, 285; censure of, 248, 343, 346; Chamberlain and, 176, 177; Dixon and, 212, 213; Fewkes and, 292; Hale and, 36–37; Hall and, 174, 175; Harrington and, 265; Haynes and, 160; Hooton and, 335; Hyde and, 292; laboratories by, 235; letter by, 347; lionizing, 8; Loubat and, 288; Mechling and, 334, 345; Parker and, 268; Powell and, 165; program by, 194; Putnam and, 242, 327; Saville and, 199; Sawtell and, 360; sociocultural anthropology and, 27; Tozzer and, 302, 303, 304–5, 346; Wilson and, 308; World's Columbian Exposition and, 236
Bodel, John Knox, Jr., 416; biographical sketch of, 440–41
Boggs, Stanley Harding, 408, 432; biographical sketch of, 410–11
Bolles, John Savage, **pl. 42**
Bond, Caroline Stewart. *See* Day, Caroline

Boston Athenaeum, 83, 157, 179
Boston Folklore Society, 260, 270
Boston Museum of Fine Arts, 135, 149, 159; Kidder and, 150; Lythgoe and, 226; Morse and, 66; Perkins and, 150; Reisner and, 228
Boston Public Library, 160, 179, 198, 259
Boston Society of Natural History (BSNH), 15, 31, 37, 38, 43, 61, 89, 105, 159, 187; Bowditch and, 283; Carr and, 95–96; Crawford and, 113; Dall and, 74; Fewkes and, 291; Goodale and, 225; Haynes and, 157; importance of, 47; Morse and, 64, 67; Putnam and, 57, 62, 76, 77, 125; Scudder and, 68; Warren and, 16; Wyman and, 28, 30
Boston University, 393, 406, 451, 452
Bowden, Aberdeen Orlando: biographical sketch of, 332
Bowditch, Charles Pickering, 57, 69, 120, 156, 198, 206, 208, 211, 212, 231, 270, 277, 285, 291, 293, 298, **pl. 27**; biographical sketch of, 281–84; Fewkes and, 292; Haynes and, 160; Hyde and, 292; Lowell and, 278; Maler and, 121; Merwin and, 319; Morley and, 321, 322; Putnam and, 190; Salisbury and, 280; Saville and, 199; Tozzer and, 302, 303
Bowditch, Henry Pickering, 29, 68, 175
Bowditch, Ingersoll, 118, 119, 210, 376; biographical sketch of, 284
Bowdoin, James: biographical sketch of, 12
Bowdoin, James, II: 12
Bowers, William Benton, II: 355; biographical sketch of, 426
Bowles, Gordon Townsend, 381, 441; biographical sketch of, 386
Braidwood, Robert, 429
Breton, Adela Catherine, **pl. 28**; biographical sketch of, 284–85
Brew, Evelyn, **pl. 54**
Brew, John Otis ("Jo"), 338, 419, 425, 426, **pl. 44**, **pl. 54**; biographical sketch of, 372–73; Byers and, 371; Claflin and, 375, 376; class by, 400, 401; Cosgroves and, 374; Hack and, 422; Haury and, 420–21; Kidder and, 368; Kidder II and, 413; MacLeish and, 451; Morley and, 323; Newton and, 403; Paul and, 412; Reed and, 421; Roberts and, 370; Schulman and, 424; Scott and, 341; Smith

and, 423, 424; Tschopik and, 404; Warner and, 445
Briggs, Lloyd Cabot, 429, **pl. 60**; biographical sketch of, 435–36
Brimmer, Martin, 153, 154, 278; biographical sketch of, 148–49
Brinton, Daniel G., 98, 158, 159, 235, 272, 287, 301; Abbott and, 90; Berendt and, 85; Carr and, 93; Flint and, 112; Morse and, 67; mound builders and, 97; Shaler and, 74
British Association for the Advancement of Sciences (BAAS), 36, 37, 67
Brues, Alice Mossie, 402; biographical sketch of, 406
Brunhouse, Robert, 316, 321, 322, 339
Bryant, Kent, **pl. 57**
BSNH. *See* Boston Society of Natural History
Bureau of American Ethnology (BAE), ix, 97, 102, 147, 155, 158, 209, 211, 300, 307, 327, 348; Agassiz and, 51–52; archives, 257; Boas and, 37; Dall and, 75; DeHass and, 145, 146; Emmert and, 106, 107; Fenton and, 274; Fewkes and, 291; Fletcher and, 108; Jones and, 262; Murdoch and, 232; Palmer and, 103, 104; Powell and, 145–46, 163, 164, 165, 166, 167; Putnam and, 80, 240; research at, 171; Roberts and, 370; Stirling and, 417
Bureau of Indian Affairs (BIA), 233–34, 269, 447; Disher and, 418; MacGregor and, 391, 455; Mekeel and, 391; Thomas and, 418
Bushnell, David Ives, Jr., 306, **pl. 29**; biographical sketch of, 307
Bussey Institute, 124, 154, 311
Butler, Mary (Mrs. Clifford Lewis III), 359; biographical sketch of, 361
Butler, Nicholas Murray, 184, 288, 292
Byers, Douglas Swain: biographical sketch of, 371–72; Johnson and, 372; Kidder and, 368; on La Farge, 362; Roberts and, 371; Rowe and, 414; Wedlock and, 379

Cammann, Schuyler van Renesselaer: biographical sketch of, 455
Campbell, Thomas Nolan, **pl. 55**; biographical sketch of, 414
Carleton, Earle Joseph, Jr., 432; biographical sketch of, 433

Carlisle Indian Industrial School, 251, 252, 253, 256, 258
Carnegie Institution of Washington (CIW), 262, 298, 323, 326, 345, 348, 351, 362; Andrews and, 410; Boggs and, 411; Franks and, 379; funding from, 409, 411; Johnson and, 372; Kidder and, 394, 419; Lothrop and, 342; Morley and, 344; Movius and, 428; Paul and, 412; Pollock and, 363, 364, 365; Putnam and, 142; Ricketson and, 364, 365; Roberts and, 370, 371; Ruppert and, 365; Smith and, 365, 366
Carpenter, Arthur Wiltse(e), 336; biographical sketch of, 339
Carpenter, Clarence Raymond, 437; biographical sketch of, 434
Carr, Lucien, 131, 146, 158, **pl. 7**; biographical sketch of, 92–99; Dunning and, 84; Fuller and, 328; Willoughby and, 220
Cary, Mary Elizabeth Cabot. *See* Agassiz, Elizabeth
Casares, David: biographical sketch of, 278–79
Catherwood, Frederick, 120, 121, 300
Catlin, George, 254, 300
Cattell, James McKeen, 68, 78, 174, 240, 346
Center for Middle Eastern Studies, 407, 429
Central Intelligence Agency (CIA), 407, 410, 415, 425, 429, 435
Central States Anthropological Society, 380
Chamberlain, Alexander Francis, 176–77; biographical sketch of, 175–76
Chang, Kwang-Chih: biographical sketch of, 354
Chapple, Eliot Dismore, 408, 447, 448, 449; biographical sketch of, 445–46
Chard, Chester Stevens: biographical sketch of, 418
Charlesworth, John Berdan, 456; biographical sketch of, 442
Charlot, Jean, **pl. 36**
Chase, George Henry, 224, 231, **pl. 20**; biographical sketch of, 230; Chi and, 354; Kidder and, 324; Merwin and, 319; Spinden and, 316; Sterns and, 333
Chávez, Ezequiel A., 207, 346
Cheng Te-k'un (Zheng Dekun), 443, 454; biographical sketch of, 432

Chi (Ji), Li, 351, 354, 355, 394, 395, **pl. 37**; biographical sketch of, 354
Child, Alice Dukes (née Blyth). *See* Blyth, Alice
Child, Francis, 300, 301
Child, Irvin Long, 408
Chute, Ruth (née Sears): biographical sketch of, 404
CIA. *See* Central Intelligence Agency
City College of New York, Jewish faculty at, 184
Civil Works Administration (CWA), 312, 370, 378, 409, 417, 421
CIW. *See* Carnegie Institution of Washington
Claflin, Helen "Haych" (daughter of W. H. Claflin Jr.), 376, **pl. 54**
Claflin, Helen (wife of W. H. Claflin Jr.), 375, 376
Claflin, William Henry, 374
Claflin, William Henry, Jr., 104, 373, **pl. 44**; biographical sketch of, 374–76; Cosgroves and, 374; Emerson and, 376; Kidder and, 368; Morss and, 379; Roberts and, 371; Wauchope and, 409
Claflin, William Henry, III: 373, 376
Claflin-Emerson Expedition, 375, 413, 425; Brew and, 373; Forbes and, 426; Roberts and, 371
Clark, Henry James, 39, 47, 52, 54, 57; biographical sketch of, 48–49
Clark, Jonas G., 174, 175
Clark University, ix, 52, 173, 186, 205; anthropology at, ix, 177; Chamberlain and, 177; Chi and, 354; financial crisis for, 175; graduate program at, 117, 177, 185; opening of, 174; Salisbury and, 281
Clarke, Esther Orne (Mrs. F. W. Putnam). *See* Putnam, Esther
Cline, Walter Buchanan, 376, 386, 436; biographical sketch of, 378
Cockerell, Theodore, 71–72
cohort effect, x, 5, 6, 7, 457
Cole, Fay-Cooper, 136, 262, 373, 410
Collier, Ellen Sewall. *See* Spinden, Ellen
Collier, John, 361, 391
Columbia University, 4, 101, 183, 210, 289, 446; Benedict and, 455; Boas and, 192, 193, 195, 212, 245, 261; department formation and, 171; Ekholm and, 410; Fewkes and, 292; Harrington and, 264; Kimball and, 447; Landgraf and, 450; Linton and, 369; Loubat and, 288; Ph.D. program at, 172, 192; Putnam and, 168, 195; Saville and, 199; Shapiro and, 383; social/cultural composition of, 184; Speck and, 271; Washburn and, 437; women students at, 397; Woodbury and, 423
Columbian Museum of Chicago, 208; A. Apache and, 252; Dorsey and, 201–2, 203; Owen and, 205; Putnam and, 237, 245; Salisbury and, 280; Thompson and, 121
Committee for the Recovery of Archaeological Remains, 372, 373
Committee on American Archaeology (AIA), 292
Committee on State Archaeological Surveys (NRC), 268, 335, 380
Committee on the Protection and Preservation of Objects of Archaeological Interest, 283
Converse, Frank Buchanan, 263, 266, 267, 271, 272
Converse, Harriet Arnot Maxwell, 266, 267, 273; biographical sketch of, 262–63; death of, 267; Parker and, 266, salon of, 246, 265, 266, 267, 271, 272, 274
Cook, Allen, 138, 197, 198, 247, 254; biographical sketch of, 200–201
Cooke, Caleb, 55, 57, 59, 71, 76, 80, 281; biographical sketch of, 63–64
Cooke, Joseph Parsons, 57, 59, 69, 72; Morse and, 64; Putnam and, 53; Wyman and, 28, 29
Coon, Carleton Stevens, 389, 414, 427, 445, **pl. 37**, **pl. 45**; biographical sketch of, 383–84; class by, 400; Dixon and, 214; Ehrich and, 430; Hooton and, 381; Howe and, 429; Putnam and, 393; Senyürek and, 440; sociocultural anthropology and, 395; Vaillant and, 367; Worman and, 432; Wulsin and, 392–93
Copan, 199, 205, 206, 207, 280, 282, 289, 293, 411, **pl. 18**, **pl. 19**; sculptures from, **pl. 17**
Cope, Edward Drinker, 59; Bickmore and, 69; Garman and, 110; Hyatt and, 61; Marsh and, 167, 257; Moore and, 286; Packard and, 70, 71

Cornell University, 241, 434; Agassiz and, 27; Cushing and, 290; graduate work at, 117, 170; Keyes and, 380; Sharp and, 454
Cosgrove, Cornelius Burton ("Burt"), Jr., 368, 375, 409, **pl. 43**, **pl. 53**; biographical sketch of, 373–74
Cosgrove, Harriet ("Hattie") Lovejoy Silliman, 368, 375, 409, **pl. 43**, **pl. 53**; biographical sketch of, 373–74
Council of Old World Archaeology, 379, 429, 455
Cox, John Hadley, 432; biographical sketch of, 433
Crane, Cornelius, 453; biographical sketch of, 456
Crawford, John: biographical sketch of, 113
Cresson, Frank Macomb, Jr., 409; biographical sketch of, 412
Cresson, Hilborne Thomson, 76, 112, 118, 119, 120, 138, 158, **pl. 13**; biographical sketch of, 114–17; Dorsey and, 201; Putnam and, 92
Crockett, Charis (née Denison), 390; biographical sketch of, 407
Culin, Stewart, 206, 231, 235, 272, 285–86, **pl. 22**; Abbott and, 90; Apache and, 253; World's Columbian Exposition and, 236
cultural anthropology, 3, 4, 5
Cummings, Byron, 322, 410, 420, 421
Cummins, Frederick: Apache and, 252
Curtiss, Edwin, 92, 95, 103, 123; biographical sketch of, 104–6; death of, 104, 105–6
Cushing, Frank Hamilton, 67, 126, 165, 235, 301, **pl. 24**; biographical sketch of, 290
Cusick, Cornelius C., 236, 250; biographical sketch of, 253–58
Cutler, Manasseh, 12; biographical sketch of, 13
Cutter, Gretchen Froehlich. *See* Sharp, Gretchen
CWA. *See* Civil Works Administration

Dakin, Albert (Albertus) Lovejoy: biographical sketch of, 221–22
Dall, Caroline Wells Healey, 74, 108
Dall, William Healey, 20, 61, 62, 63, 107, 116; biographical sketch of, 74–75
Dana, James Dwight, 33, 42, 62, 167
Darwin, Charles, 28, 29, 37, 61, 64, 87

Davenport Academy of Natural Sciences, 101, 136, 137, 222
Davis, Charlotte Elizabeth (Mrs. Grubb): biographical sketch of, 406
Davis, Dorothy Penrose. *See* Worman, Dorothy
Davis, Edward Mott, Jr., 432, **pl. 54**, **pl. 57**; biographical sketch of, 418–19
Davis, Edwin Hamilton, 18, 19, 85
Davis, George R., 232, 233, 234, 257, 258
Davis, Hester, 422
Davis, William Allison, 445, 446; biographical sketch of, 447–48
Dawkins, Sir William Boyd, 90, 91
Dawson, Helen Lucerne: biographical sketch of, 406
Day, Caroline Stewart (née Bond), 351, 394, **pl. 38**; biographical sketch of, 356–57; Harley and, 358; Post and, 386
de Booy, Theodoor, 343
de Chardin, Père Teillard, 428
de Milhau, Louis Jean de Grenon, 327, **pl. 30**; biographical sketch of, 313–14; Farabee and, 306, 307; Hastings and, 312, 313; Howe and, 328; Stefansson and, 308
de Mortillet, Gabriel, 44, 83, 90
De Valera, Eamon, **pl. 58**
DeHass, Wills, 141, 163; biographical sketch of, 144–46
Denison, Charis. *See* Crockett, Charis
Denison, John Hopkins, Jr., 409, 426; biographical sketch of, 411–12
Denver Art Museum: Sarkisian and, 433
Denver Museum of Natural History: Wormington and, 403
Department M, 233, 233–34, 235
Dexter, Ralph, 58, 117, 161, 247; Putnam and, 78, 188
Dickey, Janet McCleery (née Woods). *See* Woods, Janet
Disher, Kenneth Buchtel, 414; biographical sketch of, 417–18
Division XIV, 186, 206, 224, 225, 226, 230
Division of Anthropology and Psychology (NRC), 292, 305, 326, 348
Division of Archaeology and Ethnology (AMNH), 245

Division of Mound Exploration (Bureau of Ethnology), 102, 145, 146
Dixon, James, 42, 50, 119
Dixon, Roland Burrage, 118, 191, 193, 194, 197, 206, 207, 208, 210, 230, 231, 246, 261, 270, 298, 301, 306, 309, 316, 349, 351, **pl. 20**, **pl. 37**; Amsden and, 338; on archaeological investigations, 214; Barbour and, 314; Bates and, 331, 332; Beyer and, 329; Bingham and, 311; biographical sketch of, 211–16; Bowditch and, 284; Chi and, 354; Coon and, 383; death of, 216, 340, 377; development of, 243; Dixon and, 318; Emory and, 391; ethnographic studies and, 214; field seasons of, 212–13; Fuller and, 327, 328; Guha and, 356; Guthe and, 335; Handy III and, 340; Hulse and, 385; Hyde and, 292; Jones and, 260; Kerr and, 339; Kidder and, 324, 325; Kluckhohn and, 453; Lothrop and, 342, 343; Mechling and, 333, 334; Mekeel and, 391; Morley and, 321, 322; Phillips and, 377; recruiting by, 381, 394; Sharp and, 453; sociocultural anthropology and, 442; Spinden and, 315, 317; Stefansson and, 308; Sterns and, 333; Tangco and, 355; Tello and, 352; Tozzer and, 302, 303, 304; Utsurikawa and, 353, 354; Wilson and, 308; Woods and, 227
Dodge, David: biographical sketch of, 109
Donaldson, Henry H., 235, 236
Dorsey, George Amos, 118, 119, 123, 137, 138, 166, 191, 197, 205, 209, 212, 232, 250, 413; Apache and, 252; biographical sketch of, 201–4; Cresson and, 116; development of, 243; Jones and, 262; Newcombe and, 390; Russell and, 208; salvage ethnography and, 202; Saville and, 198; World's Columbian Exposition and, 236
Drew, Edward Bangs: biographical sketch of, 231–32
DuChane, Capt., **pl. 35**
Duker, Laura Maud (née Thompson), 359, 394; biographical sketch of, 361–62
Dunning, Edward Osborne, 92; biographical sketch of, 84–85
Dupertuis, Clarence Wesley, 381, 388, 434; biographical sketch of, 386–87

Eaton, Elizabeth S.: biographical sketch of, 404
Eckstorm, Fannie Pearson Hardy, 109
Ecole d'Anthropologie (Paris), 115, 223, 353
Edwards, Amelia B., 108, 149
Ehrich, Robert William, 427, 431, 455; biographical sketch of, 430
Ekholm, Gordon Frederick, 408, 415; biographical sketch of, 410
elective principle, 178, 179, 181
Eliot, Charles William, 39, 74, 80, 130, 148, 150, 154, 170, 171, 175, 184, 188, 194, 225, 277, 431, **pl. 4**; administration of, 181; admissions policy and, 183; Agassiz and, 52; appointment by, 172; biographical sketch of, 179–80; elective principle and, 178, 181; examination board and, 181; fundraising by, 195; graduate program and, 185, 186; Gurney and, 149; Hall and, 173; liberalization policies by, 182–83; Lyman and, 49; Norton and, 151; Shaler and, 73; special students and, 192; Ticknor and, 180; University Course of Instruction and, 185; Winsor and, 160
Eliot, Henry Ware, Jr., 404, **pl. 63**; biographical sketch of, 431
Ellis, Bruce T., 425
Ellis, Florence May (née Hawley), 425
Elliston, Harriet (née Hammond). *See* Hammond, Harriet
Emerson, Raymond A., 368, 371, 373, 375, 379; biographical sketch of, 376
Emerson-Claflin Expedition: Paul and, 412
Emmert, John W., Jr.: biographical sketch of, 106–7
Emory, Kenneth Pike, 389; biographical sketch of, 390–91
Endicott, William Crowninshield, 148; biographical sketch of, 149
Engerrand, Jorge, 304, 305
espionage by archaeologists, World War I, 323, 339, 344–47, 349
Essex Institute, 52, 53, 59, 65, 67, 76, 187, 283
ethnic diversity, 182, 183, 184, 356, 457
Everett, Edward, 24–25
Excavators' Club. *See* Harvard-Peabody Museum Excavators' Club

Faculty of the Museum, 277, 278, 280, 283, 314
Farabee, William Curtis, 193, 206, 217, 225, 230, 231, 243, 249, 270, 310, 319, 327, **pl. 30**; biographical sketch of, 305–7; de Milhau and, 313; Hastings and, 312, 313; Hellman and, 318; Hooton and, 335; Kidder and, 324; Stefansson and, 308; Tozzer and, 302
fellowships (financial): Harvard, 107, 130, 137–138, 190, 198, 201, 204, 206, 208, 210, 227, 241, 260, 270, 282, 284, 299, 303, 305, 306, 308, 311, 315, 318, 319, 322, 325, 328, 333, 339, 353, 358, 362, 370, 372–73, 377, 378, 382, 383, 384, 385, 387, 391, 392, 411, 425, 432, 433, 437, 445; Radcliffe, 359, 360, 402, 403, 408. *See also* Augustus Anson Whitney and Benjamin White Whitney Fellowship, Austin Teaching Fellowship, Hemenway Fellowship, Thaw Fellowship, Winthrop Scholarship
Felton, Cornelius C., 27, 38, 72
Feng, Han Yi (Han-chi), 443; biographical sketch of, 444
Fenollosa, Ernest F., 66
Fenton, John William, 246, 263, 267, 268; biographical sketch of, 274
Fewkes, Jesse Walter, 283, 290, 301, 327, **pl. 26**; Andrews and, 230; biographical sketch of, 291–92; Kidder and, 324; Linton and, 368; Morley and, 322; Owens and, 204
Fewkes, Vladimir Jaroslav, 427, 455, **pl. 59**; biographical sketch of, 430–31
Field, Henry, **pl. 59**; biographical sketch of, 435
Field Museum of Natural History, 137, 166, 207, 289, 434, 435; Boas and, 243; Crane and, 456; Dorsey and, 202, 203; Jones and, 262; Laufer and, 345; Linton and, 369; Mason and, 345–46; Mechling and, 334, 345, 346; Newcombe and, 390; Putnam and, 233, 237, 245; Salisbury and, 280; Smith and, 423; Thompson and, 121
fieldwork methods: archaeological, 21, 31, 75, 78, 80, 87, 120, 124, 126, 136, 138, 209, 217, 228–29, 249, 268, 325
Fiske, Ethel (née Putnam). *See* Putnam, Ethel
Fletcher, Alice Cunningham, 112, 124, 148, 156, 231, 239, 241, 242, 283, 285, **pl. 8**, **pl. 9**; biographical sketch of, 107–8; Fewkes and, 292; Nuttall and, 114; World's Columbian Exposition and, 236
Fletcher, John Gould, 321, 324; biographical sketch of, 327
Flint, Earl, 86, 92, 113, 130; biographical sketch of, 111–12
Flint, Timothy, 22; biographical sketch of, 16–17
Florimond, Joseph, Duc de Loubat, 199, **pl. 26**; biographical sketch of, 288–90
Fogg Art Museum, 159, 426, 456; Ehrich and, 430; Hammond and, 402; Lockard and, 429; Sarkisian and, 433
Foley, James L., 57, 64, 69, 72, 281
Folsom, Cora Mae, 258, 259–60, 261
Foote, Charles "Happy," **pl. 54**
Forbes, Waldo Emerson, Jr., 428; biographical sketch of, 426–27
Ford, James A., 377, 378, 417; forensic anthropology, 439
Forsythe, Scott, 256, 257
Fowler, Harold North: biographical sketch of, 147
Franks, Robert Augustus, Jr., 376; biographical sketch of, 379
Frederick Sheldon Traveling Fellowship, 353, 378, 383, 392, 432, 437
Fuller, Anne Hutchinson: biographical sketch of, 406–7
Fuller, Robert Gorham, 221, 291, 299, 303, 316, 328, 335; biographical sketch of, 327–28

Gabel, Norman Emil: biographical sketch of, 441
Gallatin, Albert: biographical sketch of, 18–19
Gamage, Abram Tarr: biographical sketch of, 109–10
Gamio, Manuel, 304, 345, 346; Engerrand and, 305; Kidder and, 325; Noguera and, 352; Vaillant and, 367
Gann, Thomas Francis William, 344–45
Garcia-Robiou, Carlos, **pl. 54**
Gardner, Burleigh Bradford, 445, 448; biographical sketch of, 446–47
Garman, Samuel Walton, 51, 123, 131, 314; biographical sketch of, 110–11
Garn, Stanley Marion, 435; biographical sketch of, 440

Garrod, Dorothy, 428, 429
Gaul, James Harvey: biographical sketch of, 428
Gebhard, Paul Henry, 414, 440; biographical sketch of, 416–17
Geological Survey of Canada, 137, 248, 333, 360
Gerrodette, Frank Honore, 138, 197, 333; biographical sketch of, 200
Gibbs, George, IV: biographical sketch of, 20–22
Gibbs, Oliver Wolcott, 20, 38, 39, 51, 71, 142
Gillin, John Philip, 411; biographical sketch of, 442–43
Gillman, Henry, 84, 92, 173; biographical sketch of, 87–88
Givens, Douglas, 230, 308, 321
Gladwin, Harold S., 312, 420, 421, 422
Glenn, Bertie, 57, 64
Glenn, Katie, 56, 57, 64
Goddard, Amory, 426, 427, 445; biographical sketch of, 428
Goddard, Pliny Earle, 241, 383
Goodale, George Lincoln, 206, 208, 210, 211, 212, 224, 283, 303, 316; biographical sketch of, 225
Goodwin, William Watson, 147, 148, 153, 179, 278; biographical sketch of, 149
Gordon, Cyrus H., 107, 253
Gordon, George Byron, 197, 205, 225, 271, 282, 285, **pl. 18**, **pl. 19**; biographical sketch of, 206–8; Dixon and, 212; Russell and, 210; Speck and, 272
Gould, Benjamin Apthorp, Jr., 38
graduate education, 182, 185–86, 195–96; development of, 169; women and, 397–98
graduate schools, 168, 169, 170, 184
Graham, David Crockett, 432, 434, 444
Graves, William Washington: biographical sketch of, 434
Gray, Asa, 8, 26, 37, 42, 43, 44, 62, 72, 79, 80, 91, 131, 149, 187, 189, **pl. 2**; Abbott and, 90; Agassiz and, 27, 38, 39, 77; Andrews and, 86, 87; Baird and, 39; Berendt and, 86; biographical sketch of, 32–33; Clark and, 48, 49; Dall and, 75; election of, 238; Gibbs and, 20; Hale and, 36; Hyatt and, 61; Lowell and, 24; Marsh and, 161; Morse and, 64; Parry and, 101; Peabody and, 45; Pickering and, 33, 35; Powell and, 166; Putnam and, 53, 188; teaching by, 23; Wyman and, 28, 29, 32
Gray, Jane Lathrop Loring (Mrs. Asa Gray), 131
Griffin, James B., 335, 377, 381, 402, 417
Grinnell, George Bird, 162
Griscom, Ludlow, **pl. 35**
Griswold, Leon Stacy: biographical sketch of, 109
Grubb, Charlotte (née Davis). *See* Davis, Charlotte
Guernsey, Isabel Hannah: biographical sketch of, 404–5
Guernsey, Samuel James, 220, 349, 366, 404, **pl. 32**, **pl. 36**, **pl. 37**; Amsden and, 338; biographical sketch of, 330–31; Byers and, 371; Claflin and, 375; Cosgroves and, 374; Fuller and, 328; Kidder and, 325; La Farge and, 362; Ricketson and, 364; Scott and, 340; Vaillant and, 367
Guha, Biraja Sankar, 351, 394, 395, **pl. 37**; biographical sketch of, 355–56
Gurney, Ephraim Whitman, 148, 153; biographical sketch of, 149–50
Guthe, Carl Eugen, 303, 325, 333, 349, 366, **pl. 34**; biographical sketch of, 334–35

Hack, John Tilton, **pl. 54**, **pl. 57**; biographical sketch of, 422
Haddon, Alfred Cost, 231; biographical sketch of, 232
Hale, Horatio Emmons, 33; biographical sketch of, 36–37
Hall, Granville Stanley, 177; biographical sketch of, 173–75
Hammond, Harriet (Mrs. William Arthur Elliston), 401, **pl. 51**; biographical sketch of, 402
Hammond, Frances, 440
Handy, Edward Smith Craighill, III: 226, 335, 391; biographical sketch of, 340
Handy, Willowdean Chatterson, 391; biographical sketch of, 340
Hansberry, Elden, 357
Hansberry, Lorraine, 357
Hansberry, William Leo, 351, 394, **pl. 38**; biographical sketch of, 357
Harding, Charles Ford, III: biographical sketch of, 449

Hardy, Manly, 31, 158; biographical sketch of, 109–10
Hargrave, Lyndon Lane, 12, 420, 423
Harley, George Way, 357, **pl. 40**; biographical sketch of, 358–59
Harp, Elmer, Jr., 414; biographical sketch of, 415–16
Harrington, Edna (née Parker). See Parker, Edna
Harrington, Mark Raymond, 246, 262, 271, 275; biographical sketch of, 263–65; Fenton and, 274; Hayden and, 311, 312; Parker and, 267, 268; Skinner and, 269, 270; Speck and, 272
Hart, Francis Russell: biographical sketch of, 412
Hartt, Charles Frederick, 27, 74, 77, 84, 92; biographical sketch of, 85
Harvard African Studies, 331, 332, 333, 360
Harvard Annex. See School for the Collegiate Instruction of Women
Harvard Anthropological Society, 226, 230, 231, 302, 317, 321
Harvard Archaeological Expedition, 403, 427
Harvard College/Harvard University, xi, 180, 183, **pl. 1**; anthropology at, ix–x, 3–4, 5, 6, 173, 178, 182, 188–89, 191, 192–93; blacks at, 182; Catholics at, 184; educational reform and, 170; founding of, 11–12; graduate education at, 170, 172, 177, 182, 185, 186, 194, 397, 398; Jewish faculty at, 184; Lawrence Scientific School and, 186; numbers of graduate students at, 399 (table); Peabody Museum and, 192, 277; Radcliffe and, 184, 194; reorganization at, 138; social environment of, 184; women students at, 184, 397
Harvard College Folklore Society, 10
Harvard Folk-Lore Club, 300, 301
Harvard Medical School, 29, 259, 293, 445; Blake and, 295; Howe and, 328; Kneeland and, 108–9; Lasker and, 439; Phillips and, 441; Ricketson and, 364
Harvard-Peabody Museum Excavators' Club, 418, 419
Harvard-Yenching Institute, 355, 386, 432, 443, 444, 454
Hastings, John Walter, 299, 306, 308, 314, **pl. 30**; biographical sketch of, 312–13

Haury, Emil Walter, 290, 312, 419, 457–58; biographical sketch of, 420–21; Gabel and, 441; Kidder and, 326; Motz and, 422; Reed and, 421
Haven, Samuel Foster, 14, 22; biographical sketch of, 19
Hawkins, Hugh, 171, 192, 224
Hawley, Florence May. See Ellis, Florence
Hay, Clarence Leonard, 282, 304, 310, 319, 326, 367; biographical sketch of, 329–30
Hayden, Irwin, 264, 265, 299, 422; biographical sketch of, 311–12
Hayden, Julian Dodge, 311, 422; biographical sketch of, 312
Haynes, Henry Harrison, 156
Haynes, Henry Williamson, 93, 116, 153, 167, 217, 218, 291, **pl. 10**; biographical sketch of, 155–60
Hearn, Katherine (née Young). See Young, Katherine
Hearst, Phoebe Apperson, 108, 114, 226, 227–28, 242, 307; biographical sketch of, 241
Held, John, Jr., 345
Hellman, Robert Richard, 213, 214, 299, 349; biographical sketch of, 318; Spinden and, 315; Will and, 317
Hemenway, Augustus, 290, 291, **pl. 24**
Hemenway, Augustus, Jr., 220, 328
Hemenway, Mary Porter Tileston, 108, 220, 291, 327, 328, 374, **pl. 24**; Cushing and, 290; Haury and, 420; Owens and, 204
Hemenway Fellowship, 137, 138, 190, 201, 206, 208, 212, 455; Brew and, 373; Farabee and, 305; Guha and, 356; Hayden and, 311; Howe and, 328; Huxley and, 299; Johnson and, 372; Kelly and, 377; Kerr and, 339; La Farge and, 362; MacGregor and, 391; Mechling and, 333; Merwin and, 318; Noguera and, 353; Owens and, 204; Roberts and, 370; Schwab and, 358; Senter and, 425; Spinden and, 315; Stefansson and, 308; Sterns and, 333
Hemenway Southwestern Archaeological Expedition, 204, 328; Cushing and, 290; Fewkes and, 291; Owens and, 204; Willoughby and, 220
Hencken, Hugh O'Neill, 224, 426, 445, 446,

pl. 58; biographical sketch of, 427; Brew and, 373; Briggs and, 436; Goddard and, 428; Howe and, 429; Morss and, 379; Newton and, 402
Henri-Martin, Leon, 218, 223, 224
Henry, Joseph, 19, 21, 38, 60, 62, 102
Henry C. Warren Fund, 208, 221, 264, 306, 319
Henshaw, Samuel, **pl. 32**
Hertzberg, Hans Theodore Edward, 381; biographical sketch of, 436
Hewett, Edgar Lee, 13, 321, 322, 323, 324, 327, 369
Heye, George Gustav, 207, 249, 264, 265, 272, 273; Pepper and, 249; Saville and, 199
Heye Foundation, 199, 207, 249, 264, 265, 270, 273, 288, 337, 342, 343
Hibben, Frank Cummings: biographical sketch of, 414–15
Higinbotham, Harlow Niles, 233, 237
Hill, Thomas, 151, 170, 185, 195; biographical sketch of, 179
Hoar, George Frisbie, 120, 174, 279, 281
Hodge, Frederick Webb, 211, 253, 270, 272, 323; Bushnell and, 307; Cosgroves and, 373, 374; on Cushing, 290; Fewkes and, 291; Pepper and, 249; Woodbury and, 423
Hodges, Nathaniel Dana Carlisle, 240
Holmes, Oliver Wendell, Sr., 28, 29, 40, 374
Holmes, William Henry, 75, 158, 159, 237, 298, 323; Fewkes and, 291, 292; Loubat and, 289; Powell and, 164, 166
Hooton, Earnest Albert, 193, 220, 298, 331, 349, 351, 370, 420, 445, 457, **pl. 37**, **pl. 46**; Andrews and, 410, 435; Angel and, 439; biographical sketch of, 335–36; Birdsell and, 439; Bodel and, 440–41; Bowles and, 386; Briggs and, 436; Carpenter and, 339; Chi and, 354; class by, 400; Cline and, 378; Coon and, 383; Crockett and, 407; data processing by, 433–34; Davis and, 406; Day and, 357; Dixon and, 215; Dupertuis and, 387; Ehrich and, 430; Field and, 435; Fuller and, 328; Garn and, 440; Guha and, 356; Guthe and, 334; Handy III and, 340; Hansberry and, 357; Howells and, 389; Hulse and, 385; Kerr and, 339; Lasker and, 439; Lessa and, 388; Lothrop and, 342; Luther and, 387, 388; Post and, 386; Radcliffe and, 401; recruiting by, 381; Reynolds and, 382; Ricketson and, 364; Sawtell and, 360; Schwab and, 358; Seltzer and, 387; Senyürek and, 440; Shapiro and, 382; Sheldon and, 434; Snow and, 438; Sterns and, 333; Tangco and, 355; Utsurikawa and, 353; Washburn and, 436–37; Williams and, 384; Willoughby and, 219; Young and, 403
Hooton Research Fund, 417
Horr, Edward Franklin, **pl. 30**
Horsford, Eben Norton, 37, 39, 50, 72, 218; biographical sketch of, 25–26
Howard, Oliver Otis, 250, 251
Howe, Bruce, 428, 436, **pl. 62**; biographical sketch of, 429
Howe, George Plummer, 299, 308; biographical sketch of, 328
Howells, William White, 381, **pl. 49**; biographical sketch of, 388–89; lab of, **pl. 48**
Hrdlička, Aleš, 224, 246, 292, 337, 348, 434
Hu, Hsien Chin ("Lottie") (Mrs. Wang), 440, 443; biographical sketch of, 408
Hughes, Byron Oroville: biographical sketch of, 437
Hulse, Frederick Seymour, 381, 393; biographical sketch of, 385
Hutchinson, Marion. *See* Tschopik, Marion
Huxley, Henry Minor, 292, 387; biographical sketch of, 299–300
Hyatt, Alpheus, 29, 55, 57, 59, 60, 70, 161, 189; Agassiz and, 58; biographical sketch of, 61–62; Dall and, 75; Morse and, 64, 67; Shaler and, 72; Verrill and, 62
Hyde, Benjamin Talbot Babbitt ("Talbot" or "B. T. B."), 249, 299, 302, 306; biographical sketch of, 292–93
Hyde, Frederick Erastus ("Fred"), Jr., 249; biographical sketch of, 292–93
Hyde Exploring Expedition, 249, 292

Icazbalceta, Joaquin García, 93, 158
Indian Anthropological Institute (Calcutta), 356
Inglis, Dorothy (née Newton). *See* Newton, Dorothy
Institute of Andean Research, 326, 342, 352, 367, 404, 405, 410, 411

Institute of Middle American Research (Tulane), 363
Institute of Social Anthropology (Smithsonian Institution), 443, 452
Instituto de Investigaciones Antropológicas (Mexico City), 353
Instituto de Investigaciones Históricas (Mexico City), 353
Instituto Nacional de Antropología e Historia (Mexico City), 353, 356
International Congress of Americanists, 67, 87, 157, 207, 215, 283, 285, 288, 304
International Congress of Anthropology, 120, 235
International School of American Archaeology and Ethnology, 346, 360; Boas and, 193; Dixon and, 215; Gordon and, 207; Hay and, 329; Mechling and, 333, 334, 345; Merwin and, 319; Tozzer and, 193, 304
Iowa Anthropological Association, 222
Iowa Archaeological Survey, 380

Jackson, Ernest, 187; biographical sketch of, 130–32
James, William, 57, 173
Jeançon, Jean Allard, 369, 370
Jefferson, Thomas, 12–13; biographical sketch of, 17–18
Jesup, Morris K., 69, 202, 206
Jesup North Pacific Expedition, 246, 248, 389
Jewish students, 182, 183, 184
Ji, Li. *See* Chi, Li
Johns Hopkins University, 52, 127, 173, 175, 450; Cammann and, 455; competition from, 185–86; graduate work at, 170, 172, 185; Hall and, 174; Jewish faculty at, 184; Ph.D. programs at, 117, 172; Post and, 386; research at, 171–72
Johnson, Frederick; biographical sketch of, 372; Brew and, 373; Kidder and, 368; Roberts and, 370, 371; Rowe and, 414; Wauchope and, 409; Wedlock and, 379
Joint Egyptian Expedition, 226, 228
Jones, Charles Colcock, Jr., 104, 374
Jones, Joseph, 104
Jones, Lombard Carter, 293; biographical sketch of, 295
Jones, William, 47, 231, 246, 250, 269, 274, 275, 329; biographical sketch of, 258–62
Journal of American Folk-Lore, 177, 260
Judd, Neil Merton, 319, 322, 348, 443; Cosgroves and, 374; Roberts and, 370; Ruppert and, 365

Katz, Milton, 389, 392; biographical sketch of, 393
Kehoe, Alice, 176, 184
Keith, Margaret Soutter (née Woods): biographical sketch of, 403
Kelley, John Charles: biographical sketch of, 414
Kelly, Arthur Randolph, 376, 385, 417; biographical sketch of, 377–78
Kelly, Daniel ("Bud"), II, 325
Kelly, William Henderson: biographical sketch of, 451
Keppler, Udo Joseph, 246, 263, 267, 268; biographical sketch of, 272–74
Kerr, Andrew Affleck, 303, 335, **pl. 37**; biographical sketch of, 339
Keyes, Charles Reuben: biographical sketch of, 380–81
Kidder, Alfred Vincent ("Ted"), 123, 143, 150, 230, 291, 300, 302, 315, 349, 414, 441, **ii**, **pl. 34**, **pl. 35**, **pl. 37**, **pl. 42**, **pl. 43**, **pl. 53**, **pl. 54**; Americanist archaeology and, 324–25; Amsden and, 337–38; Bingham and, 311; biographical sketch of, 323–26; Bowers II and, 426; Byers and, 371, 372; Claflin and, 375; Cosgroves and, 373, 374; Dixon and, 213; Fletcher and, 327; Guernsey and, 330; Guthe and, 334, 335; Haury and, 420; Hooton and, 336; Liang and, 355; Longyear and, 411; Lothrop and, 341; Morley and, 321, 322, 323; Paul and, 412; Peabody and, 219; Pollock and, 364; Reisner and, 228–29; research by, 394; Roberts and, 370; Rowe and, 414; Sawtell and, 360; Senter and, 425; Smith and, 366; Stefansson and, 308; Vaillant and, 366, 367; Wauchope and, 409; Williams and, 384; work of, 367, 419
Kidder, Alfred, II: 123, 150, 300, 315, 352, 426, 452; biographical sketch of, 413; I. Guernsey and, 404; Paul and, 411; Tschopik and, 405
Kidder, Henry Purkitt, 148; biographical sketch of, 150

Kidder, Homer Huntington, 123, 150, 226, 299, 323; biographical sketch of, 300–302; Briggs and, 436; Lothrop and, 343; Pumpelly and, 143
Kidder, Madeleine, **pl. 43**
Kimball, John Cone, 126–27, 132, 138, 187, 189, **pl. 13**; biographical sketch of, 133–135
Kimball, Moses, 135
Kimball, Solon Toothaker, 387, 445, 446, 448, **pl. 57**; biographical sketch of, 447
King, Clarence, 61, 164
Kinnicutt, Leonard P., 118
Kluckhohn, Clyde Kay Maben, 368, 445, 446, 457, **pl. 64**; Aberle and, 450; Benedict and, 454; biographical sketch of, 449–50; Child and, 408; Coon and, 384; graduate students of, 453; Kelly and, 451; Landgraf and, 450; Oliver and, 453; sociocultural anthropology and, 442; Taylor and, 425, 426; Tschopik and, 452; Whittemore and, 403; Wyman and, 452
Kneeland, Samuel: biographical sketch of, 108–9
Knowlton, F. S., 109
Knowlton, James E., 109
Kroeber, Alfred Louis, 114, 213, 216, 231, 241, 246, 326; Benedict and, 454; Boas and, 242; Dixon and, 214; Emory and, 390; Hulse and, 385; Mekeel and, 391; Putnam and, 78; Rowe and, 413; Smith and, 423; Swanton and, 210; Tangco and, 355; Thompson and, 361; Tozzer and, 302; Warner and, 444; Wilson and, 308

La Farge, Oliver Hazard Perry, 371; biographical sketch of, 362–63
La Flesche, Francis, 97
Laboratory of Anthropology, 300, 326, 425, 426, 442; Liang and, 355; Mekeel and, 391
Lancaster, Al, **pl. 54**, **pl. 57**
Landgraf, John Leslie: biographical sketch of, 450–51
Lanman, Charles Rockwell, 232; biographical sketch of, 226; Handy III and, 340; Kidder and, 325; Merwin and, 319; Sterns and, 333; Toy and, 224
Lasker, Gabriel Ward, 355; biographical sketch of, 439–40

Lattimore, Owen, 309, **pl. 60**; biographical sketch of, 443
Lawrence, Abbott, 25, 40
Lawrence Scientific School, 4, 8, 29, 32, 37, 39, 40, 54, 58, 150, 180, 189, 222, 240; Agassiz and, 24, 25, 47, 48, 50; Bickmore and, 68, 69; Clark and, 49; Cook and, 200; Dall and, 74, 75, 76; faculty of, 72; founding of, 23; Garman and, 110; Gibbs and, 20; Gordon and, 206; Harvard and, 186; Horsford and, 25, 26; Hyatt and, 61; Jeffries and, 83; Lyman and, 49; MCZ and, 47; Morse and, 64; Packard and, 70; physical/natural sciences at, 25; professors at, 26; Pumpelly and, 142; Putnam and, 47–48, 53, 57, 80; role of, 23; Scudder and, 68; Shaler and, 73, 74; Ware and, 153; Wyman and, 28
Le Conte, John L., 47, 68
Le Conte, Joseph, 47, 61
Le Plongeon, Alice Dixon, 120, 279
Le Plongeon, Augustus, 120, 279, 281
LeBaron, John Francis Patch: biographical sketch of, 106
Lesley, J. Peter, 24
Lessa, William Armand, 381; biographical sketch of, 388
Lestrade, Gerald Paul, **pl. 37**
Levy-Bruhl, Lucien, 351
Lewis, Henry Carvill, 90, 91
Lewis, Mary (née Butler). *See* Butler, Mary
Liang, Ssu-Yung (Siyong), 351, 426; biographical sketch of, 354–55
Libby, Willard, 372, 383
Lin, Yueh-Hwa ("Yaohua"), 443; biographical sketch of, 444
Lindbergh, Charles, 326, 431
Linton, Ralph, 384, 442, **pl. 42**; biographical sketch of, 368–69
Lockard, Derwood (Ted) W.: biographical sketch of, 429
Longyear, John Munro, III: 409, 443; biographical sketch of, 411
Lothrop, Eleanor, **pl. 47**
Lothrop, Samuel Kirkland, 341
Lothrop, Samuel Kirkland, Jr., 282, 290, 299, 316, 335, 349, 379, 413, **pl. 47**; biographical sketch of, 341–44; Johnson and, 372;

Longyear and, 411; Newman and, 438; Tello and, 352
Louisiana Purchase Exposition, 67, 81, 82, 328, 390
Loveridge, Arthur, **pl. 64**; biographical sketch of, 456
Lovering, Joseph, 72, 77, 238, **pl. 10**
Low, Charles F., 118
Low, Josiah Orne, 445; biographical sketch of, 448
Lowell, Abbott Lawrence, 25, 150, 181–82, 183, 208, 210, 211, 212, 278; Bingham and, 311; blacks and, 184, 356; Scott and, 341; Shaler and, 73; Tozzer and, 303
Lowell, Augustus. *See* Lowell, Joseph.
Lowell, Francis Cabot, 206, 277, 282, 283, **pl. 26**; biographical sketch of, 278
Lowell, James Russell, 173, 278
Lowell, John Amory, 28, 150; biographical sketch of, 24–25
Lowell, Joseph Augustus Peabody, 148; biographical sketch of, 150
Lowell, Perceval, 66, 67
Lowell Institute, 44, 185, 270; Agassiz and, 23; Clark and, 48; Lyon and, 225; Perkins and, 150; Wyman and, 28
Lower Mississippi Valley Survey, 377, 417, 418, 419, 422
Lowie, Robert H., 346, 418, 423
Lummis, Charles F., 283
Luther, Martin M., 309, 381, **pl. 45**; biographical sketch of, 387–88
Lyell, Charles, 15, 41, 44; Agassiz and, 24; Lowell and, 24; Marsh and, 161; Wyman and, 28
Lyman, Theodore, 47, 55, 57, 188, 189; biographical sketch of, 49; Morse and, 65; Ophiuroidea and, 54; Putnam and, 48, 52, 188
Lyon, David Gordon, 157, 206, 208, 210, 211, 212, 224, 232; biographical sketch of, 225; Reisner and, 227; Tozzer and, 303
Lythgoe, Albert Morton, 224, 228, 231, 321; biographical sketch of, 226

MacCurdy, George Grant, 218, 298, 384, 430, **pl. 20**; biographical sketch of, 222–24; death of, 427

Macgowan, Kenneth Roscoe: biographical sketch of, 381
MacGregor, Gordon, 389; biographical sketch of, 391, 455
Mack, David, 87, 92
MacLeish, Kenneth D., **pl. 56**; biographical sketch of, 451
MacNeish, Richard S., 372
Malcolm, Roy Lynden: biographical sketch of, 451
Maler, Teobert, 120, 282, 284, 319, 321, 322, **pl. 11**; biographical sketch of, 121
Mallery, Garrick, 145, 165
Marcou, Jules, 44, 47, 48, 58, 61, 142
MARI. *See* Middle American Research Institute
Marsh, Othniel Charles, 42, 43, 73, 223; biographical sketch of, 161–62; Cope and, 167, 257; Powell and, 167; Winthrop and, 41; Wyman and, 31
Martin, Paul S., 136, 421, 423
Mary Hemenway Fund for Archaeology, 229
Mason, Gregory, **pl. 35**
Mason, John Alden, 345–46, 347, 361
Mason, Otis T., 128, 145, 165, 235
Massachusetts Historical Society, 41, 42, 43, 83; Endicott and, 149; Haynes and, 157; Lowell and, 150; Winsor and, 160
Massachusetts Institute of Technology (MIT), 39, 60, 61, 446; Carpenter and, 339; Hart and, 412; Kneeland and, 109; Saville and, 198; Ware and, 153
Maudslay, Alfred P., 285
Maximilian, Archduke, 121
Maxwell Museum of Anthropology (University of New Mexico), 414
Maya archaeology, 394, 408–9, 414
Maya art, 285, 345, 371, 402, 422
Maya hieroglyphs, 117, 121, 283, 284, 321, 344
Mayo, Elton, 444, 445
McCarthy, Joseph, 309, 443
McClurg, O. T., **pl. 35**
McEvoy, Mary (née Whittemore). *See* Whittemore, Mary
McGee, William J., 61, 67, 240, 298
McKennan, Robert Addison, 389; biographical sketch of, 392
MCZ. *See* Museum of Comparative Zoology

Mead, Frances Harvey Teobert, 83, 99, 135, 236; biographical sketch of, 100
Means, James, 336, 337, 341
Means, Philip Ainsworth, 311, 341, 413, 414; biographical sketch of, 336–37
Mechling, William Hubbs, 303, 304, 343, 345, 346, 347, 360; biographical sketch of, 333–34
Mecklenberg, Duchess of, 427
Mekeel, Haviland Scudder, 389; biographical sketch of, 391
Mercer, Henry Chapman, 90
Merchants Bank, 60, 238, 239
Merriam, Clinton Hart, 63, 68, 75
Merwin, Bruce Welch, 119, 299, 336, 423; biographical sketch of, 318–20
Merwin, Raymond Edwin, 119, 212, 230, 282, 423, **pl. 29**; biographical sketch of, 318–20; Bishop and, 339; Hay and, 329, 330; Hayden and, 311; Hooton and, 336; Lanman and, 226; Tozzer and, 303, 304
Merwin, Robert, 328
Metropolitan Museum of Art, 226, 318, 331, 378
Metz, Charles Lewis, 92, 99, 111, 125–26, 133, 134, 138, 158, 200, 210, 246, **pl. 13, pl. 22**; biographical sketch of, 117–18; Cresson and, 115, 116, 117; Dixon and, 212; Hooton and, 336; Kimball and, 126–27; Nickerson and, 135; Volk and, 120; Willoughby and, 219; World's Columbian Exposition and, 236
Middle American Research Institute (MARI), 362, 405, 409, 410
Miller, Percy Chase, 230; biographical sketch of, 231
MIT. *See* Massachusetts Institute of Technology
Moens, Herman Marie Barnelot, 348
Montgomery, Ross, 424
Moore, Clara, 286
Moore, Clarence Bloomfield, 247, 298, 307, 327; biographical sketch of, 285–88; donation from, 264; Farabee and, 306; Fewkes and, 291; Stefansson and, 308; Sterns and, 333
Moore, George Foot, 231; biographical sketch of, 232
Moorehead, Singleton Peabody, 377; biographical sketch of, 366

Moorehead, Warren K., 198, 200, 235, 247, 269, 366; Cresson and, 117; on Metz, 119; World's Columbian Exposition and, 236
Morgan, Lewis Henry, 77, 146, 147, 254, 266; Hale and, 36; Hyatt and, 61; Parkman and, 154, 155
Morison, Samuel Eliot, 178, 180, 182, 411, 431
Morley, Frances Rhoads, **pl. 33**
Morley, Sylvanus Griswold, 282, 291, 316, 317, 346, 347, 349, **pl. 33, pl. 36**; Andrews IV and, 410; biographical sketch of, 320–23; Blom and, 363; Dixon and, 213; Fewkes and, 324; J. G. Fletcher and, 324, 327; Gann and, 344–45; Gates and, 363; Guthe and, 334; Hewett and, 213; Kidder and, 213, 291, 324, 326, 327; Lothrop and, 344; Mechling and, 344; Pollock and, 363, 364; Reisner and, 229; Ricketson and, 364; Smith and, 365; Spinden and, 344; spying by, 343–44; Vaillant and, 367; Vincent and, 324; Will and, 317; *see also* Small, Sylvanus Griswold
Morris, Anne Axtell, **pl. 36**
Morris, Earl H., 292, 367, **pl. 36, pl. 54**
Morrow, Anne Spencer, 431
Morrow, Dwight Whitney, Jr.: biographical sketch of, 431
Morse, Edward Sylvester, 29, 49, 54, 55, 57, 59, 60, 70, 76, 158, 239, 283; Agassiz and, 27, 58; biographical sketch of, 64–67; Bowditch and, 281; Cooke and, 63; on Cusick, 256–57; Dall and, 75; Fewkes and, 291; Hyatt and, 61; Moore and, 287; Norton and, 151; Packard and, 71, 72; Verrill and, 62; Wyman and, 31; on Zoological Club, 56
Morse, William Reginald, 432, 444; biographical sketch of, 434
Morss, Noel, 375, 376; biographical sketch of, 379
Morton, Samuel George, 27, 34, 37, 294
Mott, Lucretia, 418
Motz, John Christian Fisher, III, **pl. 55**; biographical sketch of, 422
Movius, Hallam Leonard, Jr., 426, 445, 446, **pl. 61**; biographical sketch of, 427–28; Brew and, 373; Goddard and, 428; Haury and, 420; Howe and, 429; Movius Line, 428; Newton and, 402; Shapiro and, 383

Murdoch, John, 231; biographical sketch of, 232
Museo Histórico Nacional (Lima), 342, 352
Museo Nacional de Arqueología e Historia (Mexico City), 337, 353, 412
Museum für Völkerkunde (Berlin), 143
Museum of Archaeology and Ethnography (Leningrad), 441
Museum of Comparative Anatomy, 28, 83, 84
Museum of Comparative Zoology (MCZ), 23, 26, 31, 37, 38–39, 43, 60, 61, 62, 77, 86, 124, 188, 204, 226, 231, 232, 277, 281, 313; Agassiz and, 26, 48, 50, 54, 58; Allen and, 443; Barbour and, 314, 315; Bates and, 331; Blake and, 295; Bowditch and, 282; Brues and, 406; building, 54–55; Carpenter and, 434; Clark and, 48; Cooke and, 63, 64; Dall and, 75; de Milhau and, 314; Fewkes and, 291; Garman and, 110, 111; Goodale and, 225; Griswold and, 109; Hartt and, 85; Hastings and, 313; Lawrence Scientific School and, 47; Loveridge and, 456; Lyman and, 49; MacCurdy and, 222; Morse and, 64, 65; Owens and, 204; Packard and, 70, 71; Palmer and, 102; Phillips and, 441; Putnam and, 53, 76, 80; rebellion at, 58; role of, 23; Schwab and, 358; Scudder and, 68; Slade and, 226; Ticknor and, 179; Washburn and, 436; Wulsin and, 392
Museum of Fine Arts (Boston), 16, 289, 331, 332, 404
Museum of Northern Arizona, 312, 421, 423, 425
Museum of the American Indian–Heye Foundation, 199, 207, 249, 270, 273, 288, 337, 342, 343
Mustapha, **pl. 45**

National Academy of Sciences, 26–27, 39, 60, 68, 126
National Anthropological Archives, 146
National Museum of Anthropology, 366
National Museum of the American Indian, 273
National Park Service (NPS), 368, 378, 390, 418, 421, 422
National Research Council (NRC), 268, 326, 347, 409; Boas and, 348; Fenton and, 274; Fewkes and, 292; Guthe and, 335; Kelly and, 378; Keyes and, 380; Swanton and, 211; Tozzer and, 305; Worman and, 432
National University of Mexico, founding of, 215
Nelson, Nels C., 248, 325, 383
neo-Lamarkianism, 29, 38, 61, 66, 71, 75, 161
New York State Archaeological Association, 269
New York State Museum, 268, 269, 274, 335
Newcombe, Charles Frederic: biographical sketch of, 389–90
Newell, William Wells, 260, 300
Newhall, Harvey Field, 231
Newman, Marshall Thornton: biographical sketch of, 437–38
Newton, Dorothy (Mrs. Inglis), **pl. 55**; biographical sketch of, 402–3
Nichols, Edward Hall, 231; biographical sketch of, 232
Nickerson, William Baker, 124, 132, 133, 134, 139, 187, 189; biographical sketch of, 135–37
Noguera Auza, Eduardo Guadalupe, 351, 394; biographical sketch of, 352–53
Norton, Charles Eliot, 143, 147, 156, 179, **pl. 4**; biographical sketch of, 151–53; Brimmer and, 148; death of, 151, 278; Gurney and, 149; Haynes and, 155, 160; Lowell and, 150, 278; Morse and, 66; Parkman and, 154; Putnam and, 153; report by, 152–53
Nott, Josiah C., 27, 37
NPS. *See* National Park Service
NRC. *See* National Research Council
Nuttall, Zelia Maria Magdalena, 108, 241, 242, 301, **pl. 8**, **pl. 30**; biographical sketch of, 113–14; Breton and, 285; Loubat and, 289; Morse and, 67; World's Columbian Exposition and, 236
Nye, Harold Allen, 317, 318

Office of Indian Affairs, 208–9, 417
Office of Naval Intelligence (ONI), 204, 316, 339, 370, 389, 423, 429, 435; Lothrop and, 341, 343, 344; Mechling and, 334, 345, 346; Morley and, 323, 344, 345
Office of Strategic Services (OSS), 452; Andrews and, 410; Benedict and, 455; Briggs and, 436; Carleton and, 433; Cline and, 378; Coon and, 384; Cox and, 433;

Crockett and, 407; Fuller and, 407; Gaul and, 428; Oliver and, 453; Smith and, 423; Taylor and, 425–26; Titiev and, 390; Tozzer and, 305; Vaillant and, 367; Wauchope and, 409

Ohio Company of Associates, 12, 13, 16

Oliver, Douglas Llewellyn, 456; biographical sketch of, 453

ONI. *See* Office of Naval Intelligence

Oppenheimer, Harold Laurence: biographical sketch of, 438

Ordway, Albert, 53, 54, 55, 56, 57, 62, 64; biographical sketch of, 60

Oriental Institute, 412, 428, 429

Osborn, Henry F., 61, 68, 383

OSS. *See* Office of Strategic Services

Owen, Charles Lorin: biographical sketch of, 205

Owens, John Gundy, 113, 138, 197, 198, 210, 282, 289, 291, **pl. 18**; biographical sketch of, 204–5; death of, 205, 206

Packard, Alpheus Spring, Jr., 29, 49, 57, 60, 161, 341; Agassiz and, 58; biographical sketch of, 70–72; Cooke and, 63; Hyatt and, 61; Morse and, 64; Scudder and, 68; Verrill and, 63; Wyman and, 32

Palmer, Edward, 92, 130; biographical sketch of, 101–4

Palmer-Parry Expedition, 101, 103

Papers of the Peabody Museum, 217, 300, 318, 360, 375, 379, 382, 387

Parker, Arthur Caswell, 246, 248, 254, 263, 271, 273–74, 275; biographical sketch of, 265–69; Fenton and, 274; Harrington and, 264, 265; Keppler and, 272; Skinner and, 269; Smith and, 248

Parker, Edna (Mrs. Mark Raymond Harrington), 265, 267

Parker, Ely Samuel, 254, 255, 263, 266, 267

Parker, Nicholson Henry, 266, 267

Parkman, Francis, Jr., 29, 148, 151, 152, 153, 374; biographical sketch of, 154–55

Parkman, George, 29, 154

Parry, Charles Christopher, 92, 128; biographical sketch of, 100–101

Parsons, Elsie Clews, 362

Parsons, Leavitt Cooley, 322

Parsons, Samuel Holden, 12; biographical sketch of, 13

Parsons, William Barclay, 323

Paul, Anthony Joseph Drexel, Jr., 409, 412; biographical sketch of, 411

Peabody, Alfred, **pl. 32**

Peabody, Charles, 197, 233, 270, 343, **pl. 32**; ASPR and, 224; biographical sketch of, 216–19; Farabee and, 305, 306; Haynes and, 159; Lothrop and, 343; Loubat and, 289; MacCurdy and, 222, 223, 224

Peabody, Francis, 42

Peabody, George, 30, 43, 45, 49, 216, **pl. 4**; biographical sketch of, 39–40; gift from, 41–42, 59, 195; Marsh and, 161; museum and, 83; Putnam and, 89; Queen Victoria and, 45; Russell and, 41; Winthrop and, 42–43, 45

Peabody, George Augustus, 30

Peabody, Richard Singleton, 216

Peabody Academy of Science (Peabody Museum of Salem), 42, 59, 60, 61, 62, 70; Abbott and, 88; Cooke and, 63, 64; Endicott and, 149; establishment of, 42; Morse and, 65, 67; Packard and, 71; Putnam and, 76, 77, 79, 238; Watson and, 239

Peabody Museum Association, 400

Peabody Museum Excavators' Club, 414

Peabody Museum Exploration Fund, 118

Peabody Museum method, 75, 80, 125, 136, 217, 249, 268

Peabody Museum of (American) Archaeology and Ethnology, 8, 14, 27, 28, 29, 31, 45, 47, 50, 54, 60, 62, 82, 120, 126, **2**, **pl. 5**, **pl. 17**, **pl. 25**, **pl. 32**; Abbott and, 88, 89, 90, 91; Agassiz and, 39, 42, 51; Andrews and, 86, 87, 230, 435; anthropology at, 5, 6, 141, 277, 299, 408–9; Bowditch and, 198, 282, 283, 284; Carr and, 93, 98, 99; curriculum development at, 348; Dixon and, 211, 212, 214, 215; field research and, 433; founding of, 3, 23, 41, 83; global interests at, 394; graduate program at, 362, 376, 398; Guernsey and, 330, 331, 404; Haynes and, 156, 157, 159, 160; Hooton and, 335, 336, 381, 434; Jones and, 261, 262, 295; Kidder and, 300, 301, 325, 326, 367, 373, 419; modernization at, 393–94; Moore and, 286, 287, 288; Old

World archaeology and, 394, 427; Palmer and, 102, 103, 104; Parker and, 266, 267, 268; Phillips and, 377, 418, 441; program at, 298; Putnam and, 51, 59, 76, 78, 79, 92, 100, 119, 123, 126, 128, 129, 130, 131, 135, 138, 142, 145, 154, 167, 169, 187, 189, 191, 192, 195, 197, 202, 232, 233, 238, 242, 245–46, 275, 286–87, 296; Radcliffe and, 401, 402; Reports by, 191, 214, 242, 401; Roberts and, 369, 370, 371; Salisbury and, 279, 280, 281; Smith and, 247, 366, 423, 424; students/faculty at, 297; success for, 296; Tozzer and, 302, 303, 367; Willoughby and, 219, 220, 221; women students and, 408; Wyman and, 32, 44, 83

Peabody Museum of Natural History, 42, 161, 162

Peabody Museum of Salem. *See* Peabody Academy of Science

Peabody Museum Visiting Committee, x, 130, 138, 159, 198, 264, 282, 287, 327; Bowditch and, 282; de Milhau and, 313; Fewkes and, 291; Hart and, 412; importance of, 293; Kidder and, 150; La Farge and, 363; Morss and, 379; Peabody and, 217; Phillips and, 441; Reynolds and, 382; Stone and, 405; Weld and, 190

Peabody Professor, 43

Peale, Charles Willson, 34

Peale, Titian Ramsey, 34, 35

Pecos Pueblo, 325, 334, 349; Bowers II and, 426; Byers and, 371; Cosgroves and, 374; Kidder and, 368; Reynolds and, 382; Wauchope and, 409; Williams and, 384

Peirce, Benjamin, 24, 26, 38, 39, 72, 142

Peirce, Charles Sanders, 179, 281

Pelzel, John Campbell, 432, 450; biographical sketch of, 454

Pengelly, William, 21, 159, 209

Pepper, George Hubbard, 114, 210, 246, 247, 272, 273, 275, 292, 306; biographical sketch of, 248–50; Huxley and, 299; Russell and, 208; Saville and, 199; Skinner and, 270; Tozzer and, 302

Perkins, Charles Callahan, 148, 152; biographical sketch of, 150

Phelps, Albert Irving, 92; biographical sketch of, 109–10

Philadelphia Anthropology Society, 412

Phillips, John Charles: biographical sketch of, 441

Phillips, Philip, 441, 453, **pl. 50**; biographical sketch of, 376–77; Chard and, 418; Gebhard and, 417; on Hemenway Expedition, 290; Motz and, 422; Smith and, 424; Swanton and, 211

Phillips Andover Academy, 259, 311, 325, 334, 414

Phillips Exeter Academy, 147, 216, 218, 219, 251, 252, 421

Pickering, Charles: biographical sketch of, 33–35

Pickering, John, 33; biographical sketch of, 14–15

Pitman, Theodore B., 220, 331

Plains Conference for Archaeology, 380

Pleasants, Frederick Rhodes: biographical sketch of, 455–56

Pollard, Melvin, 432; biographical sketch of, 433

Pollock, Harry Evelyn Dorr, 365, 366, **pl. 42**, **pl. 63**; biographical sketch of, 363–64

Post, Richard Howell, 381; biographical sketch of, 386

Powell, Emma Dean, 108

Powell, John Wesley, 68, 98, 104, 148, 152, 161, 257, 301; aboriginal languages and, 166; Agassiz and, 51–52; archaeology and, 164, 165–66; biographical sketch of, 162–67; Bourke and, 155; Dall and, 75; DeHass and, 145, 146; ethnographic information and, 163; Garman and, 110; Gibbs and, 22; Hyatt and, 61; Norton and, 160; Perkins and, 150; Pumpelly and, 142; Putnam and, 105; research by, 164–65; Shaler and, 73

Princeton University, 183; department formation at, 171; Jewish faculty at, 184

professionalization, x, 181, 269, 298, 394

Pumpelly, Raphael, 73, 232; biographical sketch of, 141–42

Pumpelly, Raphael Welles, 300, 301; biographical sketch of, 143–44

Putnam, Adelaide Martha (née Edmands) (first wife of F. W. Putnam), 99

Putnam, Alice Edmands (daughter of F. W. Putnam), 99, 100, 115, 175, 285, **pl. 32**; biographical sketch of, 99–100

Putnam, Charles Edwin, 222
Putnam, Eben (son of F. W. Putnam), 133, 134
Putnam, Edward Kirby, 136, 137, 230, 231, 285, 316; biographical sketch of, 222
Putnam, Elizabeth Duncan, 222, 285
Putnam, Esther Orne (née Clarke) (Mrs. F. W. Putnam), 99, 118, 285, **pl. 32**
Putnam, Ethel Appleton (Mrs. Fiske) (daughter of F. W. Putnam), 99
Putnam, Frederic Ward, 4, 8, 22, 29, 37, 48–49, 55, 56, 57, 59, 60, 148, 156, 158, **pl. 2**, **pl. 5**, **pl. 12**, **pl. 13**, **pl. 14**, **pl. 15**, **pl. 22**, **pl. 32**; Abbott and, 88, 89–90, 90–91; Agassiz and, 23, 26, 27, 50, 51, 52, 53, 58, 77, 188; Americanist anthropology and, 275, 298; Americanist archaeology and, 78, 152, 284; Andrews and, 86, 87, 230; anthropology department and, 139, 177; Apache and, 250, 251, 253; archaeological interests of, 76–77; assistants of, 236; Babbitt and, 123; on Bandelier, 155; Barbour and, 314; Bickmore and, 69; biographical sketch of, 47–48; Bowditch and, 281, 283, 284; Breton and, 285; on burial excavation, 128; Bushnell and, 306; Carr and, 93, 94, 95, 96, 97, 98–99; Chamberlain and, 175; collecting by, 119–20; Converse and, 262; Cook and, 63, 200–201; Cresson and, 114, 116; Curtiss and, 105–6; Cusick and, 256, 258; Dakin and, 221; Dall and, 75, 76; Davis and, 232; death of, 99, 100, 297; Dixon and, 211, 214, 215; Dorsey and, 201, 232; on excavating burials, 128; on exploration, 128; Farabee and, 306; fellowship support and, 137; Fewkes and, 291, 292; financial/material support for, 277; First Nations and, 274; Fletcher and, 107, 108, 111; Flint and, 112, 113; Fuller and, 327, 328; funding and, 130, 137, 277; Garman and, 110, 111; Gerrodette and, 200; Gillman and, 88; Goodale and, 225; Gordon and, 206, 207; graduate training and, 171, 190–91, 196, 212, 245; Guernsey and, 330; Harrington and, 263, 264, 265; Hartt and, 85; Hastings and, 313; Hayden and, 311; Haynes and, 157, 159, 160; Huxley and, 299; Hyatt and, 61; Hyde and, 292; institutional support and, 141; Jackson and, 130–31, 132; Jesup and, 248; Jones and, 258, 260–61, 261–62; Kidder and, 325, 368; Kimball and, 133–34; Kneeland and, 108–9; leadership of, 235, 237, 238; Loubat and, 288, 289; Lyman and, 49; Lyon and, 225; Lythgoe and, 226; MacCurdy and, 222; Marsh and, 161, 162; Mead and, 100; Mechling and, 333; methodology and, 124–25; Metz and, 118, 119, 125–26, 133, 134, 135; minority students and, 194; Moncrieff and, 122; Moore and, 286, 287; Morgan and, 153; Morley and, 320, 321, 322, 323; Morse and, 64, 65, 67; Nickerson and, 133, 135, 136, 137; Norton and, 160; Owens and, 205; Packard and, 70, 71; Palmer and, 101, 102, 103; Parker and, 266, 267, 268, 269; Parkman and, 154; Parry and, 100; Peabody and, 216, 218, 219; Pepper and, 248, 249, 250; Phelps and, 110; Powell and, 105, 166, 167; recruiting by, 132, 168, 381; research agenda of, 79, 285; Russell and, 208, 209, 210; Salisbury and, 280, 281; salvage archaeology and, 129; Saville and, 198, 199; Schumacher and, 100; Scudder and, 68; Shaler and, 73, 74; Skinner and, 271; Slade and, 124, 225; Smith and, 246–47; sociocultural development and, 127; special students and, 192; Spinden and, 316; Stefansson and, 308, 309; Sterns and, 333; Studley and, 133; Swanton and, 211; Sweet and, 123; systematic exploration and, 126, 136; Tello and, 352; Thompson and, 120–21; Thurston and, 104; Toy and, 224; Tozzer and, 302, 303; training with, 197; Verrill and, 62; vision of, 243; Volk and, 120; Wheatland and, 53; Willoughby and, 219–20; on Wilson, 176; women students and, 194; Woods and, 227; Wyman and, 31–32
Putnam, George Palmer, 453
Putnam, Joseph Duncan, 222
Putnam, Mary Louisa Duncan, 222
Putnam, Mrs. Frederic Ward. *See* Putnam, Esther
Putnam, Patrick Tracy Lowell, 358, 389, 392, **pl. 47**; biographical sketch of, 393
Putnam, Rufus, 13
Putnam Festschrift, 249, 327

Quintana, Mariano, **pl. 34**

Radcliffe Anthropological Club, 231
Radcliffe College, 27, 50, 127, 186, 281; anthropology and, 193, 194, 398; Butler and, 361; Chute and, 404; Collier and, 359; Day and, 357; Eliot and, 182; graduate students at, 398; Handy and, 340; Harley and, 358, 359; Harvard and, 184, 194; numbers of graduate students at, 399 (table); Peabody Museum and, 401, 402; Sawtell and, 360
Redfield, Robert, 407
Redway, Laurance David, 389, 436; biographical sketch of, 381
Reed, Erik Kellerman, **pl. 56**; biographical sketch of, 421
Reisner, George Andrew, 216, 224; Bates and, 331; biographical sketch of, 227–30; Goddard and, 428; Kidder and, 324–25; Lythgoe and, 226; Morley and, 321; Rowe and, 413; Vaillant and, 367
Renaud, Abel Etienne Bernardeau, 369, 370, 403, 416
research, ix, 4, 8, 170, 171–72, 173
Reynolds, Edward, 341, 371, 381, 394, 400, 441, **pl. 37**; biographical sketch of, 382
Rice, Alexander Hamilton: biographical sketch of, 293–94
Richardson, Frederick Leopold William, Jr., 427, 428, 445, 446; biographical sketch of, 448–49
Ricketson, Edith, **pl. 36**
Ricketson, Oliver Garrison, Jr., 366, **pl. 36**, **pl. 41**; biographical sketch of, 364–65
Rideout, Henry Milner, 259, 260
Rihan, Habib Yusuf, 382
Ripley, William Zebina, 224, 354
Robert S. Peabody Foundation, 216, 218, 366, 372
Roberts, Frank Harold Hannah, Jr., 326, 368, 416, 421, 432; biographical sketch of, 369–70
Roberts, Henry Buchtel, 369, 375; biographical sketch of, 370–71; Byers and, 371; Gebhard and, 416; Johnson and, 372; Kidder and, 368; Wedlock and, 379
Rose, Wilmot J., 44, 83
Ross, Denman Waldo, 66, 67, 316

Rowe, John Howland, 352; biographical sketch of, 413–14
Ruppert, Karl, 366, **pl. 36**, **pl. 42**; biographical sketch of, 365
Russell, Frank, 191, 194, 197, 206, 224, 230, 231, 261, 298; biographical sketch of, 208–10; Huxley and, 299; Slade and, 226; Woods and, 227
Russell, George Peabody, 41, 42, 43, 161, 278

SAA. *See* Society for American Archaeology
Sabloff, Jeremy, 5, 22, 92–93, 248, 269; periods and, 4
Salem Press, 59, 60, 238, 239, 240
Salem secession, vii, 26, 48, 57, 58, 61, 63, 70, 151
Salisbury, Stephen, II, 42, 174, 279, 281, **pl. 7**
Salisbury, Stephen, III ("Jr."): 19, 120, 277, 279, 282, 283, **pl. 26**; biographical sketch of, 278–81
Sapir, Edward, 248, 270, 271, 272
Sargent, Winthrop, 12, 17, 22; biographical sketch of, 13–14
Sarkisian, Harold Medill: biographical sketch of, 433
Saturday Club, 38, 48, 49, 154
Saville, Marshall Howard, 117, 118, 130, 138, 197, 231, 243, 247, 248, 249, 250, 270, 273, 282, 301, **pl. 15**; biographical sketch of, 198–200; Cook and, 200; Cresson and, 116; Dorsey and, 201; Loubat and, 288, 289; Owens and, 205; World's Columbian Exposition and, 236
Sawtell, Ruth Otis (Mrs. Wilson Dallam Wallis), 359, 394, 401; biographical sketch of, 360–61
School for the Collegiate Instruction of Women, 27, 50, 182
School of American Archaeology, 32, 108, 156, 424
School of American Research, 424
Schoolcraft, Henry Rowe, 20, 254
Schulman, Edmund: biographical sketch of, 424
Schumacher, Paul, 92, 95: biographical sketch of, 100
Schwab, George, 388, **pl. 39**: biographical sketch of, 357–58

Schwab, Jewell, **pl. 39**
Science, 174, 175, 191, 237, 239, 346; Boas and, 36, 177; Carr and, 97, 98; Cresson and, 117; Flint and, 112; Kneeland and, 109; Putnam and, 78, 240; Scudder and, 68
Scott, Donald, 299, 370, 371, 375, 382, 400, **pl. 44**, **pl. 54**; biographical sketch of, 340–41
Scott, Louise (Mrs. Donald Scott), **pl. 54**
Scott, Paul F., 376, 412, 413; biographical sketch of, 379
Scudder, Samuel Hubbard, 55, 57, 59, 60, 74, 189, 240, 291, **pl. 7**; Agassiz and, 58; biographical sketch of, 68; Bowditch and, 283; Verrill and, 62
Sears, Ruth. *See* Chute, Ruth
Second International Congress of Americanists, 87–88
Section H, Anthropology, 78, 177, 211, 239; Guthe and, 335; Linton and, 369; MacCurdy and, 223; Moore and, 287; Powell and, 165; Putnam and, 222, 241, 248, 298; Russell and, 209; Seiichi, Sotoyama, 65–66
Seler, Eduard, 207, 288, 292, 304, 321, 359
Seltzer, Carl Coleman: biographical sketch of, 387; Hooton and, 381; Howells and, 388; Huxley and, 300; Luther and, 388; Stefansson and, 309
Semitic Museum, 157, 225, 404, 430; Visiting Committee of, 281, 331
Senter, Donovan Cowgill: biographical sketch of, 424–25
Senyürek, Muzaffer Süleyman: biographical sketch of, 440
Shaler, Nathaniel Southgate, 29, 49, 53, 57, 71, 89, 91, 291; Abbott and, 90; Agassiz and, 52; biographical sketch of, 72–74; Carr and, 94, 95; Dall and, 75; on Engineer Hall, 54–55; Hyatt and, 61; Powell and, 167; Pumpelly and, 143; on students' routine, 56; Verrill and, 62; Winsor and, 160; Wyman and, 30; on Zoological Hall, 55–56
Shapiro, Harry Lionel, 381, 385, 388, 400, 434; biographical sketch of, 382–83
Sharp, Gretchen Froehlich (née Cutter): biographical sketch of, 402
Sharp, Richard Lauriston: biographical sketch of, 453–54

Shaw, Quincy Adams, 50, 154
Sheffield Scientific School, 42, 161
Sheldon, William Herbert: biographical sketch of, 434
Shogoro, Tsuboi, 66
Shop, Charles Henry Bedford Sutton, 432; biographical sketch of, 433
Shotridge, Louis, 270, 272
Sickles, Emma C., 234, 236
Simms, Stephen C., 202, 262
Skarland, Ivar, 414; biographical sketch of, 416
Skiff, Frederick J. V., 137, 237
Skinner, Alanson Buck, 221, 246, 263, 264, 272, 274, 275; biographical sketch of, 269–71; Harrington and, 265; Parker and, 267
Slade, Daniel Denison, 124, 224; biographical sketch of, 225–26
Small, Sylvanus Griswold (Morley), 320. *See also* Morley, Sylvanus Griswold
Smith, Augustus Ledyard, 363, 364, 367; biographical sketch of, 365–66
Smith, Erminnie Adele, 108, 239, 257–58
Smith, Harlan Ingersoll, 198, 200, 236, 249, 250, 262, 268, 271, 275; biographical sketch of, 246–48; Skinner and, 270
Smith, Jane ("Jennie"), 95, 214, 238, 239; biographical sketch of, 99
Smith, Robert Eliot: biographical sketch of, 365–66
Smith, Samuel Watson ("Wat"), **pl. 54**; **pl. 57**; biographical sketch of, 423–24
Smithsonian Institution, 19, 21, 22, 26, 31, 34, 36, 60, 62, 82, 83, 128, 232, 239, 273, 300, 318, 326, 337, 347, 348; Berendt and, 85, 86; Bishop and, 339; Brew and, 373; Case and, 199; Cushing and, 290; Dall and, 75; DeHass and, 146; Dorsey and, 202; Dunning and, 85; Emmert and, 106; Flint and, 111; founding of, 25; Gillin and, 443; Gillman and, 88; Guha and, 356; influence of, ix; Johnson and, 372; LeBaron and, 106; Means and, 337; Metz and, 119; Murdoch and, 232; Newman and, 437; Palmer and, 102; Paul and, 411; Powell and, 163, 164, 167; Putnam and, 79, 80; research at, 171; Roberts and, 371; Rowe and, 414; Schumacher and, 100; Taylor and, 425;

Tschopik and, 452; U.S. National Museum and, 166; Woodbury and, 423
Smithsonian Office of Anthropology, 370
Snow, Charles Ernest: biographical sketch of, 438
Society for American Archaeology (SAA), 5, 265, 269, 326, 338; Brew and, 373; Byers and, 372; Ekholm and, 410; Guthe and, 335; Roberts and, 370; Spinden and, 359; Wauchope and, 410; Wormington and, 404
Society for Applied Anthropology, 443
Society for Archaeological Research, 147
Society of American Indians, 269
sociocultural anthropology, ix, 26, 127, 212, 381, 384, 389, 442, 444, 449, 457; cohort effect and, 5; development of, 395, 433; history of, 7–8; importance of, 3; women students and, 408
Southeastern Archaeological Conferences, 378
Southwest Museum, 253, 265, 312, 338, 451
Speck, Frank Gouldsmith, 246, 263, 270, 274, 275; biographical sketch of, 271–72; Johnson and, 372; Mechling and, 333; Parker and, 267, 268
Spicer, Edward H., 447
Spier, Leslie, 386
Spinden, Ellen Sewall (née Collier), **pl. 38**; biographical sketch of, 359
Spinden, Herbert Joseph, 214, 230, 269, 282, 306, 312, 322, 343, 345, 346, 347, 348, 349, **pl. 35, pl. 37**; Barbour and, 314; Bates and, 331; biographical sketch of, 315–17; Collier and, 359; Goodale and, 225; Hellman and, 318; Morley and, 321, 344; Stefansson and, 309; Will and, 317
Spinden-Morley correlation, 316, 322
Squier, Ephraim G., 18–19, 30, 85, 151, 154, 257
Srole, Leo, 445; biographical sketch of, 448
Stallings, William Sidney, Jr., 424; biographical sketch of, 425
Standing Committee on American Archaeology (AIA), 156, 283, 284
Stanford University, 181, 222, 309, 434
Starr, Frederick, 137, 190, 203, 285
Statistical and Anthropometric Laboratory, 388, 433, 441, 457
Stefansson, Vilhjalmar: biographical sketch of, 308–9; Farabee and, 306; Howe and, 328; Kidder and, 324; Luther and, 388; Seltzer and, 387
Stephens, John Lloyd, 19, 120, 121, 300
Sterns, Frederick Henderson, 226, 230, 303, 334, 335; biographical sketch of, 332–33
Stevenson, Matilda Coxe, 107
Stevenson, Sara Yorke, 227–28, **pl. 21**
Stiles, Ezra, 12, 13
Stimpson, William, 47, 55, 57, 64; biographical sketch of, 72
Stirling, Gene McNaughton, 414; biographical sketch of, 417
Stone, Doris (née Zemurray), 398, 401, 412, **pl. 51, pl. 52**; biographical sketch of, 405
Strømsvik, Gustav, **pl. 42**
Strong, William Duncan, 352, 381, 411
Studley, Cordelia Adelaide, 75, 134, 137, 139, 187, 189, **pl. 8**; biographical sketch of, 132–33
Sturtevant, E. Lewis, 123
Swaminadhan, Subharama, 394
Swanton, John Reed, 118, 119, 197, 213, 224, 225, 243, 246, 249; biographical sketch of, 210–11; Bowditch and, 284; Dixon and, 212; Hooton and, 336; Loubat and, 289; Newcombe and, 389
Sweet, George W., 122–23
Sweet, Henry N.: biographical sketch of, 293

Tangco, Marcelo V., 351; biographical sketch of, 355
Taylor, Walter Willard, Jr., 416, 440, 450; biographical sketch of, 425–26
Tello, Julio César, 342, 394, 438, **pl. 40, pl. 47**; biographical sketch of, 351–52
Thaw, Mary Copley, 107, 190
Thaw Fellowship, 107, 137, 138, 190; Brew and, 373; Carleton and, 433; Dupertuis and, 387; Fletcher and, 107; Harley and, 358; Hulse and, 385; Nuttall and, 114; Shapiro and, 382; Williams and, 384
Thayer, Nathaniel, 50, 55, 150
Thayer, William Roscoe, 93
Thayer Expedition, 72, 85, 295
Thomas, Cyrus, 98, 106, 146, 163, 165
Thomas, Sidney Johnston, 414; biographical sketch of, 418
Thompson, Edward Herbert, 236, 284, 285, **pl. 11**; biographical sketch of, 120–21;

Bowditch and, 282; Morley and, 321; Salisbury and, 279, 280; Sweet and, 293; Tozzer and, 303

Thompson, Elizabeth Rowell, 239

Thompson, Laura Maud. *See* Duker, Laura

Thompson, Lindsay, **pl. 14**

Ticknor, George, 40, 180, 185; biographical sketch of, 178–79

Titiev, Morris ("Mischa"), 389, 407; biographical sketch of, 390

Torrey, John, 32, 33, 101

Toy, Crawford Howell, 316; biographical sketch of, 224–25

Tozzer, Alfred Marston, 193, 225, 230, 231, 249, 270, 285, 298, 306, 321, 323, 368, 394, 398, **pl. 30**, **pl. 31**, **pl. 37**; AIA fellowship and, 284; Allen and, 443; Amsden and, 338; appointment of, 367; archaeology and, 351; Barbour and, 314; Barrera-Vásquez and, 412; Bates and, 331; Beyer and, 329; biographical sketch of, 302–5; Boas and, 346; Butler and, 361; class by, 400, 401; Cline and, 378; Collier and, 359; Cresson and, 412; Dixon and, 213, 214, 215; Fuller and, 328; Guthe and, 334; Hammond and, 402; Haury and, 420; Hay and, 329–30; Hyde and, 292; Kerr and, 339; Kidder and, 324, 326; La Farge and, 362, 363; Lothrop and, 342, 343; Maya archaeology and, 408–9, 414; Mechling and, 334; Merwin and, 319; Morley and, 322; Motz and, 422; Phillips and, 377; Pollock and, 363, 364; Radcliffe and, 401; research by, 362; A. Smith and R. Smith and, 365, 366; social anthropology and, 303; Spinden and, 315, 316, 317; Sterns and, 333; Tello and, 352; Thompson and, 121; Vaillant and, 367; Washburn and, 436; Wauchope and, 409; Young and, 403

Tozzer Library, 80, 200, 213, 289, 359; Haynes and, 157; Sterns and, 333; Taylor and, 426

Tschopik, Harry Schlessinger, Jr., 352, 404, 405; biographical sketch of, 452–53

Tschopik, Marion (née Hutchinson), 352, **pl. 56**; biographical sketch of, 405

Uhle, Max, 114, 292

Underwood, Sarah, 108, 252

United Fruit Company, 411, 412, 423

U.S. Army Air Corps, 338, 364, 406, 422, 423, 428

U.S. Coast Survey, 38, 50, 75

U.S. Department of Agriculture, 386, 447, 451

U.S. Department of State, 453, 454; Amsden and, 338; Bowles and, 386; Dixon and, 215; Institute of Andean Research and, 352, 367; Lothrop and, 343

United States Exploring Expedition, 33, 34, 36, 37

U.S. Geological Survey (USGS), 159; Blake and, 295; Dall and, 75; Hack and, 422; Palmer and, 102; Powell and, 164; Pumpelly and, 142; Shaler and, 73; U.S. House of Representatives, 40, 49

U.S. National Museum (USNM), ix, 118, 222, 232, 300, 347, 348, 441; Angel and, 439; Cresson and, 115; Dall and, 75; Dorsey and, 203; Gibbs and, 21; Hrdlička and, 434; Means and, 337; Oppenheimer and, 438; Roberts and, 370; Smithsonian Institution and, 166; Taylor and, 425

U.S. Navy, 42, 87, 102, 204, 404, 416

University Museum (Harvard), Agassiz and, 50, 52

University of Arizona, 322; Boggs and, 410; Gabel and, 441; Haury and, 420, 421; Hulse and, 385; Kelly and, 451; Pleasants and, 456; Ruppert and, 365; Stallings and, 425; Woodbury and, 423

University of California–Berkeley, 242, 320; Birdsell and, 439; Hearst and, 227; Jewish faculty at, 184; Kidder and, 326; Nuttall and, 114; Putnam and, 137, 168, 195, 237, 243, 245, 306; Reisner and, 228; Rowe and, 414; Warner and, 444; Washburn and, 437; Wheeler and, 241

University of Chicago, 136, 175, 247, 429; Andrews and, 410; anthropology at, ix, x; Cutter and, 402; Davis and, 447, 448; department formation at, 171; Dorsey and, 203; Fuller and, 407; Gaul and, 428; graduate program at, 117, 172, 177, 185; Handy and, 340; Harding and, 449; Jewish faculty at, 184; Lessa and, 388; Newman and, 437; Paul and, 412; Pelzel and, 454; Putnam and, 137; Utsurikawa and, 353; Warner and, 444, 445; Winchester and, 433

University of Michigan, 33, 37, 65, 247, 248, 450; Cox and, 433; Garn and, 440; Guthe and, 334; Harrington and, 264; Hughes and, 437; Titiev and, 390
University of Michigan Museum of Anthropology: Guthe and, 335
University of Minnesota: Angel and, 439; Cline and, 378; Ekholm and, 410; Wilford and, 415; Winchester and, 433
University of New Mexico, 320; Amsden and, 338; Ellis and, 425; Hibben and, 415; Kluckhohn and, 449; Whittemore and, 403; Woods (Keith) and, 403; Wyman and, 452
University of Pennsylvania, ix, x, 14, 183, 208, 430; Abbott and, 90, 91; Cammann and, 455; Cresson and, 412; Feng and, 444; Gordon and, 207; graduate program at, 177; Hearst and, 227; Linton and, 368; Mechling and, 345; Moore and, 287; Putnam and, 168, 275; Speck and, 271–72; Tozzer and, 304; Wallis and, 350
University of Pennsylvania Museum, 14, 90, 202, 241, 249, 253, 272, 285; Abbott and, 89; Bishop and, 339; Butler and, 361; Cresson and, 412; Dorsey and, 203; Ehrich and, 430; Farabee and, 306; Gordon and, 206, 207; Harrington and, 264, 265; Kidder II and, 413; Linton and, 368; Lothrop and, 343; Mason and, 346; Mechling and, 334; Merwin and, 319; Reisner and, 227; Richardson and, 448; Speck and, 271; Vaillant and, 367; Wallis and, 360; Wulsin and, 393
University of Texas, 377; Campbell and, 414; Davis and, 419; Jewish faculty at, 184; Taylor and, 426
University of Washington: Hulse and, 385; Oppenheimer and, 438; Sharp and, 454; Taylor and, 426
University of Wisconsin, 137; Adams and, 402; Chard and, 418; Howells and, 389; Lasker and, 439; Linton and, 369; Mekeel and, 391; Sheldon and, 434
USNM. *See* U.S. National Museum
Utah Archaeological Survey, 340, **pl. 44**
Utsurikawa/Utsushikawa, Nenozo, 351, 394, 395; biographical sketch of, 353–54

Vaillant, George Clapp, 229, 349, 410, **pl. 42**; biographical sketch of, 366–67; Hay and, 330; Macgowan and, 381; Merwin and, 319; Phillips and, 377; Sterns and, 334
Varela, Cristino, **pl. 34**
Varela, Martin, **pl. 34**
Verrill, Addison Emery, 29, 55, 56, 57, 59, 60, 61, 72, 74; Agassiz and, 58; biographical sketch of, 62–63; Dall and, 75; Morse and, 64
Veysey, Laurence, 151, 183
Vishniefsky, Boris N., 441
Vogt, Evon, 305
Volk, Ernest, 118, 210, 236, 292, **pl. 11**, **pl. 13**; Abbott and, 91; biographical sketch of, 120; Cresson and, 116; Loubat and, 289; Merwin and, 319; Peabody and, 218;
Volk, George D., 403
Von Humboldt, Alexander, 18, 23, 24
Von Morlot, Adolphe, 21, 31, 32

Waldeck, Jean-Frederic Maximillien, Count de, 19
Walker, James, 41, 43
Wallis, Ruth Otis (née Sawtell). *See* Sawtell, Ruth
Wallis, Wilson Dallam: biographical sketch of, 360
Wang, Hsien Chin (née Hu). *See* Hu, Hsien
Ward, Lauriston, 299, 404, 429, **pl. 47**; biographical sketch of, 340
Ware, William Robert: biographical sketch of, 153
Warner, William Lloyd: Arensberg and, 446; biographical sketch of, 444–45; Coon and, 384; Davis and, 447, 448; Hencken and, 427; replacement of, 449; Richardson and, 448; sociocultural anthropology and, 395, 442, 444; Washburn and, 436
Warren, John Collins, 28, 295; biographical sketch of, 15–16
Warren Museum, 294, 295
WASA. *See* Women's Anthropological Society of America
Washburn, Sherwood Larned, 434, 443, **pl. 63**; biographical sketch of, 436–37
Washington University in St. Louis, 73, 384–85, 431, 434
Watson, Caroline, 238, 239

Wauchope, Robert, 326, 408, **pl. 53**; biographical sketch of, 409–10
Webb, William S., 248, 373
Webster, David Hutton: biographical sketch of, 309–10
Wedlock, Louis Lorne, 371, 372, 376; biographical sketch of, 379
Weld, Charles Goddard, 66, 67
Weld, Francis Minot, 198, 282; biographical sketch of, 190
West, Gerald M., 175, 236
Wetherill, Richard, 302, 306
Wheatland, Henry, 59, 187, **pl. 7**; biographical sketch of, 52–53
Wheatland, Richard, 47, 55, 60
Wheeler, Benjamin Ide, 108, 114, 310; biographical sketch of, 241
Wheeler, George Montague, 79, 164, 241
Wheeler, Richard Page, **pl. 55**; biographical sketch of, 421–22
Wheeler Survey, 79, 100, 164
Whiting, Beatrice Blyth, 407–8
Whiting, F., **pl. 35**
Whitney, Josiah Dwight, 95–96, 142
Whittemore, Mary (Mrs. Charles Dillon McEvoy Jr.): biographical sketch of, 403
Widener, Eleanor Elkins, 294
Wiener, Leo, 231; biographical sketch of, 232
Wilder, Burt Green, 27, 29, 32, 49, 70; Bowditch and, 281, 282
Wilford, Lloyd Alden, 410, 414; biographical sketch of, 415;
Wilkes, Charles, 33, 34, 35
Will, George Francis, 123, 213, 306, 349; biographical sketch of, 317–18; Dixon and, 214; Morley and, 321; Spinden and, 315
Willey, Gordon Randolph, 5, 22, 92–93, 248, 268, 300, 352; Bowditch and, 284; periods and, 4; Phillips and, 377; Pollock and, 363; Rowe and, 414; Smith and, 366; Stefansson and, 308; Tozzer and, 305
Williams, George Dee, 381, 382; biographical sketch of, 384–85
Williams, Stephen, 14, 315, 331, 377, 400, 434; Amsden and, 338; Haury and, 421; Hooton and, 336; Jones and, 262; Linton and, 369; Moore and, 286, 288; Shapiro and, 383; Smith and, 424; Spinden and, 317; Ward and, 340; Wilford and, 415
Williams College, 68, 309, 377, 385, 412, 447
Willoughby, Charles Clark, 197, 210, 218, 236, 270, 328, **pl. 20**, **pl. 22**, **pl. 32**, **pl. 37**; appointment of, 215; Barbour and, 314; Bates and, 331; biographical sketch of, 219–21; de Milhau and, 314; Guernsey and, 330; Hooton and, 336; Loubat and, 289; Reynolds and, 382; Sterns and, 333; Tello and, 352; undergraduate/graduate students and, 400
Wilson, Daniel, 294; biographical sketch of, 176
Wilson, Howard Barrett, 299; biographical sketch of, 208
Winchester, Harold Purcell, Jr., 432, **pl. 56**; biographical sketch of, 433
Winlock, Herbert Eustis, 331; biographical sketch of, 318
Winsor, Justin, 73, 93, 158, 167, **pl. 10**; biographical sketch of, 160
Winthrop, Robert Charles, 43–44, 45, 49, 130, 189, **pl. 6**; biographical sketch of, 40–41; Lothrop and, 341; Peabody and, 42; Salisbury and, 280; *see also* Winthrop Scholarship
Winthrop Scholarship, 44, 138, 190, 206, 208, 210, 213, 260, 261, 302; Beyer and, 329; Blom and, 363; Bowden and, 332; Brew and, 373; Chi and, 354; Dupertuis and, 387; Fullwer and, 327; Hansberry and, 357; Hayden and, 311; Mekeel and, 391; Merwin and, 318; Noguera and, 353; Ruppert and, 365; Vaillant and, 367; Wedlock and, 379; Wilson and, 308
Wissler, Clark, 216, 224, 270, 323, 452; disciplinary development and, 4; Dixon and, 214; Guthe and, 335; Saville and, 200; Vaillant and, 367
Wolcott, Joshua Roger, 188, 190
women students, ix, 184, 194, 397–98, 408
Women's Anthropological Society of America (WASA), 107, 108
Woodbury, Nathalie Ferris Sampson, 423
Woodbury, Richard Benjamin, 321, **pl. 54**, **pl. 57**; biographical sketch of, 422–23

Woods, George, 105, 106
Woods, James Haughton, 210, 212, 224; biographical sketch of, 226–27
Woods, Janet McCleery (Mrs. Dickey): biographical sketch of, 403
Woods, Margaret Soutter. *See* Keith, Margaret
Works Progress Administration (WPA), 385, 402, 421, 454–55; Angel and, 438; Cresson and, 412; Ehrich and, 431; Snow and, 438; Stirling and, 417; Wauchope and, 409
World's Columbian Exposition, 108, 117, 199, 205, 219, 232, 234, 237, 247, 250, 289, 291, 387, **pl. 22, pl. 23**; assistants at, 236; Chamberlain and, 175; Cusick and, 258; Davis and, 233; Dorsey and, 201; Higinbotham and, 233; Mead and, 100; Moncrieff and, 122; Nickerson and, 137; Nuttall and, 114; Owens and, 206; Peabody and, 216; Putnam and, 82, 93, 198, 243, 245; Thompson and, 121; Willoughby and, 219
Worman, Dorothy Penrose ("Penny") (née Davis), 418, 423, 432
Worman, Eugene Clark, Jr., 418; biographical sketch of, 432
Wormington, Hannah Marie, 402, 416, **pl. 52**; biographical sketch of, 403–4
WPA. *See* Works Progress Administration
Wright, George Frederick, 80, 91, 158, 236
Wulsin, Frederick Roelker, 389, **pl. 37, pl. 49**; biographical sketch of, 392–93
Wulsin, Janet, **pl. 49**
Wyman, Jeffries, 8, 15, 26, 37, 38, 41, 42, 43, 44, 50, 68, 72, 73, 74, 80, 149, 158, **pl. 3**; Abbott and, 88, 89; Agassiz and, 27; Americanist archaeology and, 30, 31; anatomical rooms of, **pl. 3**; Andrews and, 86, 87; Baird and, 39; Berendt and, 86; biographical sketch of, 28–32; Carr and, 95; Clark and, 49; Dall and, 75, 76; death of, 32, 79, 91, 161; directorship for, 83, 84; Dunning and, 84; Gillman and, 87; on Hartt, 85; Hyatt and, 61; Lowell and, 24; Moore and, 286, 287; Morse and, 64, 66; Parkman and, 154; Peabody and, 45; Putnam and, 53, 76, 77, 92; teaching by, 23
Wyman, Leland Clifton: biographical sketch of, 451–52

Yale University, 161, 172, 183, 274; department formation at, 171; Jewish faculty at, 184
Young, Katherine Burks (Mrs. Hearn), **pl. 51**; biographical sketch of, 403

Zemurray, Doris. *See* Stone, Doris
Zemurray, Samuel, 405, 412
Zheng Dekun. *See* Cheng Te-k'un
Zimmerman, Carle Clark, 435; biographical sketch of, 456
Zoological Club, 54, 55, 56, 60, 64
Zoological Hall, 54, 61, 62, 63, 64, 70, 72, 281; life at, 55–58
Zoological Museum. *See* Museum of Comparative Zoology
Zurich Anthropological Institute, 144